WORLD ENCYCLOPEDIA OF PEACE

WORLD ENCYCLOPEDIA OF PEACE

VOLUME 3

Honorary Editor-in-Chief
Linus Pauling

Executive Editors
Ervin Laszlo   •   Jong Youl Yoo

PERGAMON PRESS

OXFORD · NEW YORK · BEIJING · FRANKFURT
SÃO PAULO · SYDNEY · TOKYO · TORONTO

U.K.	Pergamon Press, Headington Hill Hall, Oxford OX3 0BW, England
U.S.A.	Pergamon Press, Maxwell House, Fairview Park, Elmsford, New York 10523, U.S.A.
PEOPLE'S REPUBLIC OF CHINA	Pergamon Press, Qianmen Hotel, Beijing, People's Republic of China
FEDERAL REPUBLIC OF GERMANY	Pergamon Press, Hammerweg 6, D-6242 Kronberg, Federal Republic of Germany
BRAZIL	Pergamon Editora, Rua Eça de Queiros, 346, CEP 04011, São Paulo, Brazil
AUSTRALIA	Pergamon Press Australia, P.O. Box 544, Potts Point, N.S.W. 2011, Australia
JAPAN	Pergamon Press, 8th Floor, Matsuoka Central Building, 1-7-1 Nishishinjuku, Shinjuku-ku, Tokyo 160, Japan
CANADA	Pergamon Press Canada, Suite 104, 150 Consumers Road, Willowdale, Ontario M2J 1P9, Canada

First edition 1986

Library of Congress Cataloging-in-Publication Data
World encyclopedia of peace.
Bibliography: v. 4, p.
Includes indexes.
1. Peace—Dictionaries. 2. Peace—Societies, etc.—
Dictionaries. I. Laszlo, Ervin, 1932–. II. Yu,
Chŏng-nyŏl.
JX1952.W63 1986 327.1′72′0321 86-25520

British Library Cataloguing in Publication Data

World encyclopedia of peace.
1. Peace—Dictionaries
I. Pauling, Linus II. Laszlo, Ervin
III. Yoo, Jong Youl
327.1′72′0321 JX1944

ISBN 0-08-032685-4

Printed in Great Britain by A. Wheaton & Co. Ltd., Exeter

CONTENTS

TREATIES

CONTENTS

CHRONOLOGY OF THE PEACE MOVEMENT

NOBEL PEACE PRIZE LAUREATES

CHRONOLOGY OF THE PEACE MOVEMENT

NOBEL PEACE PRIZE LAUREATES

TREATIES

The Treaties section comprises the texts of 39 treaties, agreements, conventions, and protocols of the twentieth century from 1919 to 1981. They have been selected for inclusion on the basis of their relevance to the issues of arms control, disarmament, and the prohibition of war and aggression. Treaties which conclude a war have been excluded except in cases where disarmament clauses constitute a significant element in the agreement, for example, the Treaty of Versailles. The Treaty texts have been reproduced in chronological order and the majority appear in full. In cases where treaties have been edited, summarized clauses are displayed in square brackets.

For a discussion of the nature of modern treaties, see the article in Volume 2 on *Treaties of the Modern Era*. Readers are also advised to refer to related articles in Volumes 1 and 2 on international law. For more detailed treatments of specific aspects of arms control and disarmament see the articles in Volumes 1 and 2 on *Arms Control, Evolution of*; *Multilateralism*; and *Unilateralism*. Readers are advised to refer to companion articles in Volumes 1 and 2 which discuss the significance of particular treaties; these include: *Naval Limitation Treaties Between the World Wars*; *Non-Proliferation Treaty*; *Oceans: The Common Heritage* (for discussion of the Sea-Bed Treaty); and *Conference on Security and Cooperation in Europe (CSCE)*. Readers are also advised to refer to articles on Nobel Peace Prize Laureates in Volume 3 for the significance of specific treaties of the interwar period.

Treaties

Treaty of Versailles

Date of signature: June 28, 1919
Place of signature: Versailles
Signatory states: the British Empire, France, Italy, Japan, the United States, Belgium, Bolivia, Brazil, China, Cuba, Czechoslovakia, Ecuador, Greece, Guatemala, Haiti, the Hedjaz, Honduras, Liberia, Nicaragua, Panama, Peru, Poland, Portugal, Roumania, the Serb-Croat-Slovene State, Siam, Uruguay, Germany

The United States of America, The British Empire, France, Italy and Japan.
These Powers being described in the present Treaty as the Principal Allied and Associated Powers, Belgium, Bolivia, Brazil, China, Cuba, Ecuador, Greece, Guatemala, Haiti, the Hedjaz, Honduras, Liberia, Nicaragua, Panama, Peru, Poland, Portugal, Roumania, the Serb-Croat-Slovene State, Siam, Czechoslovakia and Uruguay,
These Powers constituting with the Principal Powers mentioned above the Allied and Associated Powers, of the one part;
and Germany
of the other part;
Bearing in mind that on the request of the Imperial German Government an armistice was granted on November 11, 1918, to Germany by the Principal Allied and Associated Powers in order that a Treaty of Peace might be concluded with her, and
The Allied and Associated Powers being equally desirous that the war in which they were successively involved directly or indirectly and which originated in the declaration of war by Austria-Hungary on July 28, 1914, against Serbia, the declaration of war by Germany against Russia on August 1, 1914, and against France on August 3, 1914, and in the invasion of Belgium, should be replaced by a firm, just and durable Peace.
For this purpose the High Contracting Parties ...
Who having communicated their full powers found in good and due form have agreed as follows:
From the coming into force of the present Treaty the state of war will terminate. From that moment and subject to the provisions of this Treaty official rela-tions with Germany, and with any of the German States, will be resumed by the Allied and Associated Powers.

PART I

THE COVENANT OF THE LEAGUE OF NATIONS

The High Contracting Parties,
In order to promote international co-operation and to achieve international peace and security

by the acceptance of obligations not to resort to war,

by the prescription of open, just and honourable relations between nations,

by the firm establishment of the understandings of international law as the actual rule of conduct among Governments, and

by the maintenance of justice and a scrupulous respect for all treaty obligations in the dealings of organised peoples with one another,

Agree to this Covenant of the League of Nations.

Article 1

The original Members of the League of Nations shall be those of the Signatories which are named in the Annex to this Covenant and also such of those other States named in the Annex as shall accede without reservation to this Covenant. Such accession shall be effected by a declaration deposited with the Secretariat within two months of the coming into force of the Covenant. Notice thereof shall be sent to all other Members of the League.
Any fully self-governing State, Dominion or Col-ony not named in the Annex may become a Member of the League if its admission is agreed to by two-thirds of the Assembly, provided that it shall give effective guarantees of its sincere intention to observe its international obligations, and shall accept such regulations as may be prescribed by the League in

regard to its military, naval and air forces and armaments.

Any Member of the League may, after two years' notice of its intention so to do, withdraw from the League, provided that all its international obligations and all its obligations under this Covenant shall have been fulfilled at the time of its withdrawal.

Article 2

The action of the League under this Covenant shall be effected through the instrumentality of an Assembly and of a Council with a permanent Secretariat.

Article 3

The Assembly shall consist of Representatives of the Members of the League.

The Assembly shall meet at stated intervals and from time to time as occasion may require at the Seat of the League or at such other place as may be decided upon.

The Assembly may deal at its meetings with any matter within the sphere of action of the League or affecting the peace of the world.

At meetings of the Assembly each Member of the League shall have one vote, and may have not more than three Representatives.

Article 4

The Council shall consist of Representatives of the Principal Allied and Associated Powers, together with Representatives of four other Members of the League. These four Members of the League shall be selected by the Assembly from time to time in its discretion. Until the appointment of the Representatives of the four Members of the League first selected by the Assembly, Representatives of Belgium, Brazil, Spain and Greece shall be members of the Council.

With the approval of the majority of the Assembly, the Council may name additional Members of the League whose Representatives shall always be members of the Council; the Council with like approval may increase the number of Members of the League to be selected by the Assembly for representation on the Council.

The Council shall meet from time to time as occasion may require, and at least once a year, at the Seat of the League, or at such other place as may be decided upon.

The Council may deal at its meetings with any matter within the sphere of action of the League or affecting the peace of the world.

Any Member of the League not represented on the Council shall be invited to send a Representative to sit as a member at any meeting of the Council during the consideration of matters specially affecting the interests of that Member of the League.

At meetings of the Council, each Member of the League represented on the Council shall have one vote, and may have not more than one Representative.

Article 5

Except where otherwise expressly provided in this Covenant or by the terms of the present Treaty, decisions at any meeting of the Assembly or of the Council shall require the agreement of all the Members of the League represented at the meeting.

All matters of procedure at meetings of the Assembly or of the Council, including the appointment of Committees to investigate particular matters, shall be regulated by the Assembly or by the Council, and may be decided by a majority of the Members of the League represented at the meeting.

The first meeting of the Assembly and the first meeting of the Council shall be summoned by the President of the United States of America.

Article 6

[The permanent Secretariat to be established at Geneva.]

Article 7

[Representatives and officials to enjoy diplomatic status.]

Article 8

The Members of the League recognise that the maintenance of peace requires the reduction of national armaments to the lowest point consistent with national safety and the enforcement by common action of international obligations.

The Council, taking account of the geographical situation and circumstances of each State, shall formulate plans for such reduction for the consideration and action of the several Governments.

Such plans shall be subject to reconsideration and revision at least every ten years.

After these plans shall have been adopted by the several Governments, the limits of armaments therein fixed shall not be exceeded without the concurrence of the Council.

The Members of the League agree that the manufacture by private enterprise of munitions and implements of war is open to grave objections. The Council shall advise how the evil effects attendant upon such manufacture can be prevented, due regard being had to the necessities of those Members of the League which are not able to manufacture the munitions and implements of war necessary for their safety.

The Members of the League undertake to interchange full and frank information as to the scale of their armaments, their military, naval and air programmes and the condition of such of their industries as are adaptable to war-like purposes.

Article 9

A permanent Commission shall be constituted to advise the Council on the execution of the provisions of Articles 1 and 8 and on military, naval and air questions generally.

Article 10

The Members of the League undertake to respect and preserve as against external aggression the territorial integrity and existing political independence of all Members of the League. In case of any such aggression or in case of any threat or danger of such aggression the Council shall advise upon the means by which this obligation shall be fulfilled.

Article 11

Any war or threat of war, whether immediately affecting any of the Members of the League or not, is hereby declared a matter of concern to the whole League, and the League shall take any action that may be deemed wise and effectual to safeguard the peace of nations. In case any such emergency should arise the Secretary General shall, on the request of any Member of the League, forthwith summon a meeting of the Council.

It is also declared to be the friendly right of each Member of the League to bring to the attention of the Assembly or of the Council any circumstance whatever affecting international relations which threatens to disturb international peace or the good understanding between nations upon which peace depends.

Article 12

The Members of the League agree that if there should arise between them any dispute likely to lead to a rupture, they will submit the matter either to arbitration or to inquiry by the Council, and they agree in no case to resort to war until three months after the award by the arbitrators or the report by the Council.

In any case under this Article the award of the arbitrators shall be made within a reasonable time, and the report of the Council shall be made within six months after the submission of the dispute.

Article 13

[Disputes which cannot be settled by diplomacy to be submitted to arbitration.]

Article 14

The Council shall formulate and submit to the Members of the League for adoption plans for the establishment of a Permanent Court of International Justice. The Court shall be competent to hear and determine any dispute of an international character which the parties thereto submit to it. The Court may also give an advisory opinion upon any dispute or question referred to it by the Council or by the Assembly.

Article 15

[Disputes that are not submitted to arbitration to be submitted to the Council, who shall endeavour to effect a peaceful settlement.]

Article 16

Should any Member of the League resort to war in disregard of its covenants under Articles 12, 13 or 15, it shall *ipso facto* be deemed to have committed an act of war against all other Members of the League, which hereby undertake immediately to subject it to the severance of all trade or financial relations, the prohibition of all intercourse between their nationals and the nationals of the covenant-breaking State, and the prevention of all financial, commercial or personal intercourse between the nationals of the covenant-breaking State and the nationals of any other State, whether a Member of the League or not.

It shall be the duty of the Council in such case to recommend to the several Governments concerned what effective military, naval or air force the Members of the League shall severally contribute to the armed forces to be used to protect the covenants of the League.

The Members of the League agree, further, that they will mutually support one another in the financial and economic measures which are taken under this Article, in order to minimise the loss and inconvenience resulting from the above measures, and that they will mutually support one another in resisting any special measures aimed at one of their number by the covenant-breaking State, and that they will take the necessary steps to afford passage through their territory to the forces of any of the Members of the League which are co-operating to protect the covenants of the League.

Any Member of the League which has violated any covenant of the League may be declared to be no longer a Member of the League by a vote of the Council, concurred in by the Representatives of all the other Members of the League represented thereon.

Article 17

In the event of a dispute between a Member of the League and a State which is not a Member of the League, or between States not Members of the League, the State or States not Members of the League shall be invited to accept the obligations of Membership of the League for the purposes of such dispute, upon such conditions as the Council may deem just. If such invitation is accepted, the provisions of Articles 12 to 16 inclusive shall be applied with such modifications as may be deemed necessary by the Council.

Upon such invitation being given the Council shall immediately institute an inquiry into the circumstances of the dispute and recommend such action as may seem best and most effectual in the circumstances.

If a State so invited shall refuse to accept the obligations of membership in the League for the purposes of such dispute, and shall resort to war against a Member of the League, the provisions of Article 16 shall be applicable as against the State taking such action.

If both parties to the dispute when so invited refuse to accept the obligations of membership in the League for the purposes of such dispute, the Council may take such measures and make such recommendations as will prevent hostilities and will result in the settlement of the dispute.

Article 18

Every treaty or international engagement entered into hereafter by any Member of the League shall be forthwith registered with the Secretariat, and shall as soon as possible be published by it. No such treaty or international engagement shall be binding until so registered.

Article 19

The Assembly may from time to time advise the reconsideration by Members of the League of treaties which have become inapplicable, and the consideration of international conditions whose continuance might endanger the peace of the world.

Article 20

The Members of the League severally agree that this Covenant is accepted as abrogating all obligations or understandings *inter se* which are inconsistent with the terms thereof, and solemnly undertake that they will not hereafter enter into any engagements inconsistent with the terms thereof.

In case any Member of the League shall, before becoming a Member of the League, have undertaken any obligations inconsistent with the terms of this Covenant, it shall be the duty of such Member to take immediate steps to procure its release from such obligations.

Article 21

Nothing in this Covenant shall be deemed to affect the validity of international engagements, such as treaties of arbitration or regional understandings like the Monroe doctrine, for securing the maintenance of peace.

Article 22

To those colonies and territories which, as a consequence of the late war, have ceased to be under the sovereignty of the States which formerly governed them, and which are inhabited by peoples not yet able to stand by themselves under the strenuous conditions of the modern world, there should be applied the principle that the well-being and development of such peoples form a sacred trust of civilisation, and that securities for the performance of this trust should be embodied in this Covenant.

The best method of giving practical effect to this principle is that the tutelage of such peoples should be entrusted to advanced nations who, by reason of their resources, their experience, or their geographical position can best undertake this responsibility, and who are willing to accept it, and that this tutelage should be exercised by them as Mandatories on behalf of the League.

The character of the mandate must differ according to the stage of the development of the people, the geographical situation of the territory, its economic conditions, and other similar circumstances.

Certain communities formerly belonging to the Turkish Empire have reached a stage of development where their existence as independent nations can be provisionally recognised subject to the rendering of administrative advice and assistance by a Mandatory until such time as they are able to stand alone. The wishes of these communities must be a principal consideration in the selection of the Mandatory.

Other peoples, especially those of Central Africa, are at such a stage that the Mandatory must be responsible for the administration of the territory under conditions which will guarantee freedom of conscience and religion, subject only to the maintenance of public order and morals, the prohibition of abuses such as the slave trade, the arms traffic, and the liquor traffic, and the prevention of the establishment of fortifications or military and naval bases and of military training of the natives for other than police purposes and the defence of territory, and will also secure equal opportunities for the trade and commerce of other Members of the League.

There are territories, such as South-West Africa and certain of the South Pacific Islands, which, owing to the sparseness of their population, or their small size, or their remoteness from the centres of civilization, or their geographical contiguity to the territory of the Mandatory, and other circumstances, can be best administered under the laws of the Mandatory as integral portions of its territory, subject to the safeguards above mentioned in the interests of the indigenous population.

In every case of mandate, the Mandatory shall render to the Council an annual report in reference to the territory committed to its charge.

The degree of authority, control, or administration to be exercised by the Mandatory shall, if not previously agreed upon by the Members of the League, be explicitly defined in each case by the Council.

A permanent Commission shall be constituted to receive and examine the annual reports of the Mandatories and to advise the Council on all matters relating to the observance of the mandates.

Article 23

Subject to and in accordance with the provisions of international conventions existing or hereafter to be agreed upon, the Members of the League:

(a) Will endeavour to secure and maintain fair and humane conditions of labour for men, women and children, both in their own countries and in all countries to which their commercial and industrial relations extend, and for that purpose will establish and maintain the necessary international organisations;

(b) Undertake to secure just treatment of the native inhabitants of territories under their control;

(c) Will entrust the League with the general supervision over the execution of agreements with regard to the traffic in women and children, and the traffic in opium and other dangerous drugs;

(d) Will entrust the League with the general supervision of the trade in arms and ammunition with the countries in which the control of this traffic is necessary in the common interest;

(e) Will make provision to secure and maintain freedom of communications and of transit and equitable treatment for the commerce of all Members of the League. In this connection, the special necessities of the regions devastated during the war of 1914–1918 shall be borne in mind;

(f) Will endeavour to take steps in matters of international concern for the prevention and control of disease.

Article 24

There shall be placed under the direction of the League all international bureaux already established by general treaties if the parties to such treaties consent. All such international bureaux and all commissions for the regulation of matters of international interest hereafter constituted shall be placed under the direction of the League.

In all matters of international interest which are regulated by general conventions, but which are not placed under the control of international bureaux or commissions, the Secretariat of the League shall, subject to the consent of the Council and if desired by the parties, collect and distribute all relevant information and shall render any other assistance which may be necessary or desirable.

The Council may include as part of the expenses of the Secretariat the expenses of any bureau or commission which is placed under the direction of the League.

Article 25

The Members of the League agree to encourage and promote the establishment and co-operation of duly authorised voluntary national Red Cross organisations having as purposes the improvement of health, the prevention of disease, and the mitigation of suffering throughout the world.

Article 26

Amendments to this Covenant will take effect when ratified by the Members of the League whose Representatives compose the Council and by a majority of the Members of the League whose Representatives compose the Assembly.

No such amendment shall bind any Member of the League which signifies its dissent therefrom, but in that case it shall cease to be a Member of the League.

Annex

Original Members of the League of Nations.
Signatories of the Treaty of Peace

United States of America	China
	Cuba
Belgium	Ecuador
Bolivia	France
Brazil	Greece
British Empire	Guatemala
Canada	Haiti
Australia	Hedjaz
South Africa	Honduras
New Zealand	Italy
India	Japan

Liberia	Roumania
Nicaragua	Serb-Croat-Slovene
Panama	State
Peru	Siam
Poland	Czecho-Slovakia
Portugal	Uruguay

States Invited to Accede to the Covenant

Argentine Republic	Persia
Chili	Salvador
Colombia	Spain
Denmark	Sweden
Netherlands	Switzerland
Norway	Venezuela
Paraguay	

PART II

BOUNDARIES OF GERMANY

Article 27

[The boundaries of Germany are determined in this article.]

Article 28

[The boundaries of East Prussia are determined in this article.]

Article 29

[This article specifies that the boundaries detailed in Articles 27-28 are drawn in red on a one-in-a-million map. The map was annexed to the original Treaty but is not included here.]

In the case of any discrepancies between the text of the Treaty and this map or any other map which may be annexed, the text will be final.

PART III

POLITICAL CLAUSES FOR EUROPE

Section I

Belgium

Article 31

Germany, recognising that the Treaties of April 19, 1839, which established the status of Belgium before the war, no longer conform to the requirements of the situation, consents to the abrogation of the said treaties and undertakes immediately to recognise and to observe whatever conventions may be entered into by the Principal Allied and Associated Powers, or by any of them, in concert with the Governments of Belgium and of the Netherlands, to replace the said Treaties of 1839. If her formal adhesion should be required to such conventions or to any of their stipulations, Germany undertakes immediately to give it.

Article 32

Germany recognises the full sovereignty of Belgium over the whole of the contested territory of Moresnet (called *Moresnet neutre*).

Article 35

A Commission of seven persons, five of whom will be appointed by the Principal Allied and Associated Powers, one by Germany and one by Belgium, will be set up fifteen days after the coming into force of the present Treaty to settle on the spot the new frontier line between Belgium and Germany, taking into account the economic factors and the means of communication.

Decisions will be taken by a majority and will be binding on the parties concerned.

Section III

Left Bank of the Rhine

Article 42 .

Germany is forbidden to maintain or construct any fortifications either on the left bank of the Rhine or on the right bank to the west of a line drawn 50 kilometres to the East of the Rhine.

Article 43

In the area defined above the maintenance and the assembly of armed forces, either permanently or temporarily, and military manoeuvres of any kind, as well as the upkeep of all permanent works for mobilisation, are in the same way forbidden.

Article 44

In case Germany violates in any manner whatever the provisions of Articles 42 and 43, she shall be regarded as committing a hostile act against the Powers signatory of the present Treaty and as calculated to disturb the peace of the world.

Section IV

Saar Basin

Article 45

As compensation for the destruction of the coal mines in the north of France and as part payment towards the total reparation due from Germany for the damage resulting from the war, Germany cedes to France in full and absolute possession, with exclusive rights of exploitation, unencumbered and free from all debts and charges of any kind, the coal mines situated in the Saar Basin as defined in Article 48.

Article 48

The boundaries of the territory of the Saar Basin, as dealt with in the present stipulations, [are fixed in this article].

Article 49

Germany renounces in favour of the League of Nations, in the capacity of trustee, the government of the territory defined above.

At the end of fifteen years from the coming into force of the present Treaty the inhabitants of the said territory shall be called upon to indicate the sovereignty under which they desire to be placed.

Section V

Alsace-Lorraine

The High Contracting Parties, recognising the moral obligation to redress the wrong done by Gemany in 1871 both to the rights of France and to the wishes of the population of Alsace and Lorraine, which were separated from their country in spite of the solemn protest of their representatives at the Assembly of Bordeaux,
Agree upon the following Articles:

Article 51

The territories which were ceded to Germany in accordance with the Preliminaries of Peace signed at Versailles on February 26, 1871, and the Treaty of Frankfort of May 10, 1871, are restored to French sovereignty as from the date of the Armistice of November 11, 1918.

The provisions of the Treaties establishing the delimitation of the frontiers before 1871 shall be restored.

Article 52

The German Government shall hand over without delay to the French Government all archives, registers, plans, titles and documents of every kind concerning the civil, military, financial, judicial or other administrations of the territories restored to French sovereignty. If any of these documents, archives, registers, titles, or plans have been misplaced, they will be restored by the German Government on the demand of the French Government.

Article 60

The German Government shall without delay restore to Alsace-Lorrainers (individuals, juridical persons, and public institutions) all property, rights and interests belonging to them on November 11, 1918, in so far as these are situated in German territory.

Article 66

The railway and other bridges across the Rhine now existing within the limits of Alsace-Lorraine shall, as to all their parts and their whole length, be the property of the French State, which shall ensure their upkeep.

Section VI

Austria

Article 80

Germany acknowledges and will respect strictly the independence of Austria, within the frontiers which may be fixed in a Treaty between that State and the Principal Allied and Associated Powers; she agrees that this independence shall be inalienable, except with the consent of the Council of the League of Nations.

Section VII

Czecho-Slovak State

Article 81

Germany, in conformity with the action already taken by the Allied and Associated Powers, recognises the complete independence of the Czecho-Slovak State, which will include the autonomous territory of the Ruthenians to the south of the Carpathians. Germany hereby recognises the frontiers of this State as determined by the Principal Allied and Associated Powers and the other interested States.

Article 82

The old frontier as it existed on August 3, 1914, between Austria-Hungary and the German Empire will constitute the frontier between Germany and the Czecho-Slovak State.

Article 83

Germany renounces in favour of the Czecho-Slovak State all rights and title over the portion of Silesian territory defined [in this article].

Article 84

German nationals habitually resident in any of the territories recognised as forming part of the Czecho-Slovak State will obtain Czecho-Slovak nationality *ipso facto* and lose their German nationality.

Section VIII

Poland

Article 87

Germany, in conformity with the action already taken by the Allied and Associated Powers, recognises the complete independence of Poland, and renounces in her favour all rights and title over the territory bounded by the Baltic Sea, the eastern frontier of Germany as laid down in Article 27 of Part II (Boundaries of Germany) of the present Treaty up to a point situated about 2 kilometres to the east of Lorzendorf, then a line to the acute angle which the northern boundary of Upper Silesia makes about 3 kilometres north-west of Simmenau, then the boundary of Upper Silesia to its meeting point with the old frontier between Germany and Russia, then this frontier to the point where it crosses the course of the Niemen, and then the northern frontier of East Prussia as laid down in Article 28 of Part II aforesaid.

The provisions of this Article do not, however, apply to the territories of East Prussia and the Free City of Danzig, as defined in Article 28 of Part II (Boundaries of Germany) and in Article 100 of Section XI (Danzig) of this Part.

The boundaries of Poland not laid down in the present Treaty will be subsequently determined by the Principal Allied and Associated Powers.

A Commission consisting of seven members, five of whom shall be nominated by the Principal Allied and Associated Powers, one by Germany and one by Poland, shall be constituted fifteen days after the coming into force of the present Treaty to delimit on the spot the frontier line between Poland and Germany.

The decisions of the Commission will be taken by a majority of votes and shall be binding upon the parties concerned.

Article 91

German nationals habitually resident in territories recognised as forming part of Poland will acquire Polish nationality *ipso facto* and will lose their German nationality.

German nationals, however, or their descendants who became resident in these territories after January 1, 1908, will not acquire Polish nationality without a special authorisation from the Polish State.

Within a period of two years after the coming into force of the present Treaty, German nationals over 18 years of age habitually resident in any of the territories recognised as forming part of Poland will be entitled to opt for German nationality.

Article 93

Poland accepts and agrees to embody in a Treaty with the Principal Allied and Associated Powers such provisions as may be deemed necessary by the said Powers to protect the interests of inhabitants of Poland who differ from the majority of the population in race, language, or religion.

Poland further accepts and agrees to embody in a Treaty with the said Powers such provisions as they may deem necessary to protect freedom of transit and equitable treatment of the commerce of other nations.

Section IX

East Prussia

Article 94

In the area between the southern frontier of East Prussia, as described in Article 28 of Part II (Boundaries of Germany) of the present Treaty, and the line described below, the inhabitants will be called upon to indicate by a vote the State to which they wish to belong:

the western and northern boundary of *Regierungsbezirk* Allenstein to its junction with the boundary between the *Kreise* of Oletsko and Angerburg; thence, the northern boundary of the *Kreis* of Oletsko to its junction with the old frontier of East Prussia.

Article 95

The German troops and authorities will be withdrawn from the area defined above within a period not exceeding fifteen days after the coming into force of the present Treaty. Until the evacuation is completed they will abstain from all requisitions in money or in kind and from all measures injurious to the economic interests of the country. [. . .]

Article 98

Germany and Poland undertake, within one year of the coming into force of this Treaty, to enter into Conventions of which the terms, in case of difference, shall be settled by the Council of the League of Nations, with the object of securing, on the one hand, to Germany full and adequate railroad, telegraphic and telephonic facilities for communication between the rest of Germany and East Prussia over the intervening Polish territory, and, on the other hand, to Poland full and adequate railroad, telegraphic and telephonic facilities for communication between Poland and the Free City of Danzig over any German territory that may, on the right bank of the Vistula, intervene between Poland and the Free City of Danzig.

Section XI

Free City of Danzig

Article 101

A Commission composed of three members appointed by the Principal Allied and Associated Powers, including a High Commissioner as President, one member appointed by Germany, and one member appointed by Poland, shall be constituted within fifteen days of the coming into force of the present Treaty for the purpose of delimiting on the spot the frontier of the territory as described above, taking into account as far as possible the existing communal boundaries.

Article 102

The Principal Allied and Associated Powers undertake to establish the town of Danzig ... as a Free City. It will be placed under the protection of the League of Nations.

Article 103

A constitution for the Free City of Danzig shall be drawn up by the duly appointed representatives of the Free City in agreement with a High Commissioner to be appointed by the League of Nations. This constitution shall be placed under the guarantee of the League of Nations.

The High Commissioner will also be entrusted with the duty of dealing in the first instance with all differences arising between Poland and the Free City of Danzig in regard to this Treaty or any arrangements or agreements made thereunder.

The High Commissioner shall reside at Danzig.

Section XII

Schleswig

Article 109

The frontier between Germany and Denmark shall be fixed in conformity with the wishes of the population. [...]

Section XIII

Heligoland

Article 115

The fortifications, military establishments, and harbours of the Islands of Heligoland and Dune

shall be destroyed under the supervision of the Principal Allied Governments by German labour and at the expense of Germany within a period to be determined by the said Governments.

The term "harbours" shall include the north-east mole, the west wall, the outer and inner breakwaters and reclaimed land within them, and all naval and military works, fortifications and buildings, constructed or under construction, between lines connecting the following positions taken from the British Admiralty chart No. 126 of April 19, 1918:

(a) lat. 54° 10′ 49″ N.; long. 7° 53′ 39″ E.;

(b) lat. 54° 10′ 35″ N.; long. 7° 54′ 18″ E.;

(c) lat. 54° 10′ 14″ N.; long. 7° 54′ 00″ E.;

(d) lat. 54° 10′ 17″ N.; long. 7° 53′ 37″ E.;

(e) lat. 54° 10′ 44″ N.; long. 7° 53′ 26″ E.

These fortifications, military establishments and harbours shall not be reconstructed; nor shall any similar works be constructed in future.

Section XIV

Russia and Russian States

Article 116

Germany acknowledges and agrees to respect as permanent and inalienable the independence of all the territories which were part of the former Russian Empire on August 1, 1914.

... Germany accepts definitely the abrogation of the Brest-Litovsk Treaties and of all other treaties, conventions and agreements entered into by her with the Maximalist Government in Russia.

The Allied and Associated Powers formally reserve the rights of Russia to obtain from Germany restitution and reparation based on the principles of the present Treaty.

PART IV

GERMAN RIGHTS AND INTERESTS OUTSIDE GERMANY

Article 118

In territory outside her European frontiers as fixed by the present Treaty, Germany renounces all rights, titles and privileges whatever in or over territory which belonged to her or to her allies, and all rights, titles and privileges whatever their origin which she held as against the Allied and Associated Powers.

Germany hereby undertakes to recognise and to conform to the measures which may be taken now or in the future by the Principal Allied and Associated Powers, in agreement where necessary with third

Powers, in order to carry the above stipulation into effect.

In particular Germany declares her acceptance of the following Articles relating to certain special subjects.

Section I

German Colonies

Article 119

Germany renounces in favour of the Principal Allied and Associated Powers all her rights and titles over her oversea possessions.

Article 120

All movable and immovable property in such territories belonging to the German Empire or to any German State shall pass to the Government exercising authority over such territories . . . . The decision of the local courts in any dispute as to the nature of such property shall be final.

Section II

China

Article 128

Germany renounces in favour of China all benefits and privileges resulting from the provisions of the final Protocol signed at Peking on September 7, 1901, and from all annexes, notes and documents supplementary thereto. She likewise renounces in favour of China any claim to indemnities accruing thereunder subsequent to March 14, 1917.

Section V

Morocco

Article 141

Germany renounces all rights, titles and privileges conferred on her by the General Act of Algeciras of April 7, 1906, and by the Franco-German Agreements of February 9, 1909, and November 4, 1911. All treaties, agreements, arrangements and contracts concluded by her with the Sherifian Empire are regarded as abrogated as from August 3, 1914.

In no case can Germany take advantage of these instruments and she undertakes not to intervene in any way in negotiations relating to Morocco which may take place between France and the other Powers.

Article 142

Germany having recognised the French Protectorate in Morocco, hereby accepts all the consequences of its establishment, and she renounces the régime of the capitulations therein.

This renunciation shall take effect as from August 3, 1914.

Section VI

Egypt

Article 147

Germany declares that she recognises the Protectorate proclaimed over Egypt by Great Britain on December 18, 1914, and that she renounces the régime of the Capitulations in Egypt.

This renunciation shall take effect as from August 4, 1914.

Section VIII

Shantung

Article 156

Germany renounces, in favour of Japan, all her rights, title and privileges—particularly those concerning the territory of Kiaochow, mines and submarine cables—which she acquired in virtue of the Treaty concluded by her with China on March 6, 1898, and of all other arrangements relative to the Province of Shantung.

All German rights in the Tsingtao-Tsinanfu Railway, including its branch lines, together with its subsidiary property of all kinds, stations, shops, fixed and rolling stock, mines, plant and material for the exploitation of the mines, are and remain acquired by Japan, together with all rights and privileges attaching thereto.

The German State submarine cables from Tsingtao to Shanghai and from Tsingtao to Chefoo, with all the rights, privileges and properties attaching thereto, are similarly acquired by Japan, free and clear of all charges and encumbrances.

PART V

MILITARY, NAVAL AND AIR CLAUSES

In order to render possible the initiation of a general limitation of the armaments of all nations, Germany undertakes strictly to observe the military, naval and air clauses which follow.

Section I

Military Clauses

Chapter I

Effectives and Cadres of the German Army

Article 159

The German military forces shall be demobilised and reduced as prescribed hereinafter.

Article 160

1. By a date which must not be later than March 31, 1920, the German Army must not comprise more than seven divisions of infantry and three divisions of cavalry.

After that date the total number of effectives in the Army of the States constituting Germany must not exceed one hundred thousand men, including officers and establishments of depots. The Army shall be devoted exclusively to the maintenance of order within the territory and to the control of the frontiers.

The total effective strength of officers, including the personnel of staffs, whatever their composition, must not exceed four thousand.

2. Divisions and Army Corps headquarters staffs shall be organised in accordance with Table No. 1 . . . . [The table was annexed to this Section of the original Treaty but is not included here.]

The number and strengths of the units of infantry, artillery, engineers, technical services and troops laid down in the aforesaid Table constitute maxima which must not be exceeded.

The following units may each have their own depot:

An Infantry regiment;

A Cavalry regiment;

A regiment of Field Artillery;

A battalion of Pioneers.

3. The divisions must not be grouped under more than two army corps headquarters staffs.

The maintenance or formation of forces differently grouped or of other organisations for the command of troops or for preparation for war is forbidden.

The Great German General Staff and all similar organisations shall be dissolved and may not be reconstituted in any form.

The officers, or persons in the position of officers, in the Ministries of War in the different States in Germany and in the Administrations attached to them, must not exceed three hundred in number, and are included in the maximum strength of four thousand laid down in the third sub-paragraph of paragraph (1) of this Article.

Article 163

[How the reduction in strength of the German military forces provided for in Article 160 is to be effected.]

Chapter II

Armament, Munitions and Material

Article 164

Up till the time at which Germany is admitted as a member of the League of Nations, the German Army must not possess an armament greater than the amounts fixed in Table No. II [the table was annexed to this Section of the original Treaty but is not included here] . . . with the exception of an optional increase not exceeding one-twenty-fifth part for small arms and one-fiftieth part for guns, which shall be exclusively used to provide for such eventual replacements as may be necessary.

Germany agrees that after she has become a member of the League of Nations the armaments fixed in the said Table shall remain in force until they are modified by the Council of the League. Furthermore, she hereby agrees strictly to observe the decisions of the Council of the League on this subject.

[*Articles 165–167* specify the number of armaments and stock of munitions that Germany is allowed to maintain.]

Article 168

The manufacture of arms, munitions, or any war material, shall only be carried out in factories or works the location of which shall be communicated to and approved by the Governments of the Principal Allied and Associated Powers, and the number of which they retain the right to restrict.

Within three months from the coming into force of the present Treaty, all other establishments for the manufacture, preparation, storage or design of arms, munitions, or any war material whatever shall be closed down. The same applies to all arsenals except those used as depots for the authorised stocks of munitions. Within the same period the personnel of these arsenals will be dismissed.

Article 170

Importation into Germany of arms, munitions and war material of every kind shall be strictly prohibited.

The same applies to the manufacture for, and export to, foreign countries of arms, munitions and war material of every kind.

Chapter III

Recruiting and Military Training

Article 173

Universal compulsory military service shall be abolished in Germany.

The German Army may only be constituted and recruited by means of voluntary enlistment.

Article 177

Educational establishments, the universities, societies of discharged soldiers, shooting or touring clubs, and, generally speaking, associations of every description, whatever be the age of their members, must not occupy themselves with any military matters.

In particular they will be forbidden to instruct or exercise their members, or to allow them to be instructed or exercised, in the profession or use of arms.

These societies, associations, educational establishments and universities must have no connection with the Ministries of War or any other military authority.

Article 179

Germany agrees, from the coming into force of the present Treaty, not to accredit nor to send to any foreign country any military, naval or air mission, nor to allow any such mission to leave her territory, and Germany further agrees to take appropriate measures to prevent German nationals from leaving her territory to become enrolled in the Army, Navy or Air Service of any foreign Power, or to be attached to such Army, Navy or Air service for the purpose of assisting in the military, naval or air training thereof, or otherwise for the purpose of giving military, naval or air instruction in any foreign country.

The Allied and Associated Powers agree, so far as they are concerned, from the coming into force of the present Treaty not to enrol in nor to attach to their armies or naval or air forces any German national for the purpose of assisting in the military training of such armies, or naval or air forces, or otherwise to employ any such German national as military, naval or aeronautic instructor.

The present provision does not, however, affect the right of France to recruit for the Foreign Legion in accordance with French military laws and regulations.

Chapter IV

Fortifications

Article 180

All fortified works, fortresses and field works situated in German territory to the west of a line drawn fifty kilometres to the east of the Rhine shall be disarmed and dismantled.

Within a period of two months from the coming into force of the present Treaty such of the above fortified works fortresses and field works as are situated in territory not occupied by Allied and Associated troops shall be disarmed, and within a further period of four months they shall be dismantled. Those which are situated in territory occupied by Allied and Associated troops shall by disarmed and dismantled within such periods as may be fixed by the Allied High Command.

The construction of any new fortification, whatever its nature and importance, is forbidden in the zone referred to in the first paragraph above.

The system of fortified works of the southern and eastern frontiers of Germany shall be maintained in its existing state.

Section II

Naval Clauses

Article 181

After the expiration of a period of two months from the coming into force of the present Treaty the German naval forces in commission must not exceed:

> 6 battleships of the *Deutschland* or *Lothringen* type,
>
> 6 light cruisers,
>
> 12 destroyers,
>
> 12 torpedo boats,

or an equal number of ships constructed to replace them as provided in Article 190.

No submarines are to be included.

All other warships, except where there is provision to the contrary in the present Treaty, must be placed in reserve or devoted to commercial purposes.

Article 183

After the expiration of a period of two months from the coming into force of the present Treaty the total personnel of the German Navy, including the manning of the fleet, coast defences, signal stations, administration and other land services, must not exceed fifteen thousand, including officers and men of all grades and corps.

The total strength of officers and warrant officers must not exceed fifteen hundred.

Within two months from the coming into force of the present Treaty the personnel in excess of the above strength shall be demobilised.

No naval or military corps or reserve force in connection with the Navy may be organised in Germany without being included in the above strength.

Article 184

From the date of the coming into force of the present Treaty all the German surface warships which are not in German ports cease to belong to Germany, who renounces all rights over them.

Vessels which, in compliance with the Armistice of November 11, 1918, are now interned in the ports of the Allied and Associated Powers, are declared to be finally surrendered.

Vessels which are now interned in neutral ports will be there surrendered to the Governments of the Principal Allied and Associated Powers. The German Government must address a notification to that effect to the neutral Powers on the coming into force of the present Treaty.

Article 188

On the expiration of one month from the coming into force of the present Treaty all German submarines, submarine salvage vessels, and docks for submarines, including the tubular dock, must have been handed over to the Governments of the Principal Allied and Associated Powers.

Such of these submarines, vessels and docks as are considered by the said Governments to be fit to proceed under their own power or to be towed shall be taken by the German Government into such Allied ports as have been indicated.

The remainder, and also those in course of construction, shall be broken up entirely by the German Government under the supervision of the said Governments. The breaking-up must be completed within three months at the most after the coming into force of the present Treaty.

Article 190

Germany is forbidden to construct or acquire any warships other than those intended to replace the units in commission provided for in Article 181 of the present Treaty.

The warships intended for replacement purposes as above shall not exceed the following displacement:

Armoured ships	10,000 tons,
Light cruisers	6,000 tons,
Destroyers	800 tons,
Torpedo boats	200 tons.

Article 191

The construction or acquisition of any submarine, even for commercial purposes, shall be forbidden in Germany.

Article 195

In order to ensure free passage into the Baltic to all nations, Germany shall not erect any fortifications in the area comprised between latitudes 55° 27′ N. and 54° 00′N. and longitudes 9° 00′ E. and 16° 00′

E. of the meridian of Greenwich, nor instal any guns commanding the maritime routes between the North Sea and the Baltic. The fortifications now existing in this area shall be demolished and the guns removed under the supervision of the Allied Governments and in periods to be fixed by them. [...]

Section III

Air Clauses

Article 198

The armed forces of Germany must not include any military or naval air forces.

Germany may, during a period not extending beyond October 1, 1919, maintain a maximum number of one hundred seaplanes or flying boats, which shall be exclusively employed in searching for submarine mines, shall be furnished with the necessary equipment for this purpose, and shall in no case carry arms, munitions or bombs of any nature whatever.

In addition to the engines installed in the seaplanes or flying boats above mentioned, one spare engine may be provided for each engine of each of these craft.

No dirigible shall be kept.

Article 199

Within two months from the coming into force of the present Treaty the personnel of the air forces on the rolls of the German land and sea forces shall be demolished. Up to October 1, 1919, however, Germany may keep and maintain a total number of one thousand men, including officers, for the whole of the cadres and personnel, flying and non-flying, of all formations and establishments.

Article 200

Until the complete evacuation of German territory by the Allied and Associated troops, the aircraft of the Allied and Associated Powers shall enjoy in Germany freedom of passage through the air, freedom of transit and of landing.

Article 201

During the six months following the coming into force of the present Treaty, the manufacture and importation of aircraft, parts of aircraft, engines for aircraft, and parts of engines for aircraft, shall be forbidden in all German territory.

Section IV

Inter-Allied Commissions of Control

Article 203

All the military, naval and air clauses contained in the present Treaty, for the execution of which a time-limit is prescribed, shall be executed by Germany under the control of Inter-Allied Commissions specially appointed for this purpose by the Principal Allied and Associated Powers.

Article 204

The Inter-Allied Commissions of Control will be specially charged with the duty of seeing to the complete execution of the delivery, destruction, demolition and rendering things useless to be carried out at the expense of the German Government in accordance with the present Treaty.

They will communicate to the German authorities the decisions which the Principal Allied and Associated Powers have reserved the right to take, or which the execution of the military, naval and air clauses may necessitate.

Article 207

The upkeep and cost of the Commissions of Control and the expenses involved by their work shall be borne by Germany.

PART VI

PRISONERS OF WAR AND GRAVES

Section I

Prisoners of War

Article 214

The repatriation of prisoners of war and interned civilians shall take place as soon as possible after the coming into force of the present Treaty, and shall be carried out with the greatest rapidity.

Article 215

The repatriation of German prisoners of war and interned civilians shall, in accordance with Article 214, be carried out by a Commission composed of representatives of the Allied and Associated Powers on the one part and of the German Government on the other part.

For each of the Allied and Associated Powers a Sub-Commission, composed exclusively of Representatives of the interested Power and of Delegates of the German Government, shall regulate the details of carrying into effect the repatriation of the prisoners of war.

Article 217

The whole cost of repatriation from the moment of starting shall be borne by the German Government, who shall also provide the land and sea transport and staff considered necessary by the Commission referred to in Article 215.

Section II

Graves

Article 225

The Allied and Associated Governments and the German Government will cause to be respected and maintained the graves of the soldiers and sailors buried in their respective territories. [. . .]

Article 226

The graves of prisoners of war and interned civilians who are nationals of the different belligerent States and have died in captivity shall be properly maintained in accordance with Article 225 of the present Treaty.

The Allied and Associated Governments on the one part and the German Government on the other part reciprocally undertake also to furnish to each other:

(1) A complete list of those who have died, together with all information useful for identification;

(2) All information as to the number and position of the graves of all those who have been buried without identification.

PART VII

PENALTIES

Article 227

The Allied and Associated Powers publicly arraign William II of Hohenzollern, formerly German Emperor, for a supreme offence against international morality and the sanctity of treaties.

A special tribunal will be constituted to try the accused, thereby assuring him the guarantees essential to the right of defence. It will be composed of five judges, one appointed by each of the following Powers: namely, the United States of America, Great Britain, France, Italy and Japan.

In its decision the tribunal will be guided by the highest motives of international policy, with a view to vindicating the solemn obligations of international undertakings and the validity of international morality. It will be its duty to fix the punishment which it considers should be imposed.

The Allied and Associated Powers will address a request to the Government of the Netherlands for the surrender to them of the ex-Emperor in order that he may be put on trial.

Article 228

The German Government recognises the right of the Allied and Associated Powers to bring before military tribunals persons accused of having committed acts in violation of the laws and customs of war. Such persons shall, if found guilty, be sentenced to punishments laid down by law. This provision will apply notwithstanding any proceedings or prosecution before a tribunal in Germany or in the territory of her allies.

The German Government shall hand over to the Allied and Associated Powers, or to such one of them as shall so request, all persons accused of having committed an act in violation of the laws and customs of war, who are specified either by name or by the rank, office or employment which they held under the German authorities.

Article 229

Persons guilty of criminal acts against the nationals of one of the Allied and Associated Powers will be brought before the military tribunals of that Power.

Persons guilty of criminal acts against the nationals of more than one of the Allied and Associated Powers will be brought before military tribunals composed of members of the military tribunals of the Powers concerned.

In every case the accused will be entitled to name his own counsel.

PART VIII

REPARATION

Section I

General Provisions

Article 231

The Allied and Associated Governments affirm and Germany accepts the responsibility of Germany and her allies for causing all the loss and damage to which the Allied and Associated Governments and their nationals have been subjected as a consequence of the war imposed upon them by the aggression of Germany and her allies.

Article 232

The Allied and Associated Governments recognise that the resources of Germany are not adequate, after taking into account permanent diminutions of such resources which will result from other provisions of the present Treaty, to make complete reparation for all such loss and damage.

The Allied and Associated Governments, however, require, and Germany undertakes, that she will make compensation for all damage done to the civilian population of the Allied and Associated Powers and to their property during the period of the belligerency of each as an Allied or Associated Power against Germany by such aggression by land, by sea, and from the air, and in general all damage as defined in Annex 1 hereto [not included here]. . . .

Article 233

The amount of the above damage for which compensation is to be made by Germany shall be determined by an Inter-Allied Commissioned, to be called the *Reparation Commission* and constituted in the form and with the powers set forth hereunder and in Annexes II to VII inclusive hereto [not included here]. . . .

Article 235

In order to enable the Allied and Associated Powers to proceed at once to the restoration of their industrial and economic life, pending the full determination of their claims, Germany shall pay in such instalments and in such manner (whether in gold, commodities, ships, securities or otherwise) as the Reparation Commission may fix, during 1919, 1920, and the first four months of 1921, the equivalent of 20,000,000,000 gold marks. Out of this sum the expenses of the armies of occupation subsequent to the Armistice of November 11, 1918, shall first be met, and such supplies of food and raw materials as may be judged by the Governments of the Principal Allied and Associated Powers to be essential to enable Germany to meet her obligations for reparation may also, with the approval of the said Governments, be paid for out of the above sum. The balance shall be reckoned towards liquidation of the amounts due for reparation. Germany shall further deposit bonds as prescribed in paragraph 12 (*c*) of Annex II hereto.

Article 238

In addition to the payments mentioned above, Germany shall effect, in accordance with the procedure laid down by the Reparation Commission, restitution in cash of cash taken away, seized or sequestrated, and also restitution of animals, objects of every nature and securities taken away, seized or sequestrated, in the cases in which it proves possible to identify them in territory belonging to Germany or her allies. [. . .]

PART IX

FINANCIAL CLAUSES

Article 248

Subject to such exceptions as the Reparation Commission may approve, a first charge upon all the assets and revenues of the German Empire and its constituent States shall be the cost of reparation and all other costs arising under the present Treaty or any treaties or agreements supplementary thereto or under arrangements concluded between Germany and the Allied and Associated Powers during the Armistice or its extensions.

Up to May 1, 1921, the German Government shall not export or dispose of, and shall forbid the export or disposal of, gold without the previous approval of the Allied and Associated Powers acting through the Reparation Commission.

Article 249

There shall be paid by the German Government the total cost of all armies of the Allied and Associated Governments in occupied German territory from the date of the signature of the Armistice of November 11, 1918, including the keep of men and beasts, lodging and billeting, pay and allowances, salaries and wages, bedding, heating, lighting, clothing, equipment, harness and saddlery, armament and rolling-stock, air services, treatment of sick and wounded, veterinary and remount services, transport service of all sorts (such as by rail, sea or river, motor lorries), communications and correspondence, and in general the cost of all administrative or technical services the working of which is necessary for the training of troops and for keeping their numbers up to strength and preserving their military efficiency. [. . .]

PART X

ECONOMIC CLAUSES

Section I

Commercial Relations

Chapter I

Customs, Regulations, Duties and Restrictions

Article 264

Germany undertakes that goods the produce or manufacture of any one of the Allied or Associated States imported into German territory, from whatsoever place arriving, shall not be subject to other or higher duties or charges (including internal charges) than those to which the like goods the produce or manufacture of any other such State or of any other foreign country are subject.

Germany will not maintain or impose any prohibition or restriction on the importation into German territory of any goods the produce of manufacture of the territories of any one of the Allied or Associated States, from whatsoever place arriving which shall not equally extend to the importation of the like goods the produce or manufacture of any other such State or of any other foreign country.

PART XI

AERIAL NAVIGATION

Article 313

The aircraft of the Allied and Associated Powers shall have full liberty of passage and landing over and in the territory and territorial waters of Germany, and shall enjoy the same privileges as German aircraft, particularly in case of distress by land or sea.

Article 314

The aircraft of the Allied and Associated Powers shall, while in transit to any foreign country whatever, enjoy the right of flying over the territory and territorial waters of Germany without landing, subject always to any regulations which may be made by Germany, and which shall be applicable equally to the aircraft of Germany and to those of the Allied and Associated countries.

Article 315

All aerodromes in Germany open to national public traffic shall be open for the aircraft of the Allied and Associated Powers, and in any such aerodrome such aircraft shall be treated on a footing of equality with German aircraft as regards charges of every description, including charges for landing and accommodation.

PART XII

PORTS, WATERWAYS AND RAILWAYS

Section I

General Provisions

Article 321

Germany undertakes to grant freedom of transit through her territories on the routes most convenient for international transit, either by rail, navigable waterway, or canal, to persons, goods, vessels, carriages, wagons and mails coming from or going to the territories of any of the Allied and Associated Powers (whether contiguous or not); for this purpose the crossing of territorial waters shall be allowed. Such persons, goods, vessels, carriages, wagons and mails shall not be subjected to any transit duty or to any undue delays or restrictions, and shall be entitled in Germany to national treatment as regards charges, facilities, and all other matters.

Goods in transit shall be exempt from all Customs or other similar duties.

Section II

Navigation

Chapter I

Freedom of Navigation

Article 327

The nationals of any of the Allied and Associated Powers as well as their vessels and property shall enjoy in all German ports and on the inland navigation routes of Germany the same treatment in all respects as German nationals, vessels and property. [. . .]

Chapter III

Clauses Relating to the Elbe, the Oder, the Niemen (Russstrom-Memel-Niemen) and the Danube

Article 331

The following rivers are declared international:

the Elbe (*Labe*) from its confluence with the Vltava (*Moldau*) and the Vltava (*Moldau*) from Prague;

the Oder (*Odra*) from its confluence with the Oppa;

the Niemen (*Russstrom-Memel-Niemen*) from Grodno;

the Danube from Ulm;

and all navigable parts of these river systems which naturally provide more than one State with access to the sea, with or without transhipment from one vessel to another; together with lateral canals and channels constructed either to duplicate or to improve naturally navigable sections of the specified river systems, or to connect two naturally navigable sections of the same river.

Section III

Railways

Chapter I

Clauses relating to International Transport

Article 365

Goods coming from the territories of the Allied and Associated Powers, and going to Germany, or in transit through Germany from or to the territories of the Allied and Associated Powers, shall enjoy on the German railways as regards charges to be collected (rebates and drawbacks being taken into account), facilities and all other matters, the most favourable treatment applied to goods of the same kind carried on any German lines, either in internal traffic, or for export, import or in transit, under similar conditions of transport, for example as regards length of route. The same rule shall be applied, on the request of one or more of the Allied and Associated Powers, to goods specially designated by such Power or Powers coming from Germany and going to their territories. [. . .]

Chapter IV

Provisions Relating to Certain Railway Lines

Article 372

When as a result of the fixing of new frontiers a railway connection between two parts of the same country crosses another country, or a branch line from one country has its terminus in another, the conditions of working, if not specifically provided for in the present Treaty, shall be laid down in a convention between the railway administrations concerned. If the administrations cannot come to an agreement as to the terms of such convention the points of difference shall be decided by commissions of experts composed as provided in the preceding article.

Section IV

Disputes and Revision of Permanent Clauses

Article 376

Disputes which may arise between interested Powers, with regard to the interpretation and application of the preceding Articles shall be settled as provided by the League of Nations.

Article 377

At any time the League of Nations may recommend the revision of such of these Articles as relate to a permanent administrative régime.

Section VI

Clauses Relating to the Kiel Canal

Article 380

The Kiel Canal and its approaches shall be maintained free and open to the vessels of commerce and of war of all nations at peace with Germany on terms of entire equality.

PART XIII

LABOUR

Section I

Organisation of Labour

Whereas the League of Nations has for its object the establishment of universal peace, and such a peace can be established only if it is based upon social justice;

And whereas conditions of labour exist involving such injustice, hardship and privation to large numbers of people as to produce unrest so great that the peace and harmony of the world are imperilled; and an improvement of those conditions is urgently required: as, for example, by the regulation of the hours of work, including the establishment of a maximum working day and week, the regulation of the labour supply, the prevention of unemployment, the provision of an adequate living wage, the protection of the worker against sickness, disease and injury arising out of his employment, the protection of children, young persons and women, provision for old age and injury, protection of the interests of workers when employed in countries other than their own, recognition of the principle of freedom of association, the organisation of vocational and technical education and other measures.

Whereas also the failure of any nation to adopt humane conditions of labour is an obstacle in the way of other nations which desire to improve the conditions in their own countries;

The High Contracting Parties, moved by sentiments of justice and humanity, as well as by the desire to secure the permanent peace of the world, agree to the following:

Chapter I

Organisation

Article 387

A permanent organisation is hereby established for the promotion of the objects set forth in the Preamble.

The original Members of the League of Nations shall be the original Members of this organisation, and hereafter membership of the League of Nations shall carry with it membership of the said organisation.

Article 388

The permanent organisation shall consist of:

(1) a General Conference of Representatives of the Members and,

(2) an International Labour Office controlled by the Governing Body described in Article 393.

Article 392

The International Labour Office shall be established at the seat of the League of Nations as part of the organisation of the League.

[*Articles 393–397* specify the direction, organisation, and functions of the International Labour Office.]

[*Articles 400–420* specify the procedures for the functioning of the International Labour Office.]

Section II

General Principles

Article 427

The High Contracting Parties, recognising that the well-being, physical, moral and intellectual, of industrial wage-earners is of supreme international importance, have framed, in order to further this great end, the permanent machinery provided for in Section I and associated with that of the League of Nations.

They recognise that differences of climate, habits and customs, of economic opportunity and industrial tradition, make strict uniformity in the conditions of labour difficult of immediate attainment. But, holding as they do, that labour should not be regarded merely as an article of commerce, they think that there are methods and principles for regulating labour conditions which all industrial communities should endeavour to apply so far as their special circumstances will permit.

Among these methods and principles, the following seem to the High Contracting Parties to be of special and urgent importance:

First—The guiding principle above enunciated that labour should not be regarded merely as a commodity or article of commerce.

Second—The right of association for all lawful purposes by the employed as well as by the employers.

Third—The payment to the employed of a wage adequate to maintain a reasonable standard of life as this is understood in their time and country.

Fourth—The adoption of an eight hours day or a forty-eight hours week as the standard to be aimed at where it has not already been attained.

Fifth—The adoption of weekly rest of at least twenty-four hours, which should include Sunday wherever practicable.

Sixth—The abolition of child labour and the imposition of such limitations on the labour of young persons as shall permit the continuation of their education and assure their proper physical development.

Seventh—The principle that men and women should receive equal remuneration for work of equal value.

Eighth—The standard set by law in each country with respect to the conditions of labour should have due regard to the equitable economic treatment of all workers lawfully resident therein.

Ninth—Each State should make provision for a system of inspection in which women should take part, in order to ensure the enforcement of the laws and regulations for the protection of the employed.

Without claiming that these methods and principles are either complete or final, the High Contracting Parties are of opinion that they are well fitted to guide the policy of the League of Nations; and that, if adopted by the industrial communities who are members of the League, and safeguarded in practice by an adequate system of such inspection, they will confer lasting benefits upon the wage-earners of the world.

PART XIV

GUARANTEES

Section I

Western Europe

Article 428

As a guarantee for the execution of the present Treaty by Germany, the German territory situated to the west of the Rhine together with the bridgeheads, will be occupied by Allied and Associated troops for a period of fifteen years from the coming into force of the present Treaty.

Section II

Eastern Europe

Article 433

As a guarantee for the execution of the provisions of the present Treaty, by which Germany accepts definitely the abrogation of the Brest-Litovsk Treaty, and of all treaties, conventions and agreements entered into by her with the Maximalist Government in Russia, and in order to ensure the restoration of peace and good government in the Baltic Provinces and Lithuania, all German troops at present in the said territories shall return to within the frontiers of Germany as soon as the Governments of the Princi-

pal Allied and Associated Powers shall think the moment suitable, having regard to the internal situation of these territories. These troops shall abstain from all requisitions and seizures and from any other coercive measures, with a view to obtaining supplies intended for Germany, and shall in no way interfere with such measures for national defence as may be adopted by the Provisional Governments of Esthonia, Latvia and Lithuania.

No other German troops shall, pending the evacuation or after the evacuation is complete, be admitted to the said territories.

PART XV

MISCELLANEOUS PROVISIONS

Article 434

Germany undertakes to recognise the full force of the Treaties of Peace and Additional Conventions which may be concluded by the Allied and Associated Powers with the Powers who fought on the side of Germany and to recognise whatever dispositions may be made concerning the territories of the former Austro-Hungarian Monarchy, of the Kingdom of Bulgaria and of the Ottoman Empire, and to recognise the new States within the frontiers as there laid down.

The Present Treaty, of which the French and English texts are both authentic, shall be ratified.

The deposit of ratifications shall be made at Paris as soon as possible.

Powers of which the seat of the Government is outside Europe will be entitled merely to inform the Government of the French Republic through their diplomatic representative at Paris that their ratification has been given; in that case they must transmit the instrument of ratification as soon as possible.

A first procès-verbal of the deposit of ratifications will be drawn up as soon as the Treaty has been ratified by Germany on the one hand, and by three of the Principal Allied and Associated Powers on the other hand.

From the date of this first procès-verbal the Treaty will come into force between the High Contracting Parties who have ratified it. For the determination of all periods of time provided for in the present Treaty this date will be the date of the coming into force of the Treaty.

In all other respects the Treaty will enter into force for each Power at the date of the deposit of its ratification.

The French Government will transmit to all the signatory Powers a certified copy of the procès-verbaux of the deposit of ratifications.

Treaty Concerning the Archipelago of Spitsbergen

Date of signature: *February 9, 1920*
Place of signature: *Paris*
Signatory states: *the United States, Great Britain, Ireland and the British Dominions, India, Denmark, the French Republic, Italy, Japan, Norway, the Netherlands, Sweden*

[The Signatories]
Desirous, while recognising the sovereignty of Norway over the Archipelago of Spitsbergen, including Bear Island, of seeing these territories provided with an equitable regime, in order to assure their development and peaceful utilisation, ... have agreed as follows:

Article 1

The High Contracting Parties undertake to recognise, subject to the stipulations of the present Treaty, the full and absolute sovereignty of Norway over the Archipelago of Spitsbergen, comprising, with Bear Island or Beeren-Eiland, all the islands situated between 10° and 35° longitude East of Greenwich and between 74° and 81° latitude North, especially West Spitsbergen, North-East Land, Barents Island, Edge Island, Wiche Islands, Hope Island or Hopen-Eiland, and Prince Charles Foreland, together with all islands great or small and rocks appertaining thereto.

Article 2

Ships and nationals of all the High Contracting Parties shall enjoy equally the rights of fishing and hunting in the territories specified in article 1 and in their territorial waters.

Norway shall be free to maintain, take or decree suitable measures to ensure the preservation and, if necessary, the re-constitution of the fauna and flora of the said regions, and their territorial waters; it being clearly understood that these measures shall always be applicable equally to the nationals of all the High Contracting Parties without any exemption, privilege or favour whatsoever, direct or indirect to the advantage of any one of them.

Occupiers of land whose rights have been recognised in accordance with the terms of Articles 6 and 7 will enjoy the exclusive right of hunting on their own land: (1) in the neighbourhood of their habitations, houses, stores, factories and installations, constructed for the purpose of developing their property, under conditions laid down by the local police regulations; (2) within a radius of 10 kilometres round the head-quarters of their place of business or works; and in both cases, subject always to the observance of regulations made by the Norwegian Government in accordance with the conditions laid down in the present Article.

Article 3

The nationals of all the High Contracting Parties shall have equal liberty of access and entry for any reason or object whatever to the waters, fjords and ports of the territories specified in Article 1; subject to the observance of local laws and regulations, they may carry on there without impediment all maritime, industrial, mining and commercial operations on a footing of absolute equality.

They shall be admitted under the same conditions of equality to the exercise and practice of all maritime, industrial, mining or commercial enterprises both on land and in territorial waters, and no monopoly shall be established on any account or for any enterprise whatever.

Notwithstanding any rules relating to coasting trade which may be in force in Norway, ships of the High Contracting Parties going to or coming from the territories specified in Article 1 shall have the right to put into Norwegian ports on their outward or homeward voyage for the purpose of taking on board or disembarking passengers or cargo going to or coming from the said territories, or for any other purpose.

It is agreed that in every respect and especially with regard to exports, imports and transit traffic, the nationals of all the High Contracting Parties, their ships and goods shall not be subject to any charges or restrictions whatever which are not borne by the nationals, ships or goods which enjoy in Norway the treatment of the most favoured nation; Norwegian nationals, ships or goods being for this purpose assimilated to those of the other High Contracting Parties, and not treated more favourably in any respect.

No charge or restriction shall be imposed on the exportation of any goods to the territories of any of the Contracting Powers other or more onerous than on the exportation of similar goods to the territory of any other Contracting Power (including Norway) or to any other destination.

Article 4

All public wireless stations established or to be established by or with the authorisation of, the Norwegian Government within the territories referred to in Article 1 shall always be open on a footing of absolute equality to communications from ships of all flags and from nationals of the High Contracting Parties, under the conditions laid down in the Wireless Telegraphy Convention of July 5th, 1912, or in the subsequent International Convention which may be concluded to replace it.

Subject to international obligations arising out of a state of war, owners of landed property shall always be at liberty to establish and use for their own purposes wireless telegraphy installations, which shall be free to communicate on private business with fixed or moving wireless stations, including those on board ships and aircraft.

Article 5

The High Contracting Parties recognise the utility of establishing an international meteorological station in the territories specified in Article 1, the organisation of which shall form the subject of a subsequent Convention.

Conventions shall also be concluded laying down the conditions under which scientific investigations may be conducted in the said territories.

Article 6

Subject to the provisions of the present Article, acquired rights of nationals of the High Contracting Parties shall be recognised.

Claims arising from taking possession or from occupation of land before the signature of the present Treaty shall be dealt with in accordance with the Annex hereto, which will have the same force and effect as the present Treaty.

Article 7

With regard to methods of acquisition, enjoyment and exercise of the right of ownership of property, including mineral rights, in the territories specified in Article 1, Norway undertakes to grant to all nationals of the High Contracting Parties treatment based on complete equality and in conformity with the stipulations of the present Treaty.

Expropriation may be resorted to only on grounds of public utility and on payment of proper compensation.

Article 8

Norway undertakes to provide for the territories specified in Article 1 mining regulations which, especially from the point of view of imposts, taxes or charges of any kind, and of general or particular labour conditions, shall exclude all privileges, monopolies or favours for the benefit of the State or of the nationals of any one of the High Contracting Parties, including Norway, and shall guarantee to the paid staff of all categories the remuneration and protection necessary for their physical, moral and intellectual welfare.

Taxes, dues and duties levied shall be devoted exclusively to the said territories and shall not exceed what is required for the object in view.

So far, particularly, as the exportation of minerals is concerned, the Norwegian Government shall have the right to levy an export duty which shall not exceed 1% of the maximum value of the minerals exported up to 100,000 tons, and beyond that quantity the duty will be proportionately diminished. The value shall be fixed at the end of the navigation season by calculating the average free on board price obtained.

Three months before the date fixed for their coming into force, the draft mining regulations shall be communicated by the Norwegian Government to the other Contracting Powers. If during this period one or more of the said Powers propose to modify these regulations before they are applied, such proposals shall be communicated by the Norwegian Government to the other Contracting Powers in order that they may be submitted to examination and the decision of a Commission composed of one representative each of the said Powers. This Commission shall meet at the invitation of the Norwegian Government and shall come to a decision within a period of three months from the date of its first meeting. Its decisions shall be taken by a majority.

Article 9

Subject to the rights and duties resulting from the admission of Norway to the League of Nations, Norway undertakes not to create nor to allow the establishment of any naval base in the territories specified in Article 1 and not to construct any fortification in the said territories, which may never be used for warlike purposes.

Article 10

Until the recognition of the High Contracting Parties of a Russian Government shall permit Russia to adhere to the present Treaty, Russian nationals and companies shall enjoy the same rights as nationals of the High Contracting Parties.

Claims in the territories specified in Article 1 which they may have to put forward shall be presented under the conditions laid down in the present Treaty (Article 6 and Annex) through the intermediary of the Danish Government, who declare their willingness to lend their good offices for this purpose.

The PRESENT TREATY, of which the French and English texts are both authentic, shall be ratified.

Ratifications shall be deposited at Paris as soon as possible.

Powers of which the seat of the Government is outside Europe may confine their action to informing the Government of the French Republic, through their diplomatic representative at Paris, that their ratification has been given, and in this case they shall transmit the instrument as soon as possible.

The present Treaty will come into force, in so far as the stipulations of Article 8 are concerned, from the date of its ratification by all the signatory Powers; and in all other respects on the same date as the mining regulations provided for in that Article.

Third Powers will be invited by the Government of the French Republic to adhere to the present Treaty duly ratified. This adhesion shall be effected by a communication addressed to the French Government, which will undertake to notify the other Contracting Parties.

Convention Relating to the Non-Fortification and Neutralisation of the Aaland Islands

Date of signature: *October 20, 1921*
Place of signature: *Geneva*
Signatory states: *Germany, Denmark, Iceland, Esthonian Republic, Republic of Finland, the French Republic, Great Britain, Ireland and the British Dominions, India, Italy, Republic of Latvia, Poland, Sweden*
Ratifications: *Germany, Denmark, Finland, France, the British Empire, Sweden, Italy, Poland, Latvia*

[The signatories]
having agreed to carry out the recommendation formulated by the Council of the League of Nations in its Resolution of June 24, 1921, that a Convention should be concluded between the interested Powers with a view to the non-fortification and neutralisation of the Aaland Islands in order that these islands may never become a cause of danger from the military point of view;
Have resolved for this purpose to supplement without prejudice thereto, the obligations assumed by Russia in the Convention of March 30, 1856, regarding the Aaland Islands, annexed to Treaty of Paris of the same date;
Who, having deposited their full powers, found in good and due form, have agreed upon the following provisions:

Article 1

Finland, confirming, for her part, as far as necessary, the declaration made by Russia in the Convention of March 30, 1856, regarding the Aaland Islands, annexed to the Treaty of Paris of the same date, undertakes not to fortify that part of the Finnish Archipelago which is called "the Aaland Islands."

Article 2

[I. This article gives the geographical position of the Aaland Islands.]

II. The territorial waters of the Aaland Islands are considered to extend for a distance of three marine miles from the low-water mark on the islands, islets and reefs not permanently submerged, delimited above; nevertheless, these waters shall at no point extend beyond the lines fixed in § I of this Article.

III. The whole of the islands, islets and reefs delimited in paragraph I and of the territorial waters defined in paragraph II constitute the zone to which the following Articles apply.

Article 3

No military or naval establishment or base of operations, no military aircraft establishment or base of operations, and no other installation used for war purposes shall be maintained or set up in the zone described in Article 2.

Article 4

Except as provided in Article 7, no military, naval or air force of any Power shall enter or remain in the zone described in Article 2; the manufacture, import, transport and re-export of arms and implements of war in this zone are strictly forbidden.

The following provisions shall, however, be applied in time of peace:

(a) In addition to the regular police force necessary to maintain public order and security in the zone, in conformity with the general provisions in force in the Finnish Republic, Finland may, if exceptional circumstances demand, send into the zone and keep there temporarily such other armed forces as shall be strictly necessary for the maintenance of order.

(b) Finland also reserves the right for one or two of her light surface warships to visit the islands from time to time. These warships may then anchor temporarily in the waters of the islands. Apart from these ships, Finland may, if important special circumstances demand, send into the waters of the zone and keep there temporarily other surface ships, which must in no case exceed a total displacement of 6,000 tons.

The right to enter the archipelago and to anchor there temporarily cannot be granted by the Finnish Government to more than one warship of any Power at a time.

(c) Finland may fly her military or naval aircraft over the zone, but, except in cases of *force majeure*, landing there is prohibited.

Article 5

The prohibition to send warships into the zone described in Article 2 or to station them there shall not prejudice the freedom of innocent passage through the territorial waters. Such passage shall continue to be governed by the international rules and usages in force.

Article 6

In time of war, the zone described in Article 2 shall be considered as a neutral zone and shall not, directly or indirectly, be used for any purpose connected with military operations.

Nevertheless, in the event of a war affecting the Baltic Sea, Finland shall have the right, in order to assure respect for the neutrality of the Aaland Islands, temporarily to lay mines in the territorial waters of these islands and for this purpose to take such measures of a maritime nature as are strictly necessary.

In such a case Finland shall at once refer the matter to the Council of the League of Nations.

Article 7

I. In order to render effective the guarantee provided in the Preamble of the present Convention, the High Contracting Parties shall apply, individually or jointly, to the Council of the League of Nations, asking that body to decide upon the measures to be taken either to assure the observance of the provisions of this Convention or to put a stop to any violation thereof.

The High Contracting Parties undertake to assist in the measures which the Council of the League of Nations may decide upon for this purpose.

When, for the purposes of this undertaking, the Council is called upon to make a decision under the above conditions, it will invite the Powers which are parties to the present Convention, whether Members of the League or not, to sit on the Council. The vote of the representative of the Power accused of having violated the provisions of this Convention shall not be necessary to constitute the unanimity required for the Council's decision.

If unanimity cannot be obtained, each of the High Contracting Parties shall be entitled to take any mea-

sures which the Council by a two-thirds majority recommends, the vote of the representative of the Power accused of having violated the provisions of this Convention not being counted.

II. If the neutrality of the zone should be imperilled by a sudden attack either against the Aaland Islands or across them against the Finnish mainland, Finland shall take the necessary measures in the zone to check and repulse the aggressor until such time as the High Contracting Parties shall in conformity with the provisions of this Convention, be in a position to intervene to enforce respect for the neutrality of the islands.

Finland shall refer the matter immediately to the Council.

Article 8

The provisions of this Convention shall remain in force in spite of any changes that may take place in the present *status quo* in the Baltic Sea.

Article 9

The Council of the League of Nations is requested to inform the Members of the League of the text of this Convention, in order that the legal status of the Aaland Islands, an integral part of the Republic of Finland, as defined by the provisions of this Convention, may, in the interests of general peace, be respected by all as part of the actual rules of conduct among Governments.

With the unanimous consent of the High Contracting Parties, this Convention may be submitted to any non-signatory Power whose accession may in future appear desirable, with a view to the formal adherence of such Power.

Article 10

This Convention shall be ratified. The protocol of the first deposit of ratification shall be drawn up as soon as the majority of the signatory Powers, including Finland and Sweden, are in a position to deposit their ratifications.

The Convention shall come into force for each signatory or acceding Power immediately on the deposit of such Power's ratification or instrument of accession.

Deposit of ratification shall take place at Geneva with the Secretariat of the League of Nations, and any future instruments of accession shall also be deposited there.

In faith whereof the plenipotentiaries have signed this Convention and have annexed their seals thereto.

Done at Geneva, on the twentieth day of October, one thousand nine hundred and twenty-one, in a single copy, which shall remain in the Archives of the Secretariat of the League of Nations. A certified copy shall be sent by the Secretariat to each of the signatory Powers.

Treaty Between the United States of America, the British Empire, France, Italy and Japan, for the Limitation of Naval Armament

Also known as: *Washington Naval Treaty*
Date of signature: *February 6, 1922*
Place of signature: *Washington, DC*
Signatory states: *United States, the British Empire, France, Italy, and Japan*

[The signatories]
Desiring to contribute to the maintenance of the general peace and to reduce the burdens of competition in armament;
Have resolved, with a view to accomplishing these purposes, to conclude a Treaty to limit their respective naval armament,
Who, having communicated to each other their respective full powers, found to be in good and due form, have agreed as follows:

CHAPTER I

GENERAL PROVISIONS, RELATING TO THE LIMITATION OF NAVAL ARMAMENT

Article I

The Contracting Powers agree to limit their respective naval armament as provided in the present Treaty.

Article II

The Contracting Powers may retain respectively the capital ships which are specified in Chapter II, Part I. On the coming into force of the present Treaty, but subject to the following provisions of this Article, all other capital ships, built or building, of the United States, the British Empire and Japan shall be disposed of as prescribed in Chapter II, Part 2.

In addition to the capital ships specified in Chapter II, Part I, the United States may complete and retain two ships of the *West Virginia* class now under construction. On the completion of these two ships, the *North Dakota* and *Delaware* shall be disposed of as prescribed in Chapter II, Part 2.

The British Empire may, in accordance with the replacement table in Chapter II, Part 3, construct two new capital ships not exceeding 35,000 tons (35, 560 metric tons) standard displacement each. On the

completion of the said two ships, the *Thunderer, King George V, Ajax* and *Centurion* shall be disposed of as prescribed in Chapter II, Part 2.

Article III

Subject to the provisions of Article II, the Contracting Powers shall abandon their respective capital ship-building programmes, and no new capital ships shall be constructed or acquired by any of the Contracting Powers except replacement tonnage, which may be constructed or acquired as specified in Chapter II, Part 3.

Ships which are replaced in accordance with Chapter II, Part 3, shall be disposed of as prescribed in Part 2 of that Chapter.

Article IV

The total capital ship replacement tonnage of each of the Contracting Powers shall not exceed in standard displacement: for the United States, 525,000 tons (533,400 metric tons); for the British Empire, 525,000 tons (533,400 metric tons); for France, 175,000 tons (177,800 metric tons); for Italy, 175,000 tons (177,800 metric tons); for Japan, 315,000 tons (320,040 metric tons).

Article V

No capital ship exceeding 35,000 tons, (35,560 metric tons) standard displacement shall be acquired by, or constructed by, for, or within the jurisdiction of, any of the Contracting Powers.

Article VI

No capital ship of any of the Contracting Powers shall carry a gun with a calibre in excess of 16 inches (406 millimetres).

Article VII

The total tonnage for aircraft-carriers of each of the Contracting Powers shall not exceed in standard displacement: for the United States, 135,000 tons (137,160 metric tons); for the British Empire, 135,000 tons (137,160 metric tons); for France, 60,000 tons (60,960 metric tons); for Italy, 60,000 tons (60, 960 metric tons); for Japan, 81,000 tons (82,296 metric tons).

Article VIII

The replacement of aircraft-carriers shall be effected only as prescribed in Chapter II, Part 3, provided, however, that all aircraft-carrier tonnage in existence or building on November 12, 1921, shall be considered experimental, and may be replaced, within the total tonnage limit prescribed in Article VII, without regard to its age.

Article IX

No aircraft-carrier exceeding 27,000 tons (27,432 metric tons) standard displacement shall be acquired by, or constructed by, for, or within the jurisdiction of, any of the Contracting Powers.

However, any of the Contracting Powers may, provided that its total tonnage allowance of aircraft-carriers is not thereby exceeded, build not more than two aircraft carriers, each of a tonnage of not more than 33,000 tons (33,528 metric tons) standard displacement, and in order to effect economy any of the Contracting Powers may use for this purpose any two of their ships, whether constructed or in course of construction, which would otherwise be scrapped under the provisions of Article II. The armament of any aircraft-carriers exceeding 27,000 tons (27,432 metric tons) standard displacement shall be in accordance with the requirements of Article X, except that the total number of guns to be carried, in case any of such guns be of a calibre exceeding 6 inches (152 millimetres), except anti-aircraft guns and guns not exceeding 5 inches (127 millimetres), shall not exceed eight.

Article X

No aircraft-carrier of any of the Contracting Powers shall carry a gun with a calibre in excess of 8 inches (203 millimetres). Without prejudice to the provisions of Article IX, if the armament carried includes guns exceeding 6 inches (152 millimetres) in calibre, the total number of guns carried, except anti-aircraft guns and guns not exceeding 5 inches (127 millimetres), shall not exceed ten. If, alternatively, the armament contains no guns exceeding 6 inches (152 millimetres) in calibre, the number of guns is not limited. In either case the number of anti-aircraft guns and of guns not exceeding 5 inches (127 millimetres) is not limited.

Article XI

No vessel of war exceeding 10,000 tons (10,160 metric tons) standard displacement, other than a capital ship or aircraft-carrier, shall be acquired by, or constructed by, for, or within the jurisdiction of, any of the Contracting Powers. Vessels not specifically built as fighting ships nor taken in time of peace under Government control for fighting purposes, which are employed on fleet duties or as troop transports or in some other way for the purpose of assisting in the prosecution of hostilities otherwise than as fighting ships, shall not be within the limitations of this Article.

Article XII

No vessel of war of any of the Contracting Powers hereafter laid down, other than a capital ship, shall carry a gun with a calibre in excess of 8 inches (203 millimetres).

Article XIII

Except as provided in Article IX, no ship designated in the present Treaty to be scrapped may be reconverted into a vessel of war.

Article XIV

No preparations shall be made in merchant ships in time of peace for the installation of warlike armaments for the purpose of converting such ships into vessels of war, other than the necessary stiffening of decks for the mounting of guns not exceeding 6 inches (152 millimetres) calibre.

Article XV

No vessel of war constructed within the jurisdiction of any of the Contracting Powers for a non-Contracting Power shall exceed the limitations as to displacement and armament prescribed by the present Treaty for vessels of a similar type which may be constructed by or for any of the Contracting Powers; provided, however, that the displacement for aircraft-carriers constructed for a non-Contracting Power shall in no case exceed 27,000 tons (27,432 metric tons) standard displacement.

Article XVI

If the construction of any vessel of war for a non-Contracting Power is undertaken within the jurisdiction of any of the Contracting Powers, such Power shall promptly inform the other Contracting Powers of the date of the signing of the contract and the date on which the keel of the ship is laid; and shall also communicate to them the particulars relating to the ship prescribed in Chapter II, Part 3, Section I(b), (4) and (5).

Article XVII

In the event of a Contracting Power being engaged in war, such Power shall not use as a vessel of war any vessel of war which may be under construction within its jurisdiction for any other Power, or which may have been constructed within its jurisdiction for another Power and not delivered.

Article XVIII

Each of the Contracting Powers undertakes not to dispose by gift, sale or any mode of transfer of any vessel of war in such a manner that such vessel may become a vessel of war in the Navy of any foreign Power.

Article XIX

The United States, the British Empire and Japan agree that the *status quo* at the time of the signing of the present Treaty, with regard to fortifications and naval bases, shall be maintained in their respective territories and possessions specified hereunder:

(1) The insular possessions which the United States now holds or may hereafter acquire in the Pacific Ocean, except (a) those adjacent to the coast of the United States, Alaska and the Panama Canal Zone, not including the Aleutian Islands, and (b) the Hawaiian Islands;

(2) Hong-Kong and the insular possessions which the British Empire now holds or may hereafter acquire in the Pacific Ocean, east of the meridian of 110° east longitude, except (a) those adjacent to the coast of Canada, (b) the Commonwealth of Australia and its territories, and (c) New Zealand;

(3) The following insular territories and possessions of Japan in the Pacific Ocean, to wit: the Kurile Islands, the Bonin Islands, Amami-Oshima, the Loochoo Islands, Formosa and the Pescadores, and any insular territories or possessions in the Pacific Ocean which Japan may hereafter acquire.

The maintenance of the *status quo* under the foregoing provisions implies that no new fortifications or naval bases shall be established in the territories and possessions specified; that no measures shall be taken to increase the existing naval facilities for the repair and maintenance of naval forces, and that no increase shall be made in the coast defences of the territories and possessions above specified. This restriction, however, does not preclude such repair and replacement of worn-out weapons and equipment as is customary in naval and military establishments in time of peace.

Article XX

The rules for determining tonnage displacement prescribed in Chapter II, Part 4, shall apply to the ships of each of the Contracting Powers.

CHAPTER II

RULES RELATING TO THE EXECUTION OF THE TREATY—DEFINITION OF TERMS

Part I

Capital Ships which may be Retained by the Contracting Powers

In accordance with Article II, ships may be retained by each of the Contracting Powers as specified in this Part. [See Tables 1–5.]

Table 1

Ships which may be retained by the United States

Name :	Tonnage
Maryland	32,600
California	32,300
Tennessee	32,300
Idaho	32,000
New Mexico	32,000
Mississippi	32,000
Arizona	31,400
Pennsylvania	31,400
Oklahoma	27,500
Nevada	27,500
New York	27,000
Texas	27,000
Arkansas	26,000
Wyoming	26,000
Florida	21,825
Utah	21,825
North Dakota	20,000
Delaware	20,000
Total tonnage	500,650

On the completion of the two ships of the *West Virginia* class and the scrapping of the *North Dakota* and *Delaware*, as provided in Article II, the total tonnage to be retained by the United States will be 525,850 tons.

On the completion of the two new ships to be constructed and the scrapping of the *Thunderer, King George V, Ajax* and *Centurion*, as provided in Article II, the total tonnage to be retained by the British Empire will be 558,950 tons.

France may lay down new tonnage in the years 1927, 1929, and 1931, as provided in Part 3, Section II.

Italy may lay down new tonnage in the years 1927, 1929, and 1931, as provided in Part 3, Section II.

Part 2

Rules for Scrapping Vessels of War

The following rules shall be observed for the

Table 2

Ships which may be retained by the British Empire

Name :	Tonnage
Royal Sovereign	25,750
Royal Oak	25,750
Revenge	25,750
Resolution	25,750
Ramillies	25,750
Malaya	27,500
Valiant	27,500
Barham	27,500
Queen Elizabeth	27,500
Warspite	27,500
Benbow	25,000
Emperor of India	25,000
Iron Duke	25,000
Marlborough	25,000
Hood	41,200
Renown	26,500
Repulse	26,500
Tiger	28,500
Thunderer	22,500
King George V	23,000
Ajax	23,000
Centurion	23,000
Total tonnage	580,450

scrapping of vessels of war which are to be disposed of in accordance with Articles II and III.

I. A vessel to be scrapped must be placed in such condition that it cannot be put to combatant use.

II. This result must be finally effected in any one of the following ways:

(a) Permanent sinking of the vessel;

(b) Breaking the vessel up. This shall always involve the destruction or removal of all machinery, boilers and armour, and all deck, side and bottom plating;

(c) Converting the vessel to target use exclusively. In such case all the provisions of paragraph III of this Part, except sub-paragraph (6), in so far as may be necessary to enable the ship to be used as a mobile target, and except sub-paragraph (7), must be previously complied with. Not more than one capital ship may be retained for this purpose at one time by any of the Contracting Powers.

(d) Of the capital ships which would otherwise be scrapped under the present Treaty in or after the year 1931, France and Italy may each retain two sea-going vessels for training purposes exclusively, that is, a gunnery or torpedo schools. The two vessels retained by France shall be of the *Jean Bart* class, and of those retained by Italy one shall be the *Dante Alighieri,* the other of the *Giulio Cesare* class. On retaining these ships for the pur-

Table 3

Ships which may be retained by France

Name :	Tonnage (metric tons)
Bretagne	23,500
Lorraine	23,500
Provence	23,500
Paris	23,500
France	23,500
Jean Bart	23,500
Courbet	23,500
Condorcet	18,890
Diderot	18,890
Voltaire	18,890
Total tonnage	221,170

pose above stated, France and Italy respectively undertake to remove and destroy their conning-towers, and not to use the said ships as vessels of war.

III.

(a) Subject to the special exceptions contained in Article IX, when a vessel is due for scrapping, the

Table 4

Ships which may be retained by Italy

Name :	Tonnage (metric tons)
Andrea Doria	22,700
Caio Duilio	22,700
Conte Di Cavour	22,500
Giulio Cesare	22,500
Leonardo Da Vinci	22,500
Dante Alighieri	19,500
Roma	12,600
Napoli	12,600
Vittorio Emanuele	12,600
Regina Elena	12,600
Total tonnage	182,800

first stage of scrapping, which consists in rendering a ship incapable of further warlike service, shall be immediately undertaken.

(b) A vessel shall be considered incapable of further warlike service when there shall have been removed and landed, or else destroyed in the ship:

(1) All guns and essential portions of guns, fire-control tops and revolving parts of all barbettes and turrets;

(2) All machinery for working hydraulic or electric mountings;

(3) All fire-control instruments and range-finders;

(4) All ammunition, explosives and mines;

Table 5

Ships which may be retained by Japan

Name :	Tonnage
Mutsu	33,800
Nagato	33,800
Hiuga	31,260
Ise	31,260
Yamashiro	30,600
Fu-So	30,600
Kirishima	27,500
Haruna	27,500
Hiyei	27,500
Kongo	27,500
Total tonnage	301,320

(5) All torpedoes, war-heads and torpedo tubes;

(6) All wireless telegraphy installations;

(7) The conning-tower and all side armour, or alternatively all main propelling machinery; and

(8) All landing and flying-off platforms and all other aviation accessories.

IV. The periods in which scrapping of vessels is to be effected are as follow:

(a) In the case of vessels to be scrapped under the first paragraph of Article II, the work of rendering the vessels incapable of further warlike service, in accordance with paragraph III of this Part, shall be completed within six months from the coming into force of the present Treaty, and the scrapping shall be finally effected within eighteen months from such coming into force.

(b) In the case of vessels to be scrapped under the second and third paragraphs of Article II, or under Article III, the work of rendering the vessel incapable of further warlike service, in accordance with paragraph III of this Part, shall be commenced not later than the date of completion of its successor, and shall be finished within six months from the date of such completion. The vessel shall be finally scrapped, in accordance with paragraph II of this Part, within eighteen months from the date of completion of its successor. If, however, the completion of the new vessel be delayed, then the work of rendering the old vessel incapable of further warlike service, in accordance with paragraph III of this Part, shall be commenced within four years from the laying of the keel of the new vessel, and shall be finished within six months from the date on which such work was commenced, and the old vessel shall be finally scrapped in accordance with paragraph II of this Part, within eighteen months from the date when the work of rendering it incapable of further warlike service was commenced.

Part 3

Replacement

The replacement of capital ships and aircraft-carriers shall take place according to the rules in Section I and the tables in Section II of this Part.

Section I

Rules for Replacement

(a) Capital ships and aircraft-carriers twenty years after the date of their completion may, except as otherwise provided in Article VIII and in the tables in Section II of this Part, be replaced by new construction, but within the limits prescribed in Article IV and Article VII. The keels of such new construction may, except as otherwise provided in Article VIII and in the tables in Section II of this Part, be laid down not earlier than seventeen years from the date of completion of the tonnage to be replaced, provided, however, that no capital-ship tonnage, with the exception of the ships referred to in the third paragraph of Article II, and the replacement tonnage specifically mentioned in Section II of this Part, shall be laid down until ten years from November 12, 1921.

(b) Each of the Contracting Powers shall communicate promptly to each of the other Contracting Powers the following information:

(1) The names of the capital ships and aircraft-carriers to be replaced by new construction;

(2) The date of governmental authorisation of replacement tonnage;

(3) The date of laying the keels of replacement tonnage;

(4) The standard displacement in tons and metric tons of each new ship to be laid down, and the principal dimensions, namely, length at waterline, extreme beam at or below waterline, mean draft at standard displacement;

(5) The date of completion of each new ship and its standard displacement in tons and metric tons, and the principal dimensions, namely, length at waterline, extreme beam at or below waterline, mean draft at standard displacement, at time of completion.

(c) In case of loss or accidental destruction of capital ships or aircraft-carriers, they may immediately be replaced by new construction, subject to the tonnage limits prescribed in Articles IV and VII and in conformity with the other provisions of the present Treaty, the regular replacement program being deemed to be advanced to that extent.

(d) No retained capital ships or aircraft-carriers shall be reconstructed except for the purpose of providing means of defence against air and submarine attack, and subject to the following rules: The Contracting Powers may, for that purpose, equip existing tonnage with bulge or blister or anti-air attack deck protection, providing the increase of displacement thus effected does not exceed 3,000 tons (3,048 metric tons) displacement for each ship. No alterations in side armour, in calibre, number or general type of mounting of main armament shall be permitted except:

(1) in the case of France and Italy, which countries within the limits allowed for bulge may increase their armour protection and the calibre of the guns now carried on their existing capital ships so as not to exceed 16 inches (406 millimetres) and;

(2) the British Empire shall be permitted to complete, in the case of the *Renown,* the alterations to armour that have already been commenced but temporarily suspended.

Section II

Note Applicable to all the Tables in Section II

The order above prescribed in which ships are to be scrapped is in accordance with their age. It is understood that when replacement begins according to the . . . tables the order of scrapping in the case of the ships of each of the Contracting Powers may be varied at its option, provided, however, that such Power shall scrap in each year the number of ships above stated.

[See Tables 6 - 10.]

Part 4

Definitions

For the purposes of the present Treaty, the following expressions are to be understood in the sense defined in this Part.

Capital Ship

A capital ship, in the case of ships hereafter built, is defined as a vessel of war, not an aircraft-carrier whose displacement exceeds 10,000 tons (10,160 metric tons) standard displacement, or which carries a gun with a calibre exceeding 8 inches (203 millimetres).

Aircraft-Carrier

An aircraft-carrier is defined as a vessel of war with a displacement in excess of 10,000 tons (10,160 metric tons) standard displacement designed for the specific and exclusive purpose of carrying aircraft. It must be so constructed that aircraft can be launched therefrom and landed theron, and not designed and constructed for carrying a more powerful armament than that allowed to it under Article IX or Article X as the case may be.

Standard Displacement

The standard displacement of a ship is the displacement of the ship complete, fully manned, engined, and equipped ready for sea, including all armament and ammunition, equipment, outfit provisions and fresh water for crew, miscellaneous stores and implements of every description that are intended to be carried in war, but without fuel or reserve feed water on board.

The word "ton" in the present Treaty, except in the expression "metric tons", shall be understood to mean the ton of 2,240 pounds (1,016 kilos).

Vessels now completed shall retain their present ratings of displacement tonnage in accordance with their national system of measurement. However, a Power expressing displacement in metric tons shall be considered for the application of the present Treaty as owning only the equivalent displacement in tons of 2,240 pounds.

A vessel completed hereafter shall be rated at its displacement tonnage when in the standard condition defined herein.

Chapter III

Miscellaneous Provisions

Article XXI

If during the term of the present Treaty the requirements of the national security of any Contracting Power in respect of naval defence are, in the opinion of that Power, materially affected by any change of circumstances, the Contracting Powers will, at the request of such Power, meet in conference with a view to the reconsideration of the provisions of the Treaty and its amendment by mutual agreement.

In view of possible technical and scientific developments, the United States, after consultation with the other Contracting Powers, shall arrange for a conference of all the Contracting Powers which shall convene as soon as possible after the expiration of eight years from the coming into force of the present

Table 6

Replacement and Scrapping of Capital Ships—United States

Year	Ships laid down	Ships completed	Ships scrapped (age in parentheses)	Ships retained Summary Pre-Jutland	Post-Jutland
			Maine(20), Missouri(20), Virginia(17), Nebraska(17), Georgia(17), New Jersey(17), Rhode Island(17), Connecticut(17), Louisiana(17), Vermont(16), Kansas(16), Minnesota(16), New Hampshire(15), South Carolina(13),Michigan(13), Washington(0), South Dakota(0), Indiana(0), Montana(0), North Carolina (0), Iowa(0), Massachusetts(0), Lexington(0), Constitution(0), Constellation(0), Saratoga(0), Ranger (0), United States (0)[1]	17	1
1922		A, B[2]	Delaware(12), North Dakota(12)	15	3
1923				15	3
1924				15	3
1925				15	3
1926				15	3
1927				15	3
1928				15	3
1929				15	3
1930				15	3
1931	C, D			15	3
1932	E, F			15	3
1933	G			15	3
1934	H, I	C, D	Florida(23), Utah(23), Wyoming(22)	12	5
1935	J	E, F	Arkansas (23), Texas(21), New York (21)	9	7
1936	K, L	G	Nevada (20), Oklahoma (20)	7	8
1937	M	H, I	Arizona (21), Pennsylvania (21)	5	10
1938	N, O	J	Mississippi (21)	4	11
1939	P, Q	K, L	New Mexico (21), Idaho (20)	2	13
1940		M	Tennessee (20)	1	14
1941		N, O	California (20), Maryland (20)	0	15
1942		P, Q	West Virginia class	0	15

1 The United States may retain the *Oregon* and *Illinois,* for non-combatant purposes, after complying with the provisions of Part 2 III (b).   2 Two West Virginia class.   Note—A, B, C, D, etc., represent individual capital ships of 35,000 tons standard displacement, laid down and completed in the years specified.

Table 7

Replacement and Scrapping of Capital Ships—British Empire

Year	Ships laid down	Ships completed	Ships scrapped (age in parentheses)	Ships retained Summary Pre-Jutland	Post-Jutland
			Commonwealth(16), Agamemnon(13), Dreadnought (15), Bellerophon (12), St. Vincent (11), Inflexible (13), Superb (12), Neptune (10), Hercules (10), Indomitable (13), Temeraire (12), New Zealand (9), Lion (9), Princess Royal (9), Conquerer (9), Monarch (9), Orion (9), Australia (8), Agincourt (7), Erin (7), 4 building or projected[1]	21	1
1922	A, B[2]			21	1
1923				21	1
1924				21	1
1925		A, B	King George V (13), Ajax (12), Centurion (12), Thunderer(13)	17	3
1926				17	3
1927				17	3
1928				17	3
1929				17	3
1930				17	3
1931	C, D			17	3
1932	E, F			17	3
1933	G			17	3
1934	H, I	C, D	Iron Duke (20), Marlborough (20), Emperor of India (20), Benbow (20)	13	5
1935	J	E, F	Tiger (21), Queen Elizabeth (20), Warspite (20), Barnham (20)	9	7
1936	K, L	G	Malaya (20), Royal Sovereign (20)	7	8
1937	M	H, I	Revenge (21), Resolution (21)	5	10
1938	N, O	J	Royal Oak (22)	4	11
1939	P, Q	K, L	Valiant (23), Repulse (23)	2	13
1940		M	Renown (24)	1	14
1941		N, O	Ramillies (24), Hood (21)	0	15
1942		P, Q	A (17), B (17)	0	15

1 The British Empire may retain the *Colossus* and *Collingwood* for non-combatant purposes, after complying with the provisions of Part 2, III (b).   2 Two 35,000-ton ships, standard displacement.   Note—A, B, C, D, etc., represent individual capital ships of 35,000 tons standard displacement laid down and completed in the years specified.

Table 8
Replacement and Scrapping of Capital Ships—France

Year	Ships laid down	Ships completed	Ships scrapped (age in parentheses)	Ships retained Summary Pre-Jutland	Post-Jutland
1922				7	0
1923				7	0
1924				7	0
1925				7	0
1926				7	0
1927	35,000 tons			7	0
1928				7	0
1929	35,000 tons			7	0
1930		35,000 tons	Jean Bart (17), Courbet (17)	5	[1]
1931	35,000 tons			5	[1]
1932	35,000 tons	35,000 tons	France (18)	4	[1]
1933	35,000 tons			4	[1]
1934		35,000 tons	Paris (20), Bretagne (20)	2	[1]
1935		35,000 tons	Provence (20)	1	[1]
1936		35,000 tons	Lorraine (20)	0	[1]
1937				0	[1]
1938				0	[1]
1939				0	[1]
1940				0	[1]
1941				0	[1]
1942				0	[1]

[1] Within tonnage limitations; number not fixed.　Note—France expressly reserves the right of employing the capital-ship tonnage allotment as she may consider advisable, subject solely to the limitations that the displacement of individual ships should not surpass 35,000 tons, and that the total capital-ship tonnage should keep within the limits imposed by the present Treaty.

Table 9
Replacement and Scrapping of Capital Ships—Italy

Year	Ships laid down	Ships completed	Ships scrapped (age in parentheses)	Ships retained Summary Pre-Jutland	Post-Jutland
1922				6	0
1923				6	0
1924				6	0
1925				6	0
1926				6	0
1927	35,000 tons			6	0
1928				6	0
1929	35,000 tons			6	0
1930				6	0
1931	35,000 tons	35,000 tons	Dante Alighieri (19)	5	[1]
1932	45,000 tons			5	[1]
1933	25,000 tons	35,000 tons	Leonardo da Vinci (19)	4	[1]
1934				4	[1]
1935		35,000 tons	Giulio Cesare (21)	3	[1]
1936		45,000 tons	Conte di Cavour (21), Duilio (21)	1	[1]
1937		25,000 tons	Andrea Doria (21)	0	[1]

[1] Within tonnage limitations: number not fixed.　Note—Italy expressly reserves the right of employing the capital-ship tonnage allotment as she may consider advisable, subject solely to the limitations that the displacement of individual ships should not surpass 35,000 tons, and the total capital-ship tonnage should keep within the limits imposed by the present Treaty.

Table 10

Replacement and Scrapping of Capital Ships—Japan

Year	Ships laid down	Ships completed	Ships scrapped (age in parentheses)	Ships retained Summary	
				Pre-Jutland	Post-Jutland
			Hizen (20), Mikasa (20), Kashima (16), Katori (16), Satsuma (12), Aki (11), Settsu (10), Ikoma (14), Ibuki (12), Kurama (11), Amagi (0), Akagi (0), Kaga (0), Tosa (0), Takao (0), Atago (0), Projected programme 8 ships not laid down)[1]	8	2
1922				8	2
1923				8	2
1924				8	2
1925				8	2
1926				8	2
1927				8	2
1928				8	2
1929				8	2
1930				8	2
1931	A			8	2
1932	B			8	2
1933	C			8	2
1934	D	A	Kongo (21)	7	3
1935	E	B	Hiyei (21), Haruna (20)	5	4
1936	F	C	Kirishima (21)	4	5
1937	G	D	Fuso (22)	3	6
1938	H	E	Yamashiro (21)	2	7
1939	I	F	Ise (22)	1	8
1940		G	Hiuga (22)	0	9
1941		H	Nagato (21)	0	9
1942		I	Mutsu (21)	0	9

1 Japan may retain the *Shikishima* and *Asahi* for non-combatant purposes, after complying with the provisions of Part 2, III (b). Note—A,B,C,D, etc., represent individual capital ships of 35,000 tons standard displacement, laid down and completed in the years specified.

Treaty to consider what changes, if any, in the Treaty may be necessary to meet such developments.

Article XXII

Whenever any Contracting Power shall become engaged in a war which in its opinion affects the naval defence of its national security, such Power may after notice to the other Contracting Powers suspend for the period of hostilities its obligations under the present Treaty other than those under Articles XIII and XVII, provided that such Power shall notify the other Contracting Powers that the emergency is of such a character as to require such suspension.

The remaining Contracting Powers shall in such case consult together with a view to agreement as to what temporary modifications, if any, should be made in the Treaty as between themselves. Should such consultation not produce agreement, duly made in accordance with the constitutional methods of the respective Powers, any one of said Contracting Powers may, by giving notice to the other Contracting Powers, suspend for the period of hostilities its obligations under the present Treaty, other than those under Articles XIII and XVII.

On the cessation of hostilities the Contracting Powers will meet in conference to consider what modifications, if any, should be made in the provisions of the present Treaty.

Article XXIII

The present Treaty shall remain in force until December 31st, 1936, and in case none of the Contracting Powers shall have given notice two years before that date of its intention to terminate the Treaty, it shall continue in force until the expiration of two years from the date on which notice of termination shall be given by one of the Contracting Powers, whereupon the Treaty shall terminate as regards all the Contracting Powers. Such notice shall be communicated in writing to the Government of the United States, which shall immediately transmit a certified copy of the notification to the other Powers and inform them of the date on which it was received. The notice shall be deemed to have been given and shall take effect on that date. In the event of notice of termination being given by the Government of the United States, such notice shall be given to the diplomatic representatives at Washington of the other Contracting Powers, and the notice shall be deemed to have been given and shall take effect on the date of the communication made to the said diplomatic representatives.

Within one year of the date on which a notice of termination by any Power has taken effect, all the Contracting Powers shall meet in conference.

Article XXIV

The present Treaty shall be ratified by the Contracting Powers in accordance with their respective constitutional methods and shall take effect on the date of the deposit of all the ratifications, which shall take place at Washington as soon as possible. The Government of the United States will transmit to the other Contracting Powers a certified copy of the procès-verbal of the deposit of ratifications.

The present Treaty, of which the French and English texts are both authentic, shall remain deposited in the archives of the Government of the United States, and duly certified copies thereof shall be transmitted by that Government to the other Contracting Powers.

Convention on the Limitations of Armaments of Central American States

Date of signature: February 7, 1923
Place of signature: Washington, DC
Signatory states: Guatemala, El Salvador, Honduras, Nicaragua, Costa Rica
Ratifications: Nicaragua, El Salvador, Guatemala, Costa Rica, Honduras
Date of entry into force: November 24, 1924

[The signatories]. . .
It being their desire and interest that in the future their military policy should be guided only by the exigencies of internal order, have agreed to conclude the present Convention.

After having communicated to one another their respective full powers, which were found to be in due form, the Delegates of the five Central American Powers assembled in the Conference on Central American Affairs at Washington, have agreed to carry out the said proposal in the following manner:

Article I

The Contracting Parties having taken into consideration their relative population, area, extent of frontiers and various other factors of military importance, agree that for a period of five years from the date of the coming into force of the present Convention, they shall not maintain a standing Army and National Guard in excess of the number of men hereinafter provided, except in case of civil war, or impending invasion by another State.

Guatemala	5,200
El Salvador	4,200
Honduras	2,500
Nicaragua	2,500
Costa Rica	2,000

General officers and officers of a lower rank of the standing Army, who are necessary in accordance with the military regulations of each country, are not included in the provisions of this Article, nor are those of the National Guard. The Police Force is also not included.

Article 2

As the first duty of armed forces of the Central American Governments is to preserve public order, each of the Contracting Parties obligates itself to establish a National Guard to cooperate with the existing Armies in the preservation of order in the various districts of the country and on the frontiers, and shall immediately consider the best means for establishing it. With this end in view the Governments of the Central American States shall give consideration to the employment of suitable instructors, in order to take advantage, in this manner, of experience acquired in other countries in organizing such corps.

In no case shall the total combined force of the Army and of the National Guard exceed the maximum limit fixed in the preceding Article, except in the cases therein provided.

Article 3

The Contracting Parties undertake not to export or permit the exportation of arms or munitions or any other kind of military stores from one Central American country to another.

Article 4

None of the Contracting Parties shall have the right to possess more than ten war aircraft. Neither may any of them acquire war vessels; but armed coast guard boats shall not be considered as war vessels.

The following cases shall be considered as exceptions to this Article: civil war or threatened attack by a foreign state; in such cases the right of defence shall have no other limitations than those established by existing Treaties.

Article 5

The Contracting Parties consider that the use in warfare of asphyxiating gases, poisons, or similar substances as well as analogous liquids, materials or devices, is contrary to humanitarian principles and to international law, and obligate themselves by the present Convention not to use said substances in time of war.

Article 6

Six months after the coming into force of the present Convention each of the Contracting Governments shall submit to the other Central American Governments a complete report on the measures adopted by said Government for the execution of this Convention. Similar reports shall be submitted semi-annually, during the aforesaid period of the five years. The reports shall include the units of the army, if any, and of the National Guard; and any other information which the Parties shall sanction.

Article 7

The present Convention shall take effect with respect to the Parties that have ratified it, from the date of its ratification by at least four of the signatory States.

Article 8

The present Convention shall remain in force until the first of January, one thousand nine hundred and twenty-nine, notwithstanding any prior denunciation, or any other cause. After the first of January, one thousand nine hundred and twenty-nine, it shall continue in force until one year after the date on which one of the Parties bound thereby notifies the others of its intention to denounce it. The denunciation of this Convention by any of said Parties shall leave it in force for those Parties which have ratified it and have not denounced it, provided that these be not less than four in number. Any of the Republics of Central America which should fail to ratify this Convention, shall have the right to adhere to it while it is in force.

Article 9

The exchange of ratifications of the present Convention shall be made through communications addressed by the Governments to the Government of Costa Rica in order that the latter may inform the other Contracting States. If the Government of Costa Rica should ratify the Convention, notice of said ratification shall also be communicated to the others.

Article 10

The original copy of the present Convention, signed by all of the Delegates Plenipotentiary, shall be deposited in the archives of the Pan-American Union at Washington. A copy duly certified shall be sent by the Secretary-General of the Conference to each one of the Governments of the Contracting Parties.

Protocol for the Pacific Settlement of International Disputes

Date of signature: October 2, 1924
Place of signature: Geneva
Signatory states: Approved by the Assembly of the League of Nations on the above date

Animated by the firm desire to ensure the maintenance of general peace and the security of nations whose existence, independence or territories may be threatened;

Recognizing the solidarity of the members of the international community;

Asserting that a war of aggression constitutes a violation of this solidarity and an international crime;

Desirous of facilitating the complete application of the system provided in the Covenant of the League of Nations for the pacific settlement of disputes between states and of ensuring the repression of international crimes; and

For the purpose of realizing, as contemplated by Article 8 of the Covenant, the reduction of national armaments to the lowest point consistent with national safety and the enforcement by common action of international obligations;

The undersigned, duly authorized to that effect, agree as follows:

Article 1

The signatory states undertake to make every effort in their power to secure the introduction into the Covenant of amendments on the lines of the provisions contained in the following articles.

They agree that, as between themselves, these provisions shall be binding as from the coming into force of the present protocol and that, so far as they are concerned, the Assembly and the Council of the League of Nations shall thenceforth have power to exercise all the rights and perform all the duties conferred upon them by the protocol.

Article 2

The signatory states agree in no case to resort to war either with one another or against a state which, if the occasion arises, accepts all the obligations hereinafter set out, except in case of resistance to acts of aggression or when acting in agreement with the Council or the Assembly of the League of Nations in accordance with the provisions of the Covenant and of the present protocol.

Article 3

The signatory states undertake to recognize as compulsory, *ipso facto* and without special agreement, the jurisdiction of the Permanent Court of International Justice in the cases covered by paragraph 2 of Article 36 of the Statute of the Court, but without prejudice to the right of any state, when acceding to the special protocol provided for in the said article and opened for signature on December 16, 1920, to make reservations compatible with the said clause.

Accession to this special protocol, opened for signature on December 16, 1920, must be given within the month following the coming into force of the present protocol.

States which accede to the present protocol, after its coming into force, must carry out the above obligation within the month following their accession.

Article 4

With a view to render more complete the provisions of paragraphs 4, 5, 6, and 7 of Article 15 of the Covenant, the signatory states agree to comply with the following procedure:

1. If the dispute submitted to the Council is not settled by it as provided in paragraph 3 of the said Article 15, the Council shall endeavor to persuade the parties to submit the dispute to judicial settlement or arbitration.

2.

(a) If the parties cannot agree to do so, there shall, at the request of at least one of the parties, be constituted a Committee of Arbitrators. The Committee shall so far as possible be constituted by agreement between the parties.

(b) If within the period fixed by the Council the parties have failed to agree, in whole or in part, upon the number, the names and the powers of the arbitrators and upon the procedure, the Council shall settle the points remaining in suspense. It shall with the utmost possible despatch select in consultation with the parties the arbitrators and their President from among persons who by their nationality, their personal character and their experience, appear to it to furnish the highest guarantees of competence and impartiality.

(c) After the claims of the parties have been formulated, the Committee of Arbitrators, on the request of any party, shall through the medium of the Council request an advisory opinion upon any points of law in dispute from the Permanent Court of International Justice, which in such case shall meet with the utmost possible despatch.

3. If none of the parties asks for arbitration, the Council shall again take the dispute under consideration. If the Council reaches a report which is unanimously agreed to by the members thereof other than the representatives of any of the parties to the dispute, the signatory states agree to comply with the recommendations therein.

4. If the Council fails to reach a report which is concurred in by all its members, other than the representatives of any of the parties to the dispute, it shall submit the dispute to arbitration. It shall itself determine the composition, the powers and the procedure of the Committee of Arbitrators and, in the choice of the arbitrators, shall bear in mind the guarantees of competence and impartiality referred to in paragraph 2 (b) above.

5. In no case may a solution, upon which there has already been a unanimous recommendation of the Council accepted by one of the parties concerned, be again called in question.

6. The signatory states undertake that they will carry out in full good faith any judicial sentence or arbitral award that may be rendered and that they will comply, as provided in paragraph 3, above, with the solutions recommended by the Council. In the event of a state failing to carry out the above undertakings, the Council shall exert all its influence to secure compliance therewith. If it fails therein, it shall propose what steps should be taken to give effect thereto, in accordance with the provision contained at the end of Article 13 of the Covenant. Should a state in disregard of the above undertakings resort to war, the sanctions provided for by Article 16 of the Covenant, interpreted in the manner indicated in the present protocol, shall immediately become applicable to it.

7. The provisions of the present article do not apply to the settlement of disputes which arise as the result of measures of war taken by one or more signatory states in agreement with the Council or the Assembly.

Article 5

The provisions of paragraph 8 of Article 15 of the Covenant shall continue to apply in proceedings before the Council.

If in the course of an arbitration, such as is contemplated by Article 4 above, one of the parties claims that the dispute, or part thereof, arises out of a matter which by international law is solely within the domestic jurisdiction of that party, the arbitrators shall on this point take the advice of the Permanent Court of International Justice through the medium of the Council. The opinion of the Court shall be binding upon the arbitrators, who, if the opinion is affirmative, shall confine themselves to so declaring in their award.

If the question is held by the Court or by the Council to be a matter solely within the domestic jurisdiction of the state, this decision shall not prevent consideration of the situation by the Council or by the Assembly under Article 11 of the Covenant.

Article 6

If in accordance with paragraph 9 of Article 15 of the Covenant a dispute is referred to the Assembly, that body shall have for the settlement of the dispute all the powers conferred upon the Council as to endeavoring to reconcile the parties in the manner laid down in paragraphs 1, 2 and 3 of Article 15 of the Covenant and in paragraph 1 of Article 4 above.

Should the Assembly fail to achieve the amicable settlement:

If one of the parties asks for arbitration, the Council shall proceed to constitute the Committee of Arbitrators in the manner provided in sub-paragraphs (a), (b) and (c) of paragraph 2 of Article 4 above.

If no party asks for arbitration, the Assembly shall again take the dispute under consideration and shall have in this connection the same powers as the Council. Recommendations embodied in a report of the Assembly, provided that it secures the measure of support stipulated at the end of paragraph 10 of Article 15 of the Covenant, shall have the same value and effect, as regards all matters dealt with in the present protocol, as recommendations embodied in a report of the Council adopted as provided in paragraph 3 of Article 4 above.

If the necessary majority cannot be obtained, the dispute shall be submitted to arbitration and the Council shall determine the composition, the powers and the procedure of the Committee of Arbitrators as laid down in paragraph 4 of Article 4.

Article 7

In the event of a dispute arising between two or more signatory states, these states agree that they will not, either before the dispute is submitted to proceedings for pacific settlement or during such proceedings, make any increase of their armaments or effectives which might modify the position established by the Conference for the Reduction of Armaments provided for by Article 17 of the present protocol, nor will they take any measure of military, naval, air, industrial or economic mobilization, nor, in general, any actions of a nature likely to extend the dispute or render it more acute.

It shall be the duty of the Council, in accordance with the provisions of Article 11 of the Covenant, to take under consideration any complaint as to infraction of the above undertakings which is made to it by one or more of the states parties to the dispute. Should the Council be of opinion that the complaint requires investigation, it shall, if it deems it expedient, arrange for enquiries and investigations in one or more of the countries concerned. Such enquiries and investigations shall be carried out with the utmost possible despatch and the signatory states undertake to afford every facility for carrying them out.

The sole object of measures taken by the Council as above provided is to facilitate the pacific settlement of disputes and they shall in no way prejudge the actual settlement.

If the result of such enquiries and investigations is to establish an infraction of the provisions of the first paragraph of the present article, it shall be the duty of the Council to summon the state or states guilty of the infraction to put an end thereto. Should the state or states in question fail to comply with such summons, the Council shall declare them to be guilty of a violation of the Covenant or of the present protocol, and shall decide upon the measures to be taken with a view to end as soon as possible a situation of a nature to threaten the peace of the world.

For the purposes of the present article decisions of the Council may be taken by two-thirds majority.

Article 8

The signatory states undertake to abstain from any act which might constitute a threat of aggression against another state.

If one of the signatory states is of opinion that another state is making preparations for war, it shall have the right to bring the matter to the notice of the Council.

The Council, if it ascertains that the facts are as alleged, shall proceed as provided in paragraphs 2, 4, and 5 of Article 7.

Article 9

The existence of demilitarized zones being calculated to prevent aggression and to facilitate a definite finding of the nature provided for in Article 10 below, the establishment of such zones between states mutually consenting thereto is recommended as a means of avoiding violations of the present protocol.

The demilitarized zones already existing under the terms of certain treaties or conventions, or which may be established in future between states mutually consenting thereto, may at the request and at the expense of one or more of the conterminous states, be placed under a temporary or permanent system of supervision to be organised by the Council.

Article 10

Every state which resorts to war in violation of the undertakings contained in the Covenant or in the present protocol is an aggressor. Violation of the rules laid down for a demilitarized zone shall be held equivalent to resort to war.

In the event of hostilities having broken out, any state shall be presumed to be an aggressor, unless a decision of the Council, which must be taken unanimously, shall otherwise declare:

1. If it has refused to submit the dispute to the procedure of pacific settlement provided by Articles 13 and 15 of the Covenant as amplified by the present protocol, or to comply with a judicial sentence or arbitral award or with a unanimous recommendation of the Council, or has disregarded a unanimous report of the Council, a judicial sentence or an arbitral award recognizing that the dispute between it and the other belligerent state arises out of a matter which by international law is solely within the domestic jurisdiction of the latter state; nevertheless, in the last case the state shall only be presumed to be an aggressor if it has not previously submitted the question to the Council or the Assembly, in accordance with Article 11 of the Covenant.

2. If it has violated provisional measures enjoined by the Council for the period while the proceedings are in progress as contemplated by Article 7 of the present protocol.

Apart from the cases dealt with in paragraphs 1 and 2 of the present article, if the Council does not at once succeed in determining the aggressor, it shall be bound to enjoin upon the belligerents an armistice, and shall fix the terms, acting, if need be, by a two-thirds majority and shall supervise its execution.

Any belligerent which has refused to accept the armistice or has violated its terms shall be deemed an aggressor.

The Council shall call upon the signatory states to apply forthwith against the aggressor the sanctions provided by Article 11 of the present protocol, and any signatory state thus called upon shall thereupon be entitled to exercise the rights of a belligerent.

Article 11

As soon as the Council has called upon the signatory states to apply sanctions, as provided in the last paragraph of Article 10 of the present protocol, the obligations of the said states, in regard to the sanctions of all kinds mentioned in paragraphs 1 and 2 of Article 16 of the Covenant, will immediately become operative in order that such sanctions may forthwith be employed against the aggressor.

Those obligations shall be interpreted as obliging each of the signatory states to cooperate loyally and effectively in support of the Covenant of the League of Nations, and in resistance to any act of aggression, in the degree which its geographical position and its particular situation as regards armaments allow.

In accordance with paragraph 3 of Article 16 of the Covenant the signatory states give a joint and several undertaking to come to the assistance of the state attacked or threatened, and give to each other mutual support by means of facilities and reciprocal exchanges as regards the provision of raw materials and supplies of every kind, openings of credits, transport and transit, and for this purpose to take all measures in their power to preserve the safety of communications by land and by sea of the attacked or threatened state.

If both parties to the dispute are aggressors within the meaning of Article 10, the economic and financial sanctions shall be applied to both of them.

Article 12

In view of the complexity of the conditions in which the Council may be called upon to exercise the functions mentioned in Article 11 of the present protocol concerning economic and financial sanctions, and in order to determine more exactly the guarantees afforded by the present protocol to the signatory states, the Council shall forthwith invite the economic and financial organizations of the League of Nations to consider and report as to the nature of the steps to be taken to give effect to the financial and economic sanctions and measures of cooperation contemplated in Article 16 of the Covenant and in Article 11 of this protocol.

When in possession of this information, the Council shall draw up through its competent organs:

1. Plans of action for the application of the economic and financial sanctions against an aggressor state;

2. Plans of economic and financial cooperation between a state attacked and the different states assisting it; and shall communicate these plans to the members of the League and to the other signatory states.

Article 13

In view of the contingent military, naval and air

sanctions provided for by Article 16 of the Covenant and by Article 11 of the present protocol, the Council shall be entitled to receive undertakings from states determining in advance the military, naval and air forces which they would be able to bring into action immediately to ensure the fulfilment of the obligations in regard to sanctions which result from the Covenant and the present protocol.

Furthermore, as soon as the Council has called upon the signatory states to apply sanctions, as provided in the last paragraph of Article 10 above, the said states may, in accordance with any agreements which they may previously have concluded, bring to the assistance of a particular state, which is the victim of aggression, their military, naval and air forces.

The agreements mentioned in the preceding paragraph shall be registered and published by the Secretariat of the League of Nations. They shall remain open to all states members of the League which may desire to accede thereto.

Article 14

The Council shall alone be competent to declare that the application of sanctions shall cease and normal conditions be reestablished.

Article 15

In conformity with the spirit of the present protocol, the signatory states agree that the whole cost of any military, naval or air operations undertaken for the repression of an aggression under the terms of the protocol, and reparation for all losses suffered by individuals, whether civilians or combatants, and for all material damage caused by the operations of both sides, shall be borne by the aggressor state up to the extreme limit of its capacity.

Nevertheless, in view of Article 10 of the Covenant, neither the territorial integrity nor the political independence of the aggressor state shall in any case be affected as the result of the application of the sanctions mentioned in the present protocol.

Article 16

The signatory states agree that in the event of a dispute between one or more of them and one or more states which have not signed the present protocol and are not members of the League of Nations, such non-member states shall be invited, on the conditions contemplated in Article 17 of the Covenant, to submit, for the purpose of a pacific settlement, to the obligations accepted by the states signatories of the present protocol.

If the state so invited, having refused to accept the said conditions and obligations, resorts to war against a signatory state, the provisions of Article 16 of the Covenant, as defined by the present protocol, shall be applicable against it.

Article 17

The signatory states undertake to participate in an International Conference for the Reduction of Armaments which shall be convened by the Council and shall meet at Geneva on Monday, June 15, 1925. All other states, whether members of the League or not, shall be invited to this Conference.

In preparation for the convening of the Conference, the Council shall draw up with due regard to the undertakings contained in Articles 11 and 13 of the present protocol a general programme for the reduction and limitation of armaments, which shall be laid before the Conference and which shall be communicated to the governments at the earliest possible date, and at the latest three months before the Conference meets.

If by May 1, 1925, ratifications have not been deposited by at least a majority of the permanent Members of the Council and ten other members of the League, the Secretary-General of the League shall immediately consult the Council as to whether he shall cancel the invitations or merely adjourn the Conference until a sufficient number of ratifications have been deposited.

Article 18

Wherever mention is made in Article 10, or in any other provision of the present protocol, of a decision of the Council, this shall be understood in the sense of Article 15 of the Covenant, namely that the votes of the representatives of the parties to the dispute shall not be counted when reckoning unanimity or the necessary majority.

Article 19

Except as expressly provided by its terms, the present protocol shall not affect in any way the rights and obligations of members of the League as determined by the Covenant.

Article 20

Any dispute as to the interpretation of the present protocol shall be submitted to the Permanent Court of International Justice.

Article 21

The present protocol, of which the French and English texts are both authentic, shall be ratified.

The deposit of ratifications shall be made at the Secretariat of the League of Nations as soon as possible.

States of which the seat of government is outside Europe will be entitled merely to inform the Secretariat of the League of Nations that their ratification has been given; in that case, they must transmit the instrument of ratification as soon as possible.

So soon as the majority of the permanent members of the Council and ten other members of the League have deposited or have effected their ratifications, a *procès-verbal* to that effect shall be drawn up by the Secretariat.

After the said *procès-verbal* has been drawn up, the protocol shall come into force as soon as the plan for the reduction of armaments has been adopted by the Conference provided for in Article 17.

If within such period after the adoption of the plan for the reduction of armaments as shall be fixed by the said Conference, the plan has not been carried out, the Council shall make a declaration to that effect; this declaration shall render the present protocol null and void.

The grounds on which the Council may declare that the plan drawn up by the International Conference for the Reduction of Armaments has not been carried out, and that in consequence the present protocol has been rendered null and void, shall be laid down by the Conference itself.

A signatory state which, after the expiration of the period fixed by the Conference, fails to comply with the plan adopted by the Conference, shall not be admitted to benefit by the provisions of the present protocol.

Protocol for the Prohibition of the Use in War of Asphyxiating, Poisonous or Other Gases, and of Bacteriological Methods of Warfare

Also known as: Geneva Protocol
Date of signature: June 17, 1925
Place of signature: Geneva
Ratifications: France, Venezuela, Italy, Austria, Belgium, Egypt, Poland, Serbs, Croats and Slovenes, (Kingdom of the),

Germany, Finland, Spain, Roumania, Turkey, Denmark, Sweden, British Empire, India, Canada
Accessions: Liberia, Soviet Union, Persia, China, Union of South Africa, Australia, New Zealand

The Undersigned Plenipotentiaries, in the name of their respective Governments:

Whereas the use in war of asphyxiating, poisonous or other gases, and of all analogous liquids materials or devices, has been justly condemned by the general opinion of the civilised world; and

Whereas the prohibition of such use has been declared in Treaties to which the majority of Powers of the world are Parties; and

To the end that this prohibition shall be universally accepted as a part of International Law, binding alike the conscience and the practice of nations:

Declare:

That the High Contracting Parties, so far as they are not already Parties to Treaties prohibiting such use, accept this prohibition, agree to extend this prohibition to the use of bacteriological methods of warfare and agree to be bound as between themselves according to the terms of this declaration.

The High Contracting Parties will exert every effort to induce other States to accede to the present Protocol. Such accession will be notified to the Government of the French Republic, and by the latter to all signatory and acceding Powers, and will take effect on the date of the notification by the Government of the French Republic.

The present Protocol, of which the French and English texts are both authentic, shall be ratified as soon as possible. It shall bear to-day's date.

The ratifications of the present Protocol shall be addressed to the Government of the French Republic, which will at once notify the deposit of such ratification to each of the signatory and acceding Powers.

The instruments of ratification of and accession to the present Protocol will remain deposited in the archives of the Government of the French Republic.

The present Protocol will come into force for each signatory Power as from the date of deposit of its ratification, and, from that moment, each Power will be bound as regards other Powers which have already deposited their ratifications.

Treaty of Mutual Guarantee Between Germany, Belgium, France, Great Britain and Italy

Also known as: *Treaty of Locarno*
Date of signature: *October 16, 1925*
Place of signature: *Locarno*
Signatory states: *Germany, Belgium, French Republic, United Kingdom of Great Britain and Ireland and the British Dominions, India, Italy*

[The signatories],

Anxious to satisfy the desire for security and protection which animates the peoples upon whom fell the scourge of the war in 1914–18;

Taking note of the abrogation of the treaties for the neutralisation of Belgium, and conscious of the necessity of ensuring peace in the area which has so frequently been the scene of European conflicts;

Animated also with the sincere desire of giving to all the signatory Powers concerned supplementary guarantees within the framework of the Covenant of the League of Nations and the treaties in force between them;

Have determined to conclude a treaty with these objects, and. . .have agreed as follows:

Article 1

The High Contracting Parties collectively and severally guarantee, in the manner provided in the following Articles, the maintenance of the territorial *status quo* resulting from the frontiers between Germany and Belgium and between Germany and France, and the inviolability of the said frontiers as fixed by or in pursuance of the Treaty of Peace signed at Versailles on June 28, 1919, and also the observance of the stipulations of Articles 42 and 43 of the said Treaty concerning the demilitarised zone.

Article 2

Germany and Belgium, and also Germany and France, mutually undertake that they will in no case attack or invade each other or resort to war against each other.

This stipulation shall not, however, apply in the case of:

(1) The exercise of the right of legitimate defence, that is to say, resistance to a violation of the undertaking contained in the previous paragraph or to a flagrant breach of Articles 42 or 43 of the said Treaty of Versailles, if such breach constitutes an unprovoked act of aggression and by reason of the assembly of armed forces in the demilitarised zone, immediate action is necessary;

(2) Action in pursuance of Article 16 of the Covenant of the League of Nations;

(3) Action as the result of a decision taken by the

Assembly or by the Council of the League of Nations or in pursuance of Article 15, paragraph 7, of the Covenant of the League of Nations, provided that in this last event the action is directed against a State which was the first to attack.

Article 3

In view of the undertakings entered into in Article 2 of the present Treaty, Germany and Belgium, and Germany and France, undertake to settle by peaceful means and in the manner laid down herein all questions of every kind which may arise between them and which it may not be possible to settle by the normal methods of diplomacy:

Any question with regard to which the Parties are in conflict as to their respective rights shall be submitted to judicial decision, and the Parties undertake to comply with such decision.

All other questions shall be submitted to a conciliation commission. If the proposals of this commission are not accepted by the two Parties, the question shall be brought before the Council of the League of Nations, which will deal with it in accordance with Article 15 of the Covenant of the League.

The detailed arrangements for effecting such peaceful settlement are the subject of special Agreements signed this day.

Article 4

(1) If one of the High Contracting Parties alleges that a violation of Article 2 of the present Treaty or a breach of Articles 42 or 43 of the Treaty of Versailles has been or is being committed, it shall bring the question at once before the Council of the League of Nations.

(2) As soon as the Council of the League of Nations is satisfied that such violation or breach has been committed, it will notify its finding without delay to the Powers signatory of the present Treaty, who severally agree that in such case they will each of them come immediately to the assistance of the Power against whom the act complained of is directed.

(3) In case of a flagrant violation of Article 2 of the present Treaty or of a flagrant breach of Articles 42 or 43 of the Treaty of Versailles by one of the High Contracting Parties, each of the other Contracting Parties hereby undertakes immediately to come to the help of the Party against whom such a violation or breach has been directed as soon as the said Power has been able to satisfy itself that this violation constitutes an unprovoked act of aggression and that by reason either of the crossing of the frontier or of the outbreak of hostilities or of the assembly of armed forces in the demilitarised zone immediate action is necessary. Nevertheless, the Council of the League of Nations, which will be seized of the ques-

tion in accordance with the first paragraph of this Article, will issue its findings, and the High Contracting Parties undertake to act in accordance with the recommendations of the Council, provided that they are concurred in by all the Members other than the representatives of the Parties which have engaged in hostilities.

Article 5

The provisions of Article 3 of the present Treaty are placed under the guarantee of the High Contracting Parties as provided by the following stipulations:

If one of the Powers referred to in Article 3 refuses to submit a dispute to peaceful settlement or to comply with an arbitral or judicial decision and commits a violation of Article 2 of the present Treaty or a breach of Articles 42 or 43 of the Treaty of Versailles, the provisions of Article 4 of the present Treaty shall apply.

Where one of the Powers referred to in Article 3, without committing a violation of Article 2 of the present Treaty or a breach of Articles 42 or 43 of the Treaty of Versailles, refuses to submit a dispute to peaceful settlement or to comply with an arbitral or judicial decision, the other Party shall bring the matter before the Council of the League of Nations, and the Council shall propose what steps shall be taken; the High Contracting Parties shall comply with these proposals.

Article 6

The provisions of the present Treaty do not affect the rights and obligations of the High Contracting Parties under the Treaty of Versailles or under arrangements supplementary thereto, including the Agreements signed in London on August 30, 1924.

Article 7

The present Treaty, which is designed to ensure the maintenance of peace, and is in conformity with the Covenant of the League of Nations, shall not be interpreted as restricting the duty of the League to take whatever action may be deemed wise and effectual to safeguard the peace of the world.

Article 8

The present Treaty shall be registered at the League of Nations in accordance with the Covenant of the League. It shall remain in force until the Council, acting on a request of one or other of the High Contracting Parties notified to the other signatory Powers three months in advance, and voting at least by a two-thirds' majority, decides that the League of Nations ensures sufficient protection to the High Contracting Parties; the Treaty shall cease to have effect on the expiration of a period of one year from such decision.

Article 9

The present Treaty shall impose no obligation upon any of the British dominions, or upon India, unless the Government of such dominion, or of India, signifies its acceptance thereof.

Article 10

The present Treaty shall be ratified and the ratifications shall be deposited at Geneva in the archives of the League of Nations as soon as possible.

It shall enter into force as soon as all the ratifications have been deposited and Germany has become a Member of the League of Nations.

The present Treaty, done in a single copy, will be deposited in the archives of the League of Nations, and the Secretary-General will be requested to transmit certified copies to each of the High Contracting Parties.

FINAL PROTOCOL OF THE LOCARNO CONFERENCE

The representatives of the German, Belgian, British, French, Italian, Polish and Czechoslovak Governments, who have met at Locarno from October 5 to 16, 1925, in order to seek by common agreement means for preserving their respective nations from the scourge of war and for providing for the peaceful settlement of disputes of every nature which might eventually arise between them.

Have given their approval to the draft Treaties and Conventions which respectively affect them and which, framed in the course of the present Conference, are mutually interdependent:

Treaty between Germany, Belgium, France, Great Britain and Italy (Annex A).
Arbitration Convention between Germany and Belgium (Annex B).
Arbitration Convention between Germany and

France (Annex C).
Arbitration Treaty between Germany and Poland (Annex D).
Arbitration Treaty between Germany and Czechoslovakia (Annex E).

These instruments, hereby initialled *ne varietur*, will bear to-day's date, the representatives of the interested Parties agreeing to meet in London on December 1 next, to proceed during the course of a single meeting to the formality of the signature of the instruments which affect them.

The Minister for Foreign Affairs of France states that as a result of the draft arbitration treaties mentioned above, France, Poland and Czechoslovakia have also concluded at Locarno draft agreements in order reciprocally to assure to themselves the benefit of the said treaties. These agreements will be duly deposited at the League of Nations, but M.Briand holds copies forthwith at the disposal of the Powers represented here.

The Secretary of State for Foreign Affairs of Great Britain proposes that, in reply to certain requests for explanations concerning Article 16 of the Covenant of the League of Nations presented by the Chancellor and the Minister for Foreign Affairs of Germany, a letter, of which the draft is similarly attached (Annex F) should be addressed to them at the same time as the formality of signature of the above-mentioned instruments takes place. This proposal is agreed to.

The representatives of the Governments represented here declare their firm conviction that the entry into force of these treaties and conventions will contribute greatly in bringing about a moral relaxation of the tension between nations, that it will help powerfully towards the solution of many political or economic problems in accordance with the interests and sentiments of peoples, and that, in strengthening peace and security in Europe, it will hasten on effectively the disarmament provided for in Article 8 of the Covenant of the League of Nations.

They undertake to give their sincere co-operation to the work relating to disarmament already undertaken by the League of Nations and to seek the realisation thereof in a general agreement.

General Treaty for Renunciation of War as an Instrument of National Policy

Also known as: *Kellogg–Briand Pact, Pact of Paris*
Date of signature: *August 27, 1928*
Place of signature: *Paris*
Signatory states: *Germany, United States, Belgium, French Republic, Great Britain,*

Ireland and the British Dominions, India, Italy, Japan, Poland, Czechoslovakia
Accessions: *Afghanistan, Abyssinia, Albania, Austria, Bulgaria, Chile, China, Costa Rica, Cuba, Denmark, Free City of Danzig, Dominican Republic, Egypt, Estonia, Finland,*

Greece, Guatemala, Haiti, Honduras,
Hungary, Iceland, Latvia, Liberia, Lithuania,
Luxembourg, Mexico, the Netherlands,
Nicaragua, Norway, Panama, Paraguay, Peru,
Persia, Portugal, Roumania, Kingdom of the
Serbs, Croats and Slovenes, Siam, Spain,
Sweden, Switzerland, Turkey, Soviet Union,
Venezuela

[The signatories],
deeply sensible of their solemn duty to promote the welfare of mankind;

Persuaded that the time has come when a frank renunciation of war as an instrument of national policy should be made to the end that the peaceful and friendly relations now existing between their peoples may be perpetuated;

Convinced that all changes in their relations with one another should be sought only by pacific means and be the result of a peaceful and orderly process, and that any signatory Power which shall hereafter seek to promote its national interests by resort to war should be denied the benefits furnished by this Treaty;

Hopeful that, encouraged by their example, all the other nations of the world will join in this humane endeavour and by adhering to the present Treaty as soon as it comes into force bring their peoples within the scope of its beneficient provisions, thus uniting the civilized nations of the world in a common renunciation of war as an instrument of their national policy;

Have decided to conclude a Treaty and ... have agreed upon the following articles:

Article I

The High Contracting Parties solemnly declare in the names of their respective peoples that they condemn recourse to war for the solution of international controversies, and renounce it as an instrument of national policy in their relations with one another.

Article II

The High Contracting Parties agree that the settlement or solution of all disputes or conflicts of whatever nature or of whatever origin they may be, which may arise among them, shall never be sought except by pacific means.

Article III

The present Treaty shall be ratified by the High Contracting Parties named in the Preamble in accordance with their respective constitutional requirements, and shall take effect as between them as soon as all their several instruments of ratification shall have been deposited at Washington.

This Treaty shall, when it has come into effect as prescribed in the preceding paragraph, remain open as long as may be necessary for adherence by all the other Powers of the world. Every instrument evidencing the adherence of a Power shall be deposited at Washington and the Treaty shall immediately upon such deposit become effective as between the Power thus adhering and the other Powers parties hereto.

It shall be the duty of the Government of the United States to furnish each Government named in the Preamble and every Government subsequently adhering to this Treaty with a certified copy of the Treaty and of every instrument of ratification or adherence. It shall also be the duty of the Government of the United States telegraphically to notify such Governments immediately upon the deposit with it of each instrument of ratification or adherence.

In faith whereof the respective Plenipotentiaries have signed this Treaty in the French and English languages both texts having equal force, and hereunto affix their seals.

Anti-War Treaty (Non-Aggression and Conciliation)

Also known as: Saavedra Lamas Treaty
Date of signature: October 10, 1933
Place of signature: Rio de Janeiro
Signatory states: Argentina, Brazil, Chile,
Mexico, Paraguay, Uruguay

The States hereinafter named, in an endeavor to contribute to the consolidation of peace, and in order to express their adherence to the effort that all civilized
nations have made to further the spirit of universal harmony;

To the end of condemning aggression and territorial acquisitions secured by means of armed conquest and of making them impossible, of sanctioning their invalidity through the positive provisions of this Treaty, and in order to replace them with pacific solutions based upon lofty concepts of justice and equity;

Being convinced that one of the most effective means of insuring the moral and material benefits the world derives from peace is through the organization of a permanent system of conciliation of international disputes, to be applied 'upon a violation of the hereinafter mentioned principles;

Have decided to record, in conventional form, these aims of non-aggression and concord, through the conclusion of the present Treaty, to which end they have appointed the undersigned Plenipotentiaries, who, after having exhibited their respective full powers, which were found in good and due form, have agreed on the following provisions:

Article 1

The High Contracting Parties solemnly declare that they condemn wars of aggression in their mutual relations or against other States and that the settlement of disputes and controversies shall be effected only through the pacific means established by International Law.

Article II

They declare that between the High Contracting Parties territorial questions must not be settled by resort to violence and that they shall recognize no territorial arrangement not obtained through pacific means, nor the validity of an occupation or acquisition of territory brought about by armed force.

Article III

In case any of the States engaged in the dispute fails to comply with the obligations set forth in the foregoing Articles, the Contracting States undertake to make every effort in their power for the maintenance of peace. To that end, and in their character of neutrals, they shall adopt a common and solidary attitude; they shall exercise the political, juridical or economic means authorized by International Law; they shall bring the influence of public opinion to bear; but in no case shall they resort to intervention either diplomatic or armed. The attitude they may have to take under other collective treaties of which said States are signatories is excluded from the foregoing provisions.

Article IV

The High Contracting Parties, with respect to all controversies which have not been settled through diplomatic channels within a reasonable period, obligate themselves to submit to the conciliatory procedure created by this Treaty, the disputes specifically mentioned, and any others that may arise in their reciprocal relations, without any further limitations than those recited in the following Article.

Article V

The High Contracting Parties and the States which may hereafter accede to this Treaty may not formulate at the moment of signing, ratifying or adhering thereto limitations to the procedure of conciliation other than those indicated below:

(a) Controversies for the settlement of which pacifist treaties, conventions, covenants, or agreements, of any nature, have been concluded. These shall in no case be deemed superseded by this Treaty; to the contrary, they shall be considered as supplemented thereby insofar as they are directed to insure peace. Questions or issues settled by previous treaties are also included in the exception.

(b) Disputes that the Parties prefer to settle by direct negotiation or through submission to an arbitral or judicial procedure by mutual consent.

(c) Issues that International Law leaves to the exclusive domestic jurisdiction of each State, under its constitutional system. On this ground the Parties may object to their being submitted to the procedure of conciliation before the national or local jurisdiction has rendered a final decision. Cases of manifest denial of justice or delay in the judicial proceedings are excepted, and should they arise, the procedure of conciliation shall be started not later than within the year.

(d) Questions affecting constitutional provisions of the Parties to the controversy. In case of doubt, each Party shall request its respective Tribunal or Supreme Court, whenever vested with authority therefor, to render a reasoned opinion on the matter.

At any time, and in the manner provided for in Article XV, any High Contracting Party may communicate the instrument stating that it has partially or totally dropped the limitations set thereby to the procedure of conciliation.

The Contracting Parties shall deem themselves bound to each other in connection with the limitations made by any of them, only to the extent of the exceptions recorded in this Treaty.

Article VI

Should there be no Permanent Commission of Conciliation, or any other international body charged with such a mission under previous treaties in force, the High Contracting Parties undertake to submit their controversies to examination and inquiry by a Commission of Conciliation to be reorganized in the manner hereinafter set forth, except in case of an agreement to the contrary entered into by the Parties in each instance:

The Commission of Conciliation shall consist of five members. Each Party to the controversy shall appoint one member, who may be chosen from among its own nationals. The three remaining members shall be appointed by agreement of the Parties from among nationals of third nations. The latter must be of different nationalities, and shall not have their habitual residence in the territory of the Parties concerned, nor be in the service of either one of them. The Parties shall select the President of the Commission of Conciliation from among these three members.

Should the Parties be unable to agree, they may request a third nation or any other existing international body to make those designations. Should the nominees so designated be objected to by the Parties, or by any of them, each Party shall submit a list containing as many names as vacancies are to be filled, and the names of those to sit on the Commission of Conciliation shall be determined by lot.

Article VII

Those Tribunals or Supreme Courts of Justice vested by the domestic law of each State with authority to interpret, as a Court of sole or final recourse and in matters within their respective jurisdiction, the Constitution, the treaties or the general principles of the Law of Nations, may be preferred for designation by the High Contracting Parties to discharge the duties entrusted to the Commission of Conciliation established in this Treaty. In this event, the Tribunal or Court may be constituted by the whole bench or may appoint some of its members to act independently or in Mixed Commissions organized with justices of other Courts or Tribunals, as may be agreed by the Parties to the controversy.

Article VIII

The Commission of Conciliation shall establish its own Rules of Procedure. Those shall provide, in all cases, for hearing both sides.

The Parties to the controversy may furnish, and the Commission may request from them, all the antecedents and data necessary. The Parties may be represented by agents, with the assistance of counsellors or experts, and may also submit every kind of evidence.

Article IX

The proceedings and discussions of the Commission of Conciliation shall not be made public unless there is a decision to that effect, assented to by the Parties.

In the absence of any provision to the contrary, the Commission shall adopt its decisions by a majority vote; but it may not pass upon the substance of the issue unless all its members are in attendance.

Article X

It is the duty of the Commission to procure a conciliatory settlement of the disputes submitted to it.

After impartial consideration of the questions involved in the dispute, it shall set forth in a report the outcome of its work and shall submit to the Parties proposals for a settlement on the basis of a just and equitable solution.

The report of the Commission shall, in no case, be in the nature of a decision or arbitral award, either in regard to the exposition or interpretation of facts or in connection with juridical consideration or findings.

Article XI

The Commission of Conciliation shall submit its report within a year to be reckoned from the day of its first sitting, unless the Parties decide, by common accord, to shorten or extend that term.

Once started, the procedure of conciliation may only be interrupted by a direct settlement between the Parties, or by their later decision to submit, by common accord, the dispute to arbitration or to an international court.

Article XII

On communicating its report to the Parties, the Commission of Conciliation shall fix a period of time, which shall not exceed six months, within which the Parties shall pass upon the bases of settlement it has proposed. Once this period of time has expired the Commission shall set forth in a final act the decision of the Parties.

Should the period of time elapse without the Parties having accepted the settlement, nor adopted by common accord another friendly solution, the Parties to the controversy shall regain their freedom of action to proceed as they may see fit within the limitations set forth in Articles I and II of this Treaty.

Article XIII

From the outset of the procedure of conciliation until the expiration of the term set by the Commission for the Parties to make a decision, they shall abstain from any measure which may prejudice the carrying out of the settlement to be proposed by the Commission and, in general, from every act capable of aggravating or prolonging the controversy.

Article XIV

During the procedure of conciliation the members of the Commission shall receive honoraria in the amount to be agreed upon by the Parties to the controversy. Each Party shall bear its own expenses and a moiety of the joint expenses or honoraria.

Article XV

This Treaty shall be ratified by the High Contracting Parties, as soon as possible, in conformity with their respective constitutional procedures.

The original Treaty and the instruments of ratification shall be deposited in the Ministry of Foreign Affairs and Worship of the Argentine Republic, which shall give notice of the ratifications to the other signatory States. The Treaty shall enter into effect for the High Contracting Parties thirty days after deposit of the respective ratifications and in the order in which the same may be made.

Article XVI

This Treaty remains open to the adherence of all the States.

The adherence shall be made through the deposit of the respective instrument with the Ministry of Foreign Affairs and Worship of the Argentine Republic, which shall give notice thereof to the other States concerned.

Article XVII

This Treaty is concluded for an indefinite period, but it may be denounced by means of one year's previous notice, at the expiration of which it shall cease to be in force as regards the Party denouncing the same, but shall remain in force as regard the other States which may be Parties thereto under signature or adherence. Notice of the denunciation shall be addressed to the Ministry of Foreign Affairs and Worship of the Argentine Republic, which will transmit it to the other States concerned.

Treaty for the Limitation of Naval Armament

Also known as: London Naval Treaty
Date of signature: March 25, 1936
Place of signature: London
Signatory states: the United States, the French Republic, Great Britain, Ireland and the British Dominions, India
Ratifications: the United States, France, United Kingdom, Canada, Australia, New Zealand, India
Date of entry into force: July 29, 1937

[The signatories],
Desiring to reduce the burdens and prevent the dangers inherent in competition in naval armament;
Desiring, in view of the forthcoming expiration of the Treaty for the Limitation of Naval Armament signed at Washington on the 6th February, 1922, and of the Treaty for the Limitation and Reduction of Naval Armament signed in London on the 22nd April, 1930 (save for Part IV thereof), to make provision for the limitation of naval armament, and for the exchange of information concerning naval construction;
Have resolved to conclude a Treaty for these purposes . . .[and] have agreed as follows:

PART I

DEFINITIONS

Article 1

For the purposes of the present Treaty, the following expressions are to be understood in the sense hereinafter defined.

A.—Standard Displacement

(1) The standard displacement of a surface vessel is the displacement of the vessel, complete, fully manned, engined, and equipped ready for sea, including all armament and ammunition, equipment, outfit, provisions and fresh water for crew, miscellaneous stores and implements of every description that are intended to be carried in war, but without fuel or reserve feed water on board.

(2) The standard displacement of a submarine is the surface displacement of the vessel complete (exclusive of the water in non-watertight structure), fully manned, engined and equipped ready for sea, including all armament and ammunition, equipment, outfit, provisions for crew, miscellaneous stores and implements of every description that are intended to be carried in war, but without fuel, lubricating oil, fresh water or ballast water of any kind on board.

(3) The word "ton" except in the expression "metric tons" denotes the ton of 2,240 lb. (1,016 kilos).

B.—Categories

(1) *Capital Ships* are surface vessels of war belonging to one of the two following sub-categories:

(a) Surface vessels of war, other than aircraft-carriers, auxiliary vessels, or capital ship of sub-category (*b*), the standard displacement of which exceeds 10,000 tons (10,160 metric tons) or which carry a gun with a calibre exceeding 8 in. (203 mm.);

(b) Surface vessels of war, other than aircraft-carriers, the standard displacement of which does not exceed 8,000 tons (8,128 metric tons) and which carry a gun with a calibre exceeding 8 in. (203 mm.).

(2) *Aircraft-Carriers* are surface vessels of war, whatever their displacement, designed or adapted primarily for the purpose of carrying and operating aircraft at sea. The fitting of a landing-on or flying-off deck on any vessel of war, provided such vessel has not been designed or adapted primarily for the purpose of carrying and operating aircraft at sea, shall not cause any vessel so fitted to be classified in the category of aircraft-carriers.

The category of aircraft-carriers is divided into two sub-categories as follows:

(a) Vessels fitted with a flight deck, from which aircraft can take off or on which aircraft can land from the air;

(b) Vessels not fitted with a flight deck as described in (a) above.

(3) *Light Surface Vessels* are surface vessels of war other than aircraft-carriers, minor war vessels or auxiliary vessels, the standard displacement of which exceeds 100 tons (102 metric tons) and does not exceed 10,000 tons (10,160 metric tons), and which do not carry a gun with a calibre exceeding 8 in. (203 mm.).

The category of light surface vessels is divided into three sub-categories as follows:

(a) Vessels which carry a gun with a calibre exceeding 6.1 in. (155 mm.);

(b) Vessels which do not carry a gun with a calibre exceeding 6.1 in. (155 mm.) and the standard displacement of which exceeds 3,000 tons (3,048 metric tons);

(c) Vessels which do not carry a gun with a calibre exceeding 6.1 in. (155 mm.) and the standard displacement of which does not exceed 3,000 tons (3,048 metric tons).

(4) *Submarines* are all vessels designed to operate below the surface of the sea.

(5) *Minor War Vessels* are surface vessels of war, other than auxiliary vessels, the standard displacement of which exceeds 100 tons (102 metric tons) and does not exceed 2,000 tons (2,032 metric tons), provided they have none of the following characteristics:

(a) Mount a gun with a calibre exceeding 6.1 in. (155 mm.);

(b) Are designed or fitted to launch torpedoes;

(c) Are designed for a speed greater than twenty knots.

(6) *Auxiliary Vessels* are naval surface vessels the standard displacement of which exceeds 100 tons (102 metric tons) which are normally employed on fleet duties or as troop transports, or in some other way than as fighting ships, and which are not specifically built as fighting ships, provided they have none of the following characteristics:

(a) Mount a gun with a calibre exceeding 6.1 in. (155 mm.);

(b) Mount more than eight guns with a calibre exceeding 3 in. (76 mm.);

(c) Are designed or fitted to launch torpedoes;

(d) Are designed for protection by armour plate;

(e) Are designed for a speed greater than twenty-eight knots;

(f) Are designed or adapted primarily for operating aircraft at sea;

(g) Mount more than two aircraft-launching apparatus.

(7) *Small Craft* are naval surface vessels the standard displacement of which does not exceed 100 tons (102 metric tons).

C.—Over Age

Vessels of the following categories and sub-categories shall be deemed to be "over-age" when the undermentioned number of years have elapsed since completion:

(a) Capital ships.....26 years.

(b) Aircraft-carriers.....20 years.

(c) Light surface vessels, sub-categories (a) and (b):

(i) If laid down before 1st January, 1920.....16 years.

(ii) If laid down after 31st December, 1919.....20 years.

(d) Light surface vessels, sub-category (c).....16 years.

(e) Submarines.....13 years.

D.—Month

The word "month" in the present Treaty with reference to a period of time denotes the month of thirty days.

PART II

LIMITATION

Article 2

After the date of the coming into force of the present Treaty, no vessel exceeding the limitations as to displacement or armament prescribed by this Part of the present Treaty shall be acquired by any High Contracting Party or constructed by, for or within the jurisdiction of any High Contracting Party.

Article 3

No vessel which at the date of the coming into force of the present Treaty carries guns with a calibre exceeding the limits prescribed by this Part of the present Treaty shall, if reconstructed or modernised, be rearmed with guns of a greater calibre than those previously carried by her.

Article 4

(1) No capital ship shall exceed 35,000 tons (35,560 metric tons) standard displacement.

(2) No capital ship shall carry a gun with a calibre exceeding 14 in. (356 mm.); provided however that if any of the Parties to the Treaty for the Limitation of Naval Armament signed at Washington on the 6th February, 1922, should fail to enter into an agreement to conform to this provision prior to the date of the coming into force of the present Treaty, but in any case not later than the 1st April, 1937, the maximum calibre of gun carried by capital ships shall be 16 in. (406 mm.).

(3) No capital ship of sub-category (a), the standard displacement of which is less than 17,500 tons (17,780 metric tons), shall be laid down or acquired prior to the 1st January, 1943.

(4) No capital ship, the main armament of which consists of guns of less than 10 in. (254 mm.) calibre, shall be laid down or acquired prior to the 1st January, 1943.

Article 5

(1) No aircraft-carrier shall exceed 23,000 tons (23,368 metric tons) standard displacement or carry a gun with a calibre exceeding 6.1 in. (155 mm.).

(2) If the armament of any aircraft-carrier includes guns exceeding 5.25 in. (134 mm.) in calibre, the total number of guns carried which exceed that calibre shall not be more than ten.

Article 6

(1) No light surface vessel of sub-category (b) exceeding 8,000 tons (8,128 metric tons) standard displacement, and no light surface vessel of sub-category (a) shall be laid down or acquired prior to the 1st January, 1943.

(2) Notwithstanding the provisions of paragraph (1) above, if the requirements of the national security of any High Contracting Party are, in His opinion, materially affected by the actual or authorised amount of construction by any Power of light surface vessels of sub-category (b), or of light surface vessels not conforming to the restrictions of paragraph (1) above, such High Contracting Party shall, upon notifying the other High Contracting Parties of His intentions and the reasons therefor, have the right to lay down or acquire light surface vessels of sub-categories (a) and (b) of any standard displacement up to 10,000 tons (10,160 metric tons) subject to the observance of the provisions of Part III of the present Treaty. Each of the other High Contracting Parties shall thereupon be entitled to exercise the same right.

(3) It is understood that the provisions of paragraph (1) above constitute no undertaking expressed or implied to continue the restrictions therein prescribed after the year 1942.

Article 7

No submarine shall exceed 2,000 tons (2,032 metric tons) standard displacement or carry a gun exceeding 5.1 in. (130 mm.) in calibre.

Article 8

Every vessel shall be rated at its standard displacement, as defined in Article 1A of the present Treaty.

Article 9

No preparations shall be made in merchant ships in time of peace for the installation of warlike armaments for the purpose of converting such ships into vessels of war, other than the necessary stiffening of decks for the mounting of guns not exceeding 6.1 in. (155 mm.) in calibre.

Article 10

Vessels which were laid down before the date of the coming into force of the present Treaty, the standard displacement or armament of which exceeds the limitations or restrictions prescribed in this Part of the present Treaty for their category or sub-category, or vessels which before that date were converted to target use exclusively or retained exclusively for experimental or training purposes under the provisions of previous treaties, shall retain the category or designation which applied to them before the said date.

PART III

ADVANCE NOTIFICATION AND EXCHANGE OF INFORMATION

Article 11

(1) Each of the High Contracting Parties shall communicate every year to each of the other High Contracting Parties information, as hereinafter provided, regarding His annual programme for the construction and acquisition of all vessels of the categories and sub-categories mentioned in Article 12 (a), whether or not the vessels concerned are constructed within His own jurisdiction, and periodical information giving details of such vessels and of any alterations to vessels of the said categories or sub-categories already completed.

(2) For the purposes of this and the succeeding Parts of the present Treaty, information shall be deemed to have reached a High Contracting Party on the date upon which such information is communicated to His Diplomatic Representatives accredited to the High Contracting Party by whom the information is given.

(3) This information shall be treated as confidential until published by the High Contracting Party supplying it.

Article 12

The information to be furnished under the preceding Article in respect of vessels constructed by or for a High Contracting Party shall be given as follows; and so as to reach all the other High Contracting Parties within the periods or at the times mentioned:

(a) Within the first four months of each calendar year, the Annual Programme of construction of all vessels of the following categories and sub-categories, stating the number of vessels of each category or sub-category and, for each vessel, the calibre of the largest gun. The categories and sub-categories in question are:

Capital Ships:
  sub-category (a)
  sub-category (b)
Aircraft-Carriers:
  sub-category (a)
  sub-category (b)
Light Surface Vessels:
  sub-category (a)

  sub-category (b)
  sub-category (c)
Submarines.

(b) Not less than four months before the date of the laying of the keel, the following particulars in respect of each such vessel:

Name or designation;

Category and sub-category;

Standard displacement in tons and metric tons;

Length at waterline at standard displacement;

Extreme beam at or below waterline at standard displacement;

Mean draught at standard displacement;

Designed horse-power;

Designed speed;

Type of machinery;

Type of fuel;

Number and calibre of all guns of 3 in. (76 mm.) calibre and above;

Approximate number of guns of less than 3 in. (76 mm.) calibre;

Number of torpedo tubes;

Whether designed to lay mines;

Approximate number of aircraft for which provision is to be made.

(c) As soon as possible after the laying-down of the keel of each such vessel, the date on which it was laid.

(d) Within one month after the date of completion of each such vessel, the date of completion together with all the particulars specified in paragraph (b) above relating to the vessel on completion.

(e) Annually during the month of January, in respect of vessels belonging to the categories and sub-categories mentioned in paragraph (a) above:

(i) Information as to any important alterations which it may have proved necessary to make during the preceding year in vessels under construction, in so far as these alterations affect the particulars mentioned in paragraph (b) above.

(ii) Information as to any important alterations made during the preceding year in vessels previously completed, in so far as these alterations affect the particulars mentioned in paragraph (b) above.

(iii) Information concerning vessels which may have been scrapped or otherwise disposed of during the preceding year. If such vessels are not scrapped, sufficient information shall be given to enable their new status and condition to be determined.

(f) Not less than four months before undertaking such alterations as would cause a completed vessel to come within one of the categories or sub-categories mentioned in paragraph (a) above, or such alterations as would cause a vessel to change from one to another of the said categories or sub-categories: information as to her intended characteristics as specified in paragraph (b) above.

Article 13

No vessel coming within the categories or sub-categories mentioned in Article 12 (a) shall be laid down by any High Contracting Party until after the expiration of a period of four months both from the date on which the Annual Programme in which the vessel is included, and from the date on which the particulars in respect of that vessel prescribed by Article 12 (b), have reached all the other High Contracting Parties.

Article 14

If a High Contracting Party intends to acquire a completed or partially completed vessel coming within the categories or sub-categories mentioned in Article 12 (a), that vessel shall be declared at the same time and in the same manner as the vessels included in the Annual Programme prescribed in the said Article. No such vessel shall be acquired until after the expiration of a period of four months from the date on which such declaration has reached all the other High Contracting Parties. The particulars mentioned in Article 12 (b), together with the date on which the keel was laid, shall be furnished in respect of such vessel so as to reach all the other High Contracting Parties within one month after the date on which the contract for the acquisition of the vessel was signed. The particulars mentioned in Article 12 (d), (e) and (f) shall be given as therein prescribed.

Article 15

At the time of communicating the Annual Programme prescribed by Article 12 (a), each High Contracting Party shall inform all the other High Contracting Parties of all vessels included in His previous Annual Programmes and declarations that have not yet been laid down or acquired, but which it is the intention to lay down or acquire during the period covered by the first mentioned Annual Programme.

Article 16

If, before the keel of any vessel coming within the categories or sub-categories mentioned in Article 12 (a) is laid, any important modification is made in the particulars regarding her which have been communicated under Article 12 (b), information concerning this modification shall be given, and the laying of the keel shall be deferred until at least four months after this information has reached all the other High Contracting Parties.

Article 17

No High Contracting Party shall lay down or acquire any vessel of the categories or sub-categories mentioned in Article 12 (a), which has not previously been included in His Annual Programme of construction or declaration of acquisition for the current year or in any earlier Annual Programme or declaration.

Article 18

If the construction, modernisation or reconstruction of any vessel coming within the categories or sub-categories mentioned in Article 12 (a), which is for the order of a Power not a party to the present Treaty, is undertaken within the jurisdiction of any High Contracting Party, He shall promptly inform all the other High Contracting Parties of the date of the signing of the contract and shall also give as soon as possible in respect of the vessel all the information mentioned in Article 12 (b), (c) and (d).

Article 19

Each High Contracting Party shall give lists of all His minor war vessels and auxiliary vessels with their characteristics, as enumerated in Article 12 (b), and information as to the particular service for which they are intended, so as to reach all the other High Contracting Parties within one month after the date of the coming into force of the present Treaty; and, so as to reach all the other High Contracting Parties within the month of January in each subsequent year, any amendments in the lists and changes in the information.

Article 20

Each of the High Contracting Parties shall communicate to each of the other High Contracting Parties, so as to reach the latter within one month after the date of the coming into force of the present Treaty, particulars, as mentioned in Article 12 (b), of all vessels of the categories or sub-categories mentioned in Article 12 (a), which are then under construction for Him, whether or not such vessels are being constructed within His own jurisdiction, together with similar particulars relating to any such vessels then under construction within His own jurisdiction for a Power not a party to the present Treaty.

Article 21

(1) At the time of communicating His initial Annual Programme of construction and declaration of acquisition, each High Contracting Party shall inform each of the other High Contracting Parties of any vessels of the categories or sub-categories mentioned in Article 12 (a), which have been previously authorised and which it is the intention to lay down or acquire during the period covered by the said Programme.

(2) Nothing in this Part of the present Treaty shall prevent any High Contracting Party from laying down or acquiring, at any time during the four months following the date of the coming into force of the Treaty, any vessel included, or to be included, in His initial Annual Programme of construction or declaration of acquisition, or previously authorised, provided that the information prescribed by Article 12 (b) concerning each vessel shall be communicated so as to reach all the other High Contracting Parties within one month after the date of the coming into force of the present Treaty.

(3) If the present Treaty should not come into force before the 1st May, 1937, the initial Annual Programme of construction and declaration of acquisition, to be communicated under Articles 12 (a) and 14 shall reach all the other High Contracting Parties within one month after the date of the coming into force of the present Treaty.

PART IV

GENERAL AND SAFEGUARDING CLAUSES

Article 22

No High Contracting Party shall, by gift, sale or any mode of transfer, dispose of any of His surface vessels of war or submarines in such a manner that such vessel may become a surface vessel of war or a submarine in any foreign navy. This provision shall not apply to auxiliary vessels.

Article 23

(1) Nothing in the present Treaty shall prejudice the right of any High Contracting Party, in the event of loss or accidental destruction of a vessel, before the vessel in question has become over-age, to replace such vessel by a vessel of the same category or sub-category as soon as the particulars of the new vessel mentioned in Article 12 (b) shall have reached all the other High Contracting Parties.

(2) The provisions of the preceding paragraph shall also govern the immediate replacement, in such circumstances, of a light surface vessel of sub-category (b) exceeding 8,000 tons (8,128 metric tons) standard displacement, or of a light surface vessel of sub-category (a), before the vessel in question has become over-age, by a light surface vessel of the same sub-category of any standard displacement up to 10,000 tons (10,160 metric tons).

Article 24

(1) If any High Contracting Party should become engaged in war, such High Contracting Party may, if He considers the naval requirements of His defence are materially affected, suspend, in so far as He is concerned, any or all of the obligations of the present Treaty, provided that He shall promptly notify the other High Contracting Parties that the circumstances require such suspension, and shall specify the obligations it is considered necessary to suspend.

(2) The other High Contracting Parties shall in such case promptly consult together, and shall examine the situation thus presented with a view to agreeing as to the obligations of the present Treaty, if any, which each of the said High Contracting Parties may suspend. Should such consultation not produce agreement, any of the said High Contracting Parties may suspend, in so far as He is concerned, any or all of the obligations of the present Treaty, provided that He shall promptly give notice to the other High Contracting Parties of the obligations which it is considered necessary to suspend.

(3) On the cessation of hostilities, the High Contracting Parties shall consult together with a view to fixing a date upon which the obligations of the Treaty which have been suspended shall again become operative, and to agreeing upon any amendments in the present Treaty which may be considered necessary.

Article 25

(1) In the event of any vessel not in conformity with the limitations and restrictions as to standard displacement and armament prescribed by Articles 4, 5 and 7 of the present Treaty being authorised, constructed or acquired by a Power not a party to the present Treaty, each High Contracting Party reserves the right to depart if, and to the extent to which, He considers such departures necessary in order to meet the requirements of His national security;

(a) During the remaining period of the Treaty, from the limitations and restrictions of Articles 3, 4, 5, 6 (1) and 7, and

(b) During the current year, from His Annual Programmes of construction and declarations of acquisition.

This right shall be exercised in accordance with the following provisions:

(2) Any High Contracting Party who considers it necessary that such right should be exercised, shall notify the other High Contracting Parties to that effect, stating precisely the nature and extent of the proposed departures and the reasons therefor.

(3) The High Contracting Parties shall thereupon consult together and endeavour to reach an agreement with a view to reducing to a minimum the extent of the departures which may be made.

(4) On the expiration of a period of three months from the date of the first of any notifications which may have been given under paragraph (2) above, each of the High Contracting Parties shall, subject to any agreement which may have been reached to the contrary, be entitled to depart during the remaining period of the present Treaty from the limitations and restrictions prescribed in Articles 3, 4, 5, 6 (1) and 7 thereof.

(5) On the expiration of the period mentioned in the preceding paragraph, any High Contracting Party shall be at liberty, subject to any agreement which may have been reached during the consultations provided for in paragraph (3) above, and on informing all the other High Contracting Parties, to depart from His Annual Programmes of construction and declarations of acquisition and to alter the characteristics of any vessels building or which have already appeared in His Programmes or declarations.

(6) In such event, no delay in the acquisition, the laying of the keel, or the altering of any vessel shall be necessary by reason of any of the provisions of Part III of the present Treaty. The particulars mentioned in Article 12 (b) shall, however, be communicated to all the other High Contracting Parties before the keels of any vessels are laid. In the case of acquisition, information relating to the vessel shall be given under the provisions of Article 14.

Article 26

(1) If the requirements of the national security of any High Contracting Party should, in His opinion, be materially affected by any change of circumstances, other than those provided for in Articles 6 (2), 24 and 25 of the present Treaty, such High Contracting Party shall have the right to depart for the current year from His Annual Programmes of construction and declarations of acquisition. The amount of construction by any Party to the Treaty, within the limitations and restrictions thereof, shall not, however, constitute a change of circumstances for the purposes of the present Article. The above mentioned right shall be exercised in accordance with the following provisions:

(2) Such High Contracting Party shall, if He desires to exercise the above mentioned right, notify all the other High Contracting Parties to that effect, stating in what respects He proposes to depart from

His Annual Programmes of construction and declarations of acquisition, giving reasons for the proposed departure.

(3) The High Contracting Parties will thereupon consult together with a view to agreement as to whether any departures are necessary in order to meet the situation.

(4) On the expiration of a period of three months from the date of the first of any notifications which may have been given under paragraph (2) above, each of the High Contracting Parties shall, subject to any agreement which may have been reached to the contrary, be entitled to depart from His Annual Programmes of construction and declarations of acquisition, provided notice is promptly given to the other High Contracting Parties stating precisely in what respects He proposes so to depart.

(5) In such event, no delay in the acquisition, the laying of the keel, or the altering of any vessel shall be necessary by reason of any of the provisions of Part III of the present Treaty. The particulars mentioned in Article 12 (b) shall, however, be communicated to all the other High Contracting Parties before the keels of any vessels are laid. In the case of acquisition, information relating to the vessels shall be given under the provisions of Article 14.

PART V

FINAL CLAUSES

Article 27

The present Treaty shall remain in force until the 31st December, 1942.

Article 28

(1) His Majesty's Government in the United Kingdom of Great Britain and Northern Ireland will, during the last quarter of 1940, initiate through the diplomatic channel a consultation between the Governments of the Parties to the present Treaty with a view to holding a conference in order to frame a new treaty for the reduction and limitation of naval armament. This conference shall take place in 1941 unless the preliminary consultations should have shown that the holding of such a conference at that time would not be desirable or practicable.

(2) In the course of the consultation referred to in the preceding paragraph, views shall be exchanged in order to determine whether, in the light of the circumstances then prevailing and the experience gained in the interval in the design and construction of capital ships, it may be possible to agree upon a reduction in the standard displacement or calibre of guns of capital ships to be constructed under future

annual programmes and thus, if possible, to bring about a reduction in the cost of capital ships.

Article 29

None of the provisions of the present Treaty shall constitute a precedent for any future treaty.

Article 30

(1) The present Treaty shall be ratified by the Signatory Powers in accordance with their respective constitutional methods, and the instruments of ratification shall be deposited as soon as possible with His Majesty's Government in the United Kingdom, which will transmit certified copies of all the *procès-verbaux* of the deposits of ratifications to the Governments of the said Powers and of any country on behalf of which accession has been made in accordance with the provisions of Article 31.

(2) The Treaty shall come into force on the 1st January, 1937, provided that by that date the instruments of ratification of all the said Powers shall have been deposited. If all the above-mentioned instruments of ratification have not been deposited by the 1st January, 1937, the Treaty shall come into force so soon thereafter as these are all received.

Article 31

(1) The present Treaty shall, at any time after this day's date, be open to accession on behalf of any country for which the Treaty for the Limitation and Reduction of Naval Armament was signed in London on the 22nd April 1930, but for which the present Treaty has not been signed. The instrument of accession shall be deposited with His Majesty's Government in the United Kingdom, which will transmit certified copies of the *procès-verbaux* of the deposit to the Governments of the Signatory Powers and of any country on behalf of which accession has been made.

(2) Accessions, if made prior to the date of the coming into force of the Treaty, shall take effect on that date. If made afterwards, they shall take effect immediately.

(3) If accession should be made after the date of the coming into force of the Treaty, the following information shall be given by the acceding Power so as to reach all the other High Contracting Parties within one month after the date of accession:

(a) The initial Annual Programme of construction and declaration of acquisition, as prescribed by Articles 12 (a) and 14 relating to vessels already authorised, but not yet laid down or acquired, belonging to the categories or sub-categories mentioned in Article 12 (a).

(b) A list of the vessels of the above-mentioned categories or sub-categories completed or acquired after the date of the coming into force of the present Treaty, stating particulars of such vessels as specified in Article 12 (b), together with similar particulars relating to any such vessels which have been constructed within the jurisdiction of the acceding Power after the date of the coming into force of the present Treaty, for a Power not a party thereto.

(c) Particulars, as specified in Article 12 (b), of all vessels of the categories or sub-categories above-mentioned which are then under construction for the acceding Power, whether or not such vessels are being constructed within His own jurisdiction, together with similar particulars relating to any such vessels then under construction within His jurisdiction for a Power not a party to the present Treaty.

(d) Lists of all minor war vessels and auxiliary vessels with their characteristics and information concerning them, as prescribed by Article 19.

(4) Each of the High Contracting Parties shall reciprocally furnish to the Government of any country on behalf of which accession is made after the date of the coming into force of the present Treaty, the information specified in paragraph (3) above, so as to reach that Government within the period therein mentioned.

(5) Nothing in Part III of the present Treaty shall prevent an acceding Power from laying down or acquiring, at any time during the four months following the date of accession, any vessel included, or to be included, in His initial Annual Programme of construction or declaration of acquisition, or previously authorised, provided that the information prescribed by Article 12 (b) concerning each vessel shall be communicated so as to reach all the other High Contracting Parties within one month after the date of accession.

Article 32

The present Treaty, of which the French and English texts shall both be equally authentic, shall be deposited in the Archives of His Majesty's Government in the United Kingdom of Great Britain and Northern Ireland which will transmit certified copies thereof to the Governments of the countries for which the Treaty for the Limitation and Reduction of Naval Armament was signed in London on the 22nd April, 1930.

Convention on the Prevention and Punishment of the Crime of Genocide

Also known as: *Genocide Convention*
Date of signature: *December 9, 1948*
Place of signature: *Paris*
Signatory states: *Afghanistan, Albania, Algeria, Argentina, Australia, Austria, Bahamas, Barbados, Belgium, Brazil, Bulgaria, Burma, Byelorussia, Canada, Chile, Colombia, Costa Rica, Cuba, Czechoslovakia, Denmark, Ecuador, Egypt, El Salvador, Ethiopia, Fiji, Finland, France, Gambia, German Democratic Republic, Federal Republic of Germany, Ghana, Greece, Guatemala, Haiti, Honduras, Hungary, Iceland, India, Iran, Iraq, Ireland, Israel, Italy, Jamaica, Jordan, Kampuchea, Republic of Korea, Laos, Lebanon, Lesotho, Liberia, Luxembourg, Mali, Mexico, Monaco, Mongolia, Morocco, Nepal, Netherlands, New Zealand, Nicaragua, Norway, Pakistan, Panama, Peru, Philippines, Poland, Romania, Rwanda, Saudi Arabia, Soviet Union, Spain, Sri Lanka, Sweden, Syria, Taiwan, Tonga, Tunisia, Turkey, United Kingdom, Upper Volta, Uruguay, Venezuela, Vietnam, Yugoslavia, Zaire*
Date of entry into force: *January 12, 1951*

The Contracting Parties,
Having considered the declaration made by the General Assembly of the United Nations in its resolution 96 (I) dated 11 December 1946 that genocide is a crime under international law, contrary to the spirit and aims of the United Nations and condemned by the civilized world;
Recognizing that at all periods of history genocide has inflicted great losses on humanity; and
Being convinced that, in order to liberate mankind from such an odious scourge, international co-operation is required,
Hereby agree as hereinafter provided:

Article I

The Contracting Parties confirm that genocide, whether committed in time of peace or in time of war, is a crime under international law which they undertake to prevent and to punish.

Article II

In the present Convention, genocide means any of the following acts committed with intent to destroy, in whole or in part, a national, ethnical, racial or religious group, as such:

(a) Killing members of the group;

(b) Causing serious bodily or mental harm to members of the group;

(c) Deliberately inflicting on the group conditions of life calculated to bring about its physical destruction in whole or in part;

(d) Imposing measures intended to prevent births within the group;

(e) Forcibly transferring children of the group to another group.

Article III

The following acts shall be punishable:

(a) Genocide;

(b) Conspiracy to commit genocide;

(c) Direct and public incitement to commit genocide;

(d) Attempt to commit genocide;

(e) Complicity in genocide.

Article IV

Persons committing genocide or any of the other acts enumerated in article III shall be punished, whether they are constitutionally responsible rulers, public officials or private individuals.

Article V

The Contracting Parties undertake to enact, in accordance with their respective Constitutions, the necessary legislation to give effect to the provisions of the present Convention and, in particular, to provide effective penalties for persons guilty of genocide or of any of the acts enumerated in article III.

Article VI

Persons charged with genocide or any of the other acts enumerated in article III shall be tried by a competent tribunal of the State in the territory of which the act was committed, or by such international penal tribunal as may have jurisdiction with respect to those Contracting Parties which shall have accepted its jurisdiction.

Article VII

Genocide and the other acts enumerated in article III shall not be considered as political crimes for the purpose of extradition.

The Contracting Parties pledge themselves in such

cases to grant extradition in accordance with their laws and treaties in force.

Article VIII

Any Contracting Party may call upon the competent organs of the United Nations to take such action under the Charter of the United Nations as they consider appropriate for the prevention and suppression of acts of genocide or any of the other acts enumerated in article III.

Article IX

Disputes between the Contracting Parties relating to the interpretation, application or fulfilment of the present Convention, including those relating to the responsibility of a State for genocide or for any of the other acts enumerated in article III, shall be submitted to the International Court of Justice at the request of any of the parties to the dispute.

Article X

The present Convention, of which the Chinese, English, French, Russian and Spanish texts are equally authentic, shall bear the date of 9 December 1948.

Article XI

The present Convention shall be open until 31 December 1949 for signature on behalf of any Member of the United Nations and of any non-member State to which an invitation to sign has been addressed by the General Assembly.

The present Convention shall be ratified, and the instruments of ratification shall be deposited with the Secretary-General of the United Nations.

After 1 January 1950 the present Convention may be acceded to on behalf of any Member of the United Nations and of any non-member State which has received an invitation as aforesaid.

Instruments of accession shall be deposited with the Secretary-General of the United Nations.

Article XII

Any Contracting Party may at any time, by notification addressed to the Secretary-General of the United Nations, extend the application of the present Convention to all or any of the territories for the conduct of whose foreign relations that Contracting Party is responsible.

Article XIII

On the day when the first twenty instruments of ratification or accession have been deposited, the Secretary-General shall draw up a *procès-verbal* and transmit a copy thereof to each Member of the United Nations and to each of the non-member States contemplated in article XI.

The present Convention shall come into force on the ninetieth day following the date of deposit of the twentieth instrument of ratification or accession.

Any ratification or accession effected subsequent to the latter date shall become effective on the ninetieth day following the deposit of the instrument of ratification or accession.

Article XIV

The present Convention shall remain in effect for a period of ten years as from the date of its coming into force.

It shall thereafter remain in force for successive periods of five years for such Contracting Parties as have not denounced it at least six months before the expiration of the current period.

Denunciation shall be effected by a written notification addressed to the Secretary-General of the United Nations.

Article XV

If, as a result of denunciations, the number of Parties to the present Convention should become less than sixteen, the Convention shall cease to be in force as from the date on which the last of these denunciations shall become effective.

Article XVI

A request for the revision of the present Convention may be made at any time by any Contracting Party by means of a notification in writing addressed to the Secretary-General.

The General Assembly shall decide upon the steps, if any, to be taken in respect of such request.

Article XVII

The Secretary-General of the United Nations shall notify all Members of the United Nations and the non-member States contemplated in article XI of the following:

(a) Signatures, ratifications and accessions received in accordance with article XI;

(b) Notifications received in accordance with article XII;

(c) The date upon which the present Convention comes into force in accordance with article XIII;

(d) Denunciations received in accordance with article XIV;

(e) The abrogation of the Convention in accordance with article XV;

(f) Notifications received in accordance with article XVI.

Article XVIII

The original of the present Convention shall be deposited in the archives of the United Nations.

A certified copy of the Convention shall be transmitted to each Member of the United Nations and to each of the non-member States contemplated in article XI.

Article XIX

The present Convention shall be registered by the Secretary-General of the United Nations on the date of its coming into force.

Geneva Convention Relative to the Protection of Civilian Persons in Time of War

Date of signature: *August 12, 1949*
Place of signature: *Geneva*
Signatory states: *Afghanistan, Albania, Algeria, Argentina, Australia, Austria, Bahamas, Bahrain, Bangladesh, Barbados, Belgium, Benin, Bolivia, Botswana, Brazil, Bulgaria, Burundi, Byelorussia, Cameroon, Canada, Central African Republic, Chad, Chile, People's Republic of China, Colombia, Congo, Costa Rica, Cuba, Cyprus, Czechoslovakia, Denmark, Djibouti, Dominica, Dominican Republic, Ecuador, Egypt, El Salvador, Ethiopia, Fiji, Finland, France, Gabon, Gambia, German Democratic Republic, Federal Republic of Germany, Ghana, Greece, Grenada, Guatemala, Guinea-Bissau, Guyana, Haiti, Holy See, Honduras, Hungary, Iceland, India, Indonesia, Iran, Iraq, Ireland, Israel, Italy, Ivory Coast, Jamaica, Japan, Jordan, Kampuchea, Kenya, Democratic People's Republic of Korea, Republic of Korea, Kuwait, Laos, Lebanon, Lesotho, Liberia, Libya, Liechtenstein, Luxembourg, Madagascar, Malawi, Malaysia, Mali, Malta, Mauritania, Mauritius, Mexico, Monaco, Mongolia, Morocco, Nepal, Netherlands, New Zealand, Nicaragua, Niger, Nigeria, Norway, Oman, Pakistan, Panama, Papua New Guinea, Paraguay, Peru, Philippines, Poland, Portugal, Qatar, Romania, Rwanda, Saint Lucia, Saint Vincent and the Grenadines, San Marino, Sao Tome and Principe, Saudi Arabia, Senegal, Sierra Leone, Singapore, Solomon Islands, Somalia, South Africa, Soviet Union, Spain, Sri Lanka, Sudan, Surinam, Swaziland, Sweden, Switzerland, Syria, Tanzania, Thailand, Togo, Tonga, Trinidad and Tobago, Tunisia, Turkey, Tuvalu, Uganda, Ukraine, United Arab Emirates, United Kingdom, United States, Upper Volta, Uruguay, Venezuela, Vietnam, Yemen Arab Republic, People's Democratic Republic of Yemen, Yugoslavia, Zaire, Zambia*

Date of entry into force: *October 21, 1950*

The undersigned Plenipotentiaries of the Governments represented at the Diplomatic Conference held at Geneva from April 21 to August 12, 1949, for the purpose of establishing a Convention for the Protection of Civilian Persons in Time of War, have agreed as follows:

PART I

GENERAL PROVISIONS

Article 1

The High Contracting Parties undertake to respect and to ensure respect for the present Convention in all circumstances.

Article 2

In addition to the provisions which shall be implemented in peacetime, the present Convention shall apply to all cases of declared war or of any other armed conflict which may arise between two or more of the High Contracting Parties, even if the state of war is not recognized by one of them.

The Convention shall also apply to all cases of partial or total occupation of the territory of a High Contracting Party, even if the said occupation meets with no armed resistance.

Although one of the Powers in conflict may not be a party to the present Convention, the Powers who are parties thereto shall remain bound by it in their mutual relations. They shall furthermore be bound by the Convention in relation to the said Power, if the latter accepts and applies the provisions thereof.

Article 3

In the case of armed conflict not of an international character occurring in the territory of one of

59

the High Contracting Parties, each Party to the conflict shall be bound to apply, as a minimum, the following provisions:

(1) Persons taking no active part in the hostilities, including members of armed forces who have laid down their arms and those placed *hors de combat* by sickness, wounds, detention, or any other cause, shall in all circumstances be treated humanely, without any adverse distinction founded on race, colour, religion or faith, sex, birth or wealth, or any other similar criteria.

To this end, the following acts are and shall remain prohibited at any time and in any place whatsoever with respect to the above-mentioned persons:

(a) violence to life and person, in particular murder of all kinds, mutilation, cruel treatment and torture;

(b) taking of hostages;

(c) outrages upon personal dignity, in particular humiliating and degrading treatment;

(d) the passing of sentences and the carrying out of executions without previous judgment pronounced by a regularly constituted court, affording all the judicial guarantees which are recognized as indispensable by civilized peoples.

(2) The wounded and sick shall be collected and cared for.

Article 4

Persons protected by the Convention are those who, at a given moment and in any manner whatsoever, find themselves, in case of a conflict or occupation, in the hands of a Party to the conflict or Occupying Power of which they are not nationals.

Nationals of a State which is not bound by the Convention are not protected by it. Nationals of a neutral State who find themselves in the territory of a belligerent State, and nationals of a co-belligerent State, shall not be regarded as protected persons while the State of which they are nationals has normal diplomatic representation in the State in whose hands they are.

Article 5

[Spies and saboteurs forfeit their rights under the Convention, but shall be treated humanely.]

Article 6

[The Convention applies throughout any conflict as defined in Article 2.]

Article 7

[Protected persons' rights shall not be adversely affected by special agreements.]

Article 8

Protected persons may in no circumstances renounce in part or in entirety the rights secured to them by the present Convention, and by the special agreements referred to in the foregoing Article, if such there be.

Article 9

The present Convention shall be applied with the cooperation and under the scrutiny of the Protecting Powers whose duty it is to safeguard the interests of the Parties to the conflict. For this purpose, the Protecting Powers may appoint, apart from their diplomatic or consular staff, delegates from amongst their own nationals or the nationals of other neutral Powers. The said delegates shall be subject to the approval of the Power with which they are to carry out their duties.

Article 10

The provisions of the present Convention constitute no obstacle to the humanitarian activities which the International Committee of the Red Cross or any other impartial humanitarian organization may, subject to the consent of the Parties to the conflict concerned, undertake for the protection of civilian persons and for their relief.

Article 11

[Responsibility for protected persons may be entrusted to an organization such as the Red Cross.]

Article 12

[Disagreements over the application of the Convention shall be settled by arbitration.]

PART II

GENERAL PROTECTION OF POPULATIONS AGAINST CERTAIN CONSEQUENCES OF WAR

Article 13

The provisions of Part II cover the whole of the populations of the countries in conflict, without any adverse distinction based, in particular, on race, nationality, religion or political opinion, and are intended to alleviate the sufferings caused by war.

Article 14

[Hospitals and safety zones shall be established for the wounded, the sick, the aged, and children under fifteen.]

Article 15

Any Party to the conflict may, either direct or through a neutral State or some humanitarian organization, propose to the adverse Party to establish, in the regions where fighting is taking place, neutralized zones intended to shelter from the effects of war the following persons, without distinction:

(a) wounded and sick combatants or non-combatants;

(b) civilian persons who take no part in hostilities, and who, while they reside in the zones, perform no work of a military character.

When the Parties concerned have agreed upon the geographical position, administration, food supply and supervision of the proposed neutralized zone, a written agreement shall be concluded and signed by the representatives of the Parties to the conflict. The agreement shall fix the beginning and the duration of the neutralization of the zone.

Article 16

The wounded and sick, as well as the infirm, and expectant mothers, shall be the object of particular protection and respect.

As far as military considerations allow, each Party to the conflict shall facilitate the steps taken to search for the killed and wounded, to assist the shipwrecked and other persons exposed to grave danger, and to protect them against pillage and ill-treatment.

Article 17

The Parties to the conflict shall endeavour to conclude local agreements for the removal from besieged or encircled areas, of wounded, sick, infirm, and aged persons, children and maternity cases, and for the passage of ministers of all religions, medical personnel and medical equipment on their way to such areas.

Article 18

[Civilian hospitals shall be respected and protected at all times.]

Article 19

The protection to which civilian hospitals are entitled shall not cease unless they are used to commit, outside their humanitarian duties, acts harmful to the enemy. Protection may, however, cease only after

due warning has been given, naming, in all appropriate cases, a reasonable time limit, and after such warning has remained unheeded.

The fact that sick or wounded members of the armed forces are nursed in these hospitals, or the presence of small arms and ammunition taken from such combatants and not yet handed to the proper service, shall not be considered to be acts harmful to the enemy.

Article 20

Persons regularly and solely engaged in the operation and administration of civilian hospitals, including the personnel engaged in the search for, removal and transporting of and caring for wounded and sick civilians, the infirm and maternity cases, shall be respected and protected.

Article 21

[Hospital trains and convoys shall enjoy absolute protection.]

Article 22

[Medical relief aircraft shall not be attacked.]

Article 23

Each High Contracting Party shall allow the free passage of all consignments of medical and hospital stores and objects necessary for religious worship intended only for civilians of another High Contracting Party, even if the latter is its adversary. It shall likewise permit the free passage of all consignments of essential foodstuffs, clothing and tonics intended for children under fifteen, expectant mothers and maternity cases.

Article 24

[The rights of orphans and children separated from their families are to be protected.]

Article 25

All persons in the territory of a Party to the conflict, or in a territory occupied by it, shall be enabled to give news of a strictly personal nature to members of their families, wherever they may be, and to receive news from them. This correspondence shall be forwarded speedily and without undue delay.

Article 26

Each Party to the conflict shall facilitate enquiries made by members of families dispersed owing to the war, with the object of renewing contact with one another and of meeting, if possible. It shall encourage, in particular, the work of organizations engaged on this task provided they are acceptable to it and conform to its security regulations.

PART III

STATUS AND TREATMENT OF PROTECTED PERSONS

Section I

Provisions Common to the Territories of the Parties to the Conflict and to Occupied Territories

Article 27

Protected persons are entitled, in all circumstances, to respect for their persons, their honour, their family rights, their religious convictions and practices, and their manners and customs. They shall at all times be humanely treated, and shall be protected especially against all acts of violence or threats thereof and against insults and public curiosity.

Women shall be especially protected against any attack on their honour, in particular against rape, enforced prostitution, or any form of indecent assault.

Without prejudice to the provisions relating to their state of health, age and sex, all protected persons shall be treated with the same consideration by the Party to the conflict in whose power they are, without any adverse distinction based, in particular, on race, religion or political opinion.

However, the Parties to the conflict may take such measures of control and security in regard to protected persons as may be necessary as a result of the war.

Article 28

The presence of a protected person may not be used to render certain points or areas immune from military operations.

Article 29

The Party to the conflict in whose hands protected persons may be, is responsible for the treatment accorded to them by its agents, irrespective of any individual responsibility which may be incurred.

Article 30

Protected persons shall have every facility for making application to the Protecting Powers, the International Committee of the Red Cross, the National Red Cross (Red Crescent, Red Lion and

Sun) Society of the country where they may be, as well as to any organization that might assist them.

Article 31

No physical or moral coercion shall be exercised against protected persons, in particular to obtain information from them or from third parties.

Article 32

The High Contracting Parties specifically agree that each of them is prohibited from taking any measure of such a character as to cause the physical suffering or extermination of protected persons in their hands. This prohibition applies not only to murder, torture, corporal punishment, mutilation and medical or scientific experiments not necessitated by the medical treatment of a protected person, but also to any other measures of brutality whether applied by civilian or military agents.

Article 33

No protected person may be punished for an offence he or she has not personally committed. Collective penalties and likewise all measures of intimidation or of terrorism are prohibited.

Pillage is prohibited.

Reprisals against protected persons and their property are prohibited.

Article 34

The taking of hostages is prohibited.

Section II

Aliens in the Territory of a Party to the Conflict

Article 35

All protected persons who may desire to leave the territory at the outset of, or during a conflict, shall be entitled to do so, unless their departure is contrary to the national interests of the State. The applications of such persons to leave shall be decided in accordance with regularly established procedures and the decisions shall be taken as rapidly as possible. Those persons permitted to leave may provide themselves with the necessary funds for their journey and take with them a reasonable amount of their effects and articles of personal use.

Article 36

[The way in which such departures shall be carried out.]

Article 37

Protected persons who are confined pending proceedings or serving a sentence involving loss of liberty, shall during their confinement be humanely treated.

As soon as they are released, they may ask to leave the territory in conformity with the foregoing Articles.

Article 39

Protected persons who, as a result of the war, have lost their gainful employment, shall be granted the opportunity to find paid employment. That opportunity shall, subject to security considerations and to the provisions of Article 40, be equal to that enjoyed by the nationals of the Power in whose territory they are.

Article 40

Protected persons may be compelled to work only to the same extent as nationals of the Party to the conflict in whose territory they are.

If protected persons are of enemy nationality, they may only be compelled to do work which is normally necessary to ensure the feeding, sheltering, clothing, transport and health of human beings and which is not directly related to the conduct of military operations.

Article 44

In applying the measures of control mentioned in the present Convention, the Detaining Power shall not treat as enemy aliens exclusively on the basis of their nationality *de jure* of an enemy State, refugees who do not, in fact, enjoy the protection of any government.

Article 45

Protected persons shall not be transferred to a Power which is not a party to the Convention.

This provision shall in no way constitute an obstacle to the repatriation of protected persons, or to their return to their country of residence after the cessation of hostilities.

In no circumstances shall a protected person be transferred to a country where he or she may have reason to fear persecution for his or her political opinions or religious beliefs.

Section III

Occupied Territories

Article 47

Protected persons who are in occupied territory shall not be deprived, in any case or in any manner whatsoever, of the benefits of the present Convention by any change introduced, as the result of the occupation of a territory, into the institutions or government of the said territory, nor by any agreement concluded between the authorities of the occupied territories and the Occupying Power, nor by any annexation by the latter of the whole or part of the occupied territory.

Article 49

Individual or mass forcible transfers, as well as deportations of protected persons from occupied territory to the territory of the Occupying Power or to that of any other country, occupied or not, are prohibited, regardless of their motive.

Nevertheless, the Occupying Power may undertake total or partial evacuation of a given area if the security of the population or imperative military reasons so demand. Such evacuations may not involve the displacement of protected persons outside the bounds of the occupied territory except when for material reasons it is impossible to avoid such displacement. Persons thus evacuated shall be transferred back to their homes as soon as hostilities in the area in question have ceased.

Article 50

[Particular care is to be taken with children.]

Article 51

[Protected persons shall not be forced into military service. The nature of compulsory labour is determined.]

Article 52

No contract, agreement or regulation shall impair the right of any worker, whether voluntary or not and wherever he may be, to apply to the representatives of the Protecting Power in order to request the said Power's intervention.

Article 53

Any destruction by the Occupying Power of real or personal property belonging individually or collectively to private persons, or to the State, or to other public authorities, or to social or cooperative organizations, is prohibited, except where such destruction is rendered absolutely necessary by military operations.

Article 54

The Occupying Power may not alter the status of public officials or judges in the occupied territories, or in any way apply sanctions to or take any measures of coercion or discrimination against them, should they abstain from fulfilling their functions for reasons of conscience.

Article 55

To the fullest extent of the means available to it, the Occupying Power has the duty of ensuring the food and medical supplies of the population; it should, in particular, bring in the necessary foodstuffs, medical stores and other articles if the resources of the occupied territory are inadequate.

The Occupying Power may not requisition foodstuffs, articles or medical supplies available in the occupied territory, except for use by the occupation forces and administration personnel, and then only if the requirements of the civilian population have been taken into account. Subject to the provisions of other international Conventions, the Occupying Power shall make arrangements to ensure that fair value is paid for any requisitioned goods.

Article 56

[The Occupying Power is responsible for maintaining hospital and medical services, and for public health and hygiene.]

Article 57

[Civilian hospitals shall be requisitioned only in emergencies, and then only temporarily.]

Article 58

The Occupying Power shall permit ministers of religion to give spiritual assistance to the members of their religious communities.

The Occupying Power shall also accept consignments of books and articles required for religious needs and shall facilitate their distribution in occupied territory.

Article 59

If the whole or part of the population of an occupied territory is inadequately supplied, the Occupying Power shall agree to relief schemes on behalf of the said population, and shall facilitate them by all the means at its disposal.

Such schemes, which may be undertaken either by States or by impartial humanitarian organizations such as the International Committee of the Red Cross, shall consist, in particular, of the provision of consignments of foodstuffs, medical supplies and clothing.

All Contracting Parties shall permit the free passage of these consignments and shall guarantee their protection.

Article 62

Subject to imperative reasons of security, protected persons in occupied territories shall be permitted to receive the individual relief consignments sent to them.

Article 63

[National Red Cross and comparable societies shall be enabled to carry out their humanitarian activities.]

Article 64

The penal laws of the occupied territory shall remain in force, with the exception that they may be repealed or suspended by the Occupying Power in cases where they constitute a threat to its security or an obstacle to the application of the present Convention. Subject to the latter consideration and to the necessity for ensuring the effective administration of justice, the tribunals of the occupied territory shall continue to function in respect of all offences covered by the said laws.

Article 65

The penal provisions enacted by the Occupying Power shall not come into force before they have been published and brought to the knowledge of the inhabitants in their own language. The effect of these penal provisions shall not be retroactive.

Article 71

No sentence shall be pronounced by the competent courts of the Occupying Power except after a regular trial.

Accused persons who are prosecuted by the Occupying Power shall be promptly informed, in writing, in a language which they understand, of the particulars of the charges preferred against them, and shall be brought to trial as rapidly as possible. The Protecting Power shall be informed of all proceedings instituted by the Occupying Power against protected persons in respect of charges involving the death penalty or imprisonment for two years or more; it shall be enabled, at any time, to obtain information regarding the state of such proceedings. Furthermore, the Protecting Power shall be entitled, on request, to be furnished with all particulars of these and of any other proceedings instituted by the Occupying Power against protected persons.

Article 74

Representatives of the Protecting Power shall have the right to attend the trial of any protected person, unless the hearing has, as an exceptional measure, to be held *in camera* in the interests of the security of the Occupying Power, which shall then notify the Protecting Power. A notification in respect of the date and place of trial shall be sent to the Protecting Power.

Article 76

Protected persons accused of offences shall be detained in the occupied country, and if convicted they shall serve their sentences therein. They shall, if possible, be separated from other detainees and shall enjoy conditions of food and hygiene which will be sufficient to keep them in good health, and which will be at least equal to those obtaining in prisons in the occupied country.

They shall receive the medical attention required by their state of health.

They shall also have the right to receive any spiritual assistance which they may require.

Women shall be confined in separate quarters and shall be under the direct supervision of women.

Proper regard shall be paid to the special treatment due to minors.

Protected persons who are detained shall have the right to be visited by delegates of the Protecting Power and of the International Committee of the Red Cross, in accordance with the provisions of Article 143.

Such persons shall have the right to receive at least one relief parcel monthly.

Section IV

Regulations for the Treatment of Internees

Chapter I

General Provisions

Article 79

The Parties to the conflict shall not intern protected persons, except in accordance with the provisions of Articles 41, 42, 43, 68 and 78.

Article 80

Internees shall retain their full capacity and shall exercise such attendant rights as may be compatible with their status.

Article 81

Parties to the conflict who intern protected persons shall be bound to provide free of charge for their maintenance, and to grant them also the medical attention required by their state of health.

No deduction from the allowances, salaries or credits due to the internees shall be made for the repayment of these costs.

The Detaining Power shall provide for the support of those dependent on the internees, if such dependents are without adequate means of support or are unable to earn a living.

Article 82

The Detaining Power shall, as far as possible, accommodate the internees according to their nationality, language and customs. Internees who are nationals of the same country shall not be separated merely because they have different languages.

Throughout the duration of their internment, members of the same family, and in particular parents and children, shall be lodged together in the same place of internment, except when separation of a temporary nature is necessitated for reasons of employment or health or for the purposes of enforcement of the provisions of Chapter IX of the present Section. Internees may request that their children who are left at liberty without parental care shall be interned with them.

Wherever possible, interned members of the same family shall be housed in the same premises and given separate accommodation from other internees, together with facilities for leading a proper family life.

Chapter II

Place of Internment

Article 83

[Places of internment shall be communicated to the enemy, and shall be clearly identified from the air.]

Article 84

Internees shall be accommodated and administered separately from prisoners of war and from persons deprived of liberty for any other reason.

Article 85

The Detaining Power is bound to take all necessary and possible measures to ensure that protected persons shall, from the outset of their internment, be accommodated in buildings or quarters which afford every possible safeguard as regards hygiene and health, and provide efficient protection against the rigours of the climate and the effects of the war.

Article 86

The Detaining Power shall place at the disposal of interned persons, of whatever denomination, premises suitable for the holding of their religious services.

Article 87

Canteens shall be installed in every place of internment, except where other suitable facilities are available. Their purpose shall be to enable internees to make purchases, at prices not higher than local market prices, of foodstuffs and articles of everyday use, including soap and tobacco, such as would increase their personal well-being and comfort.

Article 88

[Air raid shelters shall be provided in all places of internment.]

Chapter III

Food and Clothing

Article 89

[Adequate food rations and supplies of drinking water shall be provided for all internees.]

Article 90

[All internees shall be provided with adequate clothing and footwear, including suitable working outfits.]

Chapter IV

Hygiene and Medical Attention

Article 91

Every place of internment shall have an adequate infirmary, under the direction of a qualified doctor, where internees may have the attention they require, as well as an appropriate diet. Isolation wards shall be set aside for cases of contagious or mental diseases.

Treatment, including the provision of any apparatus necessary for the maintenance of internees in good health, particularly dentures and other artificial appliances and spectacles, shall be free of charge to the internee.

Article 92

Medical inspections of internees shall be made at least once a month. Their purpose shall be, in particular, to supervise the general state of health, nutrition and cleanliness of internees, and to detect contagious diseases, especially tuberculosis, malaria, and venereal diseases. Such inspections shall include, in particular, the checking of weight of each internee and, at least once a year, radioscopic examination.

Chapter V

Religious, Intellectual and Physical Activities

Article 93

[Internees shall be free to practise their religious duties, and ministers of religion free to carry out their activities.]

Article 94

[Opportunities shall be provided for internees to follow intellectual, educational, and recreational pursuits.]

Article 95

[Internees shall not be employed against their wishes. Work shall not be degrading or humiliating.]

Chapter VI

Personal Property and Financial Resources

Article 97

Internees shall be permitted to retain articles of personal use. Monies, cheques, bonds, etc., and valuables in their possession may not be taken from them except in accordance with established procedure. Detailed receipts shall be given therefor.

The amounts shall be paid into the account of every internee as provided for in Article 98. Such amounts may not be converted into any other currency unless legislation in force in the territory in which the owner is interned so requires or the internee gives his consent.

Articles which have above all a personal or sentimental value may not be taken away.

A woman internee shall not be searched except by a woman.

Article 98

All internees shall receive regular allowances, sufficient to enable them to purchase goods and articles, such as tobacco, toilet requisites, etc. Such allowances may take the form of credits or purchase coupons.

Chapter VII

Administration and Discipline

Article 99

Every place of internment shall be put under the authority of a responsible officer, chosen from the regular military forces or the regular civil administration of the Detaining Power. The officer in charge of the place of internment must have in his possession a copy of the present Convention in the official language, or one of the official languages, of his country and shall be responsible for its application. The staff in control of internees shall be instructed in the provisions of the present Convention and of the administrative measures adopted to ensure its application.

The text of the present Convention and the texts of special agreements concluded under the said Convention shall be posted inside the place of internment, in a language which the internees understand, or shall be in the possession of the Internee Committee.

Regulations, orders, notices and publications of every kind shall be communicated to the internees and posted inside the places of internment, in a language which they understand.

Every order and command addressed to internees individually, must likewise, be given in a language which they understand.

Article 100

The disciplinary regime in places of internment shall be consistent with humanitarian principles, and shall in no circumstances include regulations imposing on internees any physical exertion dangerous to their health or involving physical or moral victimization. Identification by tattooing or imprinting signs or markings on the body, is prohibited.

In particular, prolonged standing and roll-calls, punishment drill, military drill and manoeuvres, or the reduction of food rations, are prohibited.

Article 101

Internees shall have the right to present to the authorities in whose power they are, any petition with regard to the conditions of internment to which they are subjected.

They shall also have the right to apply without restriction through the Internee Committee or, if they consider it necessary, direct to the representatives of the Protecting Power, in order to indicate to them any points on which they may have complaints to make with regard to the conditions of internment.

Article 102

In every place of internment, the internees shall freely elect by secret ballot every six months, the members of a Committee empowered to represent them before the Detaining and the Protecting Powers, the International Committee of the Red Cross and any other organization which may assist them. The members of the Committee shall be eligible for re-election.

Internees so elected shall enter upon their duties after their election has been approved by the detaining authorities. The reasons for any refusals or dismissals shall be communicated to the Protecting Powers concerned.

Chapter VIII

Relations with the Exterior

Article 105

Immediately upon interning protected persons, the Detaining Powers shall inform them, the Power to which they owe allegiance and their Protecting Power of the measures taken for executing the provisions of the present Chapter. The Detaining Powers shall likewise inform the Parties concerned of any subsequent modifications of such measures.

Article 106

[All internees permitted to inform their relatives of their detention, state of health, and their address.]

Article 107

[Internees permitted to send and receive letters and cards.]

Article 108

Internees shall be allowed to receive, by post or by any other means, individual parcels or collective shipments containing in particular foodstuffs, clothing, medical supplies, as well as books and objects of a devotional, educational or recreational character which may meet their needs. Such shipments shall in no way free the Detaining Power from the obligations imposed upon it by virtue of the present Convention.

Article 110

All relief shipments for internees shall be exempt from import, customs and other dues.

Article 112

The censoring of correspondence addressed to internees or despatched by them shall be done as quickly as possible.

Article 116

Every internee shall be allowed to receive visitors, especially near relatives, at regular intervals and as frequently as possible.

As far as is possible, internees shall be permitted to visit their homes in urgent cases, particularly in cases of death or serious illness of relatives.

Chapter IX

Penal and Disciplinary Sanctions

Article 117

[The laws of the territory in which they are

detained will continue to apply to internees. There shall be no double punishment.]

Article 118

The courts or authorities shall in passing sentence take as far as possible into account the fact that the defendant is not a national of the Detaining Power. They shall be free to reduce the penalty prescribed for the offence with which the internee is charged and shall not be obliged, to this end, to apply the minimum sentence prescribed.

Imprisonment in premises without daylight and, in general, all forms of cruelty without exception are forbidden.

Internees who have served disciplinary or judicial sentences shall not be treated differently from other internees.

The duration of preventive detention undergone by an internee shall be deducted from any disciplinary or judicial penalty involving confinement to which he may be sentenced.

Internee Committee shall be informed of all judicial proceedings instituted against internees whom they represent, and of their result.

Article 119

[Disciplinary punishment of internees shall not be inhuman, brutal, or dangerous for their health.]

Article 120

Internees who are recaptured after having escaped or when attempting to escape, shall be liable only to disciplinary punishment in respect of this act, even if it is a repeated offence.

Article 121

Escape, or attempt to escape, even if it is a repeated offence, shall not be deemed an aggravating circumstance in cases where an internee is prosecuted for offences committed during his escape.

Article 123

[Disciplinary punishment may be ordered only by the commandant of the place of internment.]

Article 124

Internees shall not in any case be transferred to penitentiary establishments (prisons, penitentiaries, convict prisons, etc.) to undergo disciplinary punishment therein.

The premises in which disciplinary punishments are undergone shall conform to sanitary requirements; they shall in particular be provided with adequate bedding. Internees undergoing punishment shall be enabled to keep themselves in a state of cleanliness.

Women internees undergoing disciplinary punishment shall be confined in separate quarters from male internees and shall be under the immediate supervision of women.

Article 125

[Basic rights of internees undergoing disciplinary punishment are safeguarded.]

Chapter X

Transfers of Internees

Article 127

The transfer of internees shall always be effected humanely.

Sick, wounded or infirm internees and maternity cases shall not be transferred if the journey would be seriously detrimental to them, unless their safety imperatively so demands.

If the combat zone draws close to a place of internment, the internees in the said place shall not be transferred unless their removal can be carried out in adequate conditions of safety, or unless they are exposed to greater risks by remaining on the spot than by being transferred.

Article 128

In the event of transfer, internees shall be officially advised of their departure and of their new postal address. Such notification shall be given in time for them to pack their luggage and inform their next of kin.

Chapter XI

Deaths

Article 129

[Regulations concerning the wills and death certificates of internees who die in custody.]

Article 130

The detaining authorities shall ensure that internees who die while interned are honourably buried, if possible according to the rites of the religion to which they belonged, and that their graves are respected, properly maintained, and marked in such a way that they can always be recognized.

Deceased internees shall be buried in individual graves unless unavoidable circumstances require the use of collective graves. Bodies may be cremated only for imperative reasons of hygiene, on account of the religion of the deceased or in accordance with his expressed wish to this effect. In case of cremation, the fact shall be stated and the reasons given in the death certificate of the deceased. The ashes shall be retained for safe-keeping by the detaining authorities and shall be transferred as soon as possible to the next of kin on their request.

Article 131

Every death or serious injury of an internee, caused or suspected to have been caused by a sentry, another internee or any other person, as well as any death the cause of which is unknown, shall be immediately followed by an official enquiry by the Detaining Power.

A communication on this subject shall be sent immediately to the Protecting Power. The evidence of any witnesses shall be taken, and a report including such evidence shall be prepared and forwarded to the said Protecting Power.

If the enquiry indicates the guilt of one or more persons, the Detaining Power shall take all necessary steps to ensure the prosecution of the person or persons responsible.

Chapter XII

Release, Repatriation and Accommodation in Neutral Countries

Article 132

[Internees shall be released as soon as circumstances permit.]

Article 133

Internment shall cease as soon as possible after the close of hostilities.

Internees in the territory of a Party to the conflict against whom penal proceedings are pending for offences not exclusively subject to disciplinary penalties, may be detained until the close of such proceedings and, if circumstances require, until the completion of the penalty. The same shall apply to internees who have been previously sentenced to a punishment depriving them of liberty.

Article 134

The High Contracting Parties shall endeavour, upon the close of hostilities or occupation, to ensure the return of all internees to their last place of residence, or to facilitate their repatriation.

Article 135

The Detaining Power shall bear the expense of returning released internees to the places where they were residing when interned, or, if it took them into custody while they were in transit or on the high seas, the cost of completing their journey or of their return to their point of departure.

Section V

Information Bureaux and Central Agency

Article 136

[Official Information Bureaux are to be established to receive and transmit information about internees.]

Article 137

[The Bureaux to forward information concerning protected persons, and to deal with all enquiries.]

Article 138

The information received by the national Bureaux and transmitted by it shall be of such a character as to make it possible to identify the protected person exactly and to advise his next of kin quickly. The information in respect of each person shall include at least his surname, first names, place and date of birth, nationality, last residence and distinguishing characteristics, the first name of the father and the maiden name of the mother, the date, place and nature of the action taken with regard to the individual, the address at which correspondence may be sent to him and the name and address of the person to be informed.

Likewise, information regarding the state of health of internees who are seriously ill or seriously wounded shall be supplied regularly and if possible every week.

Article 139

[The Information Bureaux to be responsible for the personal valuables left by protected persons who have been released or who have escaped or died.]

Article 140

[A Central Information Agency to be created in a neutral country.]

Article 141

The national Information Bureaux and the Central Information Agency shall enjoy free postage for all mail, likewise the exemptions provided for in Article 110, and further, so far as possible, exemption from telegraphic charges or, at least, greatly reduced rates.

PART IV

EXECUTION OF THE CONVENTION

Section I

General Provisions

Article 142

[The International Red Cross and similar agencies shall not be prevented from carrying out relief work.]

Article 143

Representatives or delegates of the Protecting Powers shall have permission to go to all places where protected persons are, particularly to places of internment, detention and work.

They shall have access to all premises occupied by protected persons and shall be able to interview the latter without witnesses, personally or through an interpreter.

Such visits may not be prohibited except for reasons of imperative military necessity, and then only as an exceptional and temporary measure. Their duration and frequency shall not be restricted.

The delegates of the International Committee of the Red Cross shall also enjoy the above prerogatives. The appointment of such delegates shall be submitted to the approval of the Power governing the territories where they will carry out their duties.

Article 144

[The Convention is to be fully disseminated in signatory countries, especially among civil, military, and police authorities.]

Article 146

The High Contracting Parties undertake to enact any legislation necessary to provide effective penal sanctions for persons committing, or ordering to be committed, any of the grave breaches of the present Convention defined in the following Article.

Article 147

Grave breaches to which the preceding Article relates shall be those involving any of the following acts, if committed against persons or property protected by the present Convention: wilful killing, torture or inhuman treatment, including biological experiments, wilfully causing great suffering or serious injury to body or health, unlawful deportation or transfer or unlawful confinement of a protected person, compelling a protected person to serve in the forces of a hostile Power, or wilfully depriving a protected person of the rights of fair and regular trial prescribed in the present Convention, taking of hostages and extensive destruction and appropriation of property, not justified by military necessity and carried out unlawfully and wantonly.

Article 148

No High Contracting Party shall be allowed to absolve itself or any other High Contracting Party of any liability incurred by itself or by another High Contracting Party in respect of breaches referred to in the preceding Article.

Article 149

At the request of a Party to the conflict, an enquiry shall be instituted, in a manner to be decided between the interested Parties, concerning any alleged violation of the Convention.

If agreement has not been reached concerning the procedure for the enquiry, the Parties should agree on the choice of an umpire who will decide upon the procedure to be followed.

Once the violation has been established, the Parties to the conflict shall put an end to it and shall repress it with the least possible delay.

Section II

Final Provisions

Article 150

The present Convention is established in English and in French. Both texts are equally authentic.

The Swiss Federal Council shall arrange for official translations of the Convention to be made in the Russian and Spanish languages.

Article 151

The present Convention, which bears the date of this day, is open to signature until February 12, 1950, in the name of the Powers represented at the Conference which opened at Geneva on April 21, 1949.

Article 152

The present Convention shall be ratified as soon as possible and the ratifications shall be deposited at Berne.

A record shall be drawn up of the deposit of each instrument of ratification and certified copies of this record shall be transmitted by the Swiss Federal Council to all the Powers in whose name the Convention has been signed, or whose accession has been notified.

Article 153

The present Convention shall come into force six months after not less than two instruments of ratification have been deposited.

Thereafter, it shall come into force for each High

Contracting Party six months after the deposit of the instrument of ratification.

Article 154

In the relations between the Powers who are bound by The Hague Convention respecting the Laws and Customs of War on Land, whether that of July 29, 1899, or that of October 18, 1907, and who are parties to the present Convention, this last Convention shall be supplementary to Section II and III of the Regulations annexed to the above mentioned Conventions of The Hague.

Article 155

From the date of its coming into force, it shall be open to any Power in whose name the present Convention has not been signed, to accede to this Convention.

Article 156

Accessions shall be notified in writing to the Swiss Federal Council, and shall take effect six months after the date on which they are received.

The Swiss Federal Council shall communicate the accessions to all the Powers in whose name the Convention has been signed, or whose accession has been notified.

Article 157

The situations provided for in Articles 2 and 3 shall give immediate effect to ratifications deposited and accessions notified by the Parties to the conflict before or after the beginning of hostilities or occupa-tion. The Swiss Federal Council shall communicate by the quickest method any ratifications or accessions received from Parties to the conflict.

Article 158

Each of the High Contracting Parties shall be at liberty to denounce the present Convention.

The denunciation shall be notified in writing to the Swiss Federal Council, which shall transmit it to the Governments of all the High Contracting Parties.

The denunciation shall take effect one year after the notification thereof has been made to the Swiss Federal Council. However, a denunciation of which notification has been made at a time when the denouncing Power is involved in a conflict shall not take effect until peace has been concluded, and until after operations connected with the release, repatriation and re-establishment of the persons protected by the present Convention have been terminated.

The denunciation shall have effect only in respect of the denouncing Power. It shall in no way impair the obligations which the Parties to the conflict shall remain bound to fulfil by virtue of the principles of the law of nations, as they result from the usages established among civilized peoples, from the laws of humanity and the dictates of the public conscience.

Article 159

The Swiss Federal Council shall register the present Convention with the Secretariat of the United Nations. The Swiss Federal Council shall also inform the Secretariat of the United Nations of all ratifications, accessions and denunciations received by it with respect to the present Convention.

The Antarctic Treaty

Date of signature: *December 1, 1959*
Place of signature: *Washington, DC*
Signatory states: *Argentina, Australia, Belgium, Chile, France, Japan, New Zealand, Norway, the Union of South Africa, the Soviet Union, the United Kingdom of Great Britain and Northern Ireland, the United States*
Ratifications: *Argentina, Australia, Belgium, Brazil, Chile, Czechoslovakia, Denmark, France, German Democratic Republic, Federal Republic of Germany, Italy, Japan, Netherlands, New Zealand, Norway, Papua New Guinea, Peru, Poland, Romania, Union of South Africa, the Soviet Union, United Kingdom of Great Britain and Northern Ireland, the United States, Uruguay*
Accessions: *Poland*

Date of entry into force: *June 23, 1961*

[The signatories],
Recognizing that it is in the interest of all mankind that Antarctica shall continue forever to be used exclusively for peaceful purposes and shall not become the scene or object of international discord;
Acknowledging the substantial contributions to scientific knowledge resulting from international cooperation in scientific investigation in Antarctica;
Convinced that the establishment of a firm foundation for the continuation and development of such cooperation on the basis of freedom of scientific investigation in Antarctica as applied during the International Geophysical Year accords with the interests of science and the progress of all mankind;

Convinced also that a treaty ensuring the use of Antarctica for peaceful purposes only and the continuance of international harmony in Antarctica will further the purposes and principles embodied in the Charter of the United Nations;

Have agreed as follows:

Article I

1. Antarctica shall be used for peaceful purposes only. There shall be prohibited, *inter alia*, any measures of a military nature, such as the establishment of military bases and fortifications, the carrying out of military maneuvers, as well as the testing of any type of weapons.

2. The present Treaty shall not prevent the use of military personnel or equipment for scientific research or for any other peaceful purpose.

Article II

Freedom of scientific investigation in Antarctica and cooperation toward that end, as applied during the International Geophysical Year, shall continue, subject to the provisions of the present Treaty.

Article III

1. In order to promote international cooperation in scientific investigation in Antarctica, as provided for in Article II of the present Treaty, the Contracting Parties agree that, to the greatest extent feasible and practicable:

(a) information regarding plans for scientific programs in Antarctica shall be exchanged to permit maximum economy and efficiency of operations;

(b) scientific personnel shall be exchanged in Antarctica between expeditions and stations;

(c) scientific observations and results from Antarctica shall be exchanged and made freely available.

2. In implementing this Article, every encouragement shall be given to the establishment of cooperative working relations with those Specialized Agencies of the United Nations and other international organizations having a scientific or technical interest in Antarctica.

Article IV

1. Nothing contained in the present Treaty shall be interpreted as:

(a) a renunciation by any Contracting Party of previously asserted rights of or claims to territorial sovereignty in Antarctica;

(b) a renunciation or diminution by any Contracting Party of any basis of claim to territorial sovereignty in Antarctica which it may have whether as a result of its activities or those of its nationals in Antarctica, or otherwise;

(c) prejudicing the position of any Contracting Party as regards its recognition or non-recognition of any other State's right of or claim or basis of claim to territorial sovereignty in Antarctica.

2. No acts or activities taking place while the present Treaty is in force shall constitute a basis for asserting, supporting or denying a claim to territorial sovereignty in Antarctica or create any rights of sovereignty in Antarctica. No new claim, or enlargement of an existing claim, to territorial sovereignty in Antarctica shall be asserted while the present Treaty is in force.

Article V

1. Any nuclear explosions in Antarctica and the disposal there of radioactive waste material shall be prohibited.

2. In the event of the conclusion of international agreements concerning the use of nuclear energy, including nuclear explosions and the disposal of radioactive waste material, to which all of the Contracting Parties whose representatives are entitled to participate in the meetings provided for under Article IX are parties, the rules established under such agreements shall apply in Antarctica.

Article VI

The provisions of the present Treaty shall apply to the area south of 60° South Latitude including all ice shelves, but nothing in the present Treaty shall prejudice or in any way affect the rights, or the exercise of the rights, of any State under international law with regard to the high seas within that area.

Article VII

1. In order to promote the objectives and ensure the observance of the provisions of the present Treaty, each Contracting Party whose representatives are entitled to participate in the meetings referred to in Article IX of the Treaty shall have the right to designate observers to carry out any inspection provided for by the present Article. Observers shall be nationals of the Contracting Parties which designate them. The names of observers shall be communicated to every other Contracting Party having the right to designate observers, and like notice shall be given of the termination of their appointment.

2. Each observer designated in accordance with the provisions of paragraph 1 of this Article shall have complete freedom of access at any time to any or all areas of Antarctica.

3. All areas of Antarctica, including all stations, installations and equipment within those areas, and all ships and aircraft at points of discharging or embarking cargoes or personnel in Antarctica, shall be open at all times to inspection by any observers designated in accordance with paragraph 1 of this Article.

4. Aerial observation may be carried out at any time over any or all areas of Antarctica by any of the Contracting Parties having the right to designate observers.

5. Each Contracting Party shall, at the time when the present Treaty enters into force for it, inform the other Contracting Parties, and thereafter shall give them notice in advance, of:

(a) all expeditions to and within Antarctica, on the part of its ships or nationals, and all expeditions to Antarctica organized in or proceeding from its territory;

(b) all stations in Antarctica occupied by its nationals; and

(c) any military personnel or equipment intended to be introduced by it into Antarctica subject to the conditions prescribed in paragraph 2 of Article I of the present Treaty.

Article VIII

1. In order to facilitate the exercise of their functions under the present Treaty, and without prejudice to the respective positions of the Contracting Parties relating to jurisdiction over all other persons in Antarctica, observers designated under paragraph 1 of Article VII and scientific personnel exchanged under subparagraph 1 (b) of Article III of the Treaty, and members of the staffs accompanying any such persons, shall be subject only to the jurisdiction of the Contracting Party of which they are nationals in respect of all acts or omissions occurring while they are in Antarctica for the purpose of exercising their functions.

2. Without prejudice to the provisions of paragraph 1 of this Article, and pending the adoption of measures in pursuance of subparagraph 1 (e) of Article IX, the Contracting Parties concerned in any case of dispute with regard to the exercise of jurisdiction in Antarctica shall immediately consult together with a view to reaching a mutually acceptable solution.

Article IX

1. Representatives of the Contracting Parties named in the preamble to the present Treaty shall meet at the City of Canberra within two months after the date of entry into force of the Treaty, and thereafter at suitable intervals and places, for the purpose of exchanging information, consulting together on matters of common interest pertaining to Antarctica, and formulating and considering, and recommending to their Governments, measures in furtherance of the principles and objectives of the Treaty, including measures regarding:

(a) use of Antarctica for peaceful purposes only;

(b) facilitation of scientific research in Antarctica:

(c) facilitation of international scientific cooperation in Antarctica;

(d) facilitation of the exercise of the rights of inspection provided for in Article VII of the Treaty;

(e) questions relating to the exercise of jurisdiction in Antarctica;

(f) preservation and conservation of living resources in Antarctica.

2. Each Contracting Party which has become a party to the present Treaty by accession under Article XIII shall be entitled to appoint representatives to participate in the meetings referred to in paragraph 1 of the present Article, during such time as that Contracting Party demonstrates its interest in Antarctica by conducting substantial scientific research activity there, such as the establishment of a scientific station or the despatch of a scientific expedition.

3. Reports from the observers referred to in Article VII of the present Treaty shall be transmitted to the representatives of the Contracting Parties participating in the meetings referred to in paragraph 1 of the present Article.

4. The measures referred to in paragraph 1 of this Article shall become effective when approved by all the Contracting Parties whose representatives were entitled to participate in the meetings held to consider those measures.

5. Any or all of the rights established in the present Treaty may be exercised as from the date of entry into force of the Treaty whether or not any measures facilitating the exercise of such rights have been proposed, considered or approved as provided in this Article.

Article X

Each of the Contracting Parties undertakes to exert appropriate efforts, consistent with the Charter of the United Nations, to the end that no one engages in any activity in Antarctica contrary to the principles or purposes of the present Treaty.

Article XI

1. If any dispute arises between two or more of the Contracting Parties concerning the interpretation or application of the present Treaty, those Contracting Parties shall consult among themselves with a view to having the dispute resolved by negotiation, inquiry,

mediation, conciliation, arbitration, judicial settlement or other peaceful means of their own choice.

2. Any dispute of this character not so resolved shall, with the consent, in each case, of all parties to the dispute, be referred to the International Court of Justice for settlement; but failure to reach agreement on reference to the International Court shall not absolve parties to the dispute from the responsibility of continuing to seek to resolve it by any of the various peaceful means referred to in paragraph 1 of this Article.

Article XII

1.

(a) The present Treaty may be modified or amended at any time by unanimous agreement of the Contracting Parties whose representatives are entitled to participate in the meetings provided for under Article IX. Any such modification or amendment shall enter into force when the depositary Government has received notice from all such Contracting Parties that they have ratified it.

(b) Such modification or amendment shall thereafter enter into force as to any other Contracting Party when notice of ratification by it has been received by the depositary Government. Any such Contracting Party from which no notice of ratification is received within a period of two years from the date of entry into force of the modification or amendment in accordance with the provisions of subparagraph 1 (a) of this Article shall be deemed to have withdrawn from the present Treaty on the date of the expiration of such period.

2.

(a) If after the expiration of thirty years from the date of entry into force of the present Treaty, any of the Contracting Parties whose representatives are entitled to participate in the meetings provided for under Article IX so requests by a communication addressed to the depositary Government, a Conference of all the Contracting Parties shall be held as soon as practicable to review the operation of the Treaty.

(b) Any modification or amendment to the present Treaty which is approved at such a Conference by a majority of the Contracting Parties there represented, including a majority of those whose representatives are entitled to participate in the meetings provided for under Article IX, shall be communicated by the depositary Government to all the Contracting Parties immediately after the termination of the Conference and shall enter into force in

accordance with the provisions of paragraph 1 of the present Article.

(c) If any such modification or amendment has not entered into force in accordance with the provisions of subparagraph 1 (a) of this Article within a period of two years after the date of its communication to all the Contracting Parties, any Contracting Party may at any time after the expiration of that period give notice to the depositary Government of its withdrawal from the present Treaty; and such withdrawal shall take effect two years after the receipt of the notice by the depositary Government.

Article XIII

1. The present Treaty shall be subject to ratification by the signatory States. It shall be open for accession by any State which is a Member of the United Nations, or by any other State which may be invited to accede to the Treaty with the consent of all the Contracting Parties whose representatives are entitled to participate in the meetings provided for under Article IX of the Treaty.

2. Ratification of or accession to the present Treaty shall be effected by each State in accordance with its constitutional processes.

3. Instruments of ratification and instruments of accession shall be deposited with the Government of the United States of America, hereby designated as the depositary Government.

4. The depositary Government shall inform all signatory and acceding States of the date of each deposit of an instrument of ratification or accession, and the date of entry into force of the Treaty and of any modification or amendment thereto.

5. Upon the deposit of instruments of ratification by all the signatory States, the present Treaty shall enter into force for those States and for States which have deposited instruments of accession. Thereafter the Treaty shall enter into force for any acceding State upon the deposit of its instrument of accession.

6. The present Treaty shall be registered by the depositary Government pursuant to Article 102 of the Charter of the United Nations.

Article XIV

The present Treaty, done in the English, French, Russian and Spanish languages, each version being equally authentic, shall be deposited in the archives of the Government of the United States of America, which shall transmit duly certified copies thereof to the Governments of the signatory and acceding States.

Declaration on the Neutrality of Laos

Date of signature: *July 23, 1962*
Place of signature: *Geneva*
Signatory states: *Burma, Cambodia, Canada,*
People's Republic of China, Democratic
Republic of Viet-Nam, France, India, Poland,
Republic of Viet-Nam, Thailand, the Soviet
Union, the United Kingdom of Great Britain
and Northern Ireland, the United States

[The signatories],
whose representatives took part in the International
Conference on the Settlement of the Laotian Question, 1961–1962;
Welcoming the presentation of the statement of neutrality by the Royal Government of Laos of July 9,
1962, and taking note of this statement, which is,
with the concurrence of the Royal Government of
Laos, incorporated in the present Declaration as an
integral part thereof, and the text of which is as
follows:

THE ROYAL GOVERNMENT OF LAOS

Being resolved to follow the path of peace and
neutrality in conformity with the interests and aspirations of the Laotian people, as well as the principles of the Joint Communiqué of Zurich dated June
22, 1961, and of the Geneva Agreements of 1954, in
order to build a peaceful, neutral, independent, democratic, unified and prosperous Laos,

Solemnly declares that:

(1) It will resolutely apply the five principles of
peaceful co-existence in foreign relations, and will
develop friendly relations and establish diplomatic
relations with all countries, the neighbouring countries first and foremost, on the basis of equality and
of respect for the independence and sovereignty of
Laos;

(2) It is the will of the Laotian people to protect and
ensure respect for the sovereignty, independence,
neutrality, unity, and territorial integrity of Laos;

(3) It will not resort to the use or threat of force in
any way which might impair the peace of other
countries, and will not interfere in the internal
affairs of other countries;

(4) It will not enter into any military alliance or into
any agreement, whether military or otherwise,
which is inconsistent with the neutrality of the
Kingdom of Laos; it will not allow the establishment of any foreign military base on Laotian territory, nor allow any country to use Laotian territory
for military purposes or for the purposes of interference in the internal affairs of other countries, nor

recognise the protection of any alliance or military
coalition, including SEATO;

(5) It will not allow any foreign interference in the
internal affairs of the Kingdom of Laos in any form
whatsoever;

(6) Subject to the provisions of Article 5 of the Protocol, it will require the withdrawal from Laos of
all foreign troops and military personnel, and will
not allow any foreign troops or military personnel
to be introduced into Laos;

(7) It will accept direct and unconditional aid from
all countries that wish to help the Kingdom of Laos
build up an independent and autonomous national
economy on the basis of respect for the sovereignty
of Laos;

(8) It will respect the treaties and agreements signed
in conformity with the interests of the Laotian people and of the policy of peace and neutrality of the
Kingdom, in particular the Geneva Agreements of
1962, and will abrogate all treaties and agreements
which are contrary to those principles.

This statement of neutrality by the Royal Government of Laos shall be promulgated constitutionally
and shall have the force of law.

The Kingdom of Laos appeals to all the States
participating in the International Conference on the
Settlement of the Laotian Question, and to all other
States, to recognise the sovereignty, independence,
neutrality, unity and territorial integrity of Laos, to
conform to these principles in all respects, and to
refrain from any action inconsistent therewith.

Confirming the principles of respect for the sovereignty, independence, unity and territorial integrity
of the Kingdom of Laos and non-interference in its
internal affairs which are embodied in the Geneva
Agreements of 1954;

Emphasising the principle of respect for the neutrality of the Kingdom of Laos;

Agreeing that the above-mentioned principles constitute a basis for the peaceful settlement of the Laotian question;

Profoundly convinced that the independence and
neutrality of the Kingdom of Laos will assist the
peaceful democratic development of the Kingdom of
Laos and the achievement of national accord and
unity in that country, as well as the strengthening of
peace and security in South-East Asia;

1. Solemnly declare, in accordance with the will of
the Government and people of the Kingdom of
Laos, as expressed in the statement of neutrality by
the Royal Government of Laos of July 9, 1962, that
they recognise and will respect and observe in every

way the sovereignty, independence, neutrality, unity and territorial integrity of the Kingdom of Laos.

2. Undertake, in particular, that

(a) they will not commit or participate in any way in any act which might directly or indirectly impair the sovereignty, independence, neutrality, unity or territorial integrity of the Kingdom of Laos;

(b) they will not resort to the use or threat of force or any other measure which might impair the peace of the Kingdom of Laos;

(c) they will refrain from all direct or indirect interference in the internal affairs of the Kingdom of Laos;

(d) they will not attach conditions of a political nature to any assistance which they may offer or which the Kingdom of Laos may seek;

(e) they will not bring the Kingdom of Laos in any way into any military alliance or any other agreement, whether military or otherwise, which is inconsistent with her neutrality, nor invite or encourage her to enter into any such alliance or to conclude any such agreement;

(f) they will respect the wish of the Kingdom of Laos not to recognise the protection of any alliance or military coalition, including SEATO;

(g) they will not introduce into the Kingdom of Laos foreign troops or military personnel in any form whatsoever, nor will they in any way facilitate or connive at the introduction of any foreign troops or military personnel;

(h) they will not establish nor will they in any way facilitate or connive at the establishment in the Kingdom of Laos of any foreign military base, foreign strong point or other foreign military installation of any kind;

(i) they will not use the territory of the Kingdom of Laos for interference in the internal affairs of other countries;

(j) they will not use the territory of any country, including their own for interference in the internal affairs of the Kingdom of Laos.

3. Appeal to all other States to recognise, respect and observe in every way the sovereignty, independence and neutrality, and also the unity and territorial integrity, of the Kingdom of Laos and to refrain from any action inconsistent with these principles or with other provisions of the present Declaration.

4. Undertake, in the event of a violation or threat of violation of the sovereignty, independence, neutrality, unity or territorial integrity of the Kingdom of Laos, to consult jointly with the Royal Government of Laos and among themselves in order to consider measures which might prove to be necessary to ensure the observance of these principles and the other provisions of the present Declaration.

5. The present Declaration shall enter into force on signature and together with the statement of neutrality by the Royal Government of Laos of July 9, 1962, shall be regarded as constituting an international agreement. The present Declaration shall be deposited in the archives of the Governments of the United Kingdom and the Union of Soviet Socialist Republics, which shall furnish certified copies thereof to the other signatory States and to all the other States of the world.

Memorandum of Understanding Between the United States of America and the Union of Soviet Socialist Republics Regarding the Establishment of a Direct Communications Link

Also known as: Hot-Line Agreement
Date of signature: June 20, 1963
Place of signature: Geneva
Signatory states: the United States, the Soviet Union

For use in time of emergency, the Government of the United States of America and the Government of the Union of Soviet Socialist Republics have agreed to establish as soon as technically feasible a direct communications link between the two governments.

Each government shall be responsible for the arrangements for the link on its own territory. Each government shall take the necessary steps to ensure continuous functioning of the link and prompt delivery of its head of government of any communications received by means of the link from the head of government of the other party.

Arrangements for establishing and operating the

link are set forth in the Annex which is attached hereto and forms an integral part hereof.

ANNEX TO THE MEMORANDUM OF UNDERSTANDING BETWEEN THE UNITED STATES OF AMERICA AND THE UNION OF SOVIET SOCIALIST REPUBLICS REGARDING THE ESTABLISHMENT OF A DIRECT COMMUNICATIONS LINK

The direct communications link between Washington and Moscow established in accordance with the memorandum, and the operation of such link, shall be governed by the following provisions:

1. The direct communications link shall consist of:

A. Two terminal points with telegraph–teleprinter equipment between which communications shall be directly exchanged;

B. One full-time duplex wire telegraph circuit, routed Washington–London–Copenhagen–Stockholm–Helsinki–Moscow, which shall be used for the transmission of messages;

C. One full-time duplex radio telegraph circuit, routed Washington–Tangier–Moscow, which shall be used for service communications and for coordination of operations between the two terminal points.

If experience in operating the direct communications link should demonstrate that the establishment of an additional wire telegraph circuit is advisable, such circuit may be established by mutual agreement between authorized representatives of both governments.

2. In case of interruption of the wire circuit, transmission of messages shall be effected via the radio circuit, and for this purpose provision shall be made at the terminal points for the capability of prompt switching of all necessary equipment from one circuit to another.

3. The terminal points of the link shall be so equipped as to provide for the transmission and reception of messages from Moscow to Washington in the Russian language and from Washington to Moscow in the English language. In this connection, the USSR shall furnish the United States four sets of telegraph terminal equipment, including page printers, transmitters, and reperforators, with one year's supply of spare parts and all necessary special tools, test equipment, operating instructions and other technical literature, to provide for transmission and reception of messages in the Russian language. The United States shall furnish the Soviet Union four sets of telegraph terminal equipment including page printers, transmitters, and reperforators, with one year's supply of spare parts and all necessary special tools, test equipment, operating instructions and other technical literature, to provide for transmission and reception of messages in the English language. The equipment described in this paragraph shall be exchanged directly between the parties without any payment being required therefor.

4. The terminal points of the direct communications link shall be provided with encoding equipment. For the terminal points in the USSR, four sets of such equipment (each capable of simplex operation), with one year's supply of spare parts, with all necessary special tools, test equipment, operating instructions and other technical literature, and with all necessary blank tape, shall be furnished by the United States to the USSR against payment of the cost thereof by the USSR.

The USSR shall provide for preparation and delivery of keying tapes to the terminal point of the link in the United States for reception of messages from the USSR. The United States shall provide for preparation and delivery of keying tapes to the terminal point of the link in the USSR for reception of messages from the United States. Delivery of prepared keying tapes to the terminal points of the link shall be effected through the Embassy of the USSR in Washington (for the terminal of the link in the USSR) and through the Embassy of the United States in Moscow (for the terminal of the link in the United States).

5. The United States and the USSR shall designate the agencies responsible for the arrangements regarding the direct communications link, for its technical maintenance, continuity and reliability, and for the timely transmission of messages.

Such agencies may, by mutual agreement, decide matters and develop instructions relating to the technical maintenance and operation of the direct communications link and effect arrangements to improve the operation of the link.

6. The technical parameters of the telegraph circuits of the link and of the terminal equipment, as well as the maintenance of such circuits and equipment, shall be in accordance with CCITT and CCIR recommendations.

Transmission and reception of messages over the direct communications link shall be effected in accordance with applicable recommendations of international telegraph and radio communication regulations, as well as with mutually agreed instructions.

7. The costs of the direct communications link shall be borne as follows:

A. The USSR shall pay the full cost of leasing the portion of the telegraph circuit from Moscow to Helsinki and 50 percent of the cost of leasing the portion of the telegraph circuit from Helsinki to London. The United States shall pay the full cost of leasing the portion of the telegraph circuit from

Washington to London and 50 percent of the cost of leasing the portion of the telegraph circuit from London to Helsinki.

B. Payment of the cost of leasing the radio telegraph circuit between Moscow and Washington shall be effected without any transfer of payments between the parties. The USSR shall bear the expenses relating to the transmission of messages from Moscow to Washington. The United States shall bear the expenses relating to the transmission of messages from Washington to Moscow.

Treaty Banning Nuclear Weapon Tests in the Atmosphere, in Outer Space and Under Water

Also known as: Limited Test Ban Treaty, Partial Test Ban Treaty
Date of signature: August 5, 1963
Place of signature: Moscow
Signatory states: Afghanistan, Algeria, Australia, Austria, Belgium, Benin, Bolivia, Brazil, Bulgaria, Burundi, Byelorussia, Cameroon, Canada, Chad, Chile, Colombia, Costa Rica, Cyprus, Czechoslovakia, Denmark, Dominican Republic, Ecuador, Egypt, El Salvador, Ethiopia, Finland, Gabon, German Democratic Republic, Federal Republic of Germany, Ghana, Greece, Guatemala, Guinea-Bissau, Haiti, Honduras, Hungary, Iceland, India, Indonesia, Iran, Iraq, Ireland, Israel, Italy, Ivory Coast, Japan, Jordan, Republic of Korea, Kuwait, Laos, Lebanon, Liberia, Libya, Luxembourg, Madagascar, Malaysia, Mali, Mauritania, Mexico, Mongolia, Morocco, Nepal, Netherlands, New Zealand, Nicaragua, Niger, Nigeria, Norway, Pakistan, Panama, Paraguay, Peru, Philippines, Poland, Portugal, Romania, Rwanda, Samoa, San Marino, Senegal, Sierra Leone, Somalia, Soviet Union, Spain, Sri Lanka, Sudan, Sweden, Switzerland, Syria, Taiwan, Tanzania, Thailand, Togo, Trinidad and Tobago, Tunisia, Turkey, United Kingdom, United States, Upper Volta, Uruguay, Venezuela, Yemen Arab Republic, Yugoslavia, Zaire
Ratifications: Afghanistan, Australia, Austria, Bahamas, Belgium, Benin, Bhutan, Bolivia, Botswana, Brazil, Bulgaria, Burma, Byelorussia, Canada, Cape Verde, Central African Republic, Chad, Chile, Costa Rica, Cyprus, Czechoslovakia, Denmark, Dominican Republic, Ecuador, Egypt, El Salvador, Fiji, Finland, Gabon, Gambia, German Democratic Republic, Federal Republic of Germany, Ghana, Greece, Guatemala, Guinea-Bissau, Honduras, Hungary, Iceland, India, Indonesia, Iran, Iraq, Ireland, Israel, Italy, Ivory Coast, Japan, Jordan, Kenya, Republic of Korea, Kuwait, Laos, Lebanon, Libya, Luxembourg, Madagascar, Malawi, Malta, Mauritania, Mauritius, Mexico, Mongolia, Morocco, Nepal, Netherlands, New Zealand, Nicaragua, Niger, Nigeria, Norway, Papua New Guinea, Peru, Philippines, Poland, Romania, Rwanda, Samoa, San Marino, Senegal, Sierra Leone, Singapore, Somalia, South Africa, Soviet Union, Spain, Sri Lanka, Sudan, Swaziland, Syria, Taiwan, Tanzania, Thailand, Togo, Tonga, Trinidad and Tobago, Turkey, Uganda, United Kingdom, United States, Uruguay, Venezuela, People's Democratic Republic of Yemen, Yugoslavia, Zaire, Zambia
Date of entry into force: October 10, 1963

[The signatories],
Proclaiming as their principal aim the speediest possible achievement of an agreement on general and complete disarmament under strict international control in accordance with the objectives of the United Nations which would put an end to the armaments race and eliminate the incentive to the production and testing of all kinds of weapons, including nuclear weapons.
Seeking to achieve the discontinuance of all test explosions of nuclear weapons for all time, determined to continue negotiations to this end, and desiring to put an end to the contamination of man's environment by radioactive substances,
Have agreed as follows:

Article I

1. Each of the Parties of this Treaty undertakes to prohibit, to prevent, and not to carry out any nuclear weapon test explosion, or any other nuclear explosion, at any place under its jurisdiction or control:

(a) in the atmosphere; beyond its limits, including outer space; or underwater, including territorial waters or high seas; or

(b) in any other environment if such explosion causes radioactive debris to be present outside the territorial limits of the State under whose jurisdiction or control such explosion is conducted. It is understood in this connection that the provisions of this subparagraph are without prejudice to the conclusion of a treaty resulting in the permanent banning of all nuclear test explosions, including all such explosions underground, the conclusion of which, as the Parties have stated in the Preamble to this Treaty, they seek to achieve.

2. Each of the Parties to this Treaty undertakes furthermore to refrain from causing, encouraging, or in any way participating in, the carrying out of any nuclear weapon test explosion, or any other nuclear explosion, anywhere which would take place in any of the environments described, or have the effect referred to, in paragraph 1 of this Article.

Article II

1. Any Party may propose amendments to this Treaty. The text of any proposed amendment shall be submitted to the Depositary Governments which shall circulate it to all Parties to this Treaty. Thereafter, if requested to do so by one-third or more of the Parties, the Depositary Governments shall convene a conference, to which they shall invite all the Parties, to consider such amendment.

2. Any amendment to this Treaty must be approved by a majority of the votes of all the Parties to this Treaty, including the votes of all of the Original Parties. The amendment shall enter into force for all Parties upon the deposit of instruments of ratification by a majority of all the Parties, including the instruments of ratification of all of the Original Parties.

Article III

1. This Treaty shall be open to all States for signature. Any State which does not sign this Treaty before its entry into force in accordance with paragraph 3 of this Article may accede to it at any time.

2. This Treaty shall be subject to ratification by signatory States. Instruments of ratification and instruments of accession shall be deposited with the Governments of the Original Parties—the United States of America, the United Kingdom of Great Britain and Northern Ireland, and the Union of Soviet Socialist Republics—which are hereby designated the Depositary Governments.

3. This Treaty shall enter into force after its ratification by all the Original Parties and the deposit of their instruments of ratification.

4. For States whose instruments of ratification or accession are deposited subsequent to the entry into force of this Treaty, it shall enter into force on the date of the deposit of their instruments of ratification or accession.

5. The Depositary Governments shall promptly inform all signatory and acceding States of the date of each signature, the date of deposit of each instrument of ratification of and accession to this Treaty, the date of its entry into force, and the date of receipt of any requests for conferences or other notices.

6. This Treaty shall be registered by the Depositary Governments pursuant of Article 102 of the Charter of the United Nations.

Article IV

This Treaty shall be of unlimited duration.

Each Party shall in exercising its national sovereignty have the right to withdraw from the Treaty if it decides that extraordinary events, related to the subject matter of this Treaty, have jeopardized the supreme interests of its country. It shall give notice of such withdrawal to all other Parties to the Treaty three months in advance.

Article V

This Treaty, of which the English and Russian texts are equally authentic, shall be deposited in the archives of the Depositary Governments. Duly certified copies of this Treaty shall be transmitted by the Depositary Governments to the Governments of the signatory and acceding States.

Treaty on the Principles Governing the Activities of States in the Exploration and Use of Outer Space, Including the Moon and Other Celestial Bodies

Also known as: Outer Space Treaty
Date of signature: January 27, 1967
Place of signature: London, Moscow, and Washington, DC
Signatory states: Afghanistan, Argentina, Australia, Austria, Belgium, Bolivia, Botswana, Brazil, Bulgaria, Burma, Burundi, Byelorussian Soviet Socialist Republic, Cameroon, Canada, Central African Republic, Chile, China, Colombia, Congo (Kinshasa), Cyprus, Czechoslovakia, Denmark, Dominican Republic, Ecuador, Egypt, El Salvador, Ethiopia, Finland, France, Federal Republic of Germany, Gambia, German Democratic Republic, Ghana, Greece, Guyana, Haiti, Holy See, Honduras, Hungary, Iceland, India,

Indonesia, Iran, Iraq, Iceland, Israel, Italy, Jamaica, Japan, Jordan, Republic of Korea, Laos, Lebanon, Lesotho, Luxembourg, Malaysia, Mexico, Mongolia, Nepal, Netherlands, New Zealand, Nicaragua, Niger, Norway, Pakistan, Panama, Peru, Philippines, Poland, Romania, Rwanda, San Marino, Sierra Leone, Somalia, South Africa, Soviet Union, Sri Lanka, Sweden, Switzerland, Taiwan, Thailand, Togo, Trinidad and Tobago, Tunisia, Turkey, Ukrainian Soviet Socialist Republics, United Arab Republic, United Kingdom, United States, Upper Volta, Uruguay, Venezuela, Republic of Viet-Nam, Yugoslavia, Zaire
Date of entry into force: *October 10, 1967*

The States Parties to this Treaty,
Inspired by the great prospects opening up before mankind as a result of man's entry into outer space,
Recognizing the common interest of all mankind in the progress of the exploration and use of outer space for peaceful purposes,
Believing that the exploration and use of outer space should be carried on for the benefit of all peoples irrespective of the degree of their economic or scientific development,
Desiring to contribute to broad international co-operation in the scientific as well as the legal aspects of the exploration and use of outer space for peaceful purposes,
Believing that such co-operation will contribute to the development of mutual understanding and to the strengthening of friendly relations between States and peoples,
Recalling resolution 1962 (XVIII), entitled "Declaration of Legal Principles Governing the Activities of States in the Exploration and Use of Outer Space", which was adopted unanimously by the United Nations General Assembly on 13 December 1963,
Recalling resolution 1884 (XVIII), calling upon States to refrain from placing in orbit around the Earth any objects carrying nuclear weapons or any other kinds of weapons of mass destruction or from installing such weapons on celestial bodies, which was adopted unanimously by the United Nations General Assembly on 17 October 1963,
Taking account of United Nations General Assembly resolution 110 (II) of 3 November 1947, which condemned propaganda designed or likely to provoke or encourage any threat to the peace, breach of the peace or act of aggression, and considering that the aforementioned resolution is applicable to outer space,
Convinced that a Treaty on Principles Governing the Activities of States in the Exploration and Use of Outer Space, including the Moon and Other Celestial Bodies, will further the Purposes and Principles of the Charter of the United Nations,
Have agreed on the following:

Article I

The exploration and use of outer space, including the moon and other celestial bodies, shall be carried out for the benefit and in the interests of all countries, irrespective of their degree of economic or scientific development, and shall be the province of all mankind.
Outer space, including the moon and other celestial bodies, shall be free for exploration and use by all States without discrimination of any kind, on a basis of equality and in accordance with international law, and there shall be free access to all areas of celestial bodies.
There shall be freedom of scientific investigation in outer space, including the moon and other celestial bodies, and States shall facilitate and encourage international co-operation in such investigation.

Article II

Outer space, including the moon and other celestial bodies, is not subject to national appropriation by claim of sovereignty, by means of use or occupation, or by any other means.

Article III

States Parties to the Treaty shall carry on activities in the exploration and use of outer space, including the moon and other celestial bodies, in accordance with international law, including the Charter of the United Nations, in the interest of maintaining international peace and security and promoting international co-operation and understanding.

Article IV

States Parties to the Treaty undertake not to place in orbit around the Earth any objects carrying nuclear weapons or any other kinds of weapons of mass destruction, install such weapons on celestial bodies, or station such weapons in outer space in any other manner.
The moon and other celestial bodies shall be used by all States Parties to the Treaty exclusively for peaceful purposes. The establishment of military bases, installations and fortifications, the testing of any type of weapons and the conduct of military maneuvers on celestial bodies shall be forbidden. The use of military personnel for scientific research or for any other peaceful purposes shall not be prohibited. The use of any equipment of facility necessary for peaceful exploration of the moon and other celestial bodies shall also not be prohibited.

Article V

States Parties to the Treaty shall regard astronauts as envoys of mankind in outer space and shall render to them all possible assistance in the event of accident, distress, or emergency landing on the territory of another State Party or on the high seas. When astronauts make such a landing, they shall be safely and promptly returned to the State of registry of their space vehicle.

In carrying on activities in outer space and on celestial bodies, the astronauts of one State Party shall render all possible assistance to the astronauts of other States Parties.

States Parties to the Treaty shall immediately inform the other States Parties to the Treaty or the Secretary-General of the United Nations of any phenomena they discover in outer space, including the moon and other celestial bodies, which could constitute a danger to the life or health of astronauts.

Article VI

States Parties to the Treaty shall bear international responsibility for national activities in outer space, including the moon and other celestial bodies, whether such activities are carried on by governmental agencies or by non-governmental entities, and for assuring that national activities are carried out in conformity with the provisions set forth in the present Treaty. The activities of non-governmental entities in outer space, including the moon and other celestial bodies, shall require authorization and continuing supervision by the appropriate State Party to the Treaty. When activities are carried on in outer space, including the moon and other celestial bodies, by an international organization, responsibility for compliance with this Treaty shall be borne both by the international organization and by the States Parties to the Treaty participating in such organization.

Article VII

Each State Party to the Treaty that launches or procures the launching of an object into outer space, including the moon and other celestial bodies, and each State Party from whose territory or facility an object is launched, is internationally liable for damage to another State Party to the Treaty or to its natural or juridical persons by such object or its component parts on the Earth, in air space or in outer space, including the moon and other celestial bodies.

Article VIII

A State Party to the Treaty on whose registry an object launched into outer space is carried shall retain jurisdiction and control over such object, and over any personnel thereof, while in outer space or on a celestial body. Ownership of objects launched into outer space, including objects landed or constructed on a celestial body, and of their component parts, is not affected by their presence in outer space or on a celestial body or by their return to the Earth. Such objects or component parts found beyond the limits of the State Party to the Treaty on whose registry they are carried, shall be returned to that State Party, which shall, upon request, furnish identifying data prior to their return.

Article IX

In the exploration and use of outer space, including the moon and other celestial bodies, States Parties to the Treaty shall be guided by the principle of co-operation and mutual assistance and shall conduct all their activities in outer space, including the moon and other celestial bodies, with due regard to the corresponding interests of all other States Parties to the Treaty. States Parties to the Treaty shall pursue studies of outer space, including the moon and other celestial bodies, and conduct exploration of them so as to avoid their harmful contamination and also adverse changes in the environment of the Earth resulting from the introduction of extraterrestrial matter and, where necessary, shall adopt appropriate measures for this purpose. If a State Party to the Treaty has reason to believe that an activity or experiment planned by it or its nationals in outer space, including the moon and other celestial bodies, would cause potentially harmful interference with activities of other States Parties in the peaceful exploration and use of outer space, including the moon and other celestial bodies, it shall undertake appropriate international consultations before proceeding with any such activity or experiment. A State Party to the Treaty which has reason to believe that an activity or experiment planned by another State Party in outer space, including the moon and other celestial bodies, would cause potentially harmful interference with activities in the peaceful exploration and use of outer space, including the moon and other celestial bodies, may request consultation concerning the activity or experiment.

Article X

In order to promote international co-operation in the exploration and use of outer space, including the moon and other celestial bodies, in conformity with the purposes of this Treaty, the States Parties to the Treaty shall consider on a basis of the equality any requests by other States Parties to the Treaty to be afforded an opportunity to observe the flight of space objects launched by those States.

The nature of such an opportunity for observation and the conditions under which it could be afforded shall be determined by agreement between the States concerned.

Article XI

In order to promote international co-operation in the peaceful exploration and use of outer space, States Parties to the Treaty conducting activities in outer space, including the moon and other celestial bodies, agree to inform the Secretary-General of the United Nations as well as the public and the international scientific community,to the greatest extent feasible and practicable, of the nature, conduct, locations and results of such activities. On receiving the said information, the Secretary-General of the United Nations should be prepared to disseminate it immediately and effectively.

Article XII

All stations, installations, equipment and space vehicles on the moon and other celestial bodies shall be open to representatives of other States Parties to the Treaty on a basis of reciprocity. Such representatives shall give reasonable advance notice of a projected visit, in order that appropriate consultations may be held and that maximum precautions may be taken to assure safety and to avoid interference with normal operations in the facility to be visited.

Article XIII

The provisions of this Treaty shall apply to the activities of States Parties to the Treaty in the exploration and use of outer space, including the moon and other celestial bodies, whether such activities are carried on by a single State Party to the Treaty or jointly with other States, including cases where they are carried on within the framework of international inter-governmental organizations.

Any practical questions arising in connection with activities carried on by international inter-governmental organizations in the exploration and use of outer space, including the moon and other celestial bodies, shall be resolved by the States Parties to the Treaty either with the appropriate international organization or with one or more States members of that international organization, which are Parties to this Treaty.

Article XIV

1. This Treaty shall be open to all States for signature. Any State which does not sign this Treaty before its entry into force in accordance with paragraph 3 of this article may accede to it at any time.

2. This Treaty shall be subject to ratification by signatory States. Instruments of ratification and instruments of accession shall be deposited with the Governments of the United States of America, the United Kingdom of Great Britain and Northern Ireland and the Union of Soviet Socialist Republics, which are hereby designated the Depositary Governments.

3. This Treaty shall enter into force upon the deposit of instruments of ratification by five Governments including the Governments designated as Depositary Governments under this Treaty.

4. For States whose instruments of ratification or accession are deposited subsequent to the entry into force of this Treaty, it shall enter into force on the date of the deposit of their instruments of ratification or accession.

5. The Depositary Governments shall promptly inform all signatory and acceding States of the date of each signature, the date of deposit of each instrument of ratification of and accession to this Treaty, the date of its entry into force and other notices.

6. This Treaty shall be registered by the Depositary Governments pursuant to Article 102 of the Charter of the United Nations.

Article XV

Any State Party to the Treaty may propose amendments to this Treaty. Amendments shall enter into force for each State Party to the Treaty accepting the amendments upon their acceptance by a majority of the States Parties to the Treaty and thereafter for each remaining State Party to the Treaty on the date of acceptance by it.

Article XVI

Any State Party to the Treaty may give notice of its withdrawal from the Treaty one year after its entry into force by written notification to the Depositary Governments. Such withdrawal shall take effect one year from the date of receipt of this notification.

Article XVII

This Treaty, of which the English, Russian, French, Spanish and Chinese texts are equally authentic, shall be deposited in the archives of the Depositary Governments. Duly certified copies of this Treaty shall be transmitted by the Depositary Governments to the Governments of the signatory and acceding States.

Treaty for the Prohibition of Nuclear Weapons in Latin America

Also known as: *Treaty of Tlatelolco*
Date of signature: *February 14, 1967*
Place of signature: *Mexico City*
Signatory states: *Argentina, Bahamas, Barbados, Bolivia, Brazil, Chile, People's Republic of China, Colombia, Costa Rica, Dominican Republic, Ecuador, El Salvador, France, Grenada, Guatemala, Haiti, Honduras, Jamaica, Mexico, Netherlands, Nicaragua, Panama, Paraguay, Peru, Suriname, Trinidad and Tobago, Soviet Union, United Kingdom, United States, Uruguay, Venezuela*
Date of entry into force: *April 22, 1968*

Preamble

In the name of their peoples and faithfully interpreting their desires and aspirations, the Governments of the States which have signed the Treaty for the Prohibition of Nuclear Weapons in Latin America,
Desiring to contribute, so far as lies in their power, towards ending the armaments race, especially in the field of nuclear weapons, and towards strengthening a world at peace, based on the sovereign equality of States, mutual respect and good neighbourliness,
Recalling that the United Nations General Assembly, in its resolution 808 (IX), adopted unanimously as one of the three points of a co-ordinated programme of disarmament "the total prohibition of the use and manufacture of nuclear weapons and weapons of mass destruction of every type",
Recalling that militarily denuclearized zones are not an end in themselves but rather a means for achieving general and complete disarmament at a later stage,
Recalling United Nations General Assembly resolution 1911 (XVIII), which established that the measures that should be agreed upon the denuclearization of Latin America should be taken "in the light of the principles of the Charter of the United Nations and of regional agreements",
Recalling United Nations General Assembly resolution 2028 (XX), which established the principle of an acceptable balance of mutual responsibilities and duties for the nuclear and non-nuclear powers, and
Recalling that the Charter of the Organization of American States proclaims that it is an essential purpose of the organization to strengthen the peace and security of the hemisphere,
Convinced:
That the incalculable destructive power of nuclear weapons has made it imperative that the legal prohibition of war should be strictly observed in practice if the survival of civilization and of mankind itself is to be assured,
That nuclear weapons, whose terrible effects are suffered, indiscriminately and inexorably, by military forces and civilian population alike, constitute, through the persistence of the radioactivity they release, an attack on the integrity of the human species and ultimately may even render the whole earth uninhabitable,
That general and complete disarmament under effective international control is a vital matter which all the peoples of the world equally demand,
That the proliferation of nuclear weapons, which seems inevitable unless States, in the exercise of their sovereign rights, impose restrictions on themselves in order to prevent it, would make any agreement on disarmament enormously difficult and would increase the danger of the outbreak of a nuclear conflagration,
That the establishment of militarily denuclearized zones is closely linked with the maintenance of peace and security in the respective regions,
That the military denuclearization of vast geographical zones, adopted by the sovereign decision of the States comprised therein, will exercise a beneficial influence on other regions where similar conditions exist,
That the privileged situation of the signatory States, whose territories are wholly free from nuclear weapons, imposes upon them the inescapable duty of preserving that situation both in their own interests and for the good of mankind,
That the existence of nuclear weapons in any country of Latin America would make it a target for possible nuclear attacks and would inevitably set off, throughout the region, a ruinous race in nuclear weapons which would involve the unjustifiable diversion, for warlike purposes, of the resources required for economic and social development,
That the foregoing reasons, together with the traditional peace-loving outlook of Latin America, give rise to an inescapable necessity that nuclear energy should be used in that region exclusively for peaceful purposes, and that the Latin American countries should use their right to the greatest and most equitable possible access to this new source of energy in order to expedite the economic and social development of their peoples,
Convinced finally:
That the military denuclearization of Latin America —being understood to mean the undertaking entered into internationally in this Treaty to keep their territories forever free from nuclear weapons—will constitute a measure which will spare their peoples from the squandering of their limited resources on nuclear

armaments and will protect them against possible nuclear attacks on their territories, and will also constitute a significant contribution towards preventing the proliferation of nuclear weapons and a powerful factor for general and complete disarmament, and

That Latin America, faithful to its tradition of universality, must not only endeavour to banish from its homelands the scourge of a nuclear war, but must also strive to promote the well-being and advancement of its peoples, at the same time co-operating in the fulfilment of the ideals of mankind, that is to say, in the consolidation of a permanent peace based on equal rights, economic fairness and social justice for all, in accordance with the principles and purposes set forth in the Charter of the United Nations and in the Charter of the Organization of American States,

Have agreed as follows:

Obligations

Article 1

The Contracting Parties hereby undertake to use exclusively for peaceful purposes the nuclear material and facilities which are under their jurisdiction, and to prohibit and prevent in their respective territories:

(a) The testing, use, manufacture, production or acquisition by any means whatsoever of any nuclear weapons, by the Parties themselves, directly or indirectly, on behalf of anyone else or in any other way; and

(b) The receipt, storage, installation, deployment and any form of possession of any nuclear weapon, directly or indirectly, by the Parties themselves, by anyone on their behalf or in any other way.

2. The Contracting Parties also undertake to refrain from engaging in, encouraging or authorizing, directly or indirectly, or in any way participating in the testing, use, manufacture, production, possession or control of any nuclear weapon.

Definition of the Contracting Parties

Article 2

For the purposes of this Treaty, the Contracting Parties are those for whom the Treaty is in force.

Definition of territory

Article 3

For the purposes of this Treaty, the term "territory" shall include the territorial sea, air space and any other space over which the State exercises sovereignty in accordance with its own legislation.

Zone of application

Article 4

1. The zone of application of the Treaty is the whole of the territories for which the Treaty is in force.

2. Upon fulfilment of the requirements of article 28, paragraph 1, the zone of application of the Treaty shall also be that which is situated in the western hemisphere within the following limits (except the continental part of the territory of the United States of America and its territorial waters): starting at a point located at 35° north latitude, 75° west longitude; from this point directly southward to a point at 30° north latitude, 75° west longitude; from there, directly eastward to a point at 30° north latitude, 50° west longitude; from there along a loxodromic line to a point at 5° north latitude, 20° west longitude; from there directly southward to a point at 60° south latitude, 20° west longitude; from there directly westward to a point at 60° south latitude, 115° west longitude; from there directly northward to a point at 0° latitude, 115° west longitude; from there along a loxodromic line to a point at 35° north latitude, 150° west longitude; from there directly eastward to a point at 35° north latitude, 75° west longitude.

Definition of nuclear weapons

Article 5

For the purposes of this Treaty, a nucler weapon is any device which is capable of releasing nuclear energy in an uncontrolled manner and which has a group of characteristics that are appropriate for use for warlike purposes. An instrument that may be used for the transport or propulsion of the device is not included in this definition if it is separable from the device and not an indivisible part thereof.

Meeting of signatories

Article 6

At the request of any of the signatories, or if the Agency established by article 7 should so decide, a meeting of all the signatories may be convoked to consider in common questions which may affect the very essence of this instrument, including possible amendments to it. In either case, the meeting will be convoked by the General Secretary.

Organization

Article 7

1. In order to ensure compliance with the obligations of this Treaty, the Contracting Parties hereby establish an international organization to be known as the "Agency for the Prohibition of Nuclear Weapons in Latin America", hereinafter referred to as

"the Agency". Only the Contracting Parties shall be affected by its decisions.

2. The Agency shall be reponsible for the holding of periodic or extraordinary consultations among member States on matters relating to the purposes, measures and procedures set forth in this Treaty and to supervision of compliance with the obligations arising therefrom.

3. The Contracting Parties agree to extend to the Agency full and prompt co-operation in accordance with the provisions of this Treaty, of any agreements they may conclude with the Agency and of any agreements the Agency may conclude with any other international organization or body.

4. The headquarters of the Agency shall be in Mexico City.

Organs

Article 8

1. There are hereby established as principal organs of the Agency a General Conference, a Council and a Secretariat.

2. Such subsidiary organs as are considered necessary by the General Conference may be established within the purview of this Treaty.

The General Conference

Article 9

1. The General Conference, the supreme organ of the Agency, shall be composed of all the Contracting Parties; it shall hold regular sessions every two years, and may also hold special sessions whenever this Treaty so provides, or, in the opinion of the Council, the circumstances so require.

2. The General Conference:

(a) May consider and decide on matters or questions covered by the Treaty, within the limits thereof, including those referring to powers and functions of any organ provided for in this Treaty.

(b) Shall establish procedures for the control system to ensure observance of this Treaty in accordance with its provisions.

(c) Shall elect the members of the Council and the General Secretary.

(d) May remove the General Secretary from office if the proper functioning of the Agency so requires.

(e) Shall receive and consider the biennial and special reports submitted by the Council and the General Secretary.

(f) Shall initiate and consider studies designed to facilitate the optimum fulfilment of the aims of this Treaty, without prejudice to the power of the General Secretary independently to carry out similar studies for submission to and consideration by the Conference.

(g) Shall be the organ competent to authorize the conclusion of agreements with Governments and other international organizations and bodies.

3. The General Conference shall adopt the Agency's budget and fix the scale of financial contributions to be paid by member States, taking into account the systems and criteria used for the same purpose by the United Nations.

4. The General Conference shall elect its officers for each session and may establish such subsidiary organs as it deems necessary for the performance of its functions.

5. Each member of the Agency shall have one vote. The decisions of the General Conference shall be taken by a two-thirds majority of the members present and voting in the case of matters relating to the control system and measures referred to in article 20, the admission of new members, the election or removal of the General Secretary, adoption of the budget and matters related thereto. Decisions on other matters, as well as procedural questions, and also determination of which questions must be decided by a two-thirds majority, shall be taken by a simple majority of the members present and voting.

6. The General Conference shall adopt it own rules of procedure.

The Council

Article 10

1. The Council shall be composed of five members of the Agency elected by the General Conference from among the Contracting Parties, due account being taken of equitable geographical distribution.

2. The members of the Council shall be elected for a term of four years. However, in the first election three will be elected for two years. Outgoing members may not be re-elected for the following period unless the limited number of States for which the Treaty is in force so requires.

3. Each member of the Council shall have one representative.

4. The Council shall be so organized as to be able to function continuously.

5. In addition to the functions conferred upon it by this Treaty and to those which may be assigned to it by the General Conference, the Council shall, through the General Secretary, ensure the proper operation of the control system in accordance with the provisions of this Treaty and with the decisions adopted by the General Conference.

6. The Council shall submit an annual report on its work to the General Conference as well as such special reports as it deems necessary or which the General Conference requests of it.

7. The Council shall elect its officers for each session.

8. The decisions of the Council shall be taken by a simple majority of its members present and voting.

9. The Council shall adopt its own rules of procedure.

The Secretariat

Article 11

1. The Secretariat shall consist of a General Secretary, who shall be the chief administrative officer of the Agency, and of such staff as the Agency may require. The term of office of the General Secretary shall be four years and he may be re-elected for a single additional term. The General Secretary may not be a national of the country in which the Agency has its headquarters. In case the office of General Secretary becomes vacant, a new election shall be held to fill the office for the remainder of the term.

2. The staff of the Secretariat shall be appointed by the General Secretary, in accordance with rules laid down by the General Conference.

3. In addition to the functions conferred upon him by this Treaty and to those which may be assigned to him by the General Conference, the General Secretary shall ensure, as provided by article 10, paragraph 5, the proper operation of the control system established by this Treaty, in accordance with the provisions of the Treaty and the decisions taken by the General Conference.

4. The General Secretary shall act in that capacity in all meetings of the General Conference and of the Council and shall make an annual report to both bodies on the work of the Agency and any special reports requested by the General Conference or the Council or which the General Secretary may deem desirable.

5. The General Secretary shall establish the procedures for distributing to all Contracting Parties information received by the Agency from governmental sources, and such information from non-governmental sources as may be of interest to the Agency.

6. In the performance of their duties, the General Secretary and the staff shall not seek or receive instructions from any Government or from any other authority external to the Agency and shall refrain from any action which might reflect on their position as international officials responsible only to the Agency; subject to their responsibility to the Agency, they shall not disclose any industrial secrets or other confidential information coming to their knowledge by reason of their official duties in the Agency.

7. Each of the Contracting Parties undertakes to respect the exclusively international character of the responsibilities of the General Secretary and the staff and not to seek to influence them in the discharge of their responsibilities.

Control system

Article 12

1. For the purpose of verifying compliance with the obligations entered into by the Contracting Parties in accordance with article 1, a control system shall be established which shall be put into effect in accordance with the provisions of articles 13–18 of this Treaty.

2. The control system shall be used in particular for the purpose of verifying:

(a) That devices, services and facilities intended for peaceful uses of nuclear energy are not used in the testing or manufacture of nuclear weapons;

(b) That none of the activities prohibited in article 1 of this Treaty are carried out in the territory of the Contracting Parties with nuclear materials or weapons introduced from abroad, and

(c) That explosions for peaceful purposes are compatible with article 18 of this Treaty.

IAEA Safeguards

Article 13

Each Contracting Party shall negotiate multilateral or bilateral agreements with the International Atomic Energy Agency for the application of its safeguards to its nuclear activities. Each Contracting Party shall initiate negotiations within a period of 180 days after the date of the deposit of its instrument of ratification of this Treaty. These agreements shall enter into force, for each Party, not later than eighteen months after the date of the initiation of such negotiations except in case of unforeseen circumstances of *force majeure*.

Reports of the parties

Article 14

1. The Contracting Parties shall submit to the Agency and to the International Atomic Energy Agency, for their information, semi-annual reports stating that no activity prohibited under this Treaty has occurred in their respective territories.

2. The Contracting Parties shall simultaneously transmit to the Agency a copy of any report they may submit to the International Atomic Energy Agency which relates to matters that are the subject of this Treaty and to the application of safeguards.

3. The Contracting Parties shall also transmit to the Organization of American States, for its information, any reports that may be of interest to it, in

accordance with the obligations established by the Inter-American System.

Special reports requested by the General Secretary

Article 15

1. With the authorization of the Council, the General Secretary may request any of the Contracting Parties to provide the Agency with complementary or supplementary information regarding any event or circumstance connected with compliance with this Treaty, explaining his reasons. The Contracting Parties undertake to co-operate promptly and fully with the General Secretary.

2. The General Secretary shall inform the Council and the Contracting Parties forthwith of such requests and of the respective replies.

Special inspections

Article 16

1. The International Atomic Energy Agency and the Council established by this Treaty have the power of carrying out special inspections in the following cases:

(a) In the case of the International Atomic Energy Agency, in accordance with the agreements referred to in article 13 of the Treaty;

(b) In the case of the Council:

(i) When so requested, the reasons for the request being stated, by any Party which suspects that some activity prohibited by this Treaty has been carried out or is about to be carried out, either in the territory of any other Party or in any other place on such latter Party's behalf, the Council shall immediately arrange for such an inspection in accordance with article 10, paragraph 5.

(ii) When requested by any Party which has been suspected of or charged with having violated the Treaty, the Council shall immediately arrange for the special inspection requested, in accordance with article 10, paragraph 5. The above requests will be made to the Council through the General Secretary.

2. The costs and expenses of any special inspection carried out under paragraph 1, sub-paragraph (b), sections (i) and (ii) of this article shall be borne by the requesting Party or Parties, except where the Council concludes on the basis of the report on the special inspection that, in view of the circumstances existing in the case, such costs and expenses should be borne by the Agency.

3. The General Conference shall formulate the procedures for the organization and execution of the special inspections carried out in accordance with

paragraph 1, sub-paragraph (b), sections (i) and (ii) of this article.

4. The Contracting Parties undertake to grant the inspectors carrying out such special inspections full and free access to all places and all information which may be necessary for the performance of their duties and which are directly and intimately connected with the suspicion of violation of this Treaty. If so requested by the Contracting Party in whose territory the inspection is carried out, the inspectors designated by the General Conference shall be accompanied by representatives of the authorities of that Contracting Party, provided that this does not in any way delay or hinder the work of the inspectors.

5. The Council shall immediately transmit to all the Parties, through the General Secretary, a copy of any report resulting from special inspections.

6. Similarly, the Council shall send through the General Secretary to the Secretary-General of the United Nations for transmission to the United Nations Security Council and General Assembly, and to the Council of the Organization of American States for its information, a copy of any report resulting from any special inspection carried out in accordance with paragraph 1, sub-paragraph (b), sections (i) and (ii) of this article.

7. The council may decide, or any Contracting Party may request, the convening of a special session of the General Conference for the purpose of considering the reports resulting from any special inspection. In such a case, the General Secretary shall take immediate steps to convene the special session requested.

8. The General Conference, convened in special session under this article, may make recommendations to the Contracting Parties and submit reports to the Secretary-General of the United Nations to be transmitted to the Security Council and the General Assembly.

Use of nuclear energy for peaceful purposes

Article 17

Nothing in the provisions of this Treaty shall prejudice the rights of the Contracting Parties, in conformity with this Treaty, to use nuclear energy for peaceful purposes, in particular for their economic development and social progress.

Explosions for peaceful purposes

Article 18

1. The Contracting Parties may carry out explosions of nuclear devices for peaceful purposes—including explosions which involve devices similar to those used in nuclear weapons—or collaborate with third parties for the same purpose, provided that

they do so in accordance with the provisions of this article and the other articles of the Treaty, particularly articles 1 and 5.

2. Contracting Parties intending to carry out, or co-operate in the carrying out of such, an explosion shall notify the Agency and the International Atomic Energy Agency, as far in advance as the circumstances require, of the date of the explosion and shall at the same time provide the following information:

(a) The nature of the nuclear device and the source from which it was obtained;

(b) The place and purpose of the planned explosion;

(c) The procedures which will be followed in order to comply with paragraph 3 of this article;

(d) The expected force of the device;

(e) The fullest possible information on any possible radioactive fall-out that may result from the explosion or explosions, and the measurfauna, and territories of any other Party or Parties.

3. The General Secretary and the technical personnel designated by the Council and the International Atomic Energy Agency may observe all the preparations, including the explosion of the device, and shall have unrestricted access to any area in the vicinity of the site of the explosion in order to ascertain whether the device and the procedures followed during the explosion are in conformity with the information supplied under paragraph 2 of the present article and other provisions of this Treaty.

4. The Contracting Parties may accept the collaboration of third parties for the purpose set forth in paragraph 1 of the present article, in accordance with paragraphs 2 and 3 thereof.

Relations with other international organizations

Article 19

1. The Agency may conclude such agreements with the International Atomic Energy Agency as are authorized by the General Conference and as it considers likely to facilitate the efficient operation of the control system established by this Treaty.

2. The Agency may also enter into relations with any international organization or body, especially any which may be established in the future to supervise disarmament or measures for the control of armaments in any part of the world.

3. The Contracting Parties may, if they see fit, request the advice of the Inter-American Nuclear Energy Commission on all technical matters connected with the application of the Treaty with which the Commission is competent to deal under its Statute.

Measures in the event of violation of the Treaty

Article 20

1. The General Conference shall take note of all cases in which, in its opinion, any Contracting Party is not complying fully with its obligations under this Treaty and shall draw the matter to the attention of the Party concerned, making such recommendations as it deems appropriate.

2. If, in its opinion, such non-compliance constitutes a violation of this Treaty which might endanger peace and security, the General Conference shall report thereon simultaneously to the Security Council and the General Assembly through the Secretary-General of the United Nations and to the Council of the Organization of American States. The General Conference shall likewise report to the International Atomic Energy Agency for such purposes as are relevant in accordance with its Statute.

United Nations and Organization of American States

Article 21

None of the provisions of this Treaty shall be construed as impairing the rights and obligations of the Parties under the Charter of the United Nations or, in the case of States members of the Organization of American States, under existing regional treaties.

Privileges and immunities

Article 22

1. The Agency shall enjoy in the territory of each of the Contracting Parties such legal capacity and such privileges and immunities as may be necessary for the exercise of its functions and the fulfilment of its purposes.

2. Representatives of the Contracting Parties accredited to the Agency and officials of the Agency shall similarly enjoy such privileges and immunities as are necessary for the performance of their functions.

3. The Agency may conclude agreements with the Contracting Parties with a view to determining the details of the application of paragraphs 1 and 2 of this article.

Notification of other agreements

Article 23

Once this Treaty has entered into force, the Secretariat shall be notified immediately of any international agreement concluded by any of the Contracting Parties on matters with which this Treaty is concerned; the Secretariat shall register it and notify the other Contracting Parties.

Settlement of disputes

Article 24

Unless the Parties concerned agree on another mode of peaceful settlement, any question or dispute concerning the interpretation or application of this Treaty which is not settled shall be referred to the International Court of Justice with the prior consent of the parties to the controversy.

Signature

Article 25

1. This Treaty shall be open indefinitely for signature by:

(a) All the Latin American Republics;

(b) All other sovereign States situated in their entirety south of latitude 35° north in the western hemisphere; and, except as provided in paragraph 2 of this article, all such States which become sovereign, when they have been admitted by the General Conference.

2. The General Conference shall not take any decision regarding the admission of a political entity part or all of whose territory is the subject, prior to the date when this Treaty is opened for signature, of a dispute or claim between an extra-continental country and one or more Latin American States, so long as the dispute has not been settled by peaceful means.

Ratification and deposit

Article 26

1. This Treaty shall be subject to ratification by signatory States in accordance with their respective constitutional procedures.

2. This Treaty and the instruments of ratification shall be deposited with the Government of the United States of Mexico, which is hereby designated the Depositary Government.

3. The Depositary Government shall send certified copies of this Treaty to the Governments of signatory States and shall notify them of the deposit of each instrument of ratification.

Reservations

Article 27

This Treaty shall not be subject to reservations.

Entry into force

Article 28

1. Subject to the provisions of paragraphs 2 and 3 of this article, this Treaty shall enter into force

among the States that have ratified it as soon as the following requirements have been met:

(a) Deposit of the instruments of ratification of this Treaty with the Depositary Government by the Governments of the States mentioned in article 25 which are in existence on the date when this Treaty is opened for signature and which are not affected by the provisions of article 25, paragraph 2;

(b) Signature and ratification of Additional Protocol I annexed to this Treaty by all extra-continental and continental States having *de jure* or *de facto* international responsibility for territories situated in the zone of application of the Treaty;

(c) Signature and ratification of the Additional Protocol II annexed to this Treaty by all powers possessing nuclear weapons;

(d) Conclusion of bilateral agreements on the application of the Safeguards System of the International Atomic Energy Agency in accordance with article 13 of this Treaty.

2. All signatory States shall have the imprescriptible right to waive, wholly or in part, the requirements laid down in the preceding paragraph. They may do so by means of a declaration which shall be annexed to their respective instruments of ratification and which may be formulated at the time of deposit of the instrument or subsequently. For those States which exercise this right, this Treaty shall enter into force upon deposit of the declaration, or as soon as those requirements have been met which have not been expressly waived.

3. As soon as this Treaty has entered into force in accordance with the provisions of paragraph 2 for eleven States, the Depositary Government shall convene a preliminary meeting of those States in order that the Agency may be set up and commence its work.

4. After the entry into force of the Treaty for all the countries of the zone, the rise of a new power possessing nuclear weapons shall have the effect of suspending the execution of this Treaty for those countries which have ratified it without waiving the requirements of paragraph 1, sub-paragraph (c) of this article, and which request such suspension; the Treaty shall remain suspended until the new power, on its own initiative or upon request by the General Conference, ratifies the annexed Additional Protocol II.

Amendments

Article 29

1. Any Contracting Party may propose amendments to this Treaty and shall submit their proposals to the Council through the General Secretary, who shall transmit them to all the other Contracting Par-

ties and, in addition, to signatories in accordance with article 6. The Council, through the General Secretary, shall, immediately following the meeting of signatories, convene a special session of the General Conference to examine the proposals made, for the adoption of which a two-thirds majority of the Contracting Parties present and voting shall be required.

2. Amendments adopted shall enter into force as soon as the requirements set forth in article 28 of this Treaty have been complied with.

Duration and denunciation

Article 30

1. This Treaty shall be of a permanent nature and shall remain in force indefinitely, but any Party may denounce it by notifying the General Secretary of the Agency if, in the opinion of the denouncing State, there have arisen or may arise circumstances connected with the content of the Treaty or of the annexed Additional Protocols I and II which affect its supreme interests and the peace and security of one or more Contracting Parties.

2. The denunciation shall take effect three months after the delivery to the General Secretary of the Agency of the notification by the Government of the signatory State concerned. The General Secretary shall immediately communicate such notification to the other Contracting Parties and to the Secretary-General of the United Nations for the information of the Security Council and the General Assembly of the United Nations. He shall also communicate it to the Secretary General of the Organization of American States.

Authentic texts and registration

Article 31

This Treaty, of which the Spanish, Chinese, English, French, Portugese and Russian texts are equally authentic, shall be registered by the Depositary Government in accordance with Article 102 of the United Nations Charter. The Depositary Government shall notify the Secretary-General of the United Nations of the signatures, ratifications and amendments relating to this Treaty and shall communicate them to the Secretary General of the Organization of American States for his information.

Transitional Article

Denunciation of the declaration referred to in article 28, paragraph 2, shall be subject to the same procedures as the denunciation of the Treaty, except that it shall take effect on the date of delivery of the respective notification.

ADDITIONAL PROTOCOL I

The. . . Plenipotentiaries, furnished with full powers by their respective Governments,
Convinced that the Treaty for the Prohibition of Nuclear Weapons in Latin America, negotiated and signed in accordance with the recommendations of the General Assembly of the United Nations in resolution 1911 (XVIII) of 27 November 1963, represents an important step towards ensuring the non-proliferation of nuclear weapons,
Aware that the non-proliferation of nuclear weapons is not an end in itself but rather a means of achieving general and complete disarmament at a later stage,
Desiring to contribute, so far as lies in their power, towards ending the armaments race, especially in the field of nuclear weapons, and towards strengthening a world at peace, based on mutual respect and sovereign equality of States,
Have agreed as follows:

Article 1

To undertake to apply the status of denuclearization in respect of warlike purposes as defined in articles 1, 3, 5 and 13 of the Treaty for the Prohibition of Nuclear Weapons in Latin America in territories for which, *de jure* or *de facto,* they are internationally responsible and which lie within the limits of the geographical zone established in that Treaty.

Article 2

The duration of this Protocol shall be the same as that of the Treaty for the Prohibition of Nuclear Weapons in Latin America of which this Protocol is an annex, and the provisions regarding ratification and denunciation contained in the Treaty shall be applicable to it.

Article 3

This Protocol shall enter into force, for the States which have ratified it, on the date of the deposit of their respective instruments of ratification.

ADDITIONAL PROTOCOL II

The. . . Plenipotentiaries, furnished with full powers by their respective Governments,
Convinced that the Treaty for the Prohibition of Nuclear Weapons in Latin America, negotiated and signed in accordance with the recommendations of the General Assembly of the United Nations in resolution 1911 (XVIII) of 27 November 1963, is an important step towards ensuring the non-proliferation of nuclear weapons,
Aware that the non-proliferation of nuclear weapons

is not an end in itself but rather a means for achieving general and complete disarmament at a later stage,

Desiring to contribute, so far as lies in their power, towards ending the armaments race, especially in the field of nuclear weapons, and towards promoting and strengthening a world at peace based on mutual respect and sovereign equality of States,

Have agreed as follows:

Article 1

The status of denuclearization of Latin America in respect of warlike purposes, as defined, delimited and set forth in the Treaty for the Prohibition of Nuclear Weapons in Latin America of which this instrument is an annex, shall be fully respected by the Parties to this Protocol in all its express aims and provisions.

Article 2

The Governments represented by the... Plenipotentiaries undertake, therefore, not to contribute in any way to the performance of acts involving a violation of the obligations of article 1 of the Treaty in the territories to which the Treaty applies in accordance with article 4 thereof.

Article 3

The Governments represented by the... Plenipotentiaries also undertake not to use of threaten to use nuclear weapons against the Contracting Parties of the Treaty for the Prohibition of Nuclear Weapons in Latin America.

Article 4

The duration of this Protocol shall be the same as that of the Treaty for the Prohibition of Nuclear Weapons in Latin America of which this Protocol is an annex, and the definitions of territory and nuclear weapons set forth in articles 3 and 5 of the Treaty shall be applicable to the Protocol, as well as the provisions regarding ratification, reservations, denunciation, authentic texts and registration contained in articles 26, 27, 30 and 31 of the Treaty.

Article 5

This Protocol shall enter into force, for the States which have ratified it, on the date of the deposit of their respective instruments of ratification.

Treaty on the Non-Proliferation of Nuclear Weapons

Also known as: *Non-Proliferation Treaty, NPT*
Date of signature: *July 1, 1968*
Place of signature: *London, Moscow, and Washington DC*
Signatory states: *Afghanistan, Australia, Austria, Barbados, Belgium, Benin, Bolivia, Botswana, Bulgaria, Cameroon, Canada, Chad, Colombia, Costa Rica, Cyprus, Czechoslovakia, Denmark, Dominican Republic, Ecuador, Egypt, El Salvador, Ethiopia, Finland, Gambia, German Democratic Republic, Federal Republic of Germany, Ghana, Greece, Guatemala, Haiti, Honduras, Hungary, Iceland, Indonesia, Iran, Iraq, Ireland, Italy, Ivory Coast, Jamaica, Japan, Jordan, Kenya, Republic of Korea, Kuwait, Laos, Lebanon, Lesotho, Liberia, Libya, Luxembourg, Madagascar, Malaysia, Maldives, Mali, Malta, Mauritius, Mexico, Mongolia, Morocco, Nepal, Netherlands, New Zealand, Nicaragua, Nigeria, Norway, Panama, Paraguay, Peru, Philippines, Poland, Romania, San Marino, Senegal, Singapore, Somalia, Sri Lanka, Sudan, Swaziland, Sweden, Switzerland, Syria, Taiwan, Togo, Trinidad and Tobago, Tunisia, Turkey, Soviet Union, United Kingdom, United States, Upper Volta, Uruguay, Venezuela, Yemen Arab Republic, People's Democratic Republic of Yemen, Yugoslavia, Zaire*
Ratifications: *Afghanistan, Australia, Austria, Bahamas, Bangladesh, Barbados, Belgium, Benin, Bolivia, Botswana, Bulgaria, Burundi, Cameroon, Canada, Cape Verde, Central African Republic, Chad, Congo, Costa Rica, Cyprus, Czechoslovakia, Denmark, Dominican Republic, Ecuador, Egypt, El Salvador, Ethiopia, Fiji, Finland, Gabon, Gambia, German Democratic Republic, Federal Republic of Germany, Ghana, Greece, Grenada, Guatemala, Guinea-Bissau, Haiti, Holy See, Honduras, Hungary, Iceland, Indonesia, Iran, Iraq, Ireland, Italy, Ivory Coast, Jamaica, Japan, Jordan, Kampuchea, Kenya, Republic of Korea, Laos, Lebanon, Lesotho, Liberia, Libya, Liechtenstein, Luxembourg, Madagascar, Malaysia, Maldives, Mali, Malta, Mauritius, Mexico, Mongolia, Morocco, Nepal, Netherlands, New Zealand, Nicaragua, Nigeria, Norway, Panama, Paraguay, Peru, Philippines, Poland, Portugal, Romania, Rwanda, Saint Lucia,*

Samoa, San Marino, Senegal, Sierra Leone, Singapore, Solomon Islands, Somalia, Sri Lanka, Sudan, Surinam, Swaziland, Sweden, Switzerland, Syria, Taiwan, Thailand, Togo, Tonga, Tunisia, Turkey, Tuvalu, Soviet Union, United Kingdom, United States, Upper Volta, Uruguay, Venezuela, People's Democratic Republic of Yemen, Yugoslavia, Zaire
Date of entry into force: *March 5, 1970*

The States concluding this Treaty, hereinafter referred to as the "Parties to the Treaty",

Considering the devastation that would be visited upon all mankind by a nuclear war and the consequent need to make every effort to avert the danger of such a war and to take measures to safeguard the security of peoples,

Believing that the proliferation of nuclear weapons would seriously enhance the danger of nuclear war,

In conformity with resolutions of the United Nations General Assembly calling for the conclusion of an agreement on the prevention of wider dissemination of nuclear weapons,

Undertaking to co-operate in facilitating the application of International Atomic Energy Agency safeguards on peaceful nuclear activities.

Expressing their support for research, development and other efforts to further the application, within the framework of the International Atomic Energy Agency safeguards system, of the principle of safeguarding effectively the flow of source and special fissionable materials by use of instruments and other techniques at certain strategic points,

Affirming the principle that the benefits of peaceful applications of nuclear technology, including any technological by-products which may be derived by nuclear-weapon States from the development of nuclear expolosive devices, should be available for peaceful purposes to all Parties to the Treaty, whether nuclear-weapon or non-nuclear-weapon States,

Convinced that, in furtherance of this principle, all Parties to the Treaty are entitled to participate in the fullest possible exchange of scientific information for, and to contribute alone or in co-operation with other States to, the further development of the applications of atomic energy for peaceful purposes,

Declaring their intention to achieve at the earliest possible date the cessation of the nuclear arms race and to undertake effective measures in the direction of nuclear disarmament,

Urging the co-operation of all States in the attainment of this objective,

Recalling the determination expressed by the Parties to the 1963 Treaty banning nuclear weapon tests in the atmosphere, in outer space and under water in its Preamble to seek to achieve the discontinuance of all test explosions of nuclear weapons for all time and to continue negotiations to this end,

Desiring to further the easing of international tension and the strengthening of trust between States in order to facilitate the cessation of the manufacture of nuclear weapons, the liquidation of all their existing stockpiles, and the elimination from national arsenals of nuclear weapons and the means of their delivery pursuant to a Treaty on general and complete disarmament under strict and effective international control,

Recalling that, in accordance with the Charter of the United Nations, States must refrain in their international relations from the threat or use of force against the territorial integrity or political independence of any State, or in any other manner inconsistent with the Purposes of the United Nations, and that the establishment and maintenance of international peace and security are to be promoted with the least diversion for armaments of the world's human and economic resources,

Have agreed as follows:

Article 1

Each nuclear-weapon State Party to the Treaty undertakes not to transfer to any recipient whatsoever nuclear weapons or other nuclear explosive devices or control over such weapons or explosive devices directly, or indirectly; and not in any way to assist, encourage, or induce any non-nuclear-weapon State to manufacture or otherwise acquire nuclear weapons or other nuclear explosive devices, or control over such weapons or explosive devices.

Article II

Each non-nuclear-weapon State Party to the Treaty undertakes not to receive the transfer from any transferor whatsoever of nuclear weapons or other nuclear explosive devices or of control over such weapons or explosive devices directly, or indirectly; not to manufacture or otherwise acquire nuclear weapons or other nuclear explosive devices; and not to seek or receive any assistance in the manufacture of nuclear weapons or other nuclear explosive devices.

Article III

1. Each non-nuclear-weapon State Party to the Treaty undertakes to accept safeguards, as set forth in an agreement to be negotiated and concluded with the International Atomic Energy Agency in accordance with the Statute of the International Atomic Energy Agency and the Agency's safeguards system, for the exclusive purpose of verification of the fulfilment of its obligations assumed under this Treaty with a view to preventing diversion of nuclear energy

from peaceful uses to nuclear weapons or other nuclear explosive devices. Procedures for the safeguards required by this Article shall be followed with respect to source or special fissionable material whether it is being produced, processed or used in any principal nuclear facility or is outside any such facility. The safeguards required by this Article shall be applied on all source or special fissionable material in all peaceful nuclear activities within the territory of such State, under its jurisdiction, or carried out under its control anywhere.

2. Each State Party to the Treaty undertakes not to provide: (*a*) source or special fissionable material, or (*b*) equipment or material especially designed or prepared for the processing, use or production of special fissionable material, to any non-nuclear-weapon State for peaceful purposes, unless the source or special fissionable material shall be subject to the safeguards required by this Article.

3. The safeguards required by this Article shall be implemented in a manner designed to comply with Article IV of this Treaty, and to avoid hampering the economic or technological development of the Parties or international co-operation in the field of peaceful nuclear activities, including the international exchange of nuclear material and equipment for the processing, use or production of nuclear material for peaceful purposes in accordance with the provisions of this Article and the principle of safeguarding set forth in the Preamble of the Treaty.

4. Non-nuclear-weapon States Party to the Treaty shall conclude agreements with the International Atomic Energy Agency to meet the requirements of this Article either individually or together with other States in accordance with the Statute of the International Atomic Energy Agency. Negotiation of such agreements shall commence within 180 days from the original entry into force of this Treaty. For States depositing their instruments of ratification or accession after the 180-day period, negotiation of such agreements shall commence not later than the date of such deposit. Such agreements shall enter into force not later than eighteen months after the date of initiation of negotiations.

Article IV

1. Nothing in this Treaty shall be interpreted as affecting the inalienable right of all the Parties to the Treaty to develop research, production and use of nuclear energy for peaceful purposes without discrimination and in conformity with Articles I and II of this Treaty.

2. All the Parties to the Treaty undertake to facilitate, and have the right to participate in, the fullest possible exchange of equipment, materials and scientific and technological information for the peaceful uses of nuclear energy. Parties to the Treaty in a position to do so shall also co-operate in contributing alone or together with other States or international organizations to the further development of the applications of nuclear energy for peaceful purposes, especially in the territories of non-nuclear-weapon States Party to the Treaty, with due consideration for the needs of the developing areas of the world.

Article V

Each Party to the Treaty undertakes to take appropriate measures to ensure that, in accordance with this Treaty, under appropriate international observation and through appropriate international procedures, potential benefits from any peaceful applications of nuclear explosions will be made available to non-nuclear-weapon States Party to the Treaty on a non-discriminatory basis and that the charge to such Parties for the explosive devices used will be as low as possible and exclude any charge for research and development. Non-nuclear-weapon States Party to the Treaty shall be able to obtain such benefits, pursuant to a special international agreement or agreements, through an appropriate international body with adequate representation of non-nuclear-weapon States. Negotiations on this subject shall commence as soon as possible after the Treaty enters into force. Non-nuclear-weapon States Party to the Treaty so desiring may also obtain such benefits pursuant to bilateral agreements.

Article VI

Each of the Parties to the Treaty undertakes to pursue negotiations in good faith on effective measures relating to cessation of the nuclear arms race at an early date and to nuclear disarmament, and on a treaty on general and complete disarmament under strict and effective international control.

Article VII

Nothing in this Treaty affects the right of any group of States to conclude regional treaties in order to assure the total absence of nuclear weapons in their respective territories.

Article VIII

1. Any Party to the Treaty may propose amendments to this Treaty. The text of any proposed amendment shall be submitted to the Depositary Governments which shall circulate it to all Parties to the Treaty. Thereupon, if requested to do so by one-third or more of the Parties to the Treaty, the Depositary Governments shall convene a conference, to which they shall invite all the Parties to the Treaty, to consider such an amendment.

2. Any amendment to this Treaty must be approved by a majority of the votes of all the Parties to the Treaty, including the votes of all nuclear-weapon States Party to the Treaty, and all other Parties which, on the date the amendment is circulated, are members of the Board of Governors of the International Atomic Energy Agency. The amendment shall enter into force for each Party that deposits its instrument of ratification of the amendment upon the deposit of such instruments of ratification by a majority of all the Parties, including the instruments of ratification of all nuclear-weapon States Party to the Treaty and all other Parties which, on the date the amendment is circulated, are members of the Board of Governors of the International Atomic Energy Agency. Thereafter, it shall enter into force for any other Party upon the deposit of its instrument of ratification of the amendment.

3. Five years after the entry into force of this Treaty, a conference of Parties to the Treaty shall be held in Geneva, Switzerland, in order to review the operation of this Treaty with a view to assuring that the purposes of the Preamble and the provisions of the Treaty are being realised. At intervals of five years thereafter, a majority of the Parties to the Treaty may obtain, by submitting a proposal to this effect to the Depositary Governments, the convening of further conferences with the same objective of reviewing the operation of the Treaty.

Article IX

1. This Treaty shall be open to all States for signature. Any State which does not sign the Treaty before its entry into force in accordance with paragraph 3 of this Article may accede to it at any time.

2. This Treaty shall be subject to ratification by signatory States. Instruments of ratification and instruments of accession shall be deposited with the Governments of the United Kingdom of Great Britain and Nothern Ireland, the Union of Soviet Socialist Republics and the United States of America, which are hereby designated the Depositary Governments.

3. This Treaty shall enter into force after its ratification by the States, the Governments of which are designated Depositaries of the Treaty, and forty other States signatory to this Treaty and the deposit of their instruments of ratification. For the purposes of this Treaty, a nuclear-weapon State is one which has manufactured and exploded a nuclear weapon or other nuclear explosive device prior to 1 January, 1967.

4. For States whose instruments of ratification or accession are deposited subsequent to the entry into force of this Treaty, it shall enter into force on the date of the deposit of their instruments of ratification or accession.

5. The Depositary Governments shall promptly inform all signatory and acceding States of the date of each signature, the date of deposit of each instrument of ratification or of accession, the date of the entry into force of this Treaty, and the date of receipt of any requests for convening a conference or other notices.

6. This Treaty shall be registered by the Depositary Governments pursuant to Article 102 of the Charter of the United Nations.

Article X

1. Each Party shall in exercising its national sovereignty have the right to withdraw from the Treaty if it decides that extraordinary events, related to the subject matter of this Treaty, have jeopardized the supreme interests of its country. It shall give notice of such withdrawal to all other Parties to the Treaty and to the United Nations Security Council three months in advance. Such notice shall include a statement of the extraordinary events it regards as having jeopardized its supreme interests.

2. Twenty-five years after the entry into force of the Treaty, a conference shall be convened to decide whether the Treaty shall continue in force indefinitely, or shall be extended for an additional fixed period or periods. This decision shall be taken by a majority of the Parties to the Treaty.

Article XI

This Treaty, the English, Russian, French, Spanish and Chinese texts of which are equally authentic, shall be deposited in the archives of the Depositary Governments. Duly certified copies of this Treaty shall be transmitted by the Depositary Governments to the Governments of the signatory and acceding States.

Treaty on the Prohibition of the Emplacement of Nuclear Weapons and Other Weapons of Mass Destruction on the Sea-Bed and the Ocean Floor and in the Subsoil Thereof

Also known as: Sea Bed Treaty
Date of signature: February 11, 1971

Place of signature: London, Moscow, and Washington, DC

Signatory states: *Afghanistan, Argentina, Australia, Austria, Belgium, Benin, Bolivia, Botswana, Brazil, Bulgaria, Burma, Burundi, Byelorussia, Cameroon, Canada, Central African Republic, Colombia, Costa Rica, Cyprus, Czechoslovakia, Denmark, Dominican Republic, Equitorial Guinea, Ethiopia, Finland, Gambia, German Democratic Republic, Federal Republic of Germany, Ghana, Greece, Guatemala, Guinea, Honduras, Hungary, Iceland, Iran, Iraq, Ireland, Italy, Jamaica, Japan, Jordan, Kampuchea, Republic of Korea, Laos, Lebanon, Lesotho, Liberia, Luxembourg, Madagascar, Malaysia, Mali, Malta, Mauritius, Mongolia, Morocco, Nepal, Netherlands, New Zealand, Nicaragua, Niger, Norway, Panama, Paraguay, Poland, Romania, Rwanda, Saudi Arabia, Senegal, Sierra Leone, Singapore, South Africa, Soviet Union, Sudan, Swaziland, Sweden, Switzerland, Taiwan, Tanzania, Togo, Tunisia, Turkey, Ukraine, United Kingdom, United States, Uruguay, Yemen Arab Republic, People's Democratic Republic of Yemen, Yugoslavia*

Ratifications: *Afghanistan, Australia, Austria, Belgium, Botswana, Bulgaria, Byelorussia, Canada, Cape Verde, Central African Republic, Congo, Cuba, Cyprus, Czechoslovakia, Denmark, Dominican Republic, Ethiopia, Finland, German Democratic Republic, Federal Republic of Germany, Ghana, Guinea-Bissau, Hungary, Iceland, India, Iran, Iraq, Ireland, Italy, Ivory Coast, Japan, Jordan, Laos, Lesotho, Malaysia, Malta, Mauritius, Mongolia, Morocco, Nepal, Netherlands, New Zealand, Nicaragua, Niger, Norway, Panama, Poland, Portugal, Qatar, Romania, Rwanda, Sao Tome, Saudi Arabia, Seychelles, Singapore, Solomon Islands, South Africa, Soviet Union, Swaziland, Sweden, Switzerland, Taiwan, Togo, Tunisia, Turkey, Ukraine, United Kingdom, United States, Vietnam, People's Democratic Republic of Yemen, Yugoslavia, Zambia*

Date of entry into force: *May 18, 1972*

The General Assembly
Recalling its resolution 2602 F (XXIV) of 16 December 1969,
Convinced that the prevention of a nuclear arms race on the sea-bed and the ocean floor serves the interests of maintaining world peace, reducing international tensions and strengthening friendly relations among States,
Recognizing the common interest of mankind in the

reservation of the sea-bed and the ocean floor exclusively for peaceful purposes,
Having considered the report of the Conference of the Committee on Disarmament, dated 11 September 1970, and appreciative of the work of the Conference on the draft Treaty on the Prohibition of the Emplacement of Nuclear Weapons and Other Weapons of Mass Destruction on the Sea-Bed and the Ocean Floor and in the Subsoil Thereof, attached to the report,
Convinced that this Treaty will further the purposes and principles of the Charter of the United Nations,

1. *Commends* the Treaty on the Prohibition of the Emplacement of Nuclear Weapons and Other Weapons of Mass Destruction on the Sea-Bed and the Ocean Floor and in the Subsoil Thereof, the text of which is annexed to the present resolution;

2. *Requests* the depositary Governments to open the Treaty for signature and ratification at the earliest possible date;

3. *Expresses the hope* for the widest possible adherence to the Treaty.

ANNEX

Treaty on the Prohibition of the Emplacement of Nuclear Weapons and Other Weapons of Mass Destruction on the Sea-Bed and the Ocean Floor and in the Subsoil Thereof

The States Parties to this Treaty,
Recognizing the common interest of mankind in the progress of the exploration and use of the sea-bed and the ocean floor for peaceful purposes,
Considering that the prevention of a nuclear arms race on the sea-bed and the ocean floor serves the interests of maintaining world peace, reduces international tensions, and strengthens friendly relations among States,
Convinced that this Treaty constitutes a step towards the exclusion of the sea-bed, the ocean floor and the subsoil thereof from the arms race,
Convinced that this Treaty constitutes a step towards a treaty on general and complete disarmament under strict and effective international control, and determined to continue negotiations to this end,
Convinced that this Treaty will further the purposes and principles of the Charter of the United Nations, in a manner consistent with the principles of international law and without infringing the freedom of the high seas,
Have agreed as follows:

Article I

1. The States Parties to this Treaty undertake not to emplant or emplace on the sea-bed and the ocean

floor and in the subsoil thereof beyond the outer limit of a sea-bed zone as defined in Article II any nuclear weapons or any other types of weapons of mass destruction as well as structures, launching installations or any other facilities specifically designed for storing, testing or using such weapons.

2. The undertakings of paragraph 1 of this Article shall also apply to the sea-bed zone referred to in the same paragraph, except that within such sea-bed zone, they shall not apply either to the coastal State or to the sea-bed beneath its territorial waters.

3. The States Parties to this Treaty undertake not to assist, encourage or induce any State to carry out activities referred to in paragraph 1 of this Article and not to participate in any other way in such actions.

Article II

For the purpose of this Treaty the outer limit of the sea-bed zone referred to in Article I shall be the coterminous with the twelve-mile outer limit of the zone referred to in Part II of the Convention on the Territorial Sea and the Contiguous Zone, signed in Geneva on 29 April 1958, and shall be measured in accordance with the provisions of Part I, Section II, of this Convention and in accordance with international law.

Article III

1. In order to promote the objectives of and ensure compliance with the provisions of this Treaty, each State Party to the Treaty shall have the right to verify through observation the activities of other States Parties to the Treaty on the sea-bed and the ocean floor and in the subsoil thereof beyond the zone referred to in Article I, provided that observation does not interfere with such activities.

2. If after such observation reasonable doubts remain conerning the fulfilment of the obligations assumed under the Treaty, the State Party having such doubts and the State Party that is responsible for the activities giving rise to the doubts shall consult with a view to removing the doubts. If the doubts persist, the State Party having such doubts shall notify the other States Parties, and the Parties concerned shall co-operate on such further procedures for verification as may be agreed, including appropriate inspection of objects, structures, installations or other facilities that reasonably may be expected to be of a kind described in Article I. The Parties in the region of the activities, including any coastal State, and any other Party so requesting, shall be entitled to participate in such consultation and co-operation. After completion of the further procedures for verification, an appropriate report shall be circulated to other Parties by the Party that initiated such procedures.

3. If the State responsible for the activities giving rise to the reasonable doubts is not identifiable by observation of the object, structure, installation or other facility, the State Party having such doubts shall notify and make appropriate inquiries of States Parties in the region of the activities and of any other State Party. If it is ascertained through these inquiries that a particular State Party is responsible for the activities, that State Party shall consult and co-operate with other Parties as provided in paragraph 2 of this Article. If the identity of the State responsible for the activities cannot be ascertained through these inquiries, then further verification procedures, including inspection, may be undertaken by the inquiring State Party, which shall invite the participation of the Parties in the region of the activities, including any coastal State, and of any other Party desiring to co-operate.

4. If consultation and co-operation pursuant to paragraphs 2 and 3 of this Article have not removed the doubts concerning the activities and there remains a serious question concerning fulfilment of the obligations assumed under this Treaty, a State Party may, in accordance with the provisions of the Charter of the United Nations, refer the matter to the Security Council, which may take action in accordance with the Charter.

5. Verification pursuant to this Article may be undertaken by any State Party using its own means, or with the full or partial assistance of any other State Party, or through appropriate international procedures within the framework of the United Nations and in accordance with its Charter.

6. Verification activities pursuant to this Treaty shall not interfere with activities of other States Parties and shall be conducted with due regard for rights recognized under international law including the freedoms of the high seas and the rights of coastal States with respect to the exploration and exploitation of their continental shelves.

Article IV

Nothing in this Treaty shall be interpreted as supporting or prejudicing the position of any State Party with respect to existing international conventions, including the 1958 Convention on the Territorial Sea and the Contiguous Zone, or with respect to rights or claims which such State Party may assert, or with respect to recognition or non-recognition of rights or claims asserted by any other State, related to waters off its coasts; including *inter alia* territorial seas and contiguous zones, or the sea-bed and the ocean floor, including continental shelves.

Article V

The Parties of this Treaty undertake to continue negotiations in good faith concerning further measures in the field of disarmament for the prevention of an arms race on the sea-bed, the ocean floor and the subsoil thereof.

Article VI

Any State Party may propose amendments to this Treaty. Amendments shall enter into force for each State Party accepting the amendments upon their acceptance by a majority of the States Parties to the Treaty and thereafter for each remaining State Party on the date of acceptance by it.

Article VII

Five years after the entry into force of this Treaty, a conference of Parties to the Treaty shall be held in Geneva, Switzerland, in order to review the operation of this Treaty with a view to assuring that the purposes of the preamble and the provisions of the Treaty are being realized. Such review shall take into account any relevant technological developments. The review conference shall determine in accordance with the views of a majority of those Parties attending whether and when an additional review conference shall be convened.

Article VIII

Each State Party to this Treaty shall in exercising its national sovereignty have the right to withdraw from this Treaty if it decides that extraordinary events related to the subject matter of this Treaty have jeopardized the supreme interests of its country. It shall give notice of such withdrawal to all other States Parties to the Treaty and to the United Nations Security Council three months in advance. Such notice shall include a statement of the extraordinary events it considers to have jeopardized its supreme interests.

Article IX

The provisions of this Treaty shall in no way affect the obligations assumed by States Parties to the Treaty under international instruments establishing zones free from nuclear weapons.

Article X

1. This Treaty shall be open for signature to all States. Any State which does not sign the Treaty before its entry into force in accordance with paragraph 3 of this Article may accede to it at any time.

2. This Treaty shall be subject to ratification by signatory States. Instruments of ratification and of accession shall be deposited with the Governments of the Union of Soviet Socialist Republics, the United Kingdom of Great Britain and Northern Ireland and the United States of America, which are hereby designated the Depositary Governments.

3. This Treaty shall enter into force after the deposit of instruments of ratification by twenty-two Governments, including the Governments designated as Depositary Governments of this Treaty.

4. For States whose instruments of ratification or accession are deposited after the entry into force of this Treaty it shall enter into force on the date of the deposit of their instruments of ratification or accession.

5. The Depositary Governments shall promptly inform the Governments of all signatory and acceding States of the date of each signature, of the date of deposit of each instrument of ratification or of accession, of the date of the entry into force of this Treaty, and of the receipt of other notices.

6. This Treaty shall be registered by the Depositary Governments pursuant to Article 102 of the Charter of the United Nations.

Article XI

This Treaty, the Chinese, English, French, Russian and Spanish texts of which are equally authentic, shall be deposited in the archives of the Depositary Governments. Duly certified copies of this Treaty shall be transmitted by the Depositary Governments to the Governments of the States signatory and acceding thereto.

Agreements to Reduce Risk of Nuclear War Between the United States and the Union of Soviet Socialist Republics

Date of signature: *September 30, 1971*
Place of signature: *Washington, DC*
Signatory states: *the United States, the Soviet Union*

The United States of America and the Union of Soviet Socialist Republics, hereinafter referred to as the Parties:
Taking into account the devastating consequences that nuclear war would have for all mankind, and recognizing the need to exert every effort to avert the risk of outbreak of such a war, including measures to guard against accidental or unauthorized use of nuclear weapons,

Believing that agreement on measures for reducing the risk of outbreak of nuclear war serves the interests of strengthening international peace and security, and is in no way contrary to the interests of any other country,

Bearing in mind that continued efforts are also needed in the future to seek ways of reducing the risk of outbreak of nuclear war,

Having agreed as follows:

Article 1

Each Party undertakes to maintain and to improve, as it deems necessary, its existing organizational and technical arrangements to guard against the accidental or unauthorized use of nuclear weapons under its control.

Article 2

The Parties undertake to notify each other immediately in the event of an accidental, unauthorized or any other unexplained incident involving a possible detonation of a nuclear weapon which could create a risk of outbreak of nuclear war. In the event of such an incident, the Party whose nuclear weapon is involved will immediately make every effort to take necessary measures to render harmless or destroy such weapon without its causing damage.

Article 3

The Parties undertake to notify each other immediately in the event of detection by missile warning systems of unidentified objects, or in the event of signs of interference with these systems or with related communications facilities, if such occurrences could create a risk of outbreak of nuclear war between the two countries.

Article 4

Each Party undertakes to notify the other Party in advance of any planned missile launches if such launches will extend beyond its national territory in the direction of the other Party.

Article 5

Each Party, in other situations involving unexplained nuclear incidents, undertakes to act in such a manner as to reduce the possibility of its actions being misinterpreted by the other Party. In any such situation, each Party may inform the other Party or request information when, in its view, this is warranted by the interests of averting the risk of outbreak of nuclear war.

Article 6

For transmission of urgent information, notifications and requests for information in situations requiring prompt clarification, the Parties shall make primary use of the Direct Communications Link between the Governments of the United States of America and the Union of Soviet Socialist Republics.

For transmission of other information, notifications and requests for information, the Parties, at their own discretion, may use any communications facilities, including diplomatic channels, depending on the degree of urgency.

Article 7

The Parties undertake to hold consultations, as mutually agreed, to consider questions relating to implementation of the provisions of this Agreement, as well as to discuss possible amendments thereto aimed at further implementation of the purposes of this Agreement.

Article 8

This Agreement shall be of unlimited duration.

Article 9

This Agreement shall enter into force upon signature.

Convention on the Prohibition of the Development, Production and Stockpiling of Bacteriological (Biological) and Toxin Weapons and on their Destruction

Also known as: Biological Weapons Convention
Date of signature: April 10, 1972
Place of signature: London, Moscow, and Washington, DC
Signatory states: Afghanistan, Argentina, Australia, Austria, Barbados, Belgium, Benin,

Bolivia, Botswana, Brazil, Bulgaria, Burma, Burundi, Byelorussia, Canada, Central African Republic, Chile, Congo, Costa Rica, Cuba, Cyprus, Czechoslovakia, Denmark, Dominican Republic, Ecuador, Egypt, El Salvador, Ethiopia, Fiji, Finland, Gabon, Gambia, German Democratic Republic, Federal

Republic of Germany, Ghana, Greece,
Guatemala, Guyana, Haiti, Honduras,
Hungary, Iceland, India, Indonesia, Iran, Iraq,
Ireland, Italy, Ivory Coast, Japan, Jordan,
Kampuchea, Republic of Korea, Kuwait, Laos,
Lebanon, Lesotho, Liberia, Luxembourg,
Madagascar, Malawi, Malaysia, Malai,
Malta, Mauritius, Mexico, Mongolia,
Morocco, Nepal, Netherlands, New Zealand,
Nicaragua, Niger, Nigeria, Norway, Pakistan,
Panama, Peru, Philippines, Poland, Portugal,
Qatar, Romania, Rwanda, San Marino, Saudi
Arabia, Senegal, Sierra Leone, Singapore,
Somalia, South Africa, Soviet Union, Spain,
Sri Lanka, Sweden, Switzerland, Syria,
Taiwan, Tanzania, Thailand, Togo, Tunisia,
Turkey, Ukraine, United Arab Emirates,
United Kingdom, United States, Venezuela,
Yemen Arab Republic, People's Democratic
Republic of Yemen, Yugoslavia, Zaire
Ratifications: Afghanistan, Argentina,
Australia, Austria, Barbados, Belgium, Benin,
Bhutan, Bolivia, Brazil, Bulgaria, Byelorussia,
Canada, Cape Verde, Chile, Congo, Cost
Rica, Cuba, Cyprus, Czechoslovakia,
Denmark, Dominican Republic, Ecuador,
Ethiopia, Fiji, Finland, German Democratic
Republic, Ghana, Greece, Guatemala, Guinea-
Bissau, Honduras, Hungary, Iceland, India,
Iran, Ireland, Italy, Jamaica, Jordan, Kenya,
Kuwait, Laos, Lebanon, Lesotho,
Luxembourg, Malta, Mauritius, Mexico,
Mongolia, Netherlands, New Zealand,
Nicaragua, Niger, Nigeria, Norway, Pakistan,
Panama, Papua New Guinea, Paraguay,
Philippines, Poland, Portugal, Qatar,
Romania, Rwanda, San Marino, Sao Tome,
Saudi Arabia, Senegal, Seychelles, Sierra
Leone, Singapore, Solomon Islands, South
Africa, Soviet Union, Spain, Sweden,
Switzerland, Taiwan, Thailand, Togo, Tonga,
Tunisia, Turkey, Ukraine, United Kingdom,
United States, Uruguay, Venezuela, Vietnam,
People's Democratic Republic of Yemen,
Yugoslavia, Zaire
Date of entry into force: *March 26, 1975*

The General Assembly,
Recalling its resolution 2662 (XXV) of 7 December
1970,
Convinced of the importance and urgency of eliminating from the arsenals of States, through effective
measures, such dangerous weapons of mass destruction as those using chemical or bacteriological (biological) agents,
Having considered the report of the Conference of the
Committee on Disarmament dated 6 October 1971,

and being appreciative of its work on the draft Convention on the Prohibition of the Development, Production and Stockpiling of Bacteriological (Biological) and Toxin Weapons and on Their Destruction,
annexed to the report,
Recognizing the important significance of the Protocol for the Prohibition of the Use in War of Asphyxiating, Poisonous or Other Gases, and of Bacteriological Methods of Warfare, signed at Geneva on 17
June 1925, and conscious also of the contribution
which the said Protocol has already made, and continues to make, to mitigating the horrors of war,
Noting that the Convention provides for the parties
to reaffirm their adherence to the principles and
objectives of that Protocol and to call upon all States
to comply strictly with them,
Further noting that nothing in the Convention shall
be interpreted as in any way limiting or detracting
from the obligations assumed by any State under the
Geneva Protocol.
Determined, for the sake of all mankind, to exclude
completely the possibility of bacteriological (biological) agents and toxins being used as weapons,
Recognizing that an agreement on the prohibition of
bacteriological (biological) and toxin weapons represents a first possible step towards the achievement of
agreement on effective measures also for the prohibition of the development, production and stockpiling
of chemical weapons,
Noting that the Convention contains an affirmation
of the recognized objective of effective prohibition of
chemical weapons and, to this end, an undertaking
to continue negotiations in good faith with a view to
reaching early agreement on effective measures for
the prohibition of their development, production and
stockpiling and for their destruction, and on appropriate measures concerning equipment and means of
delivery specifically designed for the production or
use of chemical agents for weapons purposes,
Convinced that the implementation of measures in
the field of disarmament should release substantial
additional resources, which should promote economic and social development, particularly in the
developing countries,
Convinced that the Convention will contribute to the
realization of the purposes and principles of the
Charter of the United Nations,

1. *Commends* the Convention on the Prohibition of
the Development, Production and Stockpiling of
Bacteriological (Biological) and Toxin Weapons
and on Their Destruction, the text of which is
annexed to the present resolution;

2. *Requests* the depositary Governments to open the
Convention for signature and ratification at the
earliest possible date;

3. *Expresses the hope* for the widest possible adherence to the Convention.

ANNEX

Convention on the Prohibition of the Development, Production and Stockpiling of Bacteriological (Biological) and Toxin Weapons and on Their Destruction

The States Parties to this Convention,
Determined to act with a view to achieving effective progress towards general and complete disarmament, including the prohibition and elimination of all types of weapons of mass destruction, and convinced that the prohibition of the development, production and stockpiling of chemical and bacteriological (biological) weapons and their elimination, through effective measures, will facilitate the achievement of general and complete disarmament under strict and effective international control,
Recognizing the important significance of the Protocol for the Prohibition of the Use in War of Asphyxiating, Poisonous or Other Gases, and of Bacteriological Methods of Warfare, signed at Geneva on 17 June 1925, and conscious also of the contribution which the said Protocol has aready made, and continues to make, to mitigating the horrors of war,
Reaffirming their adherence to the principles and objectives of that Protocol and calling upon all States to comply strictly with them,
Recalling that the General Assembly of the United Nations has repeatedly condemned all actions contrary to the principles and objectives of the Geneva Protocol of 17 June 1925,
Desiring to contribute to the strengthening of confidence between peoples and the general improvement of the international atmosphere,
Desiring also to contribute to the realization of the purposes and principles of the Charter of the United Nations,
Convinced of the importance and urgency of eliminating from the arsenals of States, through effective measures, such dangerous weapons of mass destruction as those using chemical of bacteriological (biological) agents,
Recognizing that an agreement on the prohibition of bacteriological (biological) and toxin weapons represents a first possible step towards the achievement of agreement on effective measures also for the prohibition of the development, production and stockpiling of chemical weapons, and determined to continue negotiations to that end,
Determined, for the sake of all mankind, to exclude completely the possibility of bacteriological (biological) agents and toxins being used as weapons,
Convinced that such use would be repugnant to the conscience of mankind and that no effort should be spared to minimize this risk,
Have agreed as follows:

Article I

Each State Party to this Convention undertakes never in any circumstances to develop, produce, stockpile or otherwise acquire or retain:

1. Microbial or other biological agents, or toxins whatever their origin or method of production, of types and in quantities that have no justification for prophylactic, protective or other peaceful purposes;

2. Weapons, equipment or means of delivery designed to use such agents or toxins for hostile purposes or in armed conflict.

Article II

Each State Party to this Convention undertakes to destroy, or to divert to peaceful purposes, as soon as possible but not later than nine months after the entry into force of the Convention, all agents, toxins, weapons, equipment and means of delivery specified in article I of the Convention, which are in its possession or under its jurisdiction or control. In implementing the provisions of this article all necessary safety precautions shall be observed to protect populations and the environment.

Article III

Each State Party to this Convention undertakes not to transfer to any recipient whatsoever, directly or indirectly, and not in any way to assist, encourage, or induce any State, group of States or international organizations to manufacture or otherwise acquire any of the agents, toxins, weapons, equipment or means of delivery specified in article I of the Convention.

Article IV

Each State Party to this Convention shall, in accordance with its constitutional processes, take any necessary measures to prohibit and prevent the development, production, stockpiling, acquisition or retention of the agents, toxins, weapons, equipment and means of delivery specified in article I of the Convention, within the territory of such State, under its jurisdiction or under its control anywhere.

Article V

The States Parties to this Convention undertake to consult one another and to co-operate in solving any problems which may arise in relation to the objective of, or in the application of the provisions of, the Convention. Consultation and co-operation pursuant to this article may also be undertaken through appropriate international procedures within the framework of the United Nations and in accordance with its Charter.

Article VI

(1) Any State Party to this Convention which finds that any other State Party is acting in breach of obligations deriving from the provisions of the Convention may lodge a complaint with the Security Council of the United Nations. Such a complaint should include all possible evidence confirming its validity, as well as a request for its consideration by the Security Council.

(2) Each State Party to this Convention undertakes to co-operate in carrying out any investigation which the Security Council may initiate, in accordance with the provisions of the Charter of the United Nations, on the basis of the complaint received by the Council. The Security Council shall inform the States Parties to the Convention of the results of the investigation.

Article VII

Each State Party to this Convention undertakes to provide or support assistance, in accordance with the United Nations Charter, to any Party to the Convention which so requests, if the Security Council decides that such Party has been exposed to danger as a result of violation of the Convention.

Article VIII

Nothing in this Convention shall be interpreted as in any way limiting or detracting from the obligations assumed by any State under the Protocol for the Prohibition of the Use in War of Asphyxiating, Poisonous or Other Gases, and of Bacteriological Methods of Warfare, signed at Geneva on 17 June 1925.

Article IX

Each State Party to this Convention affirms the recognized objective of effective prohibition of chemical weapons and, to this end, undertakes to continue negotiations in good faith with a view to reaching early agreement on effective measures for the prohibition of their development, production and stockpiling and for their destruction, and on appropriate measures concerning equipment and means of delivery specifically designed for the production or use of chemical agents for weapons purposes.

Article X

(1) The States Parties to this Convention undertake to facilitate, and have the right to participate in, the fullest possible exchange of equipment, materials and scientific and technological information for the use of bacteriological (biological) agents and toxins for peaceful purposes. Parties to the Convention in a position to do so shall also co-operate in contributing individually or together with other States or international organizations to the further development and application of scientific discoveries in the field of bacteriology (biology) for the prevention of disease, or for other peaceful purposes.

(2) This Convention shall be implemented in a manner designed to avoid hampering the economic or technological development of States Parties to the Convention or international co-operation in the field of peaceful bacteriological (biological) activities, including the international exchange of bacteriological (biological) agents and toxins and equipment for the processing, use or production of bacteriological (biological) agents and toxins for peaceful purposes in accordance with the provisions of the Convention.

Article XI

Any State Party may propose amendments to this Convention. Amendments shall enter into force for each State Party accepting the amendments upon their acceptance by a majority of the States Parties to the Convention and thereafter for each remaining State Party on the date of acceptance by it.

Article XII

Five years after the entry into force of this Convention, or earlier if it is requested by a majority of Parties to the Convention by submitting a proposal to this effect to the Depositary Governments, a conference of State Parties to the Convention shall be held at Geneva, Switzerland, to review the operation of the Convention, with a view to assuring that the purposes of the preamble and the provisions of the Convention, including the provisions concerning negotiations on chemical weapons, are being realized. Such review shall take into account any new scientific and technological developments relevant to the Convention.

Article XIII

(1) This Convention shall be of unlimited duration.

(2) Each State Party to this Convention shall in exercising its national sovereignty have the right to withdraw from the Convention if it decides that extraordinary events, related to the subject matter of the Convention, have jeopardized the supreme interests of its country. It shall give notice of such withdrawal to all other States Parties to the Convention and to the United Nations Security Council three months in advance. Such notice shall include a statement of the extraordinary events it regards as having jeopardized its supreme interests.

Article XIV

(1) This Convention shall be open to all States for signature. Any State which does not sign the Convention before its entry into force in accordance with paragraph 3 of this article may accede to it at any time.

(2) This Convention shall be subject to ratification by signatory States. Instruments of ratification and instruments of accession shall be deposited with the Governments of the Union of Soviet Socialist Republics, the United Kingdom of Great Britain and Northern Ireland and the United States of America, which are hereby designated the Depositary Governments.

(3) This Convention shall enter into force after the deposit of instruments of ratification by twenty-two Governments, including the Governments designated as Depositaries of the Convention.

(4) For States whose instruments of ratification or accession are deposited subsequent to the entry into force of this Convention, it shall enter into force on the date of the deposit of their instruments of ratification or accession.

(5) The Depositary Governments shall promptly inform all signatory and acceding States of the date of each signature, the date of deposit of each instrument of ratification or of accession and the date of the entry into force of this Convention, and of the receipt of other notices.

(6) This Convention shall be registered by the Depositary Governments pursuant to Article 102 of the Charter of the United Nations.

Article XV

This Convention, the Chinese, English, French, Russian and Spanish texts of which are equally authentic, shall be deposited in the archives of the Depositary Governments. Duly certified copies of the Convention shall be transmitted by the Depositary Governments to the Governments of the signatory and acceding States.

Agreement Between the Government of the United States of America and the Government of the Union of Soviet Socialist Republics on the Prevention of Incidents on and over the High Seas

Date of signature: May 25, 1972
Place of signature: Moscow
Signatory states: the United States, the Soviet Union

[The signatories],
Desiring to assure the safety of navigation of the ships of their respective armed forces on the high seas and flight of their military aircraft over the high seas, and
Guided by the principles and rules of international law,
Have decided to conclude this Agreement and have agreed as follows:

Article I

For the purposes of this Agreement, the following definitions shall apply:

1. "Ship" means:

(a) A warship belonging to the naval forces of the Parties bearing the external marks distinguishing warships of its nationality, under the command of an officer duly commissioned by the government and whose name appears in the Navy list, and manned by a crew who are under regular naval discipline;

(b) Naval auxiliaries of the Parties, which include all naval ships authorized to fly the naval auxiliary flag where such a flag has been established by either Party.

2. "Aircraft" means all military manned heavier-than-air and lighter-than-air craft, excluding space craft.

3. "Formation" means an ordered arrangement of two or more ships proceeding together and normally maneuvered together.

Article II

The Parties shall take measures to instruct the commanding officers of their respective ships to observe strictly the letter and spirit of the International Regulations for Preventing Collisions at Sea, hereinafter referred to as the Rules of the Road. The Parties recognize that their freedom to conduct operations on the high seas is based on the principles established under recognized international law and codified in the 1958 Geneva Convention on the High Seas.

Article III

1. In all cases ships operating in proximity to each other, except when required to maintain course and

speed under the Rules of the Road, shall remain well clear to avoid risk of collision.

2. Ships meeting or operating in the vicinity of a formation of the other Party shall, while conforming to the Rules of the Road, avoid maneuvering in a manner which would hinder the evolutions of the formation.

3. Formations shall not conduct maneuvers through areas of heavy traffic where internationally recognized traffic separation schemes are in effect.

4. Ships engaged in surveillance of other ships shall stay at a distance which avoids the risk of collision and also shall avoid executing maneuvers embarrassing or endangering the ships under surveillance. Except when required to maintain course and speed under the Rules of the Road, a surveillant shall take positive early action so as, in the exercise of good seamanship, not to embarrass or endanger ships under surveillance.

5. When ships of both Parties maneuver in sight of one another, such signals (flag, sound, and light) as are prescribed by the Rules of the Road, the International Code of Signals, or other mutually agreed signals, shall be adhered to for signalling operations and intentions.

6. Ships of the Parties shall not simulate attacks by aiming guns, missile launchers, torpedo tubes, and other weapons in the direction of a passing ship of the other Party, not launch any object in the direction of passing ships of the other Party, and not use searchlights or other powerful illumination devices to illuminate the navigation bridges of passing ships of the other Party.

7. When conducting exercises with submerged submarines, exercising ships shall show the appropriate signals prescribed by the International Code of Signals to warn ships of the presence of submarines in the area.

8. Ships of one Party when approaching ships of the other Party conducting operations as set forth in Rule 4 (c) of the Rules of the Road, and particularly ships engaged in launching or landing aircraft as well as ships engaged in replenishment underway, shall take appropriate measures not to hinder maneuvers of such ships and shall remain well clear.

Article IV

Commanders of aircraft of the parties shall use the greatest caution and prudence in approaching aircraft and ships of the other Party operating on and over the high seas, in particular, ships engaged in launching or landing aircraft, and in the interest of mutual safety shall not permit: simulated attacks by the simulated use of weapons against aircraft and ships, or performance of various aerobatics over ships, or dropping various objects near them in such

a manner as to be hazardous to ships or to constitute a hazard to navigation.

Article V

1. Ships of the Parties operating in sight of one another shall raise proper signals concerning their intent to begin launching or landing aircraft.

2. Aircraft of the Parties flying over the high seas in darkness or under instrument conditions shall, whenever feasible, display navigation lights.

Article VI

Both Parties shall:

1. Provide through the established system of radio broadcasts of information and warning to mariners, not less than 3 to 5 days in advance as a rule, notification of actions on the high seas which represent a danger to navigation or to aircraft in flight.

2. Make increased use of the informative signals contained in the International Code of Signals to signify the intentions of their respective ships when maneuvering in proximity to one another. At night, or in conditions of reduced visibility, or under conditions of lighting and such distances when signal flags are not distinct, flashing light should be used to inform ships of maneuvers which may hinder the movements of others or involve a risk of collision.

3. Utilize on a trial basis signals additional to those in the International Code of Signals, submitting such signals to the Intergovernmental Maritime Consultative Organization for its consideration and for the information of other States.

Article VII

The Parties shall exchange appropriate information concerning instances of collision, incidents which result in damage, or other incidents at sea between ships and aircraft of the Parties. The United States Navy shall provide such information through the Soviet Naval Attache in Washington and the Soviet Navy shall provide such information through the United States Naval Attache in Moscow.

Article VIII

This Agreement shall enter into force on the date of its signature and shall remain in force for a period of three years. It will thereafter be renewed without further action by the Parties for successive periods of three years each.

This Agreement may be terminated by either Party upon six months written notice to the other Party.

Article IX

The Parties shall meet within one year after the date of the signing of this Agreement to review the implementation of its terms. Similar consultations shall be held thereafter annually, or more frequently as the Parties may decide.

Article X

The Parties shall designate members to form a Committee which will consider specific measures in conformity with this Agreement. The Committee will, as a particular part of its work, consider the practical workability of concrete fixed distances to be observed in encounters between ships, aircraft, and ships and aircraft. The Committee will meet within six months of the date of signature of this Agreement and submit its recommendations for decision by the Parties during the consultations prescribed in Article IX.

Treaty Between the United States of America and the Union of the Soviet Socialist Republics on the Limitation of Anti-Ballistic Missile Systems

Also known as: Anti-Ballistic Missile, Treaty, ABM Treaty. *The first of two treaties concluding the Strategic Arms Limitation Talks (SALT I)*
Date of signature: May 26, 1972
Place of signature: Moscow
Signatory states: the United States, the Soviet Union
Date of entry into force: October 3, 1972

[The signatories], hereinafter referred to as the Parties,

Proceeding from the premise that nuclear war would have devastating consequences for all mankind,

Considering that effective measures to limit anti-ballistic missile systems would be a substantial factor in curbing the race in strategic offensive arms and would lead to a decrease in the risk of outbreak of war involving nuclear weapons,

Proceeding from the premise that the limitation of anti-ballistic missile systems, as well as certain agreed measures with respect to the limitation of strategic offensive arms, would contribute to the creation of more favorable conditions for further negotiations on limiting strategic arms,

Mindful of their obligations under Article VI of the Treaty on the Non-Proliferation of Nuclear Weapons,

Declaring their intention to achieve at the earliest possible date the cessation of the nuclear arms race and to take effective measures toward reductions in strategic arms, nuclear disarmament, and general complete disarmament,

Desiring to contribute to the relaxation of international tension and the strengthening of trust between States,

Have agreed as follows:

Article I

1. Each Party undertakes to limit anti-ballistic missile (ABM) systems and to adopt other measures in accordance with the provisions of this Treaty.

2. Each Party undertakes not to deploy ABM systems for a defense of the territory of its country and not to provide a base for such a defense, and not to deploy ABM systems for defense of an individual region except as provided for in Article III of this Treaty.

Article II

1. For the purpose of this Treaty an ABM system is a system to counter strategic ballistic missiles or their elements in flight trajectory, currently consisting of:

(a) ABM interceptor missiles, which are interceptor missiles constructed and deployed for an ABM role, or of a type tested in an ABM mode;

(b) ABM launchers, which are launchers constructed and deployed for launching ABM interceptor missiles; and

(c) ABM radars, which are radars constructed and deployed for an ABM role, or of a type tested in an ABM mode.

2. The ABM system components listed in paragraph 1 of this Article include those which are:

(a) operational;

(b) under construction;

(c) undergoing testing;

(d) undergoing overhaul, repair or conversion; or

(e) mothballed.

Article III

Each Party undertakes not to deploy ABM systems or their components except that:

(a) within one ABM system deployment area having a radius of one hundred and fifty kilometers and centered on the Party's national capital, a Party may deploy: (1) no more than one hundred ABM launchers and no more than one hundred ABM interceptor missiles at launch sites, and (2) ABM radars within no more than six ABM radar complexes, the area of each complex being circular and having a diameter of no more than three kilometers; and

(b) within one ABM, system deployment area having a radius of one hundred and fifty kilometers and containing ICBM silo launchers, a Party may deploy: (1) no more than one hundred ABM launchers and no more than one hundred ABM interceptor missiles at launch sites, (2) two large phased-array ABM radars comparable in potential to corresponding ABM radars operational or under construction on the date of signature of the Treaty in an ABM system deployment area containing ICBM silo launchers, and (3) no more than eighteen ABM radars each having a potential less than the potential of the smaller of the above-mentioned two large phased-array ABM radars.

Article IV

The limitations provided for in Article III shall not apply to ABM systems or their components used for development or testing, and located within current or additionally agreed test ranges. Each Party may have no more than a total of fifteen ABM launchers at test ranges.

Article V

1. Each Party undertakes not to develop, test, or deploy ABM systems or components which are sea-based, air-based, space-based, or mobile land-based.
2. Each Party undertakes not to develop, test, or deploy ABM launchers for launching more than one ABM interceptor missile at a time from each launcher, nor to modify deployed launchers to provide them with such a capability, nor to develop, test, or deploy automatic or semi-automatic or other similar systems for rapid reload of ABM launchers.

Article VI

To enhance assurance of the effectiveness of the limitations on ABM systems and their components provided by this Treaty, each Party undertakes:

(a) not to give missiles, launchers, or radars, other than ABM interceptor missiles, ABM launchers, or ABM radars, capabilities to counter strategic ballistic missiles or their elements in flight trajectory, and not to test them in an ABM mode; and

(b) not to deploy in the future radars for early warning of strategic ballistic missile attack except at locations along the periphery of its national territory and oriented outward.

Article VII

Subject to the provisions of this Treaty, modernization and replacement of ABM systems or their components may be carried out.

Article VIII

ABM systems or their components in excess of the numbers or outside the areas specified in this Treaty, as well as ABM systems or their components prohibited by this Treaty, shall be destroyed or dismantled under agreed procedures within the shortest possible agreed period of time.

Article IX

To assure the viability and effectiveness of this Treaty, each Party undertakes not to transfer to other States, and not to deploy outside its national territory, ABM systems or their components limited by this Treaty.

Article X

Each Party undertakes not to assume any international obligations which would conflict with this Treaty.

Article XI

The Parties undertake to continue active negotiations for limitations on strategic offensive arms.

Article XII

1. For the purpose of providing assurance of compliance with the provisions of this Treaty, each Party shall use national technical means of verification at its disposal in a manner consistent with generally recognized principles of international law.
2. Each Party undertakes not to interfere with the national technical means of verification of the other Party operating in accordance with paragraph 1 of this Article.
3. Each Party undertakes not to use deliberate concealment measures which impede verification by national technical means of compliance with the provisions of this Treaty. This obligation shall not require changes in current construction, assembly, conversion, or overhaul practices.

Article XIII

1. To promote the objectives and implementation of the provisions of this Treaty, the Parties shall establish promptly a Standing Consultative Commission, within the framework of which they will:

(a) consider questions concerning compliance with

the obligations assumed and related situations which may be considered ambiguous;

(b) provide on a voluntary basis such information as either Party considers necessary to assure confidence in compliance with the obligations assumed;

(c) consider questions involving unintended interference with national technical means of verification;

(d) consider possible changes in the strategic situation which have a bearing on the provisions of this Treaty;

(e) agree upon procedures and dates for destruction or dismantling of ABM systems or their components in cases provided for by the provisions of this Treaty;

(f) consider, as appropriate, possible proposals for further increasing the viability of this Treaty, including proposals for amendments in accordance with the provisions of this Treaty;

(g) consider, as appropriate, proposals for further measures aimed at limiting strategic arms.

2. The Parties through consultation shall establish, and may amend as appropriate, Regulations for the Standing Consultative Commission governing procedures, composition and other relevant matters.

Article XIV

1. Each Party may propose amendments to this Treaty. Agreed amendments shall enter into force in accordance with the procedures governing the entry into force of this Treaty.

2. Five years after entry into force of this Treaty, and at five year intervals thereafter, the Parties shall together conduct a review of this Treaty.

Article XV

1. This Treaty shall be of unlimited duration.

2. Each Party shall, in exercising its national sovereignty, have the right to withdraw from this Treaty if it decides that extraordinary events related to the subject matter of this Treaty have jeopardized its supreme interests. It shall give notice of its decision to the other Party six months prior to withdrawal from the Treaty. Such notice shall include a statement of the extraordinary events the notifying Party regards as having jeopardized its supreme interests.

Article XVI

1. This Treaty shall be subject to ratification in accordance with the constitutional procedures of each Party. The Treaty shall enter into force on the day of the exchange of instruments of ratification.

2. This Treaty shall be registered pursuant to Article 102 of the Charter of the United Nations.

Interim Agreement Between the United States of America and the Union of Soviet Socialist Republics on Certain Measures with Respect to the Limitation of Strategic Offensive Arms

Also known as: *Interim Agreement. The second of two treaties concluding the Strategic Arms Limitation Talks (SALT I)*
Date of signature: *May 26, 1972*
Place of signature: *Moscow*
Signatory states: *the United States, the Soviet Union*
Date of entry into force: *October 3, 1972*

[The signatories], hereinafter referred to as the Parties,
Convinced that the Treaty on the Limitation of Anti-Ballistic Missile Systems and this Interim Agreement on Certain Measures with Respect to the Limitation of Strategic Offensive Arms will contribute to the creation of more favorable conditions for active negotiations on limiting strategic arms as well as to the relaxation of international tension and the strengthening of trust between States,

Taking into account the relationship between strategic offensive and defensive arms,
Mindful of their obligations under Article VI of the Treaty on the Non-Proliferation of Nuclear Weapons,
Having agreed as follows:

Article I

The Parties undertake not to start construction of additional fixed land-based intercontinental ballistic missile (ICBM) launchers after July 1, 1972.

Article II

The Parties undertake not to convert land-based launchers for light ICBMs, or for ICBMs of older types deployed prior to 1964, into land-based launchers for heavy ICBMs of types deployed after that time.

Article III

The Parties undertake to limit submarine-launched ballistic missile (SLBM) launchers and modern ballistic missile submarines to the numbers operational and under construction on the date of signature of this Interim Agreement, and in addition to launchers and submarines constructed under procedures established by the Parties as replacements for an equal number of ICBM launchers of older types deployed prior to 1964 or for launchers on older submarines.

Article IV

Subject to the provisions of this Interim Agreement, modernization and replacement of strategic offensive ballistic missiles and launchers covered by this Interim Agreement may be undertaken.

Article V

1. For the purpose of providing assurance of compliance with the provisions of this Interim Agreement, each Party shall use national technical means of verification at its disposal in a manner consistent with generally recognized principles of international law.
2. Each Party undertakes not to interfere with the national technical means of verification of the other Party operating in accordance with paragraph 1 of this Article.
3. Each Party undertakes not to use deliberate concealment measures which impede verification by national technical means of compliance with the provisions of this Interim Agreement. This obligation shall not require changes in current construction, assembly, conversion, or overhaul practices.

Article VI

To promote the objectives and implementation of the provisions of this Interim Agreement, the Parties shall use the Standing Consultative Commission established under Article XIII of the Treaty on the Limitation of Anti-Ballistic Missile Systems in accordance with the provisions of that Article.

Article VII

The Parties undertake to continue active negotiations for limitations on strategic offensive arms. the obligations provided for in this Interim Agreement shall not prejudice the scope or terms of the limitations on strategic offensive arms which may be worked out in the course of further negotiations.

Article VIII

1. This Interim Agreement shall enter into force upon exchange of written notices of acceptance by each Party, which exchange shall take place simultaneously with the exchange of instruments of ratification of the Treaty on the Limitation of Anti-Ballistic Missile Systems.
2. This Interim Agreement shall remain in force for a period of five years unless replaced earlier by an agreement on more complete measures limiting strategic offensive arms. It is the objective of the Parties to conduct active follow-on negotiations with the aim of concluding such an agreement as soon as possible.
3. Each Party shall, in exercising its national sovereignty, have the right to withdraw from this Interim Agreement if it decides that extraordinary events related to the subject matter of this Interim Agreement have jeopardized its supreme interests. It shall give notice of its decision to the other Party six months prior to withdrawal from this Interim Agreement. Such notice shall include a statement of the extraordinary events the notifying Party regards as having jeopardized its supreme interests.

PROTOCOL

TO THE INTERIM AGREEMENT BETWEEN THE UNITED STATES OF AMERICA AND THE UNION OF SOVIET SOCIALIST REPUBLICS ON CERTAIN MEASURES WITH RESPECT TO THE LIMITATION OF STRATEGIC OFFENSIVE ARMS

[The signatories], hereinafter referred to as the Parties,

Having agreed on certain limitations relating to submarine-launched ballistic missile launchers and modern ballistic missile submarines, and to replacement procedures, in the Interim Agreement,

Have agreed as follows:

The Parties understand that, under Article III of the Interim Agreement, for the period during which that Agreement remains in force:

The US may have no more than 710 ballistic missile launchers on submarines (SLBMs) and no more than 44 modern ballistic missile submarines. The Soviet Union may have no more than 950 ballistic missile launchers on submarines and no more than 62 modern ballistic missile submarines.

Additional ballistic missile launchers on submarines up to the above-mentioned levels, in the US— over 656 ballistic missile launchers on nuclear-powered submarines, and in the USSR—over 740 ballistic missile launchers on nuclear-powered submarines, operational and under construction, may become operational as replacements for equal numbers of ballistic missile launchers of older types deployed prior to 1964 or of ballistic missile launchers on older submarines.

The deployment of modern SLBMs on any submarine, regardless of type, will be counted against the total level of SLBMs permitted for the US and the USSR.

This Protocol shall be considered an integral part of the Interim Agreement.

Basic Principles of Negotiations on the Further Limitation of Strategic Offensive Arms

Date of signature: *June 21, 1973*
Place of signature: *Washington, DC*
Signatory states: *the United States, the Soviet Union*

The President of the United States of America, Richard Nixon, and the General Secretary of the Central Committee of the CPSU, L. I. Brezhnev,

Having thoroughly considered the question of the further limitation of strategic arms, and the progress already achieved in the current negotiations,

Reaffirming their conviction that the earliest adoption of further limitations of strategic arms would be a major contribution in reducing the danger of an outbreak of nuclear war and in strengthening international peace and security,

Having agreed as follows:

First. The two Sides will continue active negotiations in order to work out a permanent agreement on more complete measures on the limitation of strategic offensive arms as well as their subsequent reduction, proceeding from the Basic Principles of Relations between the United States of America and the Union of Soviet Socialist Republics signed in Moscow on May 29, 1972, and from the Interim Agreement between the United States of America and the Union of Soviet Socialist Republics of May 26, 1972 on Certain Measures with Respect to the Limitation of Strategic Offensive Arms.

Over the course of the next year the two Sides will make serious efforts to work out the provisions of the permanent agreement on more complete measures on the limitation of strategic offensive arms with the objective of signing it in 1974.

Second. New agreements on the limitation of strategic offensive armaments will be based on the principles of the American-Soviet documents adopted in Moscow in May 1972 and the agreements reached in Washington in June 1973; and in particular, both Sides will be guided by the recognition of each other's equal security interests and by the recognition that efforts to obtain unilateral advantage, directly or indirectly, would be inconsistent with the strengthening of peaceful relations between the United States of America and the Union of Soviet Socialist Republics.

Third. The limitations placed on strategic offensive weapons can apply both to their quantitative aspects as well as to their qualitative improvement.

Fourth. Limitations on strategic offensive arms must be subject to adequate verification by national technical means.

Fifth. The modernization and replacement of strategic offensive arms would be permitted under conditions which will be formulated in the agreements to be concluded.

Sixth. Pending the completion of a permanent agreement on more complete measures of strategic offensive arms limitation, both Sides are prepared to reach agreements on separate measures to supplement the existing Interim Agreement of May 26, 1972.

Seventh. Each Side will continue to take necessary organizational and technical measures for preventing accidental or unauthorized use of nuclear weapons under its control in accordance with the Agreement of September 30, 1971 between the United States of America and the Union of Soviet Socialist Republics.

Agreement Between the United States of America and the Union of Soviet Socialist Republics on the Prevention of Nuclear War

Date of signature: *June 22, 1973*
Place of signature: *Washington, DC*
Signatory states: *the United States, the Soviet Union*

The United States of America and the Union of

Soviet Socialist Republics, hereinafter referred to as the Parties,

Guided by the objectives of strengthening world peace and international security,

Conscious that nuclear war would have devastating consequences for mankind,

Proceeding from the desire to bring about conditions in which the danger of an outbreak of nuclear war anywhere in the world would be reduced and ultimately eliminated,

Proceeding from their obligations under the Charter of the United Nations regarding the maintenance of peace, refraining from the threat or use of force, and the avoidance of war, and in conformity with the agreements to which either Party has subscribed,

Proceeding from the Basic Principles of Relations between the United States of America and the Union of Soviet Socialist Republics singe in Moscow on May 29, 1972,

Reaffirming that the development of relations between the United States of America and the Union of Soviet Socialist Republics is not directed against other countries and their interests,

Have agreed as follows:

Article I

The United States and the Soviet Union agree that an objective of their policies is to remove the danger of nuclear war and of the use of nuclear weapons.

Accordingly, the Parties agree that they will act in such a manner as to prevent the development of situations capable of causing a dangerous exacerbation of their relations, as to avoid military confrontations, and as to exclude the outbreak of nuclear war between them and between either of the Parties and other countries.

Article II

The Parties agree, in accordance with Article I and to realize the objectives state in that Article, to proceed from the premise that each Party will refrain from the threat or use of force against the other Party, against the allies of the other Party and against other countries, in circumstances which may endanger international peace and security. The Parties agree that they will be guided by these considerations in the formulation of their foreign policies and in their actions in the field of international relations.

Article III

The Parties undertake to develop their relations with each other and with countries in a way consistent with the purposes of this Agreement.

Article IV

If at any time relations between the Parties or between either Party and other countries appear to involve the risk of a nuclear conflict, or if relations between countries not parties to this Agreement appear to involve the risk of nuclear war between the United States of America and the Union of Soviet Socialist Republics or between either Party and other countries, the United States and the Soviet Union, acting in accordance with the provisions of this Agreement, shall immediately enter into urgent consultations with each other and make every effort to avert this risk.

Article V

Each Party shall be free to inform the Security Council of the United Nations, the Secretary General of the United Nations and the Governments of allied or other countries of the progress and outcome of consultations initiated in accordance with Article IV of this Agreement.

Article VI

Nothing in this Agreement shall affect or impair:

(a) the inherent right of individual or collective self-defense as envisaged by Article 51 of the Charter of the United Nations,

(b) the provisions of the Charter of the United Nations, including those relating to the maintenance or restoration of international peace and security, and

(c) the obligations undertaken by either Party towards its allies or other countries in treaties, agreements, and other appropriate documents.

Article VII

This Agreement shall be of unlimited duration.

Article VIII

This Agreement shall enter into force upon signature.

Treaty Between the United States of America and the Union of Soviet Socialist Republics on the Limitation of Underground Nuclear Weapon Tests

Also known as: *Threshold Test Ban Treaty, (TTBT)*
Date of signature: *July 3, 1974*

Place of signature: *Moscow*
Signatory states: *the United States, the Soviet Union*

[The signatories],

Declaring their intention to achieve at the earliest possible date the cessation of the nuclear arms race and to take effective measures toward reductions in strategic arms, nuclear disarmament, and general and complete disarmament under strict and effective international control,

Recalling the determination expressed by the Parties to the 1963 Treaty Banning Nuclear Weapon Tests in the Atmosphere, in Outer Space and Under Water in its Preamble to seek to achieve the discontinuance of all test explosions of nuclear weapons for all time, and to continue negotiations to this end.

Noting that the adoption of measures for the further limitation of underground nuclear weapon tests would contribute to the achievement of these objectives and would meet the interests of strengthening peace and the further relaxation of international tension.

Reaffirming their adherence to the objectives and principles of the Treaty Banning Nuclear Weapon Tests in the Atmosphere, in Outer Space and Under Water and of the Treaty on the Non-Proliferation of Nuclear Weapons,

Have agreed as follows:

Article I

1. Each Party undertakes to prohibit, to prevent, and not to carry out any underground nuclear weapon test having a yield exceeding 150 kilotons at any place under its jurisdiction of control, beginning March 31, 1976.

2. Each Party shall limit the number of its underground nuclear weapon tests to a minimum.

3. The Parties shall continue their negotiations with a view toward achieving a solution to the problem of the cessation of all underground nuclear weapon tests.

Article II

1. For the purpose of providing assurance of compliance with the provisions of the Treaty, each Party shall use national technical means of verification at its disposal in a manner consistent with the generally recognized principles of international law.

2. Each Party undertakes not to interfere with the national technical means of verification of the other Party operating in accordance with paragraph 1 of this Article.

3. To promote the objectives and implementation of the provisions of this Treaty the Parties shall, as necessary, consult with each other, make inquiries and furnish information in response to such inquiries.

Article III

The provisions of this Treaty do not extend to underground nuclear explosions carried out by the Parties for peaceful purposes. Underground nuclear explosions for peaceful purposes shall be governed by an agreement which is to be negotiated and concluded by the Parties at the earliest possible time.

Article IV

This Treaty shall be subject to ratification in accordance with the constitutional procedures of each Party. This Treaty shall enter into force on the day of the exchange of instruments of ratification.

Article V

1. This Treaty shall remain in force for a period of five years. Unless replaced earlier by an agreement in implementation of the objectives specified in paragraph 3 of Article I of this Treaty, it shall be extended for successive five-year periods unless either Party notifies the other of its termination no later than six months prior to the expiration of the Treaty. Before the expiration of this period the Parties may, as necessary, hold consultations to consider the situation relevant to the substance of this Treaty and to introduce possible amendments to the text of the Treaty.

2. Each Party shall, in exercising its national sovereignty, have the right to withdraw from this Treaty if it decides that extraordinary events related to the subject matter of this Treaty have jeopardized its supreme interests. It shall give notice of its decision to the other Party six months prior to withdrawal from this Treaty. Such notice shall include a statement of the extraordinary events the notifying Party regards as having jeopardized its supreme interests.

3. This Treaty shall be registered pursuant to Article 102 of the Charter of the United Nations.

PROTOCOL TO THE TREATY BETWEEN THE UNITED STATES OF AMERICA AND THE UNION OF SOVIET SOCIALIST REPUBLICS ON THE LIMITATION OF UNDERGROUND NUCLEAR WEAPON TESTS

[The signatories], hereinafter referred to as the Parties,

Having agreed to limit underground nuclear weapon tests,

Have agreed as follows:

1. For the purpose of ensuring verification of compliance with the obligations of the Parties under the Treaty by national technical means, the Parties shall,

on the basis of reciprocity, exchange the following data:

a. The geographic coordinates of the boundaries of each test site and of the boundaries of the geophysically distinct testing areas therein.

b. Information on the geology of the testing areas of the sites (the rock characteristics of geological formations and the basic physical properties of the rock, i.e., density, seismic velocity, water saturation, porosity and depth of water table).

c. The geographic coordinates of underground nuclear weapon tests, after they have been conducted.

d. Yield, date, time, depth and coordinates for two nuclear weapon tests for calibration purposes from each geophysically distinct testing area where underground nuclear weapon tests have been and are to be conducted. In this connection the yield of such explosions for calibration purposes should be as near as possible to the limit defined in Article I of the Treaty and not less than one-tenth of that limit. In the case of testing areas where data are not available on two tests for calibration purposes, the data pertaining to one such test shall be exchanged, if available, and the data pertaining to the second test shall be exchanged as soon as possible after a second test having a yield in the above-mentioned range. The provisions of the Protocol shall not require the Parties to conduct tests solely for calibration purposes.

2. The Parties agree that the exchange of data pursuant to subparagraphs a, b, and d of paragraph 1 shall be carried out simultaneously with the exchange of instruments of ratification of the Treaty, as provided in Article IV of the Treaty, having in mind that the Parties shall, on the basis of reciprocity, afford each other the opportunity to familiarize themselves with these data before the exchange of instruments of ratification.

3. Should a Party specify a new test site or testing area after the entry into force of the Treaty, the data called for by subparagraphs a and b of paragraph 1 shall be transmitted to the other Party in advance of use of that site or area. The data called for by subparagraph d of paragraph 1 shall also be transmitted in advance of use of that site or area if they are available; if they are not available, they shall be transmitted as soon as possible after they have been obtained by the transmitting Party.

4. The Parties agree that the test sites of each Party shall be located at places under its jurisdiction or control and that all nuclear weapon tests shall be conducted solely within the testing areas specified in accordance with paragraph 1.

5. For the purposes of the Treaty, all underground nuclear explosions at the specified test sites shall be considered nuclear weapon tests and shall be subject to all the provisions of the Treaty relating to nuclear weapon tests. The provisions of Article III of the Treaty apply to all underground nuclear explosions conducted outside of the specified test sites, and only to such explosions.

This Protocol shall be considered an integral party of the Treaty.

Protocol to the Treaty Between the United States of America and the Union of Soviet Socialist Republics on the Limitation of Anti-Ballistic Missile Systems

Date of signature: *July 3, 1974*
Place of signature: *Moscow*
Signatory states: *the United States, the Soviet Union*
Date of entry into force: *May 25, 1976*

[The signatories],
Proceeding from the basic principles of relations between the United States of America and the Union of Soviet Socialist Republics signed on May 29, 1972,
Desiring to further the objectives of the Treaty between the United States of America and the Union of Soviet Socialist Republics on the Limitation of Anti-Ballistic Missile Systems signed on May 26, 1972, hereinafter referred to as the Treaty,
Reaffirming their conviction that the adoption of further measures for the limitation of strategic arms would contribute to strengthening international peace and security,
Proceeding from the premise that further limitation of anti-ballistic missile systems will create more favorable conditions for the completion of work on a permanent agreement on more complete measures for the limitation of strategic offensive arms,
Have agreed as follows:

Article I

1. Each Party shall be limited at any one time to a single area out of the two provided in Article III of the Treaty for deployment of anti-ballistic missile (ABM) systems or their components and accordingly shall not exercise its right to deploy an ABM system or its components in the second of the two ABM system

deployment areas permitted by Article III of the Treaty, except as an exchange of one permitted area for the other in accordance with Article II of this Protocol.

2. Accordingly, except as permitted by Article II of this Protocol: The United States of America shall not deploy an ABM system or its components in the area centered on its capital, as permitted by Article III (a) of the Treaty, and the Soviet Union shall not deploy an ABM system or its components in the deployment area of intercontinental ballistic missile (ICBM) silo launchers as permitted by Article III (b) of the Treaty.

Article II

1. Each Party shall have the right to dismantle or destroy its ABM system and the components thereof in the area where they are presently deployed and to deploy an ABM system or its components in the alternative area permitted by Article III of the Treaty, provided that prior to initiation of construction, notification is given in accord with the procedure agreed to by the Standing Consultative Commission during the year beginning October 3, 1977 and ending October 2, 1978, or during any year which commences at five year intervals thereafter, those being the years for periodic review of the Treaty, as provided in Article XIV of the Treaty. This right may be exercised only once.

2. Accordingly, in the event of such notice, the United States would have the right to dismantle or destroy the ABM system and its components in the

deployment area of ICBM silo launchers and to deploy an ABM system or its components in an area centered on its capital, as permitted by Article III (a) of the Treaty, and the Soviet Union would have the right to dismantle or destroy the ABM system and its components in the area centered on its capital and to deploy an ABM system or its components in an area containing ICBM silo launchers, as permitted by Article III (b) of the Treaty.

3. Dismantling or destruction and deployment of ABM systems or their components and the notification thereof shall be carried out in accordance with Article VIII of the ABM Treaty and procedures agreed to in the Standing Consultative Commission.

Article III

The rights and obligations established by the Treaty remain in force and shall be complied with by the Parties except to the extent modified by this Protocol. In particular, the deployment of an ABM system or its components within the area selected shall remain limited by the levels and other requirements established by the Treaty.

Article IV

This Protocol shall be subject to ratification in accordance with the constitutional procedures of each Party. It shall enter into force on the day of the exchange of instruments of ratification and shall thereafter be considered an integral part of the Treaty.

Document on Confidence-Building Measures and Certain Aspects of Security and Disarmament Included in the Final Act of the Conference on Security and Cooperation in Europe

Also known as: *Helsinki Final Act, Document on Confidence-Building Measures*
Date of signature: *August 1, 1975*
Place of signature: *Helsinki*
Signatory states: *Austria, Belgium, Bulgaria, Canada, Cyprus, Czechoslovakia, Denmark, Finland, France, German Democratic Republic, Federal Republic of Germany, Greece, Holy See, Hungary, Iceland, Ireland, Italy, Liechtenstein, Luxembourg, Malta, Monaco, Netherlands, Norway, Poland, Portugal, Romania, San Marino, Soviet Union, Spain, Sweden, Switzerland, Turkey, United Kingdom, United States, Yugoslavia*

The participating States,
Desirous of eliminating the causes of tension that

may exist among them and thus of contributing to the strengthening of peace and security in the world;
Determined to strengthen confidence among them and thus to contribute to increasing stability and security in Europe;
Determined further to refrain in their mutual relations, as well as in their international relations in general, from the threat or use of force against the territorial integrity or political independence of any State, or in any other manner inconsistent with the purposes of the United Nations and with the Declaration on Principles Guiding Relations between Participating States as adopted in this Final Act;
Recognizing the need to contribute to reducing the dangers of armed conflict and of misunderstanding or miscalculation of military activities which could give rise to apprehension, particularly in a situation

where the participating States lack clear and timely information about the nature of such activities;

Taking into account considerations relevant to efforts aimed at lessening tension and promoting disarmament;

Recognizing that the exchange of observers by invitation at military manoeuvres will help to promote contacts and mutual understanding;

Having studied the question of prior notification of major military movements in the context of confidence-building;

Recognizing that there are other ways in which individual States can contribute further to their common objectives;

Convinced of the political importance of prior notification of major military manoeuvres for the promotion of mutual understanding and the strengthening of confidence, stability and security;

Accepting the responsibility of each of them to promote these objectives and to implement this measure, in accordance with the accepted criteria and modalities, as essentials for the realization of these objectives;

Recognizing that this measure deriving from political decision rests upon a voluntary basis;

Have adopted the following:

I

Prior notification of major military manoeuvres

They will notify their major manoeuvres to all other participating States through usual diplomatic channels in accordance with the following provisions:

Notification will be given of major military manoeuvres exceeding a total of 25,000 troops, independently or combined with any possible air or naval components (in this context the word "troops" includes amphibious and airborne troops). In the case of independent manoeuvres of amphibious or airborne troops, or of combined manoeuvres involving them, these troops will be included in this total. Furthermore, in the case of combined manoeuvres which do not reach the above total but which involve land forces together with significant numbers of either amphibious or airborne troops, or both, notification can also be given.

Notification will be given of major military manoeuvres which take place on the territory, in Europe, of any participating State as well as, if applicable, in the adjoining sea area and air space.

In the case of a participating State whose territory extends beyond Europe, prior notification need be given only of manoeuvres which take place in an area within 250 kilometres from its frontier facing or shared with any other European participating State, the participating State need not, however, give notification in cases in which that area is also contiguous to the participating State's frontier facing or shared with a non-European non-participating State.

Notification will be given 21 days or more in advance of the start of the manoeuvre or in the case of a manoeuvre arranged at shorter notice at the earliest possible opportunity prior to its starting date.

Notification will contain information of the designation, if any, the general purpose of and the States involved in the manoeuvres, the type or types and numerical strength of the forces engaged, the area and estimated time-frame of its conduct. The participating States will also, if possible, provide additional relevant information, particularly that related to the components of the forces engaged and the period of involvement of these forces.

Prior notification of other military manoeuvres

The participating States recognize that they can contribute further to strengthening confidence and increasing security and stability, and to this end may also notify smaller-scale military manoeuvres to other participating States, with special regard for those near the area of such manoeuvres.

To the same end, the participating States also recognize that they may notify other military manoeuvres conducted by them.

Exchange of observers

The participating States will invite other participating States, voluntarily and on a bilateral basis, in a spirit of reciprocity and goodwill towards all participating States, to send observers to attend military manoeuvres.

The inviting State will determine in each case the number of observers, the procedures and conditions of their participation, and give other information which it may consider useful. It will provide appropriate facilities and hospitality.

The invitation will be given as far ahead as is conveniently possible through usual diplomatic channels.

Prior notification of major military movements

In accordance with the Final Recommendations of the Helsinki Consultations the participating States studied the question of prior notification of major military movements as a measure to strengthen confidence.

Accordingly, the participating States recognize that they may, at their own discretion and with a view to contributing to confidence-building, notify their major military movements.

In the same spirit, further consideration will be given by the States participating in the Conference on Security and Co-operation in Europe to the question of prior notification of major military movements, bearing in mind, in particular, the experience gained by the implementation of the measures which are set forth in this document.

Other confidence-building measures

The participating States recognize that there are other means by which their common objectives can be promoted.

In particular, they will, with due regard to reciprocity and with a view to better mutual understanding, promote exchanges by invitation among their military personnel, including visits by military delegations.

* * *

In order to make a fuller contribution to their common objective of confidence-building, the participating States, when conducting their military activities in the area covered by the provisions for the prior notification of major military manoeuvres, will duly take into account and respect this objective.

They also recognize that the experience gained by the implementation of the provisions set forth above, together with further efforts, could lead to developing and enlarging measures aimed at strengthening confidence.

II

Questions relating to disarmament

The participating States recognize the interest of all of them in efforts aimed at lessening military confrontation and promoting disarmament which are designed to complement political détente in Europe and to strengthen their security. They are convinced of the necessity to take effective measures in these fields which by their scope and by their nature constitute steps towards the ultimate achievement of general and complete disarmament under strict and effective international control, and which should result in strengthening peace and security throughout the world.

III

General considerations

Having considered the views expressed on various subjects related to the strengthening of security in Europe through joint efforts aimed at promoting détente and disarmament, the participating States, when engaged in such efforts, will, in this context, proceed, in particular, from the following essential considerations:

—The complementary nature of the political and military aspects of security;

—The interrelation between the security of each participating State and security in Europe as a whole and the relationship which exists, in the broader context of world security, between security in Europe and security in the Mediterranean area;

—Respect for the security interests of all States participating in the Conference on Security and Co-operation in Europe inherent in their sovereign equality;

—The importance that participants in negotiating fora see to it that information about relevant developments, progress and results is provided on an appropriate basis to other States participating in the Conference on Security and Co-operation in Europe and, in return, the justified interest of any of those States in having their views considered.

Treaty Between the United States of America and the Union of Soviet Socialist Republics on Underground Nuclear Explosions for Peaceful Purposes

Also known as: PNE Treaty
Date of signature: May 28, 1976
Place of signature: Moscow and Washington,
DC
Signatory states: the United States, the Soviet Union

[The signatory states]
Proceeding from a desire to implement Article III of the Treaty between the United States of America and the Union of Soviet Socialist Republics on the Limitation of Underground Nuclear Weapon Tests, which calls for the earliest possible conclusion of an agreement on underground nuclear explosions for peaceful purposes,

Reaffirming their adherence to the objectives and principles of the Treaty Banning Nuclear Weapon Tests in the Atmosphere, in Outer Space and Under Water, the Treaty on Non-Proliferation of Nuclear Weapons, and the Treaty on the Limitation of Underground Nuclear Weapon Tests, and their determination to observe strictly the provisions of these international agreements,

Desiring to assure that underground nuclear explosions for peaceful purposes shall not be used for purposes related to nuclear weapons,

Desiring that utilization of nuclear energy be directed only toward peaceful purposes,

Desiring to develop appropriately cooperation in the field of underground nuclear explosions for peaceful purposes,

Have agreed as follows:

Article I

1. The Parties enter into this Treaty to satisfy the obligations in Article III of the Treaty on the Limitation of Underground Nuclear Weapon Tests, and assume additional obligations in accordance with the provisions of this Treaty.

2. This Treaty shall govern all underground nuclear explosions for peaceful purposes conducted by the Parties after March 31, 1976.

Article II

For the purposes of this Treaty:

(a) "explosion" means any individual or group underground nuclear explosion for peaceful purposes;

(b) "explosive" means any device, mechanism or system for producing an individual explosion;

(c) "group explosion" means two or more individual explosions for which the time interval between successive individual explosions does not exceed five seconds and for which the emplacement points of all explosives can be interconnected by straight line segments, each of which joins two emplacement points and each of which does not exceed 40 kilometers.

Article III

1. Each Party, subject to the obligations assumed under this Treaty and other international agreements, reserves the right to:

(a) carry out explosions at any place under its jurisdiction or control outside the geographical boundaries of test sites specified under the provisions of the Treaty on the Limitation of Underground Nuclear Weapon Tests; and

(b) carry out, participate or assist in carrying out explosions in the territory of another State at the request of such other State.

2. Each Party undertakes to prohibit, to prevent and not to carry out at any place under its jurisdiction, or control, and further undertakes not to carry out, participate or assist in carrying out anywhere:

(a) any individual explosion having a yield exceeding 150 kilotons;

(b) any group explosion:

(1) having any aggregate yield exceeding 150 kilotons except in ways that will permit identification

of each individual explosion and determination of the yield of each individual explosion in the group in accordance with the provisions of Article IV of and the Protocol to this Treaty;

(2) having an aggregate yield exceeding one and one-half megatons;

(c) any explosion which does not carry out a peaceful application;

(d) any explosion except in compliance with the provisions of the Treaty Banning Nuclear Weapon Tests in the Atmosphere, in Outer Space and Under Water, the Treaty on the Non-Proliferation of Nuclear Weapons, and other international agreements entered into by that Party.

3. The question of carrying out any individual explosion having a yield exceeding the yield specified in paragraph 2(a) of this article will be considered by the Parties at an appropriate time to be agreed.

Article IV

1. For the purpose of providing assurance of compliance with the provisions of this Treaty, each Party shall:

(a) use national technical means of verification at its disposal in a manner consistent with generally recognized principles of international law; and

(b) provide to the other Party information and access to sites of explosions and furnish assistance in accordance with the provisions set forth in the Protocol to this Treaty.

2. Each Party undertakes not to interfere with the national technical means of verification of the other Party operating in accordance with paragraph 1(a) of this article, or with the implementation of the provisions of paragraph 1(b) of this article.

Article V

1. To promote the objectives and implementation of the provisions of this Treaty, the Parties shall establish promptly a Joint Consultative Commission within the framework of which they will:

(a) consult with each other, make inquiries and furnish information in response to such inquiries, to assure confidence in compliance with the obligations assumed;

(b) consider questions concerning compliance with the obligations assumed and related situations which may be considered ambiguous;

(c) consider questions involving unintended interference with the means for assuring compliance with the provisions of this Treaty;

(d) consider changes in technology or other new circumstances which have a bearing on the provisions of this Treaty; and

(e) consider possible amendments to provisions governing underground nuclear explosions for peaceful purposes.

2. The Parties through consultation shall establish, and may amend as appropriate, Regulations for the Joint Consultative Commission governing procedures, composition and other relevant matters.

Article VI

1. The Parties will develop cooperation on the basis of mutual benefit, equality, and reciprocity in various areas related to carrying out underground nuclear explosions for peaceful purposes.
2. The Joint Consultative Commission will facilitate this cooperation by considering specific areas and forms of cooperation which shall be determined by agreement between the Parties in accordance with their constitutional procedures.
3. The Parties will appropriately inform the International Atomic Energy Agency of results of their cooperation in the field of underground nuclear explosions for peaceful purposes.

Article VII

1. Each Party shall continue to promote the development of the international agreement or agreements and procedures provided for in Article V of the Treaty on the Non-Proliferation of Nuclear Weapons, and shall provide appropriate assistance to the International Atomic Energy Agency in this regard.
2. Each Party undertakes not to carry out, participate or assist in the carrying out of any explosion in the territory of another State unless that State agrees to the implementation in its territory of the international observation and procedures contemplated by Article V of the Treaty on the Non-Proliferation of Nuclear Weapons and the provisions of Article IV of and the Protocol to this Treaty, including the provision by that State of the assistance necessary for such implementation and of the privileges and immunities specified in the Protocol.

Article VIII

1. This Treaty shall remain in force for a period of five years, and it shall be extended for successive five-year periods unless either Party notifies the other of its termination no later than six months prior to its expiration. Before the expiration of this period the Parties may, as necessary, hold consultations to consider the situation relevant to the substance of this Treaty. However, under no circumstances shall either Party be entitled to terminate this Treaty while the Treaty on the Limitation of Underground Nuclear Weapon Tests remains in force.

2. Termination of the Treaty on the Limitation of Underground Nuclear Weapon Tests shall entitle either Party to withdraw from this Treaty at any time.

3. Each Party may propose amendments to this Treaty. Amendments shall enter into force on the day of the exchange of instruments of ratification of such amendments.

Article IX

1. This Treaty including the Protocol which forms an integral part hereof, shall be subject to ratification in accordance with the constitutional procedures of each Party. This Treaty shall enter into force on the day of the exchange of instruments of ratification which exchange shall take place simultaneously with the exchange of instruments of ratification of the Treaty on the Limitation of Underground Nuclear Weapon Tests.

2. This Treaty shall be registered pursuant to Article 102 of the Charter of the United Nations.

Protocol to the Treaty Between the United States of America and the Union of Soviet Socialist Republics on Underground Nuclear Explosions for Peaceful Purposes.

[The signatories],
Having agreed to the provisions in the Treaty on Underground Nuclear Explosions for Peaceful Purposes, hereinafter referred to as the Treaty,
Have agreed as follows:

Article I

1. No individual explosion shall take place at a distance in meters, from the ground surface which is less than 30 times the 3.4 root of its planned yield in kilotons.
2. Any group explosion with a planned aggregate yield exceeding 500 kilotons shall not include more than five individual explosions, each of which has a planned yield not exceeding 50 kilotons.

Article II

1. For each explosion, the Party carrying out the explosion shall provide the other Party:

(a) not later than 90 days before the beginning of emplacement of the explosives when the planned aggregate yield of the explosion does not exceed 100 kilotons, or not later than 180 days before the beginning of emplacement of the explosives when the planned aggregate yield of the explosion exceeds 100 kilotons, with the following information to the extent and degree of precision available when it is conveyed:

(1) the purpose of the planned explosion;

(2) the location of the explosion expressed in geographical coordinates with a precision of four or less kilometers, planned date and aggregate yield of the explosion;

(3) the type or types of rock in which the explosion will be carried out, including the degree of liquid saturation of the rock at the point of emplacement of each explosive; and

(4) a description of specific technological features of the project, of which the explosion is a part, that could influence the determination of its yield and confirmation of purpose; and

(b) not later than 60 days before the beginning of emplacement of the explosives the information specified in subparagraph 1(a) of this article to the full extent and with the precision indicated in that subparagraph.

2. For each explosion with a planned aggregate yield exceeding 50 kilotons, the Party carrying out the explosion shall provide the other Party, not later than 60 days before the beginning of emplacement of the explosives, with the following information:

(a) the number of explosives, the planned yield of each explosive, the location of each explosive to be used in a group explosion relative to all other explosives in the group with a precision of 100 or less meters, the depth of emplacement of each explosive with a precision of one meter and the time intervals between individual explosions in any group explosion with a precision of one-tenth second; and

(b) a description of specific features of geological structure or other local conditions that could influence the determination of the yield.

3. For each explosion with a planned aggregate yield exceeding 75 kilotons, the Party carrying out the explosion shall provide the other Party, not later than 60 days before the beginning of emplacement of the explosives, with a description of the geological and geophysical characteristics of the site of each explosion which could influence determination of the yield, which shall include: the depth of the water table; a stratigraphic column above each emplacement point; the position of each emplacement point relative to nearby geological and other features which influenced the design of the project of which the explosion is a part; and the physical parameters of the rock, including density, seismic velocity, porosity, degree of liquid saturation, and rock strength, within the sphere centered on each emplacement point and having a radius, in meters,

equal to 30 times the cube root of the planned yield in kilotons of the explosive emplaced at that point.

4. For each explosion with a planned aggregate yield exceeding 100 kilotons, the Party carrying out the explosion shall provide the other Party, not later than 60 days before the beginning of emplacement of the explosives, with:

(a) information on locations and purposes of facilities and installations which are associated with the conduct of the explosion;

(b) information regarding the planned date of the beginning of emplacement of each explosive; and

(c) a topographic plan in local coordinates of the areas specified in paragraph 7 of Article IV, at a scale of 1 : 24,000 or 1 : 25,000 with a contour interval of 10 meters or less.

5. For application of an explosion to alleviate the consequences of an emergency situation involving an unforeseen combination of circumstances which calls for immediate action for which it would not be practicable to observe the timing requirements of paragraphs 1, 2 and 3 of this article, the following conditions shall be met:

(a) the Party carrying out an explosion for such purposes shall inform the other Party of that decision immediately after it has been made and describe such circumstances;

(b) the planned aggregate yield of an explosion for such purpose shall not exceed 100 kilotons; and

(c) the Party carrying out an explosion for such purpose shall provide to the other Party the information specified in paragraph 1 of this article, and the information specified in paragraphs 2 and 3 of this article if applicable, after the decision to conduct the explosion is taken, but not later than 30 days before the beginning of emplacement of the explosives.

6. For each explosion, the Party carrying out the explosion shall inform the other Party, not later than two days before the explosion, of the planned time of detonation of each explosive with a precision of one second.

7. Prior to the explosion, the Party carrying out the explosion shall provide the other Party with timely notification of changes in the information provided in accordance with this article.

8. The explosion shall not be carried out earlier than 90 days after notification of any change in the information provided in accordance with this article which requires more extensive verification procedures than those required on the basis of the original information, unless an earlier time for carrying out the explosion is agreed between the Parties.

9. Not later than 90 days after each explosion the

Party carrying out the explosion shall provide the other Party with the following information:

(a) the actual time of the explosion with a precision of one-tenth second and its aggregate yield;

(b) when the planned aggregate yield of a group explosion exceeds 50 kilotons, the actual time of the first individual explosion with a precision of one-tenth second, the time interval between individual explosions with a precision of one millisecond and the yield of each individual explosion; and

(c) confirmation of other information provided in accordance with paragraphs 1, 2, 3 and 4 of this article and explanation of any changes or corrections based on the results of the explosion.

10. At any time, but not later than one year after the explosion, the other Party may request the Party carrying out the explosion to clarify any item of the information provided in accordance with this article. Such clarification shall be provided as soon as practicable, but not later than 30 days after the request is made.

Article III

1. For the purposes of this Protocol:

(a) "designated personnel" means those nationals of the other Party identified to the Party carrying out an explosion as the persons who will exercise the rights and functions provided for in the Treaty and this Protocol; and

(b) "emplacement hole" means the entire interior of any drill-hole, shaft, adit or tunnel in which an explosive and associated cables and other equipment are to be installed.

2. For any explosion with a planned aggregate yield exceeding 100 kilotons but not exceeding 150 kilotons if the Parties, in consultation based on information provided in accordance with Article II and other information that may be introduced by either Party, deem it appropriate for the confirmation of the yield of the explosion, and for any explosion with a planned aggregate yield exceeding 150 kilotons, the Party carrying out the explosion shall allow designated personnel within the areas and at the locations described in Article V to exercise the following rights and functions:

(a) confirmation that the local circumstances, including facilities and installations associated with the project, are consistent with the stated peaceful purposes;

(b) confirmation of the validity of the geological and geophysical information provided in accordance with Article II through the following procedures:

(1) examination by designated personnel of research and measurement data of the Party carrying out the explosion and of rock core or rock fragments removed from each emplacement hole, and of any logs and drill core from existing exploratory holes which shall be provided to designated personnel upon their arrival at the site of the explosion;

(2) examination by designated personnel of rock core or rock fragments as they become available in accordance with the procedures specified in subparagraph 2(b)(3) or this article; and

(3) observation by designated personnel of implementation by the Party carrying out the explosion of one of the following four procedures, unless this right is waived by the other Party:

(i) construction of that portion of each emplacement hole starting from a point nearest the entrance of the emplacement hole which is at a distance, in meters, from the nearest emplacement point equal to 30 times the cube root of the planned yield in kilotons of the explosive to be emplaced at that point and continuing to the completion of the emplacement hole; or

(ii) construction of that portion of each emplacement hole starting from a point nearest the entrance of the emplacement hole which is at a distance, in meters, from the nearest emplacement point equal to six times the cube root of the planned yield in kilotons of the explosive to be emplaced at that point and continuing to the completion of the emplacement hole as well as the removal of rock core or rock fragments from the wall of an existing exploratory hole, which is substantially parallel with and at no point more than 100 meters from the emplacement hole, at locations specified by designated personnel which lie within a distance, in meters, from the same horizon as each emplacement point of 30 times the cube root of the planned yield in kilotons of the explosive to be emplaced at that point; or

(iii) removal of rock core or rock fragments from the wall of each emplacement hole at locations specified by designated personnel which lie within a distance, in meters, from each emplacement point of 30 times the cube root of the planned yield in kilotons of the explosive to be emplaced at each such point; or

(iv) construction of one or more new exploratory holes so that for each emplacement hole there will be a new exploratory hole to the same depth as that of the emplacement of the explosive, substantially parallel with and at no point more than 100 meters from each emplacement hole, from which rock cores would be removed at locations specified by designated personnel

which lie within a distance, in meters, from the same horizon as each emplacement point of 30 times the cube root of the planned yield in kilotons of the explosive to be emplaced at each such point;

(c) observation of the emplacement of each explosive, confirmation of the depth of its emplacement and observation of the stemming of each emplacement hole;

(d) unobstructed visual observation of the area of the entrance to each emplacement hole at any time from the time of emplacement of each explosive until all personnel have been withdrawn from the site for the detonation of the explosion; and

(e) observation of each explosion.

3. Designated personnel, using equipment provided in accordance with paragraph 1 of Article IV, shall have the right, for any explosion with a planned aggregate yield exceeding 150 kilotons, to determine the yield of each individual explosion in a group explosion in accordance with the provisions of Article VI.

4. Designated personnel, when using their equipment in accordance with paragraph 1 of Article IV, shall have the right, for any explosion with a planned aggregate yield exceeding 500 kilotons, to emplace, install and operate under the observation and with the assistance of personnel of the Party carrying out the explosion, if such assistance is requested by designated personnel, a local seismic network in accordance with the provisions of paragraph 7 of Article IV. Radio links may be used for the transmission of data and control signals between the seismic stations and the control center. Frequencies, maximum power output of radio transmitters, directivity of antennas and times of operation of the local seismic network radio transmitters before the explosion shall be agreed between the Parties in accordance with Article X and time of operation after the explosion shall conform to the time specified in paragraph 7 of Article IV.

5. Designated personnel shall have the right to:

(a) acquire photographs under the following conditions:

(1) the Party carrying out the explosion shall identify to the other Party those personnel of the Party carrying out the explosion who shall take photographs as requested by designating personnel;

(2) photographs shall be taken by personnel of the Party carrying out the explosion in the presence of designated personnel and at the time requested by designated personnel for taking such photographs. Designated personnel shall determine whether these photographs are in conformity with

their requests and, if not, additional photographs shall be taken immediately;

(3) photographs shall be taken with cameras provided by the other Party having built-in, rapid developing capability and a copy of each photograph shall be provided at the completion of the development process to both Parties;

(4) cameras provided by designated personnel shall be kept in agreed secure storage when not in use; and

(5) the request for photographs can be made, at any time, of the following:

(i) exterior views of facilities and installations associated with the conduct of the explosion as described in subparagraph 4(a) of Article II;

(ii) geological samples used for confirmation of geological and geophysical information, as provided for in subparagraph 2(b) of this article and the equipment utilized in the acquisition of such samples;

(iii) emplacement and installation of equipment and associated cables used by designated personnel for yield determination;

(iv) emplacement and installation of the local seismic network used by designated personnel;

(v) emplacement of the explosives and the stemming of the emplacement hole; and

(vi) containers, facilities and installations for storage and operation of equipment used by designated personnel;

(b) photographs of visual displays and records produced by the equipment used by designated personnel and photographs within the control centers taken by cameras which are component parts of such equipment; and

(c) receive at the request of designated personnel and with the agreement of the Party carrying out the explosion supplementary photographs taken by the Party carrying out the explosion.

Article IV

1. Designated personnel in exercising their rights and functions may choose to use the following equipment of either Party, of which choice the Party carrying out the explosion shall be informed not later than 150 days before the beginning of emplacement of the explosives:

(a) electrical equipment for yield determination and equipment for a local seismic network as described in paragraphs 3, 4 and 7 of this article; and

(b) geologist's field tools and kits and equipment for recording of field notes.

2. Designated personnel shall have the right in exercising their rights and functions to utilize the following additional equipment which shall be provided by the Party carrying out the explosion, under procedures to be established in accordance with Article X to ensure that the equipment meets the specifications of the other Party: portable short-range communication equipment, field glasses, optical equipment for surveying and other items which may be specified by the other Party. A description of such equipment and operating instructions shall be provided to the other Party not later than 90 days before the beginning of emplacement of the explosives in connection with which such equipment is to be used.

3. A complete set of electrical equipment for yield determination shall consist of:

(a) sensing elements and associated cables for transmission of electrical power, control signals and data;

(b) equipment of the control center, electrical power supplies and cables for transmission of electrical power, control signals and data; and

(c) measuring and calibration instruments, maintenance equipment and spare parts necessary for ensuring the functioning of sensing elements, cables and equipment of the control center.

4. A complete set of equipment for the local seismic network shall consist of:

(a) seismic stations each of which contains a seismic instrument, electrical power supply and associated cables and radio equipment for receiving and transmission of control signals and data or equipment for recording control signals and data;

(b) equipment of the control center and electrical power supplies; and

(c) measuring and calibration instruments, maintenance equipment and spare parts necessary for ensuring the functioning of the complete network.

5. In case designated personnel, in accordance with paragraph 1 of this article, choose to use equipment of the Party carrying out the explosion for yield determination or for a local seismic network, a description of such equipment and installation and operating instructions shall be provided to the other Party not later than 90 days before the beginning of emplacement of the explosives in connection with which such equipment is to be used. Personnel of the Party carrying out the explosion shall emplace, install and operate the equipment in the presence of designated personnel. After the explosion, designated personnel shall receive duplicate copies of the recorded data. Equipment for yield determination shall be emplaced in accordance with Article VI. Equipment for a local seismic network shall be emplaced in accordance with paragraph 7 of this article.

6. In case designated personnel, in accordance with paragraph 1 of this article, choose to use their own equipment for yield determination and their own equipment for a local seismic network, the following procedures shall apply:

(a) the Party carrying out the explosion shall be provided by the other Party with the equipment and information specified in subparagraphs (a)(1) and (a)(2) of this paragraph not later than 150 days prior to the beginning of emplacement of the explosives in connection with which such equipment is to be used in order to permit the Party carrying out the explosion to familiarize itself with such equipment, if such equipment and information has not been previously provided, which equipment shall be returned to the other Party not later than 90 days before the beginning of emplacement of the explosives. The equipment and information to be provided are:

(1) one complete set of electrical equipment for yield determination as described in paragraph 3 of this article, electrical and mechanical design information, specifications and installation and operating instructions concerning this equipment; and

(2) one complete set of equipment for the local seismic network described in paragraph 4 of this article, including one seismic station, electrical and mechanical design information, specifications and installation and operating instructions concerning this equipment;

(b) not later than 35 days prior to the beginning of emplacement of the explosives in connection with which the following equipment is to be used, two complete sets of electrical equipment for yield determination as described in paragraph 3 of this article and specific installation instructions for the emplacement of the sensing elements based on information provided in accordance with subparagraph 2(a) of Article VI and two complete sets of equipment for the local seismic network as described in paragraph 4 of this article, which sets of equipment shall have the same components and technical characteristics as the corresponding equipment specified in subparagraph 6(a) of this article, shall be delivered in sealed containers to the port of entry;

(c) the Party carrying out the explosion shall choose one of each of the two sets of equipment described above which shall be used by designated personnel in connection with the explosion;

(d) the set or sets of equipment not chosen for use in connection with the explosion shall be at the disposal of the Party carrying out the explosion for a period that may be as long as 30 days after the explosion at which time such equipment shall be returned to the other Party;

(e) the set or sets of equipment chosen for use shall be transported by the Party carrying out the explosion in the sealed containers in which this equipment arrived, after seals of the Party carrying out the explosion have been affixed to them, to the site of the explosion, so that this equipment is delivered to designated personnel for emplacement, installation and operation not later than 20 days before the beginning of emplacement of the explosives. This equipment shall remain in the custody of designated personnel in accordance with paragraph 7 of Article V or in agreed secure storage. Personnel of the Party carrying out the explosion shall have the right to observe the use of this equipment by designated personnel during the time the equipment is at the site of the explosion. Before the beginning of emplacement of the explosives, designated personnel shall demonstrate to personnel of the Party carrying out the explosion that this equipment is in working order;

(f) each set of equipment shall include two sets of components for recording data and associated calibration equipment. Both of these sets of components in the equipment chosen for use shall simultaneously record data. After the explosion, and after duplicate copies of all data have been obtained by designated personnel and the Party carrying out the explosion, one of each of the two sets of components for recording data and associated calibration equipment shall be selected, by an agreed process of chance, to be retained by designated personnel. Designated personnel shall pack and seal such components for recording data and associated calibration equipment which shall accompany them from the site of the explosion to the port of exit; and

(g) all remaining equipment may be retained by the Party carrying out the explosion for a period that may be as long as 30 days, after which time this equipment shall be returned to the other Party.

7. For any explosion with a planned aggregate yield exceeding 500 kilotons, a local seismic network, the number of stations of which shall be determined by designated personnel but shall not exceed the number of explosives in the group plus five, shall be emplaced, installed and operated at agreed sites of emplacement within an area circumscribed by circles of 15 kilometers in radius centered on points on the surface of the earth above the points of emplacement of the explosives during a period beginning not later than 20 days before the beginning of emplacement of the explosives and continuing after the explosion not later than three days unless otherwise agreed between the Parties.

8. The Party carrying out the explosion shall have

the right to examine in the presence of designated personnel all equipment, instruments and tools of designated personnel specified in subparagraph 1(b) of this article.

9. The Joint Consultative Commission will consider proposals that either Party may put forward for the joint development of standardized equipment for verification purposes.

Article V

1. Except as limited by the provisions of paragraph 5 of this article, designated personnel in the exercise of their rights and functions shall have access along agreed routes:

(a) for an explosion with a planned aggregate yield exceeding 100 kilotons in accordance with paragraph 2 of Article III:

(1) to the locations of facilities and installations associated with the conduct of the explosion provided in accordance with subparagraph 4(a) of Article II; and

(2) to the locations of activities described in paragraph 2 of Article III; and

(b) for any explosion with a planned aggregate yield exceeding 150 kilotons, in addition to the access described in subparagraph 1(a) of this article:

(1) to other locations within the area circumscribed by circles of 10 kilometers in radius centered on points on the surface of the earth above the points of emplacement of the explosives in order to confirm that the local circumstances are consistent with the stated peaceful purposes;

(2) to the locations of the components of the electrical equipment for yield determination to be used for recording data when, by agreement between the Parties, such equipment is located outside the area described in subparagraph 1(b)(1) of this article; and

(3) to the sites of emplacement of the equipment of the local seismic network provided for in paragraph 7 of Article IV.

2. The Party carrying out the explosion shall notify the other Party of the procedure it has chosen from among those specified in subparagraph 2(b)(3) or Article III not later than 30 days before beginning the implementation of such procedure. Designated personnel shall have the right to be present at the site of the explosion to exercise their rights and functions in the areas and at the locations described in paragraph 1 of this article for a period of time beginning two days before the beginning of the implementation of the procedure and continuing for a period of three days after the completion of this procedure.

3. Except as specified in paragraph 4 of this article,

designated personnel shall have the right to be present in the areas and at the locations described in paragraph 1 of this article:

(a) for an explosion with a planned aggregate yield exceeding 100 kilotons but not exceeding 150 kilotons, in accordance with paragraph 2 of Article III, at any time beginning five days before the beginning of emplacement of the explosives and continuing after the explosion and after safe access to evacuated areas has been established according to standards determined by the Party carrying out the explosion for a period of two days; and

(b) for any explosion with a planned aggregate yield exceeding 150 kilotons, at any time beginning 20 days before the beginning of emplacement of the explosives and continuing after the explosion and after safe access to evacuated areas has been established according to standards determined by the Party carrying out the explosion for a period of:

(1) five days in the case of an explosion with a planned aggregate yield exceeding 150 kilotons but not exceeding 500 kilotons; or

(2) eight days in the case of an explosion with a planned aggregate yield exceeding 500 kilotons.

4. Designated personnel shall not have the right to be present in those areas from which all personnel have been evacuated in connection with carrying out an explosion, but shall have the right to re-enter those areas at the same time as personnel of the Party carrying out the explosion.

5. Designated personnel shall not have or seek access by physical, visual or technical means to the interior of the canister containing an explosive, to documentary or other information descriptive of the design of an explosive nor to equipment for control and firing of explosives. The Party carrying out the explosion shall not locate documentary or other information descriptive of the design of an explosive in such ways as to impede the designated personnel in the exercise of their rights and functions.

6. The number of designated personnel present at the site of an explosion shall not exceed:

(a) for the exercise of their rights and functions in connection with the confirmation of the geological and geophysical information in accordance with the provisions of subparagraph 2(b) and applicable provisions of paragraph 5 of Article III—the number of emplacement holes plus three;

(b) for the exercise of their rights and functions in connection with confirming that the local circumstances are consistent with the information provided and with the stated peaceful purposes in accordance with the provisions in subparagraphs 2(a), 2(c), 2(d) and 2(e) and applicable provisions of paragraph 5 of Article III—the number of explosives plus two;

(c) for the exercise of their rights and functions in connection with confirming that the local circumstances are consistent with the information provided and with the stated peaceful purposes in accordance with the provisions in subparagraphs 2(a), 2(c), 2(d) and 2(e) with applicable provisions of paragraph 5 of Article III and in connection with the use of electrical equipment for determination of the yield in accordance with paragraph 3 of Article III—the number of explosives plus seven; and

(d) for the exercise of their rights and functions in connection with confirming that the local circumstances are consistent with the information provided and with the stated peaceful purposes in accordance with the provisions in subparagraph 2(a), 2(c), 2(d) and 2(e) and applicable provisions of paragraph 5 of Article III and in connection with the use of electrical equipment for determination of the yield in accordance with paragraph 3 of Article III and with the use of the local seismic network in accordance with paragraph 4 of Article III—the number of explosives plus 10.

7. The Party carrying out the explosion shall have the right to assign its personnel to accompany designated personnel while the latter exercise their rights and functions.

8. The Party carrying out an explosion shall assure for designated personnel telecommunications with their authorities, transportation and other services appropriate to their presence and to the exercise of their rights and functions at the site of the explosion.

9. The expenses incurred for the transportation of designated personnel and their equipment to and from the site of the explosion, telecommunications provided for in paragraph 8 of this article, their living and working quarters, subsistence and all other personal expenses shall be the responsibility of the Party other than the Party carrying out the explosion.

10. Designated personnel shall consult with the Party carrying out the explosion in order to coordinate the planned program and schedule of activities of designated personnel with the program of the Party carrying out the explosion for the conduct of the project so as to ensure that designated personnel are able to conduct their activities in an orderly and timely way that is compatible with the implementation of the project. Procedures for such consultations shall be established in accordance with Article X.

Article VI

For any explosion with a planned aggregate yield exceeding 150 kilotons, determination of the yield of each explosive used shall be carried out in accordance with the following provisions:

1. Determination of the yield of each individual explosion in the group shall be based on measurements of the velocity of propagation, as a function of time, of the hydrodynamic shock wave generated by the explosion, taken by means of electrical equipment described in paragraph 3 of Article IV.

2. The Party carrying out the explosion shall provide the other Party with the following information:

(a) not later than 60 days before the beginning of emplacement of the explosives, the length of each canister in which the explosives will be contained in the corresponding emplacement hole, the dimensions of the tube or other device used to emplace the canister and the cross-sectional dimensions of the emplacement hole to a distance, in meters, from the emplacement point of 10 times the cube root of its yield in kilotons;

(b) not later than 60 days before the beginning of emplacement of the explosives, a description of materials, including their densities, to be used to stem each emplacement hole; and

(c) not later than 30 days before the beginning of emplacement of the explosives, for each emplacement hole of a group explosion, the local coordinates of the point of emplacement of the explosive, the entrance of the emplacement hole, the point of the emplacement hole most distant from the entrance, the location of the emplacement hole at each 200 meters distance from the entrances and the configuration of any known voids larger than one cubic meter located within the distance, in meters, of 10 times the cube root of the planned yield in kilotons measured from the bottom of the canister containing the explosive. The error in these coordinates shall not exceed one percent of the distance between the emplacement hole and the nearest other emplacement hole or one percent of the distance between the point of measurement and the entrance of the emplacement hole, whichever is smaller, but in no case shall the error be required to be less than one meter.

3. The Party carrying out the explosion shall emplace for each explosive that portion of the electrical equipment for yield determination described in subparagraph 3(a) of Article IV, supplied in accordance with paragraph 1 of Article IV, in the same emplacement hole as the explosive in accordance with the installation instructions supplied under the provisions of paragraph 5 or 6 of Article IV. Such emplacement shall be carried out under the observation of designated personnel. Other equipment specified in subparagraph 3(b) of Article IV shall be emplaced and installed:

(a) by designated personnel under the observation and with the assistance of personnel of the Party carrying out the explosion, if such assistance is requested by designated personnel; or

(b) in accordance with paragraph 5 of Article IV.

4. That portion of the electrical equipment for yield determination described in subparagraph 3(a) of Article IV that is to be emplaced in each emplacement hole shall be located so that the end of the electrical equipment which is farthest from the entrance to the emplacement hole is at a distance, in meters, from the bottom of the canister containing the explosive equal to 3.5 times the cube root of the planned yield in kilotons of the explosive when the planned yield is less than 20 kilotons and three times the cube root of the planned yield in kilotons of the explosive when the planned yield is 20 kilotons or more. Canisters longer than 10 meters containing the explosive shall only be utilized if there is prior agreement between the Parties establishing provisions for their use. The Party carrying out the explosion shall provide the other Party with data on the distribution of density inside any other canister in the emplacement hole with a transverse cross-sectional area exceeding 10 square centimeters located within a distance, in meters, of 10 times the cube root of the planned yield in kilotons of the explosion from the bottom of the canister containing the explosive. The Party carrying out the explosion shall provide the other Party with access to confirm such data on density distribution within any such canister.

5. The Party carrying out an explosion shall fill each emplacement hole, including all pipes and tubes contained therein which have at any transverse section an aggregate cross-sectional area exceeding 10 square centimeters in the region containing the electrical equipment for yield determination and to a distance, in meters, of six times the cube root of the planned yield in kilotons of the explosive from the explosive emplacement point, with material having a density not less than seven-tenths of the average density of the surrounding rock, and from that point to a distance of not less than 60 meters from the explosive emplacement point with material having a density greater than one gram per cubic centimeter.

6. Designated personnel shall have the right to:

(a) confirm information provided in accordance with subparagraph 2(a) of this article;

(b) confirm information provided in accordance with subparagraph 2(b) of this article and be provided, upon request, with a sample of each batch of stemming material as that material is put into the emplacement hole; and

(c) confirm the information provided in accordance with subparagraph 2(c) of this article by having access to the data acquired and by observing, upon their request, the making of measurements.

7. For those explosives which are emplaced in separate emplacement holes, the emplacement shall be such that the distance D, in meters, between any explosive and any portion of the electrical equipment for determination of the yield of any other explosive in the group shall be not less than 10 times the cube root of the planned yield in kilotons of the larger explosive of such a pair of explosives. Individual explosions shall be separated by time intervals, in milliseconds, not greater than one-sixth the amount by which the distance D, in meters, exceeds 10 times the cube root of the planned yield in kilotons of the larger explosive of such a pair of explosives.

8. For those explosives in a group which are emplaced in a common emplacement hole, the distance, in meters, between each explosive and any other explosive in that emplacement hole shall be not less than 10 times the cube root of the planned yield in kilotons of the larger explosive of such a pair of explosives, and the explosives shall be detonated in sequential order, beginning with the explosive farthest from the entrance to the emplacement hole, with the individual detonations separated by time intervals, in milliseconds, of not less than one times the cube root of the planned yield in kilotons of the largest explosive in this emplacement hole.

Article VII

1. Designated personnel with their personal baggage and their equipment as provided in Article IV shall be permitted to enter the territory of the Party carrying out the explosion at an entry port to be agreed upon by the Parties, to remain in the territory of the Party carrying out the explosion for the purpose of fulfilling their rights and functions provided for in the Treaty and this Protocol, and to depart from an exit port to be agreed upon by the Parties.

2. At all times while designated personnel are in the territory of the Party carrying out the explosion, their persons, property, personal baggage, archives and documents as well as their temporary official and living quarters shall be accorded the same privileges and immunities as provided in Articles 22, 23, 24, 29, 30, 31, 34 and 36 of the Vienna Convention on Diplomatic Relations of 1961 to the persons, property, personal baggage, archives and documents of diplomatic agents as well as to the premises of diplomatic missions and private residences of diplomatic agents.

3. Without prejudice to their privileges and immunities it shall be the duty of designated personnel to respect the laws and regulations of the State in whose territory the explosion is to be carried out insofar as they do not impede in any way whatsoever the proper exercising of their rights and functions provided for by the Treaty and this Protocol.

Article VIII

The Party carrying out an explosion shall have sole and exclusive control over and full responsibility for the conduct of the explosion.

Article IX

1. Nothing in the Treaty and this Protocol shall affect proprietary rights in information made available under the Treaty and this Protocol and in information which may be disclosed in preparation for and carrying out of explosions; however, claims to such proprietary rights shall not impede implementation of the provisions of the Treaty and this Protocol.

2. Public release of the information provided in accordance with Article II or publication of material using such information, as well as public release of the results of observation and measurements obtained by designated personnel, may take place only by agreement with the Party carrying out an explosion; however, the other Party shall have the right to issue statements after the explosion that do not divulge information in which the Party carrying out the explosion has rights which are referred to in paragraph 1 of this article.

Article X

The Joint Consultative Commission shall establish procedures through which the Parties will, as appropriate, consult with each other for the purpose of ensuring efficient implementation of this Protocol

United Nations Convention on the Prohibition of Military or Any Other Hostile Use of Environmental Modification Techniques

Also known as: ENMOD Convention
Date of signature: May 18, 1977

Place of signature: Geneva
Signatory states: Australia, Belgium, Benin,

Bolivia, Brazil, Bulgaria, Byelorussia, Canada, Cuba, Cyprus, Czechoslovakia, Denmark, Ethiopia, Finland, German Democratic Republic, Federal Republic of Germany, Ghana, Holy See, Hungary, Iceland, India, Iran, Iraq, Ireland, Italy, Laos, Lebanon, Liberia, Luxembourg, Mongolia, Morocco, Netherlands, Nicaragua, Norway, Poland, Portugal, Romania, Sierra Leone, Soviet Union, Spain, Sri Lanka, Syria, Tunisia, Turkey, Uganda, Ukraine, United Kingdom, United States, Yemen Arab Republic, Zaire
Ratifications: Bangladesh, Bulgaria, Byelorussia, Canada, Cape Verde, Cuba, Cyprus, Czechoslovakia, Denmark, Finland, German Democratic Republic, Ghana, Hungary, India, Kuwait, Laos, Malawi, Mexico, Norway, Papua New Guinea, Poland, Sao Tome, Solomon Islands, Soviet Union, Spain, Sri Lanka, Tunisia, Ukraine, United Kingdom, United States, Vietnam, Yemen Arab Republic, People's Democratic Republic of Yemen
Date of entry into force: October 5, 1978

The General Assembly,
Recalling its resolutions 3264 (XXIX) of 9 December 1974 and 3475 (XXX) of 11 December 1975,
Recalling its resolution 1722 (XVI) of 20 December 1961, in which it recognized that all States have a deep interest in disarmament and arms control negotiations,
Determined to avert the potential dangers of military or any other hostile use of environmental modification techniques,
Convinced that broad adherence to a convention on the prohibition of such action would contribute to the cause of strengthening peace and averting the threat of war,
Noting with satisfaction that the Conference of the Committee on Disarmament has completed and transmitted to the General Assembly, in the report of its work in 1976, the text of a draft Convention on the Prohibition of Military or Any Other Hostile Use of Environmental Modification Techniques,
Noting further that the Convention is intended to prohibit effectively military or any other hostile use of environmental modification techniques in order to eliminate the dangers to mankind from such use,
Bearing in mind that draft agreements on disarmament and arms control measures submitted to the General Assembly by the Conference of the Committee on Disarmanent should be the result of a process of effective negotiations, and that such instruments should duly take into account the views and interests of all States so that they can be adhered to by the widest possible number of countries,

Bearing in mind that article VIII of the Convention makes provision for a conference to review the operation of the Convention five years after its entry into force, with a view to ensuring that its purposes and provisions are being realized,
Also bearing in mind all relevant documents and negotiating records of the Conference of the Committee on Disarmament on the discussion of the draft Convention,
Convinced that the Convention should not affect the use of environmental modification techniques for peaceful purposes, which could contribute to the preservation and improvement of the environment for the benefit of present and future generations,
Convinced that the Convention will contribute to the realization of the purposes and principles of the Charter of the United Nations,
Anxious that during its 1977 session the Conference of the Committee on Disarmament should concentrate on urgent negotiations on disarmament and arms limitation measures,
1. *Refers* the Convention on the Prohibition of Military or Any Other Hostile Use of Environmental Modification Techniques, the text of which is annexed to the present resolution, to all States for their consideration, signature and ratification;
2. *Requests* the Secretary-General, as Depositary of the Convention, to open it for signature and ratification at the earliest possible date;
3. *Expresses its hope* for the widest possible adherence to the Convention;
4. *Calls upon* the Conference of the Committee on Disarmament, without prejudice to the priorities established in its programme of work, to keep under review the problem of effectively averting the dangers of military or any other hostile use of environmental modification techniques;
5. *Requests* the Secretary-General to transmit to the Conference of the Committee on Disarmament all documents relating to the discussion by the General Assembly at its thirty-first session of the question of the prohibition of military or any other hostile use of environmental modification techniques.

ANNEX

The States Parties to this Convention,
Guided by the interest of consolidating peace, and wishing to contribute to the cause of halting the arms race, and of bringing about general and complete disarmament under strict and effective international control, and of saving mankind from the danger of using new means of warfare,
Determined to continue negotiations with a view to achieving effective progress towards further measures in the field of disarmament,
Recognising that scientific and technical advances

may open new possibilities with respect to modification of the environment,

Recalling the Declaration of the United Nations Conference on the Human Environment, adopted at Stockholm on 16 June 1972,

Realizing that the use of environmental modification techniques for peaceful purposes could improve the interrelationship of man and nature and contribute to the preservation and improvement of the environment for the benefit of present and future generations,

Recognizing, however, that military or any other hostile use of such techniques could have effects extremely harmful to human welfare,

Desiring to prohibit effectively military or any other hostile use of environmental modification techniques in order to eliminate the dangers to mankind from such use, and affirming their willingness to work towards the achievement of this objective,

Desiring also to contribute to the strengthening of trust among nations and to the further improvement of the international situation in accordance with the purposes and principles of the Charter of the United Nations,

Have agreed on the following:

Article I

1. Each State Party to this Convention undertakes not to engage in military or any other hostile use of environmental modification techniques having widespread, long-lasting or severe effects as the means of destruction, damage or injury to any other State Party.

2. Each State Party to this Convention undertakes not to assist, encourage or induce any State, group of States or international organization to engage in activities contrary to the provisions of paragraph 1 of this article.

Article II

As used in article I, the term "environmental modification techniques" refers to any technique for changing—through the deliberate manipulation of natural processes—the dynamics, composition or structure of the earth, including its biota, lithosphere, hydrosphere and atmosphere, or of outer space.

Article III

1. The provisions of this Convention shall not hinder the use of environmental modification techniques for peaceful purposes and shall be without prejudice to the generally recognized principles and applicable rules of international law concerning such use.

2. The States Parties to this Convention undertake to facilitate, and have the right to participate in, the fullest possible exchange of scientific and technological information on the use of environmental modification techniques for peaceful purposes. States Parties in a position to do so shall contribute, alone or together with other States or international organizations, to international economic and scientific co-operation in the preservation, improvement and peaceful utilization of the environment, with due consideration for the needs of the developing areas of the world.

Article IV

Each State Party to this Convention undertakes to take any measures it considers necessary in accordance with its constitutional processes to prohibit and prevent any activity in violation of the provisions of the Convention anywhere under its jurisdiction or control.

Article V

1. The States Parties to this Convention undertake to consult one another and to co-operate in solving any problems which may arise in relation to the objectives of, or in the application of the provisions of, the Convention. Consultation and co-operation pursuant to this article may also be undertaken through appropriate international procedures within the framework of the United Nations and in accordance with its Charter. These international procedures may include the services of appropriate international organizations, as well as of a Consultative Committee of Experts as provided for in paragraph 2 of this article.

2. For the purposes set forth in paragraph 1 of this article, the Depositary shall, within one month of the receipt of a request from any State Party to this Convention, convene a Consultative Committee of Experts. Any State Party may appoint an expert to this Committee whose functions and rules of procedure are set out in the annex, which constitutes an integral part of the Convention. The committee shall transmit to the Depositary a summary of its findings of fact, incorporating all views and information presented to the Committee during its proceedings. The Depositary shall distribute the summary to all States Parties.

3. Any State Party to this Convention which has reasons to believe that any other State Party is acting in breach of obligations deriving from the provisions of the Convention may lodge a complaint with the Security Council of the United Nations. Such a complaint should include all relevant information as well as all possible evidence supporting its validity.

4. Each State Party to this Convention undertakes to co-operate in carrying out any investigation which the Security Council may initiate, in accordance with the provisions of the Charter of the United Nations,

on the basis of the complaint received by the Council shall inform the States Parties of the results of the investigation.

5. Each State Party to this Convention undertakes to provide or support assistance, in accordance with the provisions of the Charter of the United Nations, to any State Party which so requests, if the Security Council decides that such Party has been harmed or is likely to be harmed as a result of violation of the Convention.

Article VI

1. Any State Party may propose amendments to this Convention. The text of any proposed amendment shall be submitted to the Depositary, who shall promptly circulate it to all States Parties.

2. An amendment shall enter into force for all States Parties which have accepted it, upon the deposit with the Depositary of instruments of acceptance by a majority of States Parties. Thereafter it shall enter into force for any remaining State Party on the date of deposit of its instrument of acceptance.

Article VII

This Convention shall be of unlimited duration.

Article VIII

1. Five years after the entry into force of this Convention, a conference of the States Parties to the Convention shall be convened by the Depositary at Geneva. The conference shall review the operation of the Convention with a view to ensuring that its purposes and provisions are being realized, and shall in particular examine the effectiveness of the provisions of article I, paragraph 1, in eliminating the dangers of military or any other hostile use of environmental modification techniques.

2. At intervals of not less than five years thereafter, a majority of the States Parties to this Convention may obtain, by submitting a proposal to this effect to the Depositary, the convening of a conference with the same objectives.

3. If no review conference has been convened pursuant to paragraph 2 of this article within ten years following the conclusion of a previous review conference, the Depositary shall solicit the views of all States Parties to this Convention on the holding of such a conference. If one third or ten of the States Parties, whichever number is less, respond affirmatively, the Depositary shall take immediate steps to convene the conference.

Article IX

1. This Convention shall be open to all States for signature. Any State which does not sign the Convention before its entry into force in accordance with paragraph 3 of this article may accede to it at any time.

2. This Convention shall be subject to ratification by signatory States. Instruments of ratification and of accession shall be deposited with the Secretary-General of the United Nations.

3. This Convention shall enter into force upon the deposit with the Depositary of instruments of ratification by twenty Governments in accordance with paragraph 2 of this article.

4. For those States whose instruments of ratification or accession are deposited after the entry into force of this Convention, it shall enter into force on the date of the deposit of their instruments of ratification or accession.

5. The Depositary shall promptly inform all signatory and acceding States of the date of each signature, the date of deposit of each instrument of ratification or accession and the date of the entry into force of this Convention and of any amendments thereto, as well as of the receipt of other notices.

6. This Convention shall be registered by the Depositary in accordance with Article 102 of the Charter of the United Nations.

Article X

This Convention, of which the Arabic, Chinese, English, French, Russian and Spanish texts are equally authentic, shall be deposited with the Secretary-General of the United Nations who shall send certified copies thereof to the Governments of the signatory and acceding States.

Annex to the Convention

Consultative Committee of Experts

1. The Consultative Committee of Experts shall undertake to make appropriate findings of fact and provide expert views relevant to any problem raised pursuant to article V, paragraph 1, of this Convention by the State Party requesting the convening of the Committee.

2. The work of the Consultative Committee of Experts shall be organized in such a way as to permit it to perform the functions set forth in paragraph 1 of this annex. The Committee shall decide procedural questions relative to the organization of its work, where possible by consensus, but otherwise by a majority of those present and voting. There shall be no voting on matters of substance.

3. The Depositary or his representative shall serve as the Chairman of the Committee.

4. Each expert may be assisted at meetings by one or more advisers.

5. Each expert shall have the right, through the

Chairman, to request from States, and from international organizations, such information and assistance as the expert considers desirable for the accomplishment of the Committee's work.

Guidelines on Nuclear Transfers Agreed by the Nuclear Suppliers Group

Date of signature: September 21, 1977
Place of signature: London
Signatory states: *The guidelines were agreed by the members of the Nuclear Supplier Group, known as the London Club. The members are: Belgium, Canada, Czechoslovakia, France, German Democratic Republic, Federal Republic of Germany, Italy, Japan, Poland, Soviet Union, Sweden, Switzerland, United Kingdom, United States*

COMMUNICATIONS RECEIVED FROM CERTAIN MEMBER STATES REGARDING GUIDELINES FOR THE EXPORT OF NUCLEAR MATERIAL, EQUIPMENT OR TECHNOLOGY

1. On 11 January 1978, the Director General received similar letters, all of that date, from the Resident Representatives to the Agency of Czechoslovakia, France, the German Democratic Republic, Japan, Poland, Switzerland, the Union of Soviet Socialist Republics and the United States of America, relating to the export of nuclear material, equipment or technology. In the light of the request at the end of each of those letters, the text is reproduced below as Letter I.

2. On the same day, the Resident Representatives to the Agency of Canada and Sweden also addressed analogous letters to the Director General. In the light of the request expressed at the end of each of those letters, their texts are reproduced below as Letter II and Letter III respectively.

3. On the same day, the Director General received similar letters from the Resident Representatives to the Agency of Belgium, the Federal Republic of Germany, the Netherlands and the United Kingdom of Great Britain and Northern Ireland, Members of the European Communities, relating to the export of nuclear material, equipment or technology. In the light of the request expressed at the end of each of those letters, the text is reproduced below as Letter IV.

4. On 11 January 1978 the Resident Representative to the Agency of Italy, a Member of the European Communities, addressed a letter to the Director General relating to the same subject, the text of which is reproduced below as Letter V.

5. On 11 January 1978 the Director General received complementary letters, all of that date, from the Resident Representatives to the Agency of Belgium, Czechoslovakia, the German Democratic Republic, Japan, Poland, Switzerland and the Union of Soviet Socialist Republics, the texts of which are reproduced below as Letters VI, VII, VIII, IX, X, XI and XII respectively.

6. The attachments to Letters I–V, which are in every case identical, setting forth the Guidelines for Nuclear Transfers with their Annexes, are reproduced in the Appendix.

Letter I

The Permanent Mission of . . . presents its compliments to the Director General of the International Atomic Energy Agency and has the honour to enclose copies of three documents which have been the subject of discussion between the Government of . . . and a number of other Governments.

The Government of . . . has decided that, when considering the export of nuclear material, equipment or technology, it will act in accordance with the principles contained in the attached documents.

In reaching this decision, the Government of . . . is fully aware of the need to contribute to the development of nuclear power in order to meet world energy requirements, while avoiding contributing in any way to the dangers of proliferation of nuclear weapons or other nuclear explosive devices, and of the need to remove safeguards and non-proliferation assurances from the field of commercial competition.

The Government of . . . hopes that other Governments may also decide to base their own nuclear export policies upon these documents.

The Government of . . . requests that the Director General of the International Atomic Energy Agency should circulate the texts of this note and its enclosures to all Member Governments for their information and as a demonstration of support by the Government of . . . for the Agency's non-proliferation objectives and safeguards activities.

The Permanent Mission of . . . avails itself of this opportunity to renew to the Director General of the International Atomic Energy Agency the assurances of its highest consideration.

Letter II

The Permanent Mission of Canada to the IAEA presents its compliments to the Director General and has the honour to enclose copies of three documents that have been the subject of discussion between the Government of Canada and a number of other Governments.

The Government of Canada has decided that, when considering the export of nuclear material, equipment or technology, it will act in accordance with the principles contained in the attached documents as well as other principles considered pertinent by it.

In reaching this decision, the Government of Canada is fully aware of the need to contribute to the development of nuclear power in order to meet world energy requirements, while avoiding contributing in any way to the dangers of a proliferation of nuclear weapons or other nuclear explosive devices, and of the meed to remove safeguards and non-proliferation assurances from the field of commercial competition.

The Government of Canada hopes that other Governments may also decide to base their own nuclear export policies upon these documents and such further principles as may be agreed upon.

The Government of Canada requests that the Director General of the International Atomic Energy Agency should circulate the text of this Note and its enclosures to all Member Governments for their information and as a demonstration of support by the Government of Canada for the Agency's non-proliferation objectives and safeguard activities.

The Permanent Mission of Canada to the IAEA avails itself of this opportunity to renew to the Director General the assurances of its highest consideration.

Letter III

The Permanent Mission of Sweden present their compliments to the Director General of the International Atomic Energy Agency have have the honour to enclose copies of three documents which have been the subject of discussion between the Government of Sweden and a number of other Governments.

The Government of Sweden have decided that, when considering the export of nuclear material, equipment or technology, they will act in accordance with the principles contained in the attached documents.

In reaching this decision, the Government of Sweden are fully aware of the need to avoid contributing in any way to the dangers of a proliferation of nuclear weapons or other nuclear explosive devices, and of the need to remove safeguards and non-proliferation assurances from the field of commercial competition.

The Government of Sweden hope that other Governments may also decide to base their own nuclear export policies upon these documents.

The Government of Sweden request that the

Director General of the International Atomic Energy Agency should circulate the text of this Note and its enclosures to all Member Governments for their information and as a demonstration of support by the Government of Sweden for the Agency's non-proliferation objectives and safeguards activities.

The Permanent Mission of Sweden take this opportunity to renew to the Director General of the International Atomic Agency the assurances of their highest consideration.

Letter IV

The Permanent Mission of . . . to the International Organizations in Vienna presents its compliments to the Director General of the International Atomic Energy Agency and has the honour to enclose copies of three documents which have been the subject of discussion between the . . . and a number of other Governments.

The Government of . . . has decided that, when considering the export of nuclear material, equipment or technology, it will act in accordance with the principles contained in the attached documents.

In reaching this decision, the Government of . . . is fully aware of the need to contribute to the development of nuclear power in order to meet world energy requirements, while avoiding contributing in any way to the dangers of a proliferation of nuclear weapons or other nuclear explosive devices, and of the need to remove safeguards and non-proliferation assurances from the field of commercial competition.

As a Member of the European Community, the Government of . . . so far as trade within the Community is concerned, will implement these documents in the light of its commitments under the Treaties of Rome where necessary.

The Government of . . . hopes that other Governments may also decide to base their own nuclear export policies upon these documents.

The Government of . . . requests that the Director General of the International Atomic Energy Agency should circulate the texts of this Note and its enclosures to all Member Governments for their information and as a demostration of support by the Government of . . . for the Agency's non-proliferation objectives and safeguards activities.

The Permanent Mission of . . . to the International Organizations in Vienna avails itself of this opportunity to renew to the Director General of the International Atomic Energy Agency the assurances of its highest consideration.

Letter V

The Permanent Mission of Italy present their compliments and have the honour to enclose copies of three documents which have been the subject of discussion between the Government of Italy and a number of other Governments.

The Government of Italy have decided that, when considering the export of nuclear material, equipment or technology, they will act in accordance with the principles contained in the attached documents.

In reaching this decision, the Government of Italy are fully aware of the need to contribute to the development of nuclear power in order to meet world energy requirements, while avoiding contributing in any way to dangers of a proliferation of nuclear weapons or other nuclear explosive devices, and of the need to remove safeguards and non-proliferation assurances from the field of commercial competition.

The Italian Government underline that the undertaking referred to cannot limit in any way the rights and obligations arising for Italy out of agreements to which she is a Party, and in particular those arising out of Article IV of the Non-Proliferation Treaty.

As a member of the European Community, the Government of Italy, so far as trade within the Community is concerned, will implement these documents in the light of their commitments under the Treaties of Rome where necessary.

The Government of Italy hope that other Governments may also decide to base their own nuclear export policies upon these documents.

The Government of Italy request that the Director General of the International Atomic Energy Agency should circulate the texts of this Note and its enclosures to all Member Governments for their information and as a demonstration of support by the Government of Italy for the Agency's non-proliferation objectives and safeguards activities.

Letter VI

The Permanent Mission of Belgium presents its compliments to the Director General of the IAEA and, in addition to its Note P 10-92/24 of 11 January 1978, would like to draw the attention to the following.

The Government of Belgium at present are not in a position to implement fully the principles for technology transfer set out in the documents attached to the above-mentioned Note because of the lack of appropriate laws and regulations. However, the Government of Belgium intend to implement these principles fully when appropriate laws and regulations for this purpose are put into force as necessary.

The Government of Belgium request that the Director General of the IAEA should circulate the text of this Note to all Member Governments for their information.

The Permanent Mission of Belgium take this opportunity to renew to the Director General of the IAEA the assurance of its higest consideration.

Letter VII

The Permanent Mission of the Czechoslovak Socialist Republic to the International Organizations presents its compliments to the Director General of the International Atomic Energy Agency and has the honour to refer to its Note No. 1036/78 regarding standards of the nuclear export policies which have been adopted by the members of the Nuclear Suppliers Group.

The Government of the Czechoslovak Socialist Republic greatly appreciates the role of the International Atomic Energy Agency in the sphere of control of the provisions of the Non-Proliferation Treaty. This activity has been an important instrument of preventing proliferation of nuclear weapons. Sharing the opinion that further strengthening of safeguards lies in the interest of universal peace, the Government of the Czechoslovak Socialist Republic has decided that it would deliver nuclear material, equipment and technology defined in a trigger list, to any non-nuclear-weapon State only in a case when the whole nuclear activity of a recipient country, and not only material, equipment and technology being transferred, are subject to the Agency's safeguards.

The Government of the Czechoslovak Socialist Republic expresses its opinion that this principle, if observed by all the States–nuclear suppliers, could have made a great contribution toward strengthening and universality of the Non-Proliferation Treaty.

The Permanent Mission of the Czechoslovak Socialist Republic to the International Organizations avails itself of this opportunity to renew to the Director General of the International Atomic Energy Agency the assurances of its highest consideration.

Letter VIII

The Permanent Mission of the German Democratic Republic to the International Organizations in Vienna presents its compliments to the Director General of the International Atomic Agancy and has the honour, in connection with Note No. 2/78-III addressed to the Director General of the IAEA on 11 January 1978, to state the following: in the view of the Government of the German Democratic Republic, the guidelines for nuclear exports are such as to strengthen the regime of non-proliferation of nuclear weapons and the IAEA safeguards system. The German Democratic Republic will also in future advocate agreements to the effect that nuclear exports under the trigger list mentioned in the above Note should go only to those non-nuclear-weapon States that accept IAEA safeguards for all of their nuclear activities.

The Government of the German Democratic Republic is convinced that any reinforcement of the regime of non-proliferation of nuclear weapons will promote the peaceful uses of nuclear energy and international co-operation in this area.

The Permanent Mission requests that the present text be circulated as an official document of the International Atomic Energy Agency.

The Permanent Mission of the German Democratic Republic to the International Organizations in Vienna avails itself of this opportunity to renew to the Director General of the International Atomic Energy Agency the assurances of its higest consideration.

Letter IX

The Embassy of Japan presents its compliments to the International Atomic Energy Agency and, in reference to its Note No. J.M. 78/21 of January 11, 1978, has the honour to inform the International Atomic Energy Agency of the following.

The Government of Japan at present is not in a position to implement fully the Principles for Technology Transfers set out in the documents attached to the above-mentioned Note because of the lack of appropriate laws and regulations.

However, the Government of Japan intends to implement these principles fully when appropriate laws and regulations for this purpose are put into force as necessary.

The Government of Japan requests that the Director General of the International Atomic Energy Agency be good enough to circulate the texts of this Note to all Member Governments for their information.

The Embassy of Japan avails itself of this opportunity to renew to the International Atomic Energy Agency the assurances of its highest consideration.

Letter X

The Permanent Mission of the Polish People's Republic to the International Atomic Energy Agency presents its compliments to the Director General of the IAEA and has the honour to refer to its Note No. 10-96/77 regarding standards of the nuclear export policies which have been adopted by the members of the Nuclear Suppliers Group.

The Government of the Polish People's Republic greatly appreciates the role of the International Atomic Energy Agency in the sphere of control of the provisions of the Non-Proliferation Treaty. This activity has been an important instrument of preventing proliferation of nuclear weapons. Sharing the opinion that further strengthening of safeguards lies in the interest of universal peace, the Government of the Polish People's Republic has decided that it would deliver nuclear material, equipment and technology defined in a trigger list, to any non-nuclear-weapon State only in a case when the whole nuclear activity of a recipient country, and not only

material, equipment and technology being transferred, are subject to the Agency's safeguards.

The Government of the Polish People's Republic expresses its opinion that this principle, if observed by all the States–nuclear suppliers, could have made a great contribution toward strengthening and universality of the Non-Proliferation Treaty.

The Government of the Polish People's Republic requests that the Director General of the IAEA should circulate the text of this Note to all Member Governments.

The Permanent Mission of the Polish People's Republic to the International Atomic Energy Agency avails itself of this opportunity to renew to the Director General of the IAEA the assurances of the highest consideration.

Letter XI

The Permanent Mission of Switzerland presents its compliments to the Director General of the International Atomic Energy Agency and, with reference to its to day's Note No. 003, has the honour to emphasize the following.

The Government of Switzerland at present is not in a position to implement fully the principles for Technology Transfers set out in the documents attached to the above-mentioned Note because of the lack of appropriate laws and regulations. However, the Government of Switzerland intends to implement these principles fully when appropriate laws and regulations for this purpose are put into force as necessary.

The Government of Switzerland requests that the Director General of the International Atomic Energy Agency should circulate the text of this Note to all Member Governments for their information.

The Permanent Mission of Switzerland avails itself of this opportunity to renew to the Director General of the International Atomic Energy Agency the assurances of its highest consideration.

Letter XII

With reference to Note Verbale No. 1 from the Permanent Mission of the USSR, dated 11 January 1978, I have the honour to send you the following Declaration of the Government of the USSR:

The Government of the Union of Soviet Socialist Republics emphasizes its determination to continue its efforts to secure agreement between countries supplying nuclear materials, equipment and technology on the principle that IAEA safeguards must be applied to all nuclear activities of non-nuclear-weapon States when those States receive any of the items mentioned in the initial list referred to in the above-mentioned Note Verbale. In this connection the Government of the USSR takes the view that the principle of full control is a necessary condition for ensuring effective safeguards which can prevent nuclear materials, equipment and technology from being used for manufacturing nuclear weapons or other explosive devices.

The Government requests that the text of the present letter be distributed as an official document of the IAEA.

APPENDIX

GUIDELINES FOR NUCLEAR TRANSFERS

1. The following fundamental principles for safeguards and export controls should apply to nuclear transfers to any non-nuclear-weapon State for peaceful purposes. In this connection, suppliers have defined an export trigger list and agreed on common criteria for technology transfers.

Prohibition on Nuclear Explosives

2. Suppliers should authorise transfer of items identified in the trigger list only upon formal governmental assurances from recipients explicitly excluding uses which would result in any nuclear explosive device.

Physical Protection

3.

(a) All nuclear materials and facilities identified by the agreed trigger list should be placed under effective physical protection to prevent unauthorised use and handling. The levels of physical protection to be ensured in relation to the type of materials, equipment and facilities, have been agreed by suppliers, taking account of international recommendations.

(b) The implementation of measures of physical protection in the recipient country is the responsibility of the Government of that country. However, in order to implement the terms agreed upon amongst suppliers, the levels of physical protection on which these measures have to be based should be the subject of an agreement between supplier and recipient.

(c) In each case special arrangements should be made for a clear definition of responsibilities for the transport of trigger list items.

Safeguards

4. Suppliers should transfer trigger list items only when covered by IAEA safeguards, with duration and coverage provisions in conformance with the GOV/1621 guidelines. Exceptions should be made only after consultation with the parties to this understanding.

5. Suppliers will jointly reconsider their common safeguards requirements, whenever appropriate.

Safeguards Triggered by the Transfer of Certain Technology

6.

(a) The requirements of paragraphs 2, 3 and 4 above should also apply to facilities for reprocessing, enrichment, or heavy-water production, utilizing technology directly transferred by the supplier or derived from transferred facilities, or major critical components thereof.

(b) The transfer of such facilities, or major critical components thereof, or related technology, should require an undertaking (1) that IAEA safeguards apply to any facilities of the same type (i.e. if the design, construction or operating processes are based on the same or similar physical or chemical processes, as defined in the trigger list) constructed during an agreed period in the recipient country and (2) that there should at all times be in effect a safeguards agreement permitting the IAEA to apply Agency safeguards with respect to such facilities identified by the recipient, or by the supplier in consultation with the recipient, as using transferred technology.

Special Controls on Sensitive Exports

7. Suppliers should exercise restraint in the transfer of sensitive facilities, technology and weapons-usable materials. If enrichment or reprocessing facilities, equipment or technology are to be transferred, suppliers should encourage recipients to accept, as an alternative to national plants, supplier involvement and/or other appropriate multinational participation in resulting facilities. Suppliers should also promote international (including IAEA) activities concerned with multinational regional fuel cycle centres.

Special Controls on Export of Enrichment Facilities, Equipment and Technology

8. For a transfer of an enrichment facility, or technology therefor, the recipient nation should agree that neither the transferred facility, not any facility based on such technology, will be designed or operated for the production of greater than 20% enriched uranium without the consent of the supplier nation, of which the IAEA should be advised.

Controls on Supplies or Derived Weapons-Usable Material

9. Suppliers recognize the importance, in order to advance the objectives of these guidelines and to provide opportunities further to reduce the risks of proliferation, of including in agreements on supply of nuclear materials or of facilities which produce weapons-usable material, provisions calling for mutual agreement between the supplier and the recipient on arrangements for reprocessing, storage, alteration, use, transfer or retransfer of any weapons-usable material involved. Suppliers should endeavour to include such provisions whenever appropriate and practicable.

Controls on Retransfer

10.

(a) Suppliers should transfer trigger list items, including technology defines under paragraph 6, only upon the recipient's assurance that in the case of:

(1) retransfer of such items, or

(2) transfer of trigger list items derived from facilities originally transferred by the supplier, or with the help of equipment or technology originally transferred by the supplier.

the recipient of the retransfer or transfer will have provided the same assurances as those required by the supplier for the original transfer.

(b) In addition the supplier's consent should be required for: (1) any retransfer of the facilities, major critical components, or technology described in paragraph 6; (2) any transfer of facilities or major critical components derived from those items; (3) any retransfer of heavy water or weapons-usable material.

Supporting Activities

Physical Security

11. Suppliers should promote international cooperation on the exchange of physical security information, protection of nuclear materials in transit, and recovery of stolen nuclear materials and equipment.

Support for Effective IAEA Safeguards

12. Suppliers should make special efforts in support of effective implementation of IAEA safeguards. Suppliers should also support the Agency's efforts to assist Member States in the improvement of their national systems of accounting and control of nuclear material and to increase the technical effectiveness of safeguards.

Similarly, they should make every effort to support the IAEA in increasing further the adequacy of safeguards in the light of technical developments and the rapidly growing number of nuclear facilities, and to support appropriate initiatives aimed at improving the effectiveness of IAEA safeguards.

Sensitive Plant Design Features

13. Suppliers should encourage the designers and makers of sensitive equipment to construct it in such a way as to facilitate the application of safeguards.

Consultations

14.

(a) Suppliers should maintain contact and consult through regular channels on matters connected with the implementation of these guidelines.

(b) Suppliers should consult, as each deems appropriate, with other Governments concerned on specific sensitive cases, to ensure that any transfer does not contribute to risks of conflict or instability.

(c) In the event that one or more suppliers believe that there has been a violation of supplier/recipient understandings resulting from these guidelines, particularly in the case of an explosion of a nuclear device, or illegal termination or violation of IAEA safeguards by a recipient, suppliers should consult promptly through diplomatic channels in order to determine and assess the reality and extent of the alleged violation.

Pending the early outcome of such consultations, suppliers will not act in a manner that could prejudice any measure that may be adopted by other suppliers concerning their current contacts with that recipient.

Upon the findings of such consultations, the suppliers, bearing in mind Article XII of the IAEA Statute, should agree on an appropriate response and possible action which could include the termination of nuclear transfers to that recipient.

15. In considering transfers, each supplier should exercise prudence having regard to all the circumstances of each case, including any risk that technology transfers not covered by paragraph 6, or subsequent retransfers, might result in unsafeguarded nuclear materials.

16. Unanimous consent is required for any changes in these guidelines, including any which might result from the reconsideration mentioned in paragraph 5.

Protocol I Additional to the Geneva Conventions of 1949 Relating to the Protection of Victims of International Armed Conflicts

Also known as: *Protocol I*
Date of signature: *December 12, 1977*
Place of signature: *Berne*
Signatory states: *Bangladesh, Bahamas, Botswana, Cyprus, Ecuador, El Salvador, Finland, Gabon, Ghana, Jordan, Libya, Laos, Mauritania, Niger, Sweden, Tunisia, Vietnam, Yugoslavia*
Date of entry into force: *December 7, 1978*

The High Contracting Parties
Proclaiming their earnest wish to see peace prevail among peoples,
Recalling that every State has the duty, in conformity with the Charter of the United Nations, to refrain in its international relations from the threat or use of force against the sovereignty, territorial intergrity or political independence of any State, or in any other manner inconsistent with the purposes of the United Nations,
Believing it necessary nevertheless to reaffirm and develop the provisions protecting the victims of armed conflicts and to supplement measures intended to reinforce their application,
Expressing their conviction that nothing in this Protocol or in the Geneva Conventions of 12 August 1949 can be construed as legitimizing or authorizing any act of aggression or any other use of force inconsistent with the Charter of the United Nations,
Reaffirming further that the provisions of the Geneva Conventions of 12 August 1949 and of this Protocol must be fully applied in all circumstances to all persons who are protected by those instruments, without any adverse distinction based on the nature or origin of the armed conflict or on the causes espoused by or attributed to the Parties to the conflict,
Have agreed on the following:

PART I

GENERAL PROVISIONS

Article 1

General Principles and Scope of Application

1. The High Contracting Parties undertake to respect and to ensure respect for this Protocol in all circumstances.
2. In cases not covered by this Protocol or by other international agreements, civilians and combatants remain under the protection and authority of the principles of international law derived from established custom, from the principles of humanity and from dictates of public conscience.
3. This Protocol, which supplements the Geneva Conventions of 12 August 1949 for the protection of war victims, shall apply in the situations referred to in Article 2 common to those Conventions.
4. The situations referred to in the preceding paragraph include armed conflicts in which peoples are fighting against colonial domination and alien occupation and against racist régimes in the exercise of their right of self-determination, as enshrined in the Charter of the United Nations and the Declaration on Principles of International Law concerning Friendly Relations and Co-operation among States in accordance with the Charter of the United Nations.

Article 2

Definitions

For the purposes of this Protocol:

(a) "First Convention", "Second Convention", "Third Convention" and "Fourth Convention" mean, respectively, the Geneva Convention for the Amelioration of the Condition of the Wounded and Sick in Armed Forces in the Field of 12 August 1949; the Geneva Convention for the Amelioration of the Condition of Wounded, Sick and Shipwrecked Members of Armed Forces at Sea of 12 August 1949; the Geneva Convention relative to the Treatment of Prisoners of War of 12 August 1949; the Geneva Convention relative to the Protection of Civilian Persons in Time of War of 12 August 1949; "the Conventions" means the four Geneva Conventions of 12 August 1949 for the protection of war victims;

(b) "Rules of international law applicable in armed conflict" means the rules applicable in armed conflict set forth in international agreements to which the Parties to the conflict are Parties and the generally recognized principles and rules of international law which are applicable to armed conflict;

(c) "Protecting Power" means a neutral or other State not a Party to the conflict which has been designated by a Party to the conflict and accepted by the adverse Party and has agreed to carry out the functions assigned to a Protecting Power under the Conventions and this Protocol;

(d) "Substitute" means an organization acting in place of a Protecting Power in accordance with Article 5.

Article 3

Beginning and End of Application

Without prejudice to the provisions which are applicable at all times:

(a) the Conventions and this Protocol shall apply from the beginning of any situation referred to in Article 1 of this Protocol;

(b) the application of the Conventions and of this Protocol shall cease, in the territory of Parties to the conflict, on the general close of military operations and, in the case of occupied territories, on the termination of the occupation, except, in either circumstance, for those persons whose final release, repatriation or re-establishment takes place thereafter. These persons shall continue to benefit from the relevant provisions of the Conventions and of this Protocol until their final release repatriation or re-establishment.

Article 4

Legal status of the Parties to the Conflict

The application of the Conventions and of this Protocol, as well as the conclusion of the agreements provided for therein, shall not affect the legal status of the Parties to the conflict. Neither the occupation of a territory nor the application of the Conventions and this Protocol shall affect the legal status of the territory in question.

Article 5

Appointment of Protecting Powers and of their Substitute

[At the outset of any conflict, Protecting Powers shall be designated with responsibility for supervising and implementing this Convention.]

Article 6

Qualified Persons

1. The High Contracting Parties shall, also in peacetime, endeavour, with the assistance of the national Red Cross (Red Crescent, Red Lion and Sun) Societies, to train qualified personnel to facilitate the application of the Conventions and of this Protocol, and in particular the activities of the Protecting Powers.

2. The recruitment and training of such personnel are within domestic jurisdiction.

3. The International Commitee of the Red Cross shall hold at the disposal of the High Contracting Parties the lists of persons so trained which the High Contracting Parties may have established and may have transmitted to it for that purpose.

4. The conditions governing the employment of such personnel outside the national territory shall, in each case, be the subject of special agreements between the Parties concerned.

PART II

WOUNDED, SICK AND SHIPWRECKED

Section I

General Protection

Article 8

Terminology

[This article gives definitions of the wounded, sick, shipwrecked, medical personnel, religious personnel etc.]

Article 9

Field of Application

1. This Part, the provisions of which are intended to ameliorate the condition of the wounded, sick and shipwrecked, shall apply to all those affected by a situation referred to in Article 1, without any adverse distinction founded on race, colour, sex, language, religion or belief, political or other opinion, national or social origin, wealth, birth or other status, or on any other similar criteria.

Article 10

Protection and Care

1. All the wounded, sick and shipwrecked, to whichever Party they belong, shall be respected and protected.

2. In all circumstances they shall be treated humanely and shall receive, to the fullest extent practicable and with the least possible delay, the medical care and attention required by their condition. There shall be no distinction among them founded on any grounds other than medical ones.

Article 11

Protection of Persons

1. The physical or mental health and integrity of persons who are in the power of the adverse Party or who are interned, detained or otherwise deprived of liberty as a result of a situation referred to in Article 1 shall not be endangered by any unjustified act or omission. Accordingly, it is prohibited to subject the persons described in this Article to any medical procedure which is not indicated by the state of health of the person concerned and which is not consistent with generally accepted medical standards which

would be applied under similar medical circumstances to persons who are nationals of the Party conducting the procedure and who are in no way deprived of liberty.

2. It is, in particular, prohibited to carry out on such persons, even with their consent:

(a) physical mutilations:

(b) medical or scientific experiments:

(c) removal of tissue or organs for transplantation, except where these acts are justified in conformity with the conditions provided for in paragraph 1.

3. Exceptions to the prohibition in paragraph 2 (c) may be made only in the case of donations of blood for transfusion or of skin for grafting, provided that they are given voluntarily and without any coercion or inducement, and then only for therapeutic purposes, under conditions consistent with generally accepted medical standards and controls designed for the benefit of both the donor and the recipient.

Article 12

Protection of Medical Units

1. Medical units shall be respected and protected at all times and shall not be the object of attack.
2. Paragraph 1 shall apply to civilian medical units, provided that they:

(a) belong to one of the Parties to the conflict;

(b) are recognized and authorized by the competent authority of one of the Parties to the conflict; or

(c) are authorized in conformity with Article 9, paragraph 2, of this Protocol or Article 27 of the First Convention.

3. The Parties to the conflict are invited to notify each other of the location of their fixed medical units. The absence of such notification shall not exempt any of the Parties from the obligation to comply with the provisions of paragraph 1.
4. Under no circumstances shall medical units be used in an attempt to shield military objectives from attack. Whenever possible, the Parties to the conflict shall ensure that medical units are so sited that attacks against military objectives do not imperil their safety.

Article 13

Discontinuance of Protection of Civilian Medical Units

[The protection of civilian medical units shall be discontinued, after reasonable warning, if they commit acts harmful to the enemy.]

Article 14

Limitations on Requisition of Civilian Medical Units

1. The Occupying Power has the duty to ensure that the medical needs of the civilian population in occupied territory continue to be satisfied.
2. The Occupying Power shall not, therefore, requisition civilian medical units, their equipment, their *matériel* or the services of their personnel, so long as these resources are necessary for the provision of adequate medical services for the civilian population and for the continuing medical care of any wounded and sick already under treatment.

Article 15

Protection of Civilian Medical and Religious Personnel

[Civilian medical personnel and civilian religious personnel shall be clearly identified and fully protected at all times.]

Article 16

General Protection of Medical Duties

1. Under no circumstances shall any person be punished for carrying out medical activities compatible with medical ethics, regardless of the person benefiting therefrom.
2. Persons engaged in medical activities shall not be compelled to perform acts or to carry out work contrary to the rules of medical ethics or to other medical rules designed for the benefit of the wounded and sick or to the provisions of the Conventions or of this Protocol, or to refrain from performing acts or from carrying out work required by those rules and provisions.
3. No person engaged in medical activities shall be compelled to give to anyone belonging either to an adverse Party, or to his own Party except as required by the law of the latter Party, any information concerning the wounded and sick who are, or who have been, under his care, if such information would, in his opinion, prove harmful to the patients concerned or to their families. Regulations for the compulsory notification of communicable diseases shall, however, be respected.

Article 17

Role of the Civilian Population and of Aid Societies

1. The civilian population shall respect the wounded, sick and shipwrecked, even if they belong to the adverse Party, and shall commit no act of violence against them. The civilian population and aid societies, such as national Red Cross (Red Crescent, Red Lion and Sun) Societies, shall be permitted, even on their own initiative, to collect and care for the

wounded, sick and shipwrecked, even in invaded or occupied areas. No one shall be harmed, prosecuted, convicted or punished for such humanitarian acts.

2. The Parties to the conflict may appeal to the civilian population and the aid societies referred to in paragraph 1 to collect and care for the wounded, sick and shipwrecked, and to search for the dead and report their location; they shall grant both protection and the necessary facilities to those who respond to this appeal. If the adverse Party gains or regains control of the area, that Party also shall afford the same protection and facilities for so long as they are needed.

Article 18

Identification

[This article specifies regulations concerning the identification of medical and religious personnel, and of medical units and transport.]

Article 19

Neutral and other States not Parties to the Conflict

Neutral and other States not Parties to the conflict shall apply the relevant provisions of this Protocol to persons protected by this Part who may be received or interned within their territory, and to any dead of the Parties to that conflict whom they may find.

Article 20

Prohibition of Reprisals

Reprisals against the persons and objects protected by this Part are prohibited.

Section II

Medical Transportation

Article 21

Medical Vehicles

Medical vehicles shall be respected and protected in the same way as mobile medical units under the Conventions and this Protocol.

Article 22

Hospital Ships and Coastal Rescue Craft

Protection for hospital ships and coastal rescue craft.

Article 23

Other Medical Ships and Craft

[Other medical ships and craft shall be clearly identified and shall be protected.]

Article 24

Protection of Medical Aircraft

Medical aircraft shall be respected and protected, subject to the provisions of this Part.

Articles 25–27

[Medical aircraft shall be protected; provided that prior agreement for flights over enemy territory has been obtained from the enemy.]

Article 28

Restrictions on Operations of Medical Aircraft

[Medical aircraft shall not be used for military purposes, nor for collecting or transmitting medical data.]

Article 29

Notifications and Agreements Concerning Medical Aircraft

[Notifications and agreements regarding medical aircraft.]

Article 30

Landing and Inspection of Medical Aircraft

[Medical aircraft flying over enemy territory may be ordered to land, and may be subject to inspection.]

Article 31

Neutral or other States not Parties to the Conflict

[Medical aircraft flying over neutral territory may be required to land and shall be subject to inspection.]

Section III

Missing and Dead Persons

Article 32

General Principle

In the implementation of this Section, the activities of the High Contracting Parties, of the Parties to the conflict and of the international humanitarian organizations mentioned in the Conventions and in this Protocol shall be prompted mainly by the right of families to know the fate of their relatives.

Article 33

Missing Persons

1. As soon as circumstances permit, and at the lat-

est from the end of active hostilities, each Party to the conflict shall search for the persons who have been reported missing by an adverse Party. Such adverse Party shall transmit all relevant information concerning such persons in order to facilitate such searches.

2. In order to facilitate the gathering of information pursuant to the preceding paragraph, each Party to the conflict shall, with respect to persons who would not receive more favourable consideration under the Conventions and this Protocol:

(a) record the information specified in Article 138 of the Fourth Convention in respect of such persons who have been detained, imprisoned or otherise held in captivity for more than two weeks as a result of hostilities or occupation, or who have died during any period of detention;

(b) to the fullest extent possible, facilitate and, if need be, carry out the search for and the recording of information concerning such persons if they have died in other circumstances as a result of hostilities or occupation.

3. Information concerning persons reported missing pursuant to paragraph 1 and requests for such information shall be transmitted either directly or through the Protecting Power or the Central Tracing Agency of the International Committee of the Red Cross or national Red Cross (Red Crescent, Red Lion and Sun) Societies. Where the information is not transmitted through the International Committee of the Red Cross and its Central Tracing Agency, each Party to the conflict shall ensure that such information is also supplied to the Central Tracing Agency.

4. The Parties to the conflict shall endeavour to agree on arrangements for teams to search for, identify and recover the dead from battlefield areas, including arrangements, if appropriate, for such teams to be accompanied by personnel of the adverse Party while carrying out these missions in areas controlled by the adverse Party. Personnel of such teams shall be respected and protected while exclusively carrying out these duties.

Article 34

Remains of Deceased

[The remains of the deceased shall be respected and gravesites maintained. Relatives shall be granted access to graves as soon as circumstances permit.]

PART III

METHODS AND MEANS OF WARFARE

COMBATANT AND PRISONER-OF-WAR STATUS

Section I

Methods and Means of Warfare

Article 35

Basic Rules

1. In any armed conflict, the right of the Parties to the conflict to choose methods or means of warfare is not unlimited.

2. It is prohibited to employ weapons, projectiles and material and methods of warfare of a nature to cause superfluous injury or unnecessary suffering.

3. It is prohibited to employ methods or means of warfare which are intended, or may be expected, to cause widespread, long-term and severe damage to the natural environment.

Article 36

New Weapons

In the study, development, acquisition or adoption of a new weapon, means or method of warfare, a High Contracting Party is under an obligation to determine whether its employment would, in some or all circumstances, be prohibited by this Protocol or by any other rule of international law applicable to the High Contracting Party.

Article 37

Prohibition of Perfidy

1. It is prohibited to kill, injure or capture an adversary by resort to perfidy. Acts inviting the confidence of an adversary to lead him to believe that he is entitled to, or is obliged to accord, protection under the rules of international law applicable in armed conflict, with intent to betray that confidence, shall constitute perfidy. The following acts are examples of perfidy:

(a) the feigning of an intent to negotiate under a flag of truce or of a surrender;

(b) the feigning of an incapacitation by wounds or sickness;

(c) the feigning of civilian, non-combatant status; and

(d) the feigning of protected status by the use of signs, emblems or uniforms of the United Nations or of neutral or other States not Parties to the conflict.

2. Ruses of war are not prohibited. Such ruses are acts which are intended to mislead an adversary or to induce him to act recklessly but which infringe no

rule of international law applicable in armed conflict and which are not perfidious because they do not invite the confidence of an adversary with respect to protection under that law. The following are examples of such ruses; the use of camouflage, decoys, mock operations and misinformation.

Article 38

Recognised Emblems

[Improper use shall not be made of the red cross, red crescent, or other comparable emblems.]

Article 39

Emblems of Nationality

[Improper use shall not be made of the emblems of neutral states.]

Article 40

Quarter

It is prohibited to order that there shall be no survivors, to threaten an adversary therewith or to conduct hostilities on this basis.

Article 41

Safeguard of an Enemy Hors de Combat

[An enemy who is *hors de combat* shall not be attacked.]

Article 42

Occupants of Aircraft

[No-one parachuting from an aircraft in distress shall be attacked.]

Section II

Combatant and Prisoner-of-War Status

Article 43

Armed Forces

1. The armed forces of a Party to a conflict consist of all organized armed forces, groups and units which are under a command responsible to that Party for the conduct of its subordinates, even if that Party is represented by a government or an authority not recognized by an adverse Party. Such armed forces shall be subject to an internal disciplinary system which, *inter alia*, shall enforce compliance with the rules of international law applicable in armed conflict.

2. Members of the armed forces of a Party to a conflict (other than medical personnel and chaplains covered by Article 33 of the Third Convention) are combatants, that is to say, they have the right to participate directly in hostilities.

3. Whenever a Party to a conflict incorporates a paramilitary or armed law enforcement agency into its armed forces it shall so notify the other Parties to the conflict.

Article 44

Combatants and Prisoners of War

[Combatants as defined in Article 43 who fall into enemy hands shall be treated as prisoners of war.]

Article 45

Protection of Persons who Have Taken Part in Hostilities

[A person who has taken part in hostilities and falls into enemy hands shall be presumed to be a prisoner of war.]

Article 46

Spies

1. Notwithstanding any other provision of the Conventions or of this Protocol, any member of the armed forces of a Party to the conflict who falls into the power of an adverse Party while engaging in espionage shall not have the right to the status of prisoner of war and may be treated as a spy.

2. A member of the armed forces of a Party to the conflict who, on behalf of that Party and in territory controlled by an adverse Party, gathers or attempts to gather information shall not be considered as engaging in espionage if, while so acting, he is in the uniform of his armed forces.

3. A member of the armed forces of a Party to the conflict who is a resident of territory occupied by an adverse Party and who, on behalf of the Party on which he depends, gathers or attempts to gather information of military value within that territory shall not be considered as engaging in espionage unless he does so through an act of false pretences or deliberately in a clandestine manner. Moreover, such a resident shall not lose his right to the status of prisoner of war and may not be treated as a spy unless he is captured while engaging in espionage.

4. A member of the armed forces of a Party to the conflict who is not a resident of territory occupied by an adverse Party and who has engaged in espionage in that territory shall not lose his right to the status of prisoner of war and may not be treated as a spy unless he is captured before he has rejoined the armed forces to which he belongs.

Article 47

Mercenaries

1. A mercenary shall not have the right to be a combatant or a prisoner of war.

2. A mercenary is any person who:

(a) is specially recruited locally or abroad in order to fight in an armed conflict;

(b) does, in fact, take a direct part in the hostilities;

(c) is motivated to take part in the hostilities essentially by the desire for private gain and, in fact, is promised, by or on behalf of a Party to the conflict, material compensation substantially in excess of that promised or paid to combatants of similar ranks and functions in the armed forces of that Party;

(d) is neither a national of a Party to the conflict nor a resident of territory controlled by a Party to the conflict;

(e) is not a member of the armed forces of a Party to the conflict; and

(f) has not been sent by a State which is not a Party to the conflict on official duty as a member of its armed forces.

PART IV

CIVILIAN POPULATION

Section I

General Protection Against Effects of Hostilities

Chapter I

Basic Rule and Field of Application

Article 48

Basic Rule

In order to ensure respect for and protection of the civilian population and civilian objects, the Parties to the conflict shall at all times distinguish between the civilian population and combatants and between civilian objects and military objectives and accordingly shall direct their operations only against military objectives.

Article 49

Definition of Attacks and Scope of Application

[This article gives the definition of attacks and scope of application.]

Chapter II

Civilians and Civilian Population

Article 50

Definition of Civilians and Civilian Population

[This article gives the definition of civilians and civilian populations.]

Article 51

Protection of the Civilian Population

[The civilian population shall enjoy general protection. Indiscriminate attacks on civilians and reprisals against civilians are specifically forbidden.]

Chapter III

Civilian Objects

Article 52

General Protection of Civilian Objects

1. Civilian objects shall not be the object of attack or of reprisals. Civilian objects are all objects which are not military objectives as defined in paragraph 2.

2. Attacks shall be limited strictly to military objectives. In so far as objects are concerned, military objectives are limited to those objects which by their nature, location, purpose or use make an effective contribution to military action and whose total or partial destruction, capture or neutralization, in the circumstances ruling at the time, offers a definite military advantage.

3. In case of doubt whether an object which is normally dedicated to civilian purposes, such as a place of worship, a house or other dwelling or a school, is being used to make an effective contribution to military action, it shall be presumed not to be so used.

Article 53

Protection of Cultural Objects and of Places of Worship

[Historic monuments, works of art, and places of worship are specifically protected from hostile acts.]

Article 54

Protection of Objects Indispensable to the Survival of the Civilian Population

[Starvation of civilians is forbidden. Destruction of food-stuffs, crops, livestock, or drinking water installations is forbidden.]

Article 55

Protection of the Natural Environment

[Protection of the natural environment.]

Article 56

Protection of Works and Installations Containing Dangerous Forces

1. Works or installations containing dangerous forces, namely dams, dykes and nuclear electrical generating stations, shall not be made the object of attack, even where these objects are military objectives, if such attack may cause the release of dangerous forces and consequent severe losses among the civilian population. Other military objectives located at or in the vicinity of these works or installations shall not be made the object of attack if such attack may cause the release of dangerous forces from the works or installations and consequent severe losses among the civilian population.

Chapter IV

Precautionary Measures

Article 57

Precautions in Attack

[Military attacks shall take precautions in order to minimize loss of civilian life, injury to civilians, and damage to civilian objects.]

Article 58

Precautions Against the Effects of Attacks

The Parties to the conflict shall, to the maximum extent feasible:

(a) without prejudice to Article 49 of the Fourth Convention, endeavour to remove the civilian population, individual civilians and civilian objects under their control from the vicinity of military objectives;

(b) avoid locating military objectives within or near densely populated areas;

(c) take the other necessary precautions to protect the civilian population, individual civilians and civilian objects under their control against the dangers resulting from military operations.

Chapter V

Localities and Zones Under Special Protection

Article 59

Non-defended Localities

1. It is prohibited for the Parties to the conflict to attack, by any means whatsoever, non-defended localities.

2. The appropriate authorities of a Party to the conflict may declare as a non-defended locality any inhabited place near or in a zone where armed forces are in contact which is open for occupation by an adverse Party. Such a locality shall fulfil the following conditions:

(a) all combatants, as well as mobile weapons and mobile military equipment must have been evacuated;

(b) no hostile use shall be made of fixed military installations or establishments;

(c) no acts of hostility shall be committed by the authorities or by the population; and

(d) no activities in support of military operations shall be undertaken.

Article 60

Demilitarized Zones

[Parties to the conflict shall not extend their military operations into areas that have already been designated demilitarized zones.]

Chapter VI

Civil Defence

Article 61

Definitions and Scope

[This article gives the definition and scope of civil defence.]

Article 62

General Protection

1. Civilian civil defence organizations and their personnel shall be respected and protected, subject to the provisions of this Protocol, particularly the provisions of this section. They shall be entitled to perform their civil defence tasks except in case of imperative military necessity.

2. The provisions of paragraph 1 shall also apply to civilians who, although not members of civilian civil defence organizations, respond to an appeal from the competent authorities and perfrom civil defence tasks under their control.

3. Buildings and *matériel* used for civil defence purposes and shelters provided for the civilian population are covered by Article 52. Objects used for civil defence purposes may not be destroyed or diverted from their proper use except by the Party to which they belong.

Article 63

Civil Defence in Occupied Territories

1. In occupied territories, civilian civil defence organizations shall receive from the authorities the

facilities necessary for the performance of their tasks. In no circumstances shall their personnel be compelled to perform activities which would interfere with the proper performance of these tasks. The Occupying Power shall not change the structure or personnel of such organizations in any way which might jeopardize the efficient performance of their mission. These organizations shall not be required to give priority to the nationals or interests of that Power.

2. The Occupying Power shall not compel, coerce or induce civilian civil defence organizations to perform their tasks in any manner prejudicial to the interests of the civilian population.

3. The Occupying Power may disarm civil defence personnel for reasons of security.

Article 64

Civilian Civil Defence Organizations of Neutral or other States not Parties to the Conflict and International Co-ordinating Organizations

1. Articles 62, 63, 65, and 66 shall also apply to the personnel and *matériel* of civilian civil defence organizations of neutral or other States not Parties to the conflict which perform civil defence tasks mentioned in Article 61 in the territory of a Party to the conflict, with the consent and under the control of that Party. Notification of such assistance shall be given as soon as possible to any adverse Party concerned. In no circumstances shall this activity be deemed to be an interference in the conflict. This activity should, however, be performed with due regard to the security interests of the Parties to the conflict concerned.

Article 65

Cessation of Protection

[The protection afforded to civil defence organizations shall be withdrawn, after warning, if they commit acts harmful to the enemy.]

Article 66

Identification

1. Each Party to the conflict shall endeavour to ensure that its civil defence organizations, their personnel, buildings and *matériel*, are identifiable while they are exclusively devoted to the performance of civil defence tasks. Shelters provided for the civilian population should be similarly identifiable.

2. Each Party to the conflict shall also endeavour to adopt and implement methods and procedures which will make it possible to recognize civilian shelters as well as civil defence personnel, buildings and *matériel* on which the international distinctive sign of civil defence is displayed.

3. In occupied territories and in areas where fighting is taking place or is likely to take place, civilian civil defence personnel should be recognizable by the international distinctive sign of civil defence and by an identity card certifying their status.

Article 67

Members of the Armed Forces and Military Units Assigned to Civil Defence Organizations

1. Members of the armed forces and military units assigned to civil defence organizations shall be respected and protected, provided that:

(a) such personnel and such units are permanently assigned and exclusively devoted to the performance of any of the tasks mentioned in Article 61;

(b) if so assigned, such personnel do not perform any other military duties during the conflict;

(c) such personnel are clearly distinguishable from the other members of the armed forces by prominently displaying the international distinctive sign of civil defence, which shall be as large as appropriate, and such personnel are provided with the identity card referred to in Chapter V of Annex I to this Protocol certifying their status;

Section II

Relief in Favour of the Civilian Population

Article 68

Field of Application

The provisions of this Section apply to the civilian population as defined in this Protocol and are supplementary to Articles 23, 55, 59, 60, 61 and 62 and other relevant provisions of the Fourth Convention.

Article 69

Basic Needs in Occupied Territories

1. In addition to the duties specified in Article 55 of the Fourth Convention concerning food and medical supplies, the Occupying Power shall, to the fullest extent of the means available to it and without any adverse distinction, also ensure the provision of clothing, bedding, means of shelter, other supplies essential to the survival of the civilian population of the occupied territory and objects necessary for religious worship.

2. Relief actions for the benefit of the civilian population of occupied territories are governed by Articles 59, 60, 61, 62, 108, 109, 110 and 111 of the Fourth Convention, and by Article 71 of this Protocol, and shall be implemented without delay.

Article 70

Relief Actions

1. If the civilian population of any territory under the control of a Party to the conflict, other than occupied territory, is not adequately provided with the supplies mentioned in Article 69, relief actions which are humanitarian and impartial in character and conducted without any adverse distinction shall be undertaken, subject to the agreement of the Parties concerned in such relief actions. Offers of such relief shall not be regarded as interference in the armed conflict or as unfriendly acts. In the distribution of relief consignments, priority shall be given to those persons, such as children, expectant mothers, maternity cases and nursing mothers, who, under the Fourth Convention or under this Protocol, are to be accorded privileged treatment or special protection.

2. The Parties to the conflict and each High Contracting Party shall allow and facilitate rapid and unimpeded passage of all relief consignments, equipment and personnel provided in accordance with this Section, even if such assistance is destined for the civilian population of the adverse Party.

3. The Parties to the conflict and each High Contracting Party which allows the passage of relief consignments, equipment and personnel in accordance with paragraph 2:

(a) shall have the right to prescribe the technical arrangements, including search, under which such passage is permitted;

(b) may make such permission conditional on the distribution of this assistance being made under the local supervision of a Protecting Power;

(c) shall, in no way whatsoever, divert relief consignments from the purpose for which they are intended nor delay their forwarding, except in cases of urgent necessity in the interest of the civilian population concerned.

4. The Parties to the conflict shall protect relief consignments and facilitate their rapid distribution.

5. The Parties to the conflict and each High Contracting Party concerned shall encourage and facilitate effective international co-ordination of the relief actions referred to in paragraph 1.

Article 71

Personnel Participating in Relief Actions

1. Where necessary, relief personnel may form part of the assistance provided in any relief action, in particular for the transportation and distribution of relief consignments; the participation of such personnel shall be subject to the approval of the Party in whose territory they will carry out their duties.

2. Such personnel shall be respected and protected.

3. Each Party in receipt of relief consignments shall, to the fullest extent practicable, assist the relief personnel referred to in paragraph 1 in carrying out their relief mission. Only in case of imperative military necessity may the activities of the relief personnel be limited or their movements temporarily restricted.

Section III

Treatment of Persons in the Power of a Party to the Conflict

Chapter 1

Field of Application and Protection of Persons and Objects

Article 72

Field of Application

The provisions of this Section are additional to the rules concerning humanitarian protection of civilians and civilian objects in the power of a Party to the conflict contained in the Fourth Convention, particularly Parts I and III thereof, as well as to other applicable rules of international law relating to the protection of fundamental human rights during international armed conflict.

Article 73

Refugees and Stateless Persons

Persons who, before the beginning of hostilities, were considered as stateless persons or refugees under the relevant international instruments accepted by the Parties concerned or under the national legislation of the State of refuge or State of residence shall be protected persons within the meaning of Parts I and III of the Fourth Convention, in all circumstances and without any adverse distinction.

Article 74

Reunion of Dispersed Families

The High Contracting Parties and the Parties to the conflict shall facilitate in every possible way the reunion of families dispersed as a result of armed conflicts and shall encourage in particular the work of the humanitarian organizations engaged in this task in accordance with the provisions of the Conventions and of this Protocol and in conformity with their respective security regulations.

Article 75

Fundamental Guarantees

1. In so far as they are affected by a situation

referred to in Article 1 of this Protocol, persons who are in the power of a Party to the conflict and who do not benefit from more favourable treatment under the Conventions or under this Protocol shall be treated humanely in all circumstances and shall enjoy, as a minimum, the protection provided by this Article without any adverse distinction based upon race, colour, sex, language, religion or belief, political or other opinion, national or social origin, wealth, birth or other status, or on any other similar criteria. Each Party shall respect the person, honour, convictions and religious practices of all such persons.

2. The following acts are and shall remain prohibited at any time and in any place whatsoever, whether committed by civilian or by military agents:

(a) violence to the life, health, or physical or mental well-being of persons, in particular:

(i) murder;

(ii) torture of all kinds, whether physical or mental;

(iii) corporal punishment; and

(iv) mutilation;

(b) outrages upon personal dignity, in particular humiliating and degrading treatment, enforced prostitution and any form of indecent assault;

(c) the taking of hostages;

(d) collective punishments; and

(e) threats to commit any of the foregoing acts.

3. Any person arrested, detained or interned for actions related to the armed conflict shall be informed promptly, in a language he understands, of the reasons why these measures have been taken. Except in cases of arrest or detention for penal offences, such persons shall be released with the minimum delay possible and in any event as soon as the circumstances justifying the arrest, detention or internment have ceased to exist.

4. No sentence may be passed and no penalty may be executed on a person found guilty of a penal offence related to the armed conflict except pursuant to a conviction pronounced by an impartial and regularly constituted court respecting the generally recognized principles of regular judicial procedure, which include the following:

(a) the procedure shall provide for an accused to be informed without delay of the particulars of the offence alleged against him and shall afford the accused before and during his trial all necessary rights and means of defence;

(b) no one shall be convicted of an offence except on the basis of individual penal responsibility;

(c) no one shall be accused or convicted of a criminal offence on account of any act or omission which did not constitute a criminal offence under the national or international law to which he was subject at the time it was committed; nor shall a heavier penalty be imposed than that which was applicable at the time when the criminal offence was committed; if, after the commission of the offence, provision is made by law for the imposition of a lighter penalty, the offender shall benefit thereby;

(d) anyone charged with an offence is presumed innocent until proved guilty according to law;

(e) anyone charged with an offence shall have the right to be tried in his presence;

(f) no one shall be compelled to testify against himself or to confess guilt;

(g) anyone charged with an offence shall have the right to examine, or have examined, the witnesses aginst him and to obtain the attendance and examination of witnesses on his behalf under the same conditions as witnesses against him;

(h) no one shall be prosecuted or punished by the same Party for an offence in respect of which a final judgement acquitting or convicting that person has been previously pronounced under the same law and judicial procedure;

(i) anyone prosecuted for an offence shall have the right to have the judgement pronounced publicly; and

(j) a convicted person shall be advised on conviction of his judicial and other remedies and of the time-limits within which they may be exercised.

Chapter II

Measures in Favour of Women and Children

Article 76

Protection of Women

1. Women shall be the object of special respect and shall be protected in particular against rape, forced prostitution and any other form of indecent assault.

2. Pregnant women and mothers having dependent infants who are arrested, detained or interned for reasons related to the armed conflict, shall have their cases considered with the utmost priority.

3. To the maximum extent feasible, the Parties to the conflict shall endeavour to avoid the pronouncement of the death penalty on pregnant women or mothers having dependent infants, for an offence related to the armed conflict. The death penalty for such offences shall not be executed on such women.

Article 77

Protection of Children

1. Children shall be the object of special respect and shall be protected against any form of indecent assault. The Parties to the conflict shall provide them with the care and aid they require, whether because of their age or for any other reason.

2. The Parties to the conflict shall take all feasible measures in order that children who have not attained the age of fifteen years do not take a direct part in hostilities and, in particular, they shall refrain from recruiting them into their armed forces. In recruiting among those persons who have attained the age of fifteen years but who have not attained the age of eighteen years the Parties to the conflict shall endeavour to give priority to those who are oldest.

3. If, in exceptional cases, despite the provisions of paragraph 2, children who have not attained the age of fifteen years take a direct part in hostilities and fall into the power of an adverse Party, they shall continue to benefit from the special protection accorded by this Article, whether or not they are prisoners of war.

4. If arrested, detained or interned for reasons related to the armed conflict, children shall be held in quarters separate from the quarters of adults, except where families are accommodated as family units as provided in Article 75, paragraph 5.

5. The death penalty for an offence related to the armed conflict shall not be executed on persons who had not attained the age of eighteen years at the time the offence was committed.

Article 78

Evacuation of Children

[Children shall only be evacuated to a foreign country for compelling reasons of their health or safety. Written consent of parents or guardians is required.]

Chapter III

Journalists

Article 79

Measures of Protection for Journalists

[Journalists working in areas of armed conflict shall be clearly identified and protected at all times.]

PART V

EXECUTION OF THE CONVENTIONS AND OF THIS PROTOCOL

Section I

General Provisions

Article 80

Measures for Execution

1. The High Contracting Parties and the Parties to the conflict shall without delay take all necessary measures for the execution of their obligations under the Conventions and this Protocol.

2. The High Contractng Parties and the Parties to the conflict shall give orders and instructions to ensure observance of the Conventions and this Protocol, and shall supervise their execution.

Article 81

Activities of the Red Cross and Other Humanitarian Organizations

[The Red Cross, Red Crescent, and comparable organizations shall be granted facilities to carry out their humanitarian and relief activities.]

Article 82

Legal Advisers in Armed Forces

The High Contracting Parties at all times, and the Parties to the conflict in time of armed conflict, shall ensure that legal advisers are available, when necessary, to advise military commanders at the appropriate level on the application of the Conventions and this Protocol and on the appropriate instruction to be given to the armed forces on this subject.

Article 83

Dissemination

1. The High Contracting Parties undertake, in time of peace as in time of armed conflict, to disseminate the Conventions and this Protocol as widely as possible in their respective countries and, in particular, to include the study thereof in their programmes of military instruction and to encourage the study thereof by the civilian population, so that those instruments may become known to the armed forces and to the civilian population.

2. Any military or civilian authorities who, in time of armed conflict, assume responsibilities in respect of the application of the Conventions and this Protocol shall be fully acquainted with the text thereof.

Article 84

Rules of Application

The High Contracting Parties shall communicate to one another, as soon as possible, through the depository and, as appropriate, through the Protecting Powers, their official translations of this Protocol, as well as the laws and regulations which they may adopt to ensure its application.

Section II

Repression of Breaches of the Conventions and of this Protocol

Article 85

Repression of Breaches of this Protocol

[This article gives the definition of breaches and grave breaches of this Convention. Grave breaches shall be regarded as war crimes.]

Article 86

Failure to Act

1. The High Contracting Parties and the Parties to the conflict shall repress grave breaches, and take measures necessary to suppress all other breaches, of the Conventions or of this Protocol which result from a failure to act when under a duty to do so.

2. The fact that a breach of the Conventions or of this Protocol was committed by a subordinate does not absolve his superiors from penal disciplinary responsibility, as the case may be, if they knew, or had information which should have enabled them to conclude in the circumstances at the time, that he was committing or was going to commit such a breach and if they did not take all feasible measures within their power to prevent or repress the breach.

Article 87

Duty of Commanders

[Military commanders will be responsible for ensuring that the Convention is not breached by persons under their control.]

Article 88

Mutual Assistance in Criminal Matters

1. The High Contracting Parties shall afford one another the greatest measure of assistance in connexion with criminal proceedings brought in respect of grave breaches of the Conventions or of this Protocol.

2. Subject to the rights and obligations established in the Conventions and in Article 85, paragraph 1 of this Protocol, and when circumstances permit, the High Contracting Parties shall co-operate in the matter of extradition. They shall give due consideration to the request of the State in whose territory the alleged offence has occurred.

3. The law of the High Contracting Party requested shall apply in all cases. The provisions of the preceding paragraphs shall not, however, affect the obligations arising from the provisions of any other treaty of a bilateral or multilateral nature which governs or will govern the whole or part of the subject of mutual assistance in criminal matters.

Article 89

Co-operation

In situations of serious violations of the Conventions or of this Protocol, the High Contracting Parties undertake to act jointly or individually, in co-operation with the United Nations and in conformity with the United Nations Charter.

Article 90

International Fact-Finding Commission

[This article specifies the establishment, terms of reference, and scope of an International Fact-Finding Commission. Such Commissions shall investigate grave breaches of this Convention.]

Article 91

Responsibility

A Party to the conflict which violates the provisions of the Conventions or of this Protocol shall, if the case demands, be liable to pay compensation. It shall be responsible for all acts committed by persons forming part of its armed forces.

PART VI

FINAL PROVISIONS

Article 92

Signature

This Protocol shall be open for signature by the Parties to the Conventions six months after the signing of the Final Act and will remain open for a period of twelve months.

Article 93

Ratification

This Protocol shall be ratified as soon as possible. The instruments of ratification shall be deposited with the Swiss Federal Council, depositary of the Conventions.

Article 94

Accession

This Protocol shall be open for accession by any Party to the Conventions which has not signed it. The instruments of accession shall be deposited with the depositary.

Treaty Between the United States of America and the Union of Soviet Socialist Republics on the Limitation of Strategic Offensive Arms

Also known as: *the treaty concluding the Strategic Arms Limitation Talks II (SALT II)*
Date of signature: *June 18, 1979*
Place of signature: *Vienna*
Signatory states: *the United States, the Soviet Union*

[The signatories],
Conscious that nuclear war would have devastating consequences for all mankind,
Proceeding from the Basic Principles of Relations Between the United States of America and the Union of Soviet Socialist Republics of May 29, 1972,
Attaching particular significance to the limitation of strategic arms and determined to continue their efforts begun with the Treaty on the Limitation of Anti-Ballistic Missile Systems and the Interim Agreement on Certain Measures with Respect to the Limitation of Strategic Offensive Arms, of May 26, 1972,
Convinced that the additional measures limiting strategic offensive arms provided for in this Treaty will contribute to the improvement of relations between the Parties, help to reduce the risk of outbreak of nuclear war and strengthen international peace and security,
Mindful of their obligations under Article VI of the Treaty on the Non-Proliferation of Nuclear Weapons,
Guided by the principle of equality and equal security,
Recognizing that the stregthening of strategic stability meets the interests of the Parties and the interests of international security,
Reaffirming their desire to take measures for the further limitation and for the further reduction of strategic arms, having in mind the goal of achieving general and complete disarmament,
Declaring their intention to undertake in the near future negotiations further to limit and further to reduce strategic offensive arms,
Have agreed as follows:

Article I

Each Party undertakes, in accordance with the provisions of this Treaty, to limit strategic offensive arms quantitatively and qualitatively, to exercise restraint in the development of new types of strategic offensive arms, and to adopt other measures provided for in this Treaty.

Article II

For the purposes of this Treaty:

1. Intercontinental ballistic missile (ICBM) launchers are land-based launchers of ballistic missiles capable of a range in excess of the shortest distance between the northeastern border of the continental part of the territory of the United States of America and the northwestern border of the continental part of the territory of the Union of Soviet Socialist Republics, that is, a range in excess of 5,500 kilometers.

First Agreed Statement

The term "intercontinental ballistic missile launchers," as defined in paragraph 1 of Article II of the Treaty, includes all launchers which have been developed and tested for launching ICBMs. If a launcher has been developed and tested for launching an ICBM, all launchers of that type shall be considered to have been developed and tested for launching ICBMs.

First Common Understanding

If a launcher contains or launches an ICBM, that launcher shall be considered to have been developed and tested for launching ICBMs.

Second Common Understanding

If a launcher has been developed and tested for launching an ICBM, all launchers of that type, except for ICBM test and training launchers, shall be included in the aggregate numbers of strategic offensive arms provided for in Article III of the Treaty, pursuant to the provisions of Article VI of the Treaty.

Third Common Understanding

The one hundred and seventy-seven former Atlas and Titan 1 ICBM launchers of the United States of America, which are no longer operational and are partially dismantled, shall not be considered as subject to the limitations provided for in the Treaty.

Second Agreed Statement

After the date on which the Protocol ceases to be in force, mobile ICBM launchers shall be subject to the relevant limitations provided for in the Treaty which are applicable to ICBM launchers, unless the Parties agree that mobile ICBM launchers shall not be deployed after that date.

2. Submarine-launched ballistic missile (SLBM)

launchers are launchers of ballistic missiles installed on any nuclear-powered submarine or launchers of modern ballistic missiles installed on any submarine, regardless of its type.

Agreed Statement

Modern submarine-launched ballistic missiles are: for the United States of America, missiles installed in all nuclear-powered submarines; for the Union of Soviet Socialist Republics, missiles of the type installed in nuclear-powered submarines made operational since 1965; and for both Parties, submarine-launched ballistic missiles first flight-tested since 1965 and installed in any submarine, regardless of its type.

3. Heavy bombers are considered to be:

(a) currently, for the United States of America, bombers of the B-52 and B-1 types, and for the Union of Soviet Socialist Republics, bombers of the Tupolev-95 and Myasishchev types;

(b) in the future, types of bombers which can carry out the mission of a heavy bomber in a manner similar or superior to that of bombers listed in subparagraph (a) above;

(c) types of bombers equipped for cruise missiles capable of a range in excess of 600 kilometers; and

(d) types of bombers equipped for ASBMS.

First Agreed Statement

The term "bombers," as used in paragraph 3 of Article II and other provisions of the Treaty, means airplanes of types initially constructed to be equipped for bombs or missiles.

Second Agreed Statement

The Parties shall notify each other on a case-by-case basis in the Standing Consultative Commssion of inclusion of types of bombers as heavy bombers pursuant to the provisions of paragraph 3 of Article II of the Treaty; in this connection the Parties shall hold consultations, as appropriate, consistent with the provisions of paragraph 2 of Article XVII of the Treaty.

Third Agreed Statement

The criteria the Parties shall use to make case-by-case determinations of which types of bombers in the future can carry out the mission of a heavy bomber in a manner similar or superior to that of current heavy bombers, as referred to in subparagraph 3(b) of Article II of the Treaty, shall be agreed upon in the Standing Consultative Commission.

Fourth Agreed Statement

Having agreed that every bomber of a type included in paragraph 3 of Article II of the Treaty is to be considered a heavy bomber, the Parties further agree that:

(a) airplanes which otherwise would be bombers of a heavy bomber type shall not be considered to be bombers of a heavy bomber type if they have functionally related observable differences which indicate that they cannot perform the mission of a heavy bomber;

(b) airplanes which otherwise would be bombers of a type equipped for cruise missiles capable of a range in excess of 600 kilometers shall not be considered to be bombers of a type equipped for cruise missiles capable of a range in excess of 600 kilometers if they have functionally related observable differences which dictate that they cannot perform the mission of a bomber equipped for cruise missiles capable of a range in excess of 600 kilometers, except that heavy bombers of current types, as designated in subparagraph 3(a) of Article II of the Treaty, which otherwise would be of a type equipped for cruise missiles capable of a range in excess of 600 kilometers shall not be considered to be heavy bombers of a type equipped for cruise missiles capable of a range in excess of 600 kilometers if they are distinguishable on the basis of externally observable differences from heavy bombers of a type equipped for cruise missiles capable of a range in excess of 600 kilometers; and

(c) airplanes which otherwise would be bombers of a type equipped for ASBMS shall not be considered to be bombers of a type equipped for ASBMS if they have functionally related observable differences which indicate that they cannot perform the mission of a bomber equipped for ASBMS, except that heavy bombers of current types, as designated in subparagraph 3(a) of Article II of the Treaty, which otherwise would be of a type equipped for ASBMS shall not be considered to be heavy bombers of a type equipped for ASBMS if they are distinguishable on the basis of externally observable differences from heavy bombers of a type equipped for ASBMS.

First Common Understanding

Functionally related observable differences are differences in the observable features of airplanes which indicate whether or not these airplanes can perform the mission of a heavy bomber, or whether or not they can perform the mission of a bomber equipped for cruise missiles capable of a range in excess of 600 kilometers or whether or not they can perform the mission of a bomber equipped for ASBMS. Functionally related observable differences shall be verifiable by national technical means. To this end, the Parties may take, as appropriate, cooperative measures contributing to the effectiveness of verification by national technical means.

Fifth Agreed Statement

Tupolev-142 airplanes in their current configuration, that is, in the configuration for anti-submarine warfare, are considered to be airplanes of a type different from types of heavy bombers referred to in subparagraph 3(a) of Article II of the Treaty and not subject to the Fourth Agreed Statement to paragraph 3 of Article II of the Treaty. This Agreed Statement does not preclude improvement of Tupolev-142 airplanes as an anti-submarine system, and does not prejudice or set a precedent for designation in the future of types of airplanes as heavy bombers pursuant to subparagraph 3(b) of Article II of the Treaty or for application of the Fourth Agreed Statement to paragraph 3 of Article II of the Treaty to such airplanes.

Second Common Understanding

Not later than six months after entry into force of the Treaty the Union of Soviet Socialist Republics will give its thirty-one Myasishchev airplanes used as tankers in existence as of the date of signature of the Treaty functionally related observable differences which indicate that they cannot perform the mission of a heavy bomber.

Third Common Understanding

The designations by the United States of America and by the Union of Soviet Socialist Republics for heavy bombers referred to in subparagraph 3(a) of Artilce II of the Treaty correspond in the following manner:

Heavy bombers of the types designated by the United States of America as the B-52 and the B-1 are known to the Union of Soviet Socialist Republics by the same designations;

Heavy bombers of the type designated by the Union of Soviet Socialist Republics as the Tupolev-95 are known to the United States of America as heavy bombers of the Bear type; and

Heavy bombers of the type designated by the Union of Soviet Socialist Republics as the Myasishchev are known to the United States of America as heavy bombers of the Bison type.

4. Air-to-surface ballistic missiles (ASBMS) are any such missiles capable of a range in excess of 600 kilo-

meters and installed in an aircraft or on its external mountings.

5. Launchers of ICBMS and SLBMS equipped with multiple independently targetable reentry vehicles (MIRVS) are launchers of the types developed and tested for launching ICBMS or SLBMS equipped with MIRVS.

First Agreed Statement

If a launcher has been developed and tested for launching an ICBM or an SLBM equipped with MIRVS, all launchers of that type shall be considered to have been developed and tested for launching ICBMS or SLBMS equipped with MIRVS.

First Common Understanding

If a launcher contains or launches an ICBM or an SLBM equipped with MIRVS, that launcher shall be considered to have been developed and tested for launching ICBMS or SLBMS equipped with MIRVS.

Second Common Understanding

If a launcher has been developed and tested for launching an ICBM or an SLBM equipped with MIRVS, all launchers of that type, except for ICBM and SLBM test and training launchers, shall be included in the corresponding aggregate numbers provided for in Article V of the Treaty, pursuant to the provisions of Article VI of the Treaty.

Second Agreed Statement

ICBMS and SLBMS equipped with MIRVS are ICBMS and SLBMS of the types which have been flight-tested with two or more independently targetable reentry vehicles, regardless of whether or not they have also been flight-tested with a single reentry vehicle or with multiple reentry vehicles which are not independently targetable. As of the date of signature of the Treaty, such as ICBMS and SLBMS are: for the United States of America, Minuteman III ICBMS, Poseidon C-3 SLBMS, and Trident C-4 SLBMS; and for the Union of Soviet Socialist Republics, RS-16, RS-18, RS-20 ICBMS and RSM-50 SLBMS.

Each Party will notify the other Party in the Standing Consultative Commission on a case-by-case basis of the designation of the one new type of light ICBM, if equipped with MIRVS, permitted pursuant to paragraph 9 of Article IV of the Treaty when first flight-tested; of designations of additional types of SLBMS equipped with MIRVS when first installed on a submarine; and of designations of types of ASBMS equipped with MIRVS when first flight-tested.

Third Common Understanding

The designations by the United States of America and by the Union of Soviet Socialist Republics for ICBMS and SLBMS equipped with MIRVS correspond in the following manner:

Missiles of the type designated by the United States of America as the Minuteman III and known to the Union of Soviet Socialist Republics by the same designation, a light ICBM that has been flight-tested with multiple independently targetable reentry vehicles;

Missiles of the type designated by the United States of America as the Poseiden C-3 and known to the Union of Soviet Socialist Republics by the same designation, an SLBM that was first flight-tested in 1968 and that has been flight-tested with multiple independently targetable reentry vehicles;

Missiles of the type designated by the United States of America as the Trident C-4 and known to the Union of Soviet Socialist Republics by the same designation, an SLBM that was first flight-tested in 1977 and that has been flight-tested with multiple independently targetable reentry vehicles;

Missiles of the type designated by the Union of Soviet Socialist Republics as the RS-16 and known to the United States of America as the SS-17, a light ICBM that has been flight-tested with a single reentry vehicle and with multiple independently targetable reentry vehicles;

Missiles of the type designated by the Union of Soviet Socialist Republics as the RS-18 and known to the United States of America as the SS-19, the heaviest in terms of launch-weight and throw-weight of light ICBMS, which has been flight-tested with a single reentry vehicle and with multiple independently targetable reentry vehicles;

Missiles of the type designated by the Union of Soviet Socialist Republics as the RS-20 and known to the United States of America as the SS-18, the heaviest in terms of launch-weight and throw-weight of heavy ICBMS, which has been flight-tested with a single reentry vehicle and with multiple independently targetable reentry vehicles;

Missiles of the type designated by the Union of Soviet Socialist Republics as the RSM-50 and known to the United States of America as the SS-N-18, an SLBM that has been flight-tested with a single reentry vehicle and with multiple independently targetable reentry vehicles.

Third Agreed Statement

Reentry vehicles are independently targetable:

(a) if, after separation from the booster, maneuvering and targeting of the reentry vehicles to separate aim points along trajectories which are unrelated to each other are accomplished by means of devices which are installed in a self-contained dispensing mechanism or on the reentry vehicles, and which are based on the use of electronic or other computers in combination with devices using jet engines, including rocket engines, or aerodynamic systems;

(b) if maneuvering and targeting of the reentry vehicles to separate aim points along trajectories which are unrelated to each other are accomplished by means of other devices which may be developed in the future.

Fourth Common Understanding

For the purposes of this Treaty, all ICBM launchers in the Derazhnya and Pervomaysk areas in the Union of Soviet Socialist Republics are included in the aggregate numbers provided for in Article V of the Treaty.

Fifth Common Understanding

If ICBM or SLBM launchers are converted, constructed or undergo significant changes to their principal observable structural design features after entry into force of the Treaty, any such launchers which are launchers of missiles equipped with MIRVS shall be distinguishable from launchers of missiles not equipped with MIRVS, and any such launchers which are launchers of missiles not equipped with MIRVS shall be distinguishable from launchers of missiles equipped with MIRVS, on the basis of externally observable design features of the launchers. Submarines with launchers of SLBMS equipped with MIRVS shall be distinguishable from submarines with launchers of SLBMS not equipped with MIRVS on the basis of externally observable design features of the submarines.

This Common Understanding does not require changes to launcher conversion or construction programs, or to programs including significant changes to the principal observable structural design features of launchers, underway as of the date of signature of the Treaty.

6. ASBMS equipped with MIRVS are ASBMS of the types which have been flight-tested with MIRVS.

First Agreed Statement

ASBMS of the types which have been flight-tested with MIRVS are all ASBMS of the types which have been flight-tested with two or more independently targetable reentry vehicles, regardless of whether or not they have also been flight-tested with a single reentry vehicle or with multiple reentry vehicles which are not independently targetable.

Second Agreed Statement

Reentry vehicles are independently targetable:

(a) if, after separation from the booster, maneuvering and targeting of the reentry vehicles to separate aim points along trajectories which are unrelated to each other are accomplished by means of devices which are installed in a self-contained dispensing mechanism or on the reentry vehicles, and which are based on the use of electronic or other computers in combination with devices using jet engines, including rocket engines, or aerodynamic systems;

(b) if maneuvering and targeting of the reentry vehicles to separate aim points along trajectories which are unrelated to each other are accomplished by means of other devices which may be developed in the future.

7. Heavy ICBMS are ICBMS which have a launch-weight greater or a throw-weight greater than that of the heaviest, in terms of either launch-weight or throw-weight, respectively, of the light ICBMS deployed by either Party as of the date of signature of this Treaty.

First Agreed Statement

The launch-weight of an ICBM is the weight of the fully loaded missile itself at the time of launch.

Second Agreed Statement

The throw-weight of an ICBM is the sum of the weight of:

(a) its reentry vehicle or reentry vehicles;

(b) any self-contained dispensing mechanisms or other appropriate devices for targeting one reentry vehicle, or for releasing of for dispensing and targeting two or more reentry vehicles; and

(c) its penetration aids, including devices for their release.

Common Understanding

The term "other appropriate devices," as used in the definition of the throw-weight of an ICBM in the Second Agreed Statement to paragraph 7 of Article II of the Treaty, means any devices for dispensing and targeting two or more reentry vehicles; and any devices for releasing two or more reentry vehicles or for targeting one reentry vehicle, which cannot provide their reentry vehicles or reentry vehicle with additional velocity of more than 1,000 meters per second.

8. Cruise missiles are unmanned, self-propelled, guided, weapon-delivery vehicles which sustain flight through the use of aerodynamic lift over most of their flight path and which are flight-tested from or deployed on aircraft, that is, air-launched cruise missiles, or such vehicles which are referred to as cruise missiles in subparagraph 1(b) of Article IX.

First Agreed Statement

If a cruise missile is capable of a range in excess of 600 kilometers, all cruise missiles of that type shall be considered to be cruise missiles capable of a range in excess of 600 kilometers.

First Common Understanding

If a cruise missile has been flight-tested to a range in excess of 600 kilometers, it shall be considered to be a cruise missile capable of a range in excess of 600 kilometers.

Second Common Understanding

Cruise missiles not capable of a range in excess of 600 kilometers shall not be considered to be of a type capable of a range in excess of 600 kilometers if they are distinguishable on the basis of externally observable design features from cruise missiles of types capable of a range in excess of 600 kilometers.

Second Agreed Statement

The range of which a cruise missile is capable is the maximum distance which can be covered by the missile in its standard design mode flying until fuel exhaustion, determined by projecting its flight path onto the Earth's sphere from the point of launch to the point of impact.

Third Agreed Statement

If an unmanned, self-propelled, guided vehicle which sustains flight through the use of aerodynamic lift over most of its flight path has been flight-tested or deployed for weapon delivery, all vehicles of that type shall be considered to be weapon-delivery vehicles.

Third Common Understanding

Unmanned, self-propelled, guided vehicles which sustain flight through the use of aerodynamic lift over most of their flight path and are not weapon-delivery vehicles, that is, unarmed, pilotless, guided vehicles, shall not be considered to be cruise missiles if such vehicles are distinguishable from cruise missiles on the basis of externally observable design features.

Fourth Common Understanding

Neither Party shall convert unarmed, pilotless, guided vehicles into cruise missles capable of a range in excess of 600 kilometers, nor shall either Party convert cruise missiles capable of a range in excess of 600 kilometers into unarmed, pilotless, guided vehicles.

Fifth Common Understanding

Neither Party has plans during the term of the Treaty to flight-test from or deploy on aircraft unarmed, pilotless, guided vehicles which are capable of a range in excess of 600 kilometers. In the future, should a Party have such plans, that Party will provide notification thereof to the other Party well in advance of such flight-testing or deployment. This Common Understanding does not apply to target drones.

Article III

1. Upon entry into force of this Treaty, each Party undertakes to limit ICBM launchers, SLBM launchers, heavy bombers, and ASBMs to an aggregate number not to exceed 2,400.

2. Each Party undertakes to limit, from January 1, 1981, strategic offensive arms referred to in paragraph 1 of this Article to an aggregate number not to exceed 2,250, and to initiate reductions of those arms which as of that date would be in excess of this aggregate number.

3. Within the aggregate numbers provided for in paragraphs 1 and 2 of this Article and subject to the provisions of this Treaty, each Party has the right to determine the composition of these aggregates.

4. For each bomber of a type equipped for ASBMs, the aggregate numbers provided for in paragraphs 1 and 2 of this Article shall include the maximum number of such missiles for which a bomber of that type is equipped for one operational mission.

5. A heavy bomber equipped only for ASBMs shall not itself be included in the aggregate numbers provided for in paragraphs 1 and 2 of this Article.

6. Reductions of the numbers of strategic offensive arms required to comply with the provisions of paragraphs 1 and 2 of this Article shall be carried out as provided for in Article XI.

Article IV

1. Each Party undertakes not to start construction of additional fixed ICBM launchers.

2. Each Party undertakes not to relocate fixed ICBM launchers.

3. Each Party undertakes not to convert launchers of light ICBMs, or of ICBMs of older types deployed prior to 1964, into launchers of heavy ICBMs of types deployed after that time.

4. Each Party undertakes in the process of modernization and replacement of ICBM silo launchers not to increase the original internal volume of an ICBM silo launcher by more than thirty-two percent. Within this limit each Party has the right to determine whether such an increase will be made through an increase in the original diameter or in the original depth of an ICBM silo launcher, or in both of these dimensions.

Agreed Statement

The word "original" in paragraph 4 of Article IV of the Treaty refers to the internal dimensions of an ICBM silo launcher, including its internal volume, as of May 26, 1972, or as of the date on which such launcher becomes operational, whichever is later.

Common Understanding

The obligations provided for in paragraph 4 of Article IV of the Treaty and in the Agreed Statement thereto mean that the original diameter or the original depth of an ICBM silo launcher may not be increased by an amount greater than that which would result in an increase in the original internal volume of the ICBM silo launcher by thirty-two percent solely through an increase in one of these dimensions.

5. Each Party undertakes:

(a) not to supply ICBM launcher deployment areas with intercontinental ballistic missiles in excess of a number consistent with normal deployment, maintenance, training, and replacement requirements;

(b) not to provide storage facilities for or to store ICBMs in excess of normal deployment requirements at launch sites of ICBM launchers;

(c) not to develop, test, or deploy systems for rapid reload of ICBM launchers.

Agreed Statement

The term "normal deployment requirements," as used in paragraph 5 of Article IV of the Treaty, means the deployment of one missile at each ICBM launcher.

6. Subject to the provisons of this Treaty, each Party undertakes not to have under construction at any time strategic offensive arms referred to in paragraph 1 of Article III in excess of numbers consistent with a normal construction schedule.

Common Understanding

A normal construction schedule, in paragraph 6 of Article IV of the Treaty, is understood to be one consistent with the past or present construction practices of each Party.

7. Each Party undertakes not to develop, test, or deploy ICBMs which have a launch-weight greater or a throw-weight greater than that of the heaviest, in terms of either launch-weight or throw-weight, respectively, of the heavy ICBMs, deployed by either Party as of the date of signature of this Treaty.

First Agreed Statement

The launch-weight of an ICBM is the weight of the fully loaded missile itself at the time of launch.

Second Agreed Statement

The throw-weight of an ICBM is the sum of the weight of:

(a) its reentry vehicle or reentry vehicles;

(b) any self-contained dispensing mechanisms or other appropriate devices for targeting one reentry vehicle, or for releasing or for dispensing and targeting two or more reentry vehicles; and

(c) its penetration aids, including devices for their release.

Common Understanding

The term "other appropriate devices," as used in the definition of the throw-weight of an ICBM in the Second Agreed Statement to paragraph 7 of Article IV of the Treaty, means any devices for dispensing and targeting two or more reentry vehicles; and any devices for releasing two or more reentry vehicles or for targeting one reentry vehicle, which cannot provide their reentry vehicles or reentry vehicle with additional velocity of more than 1,000 meters per second.

8. Each Party undertakes not to convert land-based launchers of ballistic missiles which are not ICBMs into launchers for launching ICBMs, and not to test them for this purpose.

Common Understanding

During the term of the Treaty, the Union of Soviet Socialist Republics will not produce, test, or deploy ICBMs of the type designated by the Union of Soviet Socialist Republics as the RS-14 and known to the United States of America as the SS-16, a light ICBM first flight-tested after 1970 and flight-tested only with a single reentry vehicle; this Common Understanding also means that the Union of Soviet Socialist Republics will not produce the third stage of that missile, the reentry vehicle of that missile, or the appropriate device for targeting the reentry vehicle of that missile.

9. Each Party undertakes not to flight-test or deploy new types of ICBMs, that is, types of ICBMs not flight-tested as of May 1, 1979, except that each

Party may flight-test and deploy one new type of light ICBM.

First Agreed Statement

The term "new types of ICBMs," as used in paragraph 9 of Article IV of the Treaty, refers to any ICBM which is different from those ICBMs flight-tested as of May 1, 1979 in any one or more of the following respects:

(a) the number of stages, the length, the largest diameter, the launch-weight, or the thrown-weight, of the missile;

(b) the type of propellant (that is, liquid or solid) of any of its stages.

First Common Understanding

As used in the First Agreed Statement to paragraph 9 of Article IV of the Treaty, the term "different," referring to the length, the diameter, the launch-weight, and the throw-weight, of the missile, means a difference in excess of five percent.

Second Agreed Statement

Every ICBM of the one new type of light ICBM permitted to each Party pursuant to paragraph 9 of Article IV of the Treaty shall have the same number of stages and the same type of propellant (that is, liquid or solid) of each stage as the first ICBM of the one new type of light ICBM launched by that Party. In addition, after the twenty-fifth launch of an ICBM of that type, or after the last launch before deployment begins of ICBMs of that type, whichever occurs earlier, ICBMs of the one new type of light ICBM permitted to that Party shall not be different in any one or more of the following respects: the length, the largest diameter, the launch-weight, or the throw-weight, of the missile.

A Party which launches ICBMs of the one new type of light ICBM permitted pursuant to paragraph 9 of Article IV of the Treaty shall promptly notify the other Party of the date of the first launch and of the date of either the twenty-fifth or the last launch before deployment begins of ICBMs of that type, whichever occurs earlier.

Second Common Understanding

As used in the Second Agreed Statement to paragraph 9 of Article IV of the Treaty, the term "different," referring to the length, the diameter, the launch-weight, and the throw-weight, of the missile, means a difference in excess of five percent from the value established for each of the above parameters as of the twenty-fifth launch or as of the last launch before deployment begins, whichever occurs earlier. The values demonstrated in each of the above parameters during the last twelve of the twenty-five launches or during the last twelve launches before deployment begins, whichever twelve launches occur earlier, shall not vary by more than ten percent from any other of the corresponding values demonstrated during those twelve launches.

Third Common Understanding

The limitations with respect to launch-weight and throw-weight, provided for in the First Agreed Statement and the First Common Understanding to paragraph 9 of Article IV of the Treaty, do not preclude the flight-testing or the deployment of ICBMs with fewer reentry vehicles, or fewer penetration aids, or both, than the maximum number of reentry vehicles and the maximum number of penetration aids with which ICBMs of that type have been flight-tested as of May 1, 1979, even if this results in a decrease in launch-weight or in throw-weight in excess of five percent.

In addition to the aforementioned cases, those limitations do not preclude a decrease in launch-weight or in throw-weight in excess of five percent, in the case of the flight-testing or the deployment of ICBMs with a lesser quantity of propellant, including the propellant of a self-contained dispensing mechanism or other appropriate device, than the maximum quantity of propellant, including the propellant of a self-contained dispensing mechanism or other appropriate device, with which ICBMs of that type have been flight-tested as of May 1, 1979, provided that such an ICBM is at the same time flight-tested or deployed with fewer reentry vehicles, or fewer penetration aids, or both, than the maximum number of reentry vehicles and the maximum number of penetration aids with which ICBMs of that type have been flight-tested as of May 1, 1979, and the decrease in launch-weight and throw-weight in such cases results only from the reduction in the number of reentry vehicles, or penetration aids, or both, and the reduction in the quantity of propellant.

Fourth Common Understanding

The limitations with respect to launch-weight and throw-weight, provided for in the Second Agreed Statement and the Second Common Understanding to paragraph 9 of Article IV of the Treaty, do not preclude the flight-testing or the deployment of ICBMs of the one new type of light ICBM permitted to each Party pursuant to paragraph 9 of Article IV of the Treaty with fewer reentry vehicles, or fewer penetration aids, or both, than the maximum number of reentry vehicles and the maximum number of penetration aids with which ICBMs of that type have been flight-tested, even if

this results in a decrease in launch-weight or in throw-weight in excess of five percent.

In addition to the aforementioned cases, those limitations do not preclude a decrease in launch-weight or in throw-weight in excess of five percent, in the case of the flight-testing or the deployment of ICBMs of that type with a lesser quantity of propellant, including the propellant of a self-contained dispensing mechanism or other appropriate device, than the maximum quantity of propellant, including the propellant of a self-contained dispensing mechanism or other appropriate device, with which ICBMs of that type have been flight-tested, provided that such an ICBM is at the same time flight-tested or deployed with fewer reentry vehicles, or fewer penetration aids, or both, than the maximum number of reentry vehicles and the maximum number of penetration aids with which ICBMs of that type have been flight-tested, and the decrease in launch-weight and throw-weight in such cases results only from the reduction in the number of reentry vehicles, or penetration aids, or both, and the reduction in the quantity of propellant.

10. Each Party undertakes not to flight-test or deploy ICBMs of a type flight-tested as of May 1, 1979 with a number of reentry vehicles greater than the maximum number of reentry vehicles with which an ICBM of that type has been flight-tested as of that date.

First Agreed Statement

The following types of ICBMs and SLBMs equipped with MIRVs have been flight-tested with the maximum number of reentry vehicles set forth below:

For the United States of America
ICBMs of the Minuteman III type—seven reentry vehicles;
SLBMs of the Poseidon C-3 type—fourteen reentry vehicles;
SLBMs of the Trident C-4 type—seven reentry vehicles.
For the Union of Soviet Socialist Republics
ICBMs of the RS-16 type—four reentry vehicles;
ICBMs of the RS-18 type—six reentry vehicles;
ICBMs of the RS-20 type—ten reentry vehicles;
SLBMs of the RSM-50 type—seven reentry vehicles.

Common Understanding

Minuteman III ICBMs of the United States of America have been deployed with no more than three reentry vehicles. During the term of the Treaty the United States of America has no plans to and will not flight-test or deploy missiles of this type with more than three reentry vehicles.

Second Agreed Statement

During the flight-testing of any ICBM, SLBM, or ASBM after May 1, 1979, the number of procedures for releasing or for dispensing may not exceed the maximum number of reentry vehicles established for missiles of corresponding types as provided for in paragraphs 10, 11, 12 and 13 of Article IV of the Treaty. In this Agreed Statement "procedures for releasing or for dispensing" are understood to mean maneuvers of a missile associated with targeting and releasing or dispensing its reentry vehicles to aim points, whether or not a reentry vehicle is actually released or dispensed. Procedures for releasing anti-missile defense penetration aids will not be considered to be procedures for releasing or for dispensing a reentry vehicle so long as the procedures for releasing anti-missile defense penetration aids differ from those for releasing or for dispensing reentry vehicles.

Third Agreed Statement

Each party undertakes:

(a) not to flight-test or deploy ICBMs equipped with multiple reentry vehicles, of a type flight-tested as of May 1, 1979, with reentry vehicles the weight of any of which is less than the weight of the lightest of those reentry vehicles with which an ICBM of that type has been flight-tested as of that date:

(b) not to flight-test or deploy ICBMs equipped with a single reentry vehicle and without an appropriate device for targeting a reentry vehicle, of a type flight-tested as of May 1, 1979, with a reentry vehicle the weight of which is less than the weight of the lightest reentry vehicle on an ICBM of a type, equipped with MIRVs and flight-tested by that Party as of May, 1 1979; and

(c) not to flight-test or deploy ICBMs equipped with a single reentry vehicle and with an appropriate device for targeting a reentry vehicle, of a type flight-tested as of May 1, 1979, with a reentry vehicle the weight of which is less than fifty percent of the throw-weight of that ICBM.

11. Each Party undertakes not to flight-test or deploy ICBMs of the one new type permitted pursuant to paragraph 9 of this Article with a number of reentry vehicles greater than the maximum number of reentry vehicles with which an ICBM of either Party has been flight-tested as of May 1, 1979, that is, ten.

First Agreed Statement

Each Party undertakes not to flight-test or deploy the one new type of light ICBM permitted to each Party pursuant to paragraph 9 of Article IV of the Treaty with a number of reentry vehicles greater than the maximum number of reentry vehicles with which an ICBM of that type has been flight-tested as of the twenty-fifth launch or the last launch before deployment begins of ICBMs of that type, whichever occurs earlier.

Second Agreed Statement

During the flight-testing of any ICBM, SLBM, or ASBM after May 1, 1979 the number of procedures for releasing or for dispensing may not exceed the maximum number of reentry vehicles established for missiles of corresponding types as provided for in paragraphs 10, 11, 12, and 13 of Article IV of the Treaty. In this Agreed Statement "procedures for releasing and for dispensing " are understood to mean maneuvers of a missile associated with targeting and releasing or dispensing its reentry vehicles to aim points, whether or not a reentry vehicle is actually released or dispensed. Procedures for releasing anti-missile defense penetration aids will not be considered to be procedures for releasing or for dispensing a reentry vehicle so long as the procedures for releasing anti-missile defense penetration aids differ from those for releasing or for dispensing reentry vehicles.

12. Each Party undertakes not to flight-test or deploy SLBMs with a number of reentry vehicles greater than the maximum number of reentry vehicles with which an SLBM of either Party has been flight-tested as of May 1, 1979, that is fourteen.

First Agreed Statement

The following types of ICBMs and SLBMs equipped with MIRVs have been flight-tested with the maximum number of reentry vehicles set forth below:

For the United States of America
ICBMs of the Minuteman III type—seven reentry vehicles;
SLBMs of the Poseidon C-3 type—fourteen reentry vehicles;
SLBMs of the Trident C-4 type—seven reentry vehicles.
For the Union of Soviet Socialist Republics
ICBMs of the RS-16 type—four reentry vehicles;
ICBMs of the RS-18 type—six reentry vehicles;
ICBMs of the RS-20 type—ten reentry vehicles;
SLBMs of the RSM-50 type—seven reentry vehicles.

Second Agreed Statement

During the flight-testing of any ICBM, SLBM, or ASBM after May 1, 1979 the number of procedures for releasing or for dispensing may not exceed the maximum number of reentry vehicles established for missiles of corresponding types as provided for in paragraphs 10, 11, 12 and 13 of Article IV of the Treaty. In this Agreed Statement "procedures for releasing or dispensing" are understood to mean maneuvers of a missile associated with targeting and releasing or dispensing its reentry vehicles to aim points, whether or not a reentry vehicle is actually released or dispensed. Procedures for releasing anti-missile defense penetration aids will not be considered to be procedures for releasing or for dispensing a reentry vehicle so long as the procedures for releasing anti-missile defense penetration aids differ from those for releasing or for dispensing reentry vehicles.

13. Each Party undertakes not to flight-test or deploy ASBMS with a number of reentry vehicles greater than the maximum number of reentry vehicles with which an ICBM of either Party has been flight-tested as of May 1, 1979, that is, ten.

Agreed Statement

During the flight-testing of any ICBM, SLBM, or ASBM after May 1, 1979 the number of procedures for releasing or for dispensing may not exceed the maximum number of reentry vehicles established for missiles of corresponding types as provided for in paragraphs 10, 11, 12 and 13 of Article IV of the Treaty. In this Agreed Statement "procedures for releasing or for dispensing" are understood to mean maneuvers of a missile associated with targeting and releasing or dispensing its reentry vehicles to aim points, whether or not a reentry vehicle is actually released or dispensed. Procedures for releasing anti-missile defense penetration aids will not be considered to be procedures for releasing or for dispensing a reentry vehicle so long as the procedures for releasing anti-missile defense penetration aids differ from those for releasing or for dispensing reentry vehicles.

14. Each Party undertakes not to deploy at any one time on heavy bombers equipped for cruise missiles capable of a range in excess of 600 kilometers a number of such cruise missiles which exceeds the product of 28 and the number of such heavy bombers.

First Agreed Statement

For the purpose of the limitation provided for in paragraph 14 of Article IV of the Treaty, there shall be considered to be deployed on each heavy bomber of a type equipped for cruise missiles capable of a range in excess of 600 kilometers the maximum number of such missiles for which any bomber of that type is equipped for one operational mission.

Second Agreed Statement

During the term of the Treaty no bomber of the B-52 or B-1 types of the United States of America and no bomber of the Tupolev-95 or Myasishchev types of the Union of Soviet Socialist Republics will be equipped for more than twenty cruise missiles capable of a range in excess of 600 kilometers.

Article V

1. Within the aggregate numbers provided for in paragraphs 1 and 2 of Article III, each Party undertakes to limit launchers of ICBMs and SLBMs equipped with MIRVs, ASBMs equipped with MIRVs, and heavy bombers equipped for cruise missiles capable of a range in excess of 600 kilometers to an aggregate number not to exceed 1,320.

2. Within the aggregate number provided for in paragraph 1 of this Article, each Party undertakes to limit launchers of ICBMs and SLBMs equipped with MIRVs and ASBMs equipped with MIRVs to an aggregate number not to exceed 1,200.

3. Within the aggregate number provided for in paragraph 2 of this Article, each Party undertakes to limit launchers of ICBMs equipped with MIRVs to an aggregate number not to exceed 820.

4. For each bomber of a type equipped for ASBMs equipped with MIRVs, the aggregate numbers provided for in paragraphs 1 and 2 of this Article shall include the maximum number of ASBMs for which a bomber of that type is equipped for one operational mission.

Agreed Statement

If a bomber is equipped for ASBMs equipped with MIRVs all bombers of that type shall be considered to be equipped for ASBMs equipped with MIRVs.

5. Within the aggregate numbers provided for in paragraphs 1, 2 and 3 of this Article and subject to the provisions of this Treaty, each Party has the right to determine the composition of these aggregates.

Article VI

1. The limitations provided for in this Treaty shall apply to those arms which are:

(a) operational;

(b) in the final stage of construction;

(c) in reserve, in storage, or mothballed;

(d) undergoing overhaul, repair, modernization, or conversion.

2. Those arms in the final stage of construction are:

(a) SLBM launchers on submarines which have begun sea trials;

(b) ASBMS after a bomber of a type equipped for such missiles has been brought out of the shop, plant, or other facility where its final assembly or conversion for the purpose of equipping it for such missiles has been performed;

(c) other strategic offensive arms which are finally assembled in a shop, plant or other facility after they have been brought out of the shop, plant, or other facility where their final assembly has been perfomed.

3. ICBM and SLBM launchers of a type not subject to the limitation provided for in Article V, which undergo conversion into launchers of a type subject to that limitation, shall become subject to that limitation as follows:

(a) fixed ICBM launchers when work on their conversion reaches the stage which first definitely indicates that they are being so converted:

(b) SLBM launchers on a submarine when that submarine first goes to sea after their conversion has been performed.

Agreed Statement

The procedures referred to in paragraph 7 of Article VI of the Treaty shall include procedures determining the manner in which mobile ICBM launchers of a type not subject to the limitation provided for in Article V of the Treaty, which undergo conversion into launchers of a type subject to that limitation, shall become subject to that limitation, unless the Parties agree that mobile ICBM launchers shall not be deployed after the date on which the Protocol ceases to be in force.

4. ASBMS on a bomber which undergoes conversion from a bomber of a type equipped for ASBMS which are not subject to the limitation provided for in Article V into a bomber of a type equipped for ASBMS which are subject to that limitation shall become subject to that limitation when the bomber is brought out of the shop, plant, or other facility where such conversion has been performed.

5. A heavy bomber of a type not subject to the limitation provided for in paragraph 1 of Article V shall become subject to that limitation when it is brought out of the 'shop, plant, or other facility where it has been converted into a heavy bomber of a type equipped for cruise missiles capable of a range in excess of 600 kilometers. A bomber of a type not subject to the limitation provided for in paragraph 1 or 2 of Article III shall become subject to that limitation and to the limitation provided for in paragraph 1 of Article V when it is brought out of the shop, plant, or other facility where it has been converted

into a bomber of a type equipped for cruise missiles capable of a range in excess of 600 kilometers.

6. The arms subject to the limitations provided for in this Treaty shall continue to be subject to these limitations until they are dismantled, are destroyed, or otherwise cease to be subject to these limitations under procedures to be agreed upon.

Agreed Statement

The procedures for removal of strategic offensive arms from the aggregate numbers provided for in the Treaty, which are referred to in paragraph 6 of Article VI of the Treaty, and which are to be agreed upon in the Standing Consultative Commission, shall include:

(a) procedures for removal from the aggregate numbers, provided for in Article V of the Treaty, of ICBM and SLBM launchers which are being converted from launchers of a type subject to the limitation provided for in Article V of the Treaty, into launchers of a type not subject to that limitation;

(b) procedures for removal from the aggregate numbers, provided for in Articles III and V of the Treaty, of bombers which are being converted from bombers of a type subject to the limitations provided for in Article III of the Treaty or in Articles III and V of the Treaty into airplanes or bombers of a type not so subject.

Common Understanding

The procedures referred to in subparagraph (b) of the Agreed Statement to paragraph 6 of Article VI of the Treaty for removal of bombers from the aggregate numbers provided for in Articles III and V of the Treaty shall be based upon the existence of functionally related observable differences which indicate whether or not they can perform the mission of a heavy bomber, or whether or not they can perform the misssion of a bomber equipped for cruise missiles capable of a range in excess of 600 kilometers.

7. In accordance with the provisions of Article XVII, the Parties will agree in the Standing Consultative Commission upon procedures to implement the provisions of this Article.

Article VII

1. The limitations provided for in Article III shall not apply to ICBM and SLBM test and training launchers or to space vehicle launchers for exploration and use of outer space. ICBM and SLBM test and training launchers are ICBM and SLBM launchers used only for testing or training.

Common Understanding

The term "testing," as used in Article VII of the Treaty, includes research and development.

2. The Parties agree that:

(a) there shall be no significant increase in the number of ICBM or SLBM test and training launchers or in the number of such launchers of heavy ICBMs;

(b) construction or conversion of ICBM launchers at test ranges shall be undertaken only for purposes of testing and training;

(c) there shall be no conversion of ICBM test and training launchers or of space vehicle launchers into ICBM launchers subject to the limitations provided for in Article III.

First Agreed Statement

The term "significant increase," as used in subparagraph 2(a) of Article VII of the Treaty, means an increase of fifteen percent or more. Any new ICBM test and training launchers which replace ICBM test and training launchers at test ranges will be located only at test ranges.

Second Agreed Statement

Current test ranges where ICBMs are tested are located: for the United States of America, near Santa Maria, California, and at Cape Canaveral, Florida; and for the Union of Soviet Socialist Republics, in the areas of Tyura-Tam and Plesetskaya. In the future, each Party shall provide notification in the Standing Consultative Commission of the location of any other test range used by that Party to test ICBMs.

First Common Understanding

At test ranges where ICBMs are tested, other arms, including those not limited by the Treaty, may also be tested.

Second Common Understanding

Of the eighteen launchers of fractional orbital missiles at the test range where ICBMs are tested in the area of Tyura-Tam, twelve launchers shall be dismantled or destroyed and six launchers may be converted to launchers for testing missiles undergoing modernization.

Dismantling or destruction of the twelve launchers shall begin upon entry into force of the Treaty and shall be completed within eight months, under procedures for dismantling or destruction of these launchers to be agreed upon in the Standing Consultative Commission. These twelve launchers shall not be replaced.

Conversion of the six launchers may be carried out after entry into force of the Treaty. After entry into force of the Treaty, fractional orbital missiles shall be removed and shall be destroyed pursuant to the provisions of subparagraph 1(c) of Article IX and of Article XI of the Treaty and shall not be replaced by other missiles, except in the case of conversion of these six launchers for testing missiles undergoing modernization. After removal of the fractional orbital missiles, and prior to such conversion, any activities associated with these launchers shall be limited to normal maintenance requirements for launchers in which missiles are not deployed. These six launchers shall be subject to the provisions of Article VII of the Treaty and, if converted, to the provisions of the Fifth Common Understanding to paragraph 5 of Article II of the Treaty.

Article VIII

1. Each Party undertakes not to flight-test cruise missiles capable of a range in excess of 600 kilometers or ASBMs from aircraft other than bombers or to convert such aircraft into aircraft equipped for such missiles.

Agreed Statement

For purposes of testing only, each Party has the right, through initial construction or, as an exception to the provisions of paragraph 1 of Article VIII of the Treaty, by conversion, to equip for cruise missiles capable of a range in excess of 600 kilometers of for ASBMs no more than sixteen airplanes, including airplanes which are prototypes of bombers equipped for such missiles. Each Party also has the right, as an exception to the provisions of paragraph 1 of Article VIII of the Treaty, to flight-test from such airplanes cruise missiles capable of a range in excess of 600 kilometers and, after the date on which the Protocol ceases to be in force, to flight-test ASBMs from such airplanes as well, unless the Parties agree that they will not flight-test ASBMs after that date. The limitations provided for in Article III of the Treaty shall not apply to such airplanes.

The aforementioned airplanes may include only:

(a) airplanes other than bombers which, as an exception to the provisions of paragraph 1 of Article VIII of the Treaty, have been converted into airplanes equipped for cruise missiles capable of a range in excess of 600 kilometers or for ASBMs;

(b) airplanes considered to be heavy bombers pursuant to subparagraph 3(c) or 3(d) of Article II of the Treaty; and

(c) airplanes other than heavy bombers which,

prior to March 7, 1979, were used for testing cruise missiles capable of a range in excess of 600 kilometers.

The airplanes referred to in subparagraphs (a) and (b) of this Agreed Statement shall be distinguishable on the basis of functionally related observable differences from airplanes which otherwise would be of the same type but cannot perform the mission of a bomber equipped for cruise missiles capable of a range in excess of 600 kilometers or for ASBMS.

The airplanes referred to in subparagraph (c) of this Agreed Statement shall not be used for testing cruise missiles capable of a range in excess of 600 kilometers after the expiration of a six-month period from the date of entry into force of the Treaty, unless by the expiration of that period they are distinguishable on the basis of functionally related observable differences from airplanes which otherwise would be of the same type but cannot perform the mission of a bomber equipped for cruise missiles capable of a range in excess of 600 kilometers.

First Common Understanding

The term "testing," as used in the Agreed Statement to paragraph 1 of Article VIII of the Treaty, includes research and development.

Second Common Understanding

The Parties shall notify each other in the Standing Consultative Commission of the number of airplanes, according to type, used for testing pursuant to the Agreed Statement to paragraph 1 of Article VIII of the Treaty. Such notification shall be provided at the first regular session of the Standing Consultative Commission held after an airplane has been used for such testing.

Third Common Understanding

None of the sixteen airplanes referred to in the Agreed Statement to paragraph 1 of Article VIII of the Treaty may be replaced, except in the event of the involuntary destruction of any such airplane or in the case of the dismantling or destruction of any such airplane. The procedures for such replacement and for removal of any such airplane from that number, in case of its conversion, shall be agreed upon in the Standing Consultative Commission.

2. Each Party undertakes not to convert aircraft other than bombers into aircraft which can carry out the mission of a heavy bomber as referred to in subparagraph 3(b) of Article II.

Article IX

1. Each Party undertakes not to develop, test, or deploy:

(a) ballistic missiles capable of a range in excess of 600 kilometers for installation on waterborne vehicles other than submarines, or launchers of such missiles;

Common Understanding to subparagraph (a)

The obligations provided for in subparagraph 1(a) of Article IX of the Treaty do not affect current practices for transporting ballistic missiles.

(b) fixed ballistic or cruise missile launchers for emplacement on the ocean floor, on the seabed, or on the beds of internal waters and inland waters, or in the subsoil thereof, or mobile launchers of such missiles, which move only in contact with the ocean floor, the seabed, or the beds of internal waters and inland waters, or missiles for such launchers;

Agreed Statement to subparagraph (b)

The obligations provided for in subparagraph 1(b) of Article IX of the Treaty shall apply to all areas of the ocean floor and the seabed, including the seabed zone referred to in Articles I and II of the 1971 Treaty on the Prohibition of the Emplacement of Nuclear Weapons and Other Weapons of Mass Destruction on the Seabed and the Ocean Floor and in the Subsoil Thereof.

(c) systems for placing into Earth orbit nuclear weapons or any other kind of weapons of mass destruction, including fractional orbital missiles;

Common Understanding to subparagraph (c)

The provisions of subparagraph 1(c) of Article IX of the Treaty do not require the dismantling or destruction of any existing launchers of either Party.

(d) mobile launchers of heavy ICBMS;

(e) SLBMS which have a launch-weight greater or a throw-weight greater than that of the heaviest, in terms of either launch-weight or throw-weight, respectively, of the light ICBMS deployed by either Party as of the date of signature of this Treaty, or launchers of such SLBMS; or

(f) ASBMS which have a launch-weight greater or a throw-weight greater than that of the heaviest, in terms of either launch-weight or throw-weight, respectively, of the light ICBMS deployed by either Party as of the date of signature of this Treaty.

First Agreed Statement to subparagraphs (e) and (f)

The launch-weight of an SLBM or of an ASBM is the

weight of the fully loaded missile itself at the time of launch.

Second Agreed Statement to subparagraphs (e) and (f)

The throw-weight of an SLBM or of an ASBM is the sum of the weight of:

(a) its reentry vehicle or reentry vehicles;

(b) any self-contained dispensing mechanisms or other appropriate devices for targeting one reentry vehicle, or for releasing or for dispensing and targeting two or more reentry vehicles; and

(c) its penetration aids, including devices for their release.

Common Understanding to subparagraphs (e) and (f)

The term "other appropriate devices," as used in the definition of the throw-weight of an SLBM or of an ASBM in the Second Agreed Statement to subparagraphs 1(e) and 1(f) of Article IX of the Treaty, means any devices for dispensing and targeting two or more reentry vehicles; and any devices for releasing two or more reentry vehicles or for targeting one reentry vehicle, which cannot provide their reentry vehicles or reentry vehicle with additional velocity of more than 1,000 meters per second.

2. Each Party undertakes not to flight-test from aircraft cruise missiles capable of a range in excess of 600 kilometers which are equipped with multiple independently targetable warheads and not to deploy such cruise missiles on aircraft.

Agreed Statement

Warheads of a cruise missile are independently targetable if maneuvering or targeting of the warheads to separate aim points along ballistic trajectories or any other flight paths, which are unrelated to each other, is accomplished during a flight of a cruise missile.

Article X

Subject to the provisions of this Treaty, modernization and replacement of strategic offensive arms may be carried out.

Article XI

1. Strategic offensive arms which would be in excess of the aggregate numbers provided for in this Treaty as well as strategic offensive arms prohibited by this Treaty shall be dismantled or destroyed under procedures to be agreed upon in the Standing Consultative Commission.

2. Dismantling or destruction of strategic offensive arms which would be in excess of the aggregate number provided for in paragraph 1 of Article III shall begin on the date of the entry into force of this Treaty and shall be completed within the following periods from that date: four months for ICBM launchers; six months for SLBM launchers; and three months for heavy bombers.

3. Dismantling or destruction of strategic offensive arms which would be in excess of the aggregate number provided for in paragraph 2 of Article III shall be initiated no later than January 1, 1981, shall be carried out throughout the ensuing twelve-month period, and shall be completed no later than December 31, 1981.

4. Dismantling or destruction of strategic offensive arms prohibited by this Treaty shall be completed within the shortest possible agreed period of time, but not later than six months after the entry into force of this Treaty.

Article XII

1. In order to ensure the viability and effectiveness of this Treaty, each Party undertakes not to circumvent the provisions of this Treaty, through any other state or states, or in any other manner.

Article XIII

1. Each Party undertakes not to assume any international obligations which would conflict with this Treaty.

Article XIV

The Parties undertake to begin, promptly after the entry into force of this Treaty, active negotiations with the objective of achieving, as soon as possible, agreement on further measures for the limitation and reduction of strategic arms. It is also the objective of the Parties to conclude well in advance of 1985 an agreement limiting strategic offensive arms to replace this Treaty upon its expiration.

Article XV

1. For the purpose of providing assurance of compliance with the provisions of this Treaty, each Party shall use national technical means of verification at its disposal in a manner consistent with generally recognized principles of international law.

2. Each party undertakes not to interfere with the national technical means of verification of the other Party operating in accordance with paragraph 1 of this Article.

3. Each Party undertakes not to use deliberate concealment measures which impede verification by national technical means of compliance with the pro-

visions of this Treaty. This obligation shall not require changes in current construction, assembly, conversion, or overhaul practices.

First Agreed Statement

Deliberate concealment measures, as referred to in paragraph 3 of Article XV of the Treaty, are measures carried out deliberately to hinder or deliberately to impede verification by national technical means of compliance with the provisions of the Treaty.

Second Agreed Statement

The obligation not to use deliberate concealment measures, provided for in paragraph 3 of Article XV of the Treaty, does not preclude the testing of anti-missile defense penetration aids.

First Common Understanding

The provisions of paragraph 3 of Article XV of the Treaty and the First Agreed Statement thereto apply to all provisions of the Treaty, including provisions associated with testing. In this connection, the obligation not to use deliberate concealment measures includes the obligation not to use deliberate concealment measures associated with testing, including those measures aimed at concealing the association between ICBMS and launchers during testing.

Second Common Understanding

Each Party is free to use various methods of transmitting telemetric information during testing, including its encryption, except that, in accordance with the provisions of paragraph 3 of Article XV of the Treaty, neither Party shall engage in deliberate denial of telemetric information, such as through the use of telemetry encryption, whenever such denial impedes verification of compliance with the provisions of the Treaty.

Third Common Understanding

In addition to the obligations provided for in paragraph 3 of Article XV of the Treaty, no shelters which impede verification by national technical means of compliance with the provisions of the Treaty shall be used over ICBM silo launchers.

Article XVI

1. Each Party undertakes, before conducting each planned ICBM launch, to notify the other Party well in advance on a case-by-case basis that such a launch will occur, except for single ICBM launches from test ranges or from ICBM launcher deployment areas, which are not planned to extend beyond its national territory.

First Common Understanding

ICBM launches to which the obligations provided for in Article XVI of the Treaty apply, include, among others, those ICBM launches for which advance notification is required pursuant to the provisions of the Agreement on Measures to Reduce the Risk of Outbreak of Nuclear War Between the United States of America and the Union of Soviet Socialist Republics, signed September 30, 1971, and the Agreement Between the Government of the United States of America and the Government of the Union of Soviet Socialist Republics on the Prevention of Incidents On and Over the High Seas, signed May 25, 1972. Nothing in Article XVI of the Treaty is intended to inhibit advance notification, on a voluntary basis, of any ICBM launches not subject to its provisions, the advance notification of which would enhance confidence between the Parties.

Second Common Understanding

A multiple ICBM launch conducted by a Party, as distinct from single ICBM launches referred to in Article XVI of the Treaty, is a launch which would result in two or more of its ICBMs being in flight at the same time.

Third Common Understanding

The test ranges referred to in Article XVI of the Treaty are those covered by the Second Agreed Statement to paragraph 2 of Article VII of the Treaty.

2. The Parties shall agree in the Standing Consultative Commission upon procedures to implement the provisions of this Article.

Article XVII

1. To promote the objectives and implementation of the provisions of this Treaty, the Parties shall use the Standing Consultative Commission established by the Memorandum of Understanding Between the Government of the United States of America and the Government of the Union of Soviet Socialist Republics Regarding the Establishment of a Standing Consultative Commission of December 21, 1972.

2. Within the framework of the Standing Consultative Commission, with respect to this Treaty, the Parties will:

(a) consider questions concerning compliance with the obligations assumed and related situations which may be considered ambiguous;

(b) provide on a voluntary basis such information as either Party considers necessary to assure confidence in compliance with the obligations assumed;

(c) consider questions involving unintended interference with national technical means of verification, and questions involving unintended impeding of verification by national technical means of compliance with the provisions of this Treaty;

(d) consider possible changes in the strategic situation which have a bearing on the provisions of this Treaty;

(e) agree upon procedures for replacement, conversion, and dismantling or destruction, of strategic offensive arms in cases provided for in the provisions of this Treaty and upon procedures for removal of such arms from the aggregate numbers when they otherwise cease to be subject to the limitations provided for in this Treaty, and at regular sessions of the Standing Consultative Commission, notify each other in accordance with the aforementioned procedures, at least twice annually, of actions completed and those in process;

(f) consider, as appropriate, possible proposals for further increasing the viability of this Treaty, including proposals for amendments in accordance with the provisions of this Treaty;

(g) consider, as appropriate, proposals for further measures limiting strategic offensive arms.

3. In the Standing Consultative Commission the Parties shall maintain by category the agreed data base on the numbers of strategic offensive arms established by the Memorandum of Understanding Between the United States of America and the Union of Soviet Socialist Republics Regarding the Establishment of a Date Base on the Numbers of Strategic Offensive Arms of June 18, 1979.

Agreed Statement

In order to maintain the agreed data base on the numbers of strategic offensive arms subject to the limitations provided for in the Treaty in accordance with paragraph 3 of Article XVII of the Treaty, at each regular session of the Standing Consultative Commission the Parties will notify each other of and consider changes in those numbers in the following categories: launchers of ICBMs; fixed launchers of ICBMs; launchers of ICBMs equipped with MIRVs; launchers of SLBMs; launchers of SLBMs equipped with MIRVs; heavy bombers; heavy bombers equipped for cruise missiles capable of a range in excess of 600 kilometers; heavy bombers equipped only for ASBMs; ASBMs; and ASBMs equipped with MIRVs.

Article XVIII

Each Party may propose amendments to this Treaty. Agreed amendments shall enter into force in accordance with the procedures governing the entry into force of this Treaty.

Article XIX

1. This Treaty shall be subject to ratification in accordance with the constitutional procedures of each Party. This Treaty shall enter into force on the day of the exchange of instruments of ratification and shall remain in force through December 31, 1985, unless replaced earlier by an agreement further limiting strategic offensive arms.

2. This Treaty shall be registered pursuant to Article 102 of the Charter of the United Nations.

3. Each Party shall, in exercising its national sovereignty, have the right to withdraw from this Treaty if it decides that extraordinary events related to the subject matter of this Treaty have jeopardized its supreme interests. It shall give notice of its decision to the other Party six months prior to withdrawal from the Treaty. Such notice shall include a statement of the extraordinary events the notifying Party regards as having jeopardized its supreme interests.

United Nations Agreement Governing the Activities of States on the Moon and Other Celestial Bodies

Opened for signature: December 5, 1979
Place of signature: New York
Ratifications: Australia, Austria, Chile, Netherlands, Pakistan, Philippines, Uruguay
Date of entry into force: July 11, 1984

The States Parties to this Agreement,
Noting the achievements of States in the exploration and use of the moon and other celestial bodies,

Recognizing that the moon, as a natural satellite of the earth, has an important role to play in the exploration of outer space,
Determined to promote on the basis of equality the further development of co-operation among States in the exploration and use of the moon and other celestial bodies,
Desiring to prevent the moon from becoming an area of international conflict,
Bearing in mind the benefits which may be derived

from the exploitation of the natural resources of the moon and other celestial bodies,

Recalling the Treaty on Principles Governing the Activities of States in the Exploration and Use of Outer Space, including the Moon and Other Celestial Bodies, the Agreement on the Rescue of Astronauts, the Return of Astronauts and the Return of Objects Launched into Outer Space, the Convention on International Liability for Damage Caused by Space Objects, and the Convention on Registration of Objects Launched into Outer Space,

Taking into account the need to define and develop the provisions of these international instruments in relation to the moon and other celestial bodies, having regard to further progress in the exploration and use of outer space,

Have agreed on the following:

Article 1

1. The provisions of this Agreement relating to the moon shall also apply to other celestial bodies within the solar system, other than the earth, except in so far as specific legal norms enter into force with respect to any of these celestial bodies.

2. For the purposes of this Agreement reference to the moon shall include orbits around or other trajectories to or around it.

3. This Agreement does not apply to extraterrestrial materials which reach the surface of the earth by natural means.

Article 2

All activities on the moon, including its exploration and use, shall be carried out in accordance with international law, in particular the Charter of the United Nations, and taking into account the Declaration on Principles of International Law concerning Friendly Relations and Co-operation among States in accordance with the Charter of the United Nations, adopted by the General Assembly on 24 October 1970, in the interests of maintaining international peace and security and promoting international co-operation and mutual understanding, and with due regard to the corresponding interests of all other States Parties.

Article 3

1. The moon shall be used by all States Parties exclusively for peaceful purposes.

2. Any threat or use of force or any other hostile act or threat of hostile act on the moon is prohibited. It is likewise prohibited to use the moon in order to commit any such act or to engage in any such threat in relation to the earth, the moon, spacecraft, the personnel of spacecraft or man-made space objects.

3. States Parties shall not place in orbit around or other trajectory to or around the moon objects carrying nuclear weapons or any other kinds of weapons of mass destruction or place or use such weapons on or in the moon.

4. The establishment of military bases, installations and fortifications, the testing of any type of weapons and the conduct of military manoeuvres on the moon shall be forbidden. The use of military personnel for scientific research or for any other peaceful purposes shall not be prohibited. The use of any equipment or facility necessary for peaceful exploration and use of the moon shall also not be prohibited.

Article 4

1. The exploration and use of the moon shall be the province of all mankind and shall be carried out for the benefit and in the interests of all countries, irrespective of their degree of economic or scientific development. Due regard shall be paid to the interests of present and future generations as well as to the need to promote higher standards of living and conditions of economic and social progress and development in accordance with the Charter of the United Nations.

2. States Parties shall be guided by the principle of co-operation and mutual assistance in all their activities concerning the exploration and use of the moon. International co-operation in pursuance of this Agreement should be as wide as possible and may take place on a multilateral basis, on a bilateral basis or through international intergovernmental organizations.

Article 5

1. States Parties shall inform the Secretary-General of the United Nations as well as the public and the international scientific community, to the greatest extent feasible and practicable, of their activities concerned with the exploration and use of the moon. Information on the time, purposes, locations, orbital parameters and duration shall be given in respect of each mission to the moon as soon as possible after launching, while information on the results of each mission, including scientific results, shall be furnished upon completion of the mission. In the case of a mission lasting more than thirty days, information on conduct of the mission, including any scientific results, shall be given periodically at thirty days' intervals. For missions lasting more than six months, only significant additions to such information need to be reported thereafter.

2. If a State Party becomes aware that another State Party plans to operate simultaneously in the same area of or in the same orbit around or trajectory to or around the moon, it shall promptly inform

the other State of the timing of and plans for its own operations.

3. In carrying out activities under this Agreement, States Parties shall promptly inform the Secretary-General, as well as the public and the international scientific community, of any phenomena they discover in outer space, including the moon, which could endanger human life or health, as well as of any indication of organic life.

Article 6

1. There shall be freedom of scientific investigation on the moon by all States Parties without discrimination of any kind, on the basis of equality and in accordance with international law.

2. In carrying out scientific investigations and in furtherance of the provisions of this Agreement, the States Parties shall have the right to collect on and remove from the moon samples of its mineral and other substances. Such samples shall remain at the disposal of those States Parties which caused them to be collected and may be used by them for scientific purposes. States Parties shall have regard to the desirability of making a portion of such samples available to other interested States Parties and the international scientific community for scientific investigation. States Parties may in the course of scientific investigations also use mineral and other substances of the moon in quantities appropriate for the support of their missions.

3. States Parties agree on the desirability of exchanging scientific and other personnel on expeditions to or installations on the moon to the greatest extent feasible and practicable.

Article 7

1. In exploring and using the moon, States Parties shall take measures to prevent the disruption of the existing balance of its environment whether by introducing adverse changes in that environment, by its harmful contamination through the introduction of extra-environmental matter or otherwise. States Parties shall also take measures to avoid harmfully affecting the environment of the earth through the introduction of extraterrestrial matter or otherwise.

2. States Parties shall inform the Secretary-General of the United Nations of the measures being adopted by them in accordance with paragraph 1 of this article and shall also, to the maximum extent feasible, notify him in advance of all placements by them of radio-active materials on the moon and of the purposes of such placements.

3. States Parties shall report to other States Parties and to the Secretary-General concerning areas of the moon having special scientific interest in order that, without prejudice to the rights of other States Parties, consideration may be given to the designation of

such areas as international scientific preserves for which special protection arrangements are to be agreed upon in consultation with the competent bodies of the United Nations.

Article 8

1. States Parties may pursue their activities in the exploration and use of the moon anywhere on or below its surface, subject to the provisions of this Agreement.

2. For these purposes States Parties may, in particular:

(a) Land their space objects on the moon and launch them from the moon;

(b) Place their personnel, space vehicles, equipment, facilities, stations and installations anywhere on or below the surface of the moon.

Personnel, space vehicles, equipment, facilities, stations and installations may move or be moved freely over or below the surface of the moon.

3. Activities of States Parties in accordance with paragraphs 1 and 2 of this article shall not interfere with the activities of other States Parties on the moon. Where such interference may occur, the States Parties concerned shall undertake consultations in accordance with article 15, paragraphs 2 and 3 of this Agreement.

Article 9

1. States Parties may establish manned and unmanned stations on the moon. A State Party establishing a station shall use only that area which is required for the needs of the station and shall immediately inform the Secretary-General of the United Nations of the location and purposes of that station. Subsequently, at annual intervals that State shall likewise inform the Secretary-General whether the station continues in use and whether its purposes have changed.

2. Stations shall be installed in such a manner that they do not impede the free access to all areas of the moon by personnel, vehicles and equipment of other States Parties conducting activities on the moon in accordance with the provisions of this Agreement or of article I of the Treaty on Principles Governing the Activities of States in the Exploration and Use of Outer Space, including the Moon and other Celestial Bodies.

Article 10

1. States Parties shall adopt all practicable measures to safeguard the life and health of persons on the moon. For this purpose they shall regard any person on the moon as an astronaut within the

meaning of article V of the Treaty on Principles Governing the Activities of States in the Exploration and Use of Outer Space, including the Moon and Other Celestial Bodies and as part of the personnel of a spacecraft within the meaning of the Agreement on the Rescue of Astronauts, the Return of Astronauts and the Return of Objects Launched into Outer Space.

2. States Parties shall offer shelter in their stations, installations, vehicles and other facilities to persons in distress on the moon.

Article 11

1. The moon and its natural resources are the common heritage of mankind, which finds its expression in the provisions of this Agreement and in particular in paragraph 5 of this article.

2. The moon is not subject to national appropriation by any claim of sovereignty, by means of use or occupation, or by any other means.

3. Neither the surface nor the subsurface of the moon, nor any part thereof or natural resources in place, shall become property of any State, international intergovernmental or non-governmental organization, national organization or non-governmental entity or of any natural person. The placement of personnel, space vehicles, equipment, facilities, stations and installations on or below the surface of the moon, including structures connected with its surface or subsurface, shall not create a right of ownership over the surface or the subsurface of the moon or any areas thereof. The foregoing provisions are without prejudice to the international régime referred to in paragraph 5 of this article.

4. States Parties have the right to exploration and use of the moon without descrimination of any kind, on a basis of equality and in accordance with international law and the terms of this Agreement.

5. States Parties to this Agreement hereby undertake to establish an international régime, including appropriate procedures, to govern the exploitation of the natural resources of the moon as such exploitation is about to become feasible. This provision shall be implemented in accordance with article 18 of this Agreement.

6. In order to facilitate the establishment of the international régime referred to in paragraph 5 of this article, States Parties shall inform the Secretary-General of the United Nations as well as the public and the international scientific community, to the greatest extent feasible and practicable, of any natural resources they may discover on the moon.

7. The main purposes of the international régime to be established shall include:

(a) The orderly and safe development of the natural resources of the moon;

(b) The rational management of those resources;

(c) The expansion of opportunities in the use of those resources;

(d) An equitable sharing by all States Parties in the benefits derived from those resources, whereby the interest and needs of the developing countries, as well as the efforts of those countries which have contributed either directly or indirectly to the exploration of the moon, shall be given special consideration.

8. All the activities with respect to the natural resources of the moon shall be carried out in a manner compatible with the purposes specified in paragraph 7 of this article and the provisions of article 6, paragraph 2, of this Agreement.

Article 12

1. States Parties shall retain jurisdiction and control over their personnel, vehicles, equipment, facilities, stations and installations on the moon. The ownership of space vehicles, equipment, facilities, stations and installations shall not be affected by their presence on the moon.

2. Vehicles, installations and equipment or their component parts found in places other than their intended location shall be dealt with in accordance with article 5 of the Agreement on Rescue of Astronauts, the Return of Astronauts and the Return of Objects Launched into Outer Space.

3. In the event of an emergency involving a threat to human life, States Parties may use the equipment, vehicles, installations, facilities or supplies of other States Parties on the moon. Prompt notification of such use shall be made to the Secretary-General of the United Nations or the State Party concerned.

Article 13

A State Party which learns of the crash landing, forced landing or other unintended landing on the moon of a space object, or its component parts, that were not launched by it, shall promptly inform the launching State Party and the Secretary-General of the United Nations.

Article 14

1. States Parties to this Agreement shall bear international responsibility for national activities on the moon, whether such activities are carried on by governmental agencies or by non-governmental entities, and for assuring that national activities are carried out in conformity with the provisions set forth in this Agreement. States Parties shall ensure that non-governmental entities under their jurisdiction shall engage in activities on the moon only under the

authority and continuing supervision of the appropriate State Party.

2. States Parties recognize that detailed arrangements concerning liability for damage caused on the moon, in addition to the provisions of the Treaty on Principles Governing the Activities of States in the Exploration and Use of Outer Space, including the Moon and Other Celestial Bodies and the Convention on International Liability for Damage Caused by Space Objects, may become necessary as a result of more extensive activities on the moon. Any such arrangements shall be elaborated in accordance with the procedure provided for in article 18 of this Agreement.

Article 15

1. Each State Party may assure itself that the activities of other States Parties in the exploration and use of the moon are compatible with the provisions of this Agreement. To this end, all space vehicles, equipment, facilities, stations and installations on the moon shall be open to other States Parties. Such States Parties shall give reasonable advance notice of a projected visit, in order that appropriate consultations may be held and that maximum precautions may be taken to assure safety and to avoid interference with normal operations in the facility to be visited. In pursuance of this article, any State Party may act on its own behalf or with the full or partial assistance of any other State Party or through appropriate international procedures within the framework of the United Nations and in accordance with the Charter.

2. A State Party which has reason to believe that another State Party is not fulfilling the obligations incumbent upon it pursuant to this Agreement or that another State Party is interfering with the rights which the former State has under this Agreement may request consultations with that State Party. A State Party receiving such a request shall enter into such consultations without delay. Any other State Party which requests to do so shall be entitled to take part in the consultations. Each State Party participating in such consultations shall seek a mutually acceptable resolution of any controversy and shall bear in mind the rights and interests of all States Parties. The Secretary-General of the United Nations shall be informed of the results of the consultations and shall transmit the information received to all States Parties concerned.

3. If the consultations do not lead to a mutually acceptable settlement which has due regard for the rights and interests of all States Parties, the parties concerned shall take all measures to settle the dispute by other peaceful means of their choice appropriate to the circumstances and the nature of the dispute. If difficulties arise in connexion with the opening of consultations or if consultations do not lead to a mutually acceptable settlement, any State Party may seek the assistance of the Secretary-General, without seeking the consent of any other State Party concerned, in order to resolve the controversy. A State Party which does not maintain diplomatic relations with another State Party concerned shall participate in such consultations, at its choice, either itself or through another State Party or the Secretary-General as intermediary.

Article 16

With the exception of articles 17 to 21, references in this Agreement to States shall be deemed to apply to any international intergovernmental organization which conducts space activities if the organization declares its acceptance of the rights and obligations provided for in this Agreement and if a majority of the States members of the organization are States Parties to this Agreement and to the Treaty on Principles Governing the Activities of States in the Exploration and Use of Outer Space, including the Moon and Other Celestial Bodies. States members of any such organization which are States Parties to this Agreement shall take all appropriate steps to ensure that the organization makes a declaration in accordance with the foregoing.

Article 17

Any State Party to this Agreement may propose amendments to the Agreement. Amendments shall enter into force for each State Party to the Agreement accepting the amendments upon their acceptance by a majority of the States Parties to the Agreement and thereafter for each remaining State Party to the Agreement on the date of acceptance by it.

Article 18

Ten years after the entry into force of this Agreement, the question of the review of the Agreement shall be included in the provisional agenda of the General Assembly of the United Nations in order to consider, in the light of past application of the Agreement, whether it requires revision. However, at any time after the Agreement has been in force for five years, the Secretary-General of the United Nations, as depository, shall, at the request of one third of the States Parties to the Agreement and with the concurrence of the majority of the States Parties, convene a conference of the States Parties to review this Agreement. A review conference shall also consider the question of the implementation of the provisions of article 11, paragraph 5, on the basis of the principle referred to in paragraph 1 of that article and taking into account in particular any relevant technological developments.

Article 19

1. This Agreement shall be open for signature by all States at United Nations Headquarters in New York.

2. This Agreement shall be subject to ratification by signatory States. Any State which does not sign this Agreement before its entry into force in accordance with paragraph 3 of this article may accede to it at any time. Instruments of ratification or accession shall be deposited with the Secretary-General of the United Nations.

3. This Agreement shall enter into force on the thirtieth day following the date of deposit of the fifth instrument of ratification.

4. For each State depositing its instrument of ratification or accession after the entry into force of this Agreement, it shall enter into force on the thirtieth day following the date of deposit of any such instrument.

5. The Secretary-General shall promptly inform all signatory and acceding States of the date of each signature, the date of deposit of each instrument of ratification or accession to this Agreement, the date of its entry into force and other notices.

Article 20

Any State Party to this Agreement may give notice of its withdrawal from the Agreement one year after its entry into force by written notification to the Secretary-General of the United Nations. Such withdrawal shall take effect one year from the date of receipt of this notification.

Article 21

The original of this Agreement, of which the Arabic, Chinese, English, French, Russian and Spanish texts are equally authentic, shall be deposited with the Secretary-General of the United Nations, who shall send certified copies thereof to all signatory and acceding States.

Convention on the Physical Protection of Nuclear Material

Date of adoption: October 10, 1979 (*Opened for signature:* March 3, 1980)
Place of signature: Vienna and New York
Signatory states: Austria, Belgium, Brazil, Bulgaria, Canada, Czechoslovakia, Denmark, Dominican Republic, European Atomic Energy Community, Finland, France, German Democratic Republic, Federal Republic of Germany, Greece, Guatemala, Haiti, Hungary, Ireland, Italy, Republic of Korea, Luxembourg, Morocco, Netherlands, Paraguay, Philippines, Poland, Romania, South Africa, Soviet Union, Sweden, United Kingdom, United States, Yugoslavia

The States Parties to This Convention,
Recognizing the right of all States to develop and apply nuclear energy for peaceful purposes and their legitimate interests in the potential benefits to be derived from the peaceful application of nuclear energy,
Convinced of the need for facilitating international cooperation in the peaceful application of nuclear energy,
Desiring to avert the potential dangers posed by the unlawful taking and use of nuclear material,
Convinced that offenses relating to nuclear material are a matter of grave concern and that there is an urgent need to adopt appropriate and effective measures to ensure the prevention, detection and punishment of such offenses,
Aware of the Need for international cooperation to establish, in conformity with the national law of each State Party and with this Convention, effective measures for the physical protection of nuclear material,
Convinced that this Convention should facilitate the safe transfer of nuclear material,
Stressing also the importance of the physical protection of nuclear material in domestic use, storage and transport,
Recognizing the importance of effective physical protection of nuclear material used for military purposes, and understanding that such material is and will continue to be accorded stringent physical protection,
Have Agreed as follows:

Article 1

For the purposes of this Convention:

(a) "nuclear material" means plutonium except that with isotopic concentration exceeding 80% in plutonium-238; uranium-233; uranium enriched in the isotopes 235 or 233; uranium containing the mixture of isotopes as occurring in nature other than in the form of ore or ore-residue; any material containing one or more of the foregoing;

(b) "uranium enriched in the 235 or 233" means uranium containing the isotopes 235 or 233 or both in an amount such that the abundance ratio of the sum of these isotopes to the isotope 238 is greater than the ratio of the isotope 235 to the isotope 238 occurring in nature;

(c) "international nuclear transport" means the carriage of a consignment of nuclear material by any means of transportation intended to go beyond the territory of the State where the shipment originates beginning with the departure from a facility of the shipper in that State and ending with the arrival at a facility of the receiver within the State of ultimate destination.

Article 2

1. The Convention shall apply to nuclear material used for peaceful purposes while in international nuclear transport.

2. With the exception of articles 3 and 4 and paragraph 3 of article 5, this Convention shall also apply to nuclear material used for peaceful purposes while in domestic use, storage and transport.

3. Apart from the commitments expressly undertaken by States Parties in the articles covered by paragraph 2 with respect to nuclear material used for peaceful purposes while in domestic use, storage and transport, nothing in this Convention shall be interpreted as affecting the sovereign rights of a State regarding the domestic use, storage and transport of such nuclear material.

Article 3

Each State Party shall take appropriate steps within the framework of its national law and consistent with international law to ensure as far as practicable that, during international nuclear transport, nuclear material within its territory, or on board a ship or aircraft under its jurisdiction insofar as such ship or aircraft is engaged in the transport to or from that State, is protected at the levels described in Annex I.

Article 4

1. Each State Party shall not export or authorize the export of nuclear material unless the State Party has received assurances that such material will be protected during the international nuclear transport at the levels described in Annex I.

2. Each State Party shall not import or authorize the import of nuclear material from a State not party to this Convention unless the State Party has received assurances that such material will during the international nuclear transport be protected at the levels described in Annex I.

3. A State Party shall not allow the transit of its territory by land or internal waterways or through its airports or seaports of nuclear material between States that are not parties to this Convention unless the State Party has received assurances as far as practicable that this nuclear material will be protected during international nuclear transport at the levels described in Annex I.

4. Each State Party shall apply within the framework of its national law the levels of physical protection described in Annex I to nuclear material being transported from a part of that State to another part of the same State through international waters or airspace.

5. The State Party responsible for receiving assurances that the nuclear material will be protected at the levels described in Annex I according to paragraphs 1 to 3 shall identify and inform in advance States which the nuclear material is expected to transit by land or internal waterways, or whose airports or seaports it is expected to enter.

6. The responsibility for obtaining assurances referred to in paragraph 1 may be transferred, by mutual agreement, to the State Party involved in the transport as the importing State.

7. Nothing in this article shall be interpreted as in any way affecting the territorial sovereignty and jurisdiction of a State, including that over its airspace and territorial sea.

Article 5

1. States Parties shall identify and make known to each other directly or through the International Atomic Energy Agency their central authority and point of contact having responsibility for physical protection of nuclear material and for coordinating recovery and response operations in the event of any unauthorized removal, use or alteration of nuclear material or in the event of credible threat thereof.

2. In the case of theft, robbery or any other unlawful taking of nuclear material or of credible threat thereof, States Parties shall, in accordance with their national law, provide cooperation and assistance to the maximum feasible extent in the recovery and protection of such material to any State that so requests. In particular:

(a) a State Party shall take appropriate steps to inform as soon as possible other States, which appear to it to be concerned, of any theft, robbery or other unlawful taking of nuclear material or credible threat thereof and to inform, where appropriate, international organizations;

(b) as appropriate, the States Parties concerned shall exchange information with each other or international organizations with a view to protecting threatened nuclear material, verifying the integrity of the shipping container, or recovering unlawfully taken nuclear material and shall:

(i) coordinate their efforts through diplomatic and other agreed channels;

(ii) render assistance, if requested;

(iii) ensure the return of nuclear material stolen or missing as a consequence of the above-mentioned events.

The means of implementation of this cooperation shall be determined by the States Parties concerned.

3. States Parties shall cooperate and consult as appropriate, with each other directly or through international organizations, with a view to obtaining guidance on the design, maintenance and improvement of systems of physical protection of nuclear material in international transport.

Article 6

1. States Parties shall take appropriate measures consistent with their national law to protect the confidentiality of any information, which they receive in confidence by virtue of the provisions of this Convention from another State Party or through participation in an activity carried out for the implementation of this Convention. If States Parties provide information to international organizations in confidence, steps shall be taken to ensure that the confidentiality of such information is protected.

2. States Parties shall not be required by this Convention to provide any information which they are not permitted to communicate pursuant to national law or which would jeopardize the security of the State concerned or the physical protection of nuclear material.

Article 7

1. The intentional commission of:

(a) an act without lawful authority which constitutes the receipt, possession, use, transfer, alteration, disposal or dispersal of nuclear material and which causes or is likely to cause death or serious injury to any person or substantial damage to property;

(b) a theft or robbery of nuclear material;

(c) an embezzlement or fraudulent obtaining of nuclear material;

(d) an act constituting a demand for nuclear material by threat or use of force or by any other form of intimidation;

(e) a threat:

(i) to use nuclear material to cause death or serious injury to any person or substantial property damage, or

(ii) to commit an offense described in subparagraph (b) in order to compel a natural or legal person, international organization or State to do or to refrain from doing any act;

(f) an attempt to commit any offense described in paragraphs (a), (b) or (c); and

(g) an act which constitutes participation in any offense described in paragraphs (a) to (f) shall be made a punishable offense by each State Party under its national law.

2. Each State Party shall make the offenses described in this article punishable by appropriate penalties which take into account their grave nature.

Article 8

1. Each State Party shall take such measures as may be necessary to establish its jurisdiction over the offenses set forth in article 7 in the following cases:

(a) when the offense is committed in the territory of that State or on board a ship or aircraft registered in that State;

(b) when the alleged offender is a national of that State.

2. Each State Party shall likewise take such measures as may be necessary to establish its jurisdiction over these offenses in cases where the alleged offender is present in its territory and it does not extradite him pursuant to article 11 to any of the States mentioned in paragraph 1.

3. This Convention does not exclude any criminal jurisdiction exercised in accordance with national law.

4. In addition to the State Parties mentioned in paragraphs 1 and 2, each State Party may, consistent with international law, establish its jurisdiction over the offenses set forth in article 7 when it is involved in international nuclear transport as the exporting or importing State.

Article 9

Upon being satisfied that the circumstances so warrant, the State Party in whose territory the alleged offender is present shall take appropriate measures, including detention, under its national law to ensure his presence for the purpose of prosecution or extradition. Measures taken according to this article shall be notified without delay to the States required to establish jurisdiction pursuant to article 8 and, where appropriate, all other States concerned.

Article 10

The State Party in whose territory the alleged offender is present shall, if it does not extradite him, submit, without exception whatsoever and without undue delay, the case to its competent authorities for the purpose of prosecution, through proceedings in accordance with the laws of that State.

Article 11

1. The offenses in article 7 shall be deemed to be included as extraditable offenses in any extradition treaty existing between States Parties. States Parties undertake to include those offenses as extraditable offenses in every future extradition treaty to be concluded between them.

2. If a State Party which makes extradition conditional on the existence of a treaty receives a request for extradition from another State Party with which it has no extradition treaty, it may at its option consider this Convention as the legal basis for extradition in respect of those offenses. Extradition shall be subject to the other conditions provided by the law of the requested State.

3. States Parties which do not make extradition conditional on the existence of a treaty shall recognize those offenses as extraditable offenses between themselves subject to the conditions provided by the law of the requested State.

4. Each of the offenses shall be treated, for the purpose of extradition between States Parties, as if it had been committed not only in the place in which it occurred but also in the territories of the States Parties required to establish their jurisdiction in accordance with paragraph 1 of article 8.

Article 12

Any person regarding whom proceedings are being carried out in connection with any of the offenses set forth in article 7 shall be guaranteed fair treatment at all stages of the proceedings.

Article 13

1. States Parties shall afford one another the greatest measure of assistance in connection with criminal proceedings brought in respect of the offenses set forth in article 7, including the supply of evidence at their disposal necessary for the proceedings. The law of the State requested shall apply in all cases.

2. The provisions of paragraph 1 shall not affect obligations under any other treaty, bilateral or multilateral, which governs or will govern, in whole or in part, mutual assistance in criminal matters.

Article 14

1. Each State Party shall inform the depositary of its laws and regulations which give effect to this Convention. The depositary shall communicate such information periodically to all States Parties.

2. The State Party where an alleged offender is prosecuted shall, wherever practicable, first communicate the final outcome of the proceedings to the States directly concerned. The State Party shall also communicate the final outcome to the depositary who shall inform all States.

3. Where an offense involves nuclear material used for peaceful purposes in domestic use, storage or transport, and both the alleged offender and the nuclear material remain in the territory of the State Party in which the offense was committed, nothing in this Convention shall be interpreted as requiring that State Party to provide information concerning criminal proceedings arising out of such an offense.

Article 15

The Annexes constitute an integral part of this Convention.

Article 16

1. A conference of States Parties shall be convened by the depositary five years after the entry into force of this Convention to review the implementation of the Convention and its adequacy as concerns the preamble, the whole of the operative part and the annexes in the light of the then prevailing situation.

2. At intervals of not less than five years thereafter, the majority of States Parties may obtain, by submitting a proposal to this effect to the depositary, the convening of further conferences with the same objective.

Article 17

1. In the event of a dispute between two or more States Parties concerning the interpretation or application of this Convention, such States Parties shall consult with a view to the settlement of the dispute by negotiation, or by any other peaceful means of settling disputes acceptable to all parties to the dispute.

2. Any dispute of this character which cannot be settled in the manner prescribed in paragraph 1 shall, at the request of any party to such dispute, be submitted to arbitration or referred to the International Court of Justice for decision. Where a dispute is submitted to arbitration, if, within six months from the date of the request, the parties to the dispute are unable to agree on the organization of the arbitration, a party may request the President of the International Court of Justice or the Secretary-General of the United Nations to appoint one or more arbitrators. In case of conflicting requests by the parties to the dispute, the request to the Secretary-General of the United Nations shall have priority.

3. Each State Party may at the time of signature, ratification, acceptance or approval of this Convention or accession thereto declare that it does not consider itself bound by either or both of the dispute settlement procedures provided for in paragraph 2. The other States Parties shall not be bound by a dispute settlement procedure provided for in paragraph 2, with respect to a State Party which has made a reservation to that procedure.

4. Any State Party which has made a reservation

in accordance with paragraph 3 may at any time withdraw that reservation by notification to the depositary.

Article 18

1. This Convention shall be open for signature by all States at the Headquarters of the International Atomic Energy Agency in Vienna and at the Headquarters of the United Nations in New York from 3 March 1980 until its entry into force.

2. This Convention is subject to ratification, acceptance or approval by the signatory States.

3. After its entry into force, this Convention will be open for accession by all States.

4.

(a) This Convention shall be open for signature or accession by international organizations and regional organizations of an integration or other nature, provided that any such organization is constituted by sovereign States and has competence in respect of the negotiation, conclusion and application of international agreements in matters covered by this Convention.

(b) In matters within their competence, such organizations shall, on their own behalf, exercise the rights and fulfill the responsibilities which this Convention attributes to States Parties.

(c) When becoming party to this Convention such an organization shall communicate to the depositary a declaration indicating which States are members thereof and which articles of this Convention do not apply to it.

(d) Such an organization shall not hold any vote additional to those of its Member States.

5. Instruments of ratification, acceptance, approval or accession shall be deposited with the depositary.

Article 19

1. This Convention shall enter into force on the thirtieth day following the date of deposit of the twenty-first instrument of ratification, acceptance or approval with the depositary.

2. For each State ratifying, accepting, approving or acceding to the Convention after the date of deposit of the twenty-first instrument of ratification, acceptance or approval, the .Convention shall enter into force on the thirtieth day after the deposit by such State of its instrument of ratification, acceptance, approval or accession.

Article 20

1. Without prejudice to article 16 a State Party may propose amendments to this Convention. The proposed amendment shall be submitted to the depositary who shall circulate it immediately to all States Parties. If a majority of States Parties request the depositary to convene a conference to consider the proposed amendments, the depositary shall invite all States Parties to attend such a conference to begin not sooner than thirty days after the invitations are issued. Any amendment adopted at the conference by a two-thirds majority of all States Parties shall be promptly circulated by the depositary to all States Parties.

2. The amendment shall enter into force for each State Party that deposits its instrument of ratification, acceptance or approval of the amendement on the thirtieth day after the date on which two-thirds of the States Parties have deposited their instruments of ratification, acceptance or approval with the depositary. Thereafter, the amendment shall enter into force for any other State Party on the day on which that State Party deposits its instrument of ratification, acceptance or approval of the amendment.

Article 21

1. Any State Party may denounce this Convention by written notification to the depositary.

2. Denunciation shall take effect one hundred and eighty days following the date on which notification is received by the depositary.

Article 22

The depositary shall promptly notify all States of:

(a) each signature of this Convention;

(b) each deposit of an instrument of ratification, acceptance, approval or accession;

(c) any reservation or withdrawal in accordance with article 17;

(d) any communication made by an organization in accordance with paragraph 4(c) of article 18;

(e) the entry into force of this Convention;

(f) the entry into force of any amendment to this Convention; and

(g) any denunciation made under article 21.

Article 23

The original of this Convention, of which the Arabic, Chinese, English, French, Russian and Spanish texts are equally authentic, shall be deposited with the Director General of the International Atomic Energy Agency who shall send certified copies thereof to all States.

ANNEX II
TABLE: CATEGORIZATION OF NUCLEAR MATERIAL

Material	Form	Category		
		I	II	III[3]
1. Plutonium[1]	Unirradiated[2]	2 kg or more	Less than 2 kg but more than 500 g	500 g or less but more than 15 g.
2. Uranium-235	Unirradiated[2]: —uranium enriched to 20% U^{235} or more —uranium enriched to 10% U^{235} but less than 20% —uranium enriched above natural, but less than 10% U^{235}.	5 kg or more	Less than 5 kg but more than 1 kg. 10 kg or more	1 kg or less but more than 15 g. Less than 10 kg but more than 1 kg. 10 kg or more.
3. Uranium-233	Unirradiated[2]	2 kg or more	Less than 2 kg but more than 500 g.	500 g or less but more than 15 g.
4. Irradiated fuel			Depleted or natural uranium, thorium or low-enriched fuel (less than 10% fissile content).[4][5]	

1 All plutonium except that with isotopic concentration exceeding 80% in plutonium-238.
2 Material not irradiated in a reactor or material irradiated in a reactor but with a radiation level equal to or less than 100 rads/hour at one metre unshielded.
3 Quantities not falling in Category III and natural uranium should be protected in accordance with prudent management practice.
4 Although this level of protection is recommended, it would be open to States, upon evaluation of the specific circumstances, to assign a different category of physical protection.
5 Other fuel which by virtue of its original fissile material content is classified as Category I and II before irradiation may be reduced one category level while the radiation level from the fuel exceeds 100 rads/hour at one metre unshielded.

ANNEX I

LEVELS OF PHYSICAL PROTECTION TO BE APPLIED IN INTERNATIONAL TRANSPORT OF NUCLEAR MATERIAL AS CATEGORIZED IN ANNEX II

1. Levels of physical protection for nuclear material during storage incidental to international nuclear transport include:

(a) For Category III materials, storage within an area to which access is controlled;

(b) For Category II materials, storage within an area under constant surveillance by guards or electronic devices, surrounded by a physical barrier with a limited number of points of entry under appropriate control or any area with an equivalent level of physical protection;

(c) For Category I material, storage within a protected area as defined for Category II above, to which, in addition, access is restricted to persons whose trustworthiness has been determined, and which is under surveillance by guards who are in close communication with appropriate response forces. Specific measures taken in this context should have as their object the detection and prevention of any assault, unauthorized access or unauthorized removal of material.

2. Levels of physical protection for nuclear material during international transport include:

(a) For Category II and III materials, transportation shall take place under special precautions including prior arrangements among sender, receiver, and carrier, and prior agreement between natural or legal persons subject to the jurisdiction and regulation of exporting and importing States, specifying time, place and procedures for transferring transport responsibility;

(b) For Category I materials, transportation shall take place under special precautions identified above for transportation of Category II and III materials, and in addition, under constant surveillance by escorts and under conditions which assure close communication with appropriate response forces;

(c) For natural uranium other than in the form of ore or ore-residue, transportation protection for quan-

tities exceeding 500 kilograms U shall include advance notification of shipment specifying mode of transport, expected time of arrival and confirmation of receipt of shipment.

Convention on Prohibitions or Restrictions on the Use of Certain Conventional Weapons Which may be Deemed to be Excessively Injurious or to Have Indiscriminate Effects

Also known as: *UN Weaponry Convention, Convention on Specific Conventional Weapons*
Date of adoption: *October 10, 1980 (Opened for signature: April 10, 1981)*
Place of signature: *Geneva*
Signatory states: *Afghanistan, Argentina, Australia, Belgium, Bulgaria, Byelorussia, Canada, People's Republic of China, Cuba, Czechoslovakia, Denmark, Ecuador, Egypt, Finland, France, German Democratic Republic, Federal Republic of Germany, Greece, Guatemala, Hungary, Iceland, India, Ireland, Italy, Japan, Laos, Liechtenstein, Luxembourg, Mexico, Mongolia, Morocco, Netherlands, New Zealand, Nicaragua, Nigeria, Norway, Pakistan, Philippines, Poland, Portugal, Romania, Sierra Leone, Soviet Union, Spain, Sudan, Sweden, Switzerland, Togo, Turkey, United Kingdom, United States, Vietnam, Yugoslavia*
Date of entry into force: *December 2, 1983*

The High Contracting Parties,
Recalling that every State has the duty, in conformity with the Charter of the United Nations, to refrain in its international relations from the threat or use of force against the sovereignty, territorial integrity or political independence of any State, or in any other manner inconsistent with the purposes of the United Nations.
Further recalling the general principle of the protection of the civilian population against the effects of hostilities,
Basing themselves on the principle of international law that the right of the parties to an armed conflict to choose methods or means of warfare is not unlimited, and on the principle that prohibits the employment in armed conflicts of weapons, projectiles and material and methods of warfare of a nature to cause superfluous injury or unnecessary suffering,
Also recalling that it is prohibited to employ methods or means of warfare which are intended, or may be expected, to cause widespread, long-term and severe damage to the natural environment,

Confirming their determination that in cases not covered by this Convention and its annexed Protocols or by other international agreements, the civilian population and the combatants shall at all times remain under the protection and authority of the principles of international law derived from established custom, from the principles of humanity and from the dictates of public conscience,
Desiring to contribute to international détente, the ending of the arms race and the building of confidence among States, and hence to the realization of the aspiration of all peoples to live in peace,
Recognizing the importance of pursuing every effort which may contribute to progress towards general and complete disarmament under strict and effective international control,
Reaffirming the need to continue the codification and progressive development of the rules of international law applicable in armed conflict,
Wishing to prohibit or restrict further the use of certain conventional weapons and believing that the positive results achieved in this area may facilitate the main talks on disarmament with a view to putting an end to the production, stockpiling and proliferation of such weapons,
Emphasizing the desirability that all States become parties to this Convention and its annexed Protocols, especially the militarily significant States,
Bearing in mind that the General Assembly of the United Nations and the United Nations Disarmament Commission may decide to examine the question of a possible broadening of the scope of the prohibitions and restrictions contained in this Convention and its annexed Protocols,
Further bearing in mind that the Committee on Disarmament may decide to consider the question of adopting further measures to prohibit or restrict the use of certain conventional weapons,
Have agreed as follows:

Article 1

Scope of Application

This Convention and its annexed Protocols shall apply in the situations referred to in Article 2 common to the Geneva Conventions of 12 August 1949 for the Protection of War Victims, including any situation described in paragraph 4 of Article 1 of Additional Protocol I to these Conventions.

Article 2

Relations with other International Agreements

Nothing in this Convention or its annexed Protocols shall be interpreted as detracting from other obligations imposed upon the High Contracting Parties by international humanitarian law applicable in armed conflict.

Article 3

Signature

This Convention shall be open for signature by all States at United Nations Headquarters in New York for a period of twelve months from 10 April 1981.

Article 4

Ratification, Acceptance, Approval or Accession

1. This Convention is subject to ratification, acceptance or approval by the Signatories. Any State which has not signed this Convention may accede to it.

2. The instruments of ratification, acceptance, approval or accession shall be deposited with the Depositary.

3. Expressions of consent to be bound by any of the Protocols annexed to this Convention shall be optional for each State, provided that at the time of the deposit of its instrument of ratification, acceptance or approval of this Convention or of accession thereto, that State shall notify the Depositary of its consent to be bound by any two or more of these Protocols.

4. At any time after the deposit of its instrument of ratification, acceptance or approval of this Convention or of accession thereto, a State may notify the Depositary of its consent to be bound by any annexed Protocol by which it is not already bound.

5. Any Protocol by which a High Contracting Party is bound shall for that Party form an integral part of this Convention.

Article 5

Entry into Force

1. This Convention shall enter into force six months after the date of deposit of the twentieth instrument of ratification, acceptance, approval or accession.

2. For any State which deposits its instrument of ratification, acceptance, approval or accession after the date of the deposit of the twentieth instrument of ratification, acceptance, approval or accession, this Convention shall enter into force six months after the date on which that State has deposited its instrument of ratification, acceptance, approval or accession.

3. Each of the Protocols annexed to this Convention shall enter into force six months after the date by which twenty States have notified their consent to be bound by it in accordance with paragraph 3 or 4 of Article 4 of this Convention.

4. For any State which notifies its consent to be bound by a Protocol, annexed to this Convention after the date by which twenty States have notified their consent to be bound by it, the Protocol shall enter into force six months after the date on which that State has notified its consent so to be bound.

Article 6

Dissemination

The High Contracting Parties undertake, in time of peace as in time of armed conflict, to disseminate this Convention and those of its annexed Protocols by which they are bound as widely as possible in their respective countries and, in particular, to include the study thereof in their programmes of military instruction, so that those instruments may become known to their armed forces.

Article 7

Treaty Relations upon Entry into Force of this Convention

1. When one of the parties to a conflict is not bound by an annexed Protocol, the parties bound by this Convention and that annexed Protocol shall remain bound by them in their mutual relations.

2. Any High Contracting Party shall be bound by this Convention and any Protocol annexed thereto which is in force for it, in any situation contemplated by Article 1, in relation to any State which is not a party to this Convention or bound by the relevant annexed Protocol, if the latter accepts and applies this Convention or the relevant Protocol, and so notifies the Depositary.

3. The Depositary shall immediately inform the High Contracting Parties concerned of any notification received under paragraph 2 of this Article.

4. This convention, and the annexed Protocols by which a High Contracting Party is bound, shall apply with respect to an armed conflict against that High Contracting Party of the type referred to in Article 1, paragraph 4, of Additional Protocol I to the Geneva Conventions of 12 August 1949 for the Protection of War Victims:

(a) where the High Contracting Party is also a party

to Additional Protocol I and an authority referred to in Article 96, paragraph 3, of that Protocol has undertaken to apply the Geneva Conventions and Additional Protocol I in accordance with Article 96, paragraph 3, of the said Protocol, and undertakes to apply this Convention and the relevant annexed Protocols in relation to that conflict; or

(b) where the High Contracting Party is not a party to Additional Protocol I and an authority of the type referred to in subparagraph (a) above accepts and applies the obligations of the Geneva Conventions and of this Convention and the relevant annexed Protocols in relation to that conflict. Such an acceptance and application shall have in relation to that conflict the following effects:

(i) the Geneva Conventions and this Convention and its relevant annexed Protocols are brought into force for the parties to the conflict with immediate effect;

(ii) the said authority assumes the same rights and obligations as those which have been assumed by a High Contracting Party to the Geneva Conventions, this Convention and its relevant annexed Protocols; and

(iii) the Geneva Conventions, this Convention and its relevant annexed Protocols are equally binding upon all parties to the conflict.

The High Contracting Party and the authority may also agree to accept and apply the obligations of Additional Protocol I to the Geneva Conventions on a reciprocal basis.

Article 8

Review and Amendments

1.

(a) At any time after the entry into force of this Convention any High Contracting Party may propose amendments to this Convention or any annexed Protocol by which it is bound. Any proposal for an amendment shall be communicated to the Depositary, who shall notify it to all the High Contracting Parties and shall seek their views on whether a conference should be convened to consider the proposal. If a majority, that shall not be less than eighteen of the High Contracting Parties so agree, he shall promptly convene a conference to which all High Contracting Parties shall be invited. States not parties to this Convention shall be invited to the conference as observers.

(b) Such a conference may agree upon amendments which shall be adopted and shall enter into force in the same manner as this Convention and the annexed Protocols, provided that amendments to this Convention may be adopted only by the High Contracting Parties and that amendments to a specific annexed Protocol may be adopted only by the High Contracting Parties which are bound by that Protocol.

2.

(a) At any time after the entry into force of this Convention any High Contracting Party may propose additional protocols relating to other categories of conventional weapons not covered by the existing annexed Protocols. Any such proposal for an additional protocol shall be communicated to the Depositary, who shall notify it to all the High Contracting Parties in accordance with subparagraph 1 (a) of this Article. If a majority, that shall not be less than eighteen of the High Contracting Parties so agree, the Depositary shall promptly convene a conference to which all States shall be invited.

(b) Such a conference may agree, with the full participation of all States represented at the conference, upon additional protocols which shall be adopted in the same manner as this Convention, shall be annexed thereto and shall enter into force as provided in paragraphs 3 and 4 of Article 5 of this Convention.

3.

(a) If, after a period of ten years following the entry into force of this Convention, no conference has been convened in accordance with subparagraph 1 (a) or 2 (a) of this Article, any High Contracting Party may request the Depositary to convene a conference to which all High Contracting Parties shall be invited to review the scope and operation of this Convention and the Protocols annexed thereto and to consider any proposal for amendments of this Convention or of the existing Protocols. States not parties to this Convention shall be invited as observers to the conference. The conference may agree upon amendments which shall be adopted and enter into force in accordance with subparagraph 1 (b) above.

(b) At such conference consideration may also be given to any proposal for additional protocols relating to other categories of conventional weapons not covered by the exisiting annexed Protocols. All States represented at the conference may participate fully in such consideration. Any additional protocols shall be adopted in the same manner as this Convention, shall be annexed thereto and shall enter into force as provided in paragraphs 3 and 4 of Article 5 of this Convention.

(c) Such a conference may consider whether provision should be made for the convening of a further conference at the request of any High Contracting Party if, after a similar period to that referred to in subparagraph 3 (a) of this Article, no conference has been convened in accordance with subparagraph 1 (a) or 2 (a) of this Article.

Article 9

Denunciation

1. Any High Contracting Party may denounce this Convention or any of its annexed Protocols by so notifying the Depositary.

2. Any such denuncitation shall only take effect one year after receipt by the Depositary of the notification of denunciation. If, however, on the expiry of that year the denouncing High Contracting Party is engaged in one of the situations referred to in Article 1, the Party shall continue to be bound by the obligations of this Convention and of the relevant annexed Protocols until the end of the armed conflict or occupation and, in any case, until the termination of operations connected with the final release, repatriation or re-establishment of the person protected by the rules of international law appplicable in armed conflict, and in the case of any annexed Protocol containing provisions concerning situations in which peace-keeping, observation or similar functions are performed by United Nations forces or missions in the area concerned, until the termination of those functions.

3. Any denunciation of this Convention shall be considered as also applying to all annexed Protocols by which the denouncing High Contracting Party is bound.

4. Any denunciation shall have effect only in respect of the denouncing High Contracting Party.

5. Any denunciation shall not effect the obligations already incurred, by reason of an armed conflict, under this Convention and its annexed Protocols by such denouncing High Contracting Party in respect of any act committed before this denunciation becomes effective.

Article 10

Depositary

1. The Secretary-General of the United Nations shall be the Depositary of this Convention and of its annexed Protocols.

2. In addition to his usual functions, the Depositary shall inform all States of:

(a) signatures affixed to this Convention under Article 3;

(b) deposits of instruments of ratification, acceptance or approval of or accession to this Convention deposited under Article 4;

(c) notifications of consent to be bound by annexed Protocols under Article 4;

(d) the dates of entry into force of this Convention and of each of its annexed Protocols under Article 5; and

(e) notifications of denunciation received under article 9, and their effective date.

Article 11

Authentic Texts

The original of this Convention with the annexed Protocols, of which the Arabic, Chinese, English, French, Russian and Spanish texts are equally authentic, shall be deposited with the Depositary, who shall transmit certified true copies thereof to all States.

APPENDIX B

PROTOCOL ON NON-DETECTABLE FRAGMENTS (PROTOCOL I)

It is prohibited to use any weapon the primary effect of which is to injure by fragments which in the human body escape detection by X-rays.

CHRONOLOGY OF THE
PEACE MOVEMENT

This section comprises a listing year-by-year of the development of the peace movement. Prominence has been given to the establishment of peace organizations and movements and to the dates of peace congresses and conferences but the most significant publications are also featured.

The chronology is selective and reflects an effort to provide a useful reference. Before an accurate and meaningful inventory can be developed much additional research must be done on both the international peace effort and on the various national and local movements. The study of the history of peace organizations and peace efforts is still somewhat underdeveloped and needs to be expanded. During the nineteenth and twentieth centuries peace organizations blossomed in great multitudes (the most recent *Guide to the Swarthmore College Peace Collection* lists over 1,500 organizations from nearly 50 nations). Just how significant some of these organizations were still needs to be determined. Moreover, a major problem in trying to develop a chronology is that peace organizations were constantly changing their names, combining with other groups to form new bodies, and producing regional and local offshoots which sometimes became more important than the original organization. Some of these changes are indicated here, but it is only a partial accounting.

For a more detailed discussion of developments in the nineteenth century see the article on *Peace Movements in the Nineteenth Century*. Readers are also advised to refer to the introductory essay *Peace "Encylopedias" of the Past and Present* and to the article on *Peace Museums*. Some of the organizations and movements displayed in this chronology have individual articles devoted to them; readers are advised to refer to the indices to access these subjects.

This chronology originally appeared in the *Biographical Dictionary of Modern Peace Leaders* (edited by Harold Josephson) and is reproduced by the kind permission of the editor and Greenwood Press, Westport, CT, USA, 1985.

Chronology of the Peace Movement

1815	New York Peace Society
	Massachusetts Peace Society
1816	Society for the Promotion of Permanent and Universal Peace (England, later known as Peace Society)
1821	Société de la morale chrétienne (France)
1828	American Peace Society
1830	La société de la paix de Genève
1838	New England Non-Resistance Society
1843	Universal Peace Congress (London)
1846	League of Universal Brotherhood (England and the United States)
1848	World Peace Congress (Brussels)
1849	World Peace Congress (Paris)
1850	World Peace Congress (Frankfurt)
1851	World Peace Congress (London)
1858	Ligue de bien public (Belgium)
1866	Universal Peace Society (United States, later renamed Universal Peace Union)
1867	Ligue internationale et permanente de la paix (Paris, becoming in 1872, Société des amis de la paix, and in 1888, Société français pour l'arbitrage entre nations)
	Ligue internationale de la paix et de la liberté (Geneva)
	Union de la paix (Le Havre)
1868	Association internationale des femmes (Geneva)
1869	Lega della pace e della libertà (Turin)
1871	Algemeen Nederlandsche Vredebond (Dutch Peace Society, after 1901, Vrede door Recht)
	Workmen's Peace Association (England, became International Arbitration League)
1873	Institute of International Law (Ghent)
	Association for the Reform and Codification of the Law of Nations
	(Brussels, reorganized as International Law Association in 1895)
1877	International Arbitration and Peace Association (England)
1878	Congres international des amis de la paix (France)
	Lega di libertà, fratellanza e pace (Milan)
1879	Women's Local Peace Association (England, became the Wisbech Local Peace Association in 1881)
1880	International Arbitration and Peace Association of Great Britain and Ireland

1882	National Arbitration League (United States)
	Society for Promotion of Danish Neutrality (first Danish peace society, later became Danish Peace Society, and still later Danish Peace and League of Nations Society)
1883	Swedish Peace and Arbitration Society
1884	Groupe des amis de la paix du Puy de Dôme (France)
1886	Christian Arbitration and Peace Society (United States)
	Liverpool and Birkenhead Women's Peace and Arbitration Association (England)
	Société de la paix du familistère du guise (France)
	Ligue internationale des femmes pour le désarmement général (Paris, became in 1900 Alliance universelle des femmes pour la paix par l'éducation)
1887–88	Association des jeunes amis de la paix (France, later La Paix par le droit)
	Società per la pace e l'arbitrato internazionale–Unione Lombarda (Milan)
	Associazione per l'arbitrato e per la pace internazionale (Rome)
	Friends Peace Committee (England)
1889	Première Conférence interparlementaire (Paris; later the Interparliamentary Union, annual meetings held until the First World War)
	World Peace Congress (Paris; peace congresses met annually with only five interruptions until the First World War)
	Nihon Heiwa-kai (first Japanese peace society)
	Société suisse de la paix (Switzerland)
	Publication of Bertha von Suttner's *Die Waffen Nieder!*
	Società della pace (Florence)
	Società della pace (Venice)
1889–90	First Pan-American Conference (Washington)
1890	Società della pace (Palermo)
1891	Österreichische Friedensgesellschaft (Austrian Peace Society)
	International Peace Bureau (Berne)
	Società della pace e l'arbitrato internazionale (Perugia)
1892	Deutsche Friedensgesellschaft (German Peace Society)
	Alliance des savants et des philanthropes (France)
1894	Société chrétienne pour la propagande de la paix (Switzerland)
1895	First Lake Mohonk Arbitration Conference (United States)
	Norwegian Peace Association
	Hungarian Peace Society
	Union internationale des femmes pour la paix I (Paris and London)
1896	National Arbitration Conference (Washington)
	Bureau française de la paix
	Ligue des femmes pour la paix et pour le désarmement international (France, later called L'Alliance universelle des femmes pour la paix et pour le désarmement)

1898	Anti-Imperialist League (United States)
	Swedish Women's Peace Association
	Association "Le paix et le désarmement par les femmes" (Paris)
1899	First Hague Peace Conference
	Association des femmes du suède pour la paix (Sweden)
	Société chrétienne des amis de la paix (France)
1900	Peace and Humanity Society (Melbourne, Australia)
1901	First Nobel Peace Prize awarded
	Société de l'éducation pacifique (France and Belgium)
	Société castraise de la paix (France)
1902	Délégation permanente des sociétés françaises de la paix
	League of Peace (Romania)
	International Museum of War and Peace (Lucerne)
1903	Groupe de l'arbitrage international (France)
1904	National Council of Peace Societies (England, became National Peace Council in 1908)
	International Anti-Militarist Union (Netherlands)
	Canadian Peace and Arbitration Society
1905	Zurich Anti-Militarism League
1906	Japan Peace Society
	Melbourne Peace Society (Australia)
	Victorian Peace Society (Australia)
	American Association for International Conciliation
	American Society for International Law
1907	Second Hague Peace Conference
	National Arbitration and Peace Congress (Washington)
	New South Wales Peace Society (Australia)
	Peace Union (Finland)
1908	Creation of Central American International Court of Justice
1909	Ligue des Catholiques français pour la paix (France)
1910	Carnegie Endowment for International Peace (United States)
	World Peace Foundation (United States)
	National Peace Council (New Zealand)
	American Society for the Judicial Settlement of International Disputes
	Publication of Norman Angell's *The Great Illusion*
	Catholic Peace Association (London)
1911	Swedish Peace Association
	Commission on International Justice and Goodwill (United States)
	Ligue internationale des pacifistes Catholiques (France)
1913	Northern Friends Peace Board (England)

1914	Church Peace Union (United States)
	No-Conscription Fellowship (England)
	Australian Peace Alliance
	Dutch Anti-War Council
	World Alliance for International Friendship Through the Churches (Geneva)
	Union of Democratic Control (England)
1915	Woman's Peace Party (United States)
	League to Enforce Peace (United States)
	Fellowship of Reconciliation (England)
	League of Nations Society (England)
	Canadian Women's Peace Party
	Women's Peace Army (Australia)
	Henry Ford's Peace Expedition (1915–16)
	Central Organization for a Durable Peace (The Hague)
	International Congress of Women (The Hague, led in 1919 to formation of Women's International League for Peace and Freedom)
1916	National Conference for Continuous Mediation (Stockholm)
	American Union Against Militarism
1917	American Friends Service Committee
	People's Council of America for Peace and Freedom
	No-Conscription League (New York)
1918	League of Nations Union (England)
	Friedensbund Deutscher Katholiken (Germany)
1919	Nie Wieder Krieg! (Never Again War!, Germany)
	League of Nations established
	Women's International League for Peace and Freedom (Zurich)
1920	Peace Union of Finland
	Peace Organization of Swedish Teachers
	League of Nations Association of Japan
	Gandhi starts first nonviolent civil disobedience campaign
1921	Women's Peace Society (United States)
	No More War Movement (England)
	War Resisters' International (originally established as PACO; became WRI in 1923)
	Washington Naval Disarmament Conference (1921–22)
	Women's Peace Society (Japan)
	International Anti-Militarist Bureau (Netherlands)
	National Council for Prevention of War (United States)
1922	Deutsche Liga für Menschenrechte (Germany)

1923	Announcement of Edward M. Bok's American Peace Award
	League of Nations Non-Partisan Association (United States, changed name to League of Nations Association in 1929)
	Antimilitaristic Union (Finland)
	Woodrow Wilson Foundation (United States)
	War Resisters League (United States)
1924	National Conference on the Cause and Cure of War (United States)
1925	Nordic Teachers' Peace Organization (Denmark)
	Union of Antimilitary Ministers in Switzerland
1927	Geneva Naval Disarmament Conference
	Catholic Association for International Peace (United States)
1928	National Anti-War League of Japan
	No More War Movement (New Zealand)
	Kellogg-Briand Peace Pact [Pact of Paris]
1929	Anti-War Congress of Intellectuals (Frankfurt)
1930	London Naval Disarmament Conference
	Second all-India nonviolent civil disobedience campaign starts
1931	Emergency Peace Committee (United States)
	Interorganization Council on Disarmament (United States)
	Ligue internationale des combattants de la paix (France)
1932	National Peace Conference (United States)
	General Disarmament Conference (Geneva, 1932–34)
	Co-operative Commonwealth Federation (Canada)
1933	Argentine Anti-War Pact
	Catholic Worker Movement (United States)
	American League Against War and Fascism (later, American League for Peace and Democracy)
1934	Peace Ballot (England)
1936	International Mennonite Peace Committee
	Peace Pledge Union (England)
	First World Peace Congress (Brussels)
	PAX (England)
	Emergency Peace Campaign (United States)
1937	No-Foreign-War Crusade (United States)
	Christian Peace Union of Switzerland
	Rassemblement international contre la guerre et le militarisme (Paris)
1938	Keep America Out of War Congress
1939	Commission to Study the Organization of Peace (United States)

1942	Congress of Racial Equality (United States)
	Publication of Quincy Wright's *A Study of War*
1943	Publication of Wendell Wilkie's *One World*
1944	Pax Christi (France)
1945	French Institute of Polemology (Paris)
	Republication of Emery Reeves' *The Anatomy of Peace*
	United Nations Organization established
1946	Swiss Peace Council
1947	United World Federalists (United States)
1948	Canadian Peace Congress
1949	Finnish Peace Committee
	Australian Peace Council
	First World Congress of Peace Partisans (Paris, launched World Council of Peace)
1951	Medical Association for Prevention of War (England)
1955	Japan Council Against Atomic Weapons
	Russell–Einstein Manifesto
1957	National Committee for a SANE Nuclear Policy (United States)
	Committee for Nonviolent Action (United States)
	(First) Pugwash Conference (on Science and World Affairs) (Pugwash, Canada)
	Journal of Conflict Resolution begins publication (United States)
1958	Campaign for Nuclear Disarmament (England)
1959	Student Peace Union (United States)
	Peace Research Institute (Oslo)
	Center for Research on Conflict Resolution (Ann Arbor, Michigan, United States)
1960	Voice of Women (Canada)
	Women Strike for Peace (United States)
	Committee of 100 (England)
1961	Turn Toward Peace (United States)
	Canadian Peace Research Institute
1962	Canadian Campaign for Nuclear Disarmament
1963	Encyclical *Pacem in Terris*
1964	*Journal of Peace Research* begins publication (Norway)
1965	International Peace Research Association Inaugural Conference (Netherlands)
	Japanese Congress Against A- and H-bombs
1966	Stockholm International Peace Research Institute
	Interchurch Peace Council (Netherlands)
1967	World Without War Council (United States)
1970	Comité national d'action pour la paix et le développement (Belgium)
1973	Nihon heiwa gakkai (Peace Studies Association of Japan)

1974	Samarbejdskomiteen for Fred og Sikkerhed (Liaison Committee for Peace and Security, Denmark)
1975	Overleg Centrum voor Vrede (Belgium)
1979	World Disarmament Campaign (England)
	Vlaams Aktic Komitee Tegen Atoomwapeds (Belgium)
1980	European Nuclear Disarmament Campaign (England)
	Kvinder for Fred (Women for Peace, Denmark)
	Nej til Tomvaben (No to Nuclear Weapons, Denmark)
1981	European Nuclear Disarmament (England)
	Movement for National Independence, International Peace and Disarmament (Greece)
1982	European Nuclear Disarmament Convention (Brussels)
	Comité pour le désarmement nucléaire en France
1983	Second European Nuclear Disarmament Convention (Berlin)

NOBEL PEACE PRIZE LAUREATES

This section comprises articles on all recipients of the Nobel Peace Prize from 1901 to 1985. There are 77 separate entries. Articles appear in chronological order by date of prize. In cases where an organization has received a prize more than once, the entry appears at the date of the first award; a cross-reference has been inserted at the appropriate date of the second or third award.

Each award has been divided into two sections: the main section relates the work of the individual or organization which led to the award of the Nobel Peace Prize; the minor section provides biographical details, placing the peace activities of the Laureate concerned in a wider context.

An attempt has been made in each article to reflect the thinking of the Nobel Committee in awarding the prize. The aim has therefore been less to provide a retrospective assessment than to examine each Laureate in the light of the contemporary preoccupations and enthusiasms of the Committee and of the peace movement itself. Readers are advised to refer to the article in Volume 1 on *Nobel Peace Prizes* for a perspective upon all the awards and upon the shifts in thinking which have influenced the decisions of the Nobel Committee.

There are a number of standard reference works for the Nobel Peace Prizes. The most important source is Frederick W. Haberman (ed.) 1972 *The Nobel Lectures, Peace*, published in three volumes by Elsevier, Amsterdam. Readers may also find the following sources useful: the work of A. Schou in the Nobel Foundation and W. Odelberg (eds.) 1972 *Nobel: The Man and His Prizes*, 3rd rev. edn. published by Elsevier, New York; M. Lipsky 1966 *The Quest for Peace*, published by Barnes and Company, South Brunswick; T. Gray 1976 *Champions of Peace*, published by Paddington Press, New York. Younger readers might be interested in the work of E. Meyer 1978 *In Search of Peace*, published by Abingdon Press, Nashville, Tennessee.

Quotations from the Nobel award ceremonies have been taken from *Les Prix Nobel*, published annually by the Imprimerie Royale, Stockholm. We are grateful to the Nobel Foundation for permission to reproduce these quotations.

Nobel Peace Prize Laureates

Henri Dunant and the Red Cross
(1901)   (1917, 1944, 1963)

Henri Dunant, founder of the Red Cross, shared the first Nobel Prize for Peace with Frédéric Passy in 1901.

The choice of Henri Dunant for the Peace Prize was greeted with heated controversy. Was it the intent of Alfred Nobel to award the mitigation of war's horrors? Nobel's personal friend of many years, Baroness von Suttner, voiced her opinion in vivid prose: "St. George rode forth to kill the dragon, not to trim its claws," she said. Von Suttner thought that allowing the monster war to develop its hideous nature freely would assure its eventual destruction from excess of evil, and she greeted this first award of the Peace Prize with scorn: "I observe that the division of the prize corresponds neither to the letter of the will nor to the testator's intention, which I know well." She did, however, applaud the choice of Frédéric Passy, founder of the Ligue Internationale et Permanente de la Paix (International and Permanent Peace League), who had been vigorously promoting peace conferences for 50 years. "Only the whole amount should have gone to him," she declared.

But the 1917, 1944, and 1963 awards to the Red Cross were destined to overrule von Suttner's objections. In its long history of assisting the victims of war, the Red Cross rescues "in the dark storm of war the idea of human solidarity and respect for the dignity of every human being, precisely at a time when the real or alleged necessities of war push moral values into the background" (Max Huber acceptance speech 1944).

The Red Cross was conceived in just such circumstances—on the plains of Northern Italy where the Battle of Solferino raged, one of the bloodiest conflicts of the nineteenth century. It was not a participant who was so fatefully moved by that awful scene, but a sensitive young Swiss businessman who had come looking for Emperor Napoleon III to discuss water rights in Algeria. All day Henri Dunant had watched from a hill through his binoculars as the battle became a massacre, with 40,000 men lying wounded or dead by nightfall.

It was not unheard of in 1859 to leave the wounded where they fell, this being accepted as their fate. But Henri Dunant was of no such mind. Commandeering men and women of the neighborhood, he worked feverishly with the few doctors there to give the wounded, from all sides, what help was possible. Without equipment, or even enough water, their aid was tragically insufficient. But the scene seered itself into his mind: Dunant's life had been changed.

Later, when he did meet with Napoleon III about the water rights, the Emperor's lack of interest and even knowledge of a drought in Algeria failed to matter to Dunant (although his indifference was not shared by his friends and associates whom he had persuaded to invest in this Algerian venture). Dunant was haunted by the battle scene, and after this nightmare had obsessed him over the next months he wrote and privately published a small book, *A Memory of Solferino* (*Un Souvenir de Solferino*) in which he proposed a plan to prevent such unnecessary suffering in the future. "Would it not be possible in time of peace and quiet," Dunant asked, "to form relief societies for the purpose of having care given to the wounded in wartime by zealous, devoted, and thoroughly qualified volunteers?" In his plan he provided that friend and foe alike, wounded and volunteers, all should have the protection of a neutral status.

Dunant had touched a universal chord of humanitarianism and people responded in such numbers that the book was twice reprinted. In Dunant's native city of Geneva a society for public service (La Société Genevoise d'Utilité Publique) appointed a committee of five, including Dunant, which arranged a conference at Geneva in October 1863 in which 16 countries participated. Here the Red Cross was born, taking its name from the reversed Swiss flag adopted as its emblem in honor of Dunant.

The Red Cross was to grow steadily in scope and stature. But such a fate was not met with by its founder. Dunant continued to invest his own resources and all of his time and energy in preparation for the next conference, traveling from country to country to extract promises of representatives. And indeed, in the next year a second Geneva conference yielded the rules of conduct regarding war-wounded and prisoners-of-war to which 12 countries became signatories. But Dunant had neglected his business and exhausted his own fortune. Suddenly he found himself facing bankruptcy, a status which carried great disgrace in his country. Shunned by friends, and even by family, he fled to Paris. There he sank into poverty and a self-imposed oblivion which he himself lifted only during the Franco–Prussian War when he once again, acting as a neutral Swiss citizen, became active on the battlefields, risking his life daily to effect the exchange of prisoners.

During this time he met with progressive Frenchmen, among them Frédéric Passy, with whom he would one day share the Nobel Prize, and he discussed with them ideas such as the rehabilitation of prisoners-of-war and training programs for soldiers for peacetime trades. They considered ways of preventing war through international arbitration courts. But though Dunant served briefly as secretary of Passy's peace society, he seemed a broken and humiliated man. At last he retired to a hospice in his native Switzerland where he lived for the rest of his life. Attempts to draw him back into active participation in the Red Cross brought limited results: he organized a Red Cross chapter in the area of his retirement; he wrote an article for Baroness von Suttner's peace paper upon her invitation. But when the news of his Nobel Prize came he sent Dr. Hans Daae to accept the award for him and directed that his share of the prize money be banked. There it stayed until his death nine years later, when, in compliance with his will, it was divided between charities in Norway and Switzerland.

A monument over his grave bears the figure of a man kneeling to offer water to a dying soldier, and a simple inscription reads: JEAN HENRI DUNANT, BORN 1828, DIED 1910. FOUNDER OF THE RED CROSS.

The Red Cross has evolved far beyond the scope of the symbol on Dunant's grave. In 1963, the year marking the centennial of the Red Cross, the Nobel Prize for Peace was divided between two sister organizations of the Red Cross: the International Committee of the Red Cross and the League of Red Cross Societies. On two previous occasions the Red Cross received the Peace Prize, both in connection with its services during military conflicts: in 1917, during the First World War and in 1944, during the closing years of the Second World War. From its celebrated beginning with Dunant's efforts to mitigate the suffering strewn in the wake of warfare, it has become an international movement concerned with the prevention and alleviation of human suffering, whether from man-made causes or natural catastrophes. It has remained independent of any government and draws much of its effectiveness through its zealously guarded neutrality.

It functions through three organizations: the International Committee of the Red Cross, the League of Red Cross Societies (which coordinates a worldwide network of national societies), and the International Conference of the Red Cross. Most countries still use the symbol of the reversed Swiss flag, a red cross on a white background, but Moslem countries use the red crescent, and Iran uses a red lion and sun.

Its highest authority rests with the International Conference of the Red Cross, a deliberative body, which calls together at four-year intervals a conference of delegates from the International Committee of the Red Cross, from the League of Red Cross Societies, and from the national Red Cross Societies (numbering 102 active societies with approximately 170,000,000 members at the time of the 1963 award), and also representatives from the governments which have signed the Geneva convention. Each delegate has one vote, and the decisions of the Conference bind the worldwide national Red Cross Societies by moral authority. A permanent International Red Cross Commission of nine members exists to discuss problems arising between conferences, and to decide when and where the next conference will be held.

The activities of the League of the Red Cross Societies and the International Committee of the Red Cross are frequently intertwined, except where the strict neutrality of the Committee separates its tasks from those of the Societies. When awarded the Nobel Prize for Peace jointly with the Committee in 1963, the League was commended for its coordinating role with the 102 active National Societies, and the resulting cooperation between people of different countries, races, creeds, and color was cited as a major contribution to international understanding and peace.

The International Committee, composed of 25 Swiss citizens, acts as intermediary between belligerents during war, and as arbitrator of disputes in times of peace. Its neutrality is of extreme importance in order that it may act free of political influences. Its members never carry weapons—they go about their tasks armed only with moral authority. The International Committee fulfills three functions which could not be performed by any other group: the protection of war victims, collecting and supplying information on missing persons, and providing relief in countries for those under duress through war.

In offering protection to war victims, Swiss delegates are sent to prisoner-of-war camps to ensure humane treatment for the captives, including adequate diet, living and detention quarters, medical care, and working conditions. They interview prisoners without the presence of witnesses. If problems are spotted, the delegates submit immediate requests for improvement. If necessary the International Committee itself will take difficulties to the higher authorities, using the principle of reciprocity as a lever. During the Second World War the International Committee's delegates carried out 11,000 camp visits. This service is now extended to civilians who are interned in wartime concentration camps where it is possible to gain admittance.

In their second function, the International Committee provides a vast network of information about prisoners-of-war and missing persons through its Central Tracing Agency. During the Second World War, with the help of thousands of volunteers, it assembled 40 million information cards in order to communicate with families anxious for news of their kin, and it communicated with as many as 6,000 families a day. Its Tracing Service at Arolsen, Germany, took on the huge and tragic task of gathering information on persons missing from concentration camps.

The Committee's third task is to supply and distribute material relief—food, clothing, medical supplies, and books. During the Second World War it organized a fleet of 14 ships which sailed under the Red Cross flag. During peacetime the Committee continues its work, gathering and distributing aid in the wake of natural disasters—earthquakes, floods, and fires—and in the aftermath of man-made catastrophes, uprisings, and myriad forms of violence.

The Committee has continued its efforts toward the development of international humanitarian law through the first Geneva Convention, written during the second Geneva conference and signed by 12 nations. Revisions of this Convention include protection during naval warfare in 1906, and for prisoners-of-war in 1929, as well as a Convention drawn up in 1949 offering protection to civilians equal to that, at least, which is extended to prisoners-of-war. It gives certain guarantees to combatants in civil wars; it prohibits executions without fair trial; it lays down humane conditions of internment and the right to protection by the International Committee. These Conventions carry only the implementation of moral authority, and sometimes the Committee faces the insurmountable difficulty of national sovereignty denying it access to a problem.

With the coming of the twentieth-century technology of nuclear physics, all Conventions are mocked until war shall yield to international law. Yet the International Committee has played a part even at the level of nuclear confrontation. During the Cuban Missile Crisis of 1962, when the United States, the Soviet Union, and Cuba engaged in a harrowing game of "brinkmanship," the Committee was asked to set up a system of 30 inspectors to ensure that no long-range atomic weapons were being delivered to Cuba. The International Committee succeeded in gaining the necessary consent to search from all three concerned powers as well as from all maritime powers whose ships called at Cuba. The crisis was resolved before the Committee was required to act, but it had proven equal to a peace-maintenance task which perhaps it alone could have performed.

Mr. Boissier, President of the International Committee, spoke of this evolution of war with the threat to all humanity posed by the hydrogen bomb. The International Committee has attempted to concentrate not on any particular weapon, he said, but on a principle which it took to the governments of the world via a draft of a proposed regulation made through the last International Red Cross Conference: "Whatever weapons are employed, the civilian population must not be harmed or at least not exposed to risks out of all proportion to the military objectives," it read. "But alas, the answer was silence," Boissier reported.

He offered hope through developing an active sense of community among people which would promote a sense of mutual responsibility for the good of humankind. "When war creates its tragic gap between nations, the Red Cross remains the last link," he said. "Its struggle against suffering is a vivid reproach to those who inflict it. It intervenes in the midst of violence, but does not have recourse thereto. The Red Cross, therefore, makes a powerful appeal, to all men, in favour of peace."

Biography of Henri Dunant

In June of 1859 Henri Dunant, a young Swiss businessman, followed Napoleon III to Italy with the intent of discussing with him water rights in Algeria. By this unlikely circumstance, Dunant happened upon the scene of the Battle of Solferino. The massacre he witnessed there turned his business trip into a personal commitment to work for a permanent, neutral, international society of volunteers, devoted to the aid of the sick and wounded during wartime.

His book, *A Memory of Solferino* [*Un Souvenir de Solferino*], recounting the affair and presenting his plan of action, galvanized society, and within a year Dunant and four members of a Geneva Committee had engineered a successful conference in Geneva with delegates attending from 16 countries. Here the Red Cross was established, choosing as its emblem the inverted flag of Dunant's native Switzerland.

Dunant set about arranging a second conference for the next year, which proved successful for the Red Cross, but financially disastrous for Dunant who had neglected his business in his feverish pursuit of his humanitarian project. From this point on, Henri Dunant suffered separation from the prospering Red Cross as he went into bankruptcy in 1867 and withdrew into a self-imposed exile which he lifted only to work on the battlefields of the Franco–Prussian War, and to work briefly with the French pacifist movement under Frédéric Passy. He returned to a hospice in Switzerland, impoverished, largely forgotten, refusing all attempts of encouragement toward rejoining society.

In 1901 he was awarded the first Nobel Prize for Peace jointly with Frédéric Passy. He did not go to receive the award, nor did he spend any of the prize money. He died nine years later, leaving a will directing the award money to charities in Norway and Switzerland.

History of the Red Cross

The Red Cross is an international movement engaged in alleviating human suffering from both natural catastrophes —floods, fires, earthquakes, famine—and man-made disasters, war and myriad violent conflicts that leave helpless victims in their wake. Its broadest aim is to improve the quality of human life throughout the world, and it accomplishes its task largely through the use of volunteers.

It was founded by a Swiss, Henri Dunant, in 1863, beginning as a neutral society with volunteers devoted to mitigating the suffering of the wounded and prisoners in wartime. It has evolved into an international organization represented by nearly all of the countries of the world and operating on a broad humanitarian basis through three organizations:

The International Conference, its highest deliberative body, holds conferences every four years with representatives from the other two Red Cross organizations and from governments signatory to the Geneva Conventions. It is here that policies and recommendations are made, and a skeletal committee of nine is maintained to function between conferences.

The International Committee of the Red Cross is composed of 25 citizens of Switzerland whose strict observance of neutrality enables them to cross international borders, during war or peace, and observe prisoner-of-war camps, run a vast network of information regarding missing persons, prisoners-of-war, and, when permitted, inmates of detention camps. Whenever possible, they assist in setting up communication between these people and their concerned families. During the Second World War, with the assistance of 4,000–5,000 volunteers, one million incoming and 900,000 outgoing messages were handled each month.

The Red Cross League facilitates cooperation between the worldwide network of 102 National Red Cross Societies, their membership numbering over 170,000,000. This is the source from which the Committee draws volunteers. Therefore the work of the Red Cross League and the International Committee often mesh. In peacetime they join together to extend disaster relief, help evacuate and resettle refugees, reunite families, and distribute relief supplies.

At the second Geneva conference in 1864 the provisions of the first Geneva Convention were signed by 12 nations, providing for relief of suffering for the wounded on battlefields. Since that time the expansion of Red Cross activities has been effected through successive similiar "Conventions," the last notable revision covering civilians throughout the world under both war and peacetime circumstances. Nearly every country of the world is now a party to these four Geneva Conventions and has a National Society. Over most of the world the emblem of the Red Cross has remained the reversed Swiss flag, a red cross on a white background, honoring its Swiss founder. Exceptions are the Moslem countries, which use the red crescent, and Iran, which uses a red lion and sun.

RUTH C. REYNOLDS

Frédéric Passy

(1901)

The first Nobel Prize for Peace was awarded to Frédéric Passy and Henri Dunant in 1901. Frédéric Passy was known as "The Apostle of Peace"—a title he richly earned. For 65 years he trod lecture platforms, put pen to paper, pouring out a prolific output from pamphlets to books, and with scholarly acumen used his training in law and economic theory in efforts to track down and destroy the causes of war.

Passy was moved by the Crimean War and the Loire flood to question why humanity could be callous to suffering in war yet feel sympathy to that caused by natural disasters. For him it was not an idle question, but rather the catalyst which thrust a generally liberal humanitarian into a lifelong commitment to a "war against war." Into this fight Passy carried two overriding weapons: a belief in free trade and a faith in arbitration. He thought that hostilities found nourishment in the acrid brew of competition, and he ardently supported the cause of free trade through which, he thought, competitors would be turned into partners in common enterprise, with the resulting environment dissolving away the cause of war.

Passy was a persuasive man. He wrote eloquent pleas in the journal *Le Temps* for peace between France and Prussia in their contest over Luxembourg in 1867, and he was widely credited for helping to avert a threatened war. In the same year he founded the Ligue Internationale de la Paix, later known as the Société Française pour l'Arbitrage entre les Nations. In 1871, following the Franco–German war, he published *Revanche ou Relèvement* (*Revenge or Retreat*), a famous appeal for a solid peace between France and Germany on the basis of voluntary arbitration, with Alsace–Lorraine as an independent neutral area.

His greatest tool for arbitration was an organization he co-founded with William Cremer (Nobel Peace Prize winner for 1903) designed to further communication, collaboration, and understanding— all tools of arbitration—between the legislators of the nations of the world. Called the Interparliamentary Union, it created regularly spaced occasions for the members of parliamentary bodies of as many nations as could be so persuaded to meet and discuss issues, to explore ways of improving collaboration between nations through their parliaments, and above all, to iron out conflicts before they could grow into "causes" in the arena of international hostilities. "It is an important assembly," Passy said, "not only on account of the number, but also the character of the members, among whom are the presidents or vice-presidents of several legislative assemblies of Europe."

Like many of Passy's projects, the Interparliamentary Union prospered. Passy recalled that the first meeting was held in a hotel parlor. Since then, he said, "they have been convened in the capitol of

Rome, and presided over by the president of the Chamber of Deputies, and at Bern in the Federal Palace . . . at The Hague, and at Brussels in the Senate Chamber." The Union functioned through the influence and character of its members, and its only means of enforcement was through moral authority.

Passy was twice elected to the French Chamber of Deputies, and while he was there he successfully urged arbitration in a dispute between France and the Netherlands over French Guiana. He also supported legislation favorable to labor, opposed the colonial policy of the government, drafted a proposal for disarmament, and presented a resolution calling for arbitration of international disputes.

Passy was capable of an unvarnished assessment of the perennial state of Europe. When he looked beyond the earnest endeavors carried on within the walls of peace conferences, beyond the work of others laboring in the field of peace, and out upon the cold reality of world events, he could speak with biting realism. In a lecture he delivered in 1891 he said, "I need hardly describe the present state of Europe to you. The entire able-bodied population is preparing to massacre one another; though no one, it is true, wants to attack and everybody protests his love of peace and determination to maintain it, yet the whole world feels that it only requires some unforeseen incident, some unpreventable accident, for the spark to fall in a flash . . . "

But when he was immersed in the most absorbing work of his life, writing of the peace congresses, the parliamentary approach to arbitration, then another side of Passy, that aspect of the man that enabled him to never yield to discouragement, emerged. In 1896 he wrote in a stunning article published in the *American Journal of Sociology* a summary of the many successes of the peace movements. He closed this article saying, "As for myself, I have labored unceasingly in this cause for thirty years, and in spite of temporary defeats and mortifications, I have never despaired of ultimate success . . . the horizon is brightening; deeds have spoken louder than words; the public mind is awakening to the necessity of arbitration. Nothing now remains for those who have fought in its behalf but a little more perseverance and hope . . . it is time to say openly . . . that the reign of violence is over and the universal conscience demands the rule of justice."

Biography

Frédéric Passy was born in 1822 in Paris, where he lived all his life. Educated as a lawyer, he left the French civil service to continue his education in the field of economics. As a theoretical economist he wrote *Mélanges économiques*, a collection of essays relating to his research. He established his scholarly reputation with his lecturing at the University of Montpellier. He belonged to the liberal tradition of the British economists Richard Cobden and John Bright, and was an ardent advocate of free trade.

He was also a firm believer in arbitration, and he worked vigorously for replacing war with arbitration as an instrument of conducting international relations. His eloquent plea for peace in *Le Temps* helped avert war between France and Prussia over Luxembourg. Following the Franco–German war he proposed arbitration between the two countries and independence for Alsace–Lorraine. As a member of the French Chamber of Deputies for terms beginning in 1881 and 1885, he successfully urged arbitration of a dispute between the Netherlands and France concerning the French Guiana–Surinam boundary. With Wil-

liam Cremer he founded the Interparliamentary Union, a vehicle for communication, collaboration, and, in case of difficulties, arbitration between members of the parliaments of all the countries who could be persuaded to participate, including countries in the New World.

His *Pour la Paix*, written when he was 87 years old, is an account of his work for international peace, including the founding of the Ligue Internationale de la Paix and the Interparliamentary Union, the development of peace congresses, and the value of the Hague Conferences.

He died in Paris on June 12, 1912.

Bibliography

Passy F 1896 Peace movement in Europe. *Am. J. Sociol.* 2(1): 1–12

RUTH C. REYNOLDS

Elie Ducommun
(1902)

The Chairman of the Nobel Peace Committee, Jorgen Gunnarson Lovland, in toasting Elie Ducommun and Charles-Albert Gobat, who shared the 1902 Peace Prize, commented on their Swiss nationality, saying that it was quite natural that three of the first four Nobel Prize winners should be Swiss because Switzerland had long been a haven for the persecuted, offering sympathy and support for peace, humanity, justice, and brotherhood among nations. Lovland thanked Ducommun for his work toward peace, done during the long, difficult years when it was received with a shaking of heads and a shrugging of shoulders, with apathy, if not with contempt.

By the close of the century, however, the peace movement had escalated beyond apathy and contempt to an increasing worldwide acceptance which Frédéric Passy, co-winner of the first Nobel Prize for Peace, described in the *American Journal of Sociology* (July 1896): "A few years ago it would have been an easy task to give an account of the peace movement in Europe, at least so far as its outward manifestations were concerned. Although there had been peace congresses held at more or less frequent intervals in Brussels, London, Frankfurt, Paris or Geneva... they seemed to have little influence. Times have changed."

"In the first place a most striking and significant fact is the ever-increasing rapidity with which these societies for the promotion of peace have sprung up." In the United Kingdom, the Peace Society was the only important one of its kind for a long time. "Today it has the satisfaction of seeing numerous

societies which have sprung up..." The story was repeated in France, and he wrote that Italy, "oppressed as it is by its military system, is a perfect hotbed for anti-military societies." Especially noteworthy progress had been accomplished in all of central Europe, in Prussia, and in Austria–Hungary. Not more than two or three years previously there had been only one peace society in Germany; "today there are at least thirty... Belgium and Holland have their own societies which are daily increasing in numbers and influence." All of these societies were putting out publications of their own, more or less widely circulated, newspapers, pamphlets, reviews, tracts, and programs. Books and periodicals were proliferating.

Such was the burgeoning nature of the international peace movement which found its first civil servant in Elie Ducommun. But the movement "was not an organic, living body," Passy said. It was only with the establishment of an authorized and permanent central information bureau for all peace work that the peace societies were united in an organic whole. Called the Bureau Internationale Permanente de la Paix (Permanent International Bureau of Peace), it was located in Bern, Switzerland, and Ducommun became its indefatigable general-secretary. Serving without pay, he organized the bureau into an institution Passy described as "the heart and brain of the whole movement, in both the old world and the new."

Passy wrote, "It has accomplished for international peace and justice that which has been done in other departments by international postal and tele-graph bureaus, and by international copyright laws. By this means all the different publications on this subject are collected, news is recorded, information obtained, doubtful or obscure questions explained, propositions forwarded and opinions received. Thus it is coming to be, under the efficient direction . . . of M. Elie Ducommun, the living soul of the great body of peacemakers all over the world" (Passy 1896).

It was a monumental undertaking, both adminis-tratively and in its sheer clerical scope, and Ducom-mun achieved it alone, including issuing a bimonthly news-sheet, *Correspondence Bimensuelle*. Despite this burden, he still found the time to edit and write numerous articles and pamphlets. In one of the most famous of these, he refuted the popular idea that war, when it came, though fearful, would necessarily be of very short duration. He argued that, on the contrary, a system of trenches and fortresses could lead to a long-drawn-out war of attrition with alter-nating advances and retreats. He foretold, with awful accuracy, the shape of things to come in the First World War.

In addition, with the help of a council of 19 mem-bers, Ducommun planned the International Peace Congresses and implemented their decisions. All of this formidable peace work was accomplished in the time he had free after other considerable pursuits. He was, for example, a member of the Grand Council in Bern for ten years. For 30 years, beginning in 1875, he was secretary-general of the Jura–Bern–Lucerne railroad, later called the Jura–Simplon line, a posi-tion that required, according to Frédéric Passy, "the rarest qualities of exactitude, order, activity, and firmness." These qualities Ducommun also devoted to directing the International Bureau of Peace, as witnessed by its progress. This organization was run single handedly by Ducommun and the work was continued by Charles-Albert Gobat with whom he shared the Peace Prize.

In his Nobel lecture Ducommun commented on one question often asked of pacifists: "Granted that war is evil, what can you find to put in its place when an amicable solution becomes impossible? The trea-ties of arbitration concluded in the past few years provide an answer," he said. "The Convention for the Pacific Settlement of International Disputes signed at The Hague in 1899 by twenty-six nations offers a solution to international conflicts by a method unknown in the ancient world, in the Middle Ages, or even in modern history—a method of set-tling quarrels between nations without bloodshed."

Biography

Elie Ducommun was born on February 19, 1833, son of a clockmaker from Neuchâtel, Switzerland. After completing his early studies in Geneva at the age of 17, he tutored in a wealthy family in Saxony for three years and perfected his German. Upon his return to Geneva, he taught in public schools for two years. He then began a career in journalism which would prove to be a distinguished one, editing first a political journal, the *Revue de Genève*, and upon moving to Bern, founding a radical journal, *Der Fortschrift* (*Progress*), which was also published in French under the title *Progrès*. He took an active part in the movement for European union, editing the news-sheet *Les États-Unis d'Europe*, pub-lished by the Ligue Internationale de la Paix et de la Liberté (International League for Peace and Freedom) founded in 1867. In 1871 he edited *Helvétie*. He also published poetry.

Ducommun held political posts of local consequence: in Geneva, prior to his leaving in 1865, he was a member of the Grand Council for nine years, becoming vice-chancellor in 1857 and chancellor of the state of Geneva in 1862. In Bern he was a member of the Grand Council for 10 years. For 30 years, beginning in 1875, he was secretary-general of the Jura–Simplon railroad line.

In 1889 Ducommun participated in the first of the regular International Peace Congresses. Two years later he became general-secretary of the newly founded International Peace Bureau, to which he devoted much time and for which he published *Correspondance Bimensuelle*. He wrote a number of articles and pamphlets for the peace movement and lectured.

Elie Ducommun died in Bern on December 7, 1906.

Bibliography

Passy F 1896 Peace movement in Europe. *Am. J. Sociol.* 2(1): 1–12

RUTH C. REYNOLDS

Charles-Albert Gobat

(1902)

The peace societies, which the Nobel Committee Chairman, Jorgen Gunnarsson Lovland, called "the popular peace movement," were doubly honored by the award of the 1902 Peace Prize to two of their strongest advocates, Charles-Albert Gobat and Elie Ducommun. Chairman Lovland congratulated Dr.

Gobat as a practitioner of a new type of diplomacy—parliamentary diplomacy. "Far from finding himself in opposition," Lovland said, "he has already demonstrated that these two kinds of diplomatic service can and do exist in cordial cooperation."

Charles-Albert Gobat was a gifted lawyer, legislator, educator, and advocate for peace. He simultaneously practiced law and taught at Bern University. He became interested in education and rose to a top administrative position as superintendent of public instruction for the Canton of Bern. He demonstrated his liberal bent by his progressive reforms in primary training, by lowering the pupil–teacher ratio, by introducing studies in living languages, and by providing vocational and professional training as alternatives to strict classical education. He demonstrated his capability as administrator by getting the budgetary means for supporting his program.

Concurrent with this activity, Gobat applied himself with customary vigor and effect to a political career. In 1882 he was elected to the Grand Council of Bern, and he was president of the cantonal government from 1886 to 1887. From 1884 to 1890 he was a member of the Council of States of Switzerland, and from 1890 until his death a member of the National Council.

Gobat was attracted to the Interparliamentary Union from its inception by two recipients of the Noble Peace Prize, William Cremer (1903) and Frédéric Passy (1901). It was a vehicle admirably suited to embrace his advocacy of peace through arbitration. The Union offered opportunities for members of parliaments from all countries to discuss international issues with each other, and thereby to enhance collaboration among nations through the means of parliamentary and democratic institutions. Transcending national boundaries without limiting the independence of any nation, or setting itself above the parliaments to which its members belonged, it was, in the words of Frédéric Passy (1896), "indeed a higher parliament, but one which possesses its influence through the weight and character of its members themselves, and which exerts a moral authority." Its most vital objective was to achieve international arbitration. In the intervals between the sessions of the Interparliamentary Union it was represented by a delegation of 15 members over whom Gobat presided. This delegation was charged with monitoring the political scene in the name of the Union.

Gobat ardently promoted arbitration. As a legislator he sponsored its application to Swiss commercial treaties wherein all treaties contained a clause which required the submission of any conflicts between the signing parties to the Permanent Court of Arbitration at The Hague.

When Gobat was presiding at the Union's fourth conference in 1892 at Bern, it established the Interparliamentary Bureau, choosing Bern as its locale. Gobat directed this Bureau for the next 17 years. Like the Permanent International Bureau of Peace, the Interparliamentary Bureau was a permanent information and administrative office. Gobat supervised the myriad details involved in listing parliamentary groups of various countries, initiating formation of groups where none existed, acting as a link between national groups, keeping track of activities in the peace movement and in the field of arbitration, attending to the administration of conferences, their agendas, and publications of proceedings, and presiding over a monthly publication for which he frequently wrote contributions. This he did almost unaided, and without remuneration.

It was decided in 1904 at the twelfth Interparliamentary Conference to call for a second Hague Peace Conference. Gobat, acting as the Union's spokesman, asked the US President, Theodore Roosevelt, to appeal to all nations to participate. Roosevelt consented, and shortly thereafter had the US Secretary of State issue a circular to the other nations.

In his Nobel lecture, Gobat described the important potentialities he visualized coming from future Hague Conferences: "Civilization and morality have not yet influenced nations to consider inviolable a promise or agreement, solemnly signed and sealed, when it becomes part of international law. Ordinary citizens are obliged and, if need be, compelled by force to meet their commitments. But let higher obligations of an international order be involved, and governments repudiate them, more often than not with a disdainful shrug of the shoulders."

This dilemma he saw amenable to a system of conciliation and mediation wherein with every possible conflict there would be an already established group of nations from which at least one could offer its good offices. "Good offices" would mean intercession between the belligerents in an effort to effect conciliation. A further step would be mediation. Whereas good offices would be limited to assuring preliminary conciliation, the mediator could go so far as to propose terms of settlement.

Gobat cited an instance in which such a procedure had actually worked. President Theodore Roosevelt (Nobel Peace Prize winner for 1906) persisted in offering his good offices to the warring Russians and Japanese. Exhausted by a terrible war, both accepted and peace was concluded. Thus President Roosevelt was the first head of state to apply the rules of the Hague Convention concerning the preservation of general peace.

Upon the death of Elie Ducommun in 1906, Gobat succeeded him as director of the International Peace Bureau, itself subsequently a Nobel Peace Prize winner in 1910.

Gobat had the privilege of living to the last moment of his life doing that in which he most believed. On March 16, 1914, while attending a meeting of the peace conference at Bern, he arose as if to speak and collapsed. He died shortly after.

Biography

Charles-Albert Gobat was born in Tramelan, Switzerland, son of a Protestant pastor. A gifted scholar, he studied at the Universities of Basle, Heidelberg, Bern and Paris, and took his law degree *summa cum laude* from Heidelberg in 1867. His legal career included both the practice of law and teaching at Bern University. He opened an office in Delemont in the Canton of Bern which became a leading legal firm.

After 15 years Gobat became interested in education and was appointed superintendent of public instruction for the Canton of Bern. During his 30 years in this position he introduced such progressive measures as lowered pupil–teacher ratio, studies in living languages, and vocational and professional training as an alternative to strict classical education.

In the 1880s he became active in cantonal and national politics, and in 1882 he was elected to the Grand Council of Bern. He was elected president of the cantonal government for the 1886–1887 term. From 1884 to 1890 he was a member of the Council of States of Switzerland, and from 1890 a lifelong member of the National Council.

From its inception in 1888, Gobat worked with the Interparliamentary Union, an organization in which members of parliaments from all nations could meet, discuss, and, it was hoped, arbitrate in disputes before they became insurmountable problems.

When the Interparliamentary Bureau was founded as an action of the fourth Union Conference, its locale placed in Bern, Gobat became its general-secretary, keeping available information about peace movements, international conciliation, and communication among national parliamentary bodies. This he did with devotion and without remuneration.

Upon the death of Elie Ducommun, who headed the Permanent International Bureau of Peace, Gobat stepped into this role.

Best known among his books on international affairs is *Le Couchemar de l'Europe* (*The Nightmare of Europe*), which he wrote in 1911.

Charles-Albert Gobat died on March 16, 1914, while in attendance at a peace conference.

Bibliography

Passy F 1896 Peace movement in Europe. *Am. J. Sociol.* 2(1): 1–12

RUTH C. REYNOLDS

William Cremer

(1903)

The 1903 Nobel Prize for Peace was awarded to William Cremer in recognition of the 34 years of effective work he devoted to the cause of peace, most notably through the initiation and organization of the Interparliamentary Union. "It has been the great object of my life to build up and endow a great peace organization which should be powerful enough to combat the forces which make for war," Cremer declared in his Nobel lecture.

That was an impressive goal to be realized by a child of an impoverished family of the working class. Cremer was born in Fareham, England, in 1828 to a coach painter and his wife. Cremer's indomitable mother raised her three children alone when the father deserted his family during Cremer's infancy. Through sacrifice and determination she sent her son to a Methodist church school, but when he was 15 his formal education ended as he entered the building trade as an apprentice carpenter.

Cremer supplemented his meager education by attending lectures, and one night he heard a lecture which powerfully affected the course of his life. The speaker suggested that international disputes could be settled by arbitration. It was an idea that found fertile soil in Cremer's mind, and he was destined for a powerful role in bringing it to successful fruition.

The young carpenter proved to be a gifted administrator. In 1858, at the age of 30, he was elected to a labor council compaigning for a nine-hour day; later that year he was one of seven who directed labor during a lock-out of 70,000 workers. He helped form a union for his trade, the Amalgamated Society of

Carpenters and Joiners. In 1870 he formed a workers' committee to promote the United Kingdom's neutrality during the Franco–Prussian conflict. This committee developed into the International Arbitration League. "We were laughed to scorn as mere theorists and utopians," he said. "The scoffers declaring that no two countries in the world would ever agree to take part in the establishment of such a court."

By then a recognized leader, Cremer went to Parliament in 1885 and remained there for the rest of his lifetime, except for the period 1895–1900 when he suffered his single defeat in the hustings. Cremer used his power as a Member of Parliament to advance his sustained work for peace.

The Hague Tribunal became a reality, with the initiating efforts of Cremer's workers' committee having played a vital role in its creation. The wealthy US industrialist Andrew Carnegie supplied funds for the construction of its home in the Palace of Peace at The Hague. In his Nobel lecture, Cremer recalled some of its successes: in 1904 a Russian fleet fired on English fishing trawlers at Dogger Bank, sinking a vessel and damaging five others, in the process killing two and wounding six. Despite the "frantic efforts of some British journals to provoke a conflict," the two governments agreed to resort to the offices of the Hague Tribunal. The affair ended with Russia paying an indemnity of £65,000.

With its peacekeeping machinery at the ready, the Hague Tribunal accomplished many friendly mediations and arbitrations. By far the most important was the dispute between the United States and the United Kingdom when the *Alabama*, a ship constructed at British shipyards for the Confederacy during the Civil War, manned by a Southern captain with a partially British crew, wreaked havoc with Northern shipping. The Hague ruled in favor of the United States, and the British accepted the decision (see Articles: *Arbitration, International*).

In 1887 Cremer felt the League came into its "proven phase" when the governments of the United Kingdom and the United States entered into a treaty which bound them to settle their differences by arbitration. It set a precedent, and within 12 months 13 similar treaties were concluded between various nations: Great Britain and France; France and Italy; Great Britain and Italy; Denmark and Holland; Great Britain and Spain; France and Spain; France and Holland; Spain and Portugal; Germany and Great Britain; Great Britain, Norway, and Sweden; Great Britain and Portugal; Switzerland and Great Britain; Sweden, Norway, and Belgium. Seven other treaties had been drafted between the United States and European countries at the time of Cremer's accounting during the Nobel award lecture.

Cremer answered skeptics about the actual use of the treaties once drawn up with the example of France and Great Britain. "All of the differences between the two countries, some of which had lasted for centuries, have been equitably adjusted," he said in a review of the first 12 months of the treaty. He was confident that under the treaties disputing nations would have time, during arbitration, to cool their tempers and the chances of war would be greatly diminished.

This "people's victory," fruit of the efforts of the British and French workers who inaugurated the first Treaty of Arbitration, excited the interest of Frédéric Passy and other French deputies, and together they expanded Cremer's efforts into a new force, called the Interparliamentary Union. The Union provided opportunities for members of parliaments from every cooperating country to meet together, discuss issues, and if any disputes were imminent, to prevent them from becoming "causes" and fanned into military conflicts.

Passy, co-winner of the first Nobel Peace Prize, described the participants of the Interparliamentary Union in an article published by the *American Journal of Sociology* (July 1896): "It is an important assembly, not only on account of the number, but also the character of the members, among whom are the presidents or vice-presidents of several legislative assemblies of Europe . . . it is indeed a higher parliament, but one which possesses its influence through the weight and character of its members themselves and which exerts a moral authority . . . "

In his Nobel lecture Cremer pointed out that the Union had not only reduced frictions between European countries, but had also brought together the United States and European countries, with resulting increased understanding between nations of the Old World and the New. "There is still a great work before us," Cremer declared in closing his lecture. "The advocates of peace are, however, no longer regarded as idle dreamers . . . our cause has, especially of late, made wonderful progress and we are nearing the goal of our hopes."

Cremer gave the money from his Nobel prize to the International Arbitration League. Thus he realized his lifelong dream of endowing a great peace organization which would combat the forces that generate war.

Biography

William Randal Cremer was born in Fareham, England, on March 18, 1828. He was the son of a coach painter who deserted his family of two daughters and the infant Cremer, and of an indomitable mother who saw that he got some education before he entered the workforce as an apprentice in the building trade. He became a leader among the workers, helping to found a union, the Amalgamated Society of Carpenters and Joiners. He realized the first step in his lifelong dream of contributing to a peaceful world by forming a workers' committee to advocate British neutrality during the Franco–Prussian War (1870–1871). This group developed into the Workmen's Peace Association, which in turn contributed to the creation of the International Arbitration League, of which Cremer became Secretary. It ultimately developed into the Hague Tribunal.

Cremer was elected to the House of Commons in 1885; with the exception of five years, from 1895 to 1900, he remained there until his death. He attracted the notice of Frédéric Passy, and in 1888 the two founded the Interparliamentary Union, a mechanism for the free communication between Members of Parliaments internationally, and for arbitration in international affairs through ongoing communication and understanding between Members of Parliaments.

Cremer married twice, his first wife dying in 1876, his second in 1884. He was knighted in 1907. He died in London in 1908.

Bibliography

Passy F 1896 Peace movement in Europe. *Am. J. Sociol.* 2(1): 1–12

RUTH C. REYNOLDS

Institute of International Law
(1904)

In 1904 the Nobel Peace Prize was awarded to the Institute of International Law (Institut de Droit International). Under its banner of *Justica et Pace* (justice and peace), this Institute of a totally private nature seeks to provide the general principles of international jurisprudence needed to underlie effective work for peace. "We cannot hope to achieve peace until law and justice regulate international as well as national relations," its president, Georg Hagerup, said in receiving the 1904 award. "*Justica et Pace* means eliminating, as far as possible, the sources of international friction which result from uncertainties and differences of opinion in the interpretation of the law. It means constructing by unremitting and patient work, block by block, the foundation that will support the rule of law over nations and peoples."

Presently located in Geneva, as of 1986 the Institute has a total of 60 members and 72 associates. It continues to promote the progress of international law wherein its range of activity covers the codification of international law, both public and private. In private international law, it strives to minimize or eliminate difficulties from differences existing in laws of different countries. In public law, it works to develop peaceful ties between nations. The organization may be credited for many previously unwritten and inexact laws now codified, legislated, and placed on statute books.

Founded in 1873 by G. Rolin-Jaquemyns, a Belgian jurist, and editor of the *Revue de droit international et de législation comparée,* with 10 distinguished jurists from as many countries, this private association of scholars from all nations who come together for the study, codification, and promotion of international law draws its members from candidates who have made a scholarly contribution in either the area of theory or of practice in international law, and who are free from political pressures. The Institute strives for a reasonably balanced representation from the nations of the world.

In his Nobel lecture, Hagerup warned against too easy an interpretation of arbitration, pointing out that careful preparatory work is required. It is in this area that the Institute of International Law has supplied invaluable services. The Institute was charged with most of the burden of preparing for the First International Arbitration Conferences at the Hague in 1899 and 1907, and these conferences utilized the Institute's studies on the laws of war, especially those on the codification of land war prepared at its 1880 session in Oxford called *Handbook of the Rules and Observances of Warfare.* Recognizing the "considerable place war occupies in the pages of history," the Institute sought in this handbook to reduce the destruction of war. During the Russo–Turkish War, it facilitated the neutralization of the Suez Canal in the event of war, under the principle of neutralizing all areas vital to international communication. Similarly, under the influence of the Institute, submarine cables were given international protection in a treaty signed by 27 states in Paris on March 14, 1884. Also, the Interparliamentary Union, founded in 1888 for the purpose of establishing and maintaining permanent lines of communication and conferences between members of parliaments from various countries over the world, acknowledged dependence upon the Institute for assistance based upon international public law.

Between 1873 and 1969, 15 directly applicable resolutions and many other indirectly applicable resolutions coming from the Institute were used in settlements of international disputes. Its range in time and subject covers from the above international treaties of the 1880s on the Suez Canal and on the submarine cable to recent discussions by the Institute on pollution of international waters providing direction for research on that pressing, contemporary problem.

The Institute has worked out general rules in the area of private international law. It formulated codifications of extradition rules, of uniform treatment of marriage, divorce and trusteeship, of rights of citizenship, of treatment of private property during wartime.

The Institute of International Law does not itself participate in the settlement of international controversies. (There is a historical exception to this rule in its adoption of a resolution in 1877 pertaining to the application of international law in the war between Russia and Turkey.)

Hagerup's closing remarks on the Institute of International Law in his 1904 Nobel lecture have proven prophetic: "If our work has had some success, it is undoubtedly because of our efforts to 'calculate the limits of the possible', as one great statesman put it; because of our patience in refusing to advocate premature solutions; and because of our belief in the necessity of developing *gradually* and *progressively* as our statutes bid us."

He said the Institute's independence of any authority or political faction constitutes its strength. The continuing study devoted to the nature of law, to the conditions of its development, and its place in the progress of human civilization in general, gave members the necessary perspective with which to judge factors holding the most promise to encourage support of international law and justice.

"All attempts to further human progress should have far-reaching aims," Hagerup said, "and those who wish to take an active part in the effort should not lose patience if the progress sometimes appears to be very slow, or even to sustain interruptions and setbacks ... but let us take heart in the discerning word spoken by Mirabeau a century ago: 'Law will one day become the sovereign of the world.'"

History

The Institute of International Law (Institut de Droit International) was founded by a group of international jurists in 1873 in recognition of the need to promote international law, in both private and public fields. Their guiding spirit and initiator was Gustave Rolin-Jaquemyns, a Belgian jurist and editor of the *Revue de droit international et de législation comparée*, who following the Franco–Prussian War of 1870–71, began a correspondence with jurists over the world to seek ways of establishing collective action toward creating a body of international law.

At his invitation 10 eminent jurists assembled for meetings in the town Hall of Ghent in September, 1873: Tobias Asser of the Netherlands (Nobel Peace Prize Winner in 1911), Wladimir Besobrasoff of Russia, J.K. Bluntschli of Germany, Carlos Calvo of Argentina, David Dudley Field of the United States, Emile de Laveleye of Belgium, James Lorimer of Great Britain, P.S. Mancini of Italy, Gustave Moynier of Switzerland, and Augusto Pierantoni of Italy. This group established the Institute, electing Mancini President. They held their first session in Geneva in 1874 at which time they established the general principles for international judicial proceedings; the next year the Institute formulated rules for the competency of the tribunals. The actual forms of procedure were dealt with in 1877 and the following year the rules were drawn up for the execution of judgments.

The participants are confined to jurists with a demonstrated record of scholarly attainment, either practical or theoretical, and who are free of political pressures. Maintaining a balanced representation from the nations of the world further influences choice of membership. The participants fall into three categories. The associates are kept at 72 in number. This group forms the source from which the members, 60 in number, are drawn. Members deal with administrative matters such as finances, regulations, and election of members and honorary members. They choose the third category of participants, honorary members, from persons distinguished in the field of law.

The president is usually selected from the country scheduled to host the next session of the Institute, and, along with the first vice-president, is elected at the end of a given session. These two officers remain in office until the close of the following session. The second and third vice-presidents are elected at the opening of each session and remain in office until the start of the next session. The secretary–general and the treasurer are elected for three sessions and may succeed themselves. These six officers form the body of the Bureau of the Institute, which holds and exercises the executive power of the Institute.

Following the Nobel Prize, and with additional grants from the Carnegie Endowment for International Peace, plus lesser gifts, the Institute has accrued the financial footing with which to reimburse members for travel expenses, to underwrite the expenses of the sessions, and to pay for publications.

The Institute conducts a continuous study of existing international law, but is does not intervene in actual international disputes. It does, however, formulate and endorse specific proposals serving the goal of creating an international community respecting law and justice.

The Institute's publication, biennial, is *Annuaire;* its present secretary–general is Nicolas Valticos, its next scheduled biennial meeting will take place in 1987.

See also: Articles: *Arbitration, International; International Law*

Bibliography

Abrams I 1957 The emergence of the International Law Societies. *Review of Politics* 19: 361–80

RUTH C. REYNOLDS

Bertha von Suttner

(1905)

The 1905 Nobel Peace Prize went to the Austrian Baroness Bertha von Suttner. Of all the peace leaders of the quarter century before 1914, she enjoyed the greatest international reputation. To her contemporaries this handsome woman of dignified presence seemed to personify the cause she served. Her fellow peace workers called her their "general-in-chief"; her detractors scoffed at "Peace-Bertha" and delighted in the cartoons that satirized the peace movement in her womanly form. Whether drawing applause, brickbats, or simply public attention, she was certainly one of the best-known women of her day.

The Peace Prize was the supreme recognition of the Baroness's many contributions to the peace cause. She was the author of the most widely read antiwar novel of the time, *Die Waffen Nieder!,* (see Articles: *Die Waffen Nieder!*), a tireless propagandist for peace by pen and in lectures throughout the Germanic countries and as far afield as the United States, a major figure at world peace congresses, an organizer and inspirer of peace societies in Germany and Austria–Hungary. More quietly, she carried the peace message in personal meetings with statesmen and diplomats.

These may seem unusual attainments for the former Countess Bertha Kinsky, a descendant of army officers, born in 1843 in the Austro–Hungarian empire, but the Countess did not remain on the conventional paths marked out for a highborn Austrian lady. After acquiring foreign languages and social graces, she very early asserted her independence. When her family fortunes were depleted, she took a job to earn her own living as governess to the daughters of the Baron von Suttner. She and the son of the family fell in love and eloped to the Caucasus. There they read widely in science, philosophy, and history and became published writers themselves. Finally

forgiven by the von Suttner family, the couple returned to Austria to take their place among the liberal intelligentsia of that center of intellectual and cultural fermentation.

As a firm believer in Immanuel Kant's ethical idealism (see Articles: *Kant, Immanuel*) and in evolution and progress, it was not unusual that Bertha von Suttner chose to write a novel on the evils of war which seemed so out of keeping with the future she envisaged. What was not to be expected was that her research on the wars of the mid-century would make her such a committed pacifist, nor that the novel would meet with such stunning success and involve her "with all my being" in the newly developing peace movement.

The novel was published in 1889, just when the modern peace movement was organizing internationally. While peace-minded deputies from national legislatures were establishing the Interparliamentary Union, representatives from peace societies emerging on the Continent were meeting with their Anglo–Saxon counterparts to take up again the world peace congresses that had not been held for many years. The Baroness soon became one of the leaders of the movement, vice-president of the Commission of the International Peace Bureau when it was established in 1892 to provide some coordination for the unofficial peace efforts in the different countries. She inspired and organized peace societies and interparliamentary groups in Central Europe and served as an important force for moderation and conciliation when political and religious differences arose.

In reading through her abundant correspondence which she carried on in three languages—letters selected for her *Memoirs,* and those unpublished but fortunately preserved in the Library of the United Nations in Geneva—one is impressed by the high regard in which she was held by her co-workers, and one marvels at the extent and variety of her exchanges with so many influential personages from all over Europe—politicians, diplomats, writers, professors, and others.

Among her friends was Alfred Nobel, the dynamite magnate, whom she had known before she became a pacifist and who had written to congratulate her after reading *Die Waffen Nieder!* The letters they exchanged tell of how the Baroness cultivated his interest in the peace movement, first enlisting his financial support for her own peace efforts and eventually contributing to his decision to endow the movement through his Peace Prize. It is clear from their correspondence and other evidence that Nobel never expected that the Baroness would have to wait until the fifth year of these awards to receive her own prize.

Suttner poured her creative energies so completely into her work for peace that after *Die Waffen Nieder!* she never wrote another successful novel, but in her writing on international events for the peace periodicals she displayed skills as a most perceptive and adept political commentator, the first woman political journalist in the German language.

In conjunction with the meeting of the First Hague Peace Conference (1899), Suttner held a salon for the delegates that was the first effective international peace lobby on record. Through their discussions with the diplomats the Baroness and the other peace advocates succeeded in persuading the conferees of the importance of establishing machinery to resolve international conflicts rather than concerning themselves exclusively with the less hopeful matter of reduction of armaments, which the Czar's original call for the conference had emphasized. It turned out that the Hague Conference produced negligible results for disarmament, but at least a first step was taken in the direction of peacekeeping machinery through the agreement to establish the Permanent Court of Arbitration at The Hague.

Although the Baroness talked of the need for a federation of Europe, it was the institutionalization of arbitration that was the more immediate objective of the Baroness and her friends. They wanted to be looked upon as practical reformers, not just visionaries, and they did not urge a fundamental change in the international order. As established members of the upper and middle classes, even further from their minds was the contention of the socialists that the only way to end war was to change the social order. The two groups agreed only on their criticisms of war and war policies. The German Social Democrats

did run *Die Waffen Nieder!* in their newspaper, but the Baroness had not written it to arouse the masses to political action.

Such was the basis of the most biting criticism of Bertha von Suttner, written by a German pacifist 10 years after her death. Carl von Ossietzky, no socialist but a staunch antimilitarist journalist (and 1935 Peace Prize laureate), blamed her for starting off the German peace movement on the wrong track with her "tearful novel." He paid her honor for her "extraordinary and honest efforts" but said that "she fought with holy water against cannon, she adored with touching childishness treaties and institutions— a priestess of sentiment, she appealed to the consciences of kings and statesmen. . . ."

It is unfortunate that Bertha von Suttner is remembered by so many only for her portrayal of human suffering in her novel. Through the years, in her day-to-day activities as pacifist and lecturer, she appealed for the exercise of reason and good sense in the conduct of foreign policy. Her commentaries on world affairs pointed again and again to the fateful consequences of ill-conceived policies. Her Nobel lecture was no sentimental denunciation of war but a reasoned appeal for peace, based upon an abiding faith in the moral evolution of humanity and a conviction that she was serving "the greatest of all causes."

This faith sustained her in the face of the abuse of the militarists and jingoists and the much more serious obstacle of general apathy. At the end of the century there had been no major war for a generation and public opinion was complacent, concerned at most with the burdens of the armed peace rather than with the fear of war. Even the measure of success that the peace leaders gained at the First Hague Conference evoked little general response. "Cold, cold are all the hearts," the Baroness lamented, noting that there was far more interest in current sports events.

It was particularly difficult to raise the flag of peace in the empires of Germany and Austria–Hungary, where military institutions were deeply rooted. Yet her activities there helped the peace forces in other countries to maintain that the movement was indeed international.

Bertha von Suttner set a precedent for the leadership that women would one day be taking in the international peace movement. The Baroness was "general-in-chief," at a time when a woman was neither expected nor encouraged to play a role as a public figure. It would take another 25 years, in fact, before the Norwegian Nobel Committee would bestow their next Peace Prize on a woman, Jane Addams.

Fate spared Bertha von Suttner from having to witness the catastrophe she had labored to prevent. She died in 1914 in Vienna, shortly before the outbreak of the First World War which brought the cancellation of the World Peace Congress that was to have met there in her honor.

The Baroness has since been honored in several countries through place names, postage stamps, and even an Austrian banknote. There is still a peace society in Vienna that keeps her memory alive. But who reads *Die Waffen Nieder!* any more? The horrors of nineteenth-century warfare which it depicted so vividly were already outpaced in the war that began the year of her death. All the same, Suttner was the first to sound the alert so convincingly in a popular medium, and she was not unheard. The coming of the war in 1914 did not invalidate what the Baroness and her friends had been saying; it confirmed their warnings. She said in her Nobel lecture in 1906 that "this question of whether violence or law shall prevail between states is the most vital of the problems of our eventful era. ... Inconceivable ... would be the consequences of the threatening world war which many misguided people are prepared to precipitate."

The mediocre statesmen who stumbled into war in the summer of 1914 do not compare very favorably with the high-minded humanitarians who had tried so hard to prevent it. If we judge such humanitarians, working for a distant aim, rather by the quality of their effort than by their success or failure in bringing the new world into being, then Bertha von Suttner must receive the very highest marks.

Biography

Baroness Bertha von Suttner was born Bertha Felicie Sophie von Kinsky, in 1843 daughter of impoverished Austrian nobility. Her father, Count Franz Josef Kinsky, an Austrian field marshal, died shortly after her birth. On her mother's side she was descended from the family of the German poet, Theodor Körner. From 1873 to 1876 she was governess in the wealthy von Suttner family. In this position she met the family scion, Baron Gundaccar Arthur von Suttner, seven years her junior, and they fell in love with one another. The family opposing the match, Bertha von Kinksy answered an advertisement written by Alfred Nobel, a wealthy inventor, for a secretary. After an exchange of correspondence, she was invited for an interview and was accepted for the position. However, she stayed only five days, and then eloped with Baron von Suttner. The couple lived in the Caucasus, earning a meager living writing, supplemented by occasional other work,

until they were received again in the von Suttner family, at which point they returned to Vienna.

Although her acquaintance with Nobel had been brief, it had lasting import, for they carried on a correspondence for the remainder of Nobel's life regarding their mutual interest in peace. It was through this correspondence that she exerted considerable influence toward his establishing the Nobel Peace Prize (see Articles: *Nobel Peace Prizes*). They met again in 1887 when the von Suttners were staying in Paris, and then in 1892 in Berne where the Baroness was attending a peace conference.

In 1888 Baroness von Suttner wrote *Das Maschinenzeitalter (The Machine Age)*, and in 1889 the novel which was to catapault her to fame, *Die Waffen Nieder!(Lay Down Your Arms!)*. Tolstoy compared her novel to *Uncle Tom's Cabin,* an American novel which greatly promoted antislavery sentiment in the United States. It is generally considered that *Lay Down Your Arms!* was one of the most influential novels of the nineteenth century.

The Baroness founded the Austrian Peace Society (*Osterreichische Friedensgesellschaft*) in 1891, and the same year took a leading role in the International Peace Congress in Rome. She helped found the International Peace Bureau and became vice president of its governing Commision. In 1892 Alfred Fried, founder of the German Peace Society (and 1911 Peace Prize co-winner), started a periodical which he named after Baroness von Suttner's famous novel, and persuaded her to become its editor-in-chief. She remained in this position until 1899. She also attended many conferences and lectured extensively.

Baroness von Suttner's pacifism had a scientific and freethinking basis, reflecting the thought of Herbert Spencer and Charles Darwin; it was intended to convince the upper and middle classes.

A prolific writer, she wrote not only on peace and social issues, but also tales of romances. Among her titles are: *Hanna* (1894), *Krieg und Frieden* (1986), *La Traviata* (1898), *Schach der Qual* (1898), *Die Haager Friedenskonferenz* (1900), and *Marthas Kinder* (1902). This last was a continuation of *Die Waffen Nieder!*.

Baroness von Suttner died in Vienna in 1914, shortly before the outbreak of the First World War.

Bibliography

Abrams I 1962 Bertha von Suttner and the Nobel Peace Prize. *Central European Affairs* XXII: 286–307

Chickering R 1975 *Imperial Germany and a World Without War: The Peace Movement and German Society, 1892–1914.* Princeton, New Jersey

Kempf B 1972 *Woman for Peace: The Life of Bertha von Suttner.* London

Lengyel E 1975 *And All Her Paths Were Peace: The Life of Bertha von Suttner.* Nashville

Pauli H 1957 *Cry of the Heart: The Story of Bertha von Suttner.* New York

Playne C E 1936 *Bertha von Suttner and the Struggle to Avert the World War.* London

Suttner B von 1972 The evolution of the peace movement. In: Haberman F W (ed.) 1972 *Nobel Lectures, Peace*, Vol. 1. Elsevier, Amsterdam, pp. 84–90

Suttner B von 1909 *Memoiren.* Stuttgart (reissued as *Lebenserinnerungen,* ed. by Fritz Böttger East Berlin 1969; English transl. 1910. *Memoirs of Bertha von Suttner: The Records of an Eventful Life,* 2 vols. Boston, Massachusetts; reissued 1972, New York with introduction by Irwin Abrams)

Suttner B von 1889 *Die Waffen Nieder! Eine Lebensgeschichte.* Dresden (English transl. 1892 *"Ground Arms!" The Story of a Life.* Chicago, Illinois; authorized transl. 1894; "revised by the authoress," 2nd edn. London; reissued 1972 as *Lay Down Your Arms! The Autobiography of Martha von Tilling.* New York, with introduction by Irwin Abrams)

IRWIN ABRAMS

Theodore Roosevelt
(1906)

The 1906 Nobel Peace Prize was awarded to Theodore Roosevelt in recognition of his successful mediation between Japan and Russia resulting in the Portsmouth Treaty in 1905. Roosevelt's award represented three new departures from previous choices: Roosevelt was the first American to receive the prize; he was the first statesman to be honored not for a lifetime of effort toward peace, but for one specific action; and his was the first award to arouse a storm of protest from peace societies on the charge of an attitude of belligerence and support of militarism.

Roosevelt was indeed on record as having eulogized war "as a necessary means of settling great national and international differences and problems." He proclaimed before the Naval War College in 1897 that "No triumph of peace is quite so great as the supreme triumphs of war . . ." He feared that his fellow Americans were growing soft and would become "an easy prey for any people which still retained those most valuable of all qualities, the soldierly virtues" (quoted in Lipsky 1966 pp. 67–69).

But some of his actions were hallmarks in arbitration practiced by a head of state: Roosevelt was among the first to submit a dispute to arbitration at The Hague when he brought an old quarrel between the United States and Mexico before the International Court; he negotiated treaties with France, Germany, Portugal, and Switzerland, and thus directed world opinion toward arbitration and influenced other nations to use the court.

However, it was not his encouragement of arbitration but his success as mediator in ending the Russo–Japanese war which the Nobel Committee cited when it announced his award. Japan, having first attempted to use arbitration over the issue of Russia's eastward expansion in search of an ice-free Pacific port, resorted to war and defeated the Russian forces repeatedly but never decisively. The American Peace Society originally asked President Roosevelt to offer his services as mediator, but this

he refused to do except by request of one of the belligerents. Japan then secretly encouraged Roosevelt to mediate. This he agreed to do, although he wrote privately to a friend, "I have not an idea whether I can or cannot get peace . . . I have done my best. I have led the horses to water, but Heaven only knows whether they will drink or start kicking one another beside the trough." At the opening meeting of the adversaries he proposed a toast to the speedy achievement of a just and lasting peace. But such was not to be, and for three weeks two sets of envoys negotiated. Roosevelt proved himself a skillful mediator, soothing injured pride on all sides, and when the Treaty of Portsmouth was finally signed both the Czar and the Japanese emperor sent messages of appreciation, as did nearly every peace society.

Roosevelt was open about his low opinion of professional peace advocates, saying that "There is no more utterly useless and often mischievous citizen than the peace-at-any-price, universal arbitration type of being who is always complaining either about war or else about the cost of armaments which act as insurance against war." He said they were demanding mutually incompatible things when they proposed peace at any price and at the same time justice and righteousness.

The pacifists viewed Roosevelt with equal scorn. Christian Lange, Nobel Laureate for 1921 and an early secretary of the Nobel Committee, observed that if one lifted the veil of Theodore Roosevelt's pan-Americanism one would find American imperialism.

Gunnar Knudsen, member of the Nobel Committee, who presided at Roosevelt's presentation ceremony, offered the award with comments which offer insight into the Committee's view on both sides of the controversy: "Twelve or fifteen years ago, Gentlemen, the cause of peace presented a very different aspect from the one it presents today. The cause was then regarded as a utopian idea and its advocates as well-meaning but overly enthusiastic idealists who had no place in practical politics, being out of touch with the realities of life. The situation has altered radically since then, for in recent years leading statesmen, even heads of state, have espoused the cause ... The United States of America was among the first to infuse the ideal of peace into practical politics. Peace and arbitration treaties have now been concluded between the United States and the governments of several countries. But what has especially directed the attention of the friends of peace and the whole of the civilized world to the United States is President Roosevelt's happy role in bringing to an end the bloody war recently waged between two of the world's Great Powers, Japan and Russia."

In his Nobel lecture Roosevelt offered some comments on peace "as a practical man," and explained that he was recommending only what he had actually tried to do during the period of his presidency. He advocated arbitration, and encouraged further development of the Hague Tribunal and of the conferences and courts at The Hague. History has borne him out in his prediction that the weakness inherent in efforts made by The Hague would be the absence of any police power to enforce the decrees of the court.

Roosevelt deplored the cost of the growth of armaments and said the Great Powers of the world should be able to reach an agreement which would put an end to such extravagance of expenditures. While he acknowledged that there was no adequate safeguard against deliberate violation of peace treaties, he still encouraged nations to conduct effective arbitration among themselves, with explicit agreement that each contracting party would respect the other's territory and their mutual sovereignties. The establishment of a sufficient number of these treaties would go a long way toward creating a world opinion which would finally find expression in the provision of methods to forbid or punish any violations, Roosevelt said.

When Roosevelt left the presidency in 1908 he stated truthfully that during his seven-year administration "we were at absolute peace, and there was no nation in the world with whom a war cloud threatened, no nation in the world whom we had wronged or from whom we had anything to fear."

The picture of Roosevelt is, then, full of paradoxes. One writer on the Nobel Peace Laureates commented, "The point is, that when the road to peace happens to coincide momentarily with the maneuvers and gyrations of the politician, such a coincidence is strictly accidental. The tactics could just as easily have coincided with war. The exigencies of the moment control" (Lipsky 1966 p. 71).

Biography

Theodore Roosevelt was born in New York City on October 27, 1858, the second of four children of Theodore Roosevelt and Martha Bulloch Roosevelt. Theodore was a spindly child owing to asthma. He adored his father, of whom he wrote, "I realize more and more every day that I am as much inferior to Father morally and mentally as physically," and he set out on a self-taught regime of riding, boxing, and shooting to conquer his ill health. Handicapped also with poor vision, Roosevelt was tutored until he entered Harvard at age 18, apparently to good effect. He won membership in Phi Beta Kappa, he excelled in sports, and he began a scholarly work, *The Naval War of 1812*, which was published two years after his graduation in 1880.

That same year he married Alice Hathaway Lee, a marriage of obvious great happiness which ended tragically four years later with Alice's death following the birth of a daughter. (The baby Alice survived and was destined to become a famous Washington observer as Alice Roosevelt Longworth.)

During the marriage Roosevelt had served in the New York State Assembly and established a sound reputation as a reformer, which he maintained during his entire political career. Following his wife's death, he invested part of his family heritage in a Wyoming ranch which he ran with great success and vigor, restoring again his own failing health and regaining his emotional equilibrium.

Roosevelt subsequently married Edith Kermit Carow, and they had four sons and a daughter. For two and a half years he continued writing and vigorously pursuing sports, until a political opportunity came with an appointment to the US civil service. There he served six years, much of the time as its head, and he again attacked corruption with a concrete program of reforms. He then left Washington for two turbulent years as president of the New York City Police Commission. Although corruption returned after he left, he accomplished some permanent reforms.

In 1897 President McKinley named Roosevelt assistant secretary of the Navy. The next year brought a war with Cuba which Roosevelt supported under his advocacy of "superior" nations exercising the right and the duty to dominate "inferior" nations in the interests of civilization; he resigned his secretaryship, accepted a colonel's rank in the 1st US Volunteer Cavalry and proceeded to ride to fame as leader of his "Rough Riders."

Upon his return to New York, Roosevelt successfully ran for governor of New York state, and he became such a success that even fiercely opposing Democrats acknowledged his sweeping and successful reforms. Indeed, some of his own party with personal interests in the corruption Roosevelt was cleaning out induced him to run on the national Republican ticket as Vice-President.

He was Vice-President for less than a year when upon the assassination of President McKinley he became President on November 14, 1901. He was re-elected in his own right in 1904 for his second term.

Roosevelt was far more prudent in his conduct of foreign policy than his previous stream of pronouncements regarding the virtues of war as an instrument in international relationships had led the peace societies to expect. He was the first national leader to call upon the power of the International Court of Arbitration at The Hague, where he asked for mediation on an old problem between Mexico and the United States.

His most controversial action centered on Panama, where he overrode the Colombian senate's rejection of his offer to buy out a French company's rights to construct a canal through Panama in 1903. He tacitly encouraged a revolution in Panama, and out of this maneuver the new Republic of Panama granted the United States full sovereignty over a ten-mile (16 km) strip through which the Panama Canal was later built.

Roosevelt's domestic program was accurately described as a "Square Deal," and he attacked a number of internal problems courageously, including racial discrimination against the black and oriental races.

In June 1905 Roosevelt accepted Japan's request to mediate a stalemated war between Russia and Japan. They met in Portsmouth, New Hampshire, and with a show of considerable skill on Roosevelt's part reached a peace treaty in September.

Theodore Roosevelt died in 1919.

Bibliography

Harbaugh W 1983 Theodore Roosevelt. In: *Encyclopedia Americana*, International edn. Danburg, Connecticut, pp. 774–81

Lipsky M 1966 *The Quest for Peace*. Barnes and Co., South Brunswick, pp. 67–69

Meyer E 1978 Theodore Roosevelt. *In Search of Peace*. Abingdon, Nashville, Tennessee, pp. 51–55

RUTH C. REYNOLDS

Ernesto Teodoro Moneta

(1907)

Teodoro Gaetano Moneta, known since childhood as Ernesto Teodoro, is remembered, above all, as being the only Italian to have won the Nobel Peace Prize. It was awarded jointly to Moneta and the French jurist Louis Renault in 1907.

Moneta was born on September 20, 1833, son of Giuseppina Muzio and Carlo Aurelio Moneta, a tradesman who lived in a Milan still under Austrian domination and rife with patriotic and humanitarian sentiments. He was little more than a child when, taking after his father, he was infused with a strong feeling of love for his country. This is shown by his behavior during the Milan insurrection of 1848: without even leaving his own home, he joined in the fighting on the side of the insurgents by dropping stones and bricks onto the Austrian patrols. In January 1849 he left Milan for the Kingdom of Sardinia and Piedmont with the intention of enlisting to fight in the first Italian War of Independence against Austria, but was rejected because he was too young.

Following the defeat of Piedmont in 1849, he returned to Milan, where, a short while later, he and his 13 brothers and sisters had to face considerable economic problems after the death of their parents. As soon as these problems had been solved, Moneta renewed his activity on behalf of the patriotic cause. Although he had adopted his father's republican principles, he nevertheless supported the plan of the Società Nazionale Italiana to unify the entire penin-

sular under a monarchy, headed by Vittorio Emanuele of Savoy.

Moneta began a military career in 1859 by enlisting in the Garibaldian company, Cacciatori delle Alpi, and fighting together with several of his brothers in the second Italian War of Independence. The following year, 1860, witnessed Garibaldi's expedition to Southern Italy, in which Moneta also took part. In 1866 he reenlisted in the regular army in order to participate in the third Italian War of Independence. This event is given particular attention by Moneta in the most interesting part of his most wide-ranging work, *Le Guerre, le Insurrezioni e la Pace nel Secolo XIX*, written in his later years when he had come to direct all his efforts to propagandizing pacifist convictions.

Moneta first became involved in journalism through his collaboration with *Unità Nazionale* and, more frequently, *Il Piccolo Corriere d'Italia*, the two organs of the patriots who wanted a united Italy. In 1867, following his abandonment of his military career, the year before, he was appointed editor of *Il Secolo*, where he stayed for almost 30 years. This innovatory, independent, and democratic newspaper would become one of the most important Italian publications of the following decades, due in large part to the efforts of Moneta. When he took up his post, the slaughter he had witnessed fighting in the battle of Custoza in 1866 was still fresh in his mind, and his conception of pacifism was already taking shape. It would subsequently find expression in his writings and, above all, in his numerous speeches. In this context, importance should be attached to his antiwar position with regard to the tension between Italy and France, resulting from the latter's occupation of Tunis (1881), and his swift condemnation of Italian colonial expansion into Eritrea.

Moneta increasingly dedicated more time to the spreading of his pacifist ideas. He began to play an active role in the international pacifist movement, especially after founding in Milan, in 1887, the Unione Lombarda per la Pace e l'Arbitrato Internazionale. In 1898 he founded *La Vita Internazionale,* of which he himself was editor. This was the official publication of the Unione Lombarda per la Pace, later entitled the Società per la Pace. It appeared twice monthly and included prestigious names amongst its contributors. In the reactionary and militarist climate of Italy at the end of the century, it was confiscated and charged with publishing an antimilitarist article by Leo Tolstoy (see Articles: *Tolstoy, Leo*). Feeling that he was also at risk, Moneta was forced to take refuge for a while in Switzerland.

The first decade of the new century still saw him undertaking long journeys, despite his age and advancing blindness, to where the International Peace Congresses were held. (These were frequently organized after the one which took place in Paris in 1889). In 1907, amid general consensus, he was awarded the Peace Prize. The high point in the life of this old pacifist from Lombardy was the Nobel lecture he gave in Oslo, in 1909, on the subject "Peace and Law in the Italian Tradition.'

The year 1911 marked the beginning of years which were to pose painful moral questions. Moneta's years of participation in the international peace movement had not led to the abandonment of his own patriotic values, which had been assimilated during his youth. This gave rise to agonizing contradictions, such as his justification of Italy's decision to undertake, in 1911, the war against Turkey for the conquest of Libya and, later on, his stand in favor of Italian intervention in the First World War against the Central Powers. For many years Moneta had been in favor of Italy remaining in the "Triple Alliance" with Germany and Austria, and a strong critic of the extremist positions of anti-Austrian patriotism. He considered the former as leading to stability and the latter as fomenting unrest. Nevertheless, in 1915, he adopted a position of "democratic interventionism," supporting France and the United Kingdom against Germany and Austria in the First World War. The led to very severe attacks on him by most exponents of the international peace movement. But in the very last days of his life he expressed his support for the program of justice and humanity in relations between peoples put forward in 1918 by US President Woodrow Wilson.

Despite its eclectic nature, the pacifism of Ernesto Teodoro Moneta had a theoretical and ethical depth of its own, and was largely based on his faith in scientific progress, which he felt would lead to greater tolerance and solidarity among nations. Unlike the typical Quaker conception of pacifism, Moneta was not opposed to the use of arms against aggression and in the case of a country losing its freedom as the result of arbitrary outside intervention. As a consequence, on the one hand a nation should be educated in the creed of universal brotherhood and also, on the other, all citizens should receive military training from the moment they attend school, so as to be ready to defend their country's freedom and independence. This is the essential element in the idea of "peace of the strong and free," which for Moneta was connected to the necessity of the "nation under arms." In a world of nations prepared only to fight defensive wars, Moneta believed that war would never actually break out because of the lack of aggressors.

Biography

Ernesto Teodoro Moneta was born on September 20, 1833, in Milan, Italy, son of aristocratic, but impoverished, parents. At 15 he fought next to his father in the Milanese insurrection of 1848 against Austrian rule. He witnessed the shooting and agonizing death of three Austrian soldiers, and their suffering planted the seeds of revulsion against war in his mind, although he continued to participate in Italy's battles for independence, fighting with Garibaldi in 1859 and 1860 and later under General Sirtori. In 1861 he joined the regular Italian army and fought in the battle of Custoza in 1866.

In 1867 he became editor of *Il Secolo,* and in the succeeding 29 years within its pages supported Italy's unification and social progress, side by side with his growing sense of pacifism. In 1887 he founded the Società Internazionale per la Pace: Unione Lombarda (International Society for Peace: Lombard League) and through it campaigned for disarmament, a league of nations, and the use of arbitration for settling international disputes. In 1890 he began an annual almanac called *L'Amico della Pace,* and in 1898 founded *La Vita Internazionale* (International Life), a successful pacifist fortnightly review.

Now an international activist, he increased his activities on behalf of pacifism. In addition to writing, he lectured and attended peace conferences. He became the Italian representative on the Commission of the International Peace Bureau in 1895. In 1906 he presided at the International Peace Conference in Milan, which led to his award of the Nobel Peace Prize in 1907.

Moneta was, however, prepared to sanction the use of military force under certain circumstances; in national self-defense, for example, and where he saw Italy's freedom at risk. Thus he supported Italy's war against Turkey on the grounds of an Italian civilizing mission in Libya, and in 1915 he advocated Italian entry into the First World War to combat the imperialist designs of the Central Powers.

Ernesto Moneta died in Milan on February 10, 1918.

Bibliography

Bauer R 1980 *Ricordo di Ernesto Teodoro Moneta, Premio Nobel per la Pace 1907* Società per la Pace e la Giustizia Internazionale Milan (Text of the commemorative speech given by Riccardo Bauer)

Colombo A 1983 L'anniversario del primo (e unico) Premio Nobel italiano nel campo politico-sociale: Ernesto Teodoro Moneta. *Corriere della Sera* September 17, 1983

Combi M 1968 *Ernesto Teodoro Moneta, Premio Nobel per la Pace 1907.* Mursia, Milan

Moneta E T 1904, 1905, 1906, 1907 *Le Guerre, le Insurrezioni e la Pace nel Secolo XIX,* 4 vols. Società Internazionale per la Pace, Milan

Moneta E T 1909 *La Pace e il Diritto nella Tradizione Italiana. Conferenza Tenuta a Cristiania il giorno 25 Agosto 1909 nel Salone dell'Istituto Nobel per la Pace.* La Compositrice, Milan

Moneta E T 1910 *L'Opera delle Società della Pace dalla loro origine ad oggi. Relazione tenuta a Como il 18 Settembre 1910 al Congresso Nazionale Pacifista.* Società Internazionale per la Pace, Milan (Extract from *La Vita Internazionale* September 20 and October 5, 1910)

ETTORE A. ALBERTONI

Louis Renault
(1907)

Louis Renault, co-winner of the 1907 Nobel Peace Prize, was foremost a professor of law. Nobel Committee Chairman Lovland called him "the guiding genius in the teaching of international law in France." He was counselor to the French Ministry of Foreign Affairs, and France's representative at all the international legal conferences to which the French government was party, and was, together with Tobias Asser (Nobel Laureate in 1911), very largely responsible for the positive results achieved at the Conferences of Private International Law at The Hague. With scholarly skill and perseverance, he fought for the concepts of law, both in his teaching and in his practice.

In the late nineteenth and early twentieth centuries many jurists met at stipulated intervals, seeking to create a system of international law which would implement improved international relationships, and eventually replace war as an ongoing mechanism for resolving conflicts. With the jurist's capacity for precise and economical summation, Renault defined their task as "the juridical organization of international life."

Few men could match Renault's preparation for this role. He had taught Roman, commercial, and international law at the Universities of Dijon and Paris and at the Sorbonne. He was among the early members of the Institut de Droit International [International Institute of Law], and one of the first judges of the Permanent Court of Arbitration at The Hague. Renault was appointed jurist consultant to

the French Foreign Ministry in 1890, and for the next 20 years, as the leading French authority on international law, he acted as its key representative at international conferences covering international private law, international transport, military aviation, submarine cables, naval affairs, the abolition of white slavery, and the revision of the Red Cross Convention of 1864. He became the single most valued authority on international law upon whom the republic relied.

Renault saw a commonality across the wide range of conferences he attended: they all sought to substitute law for the arbitrary. To resolve the difficulties that arose, he said that each country had to learn to relinquish stubborn adherence to its own ideas and to concede whatever it could without actually injuring its own essential interests.

Renault strove to produce positive results and to prevent discussions on generalities and technical formulations from protracting proceedings. He used resilience and intelligence above legal inflexibilities. For instance, he did not adhere to a fixed international democracy. He observed that while the quality of nations is juridically incontrovertible, equality, pushed to its last limits of literalness, could become absurd. For example, the United Kingdom and Luxembourg are equal states before the law. "Would it not be ridiculous if the voice of Luxembourg carried as much weight on a maritime issue as that of Great Britain?," he asked. On the other hand, he attributed a unique and vital role to small nations in these conferences: "they are most frequently the true representatives of justice precisely because they do not have the strength to impose injustice," he said.

His insight on the strengths and weaknesses of demanding unanimity foresaw some of the difficulties which would in later years plague the League of Nations and the United Nations: while, on the one hand, unanimity may lead to stalemate, on the other, it is an indispensable safeguard against hasty decisions and against coalitions of interests. He perceived that unanimity does allow compromise in the sense that a resolution can represent the will of the conference as a whole, in spite of some disagreements. "It is a matter of tact and prudence," Renault declared. "Such delicate problems are not resolved mathematically."

No nation, he felt, should be forced into anything against its will. Instead of laying down hard and fast rules, nations should limit themselves to recommendations, he said. This would not constitute a legal obligation, but rather a moral duty. Renault lay his finger upon the true source of hope over the long span of years: "It is no small matter that a moral duty be recognized by the majority of nations," he said. "By force of circumstance, it eventually becomes a part of custom and compels as much acknowledgment as if it had constituted a strict obligation in the first place."

Renault was *rapporteur* at the conferences; he drafted reports and recommendations and consequently exercised a decisive influence upon the agreements and the form they took.

When the Hague Tribunal was opened to conduct cases of international arbitration, he was named one of its 28 arbiters. During the first 14 years of its existence, Renault was chosen to be involved with six of the court's 13 cases—more than any other arbiter. His reputation for impartiality was so firmly established that during the so-called Savarkar Case between the United Kingdom and France in 1910 both parties to the dispute requested the services of Renault as a judge.

In the first Hague Peace Conference in 1899, Renault, as the reporter of the Second Commission, was concerned with naval warfare. In his Nobel lecture he pointed out some of the many difficulties presented by naval warfare, since war at sea involves the relations between the belligerents themselves and also those between belligerents and neutrals. The interests are therefore divergent. Renault said that negotiations of any sort at the Conference were an achievement, since the great seafaring nations had previously refused to be drawn into discussion on

this subject. But on this occasion great effort was made. Understanding was reached on several points, and a basis for future discussion and agreement was established.

In the second Hague Conference of 1907 his role was even more vital. He was spokesman on four problems. Renault's report in his Nobel lecture on these problems and their treatment at the Conference offers rare insight into the conferences of this period. It is interesting to note that these problems he reviewed were considered and resolved, at least in part, in 1907, just seven years before the outbreak of the First World War in 1914. They are an eloquent commentary on the hope that was basic to the international peace movement prior to that war.

Renault spoke on the following four problems:

(a) *The opening of hostilities.* For a long time people had posed the question of whether a government on the verge of war had an obligation to warn its adversary before opening hostilities. The Conference agreed unanimously that there must be a warning in the form of a reasoned declaration of war, or an ultimatum with conditional declaration of war.

(b) *Application of Geneva Convention to naval warfare.* The issue of laying automatic submarine contact mines, acknowledged to be a threat to peaceable shipping long after the end of hostilities, was discussed, but not satisfactorily resolved at this conference.

(c) *Obligations and rights of neutral countries in the case of naval warfare.* The importance of this problem lay in reducing the danger of any extension of hostilities resulting from conflicts between belligerents and neutrals. Renault reported that the Convention appeared on the whole to provide a fair settlement of the matter.

(d) *International Prize Court of Appeal.* The right to seize private property in the course of war at sea had long been a point for argument. Renault reported with surprised satisfaction that a group of great seafaring nations took the initiative in resolving this matter. A compromise was reached and a comprehensive, carefully drafted proposal was submitted to the Conference in the name of four great powers, Germany, the United States, France and Great Britain.

Renault warned against attempting to move too fast, in the belief that minds cannot be reshaped quickly. "There are some forms of resistance and even of hesitation that only time, allied with education, can overcome," he said.

"Anything that contributes to extending the domain of law in international relations contributes to peace," this distinguished jurist told his Nobel award audience. "Since the possibility of future war cannot be ignored, it is a *farsighted* policy that takes into account the difficulties created by war in the relations between belligerents and neutrals; and it is a *humanitarian* policy that strives to reduce the evils of war in the relations between the belligerents themselves and to safeguard as far as possible the interests of noncombatants and of the sick and the wounded. Whatever may be said by those who scoff at the work undertaken in this field by the Peace Conferences, wars will not become rarer by becoming more barbarous."

Biography

Louis Renault was born on May 21, 1843, at Autun. His father was a Burgundian bookseller and bibliophile. A gifted student, Renault took prizes in philosophy, mathematics, and literature before taking three law degrees in Paris, all with extraordinary honors. He taught Roman and commercial law at Dijon, criminal and international law at the University of Paris. In the latter discipline he so distinguished himself by his teaching and publications in the field, including *Introduction a l'étude du droit international*, that he was offered the chair of international law within seven years. His scholarly output of reports, notes, and articles published in law and political science journals, his books, including notably a nine-volume work of collaboration with Charles Lyon-Caen, *Traite de droit commercial*, his countless lectures, and his continued career as a foremost teacher in his field all brought him recognition as France's leading authority on international law. He was appointed a legal consultant to the Foreign Office, and became the one authority in international law upon whom France relied.

He was a key delegate to many important international meetings between 1893 and 1907, where he was responsible for the drafting of reports and recommendations. In recognition of his service he was given the titular title of Minister Plenipotentiary and Envoy Extraordinary.

Renault served on the panel of 28 arbiters for the Hague Tribunal, where he was chosen to serve in more cases than any other arbiter.

He was named to the Legion of Honor and to the Academy of Moral and Political Sciences in France, and was awarded decorations from 19 foreign nations. He received honorary doctorates from several universities, and was chosen to be president of the Academy of International Law created at The Hague in 1914.

Renault died on February 6, 1918, while still active in his career.

RUTH C. REYNOLDS

Klas Pontus Arnoldson

(1908)

It is interesting to look at the choice of the two Scandinavian award winners of the 1908 Nobel Peace Prize, Klas Pontus Arnoldson and Fredrik Bajer, in terms of the context of its time. A wave of peace movements was awash over the world. In the words of a co-winner of the first Nobel Peace Prize, Frédéric Passy, "the labors of the champions of international arbitration are not only treated with politeness and respect, but are even seriously discussed in the columns of newspapers."

The peace movements proliferated to the point of requiring a clearinghouse for information and a unifying organization to coordinate their efforts. This came about in an agency called the International Peace Bureau, and the international arbitration movement required and received the same service from the Interparliamentary Bureau.

The wars of 1864 and 1870–1871 kindled Klas Arnoldson's passion for the peace movement and he was instrumental in the founding of the Swedish Peace and Arbitration Association in 1883. He became its secretary and also the editor of *Tiden* [The Times], a medium for peace information and free debate. He resigned from *Tiden* in 1885 and became editor of *Fredsvannen* [The Friend of Peace] from 1885 to 1888 and the *Nordsvenska Dagbladet* [North Sweden Daily] from 1892 to 1894. A great part of his energies went into writing and lecturing on behalf of arbitration.

As a member of the Swedish parliament from 1882 to 1887 he put into practice his ideals in liberal political philosophy. He introduced legislation to extend the franchise and supported the extension of religious freedom. He also followed his pacifist convictions, pursuing an antimilitaristic policy and drafting a controversial resolution asking the government to investigate the possibility of guaranteed neutrality for Sweden. In 1888 he mounted a campaign for a popular petition addressed to the king favoring arbitration agreements with foreign nations. When he extended this campaign to Norway he contributed some of the impetus for the Norwegian parliament's passage of a resolution on arbitration.

In the final constitutional crisis which resulted in the dissolution of the union between Norway and Sweden in 1895, Arnoldson tended to favor Norway's claims. His attitude met with outrage in Sweden, and his award of the Peace Prize was regarded by many as an affront to the nation. "A disgrace to every Swedish man who takes pride in his national honor" with a prize paid for in Swedish money! In response the Nobel Committee pointed out that Arnoldson's candidacy had been proposed by the unanimous vote of the Swedish Group of the Interparliamentary Union.

In his Nobel lecture Arnoldson proposed the idea of a world referendum on peace in which an appeal would be issued for every adult man and woman to sign the following declaration: "If other nations will abolish their armed forces and be content with a joint police force for the whole world, then I, the undersigned, wish my own nation to do the same." To this cause, and to other causes of peace, Arnoldson contributed his Nobel Prize money. "It enables me to serve the cause of peace in yet other ways and with even stronger perseverance. So will I try to carry my burden of gratitude, and to discharge the mission to which I have been called," he pledged.

Biography

Klas Pontus Arnoldson was born in Göteborg, Sweden, the son of a caretaker. Because of the family's financial straits he was forced to leave school after his father's death when he was 16. Although he worked thereafter for a railway, Arnoldson did not cease his education but carried on, self-taught, through prolific reading and writing. It was during this period that he developed liberal ideas on religion and politics and became interested in peace.

He served in parliament from 1882 to 1887, during which time he introduced legislation to extend the franchise, favored the extension of religious freedom, and pursued an antimilitaristic policy. In 1883 he worked toward the establishment of the Swedish Peace and Arbitration Association, becoming its secretary. He edited *Tiden* [The Times], a publication on peace information and free debate. From 1885 to 1888 he edited *Fredsvannen* [The Friend of Peace], and from 1892 to 1894 the *Nordsvenska Dagbladet* [North Sweden Daily]. An ardent supporter of arbitration, in 1888 he campaigned for a petition to the king in favor of arbitration agreements with foreign countries, and in 1890 he took his cause to receptive audiences in Norway, contributing to the Norwegian parliament's passage of an arbitration resolution to the king.

Along with a lifetime of journalistic pieces, Arnoldson published a historical essay on international law, *Ar varldsfred mojlig?* [*Is World Peace Possible?*], *Religionen i forskningens ljus* [*Religion in the Light of Research*], and a history of the pacifist idea, *Seklernas hopp* [*The Hope of the Centuries*].

Klas Pontus Arnoldson died in Stockholm in 1916.

RUTH C. REYNOLDS

Fredrik Bajer

(1908)

For over 40 years Fredrik Bajer, journalist and member of the Danish parliament, lent his prolific pen, his politics, and his presence to the cause of peace and it was in recognition of this work that he was awarded the Nobel Peace Prize in 1908 alongside Klas Pontus Arnoldson.

The son of a clergyman, Bajer began his career as an army officer, serving as lieutenant in the Dragoons. Before his military career ended at the close of the 1864 war with Prussia, he had been drawn to the peace movement, and was in touch with Frédéric Passy, founder of the French peace society (and co-winner of the first Peace Prize in 1901). During the next few years he laid an important foundation for his later international activities by studying languages, mastering French, Norwegian, and Swedish. In 1872 he was elected to the Danish House of Representatives, and his efforts in the peace movement shared his attention with work toward the emancipation of women—he was among the founders of the Dansk Kvindesamfund [Danish Women's Society]—and with his dedication to the cause of Scandinavian unity. For two years he edited the journal of the Nordisk Fristats Samfund [Society of Nordic Free States].

In 1882 Bajer founded the first Danish peace society, and its title, Foreningen til Danmarks Neutralisering [Society for the Promotion of Danish Neutrality; later called the Danish Peace Association] defined his initial emphasis in working for peace. In time, however, he became increasingly interested in international peace efforts. He took an active part in the European peace movement, participating in the International Congress in Bern in 1884. He was a prominent delegate to the first Scandinavian peace conference in 1885, and in 1889 he attended the

Interparliamentary Conference held in Paris. He regularly represented the Danish Peace Association at the congresses until 1914. He founded the Danish Interparliamentary Group in 1891, acting as its secretary for 25 years, and he helped in the creation of the Scandinavian Interparliamentary Union in 1908.

Bajer's confidence and interest in arbitration grew, and he served as a member of the council controlling the Interparliamentary Union. He put his convictions into practice by guiding through the Danish parliament a proposal to establish arbitration agreements between Sweden and Norway.

In his Nobel lecture Bajer defined the range of international peace efforts by using a military metaphor: "There are three columns marching forth, the *international*, the *interparliamentary*, and the *intergovernmental*," he said. "These three columns must maintain contact with one another. In battle, it is useless to attack alone, however courageous one may be; one has to maintain contact to the left and to the right; otherwise nothing of great moment can be achieved. This contact . . . is of the utmost importance if results are to be achieved in the peace movement." It is appropriate that among Bajer's most enduring recommendations for the peace movement was its major point of "contact," the International Peace Bureau at Bern. It was at his suggestion that it was established in 1891.

The International Peace Bureau became a permanent agency for the collection and dissemination of information coming from all the peace organizations of the world. It did for those scattered efforts what satellites and computers do for information-dependent agencies today. Its first and second secretary-generals, Elie Ducommun and Charles-Albert Gobat, were both earlier Nobel Laureates (in 1903), and both worked with dedication and without pay. Bajer was president of its Board of Administration until 1907, when he declined re-election and was named honorary president.

The outbreak of the First World War in 1914 brought the International Union of Peace Societies to an abrupt end, and it diminished the role of the International Peace Bureau. However, the Bureau has continued on, and, now headquartered in Geneva, it still acts as a clearinghouse for communications between different national and international peace organizations, and between those organizations and national governments. In the place of arranging the once-proliferating peace congresses, it is more likely today to be organizing seminars on specific projects such as UN peacekeeping operations.

Bajer pinpointed another dilemma constantly present in the dissemination of information for *any* cause. Peace literature was being read mainly by the already convinced. "Up to now, we have had too much . . . preaching to the converted. We should direct special efforts toward those who remain unconverted," he said in his Nobel lecture. His solution, at least for that moment, was to offer a prize in money for the best article on the subject of peace to appear in a national newspaper. His solution was innovative, if temporary, but his observation on that dilemma has stood the test of time.

Bajer also noted in his lecture that we have long possessed the science of war, and it has been "marvelously developed." Whenever a new idea comes along, warfare immediately takes possession. On the other hand, the "waging of peace" is in its infancy. He ventured the prophecy that there would one day be ministers of peace in the cabinet, seated beside the ministers of war.

Bajer himself made many personal contributions in "waging peace." An example was his suggestion for the answer to the Nordic countries' vulnerability during wartime due to the strategic importance of the water routes around their coastlines. Bajer advocated that Nordic neutrality in the same vein as Switzerland's traditional neutrality be internationally recognized. His proposal was adopted by several international organizations, but later he became convinced that Denmark should pursue neutrality independently without relying on other states to guarantee it.

Bajer was a gifted and prolific writer. His legacy of observations from a life spent in the cause of preventing war is well-represented by this closing paragraph of his Nobel lecture:

> [Waging peace] is civilization's battle between rule by law and rule by power. In this context, pacifists should stress more and more that it is the rule of law for which they are fighting . . .
> What contributes largely to the confusion of ideas is the accepted division of the world into major powers and small states. We understand a "power" to be a state which has a large population and well-developed armed forces, army and navy, and so on. This is comparable to believing that a great man is a very tall and big man. By a great man, however, we mean a man who, because of his spiritual gifts, his character, and other qualities, deserves to be called great and who as a result earns the power to influence others. By the same token it must follow that the state we now call a small state is in reality a power if it plays such a role in the development of civilization that it marches in the front ranks and wins victories in the

fight for law which surpass those of the so-called great powers.

Biography

Fredrik Bajer was born on April 21, 1837, son of Alfred Beyer, in Vester Egede, near Naestved, Denmark. (Bajer adopted the altered spelling of his name in 1865.) Bajer served in the army as a lieutenant in the Dragoons, commanding troops in Northern Jutland during the war against Prussia and Austria in 1864. Discharged during the general reduction of troops following the end of the war, he studied languages, mastering French, Norwegian, and Swedish, and became a teacher and translator. He was dedicated to education, serving in the Pedagogical Society and participating in the first Scandinavian conference of teachers held in Göteborg in 1870.

In 1872 he was elected to the *Folketing*, the Danish House of Representatives, where he served for the next 23 years. A leading spokesman for women's rights, he supported legislation in their behalf and helped found the Danish Women's Society. Bajer promoted Nordic unity and cooperation, starting the Society of Nordic Free States, and Scandinavian unity, which he associated with neutrality and peace. He founded the first Danish peace society, the Society for the Promotion of Danish Neutrality, later called the Danish Peace Association. He attended many peace conferences, including the International Congress at Bern, where he suggested the International Peace Bureau be established. A clearinghouse for information exchange between peace organizations over the world, it was a unifying force in the peace movement and Bajer was president of its Board of Administration from its inception in 1891 until 1907. He was a delegate to the first Scandinavian peace conference in 1885 and he founded the Danish Interparliamentary Group in 1891; he helped in the creation of the Scandinavian Interparliamentary Union in 1908. A firm supporter of arbitration, he served as a member of the council controlling the Interparliamentary Union.

Fredrik Bajer died in Copenhagen in 1922.

RUTH C. REYNOLDS

Auguste Beernaert
(1909)

The 1909 Nobel Peace Prize was shared by Auguste Beernaert, whose name the Nobel Committee called renowned in the international peace conferences. He represented Belgium at the two Hague Peace Conferences, was a member of the Permanent Court of Arbitration, and honorary president of the Société de Droit International [International Law Association]. The Nobel Committee declared that Beernaert's prominent position in the international movement for peace and arbitration made his award fully in keeping with the spirit of Alfred Nobel's intentions for the prize.

Auguste Beernaert was born on July 26, 1829, son of a government functionary and a mother who herself undertook the early education of her son and daughter. The outstanding competence of both teacher and pupil is reflected in Beernaert's scholastic record at the University of Louvain (Leuven) where he took his doctorate in law in 1851 with highest distinction. He spent two years at the Universities of Paris, Heidelberg, and Berlin on a traveling fellowship, studying the status of legal education in France and Germany, and submitting his report to the Minister of the Interior.

After his admission to the bar in 1853 he first clerked for a former president of the Chamber of Representatives, after which he set up an independent practice, specializing in fiscal law. In the next 20 years he earned a reputation as a scholar for his published works in legal journals, and a comfortable income from his law practice.

In 1873 he startled legal circles by sacrificing his lucrative practice to become Minister of Public Works. Over the next five years Beernaert proved himself an able administrator and an ambitious reformer. He succeeded in improving Belgium's road, rail, and canal systems, and established new port facilities at Ostend and Anvers. He attempted, but did not succeed, to end child labor in the mines. The year 1884 saw his rise to the leadership of his government. First named Minister of the Department of Agriculture, Industry, and Public Works, four months later, following several resignations from the cabinet, King Leopold II named him Prime Minister and Minister of Finance, positions that he held for 10 years.

Under Beernaert's administration the state of the Congo was created in 1885 with Leopold as sovereign. The Congo was later to present problems to Beernaert.

In his last year of office he was instrumental in enacting constitutional reforms, including universal suffrage, the right of voting being granted to 10 times the number of citizens who had formerly enjoyed it. In 1894, on the constitutional question of proportional representation, Beernaert's cabinet fell.

Although he returned to law practice, he continued to serve the government, accepting the advisory post of Minister of State. From 1895 to 1900 his colleagues elected him the president of the Chamber of Representatives. During this period he actively worked in international attempts to abolish slavery, and he solidifed into active opposition the dismay he felt at the exploitation of the Congo.

Beernaert was a strong internationalist, and following his resignation as Prime Minister he became an active member of the Interparliamentary Union. He presided over several of its conferences, he served as president of its Council, and as president of the Executive Committee when it was formed in 1908.

As Belgium's first representative at the two Hague Conferences in 1899 and 1907 Beernaert had an opportunity to observe for himself the negative nature of the debates dealing with the question of disarmament. He expressed his grave misgivings about the de facto recognition of the principle of military occupation which came out of the two conferences.

Beernaert spearheaded proposals to unify international maritime law. While the conventions of 1885 and 1888 which met at his initiative failed to be adopted by several nations, the conventions dealing with collision and assistance at sea drawn up in 1910 under his chairmanship were signed by many nations.

At the second Hague Conference he found himself, as advocate of the principle of compulsory arbitration, placed in a dilemma over the Congo question. King Leopold was not inclined to apply this principle to the Congo dispute and Beernaert was obliged to softpedal the issue. This event cancelled some of Beernaert's effectiveness in the international field. But his contribution in establishing the positive influence which smaller nations could have on international relationships was very real.

Biography

Auguste Marie Francois Beernaert was born on July 26, 1829, in Ostend, Belgium. Educated in the first instance by his mother, a woman of outstanding intelligence, he took his doctorate in law at the University of Louvain (Leuven) in 1851 with highest honors. Following two years of study on the status of legal education in France and Germany he returned to Belgium, where he practiced law from 1853 to 1873, specializing in fiscal law, and earned a reputation as a scholar through his articles appearing in legal journals. In 1873 he became Minister of Public Works. An able administrator, he improved his country's rail, canal, and road systems, and established new port facilities. He attempted, but failed, to abolish child labor in mines.

In 1884 Beernaert became Prime Minister, having served the previous four months as Minister of the Department of Agriculture, Industry, and Public Works before resignations in the cabinet brought about his rise to leadership. During the 10 years of his administration his accomplishments were many: he balanced the budget; many domestic reforms affecting the welfare of workers were enacted; suffrage was extended to 10 times the number of citizens previously voting. The Congo, which had been developed largely under the responsibility of King Leopold II, became an independent state placed under Leopold's sovereignty.

Beernaert's cabinet fell in 1894 on the constitutional question of proportional representation, and Beernaert returned to law practice, although retaining some service in the government. He accepted the advisory post of Minister of State and served as the president of the Chamber of Representatives. He headed the·Commission of Museums and Arts.

He joined in an international opposition to slavery, including the exploitation of the Congo. A leading pacifist, he became active in the Interparliamentary Union, presiding over several conferences and serving as president of its Council after 1899 and president of its Executive Committee in 1908. He represented Belgium at the two Peace Conferences at The Hague in 1899 and 1907. He was a member of the Permanent Court of Arbitration, and frequently acted as arbiter of international disputes.

On his way home from the 1912 Geneva conference of the Interparliamentary Union he contracted pneumonia and died in a Lucerne hospital on October 6, 1912.

RUTH C. REYNOLDS

Paul Henri Benjamin Balluet,
Baron d'Estournelles de Constant de Rebecque

(1909)

"Paul Henri Benjamin d'Estournelles de Constant has become thoroughly dedicated to the movement for peace and arbitration," Chairman Lovland of the Nobel Committee declared in presenting the 1909 Peace Prize to the French co-winner with Auguste Beernaert. "D'Estournelles' work for peace has not been performed blindly," Lovland said. "As a diplomat he learned to understand international policy and has planned his efforts accordingly." Among the group of international jurists who won the Peace Prize prior to 1914, d'Estournelles was the one who turned to a political career to render his international activity more effective.

Born on November 22, 1852, at La Fleche in the Sarthe district, Paul Henri Benjamin Balluet, Baron d'Estournelles de Constant de Rebecque, was the son of a family that could trace its ancestry back to the Crusades. He was educated in law at the Lycée Louis le Grand in Paris, and in preparation for a career in the diplomatic service he studied and received a diploma there in oriental languages. He traveled widely in the Orient.

He entered the diplomatic corps in 1876 as an attaché in the consular department of the Ministry of Foreign Affairs, representing France in the next six years in Montenegro, Turkey, the Netherlands, Britain, and Tunis. Recalled to Paris in 1882, he assumed the assistant directorship of the Near Eastern Bureau of the Ministry of Foreign Affairs. He returned to London in 1890 as counselor to the Embassy, with the title of minister plenipotentiary. As chargé d'affaires he was involved in averting a threatened war between France and Britain during a French–Siamese border dispute when the British objected to a blockade imposed by the French.

The five years he spent as counselor to the Embassy convinced d'Estournelles of the general impotence of members in the diplomatic service. In 1895 he resolved to abandon the "gilded existence of the diplomatist in order to undertake the real struggle . . . against ignorance" by obtaining an elective seat in the legislature and attempting to remedy the situation in which "the silent majority allow themselves to be persuaded that they know nothing of 'Foreign Affairs'" (*International Peace* pp. 5–6).

And so, on May 19, 1895, he began his political career as deputy from Sarthe, the same constituency that had years earlier elected his famous great-uncle, the author Benjamin Constant de Rebecque. Elected senator from the same region in 1904, he held that seat as an active Radical Socialist until his death.

D'Estournelles participated at both Hague Peace Conferences, in 1899 and 1907, in the French delegation. At the first conference he led the successful struggle to strengthen the language dealing with arbitration and the court in Article 27 of Convention I, thereby securing agreement on compulsory arbitration that was recognized as being more vitally important than most countries had originally been willing

to concede. The obligation was, however, still only a moral one, and during the first few years the tribunal was systematically sabotaged by the Great Powers.

D'Estournelles countered with increased efforts to encourage the use of arbitration. One notable success was persuading Theodore Roosevelt (Nobel Peace Prize winner in 1906) to refer a US–Mexican dispute to the Hague Tribunal. He influenced Andrew Carnegie to underwrite a large amount of the cost of building a Peace Palace in The Hague, a monument eulogizing not the heroes of past wars, but the ideal of peace.

D'Estournelles sought a political solution to Europe's problems. He believed that foreign policy should ultimately be controlled by parliaments, and that consequently parliamentary arbitration groups should be developed and strengthened. In 1903 he founded a parliamentary group composed of members of the French Chamber and Senate without regard to party. Their purpose was to advance international arbitration, chiefly through the exchange of visits with foreign parliamentarians.

D'Estournelles' ultimate goal was the formation of a European Union. His immediate goal was a Franco–German *rapprochement*. However, he faced not only vengeful feelings directed against Germany, but also a violent anti-British mood which was whipped up over the Fashoda incident in 1898. He therefore worked also for a Franco–British *rapprochement*, and in 1903 he visited the British parliament at the head of the French parliamentary group for voluntary arbitration. The British paid a return visit to Paris shortly after a treaty of arbitration had been signed between the two countries. These events helped make possible the Franco–British entente in 1904, but d'Estournelles insisted that this agreement, like the Franco–Russian alliance of 1894, must not be used against Germany. The balance which these two agreements created contributed to a lessening of tensions.

In 1903 d'Estournelles also founded a Franco–German association in Munich. He agreed that past events could not be forgotten, but urged that both countries recognize that peace was an absolute imperative. "War," he declared, "drives the republics into dictatorship, the monarchies into the grip of revolution." In 1905 he founded the Association for International Conciliation in Paris, with branches abroad.

D'Estournelles observed that the rivalry between the European countries resulted in steadily increasing military expenditures, and that this weakened Europe's position in the world economy. He pointed out the advantage that would come with a European Union which would hold no threat to any important non-European power, such as the United States. D'Estournelles thought that many influential Americans were eager to see a greater measure of European cooperation. "The Americans are businessmen, and they prefer well-organized and stable conditions to the armed peace which presents a constant menace to world peace" he declared.

While he worked toward his long-range goal of the formation of a European Union, d'Estournelles also continued to pursue activities of a diplomatic and juridical nature, such as working within the Interparliamentary Union, as a member of the Permanent Court of Arbitration, and as president of the European Center of the Carnegie Endowment for International Peace.

During the First World War d'Estournelles supported his country's effort, turning his home into a hospital for the wounded. But following the war he continued his campaign for international understanding. He joined Leon Bourgeois, Nobel Peace Prize winner for 1920, in presenting a plan for the League of Nations to Clemenceau in 1918. He never ceased trying to bring together parliamentarians of various nations, especially those of France and Germany.

Biography

Paul Henri Benjamin Balluet, Baron d'Estournelles de Constant de Rebecque, was born on November 22, 1852, at La Fleche, in the Sarthe district of the Loire Valley. The son of an aristocratic family, he traced his ancestry back to the Crusades.

He was educated at the Lycée Louis le Grand in Paris, with a degree in law and a diploma from the School of Oriental Languages. As an attaché in the consular department of the Ministry of Foreign Affairs he represented France from 1876 to 1882 in Montenegro, Turkey, the Netherlands, Britain, and Tunis. In 1882 he assumed assistant directorship of the Near Eastern Bureau of the Ministry of Foreign Affairs.

In 1890 d'Estournelles became chargé d'affaires in London, and in 1893 he helped avert a war between France and Britain over a blockade during the French–Siamese border disputes. This incident sealed his conviction of the impotence within the diplomatic service, and he decided to pursue a political career in which he thought he might act

with more effect. He sought and won a seat in the legislature as deputy for Sarthe in 1895. A Radical Socialist, he was elected senator from the same region, and he held that seat for the remainder of his life.

In 1899 he served on the French delegation to the first Hague Peace Conference, seeking to strengthen arbitration. While on a lecture tour in the United States, he persuaded President Theodore Roosevelt to submit a longstanding dispute between the United States and Mexico to the Hague Tribunal.

Mutual goodwill missions under his chairmanship between London and Paris helped pave the way for the Franco–British Entente Cordiale of 1904; a visit to Munich resulted in the Franco–German Association in 1903. In 1905 he founded the Association for International Conciliation at Paris, with branches abroad.

He was an active member in the Interparliamentary Union, a delegate to the second Hague Peace Conference of 1907, a member of the Permanent Court of Arbitration and president of the European Center of the Carnegie Endowment for International Peace.

Although he supported the French effort during the First World War, following its close he continued his work toward international understanding, presenting with Leon Bourgeois a plan for the League of Nations to Clemenceau in 1918. He never ceased trying to bring together parliamentarians of various nations, particularly those of France and Germany.

D'Estournelles had tremendous energy and eclectic interests. He published translations from the classical Greek, wrote on Greek culture, won the French Academy's Prix Therouanne in 1891 with a book on French politics in Tunisia, and wrote a play based on the Pygmalion myth. His outpour of speeches and pamphlets covered topics ranging from French politics to feminism, from arbitration to aviation. Married to an American, Daisy Sedgwick-Berend, his command of English was excellent, and he became a leading French authority on the United States. He found time to engage in fencing, yachting, and painting, and when the automobile and the airplane came on the scene he pursued a keen interest in both.

D'Estournelles died in Paris on May 15, 1924 at the age of 72.

Bibliography

International Peace 1906 Baron d'Estournelles de Constant and others. Edinburgh Peace and Arbitration Society, Edinburgh

RUTH C. REYNOLDS

International Peace Bureau (IPB)
(1910)

The Nobel Peace Prize for 1910 was awarded to the International Peace Bureau (IPB) to assist it in its established work of strengthening the peace movement through disseminating information between peace societies and peace congresses spread throughout the Old and New Worlds.

In the last two decades of the nineteenth century peace societies had multiplied rapidly in a variety of countries (see Articles: *Peace Movements of the Nineteenth Century*) . Frédéric Passy, co-winner of the first Nobel Peace Prize, and a foremost peace advocate, described the peace movement in Europe in the *American Journal of Sociology* in 1896. In the United Kingdom where the Peace Society had long been the only organization of its kind, he said, it had been joined by the International Arbitration and Peace Association, the International Arbitration League, and the Women's Peace Association, to name only a few. In France the Société Francaise pour l'Arbitrage included many well-known public figures; and in its wake a variety of local Christian organizations and women's societies took up the work for peace. Italy Passy called a "perfect hotbed for anti-military societies." The story was correspondingly heartening in many other countries: Portugal, Greece, Romania, all of Central Europe—Prussia, Austria, and Hungary.

A mass of literature poured out from these organizations and Passy also observed coverage in the regular press which would have been unthinkable a few years previously. It logically followed that the number of peace congresses increased proportionately, and, from 1889 on, an international peace congress was held annually in a different city—Paris, London, Rome, Berne, Budapest, Chicago, Boston, Milan all hosted them.

Inevitably, communication between the different societies and national groups was imperfect and often slow; which caused problems when circumstances required an immediate, concerted response. Thus there was an urgent need to coordinate this burgeoning activity. Fredrik Bajer, journalist, Danish parliamentarian, and ardent pacifist (and 1908 Peace Prize co-winner), brought to the third Peace Congress in Rome held in 1891 the concept of a central office and executive organ for this purpose. The following year the Bureau Internationale et Permanente de la Paix (Permanent International Peace Bureau) was founded with its headquarters at Berne. Passy described the far-reaching results. The peace movement in spite of its occasional grand demonstrations, had not been an organic, living body. It was only after the establishment of a legally incorporated International Bureau in Switzerland that the different peace societies became united into an organic whole, and this bureau, being a center of information and activity, became the heart and brain of the whole movement in both the Old World and the New. It accomplished for international peace and justice that which had been done in other spheres by international postal and telegraph bureaus, and by international copyright laws. Different publications were collected, news was recorded, information obtained, doubtful or obscure questions explained, propositions forwarded, and opinions received—all through the auspices of the Bureau. Passy called it "the living soul of the great body of peacemakers all over the world."

Also, the Bureau handled arbitration procedures and bilateral peace treaties. Along with arranging communication between the various individuals and organizations, it published *Correspondance bimensuelle* and a yearbook, *Annuaire du mouvement pacifiste*.

All this was accomplished through the dedication and skillful services of Elie Ducommun for the first 15 years of the organization, and, following his death in 1908, by Charles-Albert Gobat—both working without recompense. These men were co-winners of the second Nobel Peace Prize in 1902, Gobat having at that time been directing a similar organization which serviced the members of the Interparliamentary Bureau.

Owing to the high quality of their administrative and clerical skills, in a happy partnership with deep and sustained dedication, Ducommun and Gobat had each run this complex, vital service on a budget of from 8,000 to 9,000 francs (US$4000 to US$4500 current rate). The Peace Prize money gave the Bureau much needed financial stabilization.

Despite this success, the First World War dealt the Bureau a near lethal blow when the International Union of Peace Societies came to an end. Following the war an international governmental body, the League of Nations came into being. Although tentative, defective, and weak, the League existed to support the ideas of arbitration and mediation which had kept the prewar peace organizations occupied and purposeful. It would seem, then, that the *raison d'être* of the IPB disappeared when a central, unifying nongovernmental organization no longer seemed necessary. But the Bureau continued on, concentrating its efforts on communication of ideas and proposals of the peace movement from outside governmental organizations to agencies within governments. It became diversified in the organizations it worked with. Now serving multiple purposes as they arose, the IPB no longer functioned as a unifying agency.

The IPB changed it locale. In order to facilitate the reconstructed activity of peace movements and to work in closer contact with the new League of Nations, the Bureau moved in 1924 to Geneva, which is still the site of its headquarters. It continued to organize annual conferences, to build up and maintain a library, and to publish a periodical.

During the Second World War the work of the Bureau again came to a halt. In 1946, the year following the close of that war, it was reeastablished as a new international organization called the International Liaison Committee of Organizations for Peace (ILCOP). After several years of negotiations, the Swiss Federal Council, which had been holding the frozen assets of the Permanent International Peace Bureau, recognized the ILCOP as the legal successor to the Bureau, and released the funds in its holding. The library went to the United Nations. Shortly after, the ILCOP readopted the name International Peace Bureau.

The Bureau still continues with much the same objectives. Its aim remains to "serve the cause of peace by the promotion of international cooperation and nonviolent solution of international conflicts." It works to facilitate communication between different national and international peace organizations, and between these organizations and governmental and intergovernmental bodies. Its established principle is one of nonalignment with such bodies. It no longer acts as a unifying agent, decision maker or mouthpiece for the peace movement as a whole. It does make the organization of international conferences the center of its activities, but such conferences are now more seminars than congresses, concentrating on different aspects of one given subject or project.

The preparation for such a project may be in considerable depth, taking two to four years for completion. The Bureau will handle a maximum of two such major projects at a time. The procedural steps are these: preparation of available documentation in a "working paper" and the conference itself, often preceded by a smaller preparatory seminar whose participants are recruited to secure attendance from three categories: (a) representatives of governments and governmental bodies, (b) peace research workers and other experts in the specific field, and (c) representatives of peace organizations and other national and international organizations concerned with the specific subject of the conference. It handles also the editing, publication, and distribution of the Conference Report, completed with any further documentation collected; and the final follow-up on the Conference findings and decisions, which in many cases involves transmitting proposals to certain governments or certain intergovernmental bodies (Herz 1969 p.4).

Today membership is open to: (a) international organizations working primarily for peace and international cooperation; (b) national peace councils or other federations coordinating the peace movement of their respective countries; (c) international organizations having the promotion of peace and international cooperation as one of their aims; (d) national and local organizations working directly for peace and international cooperation, or having the work for peace as one of their aims. Associate membership without voting rights is open to organizations and individuals who support the aim of the International Peace Bureau (Herz 1969 p.10)

History

The International Peace Bureau (IPB) was founded in Berne in 1891 with Fredrik Bajer (1908 Peace Prize co-winner) as its first president, and Elie Ducommun (1902 Peace Prize winner) its secretary–general. Its purpose was to coordinate information and answer questions. It did the planning for peace congresses, assisted with programs, implemented their decisions, and disseminated information following the congresses. It collected and issued information through a fortnightly publication, *Correspondance bimensuelle*, and a yearbook, *Annuaire du mouvement pacifiste*.

All this activity was taken care of first by Ducommun, and then, following his death in 1906, by Charles-Albert Gobat (1903 Peace Prize co-winner), who succeeded him as secretary–general. Both men worked with dedication and without pay.

The First World War had a great effect on the IPB. Following its close in 1918, and with the coming of the League of Nations, which was visualized as an organization assuming many of the functions which volunteer peace organizations had performed before the war, the Bureau changed its emphasis. It moved to Geneva to be near the League, and concentrated its efforts on gathering broad outlines of opinion within nongovernmental organizations and communicating these to governmental agencies. It continued to organize annual conferences, built up a library, and issued a periodical.

The Second World War, however, brought the IPB to a halt. Its assets were placed under the supervision of the Swiss Federal Council. Following the war the Bureau reorganized under the name of the International Liaison Committee of Organizations for Peace, (ILCOP) and after several years was recognized officially by the Swiss Federal Council as the legal successor to the International Peace Bureau, its funds being restored. The library went to the United Nations. The original name, the International Peace Bureau, was readopted soon after. Its program remains to "serve the cause of peace by the promotion of international cooperation and nonviolent solution of international conflicts." To this end is still acts as a clearinghouse for ideas, and still coordinates the activities of different peace organizations, but it no longer acts as an agent, a decision maker, or a mouthpiece for the peace movement as a whole. It cooperates with the United Nations as well as with nongovernmental bodies.

Bibliography

Herz U 1969 *The International Peace Bureau: History, Aims, Activities.* International Peace Bureau, Geneva
Passy F 1896 Peace movement in Europe. *Am. J. Sociol.* 1: 1–12

RUTH C. REYNOLDS

Tobias Asser

(1911)

Tobias Asser was co-winner with Alfred Fried of the Nobel Peace Prize in 1911. An ardent and intelligent advocate of arbitration, he made his major contribution to peace in the field of international private law. The Nobel award honored his role in the foundation of the Permanent Court of Arbitration of the first Hague Peace Conference in 1899.

Asser was an authority on international private law, and was convinced that arbitration could be accommodated by international conferences. Under his influence the Dutch government summoned four conferences at The Hague, in 1893, 1894, 1900, and 1904, for the Unification of International Private Law. Asser presided over all four. They attained the goal he had in mind, preparing the foundation for conventions which would establish uniformity in international private law, leading to greater public security and justice in future international relations. From the findings of these conventions, the responsibility then passed to participating countries to codify their national legislation accordingly.

Most of the countries of Europe sent representatives to the first two conferences, and they drew up a treaty establishing uniform international procedures for conducting civil trials. The conferences of 1900 and 1904 accomplished treaties covering family law, such as marriage, divorce, legal separation, guardianship of minors, and bills of exchange.

In collaboration with Dr. Rolin-Jaquemyns and John Westlake, Asser started the *Révue de droit international et de legislation comparée* (*Journal of International Law and Comparative Legislation*) in 1869. Four years later he was one of the founders of the Institute of International Law at Ghent, and later became its head.

On the practical side of international affairs, Asser accepted a position as legal adviser to the Netherlands Ministry of Foreign Affairs in 1875. In 1893 he resigned his professorship and retired from the bar to become a member of the Dutch Council of State, the government's highest administrative body. Beginning in 1898 he served as president of the State Commission for International Law. He was The Netherland's delegate to the Hague Peace Conferences of 1899 and 1907, where he made the practical and vital plea that the principle of compulsory arbitration be introduced into the economic area.

By now highly renowned as a negotiator, and equipped with fluent command of German, French, and English, Asser participated in virtually every treaty concluded by the Dutch government from 1875 to 1913. In the field of international law, he made a highly significant contribution to the international scene with his negotiations resulting in the neutralization of the Suez Canal. He succeeded in getting Spain and the Netherlands elected to the Suez Canal Commission as representatives of the smaller nations, along with the Great Powers.

Asser had the satisfaction of sitting as a member of the Permanent Court of Arbitration at The Hague when it heard its first case in 1902. The dispute was the United States and the Bishops of the Catholic Church versus Mexico, and the contention was over a fund set up in the eighteenth century to finance the Catholic Church in California. Following the war between the United States and Mexico in 1845 to 1848, after which the defeated Mexico ceded Upper California to the United States, Mexico refused to pay the Californian bishops monies due to them from the fund. The award was to the United States and the Bishops.

Again in 1902 Asser arbitrated a dispute, this time between the United States and Russia, over the seizure of five sealing vessels on the Bering Straits. Although the case was not taken to the Hague Tribunal, it was settled according to the code of that court.

"Asser has above all been a practical legal statesman," Jorgen Gunnarsson Lovland, Chairman of the Nobel Committee, said, and continued, "He holds a position in the sphere of international private law similar to that enjoyed by the famous French jurist Louis Renault in international public law. Indeed, his public activity has overshadowed his scholarly writing, which is of great importance in its own right. As a pioneer in the field of international legal relations, he has earned a reputation as one of the leaders in modern jurisprudence. It is therefore only natural that his countrymen should see him as successor to, or reviver of, The Netherlands' pioneer work in international law of the seventeenth century."

Biography

Tobias Michael Carel Asser was born in Amsterdam on April 28, 1838. His life was greatly influenced by his father and grandfather who were well-established lawyers and by his uncle who was a Dutch minister of justice. Asser was a brilliant student and in 1857 he won a competition with his thesis "On the Economic Conception of Value." He turned away from his business studies and took up law at the Amsterdam Athenaeum where he earned his doctorate in 1860. Later that year he was appointed a member of an international commission to abolish tolls on the Rhine River.

In 1862 he accepted a teaching appointment as professor of private law at the Athenaeum. He continued as a professor of international and commercial law when the institution was elevated to university status.

He persuaded the Dutch government to call several conferences of the European powers to design codifications of international private law. He was appointed as the presiding official for the 1893 and 1894 Hague conferences. These conferences established uniform international procedures for conducting civil trials. The treaty took effect in May 1899. He also presided over the 1900 and 1904 conferences which produced treaties governing international family law. He was soon appointed legal counselor to the Dutch Foreign Office and in 1904 he became minister of state.

He was arbitrator in the dispute between the United States and Russia on the Bering Straits, and between the United States and Mexico on the Pious Fund of the Californias. The 1902 United States and Mexico dispute was the first dispute ever to reach The Hague Arbitration Court.

Asser was co-founder of the international law journal *Revue de droit international et de législation comparée* in 1869. He took part in the Ghent Conference which established the Institute of International Law, an organization he later headed.

He was legal adviser to the Netherlands Ministry of Foreign Affairs in 1875, became a member of the Council of State in 1893, served as president of the State Commission for International Law beginning in 1898 and was a delegate to the 1899 and 1907 Hague Peace Conferences.

Asser enriched the literature of the law. His more important works are *Schets van het internationaal Privaatrecht*, written in 1877, and *Schets van het Nederlandsche Handelsrecht*, written in 1904. For his juridical scholarship with its many forms of contributions to and clarifications of international law he was awarded honorary degrees by the Universities of Edinburgh, Cambridge, Bologna, and Berlin. A library of international law which Asser gathered with the help of contributions from 20 countries is housed in the Peace Palace at The Hague; it is appropriately and simply named "The Asser Collection."

Tobias Asser died on July 29, 1913.

See also: Articles: *Arbitration, International*; *International Law*

RUTH C. REYNOLDS

Alfred Fried

(1911)

When Alfred Fried was honored as co-winner with Tobias Asser of the 1911 Nobel Prize for Peace the Nobel Committee called him "the most industrious literary pacifist in the past twenty years." It was high praise indeed for a self-educated man who left school at 15 to work as a bookseller and who applied himself to the literary arts with such diligence that he mastered scholarly writing and created what the Nobel Committee called "the best journal in the peace movement."

Fried founded the Deutsche Friedensgesellschaft (German Peace Society) and edited its major publication, *Monatliche Friedenskorrespondenz* (*Monthly Peace Correspondence*), between 1894 and 1899. A disciple of Bertha von Suttner (1905 Nobel laureate), he and the Baroness worked closely together on peace promotion projects and, like her, Fried became a popular lecturer throughout Germany and Austria. He named a pacifist journal he was starting after her famous book, *Die Waffen Nieder!* (*Lay Down Your Arms!*). Furthermore, he persuaded von Suttner to edit it. Eight years later, in 1899, it became *Die Friedenswarte* (*The Peace Watch*). Norman Angell, Peace Prize Laureate of 1933 and author of the highly successful *The Great Illusion*, called it "The most efficient periodical of the Pacifist movement in the world."

Fried edited *Die Friedenswarte* until his death, keeping its appeal toward intellectuals whose support he felt was vital to the cause of peace. He made an important contribution in influencing German views on the problems of international law, which previously had been heavily influenced by the Prussian ideology of might. The journal continues on, and is now published in Berlin. Its editorial policy under both Fried and later editors, beginning with Professor Hans Wehberg, has observed absolute objectivity in its treatment of the peace question.

Fried's goal was to go beyond questions of disarmament, which he considered only palliative, to address the causes lying behind warfare. He believed that international tension leading to wars would be alleviated by increased international understanding followed by appropriate legislation. With healthy international relations, based on legal and political orderliness replacing the existing armed peace, which Fried regarded as international anarchy, "symptoms" like military build-ups and wars would disappear automatically.

Fried contributed to the creation of the Verband für internationale Verstandigung (Society for International Understanding) in 1911. His theory of internationalism did not preclude nationalism, and he visualised a "Pan-European Bureau" modeled on the Pan-American pattern which would unite the countries of Europe while still respecting the sovereignty of each. He conceived of internationalism as based on international understanding, nourished by a central source of information on cultural, economic, and political issues. He established an annual review to promote interest in international cooperation. Called *Annuaire de la vie internationale*, it presented the example of Pan-America and also the Hague Conferences as existing steps taken in this direction.

Fried practiced truth in his journalism, and he scorned those who violated this principle for any reason. He called writers hired to beat the drums of war "priests of Philistinism," with the "pleasant task of mocking and making ridiculous the work of the Hague Conference according to the spirit of their mandates." To counter such bias in the press, he helped found the Union International de la Presse pour la Paix. Nor did he possess the usual tolerance for propaganda which inevitably accompanies war. During the First World War, although deploring and dissociating himself from the German official war policy, he openly refuted the untruths he saw about Germany in the French, British, and American press.

Fried was in Vienna in 1914 when the war broke out. Since his writing there would be subject to censorship, he availed himself of the neutrality of Switzerland and there continued publishing *Die Friedenswarte*. He also edited a periodical whose ambitious title reflected its remarkable aims in the midst of wartorn Europe: *Blätter für internationale Verstandigung und Zwischenstaatliche Organisation* (*Papers for International Understanding and Interstate Organization*). During his exile in Switzerland he kept a diary which was published following the war under the title *Mein Kriegstagebuch* (*My War Journal*). It was a monumental work in which he recorded his sentiments and activities, along with those of his colleagues, their histories, and coverage of organizations within the peace movement. In 1917 he published a collection of Baroness von Suttner's shorter writings to keep alive the cause of peace.

Prodigious though his literary output was, it far from constituted all of Fried's contribution in the peace movement. He had an impressive capacity as an organizer, and he was secretary–general of the Union Internationale de la Presse pour la Paix, a member of the Berne Peace Bureau, and secretary of the International Conciliation for Central Europe.

Fried was dismayed by the Versailles Treaty and organized a journalistic campaign protesting it; he tirelessly pressed the point that the war had proven the validity of the pacifists' analysis of world politics.

He wrote a less scholarly, but pungent evaluation of one of the graver problems challenging the peace movement, a comment which retains a ring of truth even to contemporary times: "The events of an international bicycle race are described in great detail and are eagerly swallowed up by the readers, just as the least significant comedian on the local stage is better known to the public than the people who make world history or the great events of historical importance."

The collapse of Austria–Hungary swept away the personal resources of Fried, and he died in poverty in Vienna on May 5, 1921, at the age of 57.

Biography

Alfred Hermann Fried was born in Vienna on November 11, 1864. Leaving school at 15, he first worked as a book-seller. He moved to Berlin at 24, where, self-educated, he became a distinguished and successful journalist. A disciple of Baroness Bertha von Suttner (1925 Peace Prize winner), he founded the German Peace Society (*Deutsche Friedens-gesellschaft*) and edited its major publication, *Monthly Peace Correspondence* (*Monatliche Friedenskorrespondenz*) from 1894 to 1899. He started a peace journal with von Suttner as editor called *Lay Down Your Arms!* (*Die Waffen Nieder!*) after the title of the Baroness's famous novel. Eventually this became *The Peace Watch* (*Die Frieden-swarte*) a periodical addressed to intellectuals, which has continued to the present day and is now published in Berlin. In 1905 Fried launched an annual review, *Annuaire de la vie internationale*, reflecting his interest in international cooperation.

Fried was a member of the Bern Peace Bureau, secretary of the International Conciliation for Central Europe, and secretary–general of the Union Internationale de la Presse pour la Paix. A founding member of the Society for International Understanding (Verband für internationale Verstandigung), he believed in economic cooperation and political organization among nations, with full respect of the sovereignty of each one, as the way to prevent wars rather than through disarmament.

During the First World War, which he deplored, he lived in Switzerland and continued with publication of *The Peace Watch*. He also wrote a major work on the peace movement called *My War Journal* (*Mein Kriegstagebuch*) which recorded not only his sentiments, but those of his colleagues, their history and that of the organizations of the peace movement.

Following the war Fried organized a journalistic campaign protesting against the Versailles Treaty. He lost his personal resources in the collapse of Austria–Hungary and died in poverty in Vienna on May 5, 1921.

See also: Articles: *Die Waffen Nieder!*

*ε*RUTH C. REYNOLDS

Elihu Root

(1912)

The 1912 Nobel Prize for Peace was awarded to an American statesman, Elihu Root. We have the opinion of 1931 laureate Nicholas Murray Butler, adviser to seven presidents, that "No American in the last half-century has equalled him in the field of constructive statesmanship or in intellectual grasp and power of exposition." The editors of the *New York World* agreed that Root was "one of the few living statesmen of the first intellectual rank."

Yet this Peace Prize laureate first served in the government as Secretary of War from 1899 to 1901 in the cabinets of William McKinley and Theodore Roosevelt. A case might be made that in this post, Root's work was diametrically opposed to Nobel's desire for a "reduction of standing armies and outlawing of war." With a reading of Root's outstanding Nobel lecture, however, questions about the qualifications of the man are laid to rest. It is an unflinching examination of the problems existing between humankind and permanent peace, and an eloquent statement about the philosophy behind his statesmanship which addressed these problems.

Root opened his lecture with the assertion that the humanitarian purpose behind the Peace Prize was more than a reward; it should also stimulate thought upon the means and methods best adapted, under the changing conditions of future years, to approach and ultimately attain the end Nobel so much desired. He warned that the simplicity of the subject is misleading: "The recognition of the horrors of war and the blessings of peace, the mere assemblage of peace-loving people to interchange convincing reasons for their common faith are not enough to reach or modify the causes of war ... And the mere repetition of the obvious by good people ... is subject to the drawback that the unregenerate world grows weary of iteration and reacts in the wrong direction."

He said that the limitation of this mode of promoting peace lies in the fact that war is the natural reaction of human nature in the savage state, while peace is the result of acquired characteristics, a matter primarily of development of character and the shifting of standards of conduct—a long, slow process. Root's work, both within his several government posts and his activities following his government service, was a steady effort to shift the standards of conduct wherever he might.

Root realized more clearly than most people the necessity of gaining the confidence of the Latin American states. He made a great effort as Secretary of State to overcome the considerable suspicion with which the United States was viewed by its neighbors to the south. He proposed that the Pan-American Conference of 1906 should take place deep in their territory, and his suggestion of Rio de Janeiro was well-received. Even more important was his extensive goodwill tour, visiting Uruguay, Argentina, Chile, Peru, Panama, and Colombia. He made countless addresses stressing the desire of the United States to cooperate on an equal basis. Then, the following year, he took the initiative in convoking a Central American Peace Conference at Washington and he persuaded Latin American states to participate in the Second Hague Peace Conference.

His accomplishments in Latin America continued. A complicated relationship with Colombia was settled after two years of negotiations. He was able to regularize the relationship with San Domingo, and, in cooperation with Mexico, assisted in ironing out points of difference between the Central American republics. All this patient work resulted in the establishment of a permanent court of arbitration for Central American states at Carthage, Costa Rica, and the creation of the Pan-American Bureau in Washington, DC.

In the matter of arbitration with European countries, the United States had a history of presidents interested in achieving arbitration treaties from the time of President Cleveland (1885–89 and 1893–97), and the Senate had an equally long record in setting up insurmountable obstacles. Secretary Root himself was an ardent advocate of arbitration, and spoke of it in his Nobel lecture. "There have been occasional international arbitrations from the very early times, but arbitration as a system, a recognized and customary method of diplomatic procedure rather than an exceptional expedient, had its origin in the Hague Conference of 1899," he said, "... these declarations, although enforced by no binding stipulation, nevertheless have become principles of action in international affairs because, through the progress of civilization, and the influence of many generations of devoted spirits in the cause of humanity, the world had become ready ...

"Plainly, the next advance to be urged ... is to pass on from an arbitral tribunal, the members of which are specifically selected ... for each case, and whose service is but an incident in the career of a diplomatist, to a permanent court composed of judges who devote their entire time to the performance of judicial duties ..."

Deeply convinced that the time was ripe to advance arbitration, Root succeeded in persuading the Senate to forgo their objections to treaties of arbitration with European countries, and in 1908–1909 he managed to achieve some 40 reciprocal trea-

ties of arbitration with various Latin American and European countries as well as with Japan.

Root believed there was no international controversy so serious that it could not be settled if both parties wished to settle it. Conversely, there were few controversies so trifling that they could not be made the occasion for war if the parties really wished to fight. Root pinpointed disposing causes which create an atmosphere of belligerency, among which were race and local prejudice breeding dislike and hatred between the peoples of different countries. He had opportunity to combat an instance of just such an attitude. A wave of Japanese immigration had swept over the Pacific Coast, and racial discrimination had run rampant. Japanese children were being refused admission to California schools. Root, however, persuaded California authorities to withdraw all objections to Japanese children in the schools. He negotiated a "Gentleman's Agreement" with the Japanese government by which Japan would control immigration to the United States, thereby avoiding passage of exclusionary immigration laws.

Root became a senator in 1909, serving in the Senate until 1915. As chief US Counsel before the Hague Court in 1910, he settled the US–British controversy over the North Atlantic coastal fisheries. Along with Lord Bryce, he resolved current US–Canadian problems of the time and created the Permanent American–Canadian Joint High Commission for the settlement of any future difficulties. Also while he was a senator, he had an opportunity to display an interest in justice obtained over and above nationalistic partiality by reversing the US Panama Act, a bill passed in 1912 which exempted US shipping from paying tolls to use the Panama Canal while levying charges against other nations' shipping. Under his guidance this was repealed in 1914.

He was the leading Republican supporter of the League of Nations. Despite the failure of the United States to join the League, he was granted the opportunity to contribute to his long-time dream of a permanent court furthering the role of arbitration between the community of nations. At the request of the Council of the League he served on the League's commission of jurists which framed the Statute for the Permanent Court of International Justice which was set up in 1921.

However, in 1929 after intermittent discussion between the League and the United States concerning certain reservations the Senate had insisted upon in its 1926 ratification of the Protocol of US participation in the court, Root convinced the delegates from 55 nations to accept a revised Protocol. But when he appeared before the US Senate Foreign Relations Committee to urge ratification he met an obstinate Senate which failed to act at that time and ultimately declined to ratify at all.

Root was also the first president of the Carnegie Endowment for International Peace, serving from 1910 to 1925. He helped to found its European counterpart, and worked on its programs for the advancement of pure science.

These opportunities to act upon his dedication to the cause of international arbitration did not alter Root's realism toward the long and arduous road ahead before the threat of war would yield to a major acceptance of arbitration. Nor did the reversals he encountered destroy his faith in an ultimate resolution. "The attractive idea that we can now have a parliament of men with authority to control the conduct of nations by legislation or an international police force with power to enforce national conformity to rules of right conduct is a counsel of perfection," he said. "The world is not ready for any such thing ... Human nature must come much nearer perfection than it is now, or will be in many generations, to exclude from such control prejudice, selfishness, ambition and injustice ..."

Yet it was in the inherent traits of human nature that Root placed his confidence for the ultimate permanent prevalence of peace. "There is so much good in human nature that men grow to like each other upon better acquaintance, and this points to another way in which we may strive to promote the peace of the world," he said. He recommended international conciliation through personal acquaintance between peoples, with little courtesies and kindly considerations; by the exchange of professors between universities, by exchange of students between countries, by expressions of praise and honor rather than the reverse. In sum, "by constant pressure in the right direction in a multitude of ways ..."

"Each separate act will seem of no effect," he said, "but all together they will establish and maintain a tendency towards the goal of international knowledge and broad human sympathy ...

"Not by invoking an immediate millenium, but by the accumulated effects of a multitude of efforts, each insignificant in itself, but steadily and persistently continued, we must win our way along the road to better knowledge and kindliness among the peoples of the earth which the will of Alfred Nobel describes as 'the fraternity of nations'."

Biography

Elihu Root was born on February 15, 1845, in Clinton, New York, son of Oren Root, a mathematics professor at Hamilton College. From this same college Root graduated at the age of 19, first in his class. After teaching at Rome (New York) for one year, he entered the Law School of New York University and received his law degree in 1867. He became a highly successful corporate lawyer. From 1883 to 1885 he was US district attorney for the southern district of New York. He served as legal adviser to Theodore Roosevelt during much of the latter's political career in New York.

A member of the reform element in the Republican Party, in 1899 Root accepted the post of Secretary of War in the McKinley cabinet. During the next five years he worked out arrangements for the former Spanish areas which came under US control following the Spanish–American War, devising a plan for returning Cuba to the Cubans; he eliminated tariffs on Puerto Rican goods and provided for civil government in Puerto Rico, and established US authority in the Philippines. He reorganized the administrative system of the War Department, reorganized the Army, establishing new procedures for promotion, and founded the Army War College.

In 1905 he became Secretary of State under President Theodore Roosevelt, and during his four years in this post he mended deteriorating US–South and Central American relations with a diplomatic tour, and persuaded the Latin American states to attend the second Hague Peace Conference. He brought the consular service under the Civil Service. He negotiated a "Gentleman's Agreement" with Japan in which that country agreed to limit immigration, and he influenced the West Coast to cease practices of racial discrimination against Japanese children by barring them from schools. He concluded an unprecedented number of treaties of arbitration with many Latin American and European nations as well as with Japan.

Root sponsored the Central American Peace Conference in Washington which resulted in the creation of the Central American Court of Justice, and along with Lord Bryce resolved US–Canadian problems then outstanding and created the Permanent American–Canadian Joint High Commission for settlement of future disputes. He served in the US Senate from 1909 to 1915, during which time he reversed a bill exempting US shipping from paying tolls to use the Panama Canal while other nations had to pay charges. As chief counsel for the United States before the Hague Tribunal he settled the controversy between the United States and the United Kingdom over North Atlantic coastal fisheries.

He was the leading Republican supporter of the League of Nations, recommending acceptance of the Versailles Treaty with minor reservations. He served on the League's commission of jurists which framed the statute for the Permanent Court of International Justice. Between 1910 and 1925 he was the first president of the Carnegie Endowment for International Peace, advancing pure science and peace programs, and helped to found its European counterpart.

He received many honors from many countries, including the LL.D. degree from Hamilton, Harvard, Yale, Columbia, New York University, Williams, Princeton, the University of Buenos Aires, the University of San Marcos, and the University of Lima. He won the Woodrow Wilson Foundation Medal in 1926.

Elihu Root died in New York City on February 7, 1937.

See also: Articles: *Arbitration, International*; *Pan-Americanism*

RUTH C. REYNOLDS

Henri La Fontaine

(1913)

The 1913 Nobel Prize for Peace was awarded to Henri Marie La Fontaine, whom the Nobel Committee called "the true leader of the popular peace movement in Europe." Henri La Fontaine was an internationalist whose fervent devotion to his ideals was matched by the extraordinary talents he brought to their actualization. Highly educated, he was one of Belgium's leading jurists, a zealous reformer, a professor of law, for 36 years a senator in the Belgian legislature (and the senate's vice-president for 14 of those years), a dedicated educator, and a prolific writer.

In addition, he had an immense talent and proclivity for organization. He inaugurated an ambitious bibliographical scheme wherein he established the Institut International de Bibliographie. This "House of Documentation" was a vast information retrieval scheme in which he filed, indexed, and provided information for retrieval on anything of note published anywhere in the world. With the help of a subsidy from the Belgian government, and through collaboration with Paul Otlet, he brought some of his plan to realization by developing a universal classification system and by producing reference works, particularly bibliographies of social sciences and peace. This developed into the Union of International Associations, located in Brussels. It was granted consultative status with the Economic and Social Council of the United Nations in 1951 and with UNESCO in 1952. It remains the only center in the world devoted to documentation, research, and promotion of international organizations, particularly the voluntary variety.

The peace movement before the First World War was so widespread, both in the Old World and the New, that it required a global network to unite the efforts of peace societies and the proliferating peace congresses and conferences. An organization was created to act as a clearinghouse for an ongoing exchange of information. Called the International Peace Bureau (Nobel Peace Prize winner of 1910), it was first organized and directed by the 1902 Nobel Peace Prize winner Elie Ducommun. Following his death, the co-winner of the 1902 prize, Charles-Albert Gobat, took up the leadership. La Fontaine accepted the directorship following Fredrik Bajer, co-winner of the 1908 prize.

La Fontaine also actively participated in the peace conferences. In 1889 he became secretary-general of the Société Belge de l'Arbitrage et de la Paix, and thereafter attended virtually all of the peace congresses held in the following 25 years. He was a member of the Belgian delegation to the Paris Peace Conference in 1919 and to the First Assembly of the League of Nations in 1920 and 1921. To these deliberations La Fontaine brought his uncompromising internationalism backed by his judicial expertise. He also gave his legislative support to the League of Nations, the establishment of an economic union with Luxembourg, the Locarno Pacts, the Kellogg–Briand Pact, disarmament, and the legal means of settling international disputes.

Another organization of paramount importance to La Fontaine was the Interparliamentary Union. Created in 1888 by two Nobel Prize winners, Frédéric Passy (1901) and William Cremer (1903), its purpose was to encourage and accommodate members of parliaments from nations all over the world to meet at specified intervals for discussions on matters of mutual interest. Of particular importance was the solving of problems before they became so entangled with special interests and so charged with emotion that they became difficult or impossible to arbitrate. To La Fontaine, the Union was an embryo world parliament, a supreme vehicle for arbitration, the precursor of a world government. He poured his energy and his professional acumen as a leading international jurist into making it work. He was chairman of its Juridical Committee prior to the First World War and a member of two of its important commissions, one on preparation of a model world parliament and the second on drafting a model treaty of arbitration.

Although La Fontaine's ultimate dream was of a world state, he was realistic enough to recognize that it was not coming soon, and during the First World War he wrote his best-known work, *The Great Solution: Magnissima Charta*, to sketch a "constitution" which would be appropriate for the many intervening years to come, but which would eventually be incorporated in the world state, and which in the meantime would prevent future wars. He proposed a plan for an international intellectual union, accompanied by the creation of international agencies that logically follow from the acceptance of the international idea, such as a world school and university, library, language, parliament, court, bank, and clearinghouses for labor, trade, immigration, and statistical information. In later years some of these ideas are thought to have influenced affiliated bodies of the League of Nations, such as the Institute of Intellectual Cooperation.

Also during the war he wrote "International Judicature," outlining the essentials for a supreme court of the world, but he allowed himself little hope at the time. He wrote in a letter, "The peoples are not awake . . . [There are dangers] which will render a world organization impossible. I foresee the renewal of . . . the secret bargaining behind closed doors. Peoples will be as before, the sheep sent to the slaughterhouses or to the meadows as it pleases the shepherds. International institutions ought to be, as the national ones in democratic countries, established by the peoples and for the peoples" (letter to David Starr Jordan, President of Stanford University, dated December 29, 1916).

Henri La Fontaine's letter proved prophetic within his lifetime. He lived to see his native Belgium invaded once again.

Biography

Henri Marie La Fontaine was born on April 22, 1854, in Brussels, Belgium. Besides serving in the Belgian senate for 36 years, for 14 of which he was its vice-president, this gifted scholar was also a distinguished international jurist, educator, vigorous reformer, and prolific writer. An internationalist, his overriding interest was peace through arbitration.

La Fontaine studied law at Brussels University, and was admitted to the bar in 1877. In 1893 he became professor of international law at the Université Nouvelle in Brussels.

La Fontaine supported and eventually directed the International Peace Bureau, through which he played a substan-

tive role in arranging the Hague Peace Conferences of 1899 and 1907. He also worked vigorously in the Interparliamentary Union when he became eligible for that organization through becoming a member of the Belgian senate. He was a member of the Belgian delegation to the Paris Peace Conference in 1919 and to the League of Nations Assembly in 1920, both organizations benefiting from the influence of La Fontaine's lifetime of work toward international organizations.

He founded the Centre Intellectuel Mondial which later merged into the League of Nations Institute for Intellectual Cooperation. He proposed the organization of a world school and university, a world parliament, and an international court of justice.

La Fontaine organized a vast information retrieval scheme in which he proposed to file, index, and provide information for retrieval on anything of note published anywhere. He produced a universal classification system out of this project, and some bibliographies in the fields of social sciences and peace. It ultimately led to the Union of International Associations, and became a resource center for the Economic and Social Council of the United Nations in 1951 and UNESCO in 1952.

La Fontaine was involved with education all his life; he occupied the chair of international law from 1893 to 1940, first at the Université Nouvelle when it was a branch of the Free University of Brussels, and then at the Institut des Hautes after the branch merged with the University. He offered courses of lectures on disarmament, the League of Nations, international misunderstandings, world federation, and the law in relation to political and moral crises in the world.

From his prodigious writing, these titles are outstanding works on internationalism: *Manuel des lois de la paix: Code de l'arbitrage* (*A Manual on the Laws of Peace: Code of Arbitration*), *Pasicrisie internationale: Histoire documentaire des arbitrages internationaux* (*Documentary History of International Arbitrations*), a source book of 368 documents on arbitration between 1794 and 1900, printed in whole or in part in their original languages, and *Bibliographie de la paix et de l'arbitrage internationale*, a reference work of 2,222 entries. One of his most famous titles, "*The Great Solution*," offers a set of principles for organized international relations.

He was a leading spokesman for women's rights, taking an advanced position on the place of women in the legal profession, and he was president of the Association for the Professional Education of Women.

La Fontaine enjoyed mountain climbing, and organizer that he was, he compiled an international bibliography of "Alpinism."

Henri Marie La Fontaine died in Belgium in 1943.

RUTH C. REYNOLDS

Prize Not Awarded

(1914–16)

Red Cross

(1917)

see *Henri Dunant and the Red Cross*
(1901)   *(1917, 1944, 1963)*

Prize Not Awarded

(1918)

Woodrow Wilson

(1919)

The Nobel Peace Prize for 1919 was awarded to the President of the United States, Woodrow Wilson, in recognition of his introducing "a design for a fundamental law of humanity into present-day international politics." The president of the Norwegian parliament, Anders Buen, further declared that "the basic concept of justice on which it is founded will never die, but will steadily grow in strength . . . "

In his response, President Wilson expressed his "very poignant humility before the vastness of the work still called for by this cause," adding that "if there were but one such prize, or if this were to be the last, I could not, of course, accept it. For mankind has not yet been rid of the unspeakable horror of war. I am convinced that our generation has, despite its wounds, made notable progress. But it is the better part of our wisdom to consider our work as only begun. It will be a continuing labor . . . "

Wilson entered politics in 1910, becoming Governor of New Jersey, a state that had long been dominated by corporate interests. He brought firmness and purpose to his new role, pushing through the legislature laws designed to clear up corruption and protect the public from exploitation by the big trusts. His success catapulted him into the national arena, where he won the Democratic nomination for the Presidency. Largely because Theodore Roosevelt had split the Republican vote, Wilson became President of the United States within two years of leaving Princeton.

Wilson's political philosophy was simple. He was a liberal individualist, insistent upon the right of unprivileged persons. These principles as applied to tariff and currency reform, labor legislation, and the doctrine he would later seek of self-determination for oppressed nationalities would all spring from this same source.

During his first two years he dominated Congress and achieved reforms of long-term historical significance, revising tariffs downward, creating a banking system under governmental control, and establishing a commission which checked overwhelming concentration of power in industry.

But with the coming of the First World War in 1914, Wilson's attention was chiefly directed to protecting the United States' neutrality. The British increasingly restricted US commerce, but this affected only trade. Far more serious was Germany's submarine warfare which threatened human life. By careful and patient negotiation Wilson avoided an open breach with the Germans for almost three years, even after the sinking of the liner *Lusitania* with the loss of a thousand lives, 128 of them American. Through negotiation, Wilson succeeded in persuading Germany to abandon its U-boat warfare.

In 1916 Wilson was re-elected, largely on the electorate's approval of his keeping the United States out of the war. Wilson made repeated efforts to bring the belligerents together, but his hopes were dashed when Germany declared unlimited warfare on the seas.

Wilson did not take lightly the immense responsibility of leading the American people into war. "It is a fearful thing to lead this great, peaceful people into war, into the most terrible and disastrous of all wars, civilization itself seeming to be in the balance," he told Congress as he asked for a declaration of war on April 2, 1916.

During that same month Wilson started to formulate the terms of peace when war should end. During his speech to Congress he had spoken of the reasons powerful enough to justify entering the war: "for democracy, for the right of those who submit to authority to have a voice in their own governments, for the rights and liberties of small nations, for a universal dominion of right by such a concert of free people as shall bring peace and safety to all nations and make the world itself at last free."

These were the principles he continued to visualize as basic to a lasting peace resting on a foundation of justice for all. In January, 1918, he gave his speech of the Fourteen Points. Eight of his points referred to specific national settlements; the others recommended open diplomacy, freedom of the seas, free trade, reduction of armaments, readjustment of colonial claims, and establishment of a League of Nations to enforce the peace terms and prevent future wars. As a historical scholar, he could understand Baroness von Suttner's warning, "Every war, whatever the results may be, contains within itself the seed of future wars." Wilson was determined to break the historical pattern of repeating injustices, and he saw a League of Nations as the means to that end.

It has been suggested that President Wilson unwisely assumed personal direction of the United States' part in the negotiations at the Paris Peace Conference. Certainly both party leaders in the United States opposed this. The months in Paris would put Wilson dangerously out of touch with the outlook of his own people. But Wilson felt a personal responsibility, a duty he could not delegate, to help bring about an enduring peace.

However, a first mistake was certainly his failure to include any Republicans in the group he took with him to the conference. In the congressional elections of 1918 the Republicans had won the ascendancy in Congress, and this would have been the strategic, as well as the fair, thing for President Wilson to have done. He was at the zenith of his power during this time, and he went to Paris as the herald of a new age, a universally acclaimed champion of international justice. It may have been difficult to think in terms of home politics under such circumstances, but in failing to do so Wilson unwittingly contributed to the ultimate defeat of his cherished plans for the League.

Furthermore, he soon found himself outmaneuvered by seasoned career politicans. As the deliberations progressed, old ambitions, suspicions, and prejudices surfaced, and Wilson discovered that the world's ablest diplomats were striving to advance not the cause of international justice which he had come to serve, but their separate interests and aspirations in behalf of their respective governments. He saw his Fourteen Points broken and compromised by a network of secret treaties and understandings previously unknown to him.

Wilson returned home with the first draft of the Treaty of Versailles in order to be in Washington DC when Congress adjourned. Thirty-seven Republican senators declared their opposition to the League covenant and protested its inclusion in the treaty. When Wilson returned to Paris he found that in his absence the allied premiers had passed a resolution that would have resulted in the separation of the League covenant from the treaty. In exchange for keeping the League in the treaty, the wily European diplomats succeeded in bartering away Wilson's Fourteen Points. Wilson was forced into accepting a seriously flawed treaty, imposed by the will of the victors upon the vanquished, dividing the globe into indefensible little chunks, and most seriously, crippling Germany with a plan that it should pay for the war through savage reparation demands.

Wilson lost the faith of the European peoples who had pinned upon him their hopes for a new and revolutionary kind of peace. Lloyd George wrote after Wilson's death, "I believe I may say that never have I seen such vicious, cruel vituperation as was heaped upon him at home and in Paris . . . such abuse never was leveled at any man in like position in history and it hurt him terribly."

At home, Wilson carried the Treaty of Versailles back to secure ratification by two-thirds of the Republican-controlled Senate. In this he failed by 15 votes. However, it is the opinion of many historians that Wilson could have had his treaty had he been willing to accept relatively minor changes relating to certain reservations on the collective security provisions which membership in the League would entail. His initial failure to take a high-ranking Republican with him to Paris, his loss of contact with the American public during the many months spent in Paris, his inability to countenance changes in the treaty when the Senate offered compromise, and a serious deterioration in his health following a stroke which rendered impossible his further efforts to persuade either the public or the Senate all added up to Wilson's fatal choice of taking the issue of unconditional ratification into the 1920 presidential campaign. It was his hope that the American public would vote a mandate for the treaty by electing a new Democratic president. But with the resounding defeat of the Democrats, all hopes for the treaty died.

Despite Wilson's failure to secure a just peace and the United States' entrance into the League, he must still be credited with introducing before the world a concept of international justice and morality which had lasting significance. He bequeathed his generation, and following generations, with a faith that such an order might be possible, and in the United Nations, much of Wilson's work and idealism came to fruition.

Biography

Thomas Woodrow Wilson was born in Stauton, Virginia, on December 28, 1856, son of a Presbyterian minister and a devout mother whose own father was also a Presbyterian minister. He was raised in a pious, loving, and rigidly authoritarian home.

While in college Wilson evinced an early and deep interest in government and political science. During his senior year at Princeton he wrote a paper comparing the British and US systems of government which was published in the *International Review*; at Johns Hopkins University his Ph.D. dissertation was a scholarly study of US congressional government.

In 1885 he began 25 years of teaching, first at Bryn Mawr College for two years, then at Wesleyan for two years, and finally at Princeton, where he remained until 1910. He became the president at Princeton, and brought reforms in the social and academic systems which raised Princeton to distinguished new heights among US universities.

In 1910 he entered politics, and as a reforming governor of New Jersey cleared corruption and put through legislation protecting the public from exploitation by big trusts. In 1912, as a Democratic candidate for the Presidency, he won chiefly owing to a split in the Republican party. Though plagued by a near civil war in Mexico he managed reform legislation of historical significance, but his greatest achievement was maintaining US neutrality during the First World War. This took tact and determination in the face of British and German warfare at sea, the former intrusive upon US trade and the latter, with the use of submarines, endangering American lives. Wilson repeatedly attempted mediation between the belligerent nations, but to no avail. The most severe test of his diplomacy was the German sinking of the *Lusitania* with the loss of 128 American lives among the thousand victims of that tragedy. Wilson sent a stiff note to the German government, and with persistent negotiations extracted a promise from the Germans to discontinue their U-boat warfare.

In 1916 he was re-elected, chiefly on his keeping the United States out of the war, but soon after his re-election Germany declared unlimited warfare on the seas. As a result, on April 2 the United States entered the war. Wilson proved a skillful wartime executive, but he also began a carefully constructed plan for the treaty which would come at the war's end. He wished for a peace so just that it would contain no seeds for a future war. His peace plan was the "Fourteen Points," eight of which involved more or less specific territorial and political problem solving, and six concerned with general principles of international relations: open covenants, freedom of navigation, removal of economic barriers, reduction of armaments, readjustment of colonial claims, and establishment of a League of Nations.

Wilson went to Paris to represent the United States in the negotiating of the Treaty of Versailles. There he was outmaneuvered by the seasoned diplomats Lloyd George of the United Kingdom and Clemenceau of France, whose negotiations were based upon their own national interests, upon their belief in military might, and upon their determination to crush Germany under massive reparation assessments. A vindictive document, the Treaty of Versailles retained only the League of Nations from Wilson's Fourteen Points for a peace based on justice.

Wilson's defeat was completed when he took the treaty home for congressional ratification. The Senate refused to pass an unmodified treaty; Wilson refused to compromise. Now seriously broken in health following a stroke, he unwisely carried the deadlocked issue into the 1920 presidential election. With his subsequent defeat the treaty with its vital provision for the United States' entrance into the League of Nations was never ratified.

Although he failed to get either a just peace or the United States' entrance into the League of Nations, Wilson must still be credited with a campaign for world order which had a lasting significance. He gave his generation, and following generations, the faith that such an order might be possible, and the Charter of the United Nations reflects his aspirations.

Wilson was married in 1885 to Ellen Louise Axson. They had three daughters, Margaret Woodrow, Jessie Woodrow and Eleanor Randolph Wilson. Mrs Wilson died in the

White House shortly after the outbreak of the First World War. In 1916 he married Edith Bolling Galt, who survived him by many years.

Woodrow Wilson died in Washington, DC, on February 3, 1924.

Bibliography

Current History 1924 The death of Woodrow Wilson. 19(6): 887–95

RUTH C. REYNOLDS

Leon Bourgeois

(1920)

The 1920 Nobel Peace Prize was awarded at the first ceremony to be held following the most devastating military conflict the world had seen—a "war to end all wars." The choice of France's Leon Bourgeois for the 1920 Prize, and retroactively of Woodrow Wilson of the United States for the 1919 Prize, represented the great hope vested in the League of Nations as an instrument for fulfilling this promise of lasting peace. Bourgeois was the embodiment of the continuity of this ideal, from the time of the Hague Peace Conferences of 1899 and 1907 when he laid the groundwork for the League to the gathering of its first Assembly in 1920.

Bourgeois believed that international cooperation could be achieved on the basis of the principles of arbitration and international justice that had been evolved at the Hague Conferences. The League he saw as a juridical military organization whose function would be to preserve peace, if necessary by sanctions. It would be called upon only when needed. This was the basis on which he built the case for the League when, as a necessary adjunct to arbitration, he announced somewhat prematurely in 1908 that "the League of Nations is created. It is very much alive."

The President of the Norwegian Parliament, Anders Buen, saluted Bourgeois as representative of the will for peace "through good days and bad." His praise summarized the position of countless other members of the peace movement whose activities had been in full flower at the onset of the First World War. These activists within peace and arbitration organizations over the world rallied in support of their countries through years of the very violence they had sought to prevent. But even as the war raged through 1914 to nearly the close of 1918, many were formulating a peace designed to prevent future wars.

A realist, Bourgeois viewed the position of his country as precarious without an international organization. In 1916 he had written, "We must see things as they are... Now the balance of power,

however skillful diplomats may be, results in the triumph of the greatest number and the most brutal, and not in the triumph of the noblest, the proudest, the worthiest. It is another policy, therefore, the policy of justice, which alone can give peace and security to France and the nations which do not seek to establish themselves by violence. There will be no policy of justice if the League of Nations is not set up."

A commission was established in 1917 to study the mechanisms through which the Société des Nations might work. Bourgeois was a leading contributor to the work of this commission, and it was he who submitted its conclusions to the Paris Peace Conference in January 1919.

The hope for a peace treaty based upon justice dispensed without regard to victor and vanquished was destroyed at the Paris Peace Conference with the creation of the Treaty of Versailles. The one beacon of hope now rested with the League of Nations. The Assembly of the League met for the first time on November 15, 1920, and Bourgeois was France's principal representative.

In a communication to the Nobel Committee in 1922, Bourgeois wrote of the new international law whose doctrine was uncontested by any civilized nation. He posed the question, "Have we arrived at a stage in the development of universal morality and of civilization that will allow us to regard a League of Nations as viable? What characteristics and what limitations should it have in order to adapt itself to the actual state of affairs in the world?"

Bourgeois expressed encouragement. He pointed to the immense progress already made in the political, social, and moral organization of nations: public education had spread to nearly every corner of the globe; democratic institutions were evident everywhere, with a weakening of the class prejudice so obstructive to social progress; an increasing number of social institutions now offered support to the rights of the individual, and Bourgeois believed that this would lead ultimately to the concept of the individual's responsibility for his or her conduct being in no way at odds with society itself.

He saw all these factors as preparation for the intellectual revolution that would lead people to understand the absolute necessity of having an international organization which would recognize and accommodate these principles. A fundamental necessity would be the guarantee that nothing essential could be violated by any of the contracting parties. This would require a "sovereign standard" by which each settlement could be measured and checked as needed, an absolutely impartial international law. Such a law came into being at the Hague Peace Conferences, Bourgeois maintained, and if this law was all too obviously violated in 1914 and during the war years, the Allied victory had righted the wrong done. It had been fought and won in the name of ending all wars.

As a realist, Bourgeois acknowledged the need for a means of enforcement beyond that of moral force. But he stipulated that no nation could find itself suddenly involved against its will in a military operation without the explicit consent of its government. He said that in connection with the difficult problem of limitation of armaments neither the Council nor the Assembly of the League had ever believed it possible to enact relevant statutes without the express support of every nation. He proposed that each nation would remain free to give or withhold its consent to any concerted military action. This left but one possible punishment open to the recalcitrant nation: the loss of the benefits of membership in the League.

In 1921 the Assembly of the League had adopted a resolution presented by Bourgeois concerning the establishment of the Commission on Intellectual Cooperation. Bourgeois defined intellectual cooperation as the pooling of all intellectual resources for mutual and equitable exchange. "All living organisms must have a driving force, a moving spirit," he wrote. "From all these diverse forces arising from nations and races, is it not possible to give birth to a communal soul, to a common science for a communal life, associating but not absorbing the traditions and hopes of every country in a concerted thrust for justice?"

Bourgeois concluded his message to the Nobel Committee with the acknowledgment that many years of trial must yet elapse and many retrogressions yet occur before an organization like the League of Nations could realize its potential and achieve its purpose. But he dared to hope that the "potent benefits of peace and of human solidarity will triumph . . ."

Biography

Léon Victor Auguste Bourgeois was born on May 21, 1851, in Paris, where he lived most of his life. A diligent student, he studied at the Massin Institution and the Lycée Charlemagne. Enthusiastic and with eclectic interests, his curriculum included studies in Hinduism and Sanskrit, as well as the fine arts, including music and sculpture. Following a degree from the Law School of the University of Paris he practiced law for several years. In 1876 he entered government service, in which he was destined ultimately to serve in virtually every major post in the French government. Between 1876 and 1887 he served as deputy head of the Claims Department of the Ministry of Public Works, as secretary-general of the Prefecture of the Marne, under-prefect of Reims, prefect for Tarn, secretary-general of the Seine, prefect of Haute–Garonne, director of personnel in the Ministry of the Interior, director of Departmental and Communal Affairs, and chief-commissioner of the Paris Police Department.

In 1888 Bourgeois was elected deputy from the Marne. He attended Radical Socialist congresses and became their outstanding orator. That same year he became Undersecretary of State, in 1889 the elected deputy from Reims, and in 1890 Minister of the Interior.

As Minister of Public Instruction his radical reforms encompassed primary and secondary education systems as well as universities; he regrouped university faculties and expanded the availability of postgraduate education. In 1892 he gave up his second Public Instruction portfolio to accept the Ministry of Justice portfolio.He formed his own government in 1895 and attempted to implement a general income tax, a retirement plan for workers, and plans to separate church and state, but in six months his government fell in a constitutional fight over finances.

In 1899 as chairman of the French delegation he presided over the Third Commission of the Hague Peace Conference dealing with international arbitration. Working with the British and US delegations he was party to a proposal to establish a Permanent Court of Arbitration, to which he became a member in 1903.

In 1902 he became president of the Chamber of Deputies, but resigned in 1904 for reasons of health. In 1905 he sought and won election as the senator from Marne, a position he held for the rest of his life. In 1906 he became Minister of Foreign Affairs.

As chairman of the First Commission on Arbitration at the second Hague Peace Conference in 1907, he laid the groundwork for the League of Nations, earning the accolade of being its spiritual father. In 1912 he served as Minister of Public Works, in 1914 as Minister of Foreign Affairs. He was Minister of State during the First World War and Minister of Public Works again in 1917.

Bourgeois headed a commission of inquiry on the creation of the League of Nations in 1918 and prepared a draft of the findings. As president of the French Association for the League he attended the 1919 Congress of organizations interested in its establishment. That year he also represented France in a League of Nations Commission chaired by President Woodrow Wilson of the United States.

The year 1920 saw him at the apex of his career as he became president of the French Senate and the first elected president of the Council of the League of Nations. But both health and sight were failing him, and in 1923 he retired. He died in 1925 at Chateau d'Oger, France. In recognition of his distinguished political career and statesmanship France honored Leon Bourgeois with a public funeral.

His publications include *Solidarité, La Politique de la prevoyance sociale, Le Pacte de 1919 et la société des nations,* and *L'Oeuvre de la société des nations.*

See also: Articles: *League of Nations*

RUTH C. REYNOLDS

Karl Branting

(1921)

The faith once held by members of the Nobel Committee in the peace congresses and international arbitration of pre-First World War days was transferred after the war to the League of Nations. In 1921 they chose to honor the two men primarily responsible for the admission of Sweden and Norway to the League, Karl Branting and Christian Lange. Sweden and Norway had recently accomplished a peaceful settlement of their own, and this was a microcosmic achievement of what was expected of the League of Nations. Calling Branting and Lange "worthy recipients of the Peace Prize," the Committee declared it "an honor and a pleasure for us that they should be representatives of two kindred neighboring nations determined to live at peace with each other."

Branting, Prime Minister in Sweden's first Social Democratic government in 1920, and again in 1921–1923 and 1924–1925, was Sweden's first delegate to the League, and he attended the Assembly sessions of 1920 and 1921. He soon led the cause of making the League the instrument of democracy and international understanding which it was intended to be, and he worked especially diligently in planning for an effective disarmament. This was in diametric opposition to the opinion of the Peace Laureate of the previous year, Leon Bourgeois, and by a bitter irony of fate, Bourgeois's first public speech after he had received the Prize turned out to be an attack on the limitation of armaments. Lord Robert Cecil of Britain, who would receive the Nobel Prize for Peace in 1937, was the only representative of a major power who supported Branting. It proved impossible to get even slight concessions in the limitation of armaments.

As far as national defense was concerned, while Branting was strongly opposed to unnecessarily large appropriations at the expense of social services, this did not mean that he supported "defense nihilism." It *did* mean an ordering of priorities wherein the

defense of freedom should be organized in such a way as to equalize political rights and economic benefits. Otherwise, Branting believed, even the most liberal military grants would be wasted. "Should disaster befall us, and if in the hour of danger we could only muster an army the bulk of which nourished a doubt as to *what* they really had to defend in this native land, in which all they can hope for is work and toil in days of good health and the poorhouse in their old age, then our fate would be sealed," Branting once said in a speech regarding military expenditures (Schou 1972 p. 531). Therefore, in Branting's opinion, far-reaching social reforms implied not only the best domestic policy, but also the best possible defense policy. While Branting was in public office he supported liberation of the working classes with universal suffrage, national insurance, and increased democratization. He advocated the peaceful settlement of the question of separation of Norway from Sweden's crown.

No other Nobel Laureate gave a Nobel lecture so eloquently defining the renewed hope of that postwar period for peaceful conflict resolution, this time through the League of Nations. He remarked on the similarity between Alfred Nobel's fundamental ideas and the Covenant of the League, and declared that the League was succeeding, after unparalleled devastation by the war, in opening perspectives of a durable peace and of justice between the free and independent nations of the world, both large and small. He called that devastation the birthpangs of a "*new Europe*" in which disputes between members would be solved by legal methods and not by military superiority.

He saw a further realization of Alfred Nobel's testament in the reduction of armaments called for by the League, and in the annual meetings of the League's Assembly, which he regarded as in effect the official peace congresses which Nobel had suggested. And this time they would bind the participating states to an extent that political leaders at the turn of the century would have regarded as "utopian." He recalled that Bertha von Suttner once quoted from a private communication addressed to her by Nobel saying that "It could and should soon come to pass that all states pledge themselves collectively to attack an aggressor. That would make war impossible . . . " Branting urged that the League of Nations become universal, so that it could truly fulfill such a task.

He visualized the League as an equalizer between the large powerful states and the small nations. With a fully functioning League, the power to command attention would be available to the small nations, even those who were so isolated and powerless that individually they could exert little influence on the great powers in world politics.

Branting concluded with the acknowledgment that to create an organization which would be in a position to thus protect peace in the world of conflicting interests and egotistic wills would be a frighteningly difficult task. But we must meet the obstacles whatever they may be, he said, for they pose far less than the dangers that will continue to menace civilization if present conditions persist.

Branting was a staunch supporter of state sovereignty, defending the right of a nation to shape its own destiny, free from external pressure. True internationalism he visualized as "sovereign nations in a free union." The only road to follow, he said, is that of the imperishable ideal of fraternity among free nations.

Biography

Karl Hjalmar Branting was born on November 23, 1860, in Stockholm, Sweden, son of Lars Branting. Educated at Beskow School, with a distinguished record in mathematics and Latin, he studied mathematics and astronomy at the University of Uppsala, and accepted a position in 1882 as an assistant to the director of the Stockholm Observatory. In 1883, after coming under the influence of the French socialist Paul Lafargue and the German socialist Eduard Bernstein, Branting abandoned his scientific career and joined the staff of the Stockholm paper *Tiden* [The Times] as foreign editor, becoming its editor-in-chief the next year. Upon that paper's financial demise in 1886 he became editor-in-chief of another socialist newspaper, *Socialdemokraten*. This paper became a potent force in Swedish politics during his 31 years of association with it. Branting believed in socialism based upon democracy, with the active involvement of the workers a necessity. To this end he formed workers' clubs, helped organize unions, and became one of Sweden's most forceful speakers. Known as the "father of socialism in Sweden," he was a prominent founder of the Social Democratic Labor Party in 1889, and served as its president from 1907 to his death in 1925.

Branting mobilized the working classes in support of the demand for adult, equal, and direct suffrage, but at the same time cooperated with the Liberals, resulting in a Liberal–Socialist coalition government in 1917, with Branting as Minister of Finance. This government brought about a constitutional reform of 1919 giving the right to vote to all males. However, the coalition dissolved when the Liberals refused to support the Social Democrats' demand for tax reform, unemployment insurance, and nationalization. He returned to the Prime Minister in October 1921 at which time the franchise was extended to women. He resigned in April 1923 under the impact of a combination of Liberals and Conservatives. In 1924 he once again became Prime Minister, but resigned the following year because of ill health.

Branting held a lifelong interest in international affairs. He supported the Allied position during the First World War, though maintaining Swedish neutrality. He served as Sweden's representative to the Paris Peace Conference in 1919, and led Sweden into the League of Nations, where he served as the Swedish delegate and was named to the Council of the League in 1923. Branting was chairman of the Assembly's Committee on Disarmament in 1920–1921, and a member of the Council's Committee on Disarmament in 1924. He helped with the drafting of the Geneva Protocol, a proposed international security system requiring arbitration between hostile nations.

Karl Branting died on February 24, 1925, in Stockholm.

RUTH C. REYNOLDS

Christian Lange

(1921)

Christian Lange, co-winner with Karl Branting of the 1921 Nobel Peace Prize, is unique among the Peace Prize laureates for his lifetime association with the Nobel organization, beginning with the year of its inception. In 1900 Lange was appointed first-secretary to the Norwegian Parliament's Nobel Committee and to the Norwegian Nobel Institute then in its formative stage. He assisted in planning the Institute's building, and the library of the Institute stands as a legacy to Lange's service during this period. He looked upon the Institute as a "peace laboratory, a breeding place of ideas and plans for the improvement and development of international relations."

During 1907, when the Second Hague Peace Conference convened, the Norwegian government sent Lange as one of its technical delegates. After his intense organizational activity during the formation of the Nobel Institute, he resigned his position in 1909, but continued to function as an adviser to the Institute until 1933. He then joined the Committee itself, where he remained until his death in 1938.

Lange was one of the world's foremost exponents of the theory and practice of internationalism. He worked with the Interparliamentary Union, an organization offering opportunity for the annual assembly of the members of parliaments from all over the world, often including the presidents or vice-presidents of legislative assemblies, to meet and discuss current affairs. Its primary hope was to handle any incipient problems, resolving conflicts before these could become entangled beyond solution. In the intervals between the sessions a skeletal committee of 15 members watched over the political horizon for the Union. The goal of the Union was to function as a higher parliament which, without limiting the basic independence of any nation, could function to exert a moral authority.

The Interparliamentary Union furnished Lange with his first official connection with internationalism when, in 1899, he was appointed secretary of the committee on arrangements for the Conference to be held that year in Oslo. It was his capacity for organization noted by members of the nascent Nobel organization on that occasion which brought about his appointment in their Institute and on their committee and his resulting lifelong association with the organization. Ten years later, following his resignation as first-secretary of the Nobel Institute in 1909, he returned to the Interparliamentary Union, becoming its secretary–general following Charles-Albert Gobat (1903 Peace Prize co-winner). In this position he administered the affairs of the Interparliamentary Bureau, the organizational arm of the Union through which information from over the world was collected and disseminated; he met with parliamentary groups in various countries and helped prepare the agenda for annual meetings. He edited the Union's publication and lectured and wrote on the Union.

He supervised the move of the Bureau from Berne to Brussels, and tightened its organization. However, the outbreak of the First World War in 1914 threatened its very existence as Germany overran Belgium. Lange fled to Oslo, and from his home there continued to keep international contacts alive in any way possible. The Interparliamentary Union owes its continued existence largely to Lange's efforts with the assistance of Lord Weardale, its president.

During this period Lange also taught history at the Norwegian Nobel Institute, and he started a history of the development of internationalism from its earliest days, titled *l'Histoire de l'internationalisme* (see *Peace "Encyclopedias" of the Past and Present: An Introductory Essay*). Auguste Schou, director of the Norwegian Nobel Institute, remarked that Lange's work accorded with the principles basic to the League of Nations, and that Lange had made an important contribution by participating in the work of ideological preparation for the League.

At Interparliamentary Union meetings held during the war Lange contributed greatly to the formation of plans for the revival of international cooperation at the war's end. When the war was over he convened the Council of the Union in 1919. He moved the administrative and editorial headquarters to Geneva to be close to the League of Nations, and it was there that the first conference following the war took place in 1921.

Lange was active in other organizations also. From 1916 to 1929 he was a special correspondent for the Carnegie Endowment for International Peace. He prepared a report on conditions in the warring countries, especially the Soviet Union, which was published by the *New York Times*. He also worked with a Dutch group called the "Central Organization for a Lasting Peace."

Lange spoke eloquently of internationalism in his Nobel lecture. He said he preferred the term internationalism to the term pacifism because internationalism was more positive, giving a "definite conception of how society should be organized." Internationalism in Lange's view embraced a social and political theory tackling concrete problems of how nations should organize their mutual relationships on a sound basis in economics and technology. "Today we stand on a bridge leading from the territorial state to the world community," he said. "Politically, we are still governed by the concept of the territorial state, economically and technically, we live under the auspices of worldwide communications and worldwide markets." The resulting mutual dependence between the world's peoples is the feature most to be reckoned with in present-day economics. Communications made possible simultaneous reactions to an event all over the world, creating "a common mental pulse beat for the whole of civilized mankind."

The task of politics, Lange said, is to find external organizational accommodations for what has been developed in economic, technical, and intellectual fields. The great and dominating political task of our time is to find patterns of organization which will adapt to world unity and cooperation between nations. Lange joined the internationalists of his day in looking to the League of Nations for this purpose.

From the opening of the League until his death, Lange was active in the League as a Norwegian delegate, his background in international relationships, both in theory and in practice, giving him the role which his biographer, Oscar Falnes, described as "a sort of standing adviser." A partial list of his duties in the League attests to Lange's interest in disarmament: in 1920 he provided a general orientation for the Assembly's Committee VI on Disarmament, in 1936 he chaired the Assembly's Committee III on Arms Reduction, and in 1938 he served on the Assembly's committee on armament problems.

Lange maintained that militarism goes hand in hand with nationalist economic isolationism to maintain the sovereign state against the forward march of internationalism. No state is free from it; there are merely differences of degree. "Militarism is basically a way of thinking," he said. And it is against this concept of the sovereign state that the League of Nations must now do battle, Lange argued, because through technical developments the sovereign state has become "a lethal danger to human civilization."

Lange was emphatic in his assurance that both diversity in national intellectual development and individual characteristics in local governments were wholly compatible with internationalism. "It is the political authority over *common interests* that internationalism wants to transfer to a common management," he said. "Thus, a world federation, in which individual nations linked in groups can participate as members, is the political ideal of internationalism." Before the war a first groping step was taken in this direction with the work at The Hague. Lange called the League of Nations the "first serious and conscious attempt to approach that goal."

Biography

Christian Lous Lange was born on September 17, 1869, in Stavanger, Norway. He studied history, French, and English, graduating from the University of Oslo in 1893. In 1919 he received a doctorate in the history of internationalism. He served as first-secretary to the Nobel Committee in Oslo, helping the Nobel Institute in its formative stages and establishing a distinguished research library there from 1899 to 1909, and remained as an adviser or on the Committee for the rest of his life. In 1907 he was a delegate from Norway to the Second Peace Conference at the Hague. In 1909 he became secretary–general of the Interparliamentary Union, an international organization of parliamentarians who met on a regular basis for discussions, and which had a Bureau where information between members and their legislative assemblies could be exchanged. It was largely owing to Lange's persistent dedication to keeping the Union contacts alive during the First World War that the Union survived during that period.

Lange also worked with a Dutch group, the Central Organization for a Lasting Peace and was active in the League of Nations, where he strongly supported disarmament. He was a special correspondent for the Carnegie Endowment for International Peace from 1916 to 1929.

In 1932 he received the Grotius Medal of the Netherlands.

Christian Lange died in Oslo on December 11, 1938.

RUTH C. REYNOLDS

Fridtjof Nansen and the Nansen Office

(1922)   (1938)

The 1922 Nobel Peace Prize was awarded to Fridtjof Nansen, a man beloved in his native Norway, whose Arctic explorations held the drama of a Norse saga and opened new vistas upon the Arctic and in oceanography. He was revered as few others have been for his monumental efforts to alleviate the cruel aftereffects of war upon frightened refugees beyond count, upon victims of famines, and upon prisoners of war. "The Nobel Peace Prize has in the course of the years been given to all sorts of men," a Danish journalist observed. "It has surely never been awarded to anyone who in such a short time has carried out such far-reaching *practical* peace work as Nansen" (Jens Marinus Jenson, *I Folkeforbundets Tjeneste*, Kobenhavn, 1931, p. 101).

The Nobel Peace Prize for 1938 was awarded to the Nansen Office, the organization which continued Nansen's work. Nobel Committee Chairman Stang, who presented the awards on both occasions, said the Nansen Office had continued to carry a message not only to thousands of refugees all over the world who have waited helpless and wretched, or have roamed from country to country without respite, but also a message to each of us. He admonished those fortunate enough to be secure within their respective countries not to forget that the world is much greater than their little corners of it, and to remember that humankind's children, wherever they may be and whatever they believe, are joined together by a common destiny and by an indissoluble and inflexible solidarity.

Fridtjof Nansen was born in 1861, the son of a prosperous lawyer in Christiania (Oslo). As a young man, he went on a sealing ship for a voyage into Greenland waters. When he saw the Greenland ice cap he determined that he would one day cross it. Six years later, in May 1888, he set out to do so, and his approach to planning the expedition clearly spoke of the philosophy Nansen used for surmounting obstacles. He proposed a way of no return. His party would travel from the uninhabited east to the inhabited west; thus once his party was put ashore there could be no retreat. The six men climbed to 9,000 feet above sea level, and met with storms and intense cold which forced their wintering in an Eskimo settlement. They returned in May 1889, triumphant, the first explorers to bring back information about the region's interior.

During this expedition Nansen became intrigued by the strange patterns in ocean currents. He observed that a current would carry a piece of driftwood from the Siberian coast to the Arctic Ocean, and he knew of the ill-fated ship, the *Jeanette*, caught in the pack ice off the Bering Strait, which drifted in a northwesterly direction for nearly a year before sinking. Nansen reasoned that this same drift of ice would serve as means of exploring the polar regions. If a ship were designed to ride up on the ice when the pressure enveloped its hull, the ship could likewise drift with the currents from Siberia across the Arctic Ocean toward the Greenland Sea. It would be a voyage, he thought, which would answer questions as to whether there was another continent or only an open polar sea. Nansen turned his conjecture into a well-planned expedition, building a ship appropriately named the *Fram*, which translates as "forward," and which once again described the manner in which he worked. For when it became apparent that the *Fram* would not drift right over the Pole, but would bypass it, Nansen set out with a companion, two sleds, two kayaks and 28 dogs to make a dash across the ice floes for the Pole. Although they did not reach this goal, they did reach the highest latitude anyone had ever gone. Again Nansen was forced to winter on an expedition, this time with his companion in a stone hut with polar bear and walrus meat they hunted furnishing food, and with blubber supplying fuel. In the spring the two men made their way south and rejoined their shipmates on the *Fram*. They all returned to Norway and a heroes' welcome.

Nansen then accepted a chair of oceanography at the university in Christiania (Oslo), taking part in a number of sea voyages. This might well have accounted for the rest of his life, for it suited him admirably, but as he grew older he became drawn to the problem of relations between nations. He interrupted his research in 1905 to take part in negotiations with Sweden for Norway's independence. After the desired dissolution of the Union, when Norway invited the Danish Prince Carl to become its king, Nansen was one of those chosen to escort him to his new kingdom. Nansen also served as his country's minister to the United Kingdom until May 1908. In the next few years he again led several oceanographic expeditions into polar regions, but the outbreak of the First World War in 1914 changed his life. Nansen looked on the war with horror. "The people of Europe, the 'torchbearers of civilization' are devouring one another," he said, "trampling civilization under foot, laying Europe in ruins and who will be the gainer? For what are they fighting? Power—only power."

Because the war made it impossible for Norway to import grain from the Eastern European countries, it turned to the United States. However, the United States was at war and was reluctant to sell to a neutral Norway. Nansen headed a commission appointed to persuade the United States to sell the grain. For almost a year between 1917 and 1918 negotiations dragged on, and Norway's eventual success was owing chiefly to Nansen's patience and diplomatic skill.

During the war years Nansen promoted the concept of an organization at the war's end which could bring about a secure and lasting peace. He ardently supported the League of Nations, spending the early part of 1919 in Paris as president of the Norwegian Union for the League, trying to bring influence to bear on the statesmen at the Peace Conference. He urged Norway's early entry, saying the League could be "a protection for the weak and oppressed, a judge in the disputes of its members, a force for peace and justice." From 1920 until his death he was a delegate to the League from Norway. He advocated the admission of Germany, and to this end he brought about personal contact between the Foreign Ministers of France and Germany, Aristide Briand and

Gustav Stresemann (co-winners of the 1926 Peace Prize).

It was the League of Nations which cast Nansen into his role as rescuer of the war's bereft. Frederik Stang, Chairman of the Nobel Committee, described well the difficulty of comprehending Nansen's task: "The human mind cannot visualize this enormous activity any more than it can grasp astronomical figures. One starving person, one human being lying like forgotten wreckage on a street corner, wasting away bit by bit—this we understand; here our feeling is so strong it becomes compassion. One refugee, even a crowd of refugees, pushing their children and their possessions in wheelbarrows in front of them—this we understand. But millions of these, hunted like game from country to country, behind them the fires of their burning homes, before them the emptiness of a future over which they have no control—here our minds stop dead; instead of producing images, they merely playback the statistics presented to them . . . a program whose aim is to rescue a continent's millions from misery and death, this presents proportions so immense and involves such a myriad of jumbled details that we give up and allow our minds to rest."

Nansen put it simply. He said that when one has beheld the great beseeching eyes in the starved faces of children, the eyes of agonized mothers, the ghost-like men, then one's mind can be opened to the full extent of the tragedy.

His first humanitarian task came in April 1920 when the League appointed him High Commissioner responsible for the repatriation from the Soviet Union of about 450,000 German and Austro-Hungarian prisoners of war. With minimum funds, with skill and ingenuity, Nansen approached the Soviet and German governments and concluded agreements for the delivery of the prisoners. Homeless, starved, tortured, unwanted, the prisoners had been waiting for four, five, and even six years. In September 1921 Nansen was able to report to the League of Nations that 350,000 prisoners were repatriated via the Baltic, 12,000 via Vladivostok, and 5,000 via the Black Sea.

But before he had even finished this task, Nansen was given the still more difficult task of resettling Russian refugees from all over Europe. In June 1921 the Council of the League, pressured by the International Red Cross and other organizations, appointed Nansen High Commissioner for Refugees under the auspices of the League of Nations. His assignment was to promote mutual cooperation between nations so that needy prisoners and Russian refugees could be transferred to countries where work was available.

Some nations responded favorably, but others refused to cooperate. Nansen asked, "Why were there some who did not want to help?" and he conjectured, "In all probability their motives were political. They epitomize . . . the lack of will to understand people who think differently. They call us romantics, weak, stupid, sentimental idealists, perhaps because we have some faith in the good which exists even in our opponents, and because we believe that kindness achieves more than cruelty. . ."

A large number of refugees originally from countries separated from Russia after the war were taken back home. For those stripped even of a country to call their own, Nansen invented the "Nansen Passport," a document of identification for displaced persons. It first helped the vast numbers of White Russians who had emigrated at the time of the Revolution. Nansen took on the task of resettling them in new countries where they could earn a decent living. The "Nansen Passport" came to be recognized by 52 governments, and eventually gave identity to countless thousands.

In August 1921 the Red Cross asked Nansen to undertake yet a third rescue mission. Millions of Russians were dying in the famine of 1921–22 and Nansen was asked to direct the famine relief work. While the Russians starved, there were huge quantities of grain in other countries—in the United States the wheat lay rotting for lack of buyers, and in Argentina the maize was used as fuel for railway engines. Adequate transportation was available but political differences led to arguments concerning support for the Soviet regime. Nansen answered these objections: "I do not believe that we are supporting the Soviet simply because we are showing the Russian people that there is compassion in Europe. But suppose that such aid *would* support the Soviet—is there any man who dares come forward and say: It is better to allow twenty million people to die of starvation than to support the Soviet government?" At the League assembly in September he made an urgent appeal: "We are running a race against the Russian winter," he said. "Make haste to act before it is too late to repent."

Nansen's appeal to the League was turned down, but he then repeated it to the world at large. With the help, in particular, of the American War Relief Bureau directed by Herbert Hoover, at least ten million lives were saved. Some double that estimate. But Nansen expressed deep regret at the League's failure to participate. He believed that had the League, with its great authority, lent its support the situation in the Soviet Union would have been saved, and the conditions in both the Soviet Union and Europe would have been totally different and greatly improved. Nansen warned that the future must not be built on distrust and hatred. The first prerequisite, he said, is understanding of the trends that mark our times and what is happening among the mass of the population.

In 1922 Nansen, as High Commissioner for Refugees, directed the work of aiding the victims of the Greco–Turkish War. Presented with the problem of the Greek refugees who poured into their native land from their homes in Asia Minor after the Greek army had been defeated by the Turks, Nansen arranged an exchange of about 1,250,000 Greeks living on Turkish soil for about 500,000 Turks living in Greece. He saw to their appropriate identifications and to the provisions necessary for a new start in life.

Basic to all of Nansen's success was his skill in breaking down myriad barriers which stood between the victims of misfortune and their rescuers. The Nobel Committee Chairman ventured a reason why this man could see Europe's misery at first hand, accept a sense of responsibility for alleviating it, and call forth the necessary energy, initiative, self-sacrifice, and patience to arrive at solutions. He recalled a mature man who, on the basis of his scientific knowledge, developed the theory that a current flows from east to west across the Polar Sea. Then once he had come to this conviction, he allowed his ship to be frozen into the eastern ice to be carried over the Pole. The current was there and carried him forward to his goal. "And is it not the same thing that we have now witnessed?" Chairman Stang asked. "An undercurrent has again carried Nansen forward: the deep current of human feeling which lies beneath the layer of ice in which nations and individuals encase themselves during the daily struggles and trials of life. He believed in this current, and because he did, his work has triumphed."

Fridtjof Nansen died in Oslo on May 13, 1930. His biographer, Jon Sorensen (1932), wrote, "Seldom or never has the sorrow of a nation been so much a sorrow of love. And it was more than a nation which grieved. A whole world mourned."

Fridtjof Nansen exemplified before the world a moral and universal responsibility toward those caught in the wake of the inhumane practice of war. During the early years there were times when his work advanced rapidly, not just as a result of a common compassion towards refugees, eloquent as Nansen had been in nurturing this latent virtue, but because of a shortage of labor in many countries. Refugees with sound health and skills were needed.

But during the worldwide economic depression which began in 1929 jobs became critically scarce. Countries closed their doors, placing restrictions on importation of foreign-made goods and imposing immigration barriers. Not only were refugees not allowed in; some of them were deprived of their existing work, and once again they faced the cold fate of the unwanted. Michael Hansson, president of the Nansen Office, said that refugees who had been living an uncertain existence for 20 years should have acquired a moral right to live in peace and security. The main task of the Nansen Office for some years had been to help refugees, those no longer able to work, and those dismissed from jobs in favor of the local unemployed. Somehow they must be allowed assimilation in the country of their residence. Their constant fear of being driven away once again from whatever humble homes they had created, their loss of country, of possessions, even of identity except as objects of charity represented an unfinished task begun by Nansen and taken over by the Nansen Office.

The accomplishments of the Nansen Office included construction of whole villages in Syria and Lebanon to house the Armenian refugees who were occupying Nansen's energies and concern during the last part of his life. By the end of 1935 it had settled approximately 10,000 in Erivan and 40,000 in Turkey. With minimal support from the League of Nations, always short on funds, so that some staff energies always had to be spent in seeking support, the Nansen Office had managed financial, legal, and material aid to almost a million refugees.

The rise of the Nazis to power in Germany brought critical new problems. Four thousand inhabitants of the Saar had to leave their homes when the district once more became part of the German Reich, and through the Nansen Office new homes were created for them in Paraguay. By 1935 a High Commission for Refugees from Germany had already been in existence for two years. The Norwegian government, acting out of concern for the swelling hordes of refugees coming out of Germany, suggested that this organization be merged with the Nansen Office under the authority of the League of Nations, with its seat in London. At the time this arrangement was to become operative, January 1, 1939, with Sir Herbert William Emerson the new High Commissioner, three million Jews were slowly dying of starvation in Poland, an unknown number remained in Germany, and animosity toward the Jews was spreading over southern and eastern Europe, in Hansson's words, "like a plague." He estimated that five million Jews in Europe needed the means and a place to seek a new life. In addition, he said, Europe had thousands of other political refugees.

The Nansen Office pointed out some basic, universal implications involved in its work. As well as the moral responsibility of humanitarianism, countries should recall what Nansen taught: that if intelligent human beings are abandoned and abused, bereft of work within their capabilities, their sheer desperation may be channeled into activities which could ultimately cost society sums many times the amount needed for the initial modest assistance which would have enabled them to integrate into their adopted communities. It is not only a moral step; it is also a wise one. The Nansen Office continued Fridtjof Nansen's commitment toward peace from which there is no turning back.

Hopeless as the work for refugees can seem, Hansson insisted "the one thing we must not do *is to give it up*. I feel sure that the new High Commissioner will continue this work in accordance with the traditions of the Nansen Office and in the spirit of Fridtjof Nansen." It is indicative of the ominous nature of the times in which the Nansen Office had been working that its Peace Prize award was the last made before the outbreak of the Second World War.

History

The Nansen International Office for Refugees continued the rescue work started by Fridtjof Nansen, who operated through the League of Nations as its High Commissioner for Refugees. Nansen, Norwegian scientist and explorer, had abandoned a world-renowned career in Arctic exploration and oceanography to help the refugees created by the First World War. In the early 1920s, as High Commissioner, he worked with Russians—prisoners of war, those who left Russia in the wake of the revolution there, and those living there when a major Volga crop failure brought about a devastating famine. In 1923 his mandate was extended to include Armenian refugees. Between 1924 and 1929 the International Labour Organization gave material assistance, but at all other times the High Commission, under Nansen's direction, fulfilled all functions itself. The refugee problem expanded, and the Commission's mandate correspondingly broadened to include Assyrians, Assyro–Chaldeans, and Turkish refugees.

Following Nansen's death in 1930, and the later abolition of the office of the High Commission for Refugees, the League Secretariat assumed responsibility for the refugees, while the actual assistance to them was provided by the Nansen International Office for Refugees, an autonomous body under the authority of the League.

On a diminishing scale the League provided administrative expenses for the Nansen Office, while the stream of refugees who required their assistance grew. The Office increasingly depended upon private revenues and upon fees charged for the "Nansen Certificate," an international passport devised originally by Nansen who recognized the need for identification on the part of thousands of refugees who had lost their identification with their own countries. Also, stamps were sold as a fund-raising device in France and Norway.

With the coming of the worldwide depression, the refugee problems were exacerbated by the scarcity of jobs. The Nazis in Germany, the civil war in Spain, the growing wave of anti-Semitism in Southern and Eastern Europe, and the tendency to toss helpless refugees from countries where they attempted to settle, and then prevent action on their behalf when attempted by the League of Nations—all contributed to a growing avalanche of refugees. Even so, the Nansen Office gave material, legal, and financial help to almost a million refugees. It kept the cause of the refugees alive, and achieved the adoption by 14 countries of the Refugee Convention of 1933, a modest charter of human rights. It arranged the settlement in Paraguay of 4,000 Germans required to leave Germany with the rise of the Nazis to power after 1933, and continued with the problem of Armenians in Syria and Lebanon with which Nansen had struggled, constructing villages in Turkey which housed nearly 40,000 Armenians, and resettling another 10,000 in Erivan.

With the rise of the Nazi government in Germany, the problem of refugees became so acute that the League established a High Commission for Refugees from Germany. This Commission, which also took responsibility for both Austrian and Sudetenland refugees, worked with the Nansen Office. Both were scheduled to be dissolved on December 31, 1938, to be replaced with a new agency of the League of Nations, the Office of the High Commissioner for Refugees, with headquarters in London.

Bibliography

Adams W 1939 Extent and nature of the world refugee problems. *Annals of the American Academy of Political and Social Science* 203 (May): 26–36

Sorenson J 1932 *The Saga of Fridtjof Nansen*. Norton, New York

RUTH C. REYNOLDS

Prize Not Awarded

(1923–24)

Austen Chamberlain
(1925)

The 1925 Nobel Peace Prize was awarded jointly to Austen Chamberlain of the United Kingdom and Charles Dawes of the United States after an absence of awards for two years. The announcement was delayed for still a third year and made with that of the 1926 awards. Perhaps it was the giant shadow cast by the laureate of 1922, Norway's famous explorer and humanitarian, Fridtjof Nansen, beneath which candidates for 1923 and 1924 seemed to pale. Possibly Christain Lange's advice to the Nobel Committee about waiting for a truly worthy recipient reinforced its reluctance. No explanations were given by the Nobel Committee; indeed their customary presentation speech was omitted. And none of the four laureates from the two years' awards were present or sent speeches although Gustav Stresemann delivered a delayed speech on June 29, 1927, at Olso University which was broadcast throughout Norway, Sweden, and Denmark. But the ceremony fell upon the thirtieth anniversary of Nobel's death, and Fridtjof Nansen gave a speech which paid eloquent tribute to the Committee's choice. The four laureates, Charles Dawes of the US and Austen Chamberlain of Great Britain for 1925, Aristide Briand of France and Gustav Stresemann of Germany for 1926, created two international pacts: the Dawes Plan, which bears its chief architect's name, and the Treaty of Locarno drawn up by the other three. Nansen said the Dawes plan was the first dawning of the day after a long darkness, marking the beginning of the policy of reconciliation which led to the Locarno agreements. And the Locarno agreements, he said, introduced a radical and complete change in European politics, transforming the relations between the former antagonists in the war and infusing them with an entirely new spirit—one deriving from the almost unprecedented attempt to base politics on the principle of mutual friendship and trust.

Nansen said it was neither idealism nor altruism but a sense of necessity which prompted these men to their accomplishments, and he further noted that none of them were "idealistic pacifists" but realistic politicians and responsible statesmen who recognized that the only chance of creating a future for humankind was to unite in a desire to work together.

The award to Chamberlain had indeed aroused its share of objections. He was called "a national politician thrust upon the world scene." A review of the circumstances surrounding the events leading to the Locarno agreements, however, might occasion gratitude that that was indeed the case. It was Chamberlain who first heeded Germany's proposals for such a pact, and he played the decisive part in achieving its fruition. At the end of 1922 the German Chancellor, Wilhelm Cuno, had proposed that the powers with interests along the Rhine should agree not to make war on one another for a period of 30 years unless such action was decided upon by plebiscite, but this was rejected by the French. In the next year the Germans came up with another proposal, this time based on a treaty of arbitration, but again without success. In February 1925 the German government, with Stresemann as Foreign Minister, tried again, this third time suggesting a pact expressly guaranteeing the Rhine frontiers by means of a collective and individual pledge. Yet again France's response was cool, but Chamberlain, as UK Secretary of State for Foreign Affairs, expressed enthusiastic interest. When France's government changed and Briand became its Foreign Minister, the longed-for meeting was arranged to follow the close of the sixth assembly of the League of Nations in September 1925.

It was agreed later that at the conference Chamberlain supplied the main motivating spirit. The atmosphere was kept friendly, as attested to by Chamberlain's brief message when accepting the Nobel Prize in which he acknowledged his colleagues as "statesmen both remarkable for the magnanimity of their spirit, for the independence of their judgment, and for their love of peace," and said,"Without their help, I would have been able to do nothing." Throughout the conference, where representatives of seven powers—the United Kingdom, Germany, France, Belgium, Italy, Poland, and Czechoslovakia—met at Locarno in southern Switzerland, words like "allies" and "enemies" were never used, and the old hostilities associated with such words dropped away. Major powers surrendered their absolute right to make war—an event without historical precedent. And this was localized around the Rhine. "For the first time since Louis XIV, King of France between 1643 and 1715, the Rhine had ceased to be a cause of dissension in European politics. So closes a chapter in history," Nansen exulted in his Nobel ceremony speech.

Under the Treaty Germany, Belgium, France, the United Kingdom, and Italy mutually guaranteed the peace in Western Europe, and Germany undertook to arbitrate in disputes with France, Belgium, Poland, and Czechoslovakia. The United Kingdom and Italy committed themselves to declare war on Germany if Germany attacked France, and to declare war on France if France attacked Germany. The German–Belgian and the German–French frontiers were guaranteed inviolable as established by the Versailles Treaty through a Security Pact.

An important part of Germany's acceptance back into the community of nations was its admission to the League of Nations. This Stresemann had requested in 1919, but only to be rejected. The Treaty of Locarno approved the admission of Germany to the League, and this was to provide a place for continued friendly and valuable interchange between the statesmen who created the Locarno agreements.

Circumstances provided a final and appropriate tribute to the statesman who had led the way in accepting Germany's proposal for attempting these negotiations: it was on Chamberlain's birthday, October 16, in 1925 that the Foreign Ministers initialed the documents known as the Treaty of Locarno

With the advantage of hindsight it can be seen that the agreements came too late to provide a lasting solution to complex problems, many of them deeply rooted in history, others the direct heritage of the Versailles Trety. Within 10 years Germany, Italy, and Japan had withdrawn from the League of Nations, and Germany had formally and unilaterally repudiated the Treaty of Versailles and had violated the Treaty of Locarno by reoccupying the Rhineland. Nevertheless, the four statesmen had presented to the world an enlightened attempt to base international relations on the principles of friendship and mutual trust.

Biography

Joseph Austen Chamberlain was born in Birmingham on October 16, 1863, the eldest son of Joseph Chamberlain, the British statesman known as the "Empire-builder." His half-brother, Neville Chamberlain, was Prime Minister from 1937 to 1940. Austen Chamberlain's schooling included Rugby and Cambridge, plus nine months at the Ecole des Sciences Politiques in Paris and twelve months in Berlin. Upon his return to Birmingham he became his father's private secretary, a further preparation for a political career which began in 1887 when he took a seat in the House of Commons, representing East Worcestershire. His maiden speech there drew praise from William Gladstone. When his father died in 1914, Chamberlain succeeded him in the seat for West Birmingham, and remained there for the rest of his life.

His 45 years in the House of Commons fall into two periods: the first, from 1892 to 1922, dealing primarily with domestic questions, the second, from 1922 to his death in 1937, with international questions. He held a series of responsible posts from 1895 to 1906: Civil Lord of the Admiralty, financial secretary to the Treasury, Postmaster-General, and Chancellor of the Exchequer.

Under Asquith's coalition government Chamberlain served for two years as Secretary of State for India, resigning in 1917. The next year Lloyd George made him his Chancellor of the Exchequer. From 1919 to 1921 Chamberlain saw to it that the enormous debts accumulated during the war were paid, and maintained a stable currency and strengthened the national credit.

Chamberlain succeeded Bonar Law as leader of the Conservative Party in 1921, staying its head for 18 months until the withdrawal of the Conservatives from Lloyd George's coalition, at which time he chose to stand by the Prime Minister.

In the Baldwin government of 1924 to 1929 Chamberlain was Secretary of State for Foreign Affairs. Here he reflected his father's training, combining a realistic philosophy with a moral fearlessness, and bringing patience, determination, and resourcefulness to his task. His first important act as Foreign Secretary was to reject the proposed Geneva Protocol, not because of its requirement for compulsory arbitration of international disputes, but because it was the Council of the League of Nations which was deciding what action member states should take to enforce the authority of the League in time of crisis. This was a contested procedure in some diplomatic circles, and Chamberlain offered the tempering suggestion that the best way in theory to deal with situations as they arose was to "supplement the Covenant by making special arrangements in order to meet special needs."

The apogee of his career as Foreign Secretary was the Treaty of Locarno. Composed of eight agreements, it included the Rhine Guarantee Pact with Germany, Belgium, France, the United Kingdom, and Italy as signatories; individual treaties of arbitration between Germany and former enemy nations; guarantee treaties involving France, Poland, and Czechoslovakia; and a collective note on the entry of Germany into the League of Nations.

When he returned to London, Chamberlain received a triumphant welcome, and was knighted.

During his later years in the Foreign Office Chamberlain dealt with problems with China and Egypt. He attempted in vain to defend British interests against the encroachments of the Chinese Nationalists, but lacked the necessary support from the United States and Japan. He prepared the way for a treaty on Anglo–Eyptian relations which was signed in the mid-1930s.

Chamberlain saw early the dangerous threat posed by Adolf Hitler. He favored both the imposition of sanctions against Italy during the Abysinnian crisis and their removal when they failed to prevent an Italian victory.

He wrote *Down the Years*, a reminiscence with character studies and essays, and *Politics from Inside*, consisting chiefly of letters he wrote from 1906 to 1914 to keep his ailing father informed of governmental and diplomatic events.

Sir Austen Chamberlain died on March 17, 1937.

RUTH C. REYNOLDS

Charles Dawes

(1925)

Charles G. Dawes, American financier and Vice-President of the United States was co-winner (with Austen Chamberlain of the United Kingdom) of the 1925 Nobel Peace Prize for his leadership in preparing a plan which stabilized a wildly inflationary German economy and led to the acceptance of Germany into the European community as a nation in good standing. Nobel Laureate Fridtjof Nansen, called the Dawes Plan the first light shed in the darkness of postwar Europe.

The circumstance of the awarding of the 1925 Prize was notably irregular. The Prize was the first to be awarded since that of Fridtjof Nansen in 1922. Its announcement was delayed a year, and took place at the same time as that of the 1926 awards. No presentation speech was made for the 1925–26 awards by a member of the Nobel Committee, although a distinguished audience at the ceremony, which marked the thirtieth anniversary of Alfred Nobel's death, were fortunate in hearing a stirring address by Fridtjof Nansen. None of the four co-winners were present at the ceremony, nor did they send a written speech as was often done in the event of absence. (Germany's Gustav Stresemann did deliver a Nobel lecture, but not until June 1927.) Most unusual of all, however, was the fact that none of the co-winners were known for their work in peace. But they had participated in the creation of two international pacts, the Dawes Plan and the Locarno Treaty, which brought partial restoration to a critically ill world economy and a consequent hope for international harmony in an extremely tense world. It may be said that these two important pacts were the objects of honor in both years' prizes. It may also be noted that they affected the careers of their statesmen–architects, directing their policies thereafter toward internationalism. In his lecture at the 1926 Prize ceremony Nansen called the Dawes Plan important both economically and politically for Europe and the United States. But its great significance, he said, lay in its indication of a psychological change in European mentality. The Plan's peaceful policy of reconciliation opened the way to the Locarno agreements.

The Treaty of Versailles following the First World War placed a moral responsibility upon Germany for all damage done to the populations of the Allied countries, but it did not deal directly with the financial aspects of the reparations. It provided for a Reparations Commission to translate the Treaty's provisions into actual figures through assessments of damage, and to establish the method and schedule of payment by May 1921. Such a Commission did attempt to comply, but it provided only a computation of legal liability and a suggested schedule of payment, and made no attempt to assess German's capacity to meet such payments. Germany could not begin to meet the amounts and schedule indicated, and defaulted on its payments altogether in 1923. Thereupon Belgium and France occupied the Ruhr, Germany's major coal mining and industrial center. The population of the Ruhr responded with passive resistance, and the German government suspended deliveries. These events destabilized European industrial production, and ignited a wild inflation of the Reichsmark threatening the total disintegration of Germany's economy and endangering Germany's whole constitutional fabric.

The Allied Reparations Commission was ready for the assistance of experts. The United States was affected by Germany's economic difficulties, whose effects were now being felt beyond Europe; and US Secretary of State Hughes suggested that Germany's capacity to pay reparations should be investigated. A competent committee for this purpose was formed in late 1923. The United States sent General Charles G. Dawes and Owen D. Young. The United Kingdom, France, Italy, and Belgium also sent personnel for the committee. It began its meetings in Paris on January 14, 1924, and made its report—the Dawes Plan—on April 9, 1924. It was recognized in the first place that as long as the occupation of the Ruhr continued, Germany was not a complete fiscal unit and that there could be no guarantee of it having a balanced budget. Second, the reparation liabilities under the Versailles Treaty figured among the budgetary expenses, and if they were in excess of budgetary possibilities it became impossible to guarantee that steps taken for the stability of the currency would be permanent. The Committee adopted a business attitude and considered political factors only insofar as they affected the practicability of the Plan. It sought the recovery of the debt, not the imposition of penalties, and it insisted that success in stabilizing Germany's economy and balancing its budget depended upon the return of the Ruhr to Germany. The country's finances were to be reorganized with the assistance of loans from European and US investors with repayments guaranteed by mortgages on the German railways and on German industries.

The Plan salvaged Europe's economy, although it was not a permanent solution. Most importantly, it halted, at least temporarily, the endless conflicts about Germany's reparations which had contributed to the anxiety and insecurity among Europe's nations during their first five years of peace. The last of the Belgian and French troops departed from the Ruhr on July 31, 1925.

Charles Dawes was well-qualified for this mission he accomplished so successfully. Trained in law, he had turned his hand rather to business ventures, administrating 28 gas and electric plants with his brothers, and moved successfully into banking. He had entered government service as a comptroller of the currency under President William McKinley. He had integrated the system of supply procurement and distribution for the entire US Expeditionary Force, and later performed the same service for the Allies by devising a central purchasing board, as well as a unified distribution authority. He had opposed many members of his Republican Party by strongly urging Congress to accept the Treaty of Versailles and the League of Nations. He had instigated a stringent and highly successful reform within the US government which demanded adherence to a budget within each department and unified purchasing.

He donated the Nobel Peace Prize award money to the endowment of the newly established Walter Hines Page School of International Relations at Johns Hopkins University.

Biography

Charles Gates Dawes was born on August 27, 1865, into a family with a history of distinguished service to its country which ranged over seven generations, from his father's service as a brevet brigadier–general in the Civil War to General William Dawes, who rode with Paul Revere in 1775 to warn fellow colonists of the British advance at the opening of the American Revolution, and then to the first William Dawes, who in 1628 had been among the Puritans who came to America. Charles Dawes himself was Vice-President of the United States at the time of his Nobel Peace Prize award in 1925, a prize he shared with Austen Chamberlain.

Educated at Marietta College, Dawes also studied for two years at the Law School of the University of Cincinnati. He did not practice law, although he may well have applied it to his advantage in his many highly profitable business ventures: he controlled a city block of business offices in Lincoln, Nebraska, and a meat-packing company; he invested in land and in bank stocks and directed a bank in Nebraska. He amassed his large personal fortune when he purchased control of a plant manufacturing artificial gas in Wisconsin, and another north of Chicago, thus beginning a gas and electric plant empire of 28 plants between himself and his brothers. He founded and became president of the Central Trust Company of Illinois.

Dawes turned this talent into service for his government, beginning with the comptrollership of the currency under President McKinley. During the First World War, while on General Pershing's staff, he integrated the system of supply procurement and distribution for the entire US Expeditionary Force, and later repeated a like service for the Allies by creating a central purchasing board and a unified distribution authority; rising eventually to the rank of General. Appointed to the newly inaugurated position of Director of the Budget following the war in 1920, he reformed budgetary procedures throughout the federal government.

In 1923 the League of Nations invited Dawes to chair a committee to analyze and recommend appropriate action on the problem of German reparations. The outcome of the work of this committee was the Dawes Plan.

From 1924 to 1932 Dawes devoted his entire attention to public service: as Vice-President from 1925 to 1929, as adviser to the Dominican Republic on financial operations in 1929, as ambassador to the United Kingdom from 1929 to 1932, as delegate to the London Naval Conference in 1930. During the Depression he chaired the Reconstruction Finance Corporation, a governmental agency empowered to lend money to banks, railroads, and other businesses to prevent economic collapse.

A gifted as well as a disciplined man, he wrote books, played the flute and piano, and established grand opera in Chicago while devoting time to both family life and civic duties. His published works include *A Journal of the Great War*, *Notes as Vice President*, and *A Journal of Reparations*.

Charles Dawes died at his home in Evanston, Illinois, on April 23, 1951.

RUTH C. REYNOLDS

Aristide Briand

(1926)

The 1926 Nobel Peace Prize was shared by Aristide Briand of France and Gustav Stresemann of Germany. Co-architects with the United Kingdom's Austen Chamberlain of the Locarno Treaty, they created an international pact which broke the deadlock of confusion and hostilities in postwar Europe.

The ruinous First World War brought devastation unparalleled in history to the peoples of Europe, and its cruelty infected the peace which followed. Despite the efforts of some enlightened statesmen who fought for a treaty designed to secure a peaceful future, the bitterly contested Versailles Treaty degenerated into an instrument of vengeance. Reparations were demanded of Germany beyond its capacity to pay. Endless conflicts about the reparations produced tensions and insecurity among the nations of Europe for four years following the war and Germany's efforts to meet payments plunged that country into a runaway inflation, paralyzing its economy and endangering its constitutional government. When Germany defaulted altogether in 1923, France and Belgium sent troops into the Ruhr, Germany's coal mining and industrial center, and to the districts between the bridgeheads on the right bank of the Rhine. German officials and leading citizens were expelled from the region. The repercussions of this occupation sent shock waves through Germany; the population engaged in passive resistance, and their supportive government suspended deliveries. Germany's remaining financial resources were completely drained and production lagged all over Europe, threatening its precarious political equilibrium. At this critical juncture a committee was sent to review the reparations in relation to Germany's capacity to pay. Known as the Dawes Plan, the findings of this committee, headed by Charles Dawes, American financier and co-winner of the 1925 Nobel Prize, introduced some sanity into the situation with a nonpolitical, soundly based review of Germany's financial situation, and assistance devised accordingly. It secured a breathing space for Germany, but a temporarily averted crisis could not offer permanent solutions to myriad and complex problems still outstanding, and Germany made a series of overtures for further arbitration.

The last proposal, centering on vexed questions about the Rhineland, was presented by Gustav Stresemann, then Chancellor. Following the war, French policy aimed at detaching the left bank of the Rhine including Alsace, cutting away from Germany 8 percent of its territory, 11 percent of its population, 12 percent of its coal supply, and 80 percent of its iron ores.

Stresemann was eager for diplomatic dialogue on the problem. This was the situation into which Aristide Briand stepped as an incoming Foreign Minister. Briand saw a hope that with the principal grievances removed a new democratic Germany might emerge. Briand's open reception to Stresemann's overture for negotiation marked a reversal of tenacious hostilities and opened the way to the Locarno agreements. The Treaty of Locarno, negotiated throughout 1925, was finally signed on December 1. It was a pact of nonaggression between France, Germany, and Belgium, guaranteed by the two supposedly impartial powers, Great Britain and Italy. The Treaty brought about a radical change in European politics. The hostile and protracted stalemate in relations between European nations yielded to an unprecedented attempt to base politics on the principles of mutual recognition of the common need for security.

Briand, Stresemann, Chamberlain, and Dawes were not the pacifists customarily associated with the Peace Prize. They were practical, high-level politicians with strong nationalistic outlooks. But they were realists. Briand aptly remarked, "The war has taught us one thing, namely, that a common fate binds us together. If we go under, we go under together. If we wish to recover, we cannot do so in conflict with each other, but only by working together." Whatever doubts existed about their personal qualifications as Peace Prize laureates—and many were expressed—there was no hesitation in welcoming the Dawes Plan and the Locarno Pact as, in Fridtjof Nansen's words, "the first dawning of the day after long darkness." Arthur Balfour called Locarno, "The symbol and cause of a great amelioration in the public feeling of Europe." The two initiatives may well be construed as the true recipients of the 1925 and 1926 Peace Prizes. It is certainly notable that all four of the statesmen responsible for these diplomatic instruments were awarded their prizes simultaneously, the 1925 Prize being given retroactively.

Briand, Stresemann, and Chamberlain made careful preparations for the conference in Locarno scheduled to take place following the closing of the Assembly of the League of Nations in September 1925. They came from diverse backgrounds, but they were bound by the common goal of seeking a general security wherein political and economic stability could be achieved. They shed the vocabulary of a decade—the words "allies" and "enemies" were never used throughout the conference—and tensions and hostilities gave way to a spirit of sober negotiation and arbitration. For the first time in history, major powers surrendered their absolute right to make war. Furthermore, the surrender was localized to that historical storm center, the Rhine. After the evacuation of the Ruhr, Germany suggested a pact between the powers interested in the Rhine which would give a mutual guarantee for the existing frontiers. In the Locarno Pact this mutual guarantee was given with Germany's promise not to try to recover Alsace–Lorraine.

The Locarno Treaty was a series of diplomatic agreements for peace and arbitration. Germany, Belgium, France, the United Kingdom and Italy together guaranteed the peace in Western Europe, and Germany undertook to arbitrate about disputes with France, Belgium, Poland, and Czechoslovakia. The United Kingdom and Italy were committed to declare war on Germany if Germany attacked France, and to declare war on France if France attacked Germany.

Germany's entry into the League of Nations was a condition for putting the Locarno agreements into effect. This carried the enormous import of restoring Germany into the European community as a nation in good standing, and it was a privilege which had been previously denied it when Stresemann had made application for Germany's membership in the League in 1919.

Germany's admission was welcomed in a speech by Briand. Among other things, he said: "No more war! . . . From now on it will be for the judge to decide what is right. Just as individual citizens settle their disagreements before a judge, so shall we also resolve ours by peaceful means. Away with rifles, machine guns, cannons. Make way for conciliation, arbitration, peace!"

Briand continued for the next five years to direct foreign policy on the basis of law replacing discord and an increasing belief in the international approach. Possessed all his life of a sharp eye for reality and political acumen—some would say political opportunism—it reflected his increasing belief in internationalism that he proposed a sweeping concept of a European Union at the League of Nations in May 1930. But the one-time Gallic nationalist politician had moved ahead of his peer statesmen, and his proposal was rejected.

Far more tragic was the fate of the Treaty of Locarno. In his acceptance message for the Nobel Peace Prize Briand had declared, "My ambition is that ten years hence the people will say that we deserved this award." Ten years later, however, Germany, Italy, and Japan had withdrawn from the League of Nations and Germany had violated the Pact by reoccupying the Rhineland.

It is the opinion of certain international observers that the history of that decade would have been better served if Briand and Stresemann had lived longer. For instance, in the year that brought the Second World War, Nicholas Murray Butler, Peace Prize co-winner in 1931, ventured his opinion: "It will always remain my firm conviction that had Stresemann and Briand been spared for another decade to maintain and to strengthen their mutual confidence and their commanding leadership in their respective countries, conditions in Europe and the world would be very different today from what they unhappily are."

Biography

Aristide Briand was born in Nantes on March 28, 1862. As a law student he became interested in politics and wrote for *Le Peuple* and *La Petite République*. He was a cofounder of *L'Humanité*. A member of the Unified Socialist party, in 1902 he was elected to the Chamber of Deputies as deputy for Loire. He served as *rapporteur* on a committee charged with writing a law on the separation of church and state, and served on the portfolio of public instruction and worship under the Sarrien ministry in 1906. His acceptance of this post in a bourgeois ministry led to his expulsion from the Unified Socialist Party. Briand also served in this post under Clemenceau.

He formed his first cabinet, the first of his spells as Premier, in July 1909, taking the portfolio of the interior and worship himself. In October 1910 he responded to a threatened strike on the railways by mobilizing all railroad workers who were still subject to military service and dismissed those who disobeyed, and he had the members of the strike committee arrested. Following the fall of his government in 1911, he became Minister of Justice in Poincaré's cabinet in January 1912. When Poincaré was elected President of the Republic in January 1913, Briand succeeded him as Premier. This government was quickly brought down over questions of electoral reform.

In August 1914, during the First World War, Viviani offered Briand the portfolio of justice. Then, when Viviani's cabinet fell in October 1915, Briand formed a government in which he held the portfolio of foreign affairs. He made its character one of a national coalition by including as ministers without portfolio the Socialist Guesde, the Catholic Conservative Cochin, and the three former ministers de Freycinet, Combes, and Bourgeois (the latter the Peace Prize winner for 1920). By the summer of 1916 he was accused of lack of vigor in prosecution of the war, and he formed a new cabinet. This government fell in 1917 over a difference of opinion between the Chamber of Deputies and the Minister of War, Lyautey.

For three years Briand took little part in government affairs. In September 1917 he was approached by von der Loucken, civil commissioner of Germany in Brussels, with a proposal for a meeting to discuss peace. Briand was favorably inclined to accept but was dissuaded by the Minister of Foreign Affairs.

In 1921 he again formed a government and took charge of foreign affairs. His special concern was application of the Treaty of Versailles, especially regarding Germany's war reparations. In the autumn of that year he went to Washington as the French representative to a conference on naval disarmament.

In 1922 Briand discussed with Lloyd George in London the question of an Anglo–French defensive pact. Upon his return to Paris he found he had lost support for the pact and resigned as Premier in January 1922.

In 1925 he took the portfolio of foreign affairs in Painlevé's cabinet and began the most successful years of his career with his participation in bringing about the Locarno agreements in 1925. On November 22 he became the new head of government, but the following March his ministry fell over an issue of a financial measure the Chamber refused to support. He accepted the office again, but with the depreciation of the franc the situation deteriorated

and the government fell in June. Once more Briand reconstructed a ministry, bringing in Caillaux as Minister of Finance, but a month later it too was defeated. In the succeeding coalition Briand again became Minister of Foreign Affairs. He directed the government of France on the basis of European consolidation and reconstruction.

In 1927 Briand offered the US Secretary of State, Frank Kellogg, a proposal for a treaty renouncing war as an instrument of national policy. He visualised it as a precedent for other nations to observe and follow. Kellogg, however, preferred to get the support of other nations from the beginning and this was done. Known as the Kellogg–Briand Pact, it gathered 63 signatories, including all the major nations.

Briand's last proposal was a concept put forth at the United Nations for a European Union. But when he failed to get the post of Foreign Minister with the next government, the proposal languished.

Briand occupied the French Foreign Office longer than any other diplomat since Talleyrand. He was Premier more often than any other politician in France. He was a member of 25 different minorities, and was in office for 16 years and 5 months. Politically he moved from his original leftist position to the right, but at the same time from his original nationalistic views to internationalist.

His published works include *La Séparation des églises et de l'état* and *Paroles de paix*. Aristide Briand died on March 6, 1932.

RUTH C. REYNOLDS

Gustav Stresemann

(1926)

The Nobel Committee looked upon the Treaty of Locarno as a longed-for release from postwar hostilities and the entrance into a fresh diplomacy of arbitration and peace. Of central importance was its establishment of a new and better relationship between France and Germany. Therefore the 1926 Peace Prize honored the German and French statesmen–architects of the Locarno agreements, Gustav Stresemann and Aristide Briand.

The First World War, unparalleled in history for suffering wreaked upon whole populations, had ended in the bitterly contested Versailles Treaty which had heaped upon the defeated Germans a crushing load of reparations for damages inflicted upon the Allied populations. But it assigned no monetary assessment to these reparations, instead providing for a Reparation Commission to translate these reparations into Reichsmarks by 1921. The Commission did so, but without regard to Germany's

capacity to meet the recommended cost of the expiation demanded of it. As a consequence, though Germany made efforts, it fell short; by 1923 it was apparent the wild inflation of the Reichsmark made the assessment impossible to meet and Germany defaulted altogether. This brought on the French–Belgian occupation of the Ruhr, Germany's vital coal mining and industrial center. The expulsion of German officials touched a keen nerve center in Germany, and the German government suspended deliveries and supported the area's population in a policy of passive resistance. Only the Dawes Plan of 1924, drawn up by one of the United States' leading financiers, Charles Dawes (1925 Peace Prize co-winner) in cooperation with representatives from the United Kingdom, France, and Belgium, saved Germany from economic and political disaster, and prevented corresponding havoc spreading throughout the world's economy. The Plan adjusted the reparations to meet Germany's capacity to pay. Germany received an international loan, its finances were stabilized with the reorganization of the Reichsbank under Allied supervision, and recognition was made of the economic necessity to return the Ruhr. This constituted a progression from hostility to cooperation between Germany and the other nations of the European community. Gustav Stresemann had been present each step of the way.

A glance at Stresemann's biography might raise questions about his suitability as a Peace Prize candidate. He was an ardent German patriot, supporting prewar German policy, and fiercely loyal to the Kaiser. He approved unrestricted submarine warfare, having argued as early as 1907 in favor of a creation of a strong navy. It may be said to his credit, however, that in 1917 when he became the leader of the National Liberal Party, although supporting the war, he also urged that Germany should be prepared for peace if acceptable peace terms were offered. He believed in force, in authority, in discipline.

Stresemann's great value was his realism. He began to see that Imperial Germany had believed in force without possessing adequate force to back up its policies. A month after the armistice of November 11, 1918, Stresemann formed the German People's Party as successor to the National Liberal Party. This party was at first monarchist, but gradually changed to republicanism, as did Stresemann himself. He was elected to the national assembly at Weimar to frame a new constitution in 1919, gained a seat in the new Reichstag in 1920, and was a member of the opposition until 1923, when he became Chancellor of a coalition government. It was a chaotic time: inflation had taken the Reichsmark from 4.2 to the dollar to 4,200,000,000,000 to the dollar. Stresemann's administration was short—just two months, during which time he dealt firmly with an insurrection in Saxony, restored order after Hitler's attempted *Putsch* failed, ended the passive resistance of Germans in the Ruhr to the French occupying forces, and turned to stabilizing the German currency. After resigning his Chancellor's portfolio, Stresemann became Secretary of Foreign Affairs in the following administration, and held this position with distinction under four governments. Against this background, Stresemann welcomed the Dawes Plan.

Stresemann worked well with Briand of France and Austen Chamberlain of the United Kingdom (1925 Nobel laureate), and they made careful preparations for the conference which was to meet at Locarno, Switzerland, to draw up mutual security pacts. These statesmen came from different backgrounds, but they arrived with a common goal: to provide general security so that political and economic stability could be achieved. In the words of Fridtjof Nansen (1922 Nobel laureate), the men who met at Locarno were not idealistic pacifists; they were realistic politicians and responsible statesmen who, having originally pursued directly conflicting policies, had come to the realization that the only chance of creating a real future for humankind was to stand united in a sincere desire to work together.

The words "allies" and "enemies" were never uttered by any delegate throughout the conferences. Under these cirumstances old hostilities lost their hold and, for the first time in history, major powers surrendered their absolute right to make war. The surrender localized around one particuar storm center, the Rhine. The Treaty of Locarno, which was signed on December 1, 1925, was a pact of nonaggression between France, Germany, and Belgium, guaranteed by two supposedly impartial powers, Great Britain and Italy.

By the Pact, the United Kingdom and Italy were committed to declare war on Germany if Germany attacked France, and to declare war on France if France attacked Germany. A treaty of mutual guarantee, or security pact, guaranteed the inviolability of the German–Belgian and the German–French frontiers as established by the Versailles Treaty. Stresemann can be credited here as working side by side with Chamberlain and Briand on integrating Germany into a new, peaceful European League.

Entry into the League of Nations was a condition for putting the Locarno Pact into effect. This was a trimph for Stresemann, who had tried to secure entrance into the League for Germany in 1919 but had been rejected.

Stresemann appealed in a national broadcast for support of the Treaty saying, "Locarno may be interpreted as signifying that the States of Europe at last realize that they cannot go on making war upon each other without being involved in common ruin."

Stresemann's comments upon the Locarno Pact in his Nobel lecture express a spirit commensurate with the qualities of a man of peace. He offered a rare and honest insight into the soul of a vanquished people: "Germany had to assume superhuman reparations which the people would never have borne had there not existed an ageless legacy of service to the state... I am speaking of the middle classes who saw the fruits of a lifetime of work vanish and who had to start from scratch to earn a bare livelihood... Theirs was an economic uprooting. But there was a mental and political uprooting, as well... [they] were now without a solid foundation for their thinking and emotions."

Stresemann told them that the Locarno agreements represented a policy for the future: "Germany faces this future with a stable nation which has been based upon hard work, upon an economy which will give increasing millions income and security. . .and upon a vital spirit which strives for peace. . .," he said.

Stresemann looked beyond his nation, and for him the Treaty of Locarno transcended old boundaries, both spiritual and geographic: "I do not think of Locarno only in terms of its consequences for Germany," he said. "Locarno means much more to me. It is the achievement of lasting peace on the Rhine, guaranteed by the formal renunciation of force by the two great neighboring nations and also by the commitment of other states. . . It can and it ought to be the basis for a general cooperative effort among these nations to spread peace wherever their material power and moral influence reach. . . *Treuga Dei*, the peace of God, shall reign where for centuries bloody wars have raged." More prosaically, his comments were echoed by Arthur Balfour who called Locarno "The symbol and cause of a great amelioration in the public feeling of Europe."

Stresemann's hope did not pass the test of history. Within 10 years Germany, Italy, and Japan had withdrawn from the League of Nations, and Germany had formally and unilaterally repudiated the Treaty of Versailles and had violated the Locarno agreements by reoccupying the Rhineland. It is, however, the opinion of certain international observers that the history of that decade would have been different if Stresemann and Briand had lived longer. For instance, in 1939, the year which brought the opening of the Second World War, Nicholas Murray Butler (1931 Peace Prize co-winner) voiced this opinion: "It will always remain my firm conviction that had Stresemann and Briand been spared for another decade to maintain and to strengthen their mutual confidence and their commanding leadership in their respective countries, conditions in Europe and the world would be very different today from what they unhappily are."

Biography

Gustav Stresemann was born in Berlin on May 10, 1878, son of Ernst Stresemann, a prosperous tavern keeper. He was educated at the Andreas Real Gymnasium in Berlin, and at the Universities of Berlin and Leipzig. His doctoral dissertation was an economic investigation of the bottled beer trade in Berlin, combining the practical and the theoretical by assessing the pressures of big business capitalism on the independent middle class of Berlin.

In 1901 he entered commerce as a clerk in the Association of German Chocolate Manufacturers, and a year later took over the management of a local branch of the Manufacturers Alliance. Through his organizational ability and persuasiveness, he increased membership in the Alliance from 180 in 1902 to 5,000 in 1912—a clear demonstration of the executive ability he was to carry into his political career. Other talents which would carry him to the highest level of government posts were early visible—his leadership and his eloquent persuasiveness were evident in his school years.

From 1906 to 1912 he held a seat on the town council of Dresden, in 1907 he won election to the Reichstag, and in 1917 he was elected leader of the National Liberal Party. He supported German prewar policy, and during the war supported unrestricted submarine warfare, but he urged Germany to accept a peace if a reasonable offer was made. He helped defeat the Bethmann–Hollweg government.

After the Armistice in November 1918, Stresemann formed the German People's Party as successor to the National Liberal Party. His newly formed party was monarchistic in the beginning but grew progressively more republican, as did Stresemann himself. He was Chancellor briefly of a coalition government, August 13 to November 23, 1923. During this period inflation was out of control, Hitler attempted his notorious *Putsch* in Bavaria, and there was an insurrection in Saxony. Stresemann dealt firmly with all these crises, but was forced to resign as Chancellor when his vigorous measures against the communists in Saxony caused him to forfeit the support of the Social Democrats. Thereafter he held a post of Secretary of Foreign Affairs through four governments, with a record of distinction.

He participated in administrating the Dawes Plan, which restructured reparations on the basis of Germany's ability to pay, and negotiated successfully with the Western Allies over the question of maintaining national boundaries established at Versailles. Stresemann was a major architect along with the United Kingdom's Austen Chamberlain (1925 Nobel laureate) and France's Aristide Briand of the several international agreements called the Treaty of Locarno. The Treaty was the first international agreement of major nations in which they surrendered the right to make war as they wished, substituting instead a series of pacts which they thought would offer mutual security and secure the peace.

Stresemann signed a rapprochement with the Soviet Union, the Treaty of Berlin, in 1926. That same year he saw Germany at last accepted into the League of Nations, and he served as delegate there from 1926 to 1929. As German delegate, he was one of the first to declare his readiness to sign the Kellogg–Briand Pact, renouncing war as an instrument of national policy.

In 1929 at The Hague, Stresemann accepted the Young Plan for the evacuation of the Ruhr; but he did not live to see it implemented.

Gustav Stresemann died in Berlin on October 3, 1929.

RUTH C. REYNOLDS

Ferdinand Buisson

(1927)

Ferdinand Buisson was 87 at the time he received the 1927 Nobel Prize for Peace as co-winner with Ludwig Quidde. For many decades Buisson had undertaken the task of reorienting public opinion away from war and to the higher ideal of peaceful cooperation among nations and the award was made for a lifetime of work devoted to this ideal. Sixty years previously he had helped Frédéric Passy, co-winner of the first Peace Prize (1901), form the Bureau Internationale et Permanente de la Paix (Permanent International Bureau of Peace). The same year, 1867, he had attended the First International Peace Conference at Geneva, where he advocated a United States of Europe. Known as "the world's most persistent pacifist," Buisson wrote literally thousands of articles and stood before countless lecterns speaking for the cause of peace.

Though fundamentally opposed to war, Buisson firmly believed that France was rightfully defending itself in the First World War. He believed that the defeat of Germany was necessary to ensure peace and justice in Europe. But he was bitterly disappointed with the Treaty of Versailles, and together with many other advocates of peace believed that hope now rested with the League of Nations. He was convinced that it was necessary to counteract the dangerous element of vengeance in the peace treaty by establishing friendship and understanding between France and Germany.

Buisson was born in Paris and was educated at the Lycée Bonaparte. He left school at 16 to help support his family upon the death of his father. His first job in his long career in education began at that time as a tutor in Paris. He later completed his education at the University of Paris, successfully passing the state teachers' examination in philosophy. However, Buisson's sharp sense of political justice kept him from taking the necessary oath of allegiance to Napoleon III in order to teach in his own country. He went into political exile in Switzerland, and there he held the chair of philosophy at the Academy of Neuchatel from 1866 to 1870.

He attended the First Geneva Congress of Peace and joined the Ligue Internationale de la Paix et de la Liberté (International League of Peace and Liberty) founded by Charles Lemonnier in 1867. He wrote articles denouncing militarism and began his lifelong campaign for the intensive education of the masses as the way to put an end to war.

With the establishment of the Third Republic in France Buisson was free to return there in the latter part of 1870. He was appointed inspector of elementary education, but the new government which soon came to power looked askance at his advocacy of secularization of schools, and he lost this post. With the coming of a more liberal ministry, however, Buisson came back into service as inspector–general of elementary education. He held this post from 1878 to 1896, and made many reforms in the French primary system of education. In 1896 he was appointed to the faculty at the Sorbonne as professor of the science of education. Buisson turned his prolific pen to pedagogy, and among many books wrote his major four-volume work, *Dictionnaire de pédagogie et d'instruction primaire*. He was also editor-in-chief of a leading educational journal, *Manuel général d'instruction primaire*.

The Dreyfus case outraged his sense of justice and Buisson campaigned to reverse the Dreyfus decision and helped found the Ligue des Droits des Hommes (League of the Rights of Man), serving as its president for 13 years beginning in 1898, and after his retirement from active work remaining its honorary president for life.

In 1902 he was elected to the Chamber of Deputies as a Radical Socialist. There he presided over the commission for the separation of church and state. He worked tirelessly for the League of Nations. He protested the French Ruhr policy and supported reconciliation with the Germans. He sat in the Chamber until 1914 and reentered it in 1919.

At the time of the Ruhr dispute following the Franco–Belgian occupation Buisson went on speaking tours across France protesting the French policy and advocating Franco–German reconciliation. At the age of 84 he engaged in a speaking tour of Germany, and during one address said, "A force exists which is far greater than France, far greater than Germany, far greater than any nation, and that is mankind. But above mankind itself stands justice, which finds its most perfect expression in brotherhood."

Biography

Ferdinand Edouard Buisson was born in Paris on December 20, 1841, the son of a Protestant judge of the St Etienne Tribunal. Educated at the Collège d'Argentan and the Lycée St Etienne, he left school at 16 in order to support his family. He subsequently completed his secondary education at the Lycée Condorcet and took a degree at the University of Paris. At the age of 51 he received his doctorate in literature.

In 1866 he took his first teaching post, at Switzerland's Academie de Neuchatel. He participated in the Geneva Peace Congress which founded the Ligue Internationale de la Paix et de la Liberté, and during this period he began writing. He was instrumental in the founding of the journal *Les États-Unis d'Europe*, which first appeared in 1867; and his contributions included the influential *L'Abolition de la guerre par l'instruction* (Abolishing war through education).

With the establishment of the Third Republic, Buisson returned to France and became inspector of primary education, from which position he resigned over the outcry regarding his stance in favor of secular education. Later he became secretary of the Statistical Commission on Primary Education, and in 1878 inspector–general of primary education in France. In the following year he became director of primary education, and during the 18 years he held this position he established free, compulsory, secular primary education and participated in its implementation.

A scholar as well as an administrator, from 1896 to 1902 he was professor of education at the Sorbonne. He authored a four-volume work, *Dictionnaire de pédagogie et d'instruction primaire*, and became editor-in-chief of *Manuel général d'instruction primaire*, a journal of education.

He wrote and spoke supporting the reversal of the Dreyfus decision, in connection with which he helped found the League of the Rights of Man in 1898, serving as its president for 13 years, and remaining honorary president for life.

From 1902 to 1914 Buisson sat in the Chamber of Deputies as a Radical Socialist, supporting compulsory, secular schooling, chaired a commission on the issue of separation of church and state, and served as vice-chairman of a commission on proposals for social welfare legislation. He sat on the Commission for Universal Suffrage and supported the principle of proportional representation.

He returned to the Chamber in 1919 and served until 1924. He donated the proceeds of the Nobel Peace Prize to pacifist programs.

Ferdinand Buisson died at his home in Thieuloy-Saint-Antoine on February 16, 1932.

RUTH C. REYNOLDS

Ludwig Quidde

(1927)

The 1927 Nobel Peace Prize went to Ludwig Quidde, co-winner with Ferdinand Buisson. Quidde was a distinguished historian whose scholarly gifts infused all that he did in a long career as a pacifist.

From a country so resolutely war-oriented as Germany, Quidde's antimilitaristic stand made him the more remarkable among the peace advocates honored by the Nobel Prize. Fredrik Stang, Chairman of the Nobel Committee, said that Quidde's interest in the peace movement grew out of a combination of his historical studies, his ethical ideals, his distrust of the military, and the urging of his wife, Margarethe, whom he married in 1882. Stang called Quidde's political ideology "a direct heritage from the Enlightenment," and said that Quidde strove to imbue the German people with a sense of justice which would of itself generate social reform.

Certainly Quidde had the courage of his convictions. He delivered a political speech in 1896 for which he was accused of lese-majesty; he was tried, convicted, and sentenced to three months in the Munich prison Stadelheim. This was following an experience of publishing anonymously an attack on German militarism, and, in quick succession, his famous *Caligula*, ostensibly a historical study and this time published openly under his own name. Done with scholarly care for detail, it was in truth a thinly disguised and scathing attack on Kaiser Wilhelm II and the Byzantine nature of the Prussian society over which he reigned. The ruthless use of power, his vanity as an actor, his conceit as an orator —all these attributes of the Emperor were satirized. Was the Emperor first-century Roman or twentieth-century German? Quidde denied an intended analogy, thus leaving the proof of intended similarity to the prosecution, a project too embarrassing to pursue. By his own cleverness Quidde had outwitted his prosecutors, and he thus escaped conviction on the charge of lese-majesty.

Quidde threw himself into political activity, much of it centered around peace. The oldest son of a wealthy Bremen merchant, he was of independent means and could therefore give his undivided time and energy where he wished. He filled a position on the council of the International Peace Bureau in Berne where Elie Ducommun, Nobel laureate in the second year of the awards (1902), served as secretary-general. Quidde rose to a position of leadership in the World Peace Congress in Glasgow in 1901, and in 1905 he joined Frédéric Passy, co-winner of the first Nobel award (1901), at the Lucerne Congress held to achieve a rapprochement between Germany and France. In 1907 he supervised the organization of the World Peace Congress and in 1914 became president of the German Peace Society, remaining in that position for 15 years.

With the outbreak of the First World War Quidde fled to The Hague. He tried to maintain contact with the English and French peace associations but his attempts were fruitless and won him only an accusation of treason when he returned to Germany. The charges were dropped, but he was under close observation for months and endured censorship of his mail and confiscation of his pamphlets.

Despite this mistrust, in 1919 Quidde was elected to the Weimar National Assembly. There he argued against Germany's accepting the Treaty of Versailles. He approved and supported the League of Nations, and favored Germany's entry into it.

Quidde tried to revive the German peace movement and headed the German Peace Cartel. In 1924 he was arrested for writing an article protesting against secret military training and was imprisoned in Munich under the emergency regulations then in force in Bavaria.

Quidde did not believe that disarmament was the answer to securing peace. Armaments are necessary, he said in his Nobel lecture, only because of the real or imagined danger of war. He subscribed to the theory that disarmament will be the result of secure peace rather than the means of obtaining it. The security he spoke of is that attained by the development of international law through an international organization based on the principles of law and justice. But psychology is more powerful in life than logic, he said. When distrust exists between governments, when there is a danger of war, the governments would not be willing to disarm even when logic indicates that disarmament would not affect military security at all. Hence the observation that without a secure peace, even if all countries disarmed proportionately, military security would not be served. But the limitation of armaments is worthwhile quite apart from reasons of security, in that armaments place an enormous burden on the economic, social, and intellectual resources of a nation.

Quidde also pointed out that every success in limiting armaments is a sign that the will to achieve mutual understanding exists, and every such success supports the fight for international law and order. One important step to international justice comes

through mediation, he said. "We pacifists can boast of having been among the first to recognize the necessity of setting up a system for mediation alongside that for arbitration. The Lucerne Congress of 1905 passed the Fried–Quidde motion calling attention to the importance of an organized means of mediation... Arbitration courts can be used for those cases which are suitable for litigation. But the most serious and dangerous disputes arise over conflicts of interest which are not subject to the rules of legal process. In such cases, mediation is needed to decide what is equitable and fair... International mediation needs to be organized just as much as does arbitration."

Quidde warned that we must learn that we have a choice only between total devastation that will result from a future war and a peace secured by rule of law. He turned to Immanuel Kant's *Zum ewigen Frieden*, (Perpetual Peace) a discussion about how it might be possible to ensure peace. "He did not present the point of view of the moral philosopher who bases his hopes on an improvement in mankind," Quidde said. "Oh, no! Kant found the only assurance for peace in the idea that war would become so terrible and unbearable that human beings, even though they remain as morally weak as they now are, would be forced to work together for peace" (see Articles: *Perpetual Peace*).

Quidde followed with an observation on a higher ethical level: "The same technology which has made war so terrible has given us the means to bring the whole world within one international organization. The moral basis of such an organization must not be merely the fear of war. It must be the conviction that it is a moral duty to do away with war and to secure peace. Only on this basis can we hope to reach complete disarmament and a peace secured by treaties."

Biography

Ludwig Quidde was born in Bremen in 1858. A distinguished historian educated at Strasbourg and Gottingen, he specialized in German history in the Middle Ages. In 1889 he founded the *Deutsche Zeitschrift für Geschichtswissenschaft* (German Review of Historical Science), and edited it until 1896. He spent 1890–92 as a staff member of the Prussian Historical Institute in Rome. He later taught history at the University of Munich.

A dissenter who opposed Germany's militarism, Quidde served three months in a Munich prison for a political speech in 1896. Undaunted, he wrote a satire on Caligula, a thinly disguised attack on Kaiser Wilhelm II. Though tried for lese-majesty, he was not convicted and the work enjoyed tremendous success.

An ardent pacifist, he worked with the International Peace Bureau in Bern, led the World Peace Congress in Glasgow in 1901, and joined Frédéric Passy (1901 Peace Prize co-winner) at the 1905 Lucerne Congress in an effort to achieve Franco–German rapprochement. He supervised the organization of the Second World Peace Congress at Geneva in 1907 and was president of the German Peace Society for 15 years.

Quidde spent the First World War in The Hague. Upon his return to Germany he was elected to the Weimar National Assembly. There he argued against Germany accepting the Treaty of Versailles and supported the League of Nations and Germany's entrance into it. He tried to revive the German peace movement and headed the German Peace Cartel.

Quidde did not believe disarmament would secure peace. He believed in the development of international law through an international organization based on the principles of law and justice.

With the coming of Hitler to power in 1933 he again went into exile, this time in Geneva. He wrote and attended Peace Congresses and founded the Comité de Secours aux Pacifistes Exiles to care for fellow political exiles from Germany.

Ludwig Quidde died in March 1941 in his eighth year of exile.

See also: Articles: *Arbitration, International; Mediation*

RUTH C. REYNOLDS

Prize Not Awarded
(1928)

Frank Kellogg
(1929)

The 1929 Nobel Peace Prize was awarded to Frank Kellogg, US Secretary of State, for his part in drawing up the Kellogg–Briand Pact (1928) condemning recourse to war as a solution to international discord. The pact was signed by 63 countries, including all the major nations, and the Nobel Committee pronounced it not only a noteworthy example of the efforts of the United States, but also a sound and conscientious collaboration on the part of the international front for the advancement of peace.

The actual idea of abolishing war as a juridical institution by means of treaties was indeed an American one, originating in 1923 with a Chicago lawyer, S. O. Levinson, who had begun an "Outlawry of War" movement in the United States, likening the abolition of war to that of dueling and slavery. Nicholas Murray Butler (Peace Prize co-winner in 1931) had taken an interest in the movement as part of his crusade to create a truly "international mind." He mentioned to the French Foreign Minister, Aristide Briand (Peace Prize co-winner in 1926), in a meeting in June 1926 that he thought the time had now come for nations to renounce war through a voluntary agreement. Briand chose a memorable date for Americans on which to respond with a declaration of his interest in the movement. On the tenth anniversary of the entry of the United States into the First World War, a devastating conflict which was still generating intense efforts to find a path to lasting peace, he wrote in an open letter to the press on April 6, 1927, "If there were any need between these two great democracies to testify more convincingly in favor of peace and to present to the peoples a more solemn example, France would be ready publicly to subscribe, with the United States, to any mutual engagement in Paris a draft of a treaty of perpetual friendship between the two countries, proposing that the two parties would solemnly declare that they condemned war and renounced it as an instrument of their national policies."

At first, Secretary Kellogg fought shy of the proposal, partly fearful of a two-nation entanglement. But Nicholas Murray Butler did not share his hesitation. In a letter to the *New York Times* he initiated a campaign arousing public opinion in its favor. With the idea of elevating the French bilateral proposal to a multilateral pact which would draw in the nations of the world, Kellogg became persuaded. He replied in a note to Briand on December 28 that the government of the United States was prepared to consult with the government of France with a view to the conclusion of a treaty among the principal powers of the world, open to signature by all nations, to condemn war and renounce it as an instrument of national policy in favor of peaceful settlement of international disputes. From this day forward Kellogg gave it his every attention. It entailed a considerable amount of work and diplomatic skill to coordinate the various views, but the pact was signed in Paris on August 27, 1928. The signatory powers were the United States, Great Britain, France, Italy, Japan, Germany, Belgium, Poland, and Czechoslovakia; but it was later endorsed by 63 nations, among them all the major powers.

Frank Kellogg would seem to have been an unlikely candidate for a Peace Prize laureate. He had never made any claim to being a peace lover or an internationalist—indeed he was an isolationist—but, in his favor, it may be noted that he *had* voted as a senator against the ratification of the short-sighted Treaty of Versailles.

Kellogg was appointed Secretary of State in 1925, in which position he served until 1929. During his secretaryship he improved US relations with Mexico, tranquilized an impending conflict between Chile and Peru, and achieved conciliatory treaties with all the Latin American nations except Argentina, and with 15 other powers. All in all he signed 80 treaties of various kinds, but none was so important to him as the Pact of the Paris, commonly called the Kellogg–Briand Pact.

Kellogg had shown diplomatic skill in resolving the conflict between the initial view of the French that the treaty should first be bilateral, with the United States and France working out a pattern for other nations to follow, and the view of the United States that the pact should include as many nations as possible. He never lost faith in the underlying concept, the renunciation of war as an instrument of national policy; but the failure to make provision for enforcement was an obvious shortcoming. In his Nobel lecture Kellogg said he knew there were those who believed that peace would not be attained until some supertribunal was established to punish the violaters of such treaties, "but I believe," he said, "that in the end the abolition of war, the maintenance of world peace, the adjustment of international questions by pacific means will come through the force of public opinion, which controls nations and peoples—that public opinion which shapes our destinies and guides the progress of human affairs."

Biography

Frank Billings Kellogg was born in Potsdam, New York, on December 22, 1858, son of Asa Kellogg and Abigail Billings Kellogg. When he was nine years old his family moved to a farm in Olmstead, Minnesota. With only five more years of schooling before he was taken out to help his father on the farm, he nonetheless continued via self-education with borrowed textbooks, and with a two-year apprenticeship in a law office he passed to the Bar in 1877.

In the next 20 years Kellogg became highly successful, counting among his clients railroads, iron-mining companies and steel-manufacturing firms, and counting among his friends Andrew Carnegie, John D. Rockefeller, and James J. Hill. Despite these associations, however, he first attained national fame as a "trustbuster" lawyer, carrying out the enthusiastic antitrust policy of President Theodore Roosevelt. He was named president of the American Bar Association in 1912 and 1913. He was a member of the National Committee of the Republican Party from 1904 to 1912, and three times a delegate to its national conventions. In 1916 he was elected to the US Senate, serving until 1922. In March 1923 he went as a delegate to the fifth Pan-American Conference in Chile, and later that year President Coolidge named him ambassador to the United Kingdom. While on that assignment he worked on reparation questions and the acceptance of the Dawes Committee report. Between 1925 and 1929 he was Secretary of State in Coolidge's cabinet, during which time he saw critical problems with Mexico on oil and land expropriation solved by legal rather than military means, and his Caribbean and South American nations policies received mixed reviews, with liberals calling them too aggressive, but the middle opinion finding them a "retreat from imperialism." Toward China, with whom relations were troubled by attacks against foreigners in Shanghai and Nanking, and by problems of tariff autonomy and abolition of extraterritoriality, his policy was recognized as carried out "in goodwill."

During his secretaryship he signed 80 treaties of various kinds, a record set for that time. In pursuance of his belief in the efficacy of the legal arbitration of disputes, 19 of them were bilateral treaties with foreign nations. No treaty was so important to Kellogg as the Pact of Paris, commonly known as the Kellogg–Briand Pact.

He was, toward Europe, basically an isolationist, although following his bringing the Kellogg–Briand Pact to a successful conclusion with 63 signatories he served as judge of the Permanent Court of International Justice at The Hague from 1930 to 1935.

Kellogg received many honors, among them the French Legion of Honor and honorary degrees from Carleton College, Lawrence University, Harvard, the University of Minnesota, Princeton, Trinity College, and Oxford University.

He married Clara M. Cook of Rochester, Minnesota, in 1896.

Frank Kellogg died at St Paul, Minnesota on December 21, 1937.

RUTH C. REYNOLDS

Nathan Söderblom

(1930)

The Nobel Peace Prize of 1930 was awarded to Sweden's Archbishop Nathan Söderblom. He was a primate in the cause of world peace as he was a primate in his own church in Sweden. The Nobel Committee stated, in presenting the award, that Söderblom understood the enormous importance of the church in the fight for peace, and the powerful influence which the church could bring with it. "The Christian church has sinned grievously and often against the teaching of Him whose first commandment to men was that they should love one another. This church surely has a unique opportunity now of creating that new attitude of mind which is necessary if peace between nations is to become reality," Committee member Mowinckel said.

Söderblom came superbly qualified for this task by training and through personal dedication. During his undergraduate studies at Uppsala University he began a formidable mastery of languages with honors in Greek and competency in Hebrew, Arabic, and Latin. For the next six years he studied theology and probed into the history of religions, learning whatever languages necessary to do so. His Doctor of Theology degree at the Protestant Faculty of the Sorbonne stands as an eloquent testament to his in-depth studies continued while a pastor at the Swedish Church in Paris, for his was the first such degree ever granted to a foreigner.

While attending a Christian student conference in New England, Söderblom heard a lecture which prompted an entry into his diary prophetically descriptive of his destined dedication: "Lord, give me humility and wisdom to serve the great cause of the free unity of thy church." This was to become his great contribution to the search for peace. Even before the war, he had made a beginning in his work of uniting the church communities of the world, and thus promoting international understanding.

It was a long road from the spiritual wreckage left in the wake of the First World War to an Ecumenical Council which Söderblom called "as magnificent an achievement as the League of Nations." He shared that experience of many years in his Nobel lecture, offering a moving and descriptive history of the ecumenical movement. The account given below closely follows that lecture, distilled to include only the major stations along the road.

During the war Christians were filled with anguish; they asked themselves whether the church, which had been called the "Prince of Peace," had fulfilled its duty. Many of the clergy, of different countries and different creeds, in both the Old World and the New, increasingly felt the need for a Christendom which was united in at least the essential principle of living according to the commandment of love. Thus united, they would constitute a more powerful crusade for peace. During the war, in the summer of 1917, a congress was called of those churches whose nations would grant passports for travel with the purpose of declaring Christian unity, and to express before the world the belief that the values of Christendom transcended those of individual nations.

Agreeing not to discuss the war, or purely political measures for achieving peace, they examined what the different churches could accomplish in the struggle against war, and how they could bring about the proper state of mind needed for better international understanding. Reckless nationalism had to be replaced by Christian brotherhood that would transcend national boundaries. The outcome of the congress, called the Conference of Churches in Neutral Countries, was a threefold set of statements designed for consideration by the body of churches, and as a guide for its work: (a) the unity of Christians; (b) Christians and the life of society; and (c) Christians and the law. The supranational character of the Conference had immense effect as a harbinger and implement of peace—embodying a spiritual entity that addressed people as human beings and not as speakers of given languages and members of given races and nationalities.

The Evangelical Church, war weakened and discordant though it was, became the first community of people in the world who brought together responsible men and women from both camps after the Great War. It met at the International Committee of the World Alliance at Oud Wassenaar in October 1919. There Söderblom proposed the international ecumenical conference which was eventually held at Stockholm in 1925.

The breakthrough occurred in 1925 at Stockholm. The Ecumenical Council which came into being represented, officially or semiofficially, the larger part of Christendom. By meeting to discuss precisely those matters about which they differed, doctrinal differences were diminished; and in the process there emerged a sense of the essential spiritual and religious unity throughout the whole Evangelical Church.

However, Söderblom said, Christians should not wait for full agreement before they start practicing the duty of love imposed by the Master. While discussions concerning doctrinal matters and the church ordinances may be long-ranged, Christians must follow immediately the divine command to love one another. No result of the Stockholm meeting has been more obvious and noteworthy, he said, than the realization that, according to the Gospel, God must be first in people's hearts and must thus also rule over the people, over groups in society, and over nations themselves.

The ecumenical revival does not belong just to the circle of priests and laymen, he said. It must force its way outward and become the property of society, a concern of all churches and of all people.

Three essential tasks toward the cause of peace emerged from these ecumenical meetings: (a) To instill the spirit of fraternity and truth into the heart of humankind. (b) The church itself must realize and impress upon others the absolute nature of God's commandments which extend justice beyond the boundaries of nations, thereby substituting cooperation for self-assertion. (c) It follows from the point just made that the armed forces must be stripped of their previous role, which has been fostered by fear, by lust for power, and by serving Mammon. Söderblom said we must instead make them the safeguard of security, peace, and liberty, just as the police force is the safeguard within the state.

If efforts toward peace are to get anywhere, he said, they must be more realistic than in the past. The question is not whether one is orthodox in conforming to some peace formula or other, but whether one does something to promote peace. We must not allow ourselves to be lulled into any simplistic peace dream. We must struggle to win peace, struggle against schism, against hatred and injustice. This fight must be directed primarily toward the primitive human within us. Impatient minds may perhaps find such a concept hopeless, pessimistic, and old fashioned but, Söderblom insisted, we must face reality. The noble and practical measures for world peace will be realized only to the extent to which the supremacy of God conquers the heart of humankind.

At the Ecumenical Council held at Eisenach in 1928 four points were evolved in the "Eisenach Resolution":

(a) A wholehearted welcome extended to the solemn declaration made by the leading statesmen of the world in the names of their nations that they condemn war as a means of settling international disputes and denounce it as a tool of international power politics.

(b) The belief that the settlement of international disputes by war is irreconcilable with the spirit of Christ, and therefore irreconcilable with the spirit and conduct of His church.

(c) The conviction that the time must come when existing treaties have to be revised in the interest of peace, but maintaining that all international disputes and conflicts which cannot be solved through diplomacy or mediation must be settled through arbitration by the International Court of Justice or some other court of law acknowledged by all parties involved.

(d) The legal system being the work of God, the duty of the church is to stress its sanctity and to work for its extension beyond national boundaries. The church must uphold the binding nature of any contract obliging nations to settle disputes through arbitration or legal channels. Thus, if the government of a church's own country disregards this obligation to submit a dispute to such a procedure, that church must condemn any war developing from this situation, and must disclaim, in both word and action, any connection with it.

What we are recommending, Söderblom said, is not a breach of loyalty; on the contrary, it is obedience to a higher obligation. A supranational judicial system is being built. Binding treaties between nations who are committed to conciliation or arbitration when disputes arise rather than to war represent the foundations of a larger edifice of the rule of law. What we do advocate is obedience to the rule of Christ and His apostles instructing us to respect civic law. All people and all nations must participate in the construction of a supranational legal system, which, according to Christian doctrine, is a continuation of God's creation.

In due course, the Life and Work Movement of which Söderblom was the inspiration came to join forces with the other great wing of the ecumenical movement, the predominately Anglican Faith and Order Movement. Their fusion led in 1948 to the formulation of the World Council of Churches. This organization with its headquarters in Geneva is active worldwide in its continuing efforts to unify the world's churches in the struggle for universal peace (see Articles: *World Council of Churches (WCC)*).

Apart from the ethical values of Christianity, Söderblom believed that the Christian way of life was in itself of great value to the cause of peace. In a sermon in 1917 he emphasized two factors: first the Christian belief in the impossible and the fact that faith "took the long view," and the other, the ability of the Christian way of life to strengthen confidence in the community based on law.

Biography

Nathan Söderblom (named Lars Olof Jonathan) was born in Trono, in the Swedish province of Halsingland, son of Jonas Söderblom, a pietistic pastor, and Sophia Blume Söderblom. He took his bachelor's degree at the School of Theology in Uppsala in 1886, after which he continued his studies there and (from 1888 to 1893) edited the Student Missionary Association review (*Meddelanden*). In 1893 he was ordained a priest, taking first a position as a chaplain in a mental hospital in Uppsala, following which he accepted a call to the Swedish Church in Paris in 1894, where he stayed until 1901. He continued his studies, mastering ten languages to pursue the origins and history of Asiatic religions including translations from Sanskrit, Persian, and Chinese. The Sorbonne made him a Doctor of Theology, the first foreigner ever to receive that honor. From 1901 to 1914 Söderblom occupied a chair in the School of Theology at Uppsala University, and concurrently from 1912 to 1914 was professor of comparative theology at the University of Leipzig. In 1914 he was elected as Archbishop of Uppsala, by virtue of which he also became primate of the Church of Sweden. He was elected a member of the Swedish Academy in 1921.

In 1923 he visited the United States under the auspices of the World Alliance for Promoting International Friendship, delivering a series of lectures at Harvard, Yale, and other universities and being received at the White House by President Coolidge.

Internationally Söderblom was known as one of the architects of the ecumenical movement of the twentieth century. As early as 1909 he was working toward intercommunion between the Swedish Church and the Church of England. The culmination of his efforts took place at the Stockholm Conference held in 1925 between Anglican, Protestant, and Orthodox Christians.

In 1927 he was a member of the World Conference on Faith and Order at Lausanne. This conference culminated in a final report which established common ground on a number of key doctrinal questions.

His theological writings include studies of the origins of religions, religious history, the character of the Church of Sweden, and Indian modes of worship.

He was married to Anna Forsell and they had 13 children.

He was in the midst of a famous lectureship, the Gifford Lectures in Edinburgh in 1931, at the time of his death on July 12.

RUTH C. REYNOLDS

Jane Addams

(1931)

The Nobel Prize for Peace in 1931 was awarded to Jane Addams and Nicholas Butler for their assiduous work of many years toward reviving the ideal of peace in their own nation and the whole of humanity. "In honoring Jane Addams," the Nobel Committee said, "we also pay tribute to the work which women can do for peace and fraternity among nations . . . Jane Addams combines all the best feminine qualities which will help us to develop peace on earth."

Jane Addams was a powerful moving force from the laissez-faire of unrestricted capitalism to a consideration of responsibilities toward the individuals within capitalist society. She asked for a "social ethic" to take the place of an "individualistic ethic." And people listened to her because for 40 years she translated her social ideals into action through Hull House.

Much has been written about Addams as "the Angel of Hull House." She is pictured as a feminine version of St. Francis, sacrificing comfort, security, and all the amenities of life which her well-to-do family had offered her, in order to lose herself in the poverty of a Chicago tenement district. But this is a poor exchange for the reality: a capable administrator, a complex, intelligent woman of immense persuasive ability who participated in almost every major reform of her era. Addams had no desire to descend to the poverty level. Her interests were to lift the level all about her out of poverty.

She learned her basics in sociology from what she found about her. She learned from young working girls in factories and sweatshops. She learned from garbage, from suicide, from dirt. She learned from children things she had not known in her own childhood. She read voraciously. Then, from what she learned, she developed a program centered upon the question: how could the quality of life be raised? Under her hand, Hull House was always a place where beauty was cultivated, and it was home to a multicultural spread of interests and activities.

She was intensely practical when that best served the purpose, insisting that the fullest possible good be required from existing public and social agencies, and demanding new agencies when the old had been proven inadequate. She went through the streets of Chicago's tenement district as the duly commissioned inspector of streets and alleys, determined to make the agencies of government act to the benefit of the dwellers in those underprivileged areas. Her great administrative genius was to deal with people on the level of their highest potential.

Year after year Addams saw nearly all the migrant races of the world pass by her doorstep. Living among them, she entered their psychology, learned their point of view, and appreciated their racial contribution to the national culture. She developed many ways of promoting justice through understanding. She used hospitality to bring together guests who might exchange differing points of view. Hull House was a living demonstration that neighborliness between men and women of different classes was possible. She endowed it with her own brand of caring. "It was that word 'with' from Jane Addams," said a working-woman, "that took the bitterness out of my life. For if she wanted to work with me and I could work with her, it gave my life new meaning and hope."

Hull House grew into a center of several buildings accommodating cultural enrichment of the people of that impoverished area. It helped them learn to look after their interests. It became a friendly center for organizing against sweatshop working conditions, and this culminated in legislation passed against exploitive work practices.

Finding ways of giving stability to the immigrant family was the earliest and one of the most lasting Hull House goals. The Immigrants Protective League had its inception there. The nursery and kindergarten, and the clubs for boys and girls which were established there freed mothers who had to work outside the home. Hull House arts and crafts gave the immigrants a sense of tradition, of recognition of their various skills, a feeling of social stability and personal value.

Hull House stood first of all for social democracy. Addams' experiences there persuaded her of the necessity for progressive social legislation to bring democracy into areas where it had not been practiced before. Hull House participated in establishing juvenile courts, creating public baths in the tenements, instituting medical inspection in the schools. It served to awaken the nation's conscience to the desperate plight of the underprivileged in US cities.

Addams became intent upon improving the social system beyond her Chicago neighborhood. Her public career expanded to state and national legislation, seeking to improve working conditions of women and children everywhere, guaranteeing compensation for injuries to the heads of families. Increasingly she participated in mediation, particularly in the field of labor disputes. In a strike of the Amalgamated Clothing Workers of America she helped bring about an agreement in 1910 which laid a foundation for industrial peace in an industry nationally known for its "sweatshop practices." She influenced the settlement of the great Pullman strike of 1894 through arbitration, out of which grew a public demand for the State Board of Arbitration and Conciliation.

During the 40 years she lived at Hull House she sought, above all else, a moral change which would create peace and contentment where there had previously been only divisive exploitation. Addams fell far short of this goal, but she created shifting US attitudes toward poverty and reform, and toward a social order responsive to the needs of far more of its people.

She carried her passionate concern for understanding between peoples to the international scene. It was a natural series of steps from municipal ordinances, state and national legislation to the means for establishing a peaceful world order.

Addams was a pacifist. In her view the worst thing about war was its total prevention of the mutual understanding of peoples. Living in Hull House among representatives of a score of nations had convinced her that in each human being there are universal emotions which transcend national and cultural boundaries. She sought the means to express these universal emotions. She had repeatedly witnessed her immigrant neighbors modifying their provincialism and taming the ferocity of their nationalism. Entries in her notebooks show that she hoped this "internationalism" would be the forerunner to developing a similar instrument in the cause of world peace. As late as 1913 she spoke at a meeting in Carnegie Hall of a "rising in the cosmopolitan centers of America of a sturdy and unprecedented international understanding which in time would be too profound to lend itself to war." The applause of the audience was overwhelming. But one year later the First World War came, and Addams witnessed the revitalization of old antagonisms between the very neighbors who had inspired her dream.

Addams never supported the United States' entry into the war, despite abuses and insults. She accepted an invitation to become president of the International Congress of Women meeting at The Hague in 1915. It was typical of her active pacifism that she would join in planning for a wise peace to have in readiness for the war's end. In reading the resolutions which came out of this conference, it is striking how they anticipated the 14 points introduced by President Wilson of the United States. Afterwards Addams, with other delegates, visited both the warring and neutral countries to promote the idea of a conference of neutrals which would offer continuous mediation to the belligerents. She supported the League of Nations, the World Court, disarmament and education for peace.

The Congress of Women met in 1919 in Zurich and founded the Women's International League for Peace and Freedom. This is a permanent federation of women with organized sections in 25 countries and a worldwide membership. It operates to promote new methods in international relations for removing animosities and righting wrongs without resort to war. Addams served as its president until 1929, and as honorary president for the remainder of her life.

Addams' long career in pacifism is beautifully summarized by one of her biographers, James Linn: "It was a struggle long-continued and brave. It involved, and finally concentrated, the help of thousands of other women in many countries, finally in almost all countries. It engaged the attention, admiration, and in the end, the genuine conviction of many statesmen. It led her through first the patronizing commendation of millions, then through their obloquy and insult. It culminated, three weeks before she died, in a celebration personally triumphant, in which were joined not only some of the best known men and women of her own country, but the ambassadors of England, France, Russia and Japan, praising her as no American woman had ever before been internationally praised. But it was a struggle based not on emotion, and not on economic principles, but on understanding" (Linn 1935 p. 285).

Biography

(Laura) Jane Addams was born in Cedarville, Illinois, on Setember 6, 1860, daughter of John H. and Sarah (Weber) Addams. Her father was a successful businessman and served as a state senator for 16 years. She graduated from the Rockford Female Seminary in 1881 as valedictorian and was granted a bachelor's degree. She entered the Women's Medical College of Philadelphia, but frail health owing to a congenital spinal curvature forced her withdrawal. She spent the next two years in Europe studying the poor districts in European cities, and her visit to Toynbee Hall, a settlement house in London, inspired her to plan a similar house for the underprivileged in Chicago. In 1889 she and

her friend, Ellen G. Starr, leased the former mansion of Charles Hull and established a center providing for a higher civic and social life and improved conditions in the industrial districts of Chicago. These included juvenile courts, public baths, industrial education, and medical inspection in schools. Addams undertook to supervise the cleaning of streets in the Hull House neighborhood and was appointed garbage inspector for this purpose by the mayor.

Addams and Starr put great effort into soliciting financial aid as well as interest and participation in furthering the cause of social welfare. By its second year Hull House was host to 2,000 people every week. Addams' reputation grew and she went into larger fields of civic responsibility. She was one of the founders of the NAACP (National Association for the Advancement of Colored People), and was vice-president of the Woman Suffrage Association. In 1905 she was appointed to Chicago's Board of Education and thereafter chaired the School Management Committee. She participated in the founding of the Chicago School of Civics and Philanthropy in 1908, and during the ensuing year became the first woman president of the National Conference of Charities and Corrections.

A feminist, Addams believed that women must participate fully in society and exercise the right of suffrage. She worked tirelessly towards preventing war, and in 1906 she gave a series of lectures at the University of Wisconsin which were published under the title *Newer Ideals of Peace*. She spoke at a ceremony commemorating the building of the Peace Palace at The Hague in 1913. During the next two years, as a lecturer sponsored by the Carnegie Foundation, she spoke against the United States' participation in the First World War.

In 1915 she became chairwoman of the Women's Peace Party and president of the International Congress of Women convened at The Hague, and in 1919 at Zurich, where the congress founded the Women's International League for Peace and Freedom. Addams served as its president until 1929, when she assumed honorary presidency until her death in 1935.

Her publications are: *Democracy and Social Ethics* (1904), *Newer Ideals of Peace* (1907), *The Spirit of Youth in the Streets* (1909), *Twenty Years at Hull House* (1910), *A New Conscience and an Ancient Evil* (1912), *The Long Road of Woman's Memory* (1916), and *Peace and Bread in the Time of War* (1922). She held the honorary degrees of LL.D. from eight universities, among them the University of Wisconsin (1904) and Smith College (1910), and the M.A. of Yale (1910).

Bibliography

Christian Century 1935 Jane Addams. 52 (June 5): 751–53

Davis A 1973 *American Heroine*, Oxford University Press, New York

Farrel J 1967 *Beloved Lady*, John Hopkins Press, Baltimore, Maryland

Kellogg P 1935 Jane Addams, 1860–1935. *The Survey* 71 (June): 175

Levine D 1971 *Jane Addams and the Liberal Tradition*. State Historical Society of Wisconsin, Madison, Wisconsin

Linn J 1935 *Jane Addams*. Appleton-Century, New York

Lovett R 1930 Jane Addams at Hull House. *The New Republic* 62 (May 14): 349-51

Taylor G 1935 Jane Addams, the great neighbor. *Survey Graphic* 24 (July): 338-41

RUTH C. REYNOLDS

Nicholas Murray Butler

(1931)

In naming Nicholas Murray Butler a co-winner of the 1931 Nobel Peace Prize, the Nobel Committee honored his efforts of a lifetime spent in promoting peace through heightened international understanding between people and nations. President of Columbia University, Dr. Butler worked as an educator and as an adviser to seven presidents. As a friend of statesmen of foreign nations and as an advocate of internationalism, he was the living embodiment of his own concept, the "international mind." Butler chaired the Lake Mohonk Conferences on International Arbitration which met periodically between 1907 and 1912, was president of the US branch of Conciliation Internationale, and headed the section on international education and communication in the Carnegie Endowment for International Peace.

The Nobel Committee praised Butler as an educator who stimulated popular thought and then translated public will into positive action. His every specific idea implanted in the popular will brought us another step along the road to a new society, the Committee said.

Butler was drawn from his preoccupation as an educator and highly successful president of Columbia University to embrace a second role as internationalist peace worker by Baron d'Estournelles de Constant (Paul Henri Benjamin Balluet), winner of the 1907 Peace Prize. Baron d'Estournelles interested Butler in Conciliation Internationale. Committee member Koht described this organization at the award ceremony: "In my opinion it would be difficult to name another peace organization which has persisted in such effective, tenacious, and steady work for the cause of peace as has this American group under the presidency of Butler." Butler was a fine administrator, and a persuasive man. It was Butler's influence which prompted Andrew Carnegie, the American philanthropist, to donate US \$10 million in 1910 to establish the Carnegie Endowment for International Peace. This organization financed visits of professors, economists, and outstanding authorities to make "peoples hitherto strange and remote" more familiar with each other through personal contact with representatives from each of their cultures.

Carnegie chose Butler to develop the Endowment's division for education and publicity. Butler set up lecture courses, international relations clubs, conferences, and study programs in an effort to create an enlightened and sympathetic public opinion toward international affairs. It was a striking example of the combination of his skill as an educator and the responsible use of politics to achieve world peace through expanding horizons of international understanding and cooperation.

To such a staunch internationalist as Butler the First World War came as a great shock, as it did to many who were working within the peace movements of that period. But following the war, Butler renewed his efforts through the organization to addressing the problems that might imperil international peace in the future. He sent experts to examine potential causes of war in the Balkans, the Far East, and Mexico, and compiled reports on points of potential political danger. International relations clubs were organized in Britain, Australia, Canada, South Africa, India, China, Japan, the Philippines, and various South American countries. After the war the ravaged libraries of Rheims, Belgrade, and the University of Louvain were rebuilt.

The Carnegie Endowment also financed the reconstruction of the commune of Fargniers in Aisne, which had been designated by the French government as the village which had suffered most during the war. It also underwrote the administrative costs of several international conferences, notably the Balkan Conferences of 1930 to 1934. It sponsored studies of international law, the history of the First World War, of the Saar conflict, and of international relations generally. The Endowment maintained a large library and compiled treaty texts and diplomatic documents; it also issued a periodical, *International Conciliation*. Butler later succeeded to the presidency of the Endowment.

Butler's goal was to create what he called an "international mind." Taken from the title of a book of Butler's addresses made at the Lake Mohonk Conferences, it was defined by its author as the habit of thinking of the nations of the civilized world as friendly and cooperative equals. Thus he attempted to educate Americans out of their isolationism and to convince them to take their overseas responsibilities more seriously. He believed that no civilized nation could live in isolation. "When private citizens and public officials look upon international obligations and international relations as the upright man looks upon his personal promises and personal relationships, the peace of the world will be secure," he said.

His persuasion of the American people to overcome their isolationism resulted in the Kellogg–Briand Pact (1928), an agreement between France and the United States to outlaw war. Ratification of the United States and France was followed by practically all the world powers. Unfortunately, the pact lacked the authority of enforcement, and left the door open to so-called "wars of defense." The ink was hardly dry on the pact before Butler was lamenting: "No sooner had it been ratified by sixty-three governments than at least one-half of them began arming for war under the pretense of arming for defense, at a rate that had never been equalled in all history."

But it did make one more contribution toward the development of a public concept about the responsibilities inherent in the maintenance of peace. "Those who set their sights on awakening and educating public opinion cannot expect swift victories of the kind that win popular acclaim," the Nobel Committee said. Butler's patient groundwork in developing a desire and will for peace on the part of many people is necessary before concrete accomplishments can come into being. "Nothing in society ever moves forward of its own momentum; progress must always be sustained by the human thought, human will, and human action to transmute the need into a living social form." The Committee declared that it was for just such effort over the course of a long career that it was paying tribute to Butler.

For another 10 years after receiving the award, Butler continued to work actively, encouraging international understanding between nations and peoples. Only the onset of blindness slowed his vast correspondences, his lectures, and his use of the political forum to promote the "international mind."

Biography

Nicholas Murray Butler was born in Elizabeth, New Jersey, son of Henry L. Butler, a manufacturer, and Mary Murray Butler. In 1882 he received his bachelor's degree in philosophy from Columbia College, in 1883 a master's degree, and in 1884 a doctorate, also from Columbia College (later to become Columbia University). In 1884–1885 he studied in Paris and Berlin, and in the fall of 1885 he joined the faculty of Columbia in the department of philosophy. He remained at Columbia for 60 years; there he established the Teachers College and founded the *Educational Review*, which he edited for 30 years.

A distinguished educator, he served on the New Jersey Board of Education from 1887 to 1895, and participated in creating the College Entrance Examination Board in 1893. He became acting president of Columbia in 1901 and president in 1902, a position he maintained until his retirement in 1945. He was president of Bernard College and Teachers College from 1901 to 1945. Under his presidency Columbia University became a major educational institution.

Butler served in politics with equal distinction, both at home and abroad. He was a delegate to the Republican convention, for the first time in 1888 and the last time in 1936. With Eliho Root, whom he met when studying abroad in Paris and Berlin following his doctoral degree in 1884, and William Howard Taft and Theodore Roosevelt, Butler constituted a fourth in a powerful political quartet in the early part of the nineteenth century. It was the split of this group in 1912, with Roosevelt running for the Presidency as candidate of the Progressive Party, and Taft for the Republican Party with Butler as Vice-President, which resulted in the victory of the Democratic candidate, Woodrow Wilson.

Butler worked as an educator in a lifetime effort to bring about world peace through international cooperation and the education of the body politic through an enlightened electorate. He chaired the Lake Mohonk Conferences on International Arbitration from 1907 to 1912, where he coined the concept of "international minded-ness" wherein all nations are conceived as working together as friendly and cooperative equals.

He was appointed president of the US branch of Conciliation Internationale, founded by Baron d'Estournelles, himself a Nobel Peace Prize winner in 1909. He persuaded Andrew Carnegie to endow US $10 million toward the Carnegie Endowment for International Peace, which he finally linked to the US branch of Conciliation Internationale. Butler served first on the Endowment's section for international education and communication, then founded the European branch of the Endowment, with headquarters in Paris. Later, in 1925, he became president of the Endowment, a post he held until 1945.

Butler held honorary degrees from 37 colleges and universities, including Yale, Harvard, Princeton, Johns Hopkins, Chicago, St. Andrews, Manchester, Oxford, Cambridge, and California. He was the recipient of decorations from 15 foreign governments and a member of more than 50 learned societies and 20 clubs.

He wrote *The Meaning of Education* (1898, revised edition 1915), *True and False Democracy* (1907), *The American as He Is* (1908), *Education in the United States* (1910), *The International Mind* (1913), *A World in Ferment* (1918), *The Faith of a Liberal* (1924), *The Path to Peace* (1930), *Between*

Two Worlds (1934), an autobiography entitled *Across the Busy Years* (1939), *Why War?* (1940), *Liberty, Equality, Fraternity* (1942), and *The World Today* (1946).

Butler married Susanna Edwards Schuyler in 1887. They had one daughter, Sarah Schuyler. Susanna Butler died in 1903. In 1907 Butler married Kate La Montagne.

He died on December 7, 1947.

RUTH C. REYNOLDS

Prize Not Awarded

(1932)

Norman Angell

(1933)

The 1933 Nobel Prize for Peace was awarded to Norman Angell, journalist and author, whom the Nobel Committee called "the great educator of public opinion," and said that, as a writer, he had done as much as anyone in our time to "remove the wrong conception that war benefits anyone."

"Norman Angell speaks to the intellect," said Committee Chairman Christian Lange (1921 Peace Prize co-winner). "He is cool and clear. He has a profound belief in reason and in rationalism. He is convinced that at long last reason will prevail when we succeed in sweeping away the mists of illusion and intellectual error."

Norman Angell spent a lifetime of continuous and concentrated attack upon the misconceptions that make war possible—misconceptions held by the populace and leaders alike. He asked people to ponder why nations have so often followed policies with peaceful intent, only to have war as the outcome. He asked them as individual citizens to probe their role in this process.

Angell was catapulted to international fame through an early book, *The Great Illusion*, published in 1910. It sold over two million copies and was translated into 25 languages. From that time forward he reached an audience of millions through his books, which numbered 41 in all, through years as a journalist in Europe and the United Kingdom, and at lecture halls in the Old World and the New. He thought of those millions in terms of the individuals represented, and it was to the individual that he made his appeal.

This was his approach to *all* groups of peoples. During the two world wars he supported his country in the war effort. He took exception to pacifists, who,

he said, perhaps did not see very clearly that the refusal to endow law with power did not diminish the total amount of force in the world, but left it in the hands of the lawless, the most violent. But his participation in the wars against Germany did not lead him into sterotyped images of the enemy. He was revolted by those who saw the German not as a person at all, but as an abstraction. To Angell Germany was "an entity which included underfed children, old women and ignorant peasants as well as besotted high-collared officers."

Therefore his overwhelming question of *all* peoples was why, and in what manner, had the public mind been at fault, and in what ways, through each individual unit, might it create a change. He was convinced that the large measure of public support given to policies making for international conflict came not from a lack of specialist or technical knowledge on the part of the public, but from misapplication of the knowledge they had. He illustrated this common occurrence through the attitudes often held about the League of Nations. "We who urge a League of Nations are told so often that we forget human nature, that we overlook the fact that men are naturally quarrelsome. The fact that men are naturally quarrelsome is presumed to be an argument against such institutions as the League. But it is precisely the fact of the natural pugnacity of man that makes such institutions necessary. If men were naturally and easily capable of being their own judges, always able to see the other's case, never got into panics, never lost their heads, never lost their tempers and called it patriotism—why then we should not want a League. But neither should we want most of our national apparatus of government either—parliaments, congresses, courts, police, ten commandments. These are all means by which we deal with the unruly element in human nature . . . ."

"You cannot change human nature" is an illusion that destroys clear thinking. Angell pointed out that what we call "human nature" is in fact not a constant factor, but alters with changes in cultures. The field of peace itself holds concrete examples of changed behavior: wars based on religious motives are a thing of the past, as are violent conflicts such as dueling or blood feuds.

Angell told his audiences that humankind's deep tragedy is that it so rarely sees reality. We see what we desire to see. We have before our eyes mists, stereotypes inherited from our parents, from our grandparents, and they from theirs. Intellectually we are wearing the cast-off clothes of our ancestors, and we do not see that they no longer fit us. Political leaders frequently labor under the same misconceptions.

Angell had intimate knowledge of public opinion in three of the big powers of the world. He began his life as Ralph Norman Angell Lane in a well-to-do but unpretentious Victorian household in Holbeach in Lincolnshire, England, one of six children of Thomas Angell Lane and Mary Brittain Lane. A precocious boy, he was reading Herbert Spencer, T. H. Huxley, Voltaire, Darwin, and John Stuart Mill by the time he was sent, at the age of 12, to the Lycée de St. Omer in France by his father, who believed in international education. Angell recalled Mill's essay *On Liberty* as his prime source of intellectual excitement during those years. After attending a business school in London he went to Geneva, where he studied at the University and edited a biweekly English paper. A year later, however, he set off for the United States, convinced that Europe was hopelessly enmeshed in insoluble problems. He settled in the western part of the United States, and for seven years worked at varying jobs: as a vine planter, an irrigation ditch digger, a cowboy, and a prospector, ending up as a journalist, reporting for the St. Louis *Globe-Democrat* and later the San Francisco *Chronicle*.

"My first prompting to the importance of the international problem came from my experience out West," Angell once told an interviewer. "The folklore of the West and Mid-West was deeply anti-British . . . the Redcoat was the villain and all that. Riding over the range with other cowboys, I learned that I was a cruel, imperialist oppressor, that the British were blood-suckers. Well, I knew that England was I multiplied 40 million times and that it simply wasn't so. I said to myself, 'this is the danger to mankind—

not just Anglophobia, but the ease with which fantasies, fables and myths can possess a whole people.'"

He returned to France, where over the years he worked for the *Daily Messenger* (an English-language paper), *Éclair* and the Paris edition of the British *Daily Mail*. In 1912, after receiving public acclaim through *The Great Illusion*, he resigned his newspaper work to dedicate himself to writing and lecturing on the futility of war and on internationalism.

Having returned to England, Angell was briefly involved in politics, serving as a Labour Member of Parliament for one term from 1929 to 1931. But he preferred to work for internationalism outside the parliamentary arena, and did not pursue his political career. He worked with groups promoting internationalism: the Council of the Royal Institute of International Affairs, and the League of Nations Union. He was knighted for public service in 1931.

Angell devoted his life to stripping away cultural and emotional myths destructive to clear thinking. He passionately believed that common sense and rational thought on the part of the populace were the *sine qua non* of attaining permanent peace. "A decision has to be taken," he said. "It has to be taken, not only by the experts, the trained economists, the academic specialists, but by the voting millions of over-driven professional men, coal heavers, dentists, tea-shop waitresses, parsons, charwomen, artists, country squires, chorus girls who make and unmake governments, who do not hesitate, as we have seen, again and again, to override the specialist or expert and impose their opinion upon him. With them rests the final verdict."

He vigorously attacked the illusion of the profitability of war in the modern world of interdependent nations. The truth, illustrated by history observable by all, is that even the so-called winners have become losers, not only in terms of human life, but in terms of economic and general well-being. Angell pointed out that if "victorious" wars were economically advantageous, then citizens of those big powers which have built their world empires through wars would be economically better off than the citizens of small peaceful nations. But, he said, a review of capital and revenues in these two categories of nations furnished proof that this was not so. In 1933 Dutch, Swedish, Swiss and Norwegian stocks stood higher on the world's exchanges than did those of the United Kingdom, of France, and of Germany.

Angell warned that to shut our eyes to the role that the individual plays in the perpetuation of policies that lead to war is to perpetuate victimization. A few score officials, or capitalists, cannot by their physical power compel hundreds of millions of individuals year after year to go on paying taxes, to take vast risks with their own welfare, and to jeopardize their society if those millions are persuaded that the taxes, the risks, and the sacrifices are quite unnecessary and, indeed, harmful. The only means by which the individual can be liberated from the potential power of exploitive groups is through insight into the nature of those impulses and motives to which the exploiters so successfully appeal.

He pointed out that the Nazis began as a party of ten persons. Ten persons had no force against the power of the German nation. The latent strength of that party of ten persons rested in its potential power to reach the public mind. Without that popular appeal it could never have come into being. Similarly, war would be impossible without the acquiescence of large sections of the public.

Nationalism can assume forms that are demonstrably dangerous to the community of nations precisely because it strikes responsive chords deep in human impulses and instincts. Thus, "Until we are taught to recognize—what our history books do not teach—that the fault is usually ours as much as some other nation's, we have not taken the first step to that wisdom which alone can save us," Angell said. In the same way that we have come to see that it is irrelevant and unworthy to fight about religion, so we must come to see that it is irrelevant and self-defeating to fight about our nationalisms. Angell pleaded for a "world philosophy" and a "world conscience" through which nationalisms would give way to a "community of nations." He assured his audiences, "We can still make a cosmos out of this chaos by taking thought."

Angell traveled widely in the United States, giving lectures. He worked with President Woodrow Wilson in the development of Wilson's plan for a League of Nations founded upon the principles of collective security. Angell held collective security to be a cornerstone in internationalism. In a statement of principles he wrote in 1918 he said that under any system in which adequate defense rests upon the individual nation's preponderance of power, the security of that one nation must involve the insecurity of other less powerful nations.

He declared that if we will not defend other nations in their right to life, then inevitably the time will come when it will be impossible to defend the right to life for our own nation. If each is to be his or her own and sole defender, then any minority which can make itself stronger than any single nation can

place not one but all at its mercy. A little gang of ruthless men could overcome 20 nations because when one was attacked the others remained indifferent.

Angell's words proved prophetic. This was the story of the fall of the League of Nations.

After the two atomic bombs fell upon Japanese cities in the violent end to a war and in the opening of a new—and irreversible—era Angell wrote that a new alternative had been established: "We prevent war, or we perish."

In summing up his life in his autobiography, Angell wrote: "The end I chose—elimination of war —I would without any hesitation whatsoever choose again. No other single task would be more worth the efforts of a lifetime."

Biography

Ralph Norman Angell Lane was born on December 26, 1872, one of six children of Thomas Angell Lane and Mary Brittain Lane. Raised in Holbeach in Lincolnshire, England, he attended British elementary schools, the Lycée de St. Omer in France, and a business school in London, before spending one year at the University of Geneva. At this point his education took another tack as he left Europe, which he found hopelessly entangled in social problems, and went to the westernmost part of the United States. There he pursued many trades—ranch-hand, cowboy, prospector among them—finally becoming a reporter, first for the St. Louis *Globe-Democrat* and later the San Francisco *Chronicle*.

In 1898 Angell went to Paris, where he was subeditor of the English-language *Daily Messenger*, then staff contributor to *Éclair*. He covered the Dreyfus case for American papers. In 1905 he became editor of the Paris edition of Lord Northcliffe's *Daily Mail*. In 1912 he resigned to devote himself completely to writing and lecturing on the theme of the futility of war, and to educate public opinion about the need to replace competitive nationalism with "a community of nations."

In 1910 *The Great Illusion* was published under the name Norman Angell, which he later legalized. It sold over two million copies and was translated into 25 languages. In 1933 he updated the book, applying the thesis of 1909 to 1933 and stated the case for cooperation as the basis for civilization; in 1938 he again updated it under the title *The Great Illusion—Now*, in which he documented his theses with events of the previous five years.

Angell was not a rigid pacifist; he supported his country in both world wars. His quarrel was with armed aggression and the illusion that war could ever be profitable.

From 1929 to 1931 he was a Labour member of the House of Commons, representing Bradford North. He chose to leave politics to take his case for internationalism directly to the people without hindrance from party ties.

He wrote regularly for newspapers and journals and edited *Foreign Affairs* from 1928 to 1931. He was knighted for public service in 1931 upon the recommendation of Ramsey MacDonald.

In 1932, *The Unseen Assassins* was published. It attracted wide attention for its discussions of imperialism, nationalism, and effective education of the common man.

He was a member of the Council of the Royal Institute of International Affairs, an executive of the Comité mondial contre la guerre et le fascisme (World Committee against War and Fascism), an active member of the Executive Committee of the League of Nations Union, and president of the Abyssinia Association.

He traveled the lecture circuit almost every year, and at the age of 90 went on a two-month lecture tour of the United States.

Sir Norman Angell died on October 7, 1967, at the age of 94.

Bibliography

Christian Century 1934 Nobel Peace Prizes for Angell and Henderson. 51 (December 19): 1612

Miller J D B 1986 *Norman Angell and the Futility of War: Peace and the Public Mind*. Macmillan, London

New York Times 1967 Sir Norman Angell dies at 94; Won Nobel Peace Prize in '33. (October 9)

RUTH C. REYNOLDS

Arthur Henderson

(1934)

The 1934 Nobel Peace Prize went to Arthur Henderson, British parliamentarian, Foreign Secretary in MacDonald's cabinet, delegate to the Assembly of the League of Nations, and president of the World Disarmament Conference at Geneva. As he received this honor, the Conference was tottering on the edge of disaster. Equally at risk stood the League of Nations, that bulwark from which a lasting peace was to be launched, and the Nobel Committee called Arthur Henderson "among the bravest and most faithful on this bulwark."

The Committee presented the award with a tribute to Henderson's endeavors in behalf of that Conference: "Not many would have been able to hold out so long; not many would even have been strong enough, and still fewer would have possessed the necessary authority. If the Conference is still alive and if there is still a thin thread of hope, it is primarily because of Mr. Arthur Henderson."

Lloyd George once said, "Disarmament would be regarded as the real test of whether the League of Nations was a farce or whether business was meant." Henderson became the embodiment of the League's disarmament effort. He had been in Parliament almost continuously after 1903, and until the First World War his efforts had been almost exclusively in behalf of labor. But, as that war drew to a close, Henderson's thinking took on an international dimension. In 1917 he went to Russia as an official observer for the British government. In 1918 he initiated a conference at Bern, with delegates from the defeated and neutral countries joining the victorious

ones, to produce recommendations to send to Versailles where the Allies were drawing up the terms of the peace. In 1924, while Home Secretary in MacDonald's cabinet, Henderson spent most of his time on two international problems: the implementation of the Dawes Plan to introduce some reason into the reparations demanded of the Germans, and the drafting of the Geneva Protocol on the ultimate settlement of international disputes by arbitration.

Henderson had some concrete successes. During his two years as Foreign Secretary in MacDonald's government from 1929 to 1931 he brought about the United Kingdom's resumption of diplomatic relations with the Soviet Union which had been severed since 1917, he maneuvered acceptance of the Young Plan for German reparations by the creditor nations and Germany, he arranged with France's Foreign Minister, Briand (1926 Peace Prize co-winner), for the evacuation of French troops from the Rhineland prior to the date stipulated in the Treaty of Versailles, and he furthered the cause of Egyptian independence, which was achieved in 1936. Henderson also attended the entire sessions of the Tenth and Eleventh Assemblies of the League of Nations. Lord Cecil (1937 Peace Prize winner) called him "the most successful foreign minister we have had since 1918, with no brilliant and shiny qualities, but with that faculty for being right which Englishmen possess. His political courage was great—almost the rarest and the most valuable quality for a statesman." It was a virtue Henderson was in need of frequently.

Following the First World War, many statesmen as well as peace advocates understood the vital need for solving the cyclic nature of arms build-up and wars. Woodrow Wilson's Point Four wanted adequate guarantees given and taken that national armaments would be reduced to the lowest point consistent with domestic safety. Germany's greatest misgiving about the Treaty of Versailles concerned its required unilateral disarmament, and the German government wrote to the Paris Peace Conference: "Germany is prepared to agree to her proposed disarmament provided this is a beginning of a general reduction of armaments." France's Clemenceau replied: "The Allied and Associated Powers wish to make it clear that their requirements in regard to German armaments were not made solely with the object of rendering it impossible for her to resume her policy of aggression. They are also the first step toward that general reduction and limitation of armaments which they seek to bring about as one of the most fruitful preventatives of war and which it will be one of the first duties of the League of Nations to promote."

The connection made between the fate of humankind and successful disarmament was not confined to statesmen and diplomats. Twelve million signatures were presented to the Disarmament Conference by The Women's Societies on a document declaring that the delegates must choose between "world disarmament or world disaster." A questionnaire by Lord Cecil, which he called the "Peace Ballot" and which was sent out unofficially, received a return of eleven and a half million replies, out of which the massive majority of eleven million were in favor of arms reduction by international agreement.

But the commission charged with the formulation of a definite plan for disarmament by the League of Nations was doomed to failure from the beginning. The commission provoked the opposition of the various national bureaucracies because commission members were appointed by the League and were not official representatives of the various governments. Called the "Temporary Mixed Commission," it worked for five years making studies, condemning private manufacture of munitions, and pressing for control of the traffic in arms, before it came to an end in 1925 when the United Kingdom refused to have anything further to do with it.

The League created a new Preparatory Commission to work toward an international conference. It worked without noticeable effect for five years. Meanwhile the familiar pattern of arms build-up described by Lord Grey, British foreign minister,

grew apace: "The increase of armaments that is intended in each nation to produce consciousness of strength and a sense of security does not produce these effects. On the contrary, it produces a consciousness of the strength of other nations and a sense of fear. Fear begets suspicion and distrust and evil imaginings of all sorts till each government feels it would be criminal not to take every precaution; while every government regards every precaution of every other government as evidence of hostile intent."

It was Henderson's efforts which were largely responsible for the creation of the Disarmament Conference in 1932. In recognition of this he presided over its opening sessions despite the fall of the government in which he, as British Foreign Secretary, had first scheduled the Conference. He interpreted his election to the office of president as a mark of trust in him personally; but this circumstance had the unfortunate consequence of the British delegation working quite independently of Henderson. Sir John Simon, now the British Foreign Secretary in MacDonald's National Coalition Government, looked askance at the idea of real collective security and disarmament under international control, and the negative and arbitrary policy of the British delegation must bear some of the responsibility for the collapse of the Conference.

At the opening of the Conference Japan was committed to an act of war, and Hitler withdrew Germany from it in 1933. It was only Henderson's patience and his deep conviction that there could be no real disarmament except on the basis of the collective security system within the League of Nations that kept the Conference going through 1934. He believed the Conference to be a focal point of a struggle between anarchy and world order, between those who would think in terms of inevitable armed conflict and those who sought to build a durable peace.

Henderson's Nobel lecture did not carry the tone of one whose task is well on its appointed way. "Men and women everywhere are once more asking the old question: is it peace?," he began. "They are asking it with anxiety and fear; for, on the one hand, there has never been such a longing for peace and dread of war as there is today. On the other hand, there have never been such awful means of spreading destruction and death as those that are now being prepared in well nigh every country."

He told his Nobel audience that a policy of international cooperation which would effectively guarantee world peace would require a political commitment wherein each nation would cease judging its own rights for itself, and participate in a system of world law and order. Nations must subordinate in some measure national sovereignty in favor of world-wide institutions and obligations: "The establishment of a world commonwealth is, in the long run, the only alternative to a relapse into a world war. The psychological obstacles are formidable but not insurmountable," he said. " ... It will be no light and simple task ... it is, on the contrary, perhaps the greatest and most difficult enterprise ever imagined by the audacious mind of man. But it is a task which has become a necessity."

The failure of the Disarmament Conference foreshadowed the Second World War, but Henderson's biographer, Mary A. Hamilton (1938), states, "If any man is clear of responsibility, it is Arthur Henderson."

Biography

Arthur Henderson was born on September 13, 1863, in Glasgow, Scotland, son of David Henderson, a manual worker, who died nine years later, leaving the family in poverty. Arthur left school to help earn himself and his family a living. Upon his mother's remarriage he returned to school, but for three years only. His education continued, however, in sprightly conversations during the lunch hour of the General Foundry works where he worked as an apprentice, and through reading newspapers. He held membership in the Ironfounders' Union all his life. In 1896 he was chosen district delegate of his union, a salaried full-time position.

Skill in speaking learned in a debating society and in work as a lay preacher in the Salvation Army and later in the Methodist Church helped launch him into a political career begun as town councillor in 1892. In 1896 he moved to Darlington, and there he was elected to the Durham County Council. In 1903 he became the first Labour mayor of Darlington.

All his life Henderson supported Labour. He won election to Parliament in 1903 under the sponsorship of the Labour Representation Committee, he chaired the conference in 1906 which formed the Labour Party, and he was its secretary from 1911 to 1934.

Henderson served almost continuously in Parliament after 1903, sometimes through general elections and other times by regaining a seat through by-elections. He was chairman of the Parliamentary Labour Party, chief whip three times, president of the Board of Education 1915–16,

Paymaster-General in Asquith's government in 1916, and a minister without portfolio, acting primarily as an adviser on labor questions, in Lloyd George's government.

Following the First World War Henderson's activities took on an international bent. In 1917 he went to Russia as an official observer for the United Kingdom, and in 1918 he initiated the call for a conference at Bern to formulate recommendations for the delegates then drawing up the Peace Treaty at Versailles.

In 1923 he was chairman of the Labor and Socialist International at Hamburg. The next year he was Home Secretary in MacDonald's cabinet, during which time he worked on the implementation of the Dawes Plan for German reparations and on the drafting of the Geneva Protocol on the ultimate settlement of international disputes by arbitration.

He became Foreign Secretary in the MacDonald government in 1929. During his two years in office he brought about resumption of diplomatic relations with the Soviet Union, severed since 1917, he maneuvered acceptance of the Young Plan for German reparations by Germany and creditor nations, and arranged for the early evacuation of French troops from the Rhineland. He furthered the cause of Egyptian independence, which took place in 1936. He attended the entire sessions of the Tenth and Eleventh Assemblies of the League of Nations. A dedicated supporter of the League's disarmament effort, he served as president of the ill-fated Disarmament Conference in Geneva beginning in February 1932 and ending in 1935.

Henderson married Eleanor Watson in 1888. They had a daughter and three sons. The sons all served in the armed forces in the First World War, and the eldest was killed in action. The other two became Henderson's colleagues in the House of Commons in the last part of his life.

He was awarded the Wateler Peace Prize of the Carnegie Foundation in 1933 for the "energy, persistence, ability and impartiality" with which he had presided over the Disarmament Conference.

Arthur Henderson died on October 20, 1935.

Bibliography

Hamilton M 1938 *Arthur Henderson: A Biography*. Heinemann, London

New York Times 1934 Henderson to get Nobel Peace Prize. December 9, p. 24

New York Times 1934 Many shifts made in London policies: Henderson Prize ignored. Peace award to one outside government wins but scant mention and less praise. December 16, p. E3

The Times 1935 Eulogy in House of Commons. October 23, p. 9

RUTH C. REYNOLDS

Carl von Ossietzky

(1935)

The award of the 1935 Nobel Peace Prize to Carl von Ossietzky brought a storm of protest upon the heads of the Nobel Committee, but also intense support. During the period of von Ossietsky's candidacy a great many people felt that Alfred Nobel's injunction that the Prize go to "the person who shall have done the most or the best work for fraternity between peoples" could hardly apply to an imprisoned and defeated member of a powerless peace society in a dictatorship seemingly bent on war, and they regarded him as at most a symbol in the struggle for peace rather than a champion. More vehement voices joined this chorus with the objection that such a choice would antagonize Germany to no good purpose. Finally, from Germany itself came the warning not to provoke the German people by "rewarding this traitor to our country."

But peace advocates struggling in the midst of ever-increasing international tensions looked upon this martyred journalist as a supreme fighter for "fraternity among peoples." In a worldwide campaign they urged the favorable consideration of his candidacy for the award. Six previous recipients of the Peace Prize joined them. One of them wrote, "All of us have in some way or other tried to do something for peace, but we say that he has done more than any of us."

As petitions in behalf of von Ossietsky continued to pour in, the Nobel Committee arrived at a solution. The two Committee members who had, either presently or in the past, held government positions, resigned and were replaced by substitutes. Thereupon the Committee was a separate entity from the government, and it announced the award to Carl von Ossietzky. When the German minister to Norway protested, he was told, "The Norwegian government is in no way concerned. Kindly address yourself to the Nobel Committee."

In bestowing the award on von Ossietzky *in absentia*, the Chairman of the Nobel Committee addressed the question regarding von Ossietzky's status as only a symbol in the struggle for peace. "In my opinion this is not so," he said. "Carl von Ossietzky is not just a symbol. He is something quite different and something more. He is a deed and he is a man. It is on these grounds that Ossietzky has been awarded the Nobel Peace Prize, and on these grounds alone . . . The wish of the Nobel Committee has always been to fulfill its task and its obligation, namely to

reward work for peace. That and nothing else . . . . In awarding the Nobel Peace Prize to Carl von Ossietzky we are therefore recognizing his valuable contribution to the cause of peace—nothing more, and certainly nothing less."

Carl von Ossietzky's fight for peace was waged with a honed and talented pen. He was an outstanding stylist—trenchant, witty, and elegant. He carried on his fight for democratic principles in a Europe already consorting with dictatorial doctrines as a cure for the harsh harvest of the vengeful Treaty of Versailles, and he correctly divined that the suppression of free opinion and a free press was closely connected with Germany's distress during the postwar period.

Von Ossietzky had been an ardent pacifist even before his experiences as a front-line soldier in the First World War. As a young journalist he drew charges of "insult to the common good" from the Prussian War Ministry for his article criticizing a promilitary court decision in *Das Freie Volk* (*The Free People*). When called to make a court appearance, his fine was secretly paid by his young English wife, Maud Wood, whom he had married on May 22, 1914.

In 1916 he fought in the Bavarian Pioneer Regiment. The effect of this experience was to crystallize his lifelong pacifism into a personal commitment from which there was no turning back. He would instill into his fellow Germans a "peace mentality." While secretary of the German Peace Society he helped found the *Nie Wieder Krieg* (No More War) movement. But he had little taste for clerical work and organization. The well-chosen phrase was the weapon of his choice. He edited and wrote for liberal papers urging the German people to create a progressive nation under civilian, not military, leadership.

A fellow journalist, Hubert Herring (1936), described him and the events which led to his imprisonment: "I knew Carl von Ossietzky well in 1923. He and his wife and daughter lived in a dingy tenement in an unfashionable street in Berlin . . . He was a man of wrath uncorrupted by bitterness. He denounced with fury the willful sinfulness of the Allies who in their blindness had seared Germany with the brand of unforgettable guilt, and who, by the branding, had persuaded Germany that her only road of salvation lay in the creation of a Germany which could meet might with might . . .

"With even more vigor, he turned his fury upon those who were working corruption within the German republic. Ossietzky was a devout republican, but he saw the German republic eaten away by the disease which was the inheritance of Versailles. He threw his fragile strength against the insolence without and the poison within. The French were in the Ruhr that summer, and the Allies were busily devising ways for collecting the uncollectable debt incurred under the terms of the fictitious peace. Ossietzky was as harsh in his judgment upon the Allies as any other German, but his deeper sorrow sprang from the recognition of the lack of moral grandeur in the men who were leading Germany from disaster to disaster . . . Ossietzky knew that German arms and armaments would never bring redress, that the redemption of Germany must come by the plotting of new ways of national living.

"In 1931, shortly before Hitler came to power, the republic jailed him as a traitor for his attacks upon the development of the German military air force. He was released, and after Hitler's accession his friends urged him to escape. He refused indignantly. 'A man,' he said, 'speaks with a hollow voice across a national border. As a prisoner for the cause of freedom I would serve the struggle for peace better than as a free man outside of Germany.'"

Von Ossietzky spoke his mind about Hitler. Unlike many around him, he never underestimated Hitler and his movement. He realized the strong appeal which the movement had for the German middle classes that had always held aloof from real liberalism. On February 26, 1933, he gave a lecture in which he discussed the possibilities of a united front against Nazism. On February 27 the Reichstag fire took place, and the same night he was arrested and began his long and tortured years in various concentration camps. Never robust, the misery and the cruelty of those Nazi camps broke what little he had left of health.

Nothing official was told about von Ossietzky's fate, although a Vienna paper quoted a co-prisoner who said von Ossietzky had been badly treated by storm-troopers and that his teeth had been knocked out with a revolver butt.

He was transferred from Sonnenburg concentration camp to the camp of Esterwegen–Papenburg, and it was there, due to the persistence of Wickham Steed and Romain Rolland, that they, with a few other international journalists, were allowed to visit.

They found him broken in health and spirit and he declined to speak freely.

After the German minister in Norway had been informed of the award, the Nazis moved von Ossietzky from the camp to a Berlin hospital. There the tubercular, 47-year-old pacifist received the news of his $39,303 award. He sent a message that said, in part, "I am surprised and glad . . . The time has come when nations will agree to sit around a green table and put a halt to [the rearmament] insanity."

Journalists requested authorization to interview the laureate. German officials were present during the interview granted them, in which von Ossietzky said, "I count myself as belonging to a party of sensible Europeans who regard the armaments race as insanity. If the German government will permit, I will be only too pleased to go to Norway to receive the Prize and in my acceptance speech I will not dig up the past or say anything which might result in discord between Germany and Norway."

This wish was not fulfilled. Despite the declaration of the German Propaganda Ministry that von Ossietzky was free to go, documents of the secret police have since revealed that he was refused a passport. Although in a civilian hospital, von Ossietzky was kept under surveillance until his death.

His award had tremendous repercussions in the press. Radicals and socialists rejoiced, but the news was received by Germany with rage that percolated from Hitler down. Calling it a "brazen challenge and insult to the New Germany," it demanded that von Ossietzky refuse the prize. This he would not do. Hitler then decreed that no German thereafter should accept a Nobel Prize.

For some time the whereabouts of the prize money was a mystery. Norway at first could not get in touch with von Ossietzky. When they eventually received a message from him that he was free to receive the prize money, they placed the funds at his disposal in a bank. Since von Ossietzky was not permitted to leave the hospital, the power of attorney was given to his lawyer, who delivered still another blow to von Ossietzky by embezzling the money. Von Ossietzky's last public appearance was at a court hearing where the lawyer was sentenced to two years' hard labor. Only 16,500 Reichsmarks were left, and this the German government took for his "board and room" of the last four years. His wife received nothing. In 1954 the government of the Federal Republic of Germany awarded their daughter 5 Deutschmarks ($1.92).

Herbert Herring (1936) called him "an inconspicuous man with a weak voice, a delicate body and a flaming eye, but history and Adolf Hitler have made that voice overtop the pounding of studded boots on the pavements of Unter den Linden."

Biography

Carl von Ossietzky was born in Hamburg on October 3, 1889, son of a civil servant who died when he was two. His mother married Gustav Walter, a Social Democrat, when Carl was nine. His stepfather proved influential in shaping von Ossietzky's later political attitudes.

As a young journalist von Ossietzky first worked for *Das Freie Volk* (*The Free People*), the weekly organ of the Democratic Union. In 1913 an article criticizing a promilitary court decision drew charges of "insult to the common good" from the Prussian War Ministry.

In the First World War von Ossietzky fought in the Bavarian Pioneer Regiment. His pacifism intensified by the war, he returned to Hamburg determined to educate people to a "peace mentality." He held a position as secretary of the German Peace Society, creating the monthly *Mitteilungsblatt* (*Information Sheet*), and became a regular contributor to *Monisten Monatsheften* (*Monists' Monthly*). He helped to found the *Nie Wieder Krieg* (No More War) organization in 1922. He was also foreign editor on the *Berliner Volkzeitung* (*Berlin People's Paper*).

In 1926 the founder and editor of *Die Weltbuhne* (*The World Stage*), Siegfried Jacobsohn, offered him a position on the editorial staff. Following the death of Jacobsohn, von Ossietzky continued his former editor's efforts to publicize the secret rearmament of Germany. He was tried for libel, found guilty, and sentenced to one month in prison.

In March 1929 he published an article by Walter Kreiser further exposing Germany's rearming. Accused of treason, he was sentenced in November 1931 to 18 months in prison, but was amnestied in December 1932.

He refused to leave Germany despite the growing danger posed by the Nazis, saying a man speaks with a hollow voice across a border. On February 27, the evening following the Reichstag fire, he was arrested and thrown into prison, and then into concentration camps at Sonnenburg and at Esterwegen–Papenburg, where cruel treatment broke his health.

He was awarded the Nobel Prize for Peace in 1935, but he was not granted a passport to attend the presentation ceremony. Germany interpreted the award as an insult to the "New Germany," and decree was passed in January 1937 forbidding Germans to accept any Nobel Prize.

Ridden with tuberculosis, von Ossietzky was kept in a civilian hospital following the award, but under constant surveillance. His lawyer embezzled the prize money.

Carl von Ossietzky died, at the age of 48, of meningitis, on May 4, 1938. He left a widow, Maud Wood, whom he had married on May 22, 1914, and a daughter, Rosalinde Ossietzky–Palm.

Bibliography

Herring H 1936 Both win the Nobel Prize! *Christian Century* 53 (December 16): 1687–88

New York Times 1936 Germany enraged by Ossietzky Prize. November 25, p. 1

New York Times 1938 Von Ossietzky dies in Berlin hospital. May 5, p. 23

Newsweek 1936 Germany: Inventor of dynamite posthumously rewards 'traitor.' December 5, p. 12

Time 1936 International—Nobel Prize prisoner. 28 (December 7): 18

Ruth C. Reynolds

Carlos Saavedra Lamas

(1936)

The 1936 Nobel Prize for Peace was awarded to the Argentinian Carlos Saavedra Lamas. International lawyer, practical statesman, skilled mediator, educator, and academician, Dr. Carlos Saavedra Lamas was an architect of treaties who put the keystone into place for every South American diplomatic triumph devised in the mid-1930s. Urbane, son of a family rich in the tradition of public service, he had acquired a thorough grounding in academic training. He put these attributes to the delicate tasks of mediation, arbitration, and other creative means for settling international conflicts.

Saavedra Lamas entered politics early. It was as a young man that he first displayed his flair for diplomacy by saving Argentina's floundering arbitration treaty with Italy in 1908–09. As a member of the

Argentine Chamber of Deputies, long before he was to take the post as Foreign Minister he became the unofficial adviser to both the legislature and the Foreign Office on the analysis and implications of proposed treaties. His first government post of importance, held before he was 30, was as national Minister of Justice and Public Education in 1915. He proved himself a progressive educator.

Saavedra Lamas was an aristocrat, a descendant of Don Corucho Saavedra, the first President of Argentina. He was a distinguished student, receiving his Doctor of Laws degree *summa cum laude*, and continuing his studies in Paris. He was widely traveled. He began an academic career destined to span 40 years by accepting a professorship of law and constitutional history at the University of La Plata.

Later he inaugurated a course in sociology at the University of Buenos Aires; he taught political economy and constitutional law at the Law School of the University and eventually became its president.

He led as an Argentinian academician in the field of labor legislation. He was the first university professor to lecture in Argentina in that field. He wrote treatises on the existing system and the need for a universally recognized doctrine on the treatment of labor. Notable particularly were his *Centro de legislacion social y del trabajo* (Center of Social and Labor Legislation) in 1927 and the three-volume *Codigo nacional del trabajo* (National Code of Labor Law) in 1933.

On the international labor scene, Saavedra Lamas supported the founding of the International Labour Organization in 1919 and was unanimously elected president of its 1928 Geneva conference. On a local and practical level, he drafted labor legislation in Argentina. In his Nobel lecture he said that social peace must be erected on the basis of greater social justice. "Unemployment is a great tragedy," he said. "The man who goes about hopelessly seeking work in order to earn bread for his children is a living reproach to civilization."

International law also captured his interest, and his scholarly output in this field included *La Crise de la codification et de la doctrine argentine de droit internationale* (The Crisis of Codification and the Argentine Doctrine of International Law) in 1931. Saavedra Lamas authored legislation on many subjects with international ramifications, including asylum, colonization, immigration, arbitration, and international peace.

In 1932 General Agustin P. Justo, the incoming President of Argentina, chose Saavedra Lamas as his Foreign Minister. One of Saavedra Lamas' early accomplishments in this position was persuading Argentina to rejoin the League of Nations after an absence of 13 years. He was an ardent supporter of the League, and he represented Argentina at every important international meeting during this period. He initiated the 1932 declaration in which the American republics agreed not to recognize any change of territory in the Americas resulting from a force of arms. The Pan-American Society of New York in 1933 awarded him its medal in recognition of his international work.

In his first year as Foreign Minister he began work on his Antiwar Pact, which would contain some of the merits of the Kellogg–Briand Pact, an international statement outlawing war except as a defensive measure against aggression. Saavedra Lamas visual-

ized his pact coordinated with the existing Pan-American Union and the US–Latin American relationship. Upon the latter relationship Saavedra Lamas had previously made major diplomatic impact by influencing the United States to rethink its interpretation of the Monroe Doctrine (see Articles: *Monroe Doctrine*). This doctrine, originally written by President Monroe in 1823 to discourage future colonization by European powers in the Americas, and to forbid European intervention in American affairs, had unfortunately come to be seen as an accommodation for American imperialism by securing the interests of the North American business community in its South American financial ventures. Saavedra Lamas launched vigorous opposition to such imperialistic intervention, and he had the satisfaction of seeing a policy change come about, particularly under US Secretary of State Cordell Hull (1945 Peace Prize laureate) and President Franklin D. Roosevelt.

In his Antiwar Pact Saavedra Lamas hoped to coordinate these three factors: the Pan-American Union, the League of Nations, and a noninterventionist United States. The particular feature of his pact was that, unlike the Kellogg–Briand Pact, which called for the outlawry of war on a moral basis, his pact would provide sanctions which could be used against an aggressor. Another feature unique to this pact was a provision for procedures *during* a conflict. It provided for the reestablishment of peace, while at the same time maintaining the principle of neutrality. This was to be accomplished through carefully formulated and guaranteed international cooperation among the neutral nations.

The conclusion of Saavedra Lamas' Antiwar Pact was doubly successful: it was signed by Argentina, Brazil, Mexico, Chile, Uruguay, and Paraguay in October 1933 and eight months later by 14 Spanish American States, the United States, and Italy. Within a year, the treaty was actually put to the test. One of the signatory powers, Paraguay, was the victim of an aggression on the part of Bolivia. The subject of the dispute was the northern portion of the Gran Chaco country where frontiers had not been properly fixed since the end of Spanish rule. A military deadlock had set in which the League of Nations had been unable to break. In May 1935 Saavedra Lamas took the course of action outlined in his Antiwar Pact, approaching the Brazilian, Chilean, and Peruvian diplomatic representatives in Buenos Aires about setting up a mediatory operation. A commission was created using these nations along with the United States and Uruguay. Saavedra Lamas served as chairman. The two belligerents accepted a proffered settlement, and on June 12, 1935, the armistice protocol was signed. Saavedra Lamas' Antiwar Pact had operated successfully on a South American controversy, under his leadership. At the peace negotiations which were initiated shortly afterwards Saavedra Lamas also played a leading role. He presented his Antiwar Pact to the League of Nations, where it was well-received and signed by 11 countries. In 1936 he was elected president of the Assembly of the League.

At this Assembly, when Saavedra Lamas alluded to the six American states whose work of conciliation had succeeded in ending the war in South America, he gave careful emphasis to the fact that two of the six, the United States and Brazil, were not members of the League. From this he made the hopeful extrapolation that the possibility therefore existed in future mediation cases of winning the cooperation of nations *outside* the League. "I see this as a significant signpost for the diplomacy of peace," he said. "We must regard it not as an isolated or exceptional occurrence, but as one which will become the rule."

Saavedra Lamas retired as Foreign Minister in 1938 and returned to academic life. Between 1941 and 1943 he accepted the presidency of the University of Buenos Aires, and, following that, completed his academic career as a professor for an additional three years.

He was awarded the Grand Cross of the Legion of Honor of France and similar honors from Brazil, Chile, Bolivia, Colombia, Portugal, Spain, Poland, Bulgaria, Belgium, and Yugoslavia. He accepted, in 1935, the Star of the German Red Cross. This was from the same country whose government raged against the award of the 1935 Nobel Peace Prize to its imprisoned journalist, Carl von Ossietzky, whose crime was to protest publicly against the remilitarization of Germany. Von Ossietzky's award, given a year late, was presented at the same ceremony with Saavedra Lamas. The two recipients could scarcely have made more contrasting contributions to peace. But they had one thing in common: neither one attended the ceremony—Saavedra Lamas because he was presiding at the Inter-American Conference for the Maintenance of Peace meeting in Buenos Aires, and Ossietzky because as a prisoner for life in the Nazi prison system he was denied the privilege of attending the ceremony.

In a radio address given in response to the award, Saavedra Lamas said: "We are living in the aftermath of a great war. The fabric which civilization has been weaving in its efforts of centuries, once broken, is difficult to reconstruct. Under its broken web there appears to be a native barbarism ... War of aggression, war which does not imply defense of one's country, is a collective crime. In its consequences on the mass of the poor and humble, it does not possess even that blaze of valor, or of heroism, that leads to glory. War implies a lack of comprehension of mutual national interests; it means the undermining and even the end of culture. It is the useless sacrifice of courage erroneously applied, opposed to that other silent courage that signifies the effort to aid others to improve existence by raising all in this fleeting moment of ours to higher levels of existence."

Biography

Carlos Saavedra Lamas was born in Buenos Aires on November 1, 1878, into an aristocratic Argentine family descended from Argentina's first President, Don Corucho Saavedra. He was educated at Lacordaire College and the University of Buenos Aires, where he received the Doctor of Laws degree *summa cum laude*, subsequently continuing his studies in Paris. Educator as well as statesman and lawyer, during an academic career which spanned 40 years, Saavedra Lamas taught law and constitutional history at the University of La Plata, sociology at the University of Buenos Aires, and constitutional law and political economy at the Law School of the University, as well as serving as its president in 1941–43.

He was a leading academician in labor legislation and international law. In the former capacity he was the first Argentinian professor to lecture in that field, and his publications included *Centro de legislacion social y del trabajo*, (1927), *Trites internationaux de type sociale* (1924), and *Codigo nacional del trabajo*, a three-volume work (1933). In the field of international law he published *La Crise de la codification et de la doctrine argentine de droit internationale*. He also drafted legislation in many areas of international application: asylum, colonization, immigration, arbitration, and peace.

He held the following governmental posts: director of Public Credit, 1906, secretary–general for the muncipality of Buenos Aires, 1907. In 1908 he served two successive terms in parliament; in 1915 he was Minister of Justice and Education and in 1932 became Foreign Minister.

He was responsible for most of the South American diplomatic successes of the 1930s, including achieving improved South American relations with North America by working, most notably with US Secretary of State Cordell Hull (1945 Peace Prize laureate) and President Franklin D. Roosevelt, toward less imperialism from North America. He initiated in Washington, DC, the Declaration of August 3, 1933 which put the American states on record as refusing to recognize any territorial change in the hemisphere brought about by force. He drew up a Treaty of Nonaggression and Conciliation which was signed by six South American countries in October 1933, and by all of the

American countries at the Seventh Pan-American Conference at Montevideo two months later. He wrote the Antiwar Pact and guided its successful application to ending the stalemated conflict between Paraguay and Bolivia. He presented the Antiwar Pact to the League of Nations, where it was signed by 11 countries in 1936. That year he was elected president of the Assembly of the League.

The Pan-American Society of New York awarded him its medal in recognition of his international work in 1933. He was awarded the Grand Cross of the Legion of Honor of France and similar honors from Brazil, Chile, Bolivia, Colombia, Portugal, Spain, Poland, Bulgaria, Belgium, and Yugoslavia. He received the Star of the German Red Cross for his work for world peace in 1935, and won the Nobel Prize for Peace in 1936.

Carlos Saavedra Lamas died on May 5, 1959, in Buenos Aires. He left a wife, Rosa Saenz Pena de Saavedra Lamas, and a son, Carlos Roque.

Bibliography

Herring H 1936 Both win the Nobel Prize! *Christian Century* 53 (December 16): 1687–88

New York Times 1936 Saavedra Lamas wrote Peace Pact. November 25, p. 5

New York Times 1959 Dr. Saavedra Lamas dies at 80; Won Nobel Peace Prize in 1936. May 6, p. 39

RUTH C. REYNOLDS

Robert Cecil

(1937)

The 1937 Nobel Prize for Peace went to Viscount Cecil of Chelwood, British parliamentarian and cabinet minister, one of the architects of the League of Nations and its faithful defender. From the inception of the League until 1946 when it ceased to function, he devoted almost his entire public life to this international instrument for maintaining peace. Three British Prime Ministers, Ramsay MacDonald, Stanley Baldwin, and David Lloyd George, representing the three major parties in the United Kingdom, paid him a rare tribute: "The formation and maintenance of the League of Nations are due to the labours of many distinguished men of many nationalities, but it has fallen to Lord Cecil to devote himself single-mindedly to strengthening the League and promoting an intelligent understanding of its work among all classes of his fellow citizens."

Edgar Algernon Robert Gascoyne Cecil was born in 1864 into one of England's most distinguished families among the landed aristocracy. He was the third son of the Marquess of Salisbury, leader of the Conservative Party and three times Prime Minister between 1885 and 1902. The education which Cecil received at home until he was 13 was far more interesting, he wrote in his autobiography, than his subsequent four years at Eton. It was an upbringing remote from pacifism as his father accepted the legacy of Disraeli and continued the United Kingdom's imperialist policy.

Cecil read law at Oxford and was called to the Bar in 1887. He became an accomplished advocate and, in due time, a Queen's Counsel. In 1906 he was

elected to parliament and sat on the Conservative benches.

With the outbreak of the First World War in 1914 he joined the Red Cross and went to Paris to organize the Department of Wounded and Missing. The experience left him with an abhorrence of war. In 1915, in Asquith's coalition government, he became Undersecretary for Foreign Affairs under Sir Edward Grey, and the following year, in Lloyd George's government, he became Minister of Blockade, serving in this position from 1916 to 1918. In the course of these posts Cecil was introduced to concepts of pacifism through collaboration with leading Liberals such as Asquith and Grey. In 1915 a League of Nations Society was founded, probably the first organization to use that name. Cecil joined in this work in 1916, and it became the predominant influence in his life. The conversion from his youthful unawareness of the problems of peace to a conviction which dominated his life had begun.

In 1918 Cecil initiated through Lord Grey, then the Foreign Secretary, a commission to draw up the first British draft of a Covenant for the proposed League of Nations. Cecil was its driving force, and together with his long-time friend, General Jan Smuts, composed much of the draft. It was Cecil who originated the plan of having the League handle social, economic, and humanitarian functions, while Smuts suggested the Secretariat and the concept of mandates. This became the working draft of the Covenant, and Cecil and Smuts, together with Woodrow Wilson, are considered the authors of the Covenant in its final form.

On November 12, 1918, the day following the Armistice, Cecil spoke at the University of Birmingham about plans for the League of Nations. He said the victors had a moral obligation to construct a lasting peace through an instrument designed for international cooperation and arbitration. As early as June 1919 he called for the admission of Germany and the Soviet Union into the League. That same year he became president of the League of Nations Union. He also became president of the International Federation of the League of Nations Societies. Both of these organizations were means for educating people about the League, one national, the other international.

The dynamic force upon which the League should rest, Cecil urged, was that of vigilant and informed public opinion. He said that publicity was the very lifeblood of the League of Nations. When the inevitable conflicts arise, and a peaceful solution by legal judgment or arbitration and mediation is sought, public opinion should be given a voice. Cecil insisted that the Assembly should meet annually, and that the meetings should be open to the public. A unique attribute which Cecil added, new to international politics, was opening the Assembly's sessions each year with a general debate. The Assembly thus became a free tribune.

Cecil seemed tireless in his work on behalf of the League. At the Paris Peace Conference he was the British representative in charge of negotiations for a League of Nations. At the first three assemblies he served as delegate for the Union of South Africa by choice of General Smuts. In 1923 he made a five-week tour of the United States explaining the League to American audiences. From 1923 to 1927 he was the minister responsible, under the jurisdiction of the Foreign Secretary, for British activities in League affairs.

Cecil pleaded for the fundamental moral principles necessary for the effective work of the League. "Do not let us be afraid of our power," he said. "Let us go on from strength to strength. It is not by doing too much that the League is in any danger. The one danger that threatens the League is that it may gradually sink down into a position of respectable mediocrity and useless complication with the diplomatic machinery of the world . . . We must be ready to take a bold line in the great work of reconciliation and pacification that lies before us."

The very hesitancy that he spoke against seemed to Cecil increasingly to be the policy of the Conservative Party. In 1927 at great personal cost he severed the official ties which bound him to the Party. He wrote, "As time went on I became increasingly conscious that that view was not really accepted by most Conservative politicians and was indeed hotly and violently rejected by large numbers of the right wing of the Party. Not only indeed did they reject in their hearts the League of Nations, but they did not propose to take any step for getting rid of war. Clearly, they and I could not honestly belong to the same party."

The very weakness that he feared drove its first shaft into the heart of the League in 1931–32 when the League failed to take action against Japan upon that member country's armed intervention in Manchuria. Sanctions which were urged in many quarters were not used because the Great Powers on whom the burden of enforcement would rest refused to run the risk of war with Japan to compel it to observe its Covenant obligations.

Cecil delivered a dynamic speech on the relevance of disarmament to what had happened. Disarmament, he said, was the touchstone for the will to peace. If disarmament were once carried through, the international atmosphere would suddenly be transformed. The nations would have cast their ultimate vote for peace. If, on the other hand, they rejected disarmament, the world would sink back into dependence upon military might as Japan had just done.

Another contributing factor to the failure to face up to the potential strength of the League through concerted action on the part of its members lay with the old traditional diplomats. They believed that foreign affairs are a matter which only those who have had special training can handle. Debate carried on openly, with little regard for the technical phraseology of diplomacy, would offend their every instinct.

Cecil launched two major attempts to mobilize UK public opinion behind a strong League, decisive in action. The first was a national voluntary referendum in the form of a questionnaire called the "Peace Ballot." The respondent was asked to comment upon the desirability of the League of Nations, on disarmament, on economic sanctions against aggressors, and on military sanctions. The optimists had hoped to receive four to five million replies. In fact eleven and a half million replies poured in, out of which an overwhelming majority, eleven million, were in favor of the League of Nations, ten and a half million for disarmament, ten million for the use of economic sanctions against an aggressor, and 6,780,000 for military sanctions. It happened during the time of a general election, and the Baldwin government proclaimed its firm support for the Peace Ballot findings.

Meanwhile, the Ethiopian crisis loomed, with Italy, a member country, committing an act of overt military aggression on Ethiopia. Once the election was over, the Baldwin government retreated from its stated position and chose to abandon the sanctions, embarking instead upon the largest rearmament program in British history. So Cecil again went to the people. This time, together with the French politician Pierre Cot, he planned the *Rassemblement universel pour la paix* (International Peace Campaign). Founded in March, 1936, its object was to unite peace efforts into an international common front in order to promote concentrated action against violence. It, too, received heartening response from the populace. But Cecil later was to look back and perceive that they had attached too much hope to the conception that no nation would be so rash or so arrogant as to set itself against the public opinions of the world.

In his Nobel address Cecil conjectured that the failure to check Italy had its roots in the League's initial failure to check Japan. Aggressive nations throughout the world were able to observe that, in spite of the League and its Covenant, the old military policies could be successfully reinstated. The consequences were rapid and fatal to the League. Germany forcibly reoccupied Rhineland provinces in 1936. In the civil war in Spain which started in the same year, outside nations intervened—Italy and Germany sent troops and military supplies to support the Nationalist rebels and the Soviet Union provided assistance to the Republican forces. Austria was absorbed by Germany on April 10, 1938. Japan, now out of the League, intensified its campaign against China in 1937.

It was evident that the League was faltering. Germany, Japan, and Italy had withdrawn and the Soviet Union had been expelled. Only 46 of the 63 member states remained. Cecil contended that the League itself had been valid in concept; it was the governments which had failed. Anthony Eden agreed: The Council of the League was "as serviceable a piece of diplomatic machinery as I have ever known," he said. Perhaps the most tragic comment of all came from Winston Churchill: during the Second World War he told Cecil, "This war could easily have been prevented if the League of Nations had been used with courage and loyalty by the associated nations."

Cecil concluded that the great question posed by the League's failure was whether the revival of the old ideas was going to make its way amongst the nations of the world. "Do not let us underrate the danger," he said. "It threatens everything we care for ... Let me say that in my view it is quite certain that we can prevent it. I have myself no doubt on that point at all. The vast majority of the peoples of the world are against war and against aggression. If they make their wishes known and effective, war can be stopped. It all depends upon whether they are willing to make the effort necessary for the purpose."

Cecil was created first Viscount of Chelwood in 1923. His work for world peace was commemorated on his coat of arms. The two supporting lions have olive branches on their shoulders.

Biography

Viscount Cecil of Chelwood was born Edgar Algernon Robert Gascoyne Cecil in London in 1864, son of the Marquess of Salisbury, leader of the Conservative Party and three times Prime Minister between 1885 and 1902. He was educated at Eton and at University College, Oxford, where he studied law. He was called to the Bar in 1887. He was a Conservative Member of Parliament for Marylebone East from 1906 to 1910, and for the Hitchin Division of Hertfordshire from 1911 to 1923.

Cecil served with the Red Cross during the First World War, was Undersecretary for Foreign Affairs, 1915–1916, and Minister of Blockade from 1916 to 1918. He became Assistant Secretary of State for Foreign Affairs in 1918.

Cecil's public life was devoted to the League of Nations. With General Jan Smuts he wrote the British draft of the Covenant of the League, which proved to be the working draft from which the final Covenant was written with the co-authorship of US President Woodrow Wilson. At the Paris Peace Conference he was the British representative in charge of negotiations for a League of Nations. From 1920 to 1922 he represented the Dominion of South Africa in the League Assembly. He was Lord Privy Seal, 1923–24, and Chancellor of the Duchy of Lancaster, 1924–27, during which two posts he was the minister responsible, under the jurisdiction of the Foreign Secretary, for British activities in League affairs.

In 1927 he left the Conservative Party owing to differences regarding the League about which he found many Conservative politicians were distinctly unenthusiastic; and thereafter worked independently to promote public opinion in support of the League. He was president of the British League of Nations Union from 1923 to 1945, and joint founder with Pierre Cot, French politician, of the International Peace Campaign (*Rassemblement universel pour la paix*) in 1936.

Cecil was awarded many honors. He was created first Viscount of Chelwood in 1923 and made a Companion of Honor in 1956. He was elected the chancellor of Birmingham University, 1918–44, and rector of the University of Aberdeen, 1924–27. He won the Peace Award of the Woodrow Wilson Foundation in 1924. He was presented with honorary degrees by the Universities of Edinburgh, Oxford,

Cambridge, Manchester, Liverpool, St. Andrews, Aberdeen, Princeton, Columbia, and Athens.

His publications include: *Principles of Commercial Law, Our National Church, The Way of Peace, A Great Experiment, A Real Peace,* and *All the Way.*

He married Lady Eleanor Lambton, daughter of the Second Earl of Durham, in 1889.

Viscount Cecil of Chelwood died on November 24, 1958, at the age of 94.

RUTH C. REYNOLDS

Nansen Office

(1938)

see *Fridtjof Nansen and the Nansen Office*
(*1922*)　　　　　　　(*1938*)

Prize Not Awarded

(1939–43)

Red Cross

(1944)

see *Henri Dunant and the Red Cross*
(*1901*)　　　　(*1917, 1944, 1963*)

Cordell Hull

(1945)

The 1945 Nobel Prize for Peace was awarded to Cordell Hull for his long and indefatigable work toward promoting understanding between nations. During his nearly half-century of service to his government, Hull's single most pressing goal was the stabilization of international relations based on a fair economic interchange between nations. This he believed to be fundamental to the cause of world peace. It was "the driving spirit behind his fight against isolationism at home, his efforts to create a peace bloc of states on the American continents, and his work for the United Nations Organization," the Nobel Committee said.

Born in a log cabin in the mountains of Tennessee in 1871, Hull is associated with both the real and the mythological values of the American frontier. It is a

tradition that marked his long career, and it offers insight into the character of the man. Benjamin Stolberg, in the *American Mercury* (April 1940) offered an illuminating profile: "Hull comes from the land of the great frontier border leaders—Andrew Jackson, Henry Clay, Lincoln, Andrew Johnson...its families represented the only social phenomenon which is distinctly American—the rise of the Common Man and his folk democracy. It is this tradition which gives Hull the characteristic folk outlook of the frontier, and above all, the personal traits which it developed...always principled...suspicious of the human animal, without moral indignation and without cynicism...and when necessary, fearless."

After graduating from Mount Vale Academy in Celina, Tennessee, Hull attended the National Normal University in Ohio for a winter, and from there he went to Cumberland University Law School, known for its "short order" law curriculum. By 19 years of age he was admitted to the bar. Following his brief schooling, Hull's education continued on, self-taught. With his native intelligence and tireless industry, he acquired expertise in his chosen field of economics, and in time he became a leading authority on taxation and tariff.

In 1893, when he was 21, Hull was elected to the Tennessee state legislature, where he served until the Spanish–American war in 1897. The following year he returned to Celina and resumed the practice of law until 1907, when, at the age of 30, he was appointed Judge of the Fifth Tennessee Circuit. The vigorous young judge turned out to be "so tough on the sinful that crime lost much of its allure and nearly all of its profits."

Four years later Hull returned to the call of politics, and after a campaign in which he "stunned the mountaineers with tax talk," he went to Congress from the Fourth Tennessee District on a margin of 17 votes. It was the beginning of a long and sustained career in public service during which Hull put into practice the principles of fairness and steadfastness of purpose he had absorbed in his frontiersman youth.

Hull renewed interest in the income tax law originally introduced by his mentor, Congressman McMillin, and subsequently killed by the Supreme Court. Hull wrote a modern draft which became the First Federal Income Tax Act in 1913, in which Hull was convinced that the direct taxation of wealth, rather than indirect taxation of the consumer, would shift the heaviest burden to the rich and away from those less able to bear it. This same drive for fairness was to guide Hull's approach to international relations, and determine his foreign policy. At the time of his Peace Prize award, the Committee said, "We see him as representative of all that is best in liberalism, a liberalism with a strong social implication."

On all levels, individual, national, and international, Hull acted on his belief that the practice of mutual cooperation would resolve tensions. He held that high tariffs were barriers obstructing fairness in trade, and therefore posed a threat to lasting international peace. In a speech Hull made before Congress on September 10, 1918, he explained these views: "Believing as I have that the best antidote against war is the removal of its causes rather than its prevention after the causes once arise, and finding that trade retaliation and discrimination in its more vicious forms have been productive of bitter eco-

nomic wars which in many cases have developed into wars of force, I introduced the resolution in the House of Representatives congress [providing for] the organization of an international trade-agreement to eliminate by mutual agreement all possible methods of retaliation and discrimination in international trade" (Hinton 1942 p. 112).

The League of Nations took up the task of reducing trade restrictions, and its efforts culminated at the World Monetary and Economic Conference held in London in 1933 which Hull attended as Secretary of State. Faithful to his conviction that economic imbalance was the root of most wars, Hull headed the United States delegation to the Conference only to see the stability he sought blasted by President Roosevelt, who rejected Hull's plan for currency stabilization on the grounds that a nation's prosperity depended more upon healthy internal economic structure than upon the price of its currency in relation to the price of currencies of other nations. Hull did not believe in this move toward economic nationalism. In a speech given two months later he declared, "The world is still engaged in wild competition, in economic armaments which constantly menace both peace and commerce."

Hull carried his campaign for free and reciprocal trade to the Pan-American Conference in Montevideo. There, with his homespun simplicity, he overcame initial suspiciousness and won the Latin Americans' confidence by abandoning traditional diplomatic protocol and approaching each statesman on an individual and personal level. An agreement was successfully drafted which defined the rights and obligations of each nation. By the time of the subsequent Buenos Aires and Lima Conferences, in 1936 and 1938, the outlook in Europe had become more ominous. One major stumbling block before which Hull was helpless was that the South American countries were members of the League of Nations and the United States was not. But the success that was achieved by the Good Neighbor Policy in Latin American initiated by Roosevelt was built upon the groundwork of Hull's skillful replacement of "dollar diplomacy" with an establishment of trust within the Latin American countries.

Despite the setback of the London Conference of 1933, Hull was able the next year to secure the Trade Agreements Act which empowered the President to lower tariffs by 50 percent and to reduce import restrictions for countries who would reciprocate. On the basis of this bill Hull concluded 27 trade agreements. This marked a radical change in the economic policy of the United States, one that Hull saw as an important step toward improved international relations.

As Secretary of State, Hull had to face the Axis powers just as a wave of isolationism swept the United States. While the isolationists regarded peace primarily as peace for the United States, Hull thought in terms of a flexible form of neutrality which would permit the United States to cooperate with other countries in maintaining peace. The United States cannot unilaterally proclaim peace for herself alone, Hull said.

With the coming of the Second World War, Hull devoted himself to the cause of defeating the aggressive Axis powers, but he also looked ahead to problems which would arrive with peace. He drafted six clauses governing the future policy of the four allied powers which were adopted at the Moscow Conference of 1943.

His greatest contribution to world peace, to which he devoted his final efforts in the face of failing health, was setting up the United Nations. He visualized a postwar organization within which international cooperation might at last dominate the world scene. President Roosevelt called Hull the "Father of the United Nations." When he received Hull's resignation by reason of illness, the President expressed the hope that Hull might preside over the UN's first session "as the one person in all the world who has done the most to make this great plan for peace an effective fact." The President continued his message with words which serve well as a summary of Cordell Hull's long and distinguished career: "In so many different ways you have contributed to friendly relations among nations that even though you may not remain in a position of executive administration, you will continue to help the world with your moral guidance."

Biography

Cordell Hull was born in 1871 in a log cabin built by his father in the mountains of Tennessee, one of five sons of William Hull and Elizabeth Riley Hull. Raised in the backwoods, Hull absorbed the democracy practiced by the frontiersmen who gathered at the local schoolhouse to learn about government affairs and to discuss politics. At 16 he went to Mount Vale Academy at Celina, Tennessee, where he was greatly influenced by Congressman Benton McMillin, brother of the headmaster. Following graduation from Mount Vale Academy, a whirlwind education of one winter at National Normal University in Ohio, and a course in law at Cumberland University, Hull was admitted to the bar at 19. He continued his education on his own and acquired expertise in taxation and tariff.

In 1893 at the age of 21, Hull was elected to the Tennessee State Legislature, but his career was interrupted by the Spanish–American War in which he served briefly as a captain in the Fourth Tennessee Regiment. Upon his return to Celina, he resumed practicing law until appointed a judge of the Fifth Tennessee District, where he earned a reputation for fairness and common sense.

Four years later he yielded to the call of politics and successfully ran for a seat in the House of Representatives, where he served until 1931 (with a two-year hiatus, 1920–22, during which he was pressed into service as Chairman of the National Executive Committee of the Democratic Party). In Congress he became known for his belief in Jeffersonian free trade policies, and for his taxation programs, the former designed to encourage worldwide economic health, and the latter to distribute the burden of revenue costs in terms of the citizens' ability to pay. To this end he authored the federal income tax system of 1913, and its revision of 1916.

In 1931 he was elected to the Senate, and when Franklin Roosevelt became President two years later, Hull became his Secretary of State, a position he held for a record 12 years. During this time he implemented Roosevelt's Good Neighbor Policy in the Latin American countries, resulting in an agreement that "no state has the right to intervene in the internal or external affairs of another."

Although Hull's design for international economic stability which he carried as head of the US delegation to the Monetary and Economic Conference in London in 1933 was overruled by Roosevelt's decision in favor of economic nationalism, by the next year Hull had sufficiently gained the confidence of the President to allow passage of the Trade Agreements Act, providing the President with authority to lower existing tariff rates by as much as 50 percent to those countries willing to make reciprocal concessions. This was a great triumph for Hull's dream of an international commerce so healthy and so unhampered by barriers of nationalism that the root cause of war could thereby be addressed.

As an internationalist, Secretary of State Hull had a difficult role with regard to the growing isolationism within his own country and the aggressiveness of the Axis powers without. He correctly read the increased need for military defense, and recognized the possibility of a future surprise attack by the Japanese whom he condemned for their moves in Indochina. He played a prominent part in the Pan-American Conference in Havana in 1940 in which an arrangement was devised to ready the Americas to meet unitedly any threat from abroad.

During the Second World War, Hull gave forward-looking attention to the problems that would come with peace. To this end he drafted six clauses governing the future policy of the United States, the Soviet Union, the United Kingdom, and China, which were adopted at the Moscow Conference of 1943.

His crowning achievement was his preparation of a blueprint for the United Nations, which Hull saw as a major step toward the creation of a "world order under law." For this great service to which Hull gave his strenuous and final efforts as Secretary of State, President Roosevelt called him the "Father of the United Nations."

Illness forced his resignation from public service, but Hull was able to attend the first session of the United Nations in San Francisco in 1945 as a senior advisor to and member of the United States delegation. He was awarded the Theodore Roosevelt Distinguished Service Medal in 1945.

Cordell Hull's *Memoirs* was published in 1950. He was married to Rose Francis Whitney in 1917. He died on July 23, 1955.

Bibliography

Basso H 1940 "Jedge" Hull of Tennessee. *The New Republic* 102 (May 27): 720–23
Hinton H 1942 *Cordell Hull: A Biography*. Hurst and Blackett, London
Newsweek 1940 Tug of war pressure on US increasing, but Secretary Hull holds firm. 16 (October 14): 21–22
Stolberg B 1940 Cordell Hull: The vanishing American. *American Mercury* 49 (April): 391–99

RUTH C. REYNOLDS

Emily Balch

(1946)

The Nobel Peace Prize for 1946 was awarded to John Mott and Emily Greene Balch. Balch shared the prize in recognition of her lifelong, indefatigable contributions to the cause of justice and peace, and for the rich sense of ethics she introduced to this work. "International unity is not in itself a solution," she declared. "Unless it has a moral quality, accepts the discipline of moral standards, and possesses the quality of humanity, it will not be the unity we are interested in."

Emily Balch, daughter of a successful lawyer, was raised in an intellectual home; the influence was reflected throughout her life. A member of the first graduation class at Bryn Mawr in 1889, she furthered her education in Paris, studying economics on a Bryn Mawr fellowship in 1890–91, out of which she wrote *The Poor in France*. She completed her studies with courses taken at Harvard and the University of Chicago, and with an additional year spent studying economics in Berlin, from 1895 to 1896.

Later in 1896 she joined the faculty at Wellesley, and by 1913 she headed the department of economics and sociology. She believed in personal research and application of what was learned. This made her an outstanding teacher, and she encouraged students to investigate social conditions on their own to augment their reading. She herself acted on the same principle. As a student she had become familiar with the poverty and slums existing in the same city as her own comfortable home. She worked in a social center, the Denison House, in the South Cove District of Boston during its first winter.

Balch was the first college professor to introduce the problems of America's immigrants into college courses. Her work on the Slavic immigrants was outstanding. The Nobel Committee Chairman, Gunnar

Jahn, called it "a landmark in the scientific analysis of immigration problems" and one which illustrated her practice of thorough preparation. She visited Slav centers in the United States and she did a year's research in the regions of Austria–Hungary from where many Slavic immigrants came.

Balch pioneered in trade unionism and was a founder of the Women's Trade Union. She chaired the Massachusetts Minimum Wage Commission and was a guiding spirit in drafting the United States' first minimum wage law. She became a disciple of Jane Addams (Nobel Peace Prize winner for 1931), and like her, Balch persisted in a lifetime allegiance to her vision of justice.

In 1915, early in the First World War, she went as a delegate to the International Congress of Women at The Hague. There she took a fateful step: she helped to found the Women's International Committee for Permanent Peace, which became the Women's International League for Peace and Freedom (WILPF), and in so doing, she participated in creating the organization in which she was to work for the rest of her life. It was symbolic of her dedication to WILPF that she gave her Nobel Peace Prize money to it.

At The Hague, the women in the new organization prepared peace proposals to take to officials of the nations at war, neutral and belligerent alike. (Such a procedure was possible, Chairman Jahn explained, because "the monstrous beast of war had not yet fully bared his fangs.") Balch went to Russia and the Scandinavian countries. When she returned home she talked with President Wilson and Secretary Lansing. Balch later wrote of these conferences, "For one brief . . . moment in my life I consorted with men in the seats of power."

The soundness and practicality of these proposals was attested by President Woodrow Wilson of the United States: "Without any doubt the best which have so far been proposed," he said of them. Parts of these proposals were later incorporated in the League of Nations Covenant. Balch had made a principal contribution to this proposal out of her wealth of knowledge and her innate sense of practicality.

Her opposition to the war cost Balch her teaching post at Wellesley in 1918 when the faculty declined to renew her contract. She wrote of that ordeal, "It is a hard thing to stand against the surge of war-feeling, against the endless reiteration of every printed word, of the carefully edited news, of posters, parades, songs, speeches, sermons . . . where is the line," she asked herself introspectively, "dividing inner integrity from fanatical self-will?"

The dismissal left Balch at 52 with her professional life cut short and no particular prospects. But she was not destined to be idle. The *Nation* magazine offered her a position on its editorial staff, and she also wrote *Approaches to the Great Settlement* during this period. During the years between the two world wars, she participated in most of the nine congresses WILPF held. They ranged over a wide area of concerns: drug control, minority problems, and, as always, work toward disarmament.

The Second World War plunged Balch into a long and painful struggle as she sought to reconcile her pacifist convictions with the terrifying excesses of the Nazi regime. Her decision to support the war brought her into disagreement with organizations which she had long supported: the Quakers, the Fellowship of Reconciliation, and the War Resisters' League. Characteristically, much of her work took the form of looking ahead to the problems which would follow the war: she studied and wrote proposals for internationalization of defense bases, of the polar regions and of all important waterways; in 1944 she drafted a set of peace terms based upon constructive international settlements, and this was publicized by the United States WILPF. Sensitive as always to the face of injustice, she also sought aid for the victims of the Fascist regimes, and for the American Japanese who were forced into relocation camps and stripped of their basic rights as American citizens.

The WILPF scheduled its second conference in Zurich immediately following the war while the Allies were discussing the peace treaty in Paris. The women studied the emerging treaty and offered resolutions of which the Nobel Committee Chairman,

Gunnar Jahn, said it would have been judicious to have heeded.

After the Zurich conference, Balch stayed on in Geneva as the secretary-general of the International Women's League until 1922. She returned in 1934 for a year and a half, donating her services as acting international secretary to the financially hard-pressed WILPF.

Balch gave years of relentless effort to WILPF. "She never embarked on a campaign until she was sure of the facts," Chairman Jahn remarked. He cited an example which proved successful. In 1926 the American branch of the League endeavored to secure the withdrawal of US troops from Haiti after 11 years of occupation. As a representative of the American branch of WILPF, Balch first traveled to Haiti with a delegation and studied the situation. With Balch as principal author, they drew up a report, *Occupied Haiti*, which Jahn pronounced "conclusive proof of her ability to get to the root of the problem and of her consummate skill in devising a practical and democratic solution that would greatly benefit the people." Balch implemented the study with a campaign for the cessation of American intervention in the island's affairs. When the American government did indeed withdraw the troops, it used many suggestions from the study.

William E. Hocking, historian, offers a summary of the unique quality of Emily Balch: "No other life known to me has been so consistently and almost exclusively devoted to the cause of peace and with such pervasive good judgment and effect . . . Her own thought was recognized as responsible . . . and won its way to the minds of those who were making decisions. It will be long before the sum of her labors can be gathered, but when it is done, its achievements will be recognized as the more remarkable because its methods have been so much the quiet ways of friendly reason" (quoted in Lipsky 1966 p. 151).

Biography

Emily Greene Balch was born on January 8, 1867, in Jamaica Plain, Massachusetts, daughter of Francis V. Balch and Ellen Noyes Balch. She graduated in the first class of Bryn Mawr College in 1889 and continued her studies in economics and social sciences in Paris, at Harvard and the University of Chicago, and in Berlin. She taught economics and sociology at Wellesley College from 1896 until 1915, at which time she headed the department of economics and sociology.

In 1915, with the First World War then in its first year, she attended a convention of the International Congress of Women at The Hague, where she participated in the founding of the Women's International Committee for Permanent Peace, later named the Women's International League for Peace and Freedom (WILPF), in which she was to devote most of her efforts toward peace and justice throughout her life.

From the womens' conference at The Hague, two delegations visited nuetral and belligerent countries, one of them headed by Balch, where they were accorded polite, but inconclusive, interviews with statesmen. She also participated in a Neutral Conference for Continuous Mediation sponsored by Henry Ford, joined the Collegiate Anti-Militarism League, and sat on the council of the Fellowship of Reconciliation. These anti-war activities cost Balch her teaching position at Wellesley and she joined the staff of *Nation*, a weekly magazine sympathetic to the twin causes of peace and justice. In this same period she wrote *Approaches to the Great Settlement*.

Balch attended the second WILPF conference in Zurich following the war's end in 1919, where the women delegates studied the peace proposals and made recommendations. She became secretary-general of the international section of WILPF, a post she held until 1922 and again in 1934–35.

Balch continued her work for peace and justice chiefly through WILPF, but also through service to other international organizations and commissions, including the League of Nations. Her investigations into the US occupation of Haiti exemplify a successful venture in which the League succeeded, again under the leadership of Balch, in getting the US troops withdrawn.

Balch reluctantly supported the Second World War out of horror at the excesses of the Nazi regime. She wrote proposals for a constructive peace treaty, she vigorously supported the United Nations, and she worked to assist the victims of the Nazi regime and in behalf of the American Japanese who were interned and stripped of their rights as citizens during the war.

Balch always espoused the concept that practical solutions, no matter how technically refined, count for nothing unless they have an ethical foundation. Throughout her life she served the causes of humanitarianism, justice, and peace in myriad ways: through service on immigration boards and on industrial education boards; she fought for regulation of child labor; she participated in the struggle for women's suffrage; she combated racial discrimination; she worked in the United Nations, the Society of Friends, and the Fellowship of Reconciliation. Through application of her expertise in economics and social science she made valuable studies: *Public Assistance of the Poor in France*, *Outline of Economics*, *A Study of Conditions of City Life*, *Our Slavic Fellow Citizens*, *Approaches to the Great Settlement*, *Occupied Haiti*, *Refugees as Assets*, *The Miracle of Living* (poems), and *Vignettes in Prose*.

Emily Greene Balch died on January 9, 1961.

Bibliography

Lipsky M 1966 *The Quest for Peace*. Barnes and Co., South Brunswick

RUTH C. REYNOLDS

John Mott
(1946)

The 1946 Nobel Peace Prize was given to John Raleigh Mott and Emily Greene Balch. Mott received the award in recognition of his creation of worldwide organizations uniting millions of young people in work for ideals of peace and tolerance among nations. "Mott's work has been devoted to the most fundamental issue of all . . . he has prepared the soil in which the hope of the world will grow," the Nobel Committee said.

The son of an Iowa timber merchant, Mott grew up surrounded by books; his family and church exerted a strong religious influence, and his mother imparted to him an early love of European history. His first year in college was spent at a Methodist preparatory school, but he transferred to Cornell University to take advantage of its wider curriculum. Though he belonged to the Cornell Young Men's Christian Association (YMCA), Mott was not intensely interested in religion during his first year.

But during his second year he came into an auditorium just as a guest lecturer thundered, "Seekest thou great things for thyself? Seek them not. Seek ye first the Kingdom of God." It was a fateful moment for Mott. "On those few words," he wrote later, "hinged my life-investment decision." Mott entered upon a period of intense Bible study which he characteristically translated into action by doing religious work in the county jail. Caught up in foreign missionary enthusiasm among the student body, he was chosen to be their representative at the first interdenominational Christian Student Conference of 251 young men from 89 United States and Canadian colleges. He was elected president of the Cornell YMCA, and, displaying a gift for inspiring and organizing, he developed within Cornell one of the largest and best organized student religious societies in the world.

Mott graduated Phi Beta Kappa, with a degree in history and political science. Now certain of his commitment to Christian missionary work, he accepted a traveling secretary's position with the national YMCA. This began a lifetime career in which he became, in the words of the Nobel Committee, a "living force, opening young minds to the light which . . . can lead the world to peace and bring men together in understanding and goodwill."

It is not a simple matter to trace all of the organizations served by this zealous and capable man. Certainly the YMCA was central in his career. He held the student secretaryship and the foreign secretaryship of the international committee of the YMCA before assuming its general-secretaryship and finally its presidency. His name, more than that of any other, became associated with the YMCA movement. But Mott could serve as an executive officer of more than one major and international organization at once because he had the genius of the executive who can select competent assistants and skillfully delegate administrative details to them. During the 27 years that he traveled among colleges over the world for the YMCA, collaborating with the student leaders in planning complete programs of activity, he also worked as chairman of the faltering Student Volunteer Movement for Foreign Missions. Working with the YMCA, Young Women's Christian Association (YWCA), and Interseminary Missionary Alliance, he revitalized student groups, and under his directorship over 10,000 student volunteers were sent abroad.

Mott's success can better be understood in terms of his preparation for any task undertaken. When he was to visit a country he first studied its culture, its customs, and its religious and political background. He was able to talk with those he would meet as a friend who knew the country, the people, and their way of life. He met new situations with an open mind, receptive to other ways of thinking.

Mott defined the purpose of all his work as weaving together Christian forces all over the world. In 1893 he organized the Foreign Missions Conference of North America, uniting the missionary units of the entire North American continent. In 1895, with Karl Fries, he founded the World's Student Christian Federation with delegates from five student units representing ten countries present at its first meeting. Mott toured in its behalf for the next two years and doubled its membership. He was able to organize national student movements in India, China, Japan, Australia, New Zealand, and parts of Europe and the Near East as well as to establish 70 local Christian units. By 1920 the World's Student Christian Federation was estimated as having a membership of

300,000 young men and women in more than 3,000 educational institutions in 27 countries.

In 1910 Mott was chosen to be the presiding officer of the World Missionary Conference. He toured the Far East holding regional missionary conferences in India, China, Japan, and Korea. He used his time to a creative maximum, spending his days organizing this work and his evenings speaking to huge audiences of native students. Over the years the conferences attracted more and more delegates, and Mott took an active part in the leadership of all the gatherings. The students who flocked to Mott's organization were not only Protestants—they came from the Roman Catholic and Orthodox churches, from the Thomist Christians in India, from the Nestorian, Syrian, and Coptic churches. Mott's aim was to give the Christian world new leaders whose love and tolerance would transcend the old frontiers which had previously separated people.

During the First World War the YMCA undertook wide relief activities, both material and spiritual, for the Allied armies in the field, and for prisoners of war on both sides. Nobel Committee Chairman Ingebretsen described this humanitarian work as a "gathering of the resources of his organizations in a mighty effort to span the abyss of hatred of those days . . . Mott himself was always on the move, traveling from country to country and visiting the fronts, entering into negotiations with statesmen in belligerent as well as in neutral states, recruiting suitable helpers for this vast project, for which he collected no less than two hundred and fifty million dollars." Mott's YMCA, with 25,000 volunteers, worked to render captivity for the prisoners mentally and physically bearable, so they might be better prepared to return to normal life after the war.

After the armistice, Mott turned his attention to rehabilitation programs with a success that brought about an invitation to Mott and his assistants to bring their program to Poland, Czechoslovakia, Greece, Bulgaria, Rumania, Estonia, Latvia, and Lithuania. President Taft of the United States called it "one of the greatest works of peace ever carried out in the entire history of war," adding that it was chiefly due to Mott's organizing genius and inspiring leadership. Mott received the Distinguished Service Medal for this work.

In 1913 President Wilson had offered Mott the ambassadorship to China. "I do not know when I have been so disappointed," the President had remarked upon receiving Mott's refusal. However, in 1916, when a serious conflict arose between the United States and Mexico, Mott served on a delegation sent to Mexico to resolve difficulties. And he joined an American diplomatic mission to Russia in 1917.

During the Second World War the YMCA once again worked in prisoner-of-war camps. And at the war's end, the 80-year-old Mott set out on worldwide travels to reestablish international links which the war had broken. He arranged the first world conference of the YMCA, held in Geneva that summer.

Mott combated racial prejudice wherever he found it the world over. The Nobel Committee called his work to subdue racial antagonism "a link in the chain of peace which he tried to forge around the world." This included Mott's own country, where racial prejudice blighted the lives of thousands of American citizens. Mott formed associations in the southern states composed of members of whites and blacks together. In 1914 the first congress ever held for black and white Christians from northern and southern states was organized under Mott's chairmanship. "This is the principle that has governed all of Mott's work among the different churches and missions, among races and nations," Committee Chairman Ingebretsen said. "The three great world organizations which have flourished under his leadership for a generation, the Student Federation, the YMCA, and the International Missionary Council have in his hands been instruments for creating that spirit of Christian tolerance and love which can give peace to the world."

The *Christian Century* (February 1955) summarized Mott's long and distinguished career. Declaring that Mott stood alone, unmatched by any of his contemporaries, an editorial read, "He saw with prophetic clarity the first signs of a new world being born, and he set into motion the ecumenical forces by which Christian churches East and West marshaled their forces to face the changing order ... he was an embodiment of a whole cycle of Christian history."

Biography

John Raleigh Mott was born in Livingston Manor, New York, on May 25, 1865, son of John S. Mott and Elmira Dodge Mott. His family moved to Postville, Iowa, where his father, a timber merchant, was elected the first mayor of the town. Mott's childhood was influenced by affectionate, cultured, and religious parents, and the Methodist Church. He started college at a Methodist preparatory school and then transferred to Cornell University. There three sentences he heard from a visiting Cambridge lecturer, J. Kynaston Studd, set the course of his life: "Seekest thou great things for thyself? Seek them not. Seek ye first the Kingdom of God."

Mott became vice-president of the Cornell YMCA, and in the summer of 1886 he represented Cornell at the first Christian Student Conference, where 251 young men from 89 American and Canadian colleges met. This sealed Mott's determination to enter a career as a Christian missionary. He showed outstanding aptitude during the following year when he was elected president of the YMCA, and after his graduation from Cornell in 1888 with a degree in history and political science, he became secretary of the International Committee of the YMCA. He continued in this career, traveling to institutions of education throughout the world and influencing millions of young people toward work for Christian ideals of tolerance, understanding, and goodwill between individuals and between nations.

At the same time, Mott accepted an administrative post at the faltering Student Volunteer Movement for Foreign Missions, uniting the intercollegiate YMCA, YWCA and Interseminary Missionary Alliance, and under his directorship it became strong, disciplined, and dependable, recruiting over 10,000 United States and Canadian student volunteers.

In 1885 he turned his remarkable talents of inspiring and organizing to the Foreign Missions Conference of North America, uniting missionary units over the North American continent. In 1895, with Karl Fries of Sweden, Mott organized the World's Student Christian Federation with delegates representing 10 countries present at its first meeting. Following Mott's tour of promotion over the next two years, it doubled that number. He organized 70 local units and student movements in India, China, Japan, Australia, New Zealand, and parts of Europe and the Near East. By 1925 the World's Student Christian Federation had a membership of 300,000 students in more than 3,000 schools in 27 countries.

Mott worked on many projects simultaneously. After he was chosen presiding officer of the World Missionary Conference, he toured the Far East, holding missionary conferences in India, China, Japan, and Korea during the days and speaking to huge audiences of students in the evenings. By delegation of authority to skillfully chosen assistants, and by maximum use of his own time, he was able to hold the student secretaryship and the foreign secretaryship of the International Committee of the YMCA until 1915, its general-secretaryship until 1928, and its presidency from 1926 to 1937, while over the years simultaneously providing leadership to other organizations.

During the First World War the YMCA carried relief and spiritual guidance to the Allied armies and to prisoners-of-war on both sides under Mott's direction as General-Secretary of the National War Work Council and leader of the United War Work Campaign. In the Second World War the 80-year-old Mott showed his characteristic zeal in administering similar programs.

In 1947 Mott resigned from the World's Alliance of Young Men's Christian Associations.

Mott married Leila Ada White in 1891; they had two sons and two daughters. He died in 1955 at his home in Orlando, Florida, at the age of 89.

Bibliography

Christian Century 1928 John R. Mott. November 8, pp. 1354–56

Christian Century 1955 John R. Mott. 72(February): 1908–1920
Time 1946 A for effort. November 25, p. 33

RUTH C. REYNOLDS

The Quakers
(1947)

The Nobel Peace Prize for 1947 was awarded to the Quakers, represented by their two relief organizations, the Friends Service Council (FSC) in London and the American Friends Service Committee (AFSC) in Philadelphia. The Chairman of the Award Committee, Gunnar Jahn, said, "The Quakers have shown us that it is possible to translate into action what lies deep in the hearts of many: compassion for others and the desire to help them—that rich expression of the sympathy between all men, regardless of nationality or race, which, transformed into deeds, must form the basis for lasting peace. For this reason alone the Quakers deserve to receive the Nobel Prize today."

The Quakers' full name is "The Religious Society of Friends," and they were conceived during the English Revolution in the seventeenth century. Religious organizations have often fought heroically for their freedom, but less often have they been willing to defend the freedom of others once they have won their own struggle. The principle fought for is thus reduced from the high level of freedom to the lesser level of a given system of beliefs defended. The Quakers extend total tolerance toward other religions, they have never considered dogmas and fixed forms as important to them, and they have remained as they began—a religious community acting upon the belief that there is a measure of the divine in human beings, and this fundamental goodness, universal to all, they seek to translate into action.

Quaker pacifism is not passive nor negative, Henry J. Cadbury, AFSC Chairman, told the Nobel award audience. "It is part of a positive policy. The prevention of war is an essential part of that policy." Dr. Cadbury, American theologian, one of the founders of the AFSC, as well as its chairman from 1928 to 1934 and from 1944 to 1960, said that the Friends believe they must work for the prevention of war by all means in their power: by influencing public opinion in peacetime, by interceding with governments, by encouraging international organization, and by setting an example.

Their work began in prisons, and they have worked for social justice throughout the world, alle-

viating suffering wherever they found it. This includes the AFSC's work with the American deprived —the black, the American Indian, the Mexican–American, the migrant worker, the Virginia miner— augmenting their 300-year history of aid worldwide. Perhaps, though, the Quakers are associated most with their work of relief and rehabilitation for the victims of war. They were to be found on the scene during many armed conflicts since their inception, administering aid without regard for political creed —in the Napoleonic Wars, the Crimean War, the Boer war, and during the period of American slavery.

In the First World War, young Quaker men and women worked in France caring for children, providing refugees with the necessities for beginning over again, and rebuilding homes. Following that war, Quaker teams crossed previous barriers of nationalities, politics, and creeds to fight the awesome suffering left in its wake: homelessness, famine, and disease, in the Soviet Union, Poland, Serbia, Germany. In a few short years they were aiding refugees escaping Hitler's Germany, Spain's helpless children in the Civil War, Japanese in concentration camps in the United States, the British during the London blitz. Following the Second World War the Quakers engaged in such wide and vast programs—covering Arab refugees on the Gaza Strip, relief programs in India, China, and Japan as well as the countries of Europe—that the very magnitude of their accomplishment testifies to the outside help this relatively small group of about 200,000 members attracts. Through their inspiring example, the Quakers have long brought out the latent humanitarianism in others.

But this international service goes beyond humanitarianism; it is more than merely mopping up, cleaning up the world after war, Cadbury explained. It is the Quakers' witnessing for peace. "It is aimed at creating peace by setting an example of a different way of international service," he said. The Quakers' relief programs are designed to lead people on to self-help, and from there to paths they can take toward creating a peaceful world.

In their service to others, the members of the Friends reach for empathy with those whom they would help. Margaret A. Backhouse, Chairman of the Friends Service Council, as well as Vice-Chairman of the Friends Relief Service, talked about training oneself "to enter into the condition of others." Not satisfied to be administrators of assistance from a distance, the Friends seek personal contact with those whom they help. They desire to share knowledge, and out of this flow of increased mutual understanding they hope to draw from those with whom they are working the will first to strive for their own betterment, and then to give of themselves to helping others. "Self-interest can reestablish a man's self-esteem, but it is only the first step toward the realization of the brotherhood," she said, " . . . By sharing his goods and, better still, sacrificing his time and energy, he can break down barriers and enter into the lives of others, developing the good within himself."

" . . . This appeal to the good in people can cut across deep-rooted prejudices and break down political, national, and credal enmities," Backhouse declared, " . . . men must learn to live in the life and power which takes away the occasion of all wars."

In the spirit of appealing to the reasonableness in humankind, the Friends have inaugurated a series of Quaker International Centers. Known as "Quaker Embassies," and staffed by people from at least three or more countries, they invite men and women to come and discuss conflicting views on neutral grounds and in friendship. Besides offering the Quaker message, these centers provide a training ground for Quaker ambassadors of peace, and a base from which these people can operate during crises. The Quakers also hold conferences for diplomats, and maintain international affairs representatives in key cities all over the world and at the United Nations.

"Today the Quakers are engaged in work that will continue for many years to come," Chairman Jahn said in closing his presentation address, "but . . . it is not in the extent of their work or in its practical form that the Quakers have given most to the people they have met. It is in the spirit in which this work is performed . . . they have shown us the strength to be derived from faith in the victory of the spirit over force. And this brings to mind a verse from one of Arnulf Overland's poems . . . I know of no better salute:

The unarmed only
can draw on sources eternal.
The spirit alone gives victory.

History

The Religious Society of Friends (Quakers) was founded in 1647 by George Fox in England in the midst of the English Revolution. In 1660 the Society sent a manifesto to Cromwell: "We utterly deny all outward wars and strife, and fightings with outward weapons, for any end, or under any pretense whatever; this is our testimony to the world . . . and we certainly know and testify to the world that the Spirit of Christ, which leads us into all truth, will never move us to fight and war against any man with outward weapons, either for the kingdom of Christ, nor for the kingdom of this world. Therefore, we cannot learn war anymore." These words have continued to define the Quakers' attitude toward war. They believe in the goodness present in every human being, and seek to translate this "inner light" into good works performed selflessly and across all barriers of nationality, religion, or creed. As vehicles for such action, the Service Council of the British Society of Friends (FSC) was founded in 1850, and the American Friends Service Committee (AFSC) was founded in 1917. Initially the AFSC served to provide young American Friends with a means to serve as conscientious objectors during the First World War in ways commensurate with their love of humankind and their abhorrence of war. All too soon they were similarly engaged in like services in the Second World War. Between the two wars and following them, they acted as the American arm of a religious community serving the Quaker tenet of "God in every man," and acting upon the faith taught by their founder that the power of love can take away the occasion for all wars.

Most widely known for its work in relieving the suffering and ravages of war and the cruel period which inevitably follows, the AFSC has had a tragically ample demand for such endeavors: communal rioting upon the partition of India, relief for Arab refugees on the Gaza Strip, the Korean War, the Hungarian Revolution, the Algerian War, the war in Vietnam, the Nigerian–Biafran War. Whenever possible, the Friends work with people caught in conflict on both sides, without regard for defining friend and foe.

These activities have been accompanied by programs designed to ease the tensions which lead to wars. Since poverty existing side by side with opulence provides cause for such tensions, with nations as with individuals, the Friends have increased their aid to include social and technical assistance in developing nations, among them Pakistan, India, Zambia, Peru, Mexico, and Algeria. Family planning is included in many of these projects.

Since the early 1950s, the AFSC has brought mid-career diplomats to off-the-record conferences where they may make informal exchanges released from the strictures of protocol. The program has been expanded geographically to include Africa and parts of Asia, and expanded in personnel to include young people outside of diplomacy who might be in a position to help prevent situations of tension from developing between their countries; they provide training in spreading goodwill and understanding.

With similar purpose in dispelling tension, the AFSC has attacked both injustice and poverty in their own country: among Indians, Mexican–Americans, migrant workers, prisoners, blacks, and the poor.

The AFSC works continually on creating an informed public opinion on issues of war and peace. Through speaking tours, publications of peace literature, vigils, and participation in demonstrations and protests of like-minded groups, by a campaign to end the draft, the Committee works to arouse fellow Americans about the growth of the military–industrial complex in the United States.

"A good end cannot sanctify evil means; nor must we ever do evil, that good may come of it," wrote William Penn, the Quaker who founded Pennsylvania; "let us then try what love can do." When the AFSC celebrated its fiftieth anniversary in 1967, "To See What Love Can Do" became its motto.

See also: Articles: *Penn, William*; *Quakerism*

RUTH C. REYNOLDS

Prize Not Awarded
(1948)

John Boyd Orr
(1949)

The Nobel Peace Prize for 1949 was awarded to Lord Boyd Orr of Brechin, farmer, scientist, physician, and humanitarian, who applied his combined skills to a lifetime dream of removing hunger from the face of the Earth. Early in life he began research on the relationship between nutrition and metabolism. He saw a connection between this nutritional research and hunger. Pointing out that the Chinese word for peace is "ho-ping," which means food for all, Boyd Orr believed that cooperation by the nations in a common war against want would be the key to ultimate collaboration on international political issues. For Boyd Orr, the application of his research was always in behalf of his vision of a world without hunger, a world which would thereby have taken a vast step toward permanent peace.

The son of a Scottish farmer, John Boyd Orr earned his way through the University of Glasgow and taught long enough to accumulate funds for further education. He demonstrated an interest in a wide area of subjects, and unusual capability. He graduated with a background in theology, a doctorate in science, and an M.D. degree. After a brief career in the military in the First World War, in which he did research in military dietetics, he returned to Aberdeen where he had just begun establishing the Rowett Institute. During his 25 years as its director he founded and directed the Imperial Bureau of Animal Nutrition, he served as editor-in-chief of the journal he created there, *Nutritional*

Abstracts and Reviews, and Rowett became world famous as a British Empire clearinghouse of information.

Boyd Orr's years at the Rowett Institute were devoted to both animal and human nutrition. A flourishing 1,000-acre stock farm demonstrated the success of ongoing animal research, and during that time he did a series of studies on the diet of the people of Britain. One of them, titled *Food, Health and Income*, revealed an "appalling amount of malnutrition" among the people of England regardless of economic status.

In 1935 he was knighted for his services to agriculture. He was a member of the British Nutrition Committee, served on the Colonial Agriculture and Animal Health Council, and was Chairman of the Scottish Scientific Advisory Committee advising the government on the health of the people of Scotland.

In the Second World War the application of nutritional ideas Boyd Orr had pioneered resulted in a diet in wartime England which, though under the strictures of rationing, produced a level of health beyond all expectations.

Boyd Orr's nutritional concern encompassed hungry people everywhere. "Hunger and want in the midst of plenty are a fatal flaw," he said, "constituting one of the fundamental causes of war." He observed that the opulence of the few can no longer be hidden in a world which science had shrunk to a point where, "measured in time of transport and communication, the whole round globe is now smaller than a small European country of a hundred years ago."

Boyd Orr was convinced that the United Nations offered the world the necessary vehicle through which nations could cooperate to apply science to developing the food supply, and to creating the World Bank necessary to solving the economic complexities of food distribution. In 1945, now retired from Rowett, although serving as a rector of Glasgow University and occupying a seat in the House of Commons, he still took time to give vital assistance in the planning of the Food and Agriculture Organization (FAO). This specialized agency within the UN held the promise for Boyd Orr of carrying out much of his lifelong work, and he became its first Director-General.

"The world would be a much safer place for our children if there were fewer soldiers thinking of armaments for the next war and more statesmen thinking of food for the next generation," he said, and he worked zealously for a cooperation between nations in a common war against want. "It is difficult to get nations to cooperate on a political level," he said, "The world is torn by political strife. But through the FAO the nations are cooperating. Here at the council table representatives of governments are not talking about war ... they are planning for the greatest movement that will make for peace—increased food production, the strengthening of agriculture and food for the people of the world." But he was often frustrated by the lack of authority and funds needed to implement the FAO's planning.

The most important function of the FAO was to assist in agricultural production throughout the world, and under Boyd Orr's direction it became the most efficient organization in this field, addressing a series of technical and economic problems which had to be solved before any real progress in the development of agriculture could be made. Besides the vast undertaking of teaching farmers modern methods, particularly in the developing countries where primitive methods were still being practiced, Orr saw the need to plan for worldwide food distribution. He proposed the creation of a World Food Board which would stabilize food prices, create reserves of food to meet shortages, raise capital to finance the sale of surpluses to the countries in the greatest need, and finally, establish a World Bank to provide credit for the development of world agriculture. He traveled extensively to generate support for his comprehensive food plan.

To Boyd Orr's bitter disappointment, neither the United Kingdom nor the United States would support the World Food Board, and an advisory body with no executive authority, the World Food Council, was established instead. Boyd Orr declared in his Nobel lecture, "If the sixty governments which adhere to these specialized agencies and have given them a great deal of cooperation and lip service would agree to devote to them one unit of their currency for every one hundred they are devoting to preparation for war, and allow them freedom of action, I venture to predict that within a few years the political issues which divide nations would become meaningless and the obstacles to peace would disappear."

In April 1948 he resigned from his directorship and gave his full attention to leadership in other areas of peace activities: he served as President of the British Peace Council, of the World Federalist Association, and of the World Peace Association.

Boyd Orr said that any change in science brings about changes in the structure of society, and these changes involve conflict and confusion. "The most important question today," he asserted in his autobiography, *As I Recall*, "is whether man has attained the wisdom to adjust the old systems to suit the new powers of science and to realize that we are now one world in which all nations will ultimately share the same fate."

Boyd Orr spent his long life defining the problems and solutions created by a science to which he himself made valuable contributions, and he simultaneously gave of his creative energies to search for means to "adjust old systems" to meet the challenge of that science.

Biography

John Boyd Orr, farmer, educator, scientist specializing in nutrition, medical doctor, and humanitarian, was born on September 23, 1880, in Kilmaurs, Ayrshire, Scotland, one of seven children of R. C. Orr, a farmer. His family was poor, therefore Boyd Orr had not only to earn his own education, but to help pay for the schooling of brothers and sisters. After graduating from the University of Glasgow, which he attended on a scholarship following schooling in his village, Boyd Orr taught long enough to accumulate funds for his own further education. He demonstrated an eclectic appetite for education, matriculating first in theology, then entering into the sciences out of interest in Darwin's revolutionary theories which Boyd Orr wished to judge for himself. When he graduated from Glasgow he had both an M.D. degree and a doctorate degree in science, having earned a Bellahouston Gold Medal and a Barbour research scholarship. During his lifetime Boyd Orr was to put all these academic disciplines to distinguished use.

He began his career with a position he called "humble and poorly paid" at Aberdeen University working in a basement laboratory as Director of Animal Nutrition Research. Out of this experience he was later to become the director of the Rowett Institute of Research, and in 25 years he brought it from the initial planning stage on paper to world fame as a British Empire clearinghouse of information.

Boyd Orr's primary interest was in nutrition, and he conducted first animal studies, the success of which was reflected in a flourishing 1,000-acre stock farm connected with the Rowett Institute. His study on early pioneering work at the Institute in mineral metabolism, *Minerals in Pastures and their Relation to Animal Nutrition*, became a classic.

By the mid-1920s Boyd Orr was a member of the Colonial Advisory Council of Agriculture and Animal Health, and did research in pastural problems in Australia. For the British Empire Marketing Board research committee he did a study on two African tribes, one meat-eaters and blood drinkers, the other consuming milk and cereals.

From this point on, Boyd Orr turned his attention to human nutrition. He made a pioneering and permanent imprint in this field. In 1935 he was knighted for his services to agriculture, and that same year he was appointed to a League of Nations Committee to investigate world nutrition. He was Chairman of the Scottish Scientific Advisory Committee which advised the government on matters affecting the health and welfare of the people of Scotland. His study on the diet of the people of Britain, *Food, Health and Income*, revealing an appalling level of malnutrition among the British, served as the basis for the British policy on food in the Second World War and resulted in a healthy diet even under the strictures of wartime rationing.

In 1945 while he was serving as rector at Glasgow University, and as one of three elected representatives of Scottish universities seated in the British Parliament, he was unanimously elected Director-General of the Food and Agriculture Organization (FAO), a specialized agency within the UN. The FAO was the embodiment of much of Boyd Orr's lifetime work, and he left Parliament after a year and a half to give it his full energy.

His devotion to the FAO was based on his conviction that an adequate worldwide food supply, delivering people from want, would be a basis for peaceful cooperation between classes, nations, and races. To this end he worked for the FAO on a comprehensive plan which would cover all contingencies of food production and distribution. It began with a program to train farmers, particularly in developing countries, a formidable task designed to assist them in the leap from primitive farming to twentieth-century techniques. The plan included establishing a World Food Board which would stabilize food prices and create reserves to meet shortages—Boyd Orr saw no place for restrictive farming in a world containing hungry people. The plan also included the establishment of a World Bank which would help finance all aspects of world food production and distribution. To his bitter disappointment, neither the United Kingdom nor the United States would support the World Food Board, and a World Food Council, an advisory body without means of implementing any program advised, was established.

In April 1948 Boyd Orr resigned from his directorship and gave his attention to his other posts in peace activities: President of the British Peace Council, of the World Federalist Association, and of the World Peace Association.

Lord Boyd Orr received many honors and awards. He was a Fellow of the Royal Society, elected for his fundamental research in physiology; he was an Honorary Graduate LL.D. of St. Andrews and Edinburgh Universities, Scotland, and of Princeton University, United States.

He and his wife, the former Elizabeth Pearson, had one son and two daughters.

He died at his home in Scotland in June 1971 at the age of 90.

RUTH C. REYNOLDS

Ralph Bunche
(1950)

A distinguished US official in the United Nations who succeeded in achieving an armistice between the Arabs and the Israelis won the Nobel Prize for Peace in 1950. Ralph Bunche, one of the youngest laureates honored with the Peace Prize, was first a distinguished scholar in the subject of international relations, then an educator, and finally an official in the US government and in the United Nations.

Ralph Johnson Bunche was born on August 7, 1904, in Detroit, Michigan, one of three children of Fred Bunche, a barber, and Olive Johnson Bunche, an amateur musician. Bunche was raised in a closely knit family kept strong and supportive by his grandmother, Lucy Johnson. She was raised in slavery, and Bunche recalls her as "the strongest woman I ever knew." "Nana" Johnson was the dominant influence in his growing years.

At an early age Bunche began to contribute to the family's support, starting as an errand boy when he was seven. Bunche's mother and father both died in his tenth year, and Nana took the family to live in Los Angeles. By the age of 12 he was working long hours in a bakery, often until 11 or 12 o'clock at night. "Life was no idyll," recalled Bunche. "I was learning what it meant to be a Negro. ... But I wasn't embittered by such experiences, for Nana had taught me to fight without rancor. She taught all of us to stand up for our rights, to suffer no indignity, but to harbor no bitterness toward anyone, as this would only warp our personalities ... she instilled in us a sense of personal pride strong enough to sustain all external shocks, but she also taught us understanding and tolerance. ...." Her words formed the foundation upon which Bunche was to build a distinguished career in interracial and international relationships.

Although always obliged to combine work with school, Bunche showed early his formidable intellectual gifts. He won a prize in history and another in English in his elementary school years; in high school he was a skilled debater and all-round athlete. He graduated valedictorian of his class in Jefferson High School in Los Angeles. At the University of California at Los Angeles he paid his way through college by working as janitor, part-time carpet layer, petty-officer's messman, and teaching assistant in political science. He showed an unusual blend of talents. He performed with academic distinction, developing an interest in the field of race relations while majoring in international relations. He was a star guard on three championship varsity basketball teams, played football and baseball, he was sports editor of the college yearbook, and took part in oratorical and debating contests. A member of Phi Beta Kappa, he graduated *summa cum laude* in 1927, with a scholarship to Harvard in hand. His community expressed its pride in this talented young man in a concrete fashion, sending him to Harvard with a gift of a thousand dollars to augment his scholarship.

Bunche completed a masters degree in political science at Harvard during 1928, after which he taught at Howard University for four years. In 1932 he returned to Harvard for his doctorate, alternating study with continued teaching. For his doctoral thesis he decided on comparing the rule of a mandated area, French Togoland, with a colony, Dahomey in French West Africa. Funded for the necessary travels through two fellowships, the Ozias Goodwin and the Rosenwald Field, he set off in Africa with a native truck, determined to conduct his own investigations, and disdaining customary practices of reliance on official reports. The resulting thesis won Bunche the Toppan Prize as the best thesis in the social sciences.

After two more years at Howard University, Bunche was awarded a two-year postdoctoral fellowship in anthropology and colonial policy from the Social Science Research Council. He studied at Northwestern University in 1936 and the London School of Economics in 1937. Then he applied to South Africa's Capetown University. Once he had convinced the authorities that his purpose was not to incite the natives to revolt, he was admitted and began a study on African tribes in the Kenya highlands. This time traveling in a second-hand Ford, he lived for three months among the Kikuyus as an honorary tribal citizen. Native drums would announce his arrival before each stop and he would be greeted with ceremony and feasting.

Out of his researches Bunche wrote *A World View of Race,* exposing myths about races which, in the hands of ignorant or unscrupulous politicians, were exploited to further their own ends. He analyzed British and French colonial policies, which, though different, each committed the grievous policy of denying the natives an opportunity to develop their potential.

Bunche regarded racial problems as a part of the larger problem of the haves and the have-nots, expanding internationally to intricate difficulties between the prosperous established countries and the underdeveloped countries. Bunche did not see the problem as lying with the individuals within a nation or a group. "Most of us, I believe, would be quite tractable if the pressures exerted by groups or by society would give us the chance," he once wrote. "But relations between people are never governed by individuals ... for the individual is subordinated to the group in all important questions."

In 1936 Bunche served as a codirector of the Institute of Race Relations at Swarthmore College, and from 1938 to 1940 as a staff member of the Carnegie Corporation of New York. In the latter capacity he served as chief aid to the Swedish sociologist (and Nobel Prize winner) Gunnar Myrdal in conducting a survey on the conditions of the Negro in America (see Articles: *Myrdal, Gunnar*). While collecting their data the two were "run out" of Southern towns three times.

With the coming of the Second World War, Bunche, in 1941, began working for the government as Senior Social Science Analyst in Africa and the Far East, in the Office of the Coordinator of Information. The next year found him Principal Research Analyst for Africa and the Far East for the same branch of the government, now called the Office of Strategic Services (OSS), and the following year Chief of the Africa Section of the Research and Analysis Branch of OSS. From there he transferred to the State

Department, where his rise was equally rapid. On February 1, 1945, he became Acting Associate Chief of the Division of Dependent Area Affairs, "which means," the *Christian Science Monitor* commented, "that he knows about all there is to know on this subject." He was the first black man to break through the racial barriers and hold the post of Acting Chief in the State Department Office.

By this time Bunche had attended nine international conferences, serving as adviser or delegate, within four years. He had helped draw up the non-self-governing territories and trusteeship sections of the United Nations Charter and worked on plans for the disposal of the Italian colonies.

Bunche officially entered the United Nations "on loan" from the State Department in May 1946 when he joined the UN Secretariat as Director of the Trusteeship Division which he had helped organize. "He is as well qualified as is humanly possible for the post," the New York *Herald Tribune* declared. "Americans must regard [him] with pride and humility." It was the opening to the most important assignment of his career. From June to September 1947 he was in Palestine as special assistant to the representative of the Secretary-General of the UN Special Committee on Palestine. Bunche was credited with contributing a large part in the drafting of the Committee's historic report.

On December 3, 1947, Bunche was appointed the Principal Secretary of the United Nations Palestine Commission. The *New York Times* commented that his "experience, understanding, and character should be of inestimable value to the new commission as it takes up its complicated and critical task." The Committee had recommended dividing the country into Jewish and Arab states. In early 1948, while fierce fighting persisted between the Jews and Arabs, the Commission, directed by Bunche, reached an informal agreement to ask the UN Security Council for an international armed force to effect the partition of the Holy Land. The UN appointed Count Folke Bernadotte as mediator and Ralph Bunche as his chief aide, their first task being to secure a truce. They succeeded in obtaining a truce lasting from June 11 to July 9. But on July 10 hostilities broke out once more.

The Chairman of the Nobel Committee, Gunnar Jahn, described the incident, which contributed so vitally to the Peace Prize award, in his presentation speech.

The two men who met in 1948 to undertake this common task could hardly have been more unlike. . . . On the one hand, Folke Bernadotte, grandson of King Oscar II of Sweden and nephew of Sweden's reigning monarch, steeped in all the traditions of a royal family; on the other, Bunche, whose grandmother had been born in slavery, who had been brought up in poverty, who was entirely a self-made man.

Folke Bernadotte was scantily informed on the Palestine conflict . . . Bunche, Head of the Trusteeship Department of the United Nations, had back of him an education and training directed precisely at recognizing and understanding the problems raised by international disputes.

Yet the two men had one thing in common: they both believed in their mission.

Bernadotte was assassinated on September 17, 1948, and Bunche became his successor as the acting mediator. He immediately endorsed the Bernadotte plan for settling the Palestine dispute by awarding Galilee to the Jews, the Negev desert area to the Arabs, and the city of Jerusalem to the United Nations, and he appealed to the UN Security Council to order a ceasefire to allow both parties to try to reach an agreement on an armistice as a preliminary to a final settlement. His proposal was approved by the Security Council on November 16.

It was a daring proposal, Chairman Jahn explained, for an armistice is more than a ceasefire; it is in effect a preliminary to peace. It turned out that Bunche had judged the situation correctly. Negotiations between the Arab states and Palestine dragged on for 11 months, and required the greatest demands on the mediator, for the Arabs did not want to sit at the same table with the Jews. Bunche was compelled to negotiate separately with each side, constantly having to clear away the mutual distrust. This was not mediation between two parties, but between Palestine on the one hand, and seven Arab states on the other, and agreements had to be concluded separately with each of the seven. By exercising infinite patience, Bunche succeeded in persuading all parties to accept an armistice. When asked how he managed it, Bunche replied,

Like every Negro in America, I've been buffeted about a great deal. I've suffered many disillusioning experiences. Inevitably, I've become allergic to prejudice. On the other hand, from my earliest years I was taught the virtues of tolerance; militancy in the fight for rights, but not bitterness. And as a social scientist I've always cultivated a coolness of temper, an attitude of objectivity when dealing with human sensitivities and irrationalities, which has always proved invaluable—never more so than in the Palestine negotiations. Success there was dependent upon maintaining complete objectivity.

Throughout the endless weeks of negotiations I was bolstered by an unfailing sense of optimism. Somehow, I knew we had to succeed.... (*American Magazine*, February 1950 p. 125)

Bunche's reply, Chairman Jahn said, described the man: his childhood heritage from his grandmother, the knowledge, education, and experience he gained in a life dedicated to service. It was the sum of all these factors which created the skilled mediator who succeeded in getting these hostile parties to lay down their arms. "The outcome was a victory for the ideas of the United Nations ... but it was one individual's efforts that made the victory possible," Jahn said.

Chairman Jahn acknowledged that there remained "even greater challenges than before." Bunche continued to meet that challenge. "The objective of any who sincerely believe in peace clearly must be to exhaust every honorable recourse in the effort to save the peace," he observed. Bunche served as Undersecretary-General for Special Political Affairs from 1955 to 1967, and as Under-Secretary-General of the UN from 1968 to 1971.

Biography

Ralph Johnson Bunche was born in Detroit, Michigan, on August 7, 1904, one of three children of Fred and Olive Johnson Bunche. After his parents' death when he was a young child, he was raised by his grandmother, Lucy Johnson, an indomitable woman, raised in slavery, who influenced young Ralph with a lasting sense of self-worth, integrity and the capacity for hard work, intelligently directed. His intellectual gifts surfaced early, and while working to help augment the family income from elementary school on he distinguished himself with continuous awards. He graduated valedictorian of his class at Jefferson High School in Los Angeles. A member of Phi Beta Kappa, he graduated *summa cum laude* from the University of California at Los Angeles in 1927. With a series of scholarships and fellowships he earned his masters degree in political science at Harvard, in 1928, and after four years on the faculty of Howard University he returned to Harvard to earn his Ph.D. in 1934, writing a dissertation on "French Administration in Togoland and Dahomey" for which he won the Toppan Prize for the best dissertation in the social sciences. He did postdoctoral work at Northwestern University in anthropology in 1936, at the London School of Economics studying anthropology and colonial policy in 1937, and the same year at the University of Capetown, South Africa, where he did several months of field work among the Kikuyus in the Kenya highlands. The fellowships which helped finance his education were: University Scholarship, Harvard, 1927–28; Ozias Goodwin Memorial Fellowship, Harvard, 1929–30; Rosenwald Fellowship, 1932–33; Toppan Prize, Harvard, 1934; Social Science Research Council Fellowship, 1936–38.

Throughout his career Bunche maintained strong ties with education. He chaired the Department of Political Science at Howard University from 1928 until 1950; he served as codirector of the Institute of Race Relations, Swarthmore College, in 1936; he taught at Harvard University from 1950 to 1952; he served on the New York City Board of Education, 1958–64; on the Board of Overseers of Harvard University, 1960–65; on the Board of the Institute of International Education; and as a trustee of Oberlin College, Lincoln University, and New Lincoln School.

Bunche was active in the Civil Rights Movement in America. He participated in the Carnegie Corporation's survey of the Negro in America with Gunnar Myrdal; he was a member of the "Black Cabinet" consulted on minority problems by the Roosevelt Administration; he declined President Truman's offer of the position of assistant secretary of state because of the segregated housing in Washington, DC; he helped to lead the civil rights march organized by Martin Luther King Jr. in Alabama in 1965; he supported the action programs of the National Association for the Advancement of Colored People (NAACP) and of the Urban League.

After the start of the Second World War he entered government service and held the following posts: Senior Social Science Analyst, Africa and the Far East; Office of the Coordinator of Information [later known as the Office of Strategic Services (OSS)], 1941–42; Principal Research Analyst, Africa and the Far East, OSS, 1942–43; Chief, Africa Section, Research and Analysis Branch, OSS, June 1943–January 1944; Divisional Assistant, Colonial Problems, Division of Political Studies, Department of State, January–July 1944; Area Specialist, Expert on Africa and Dependent Areas, Division of Territorial Studies, Department of State, July 1944–February 1945.

In the Division of Dependent Area Affairs, Office of Special Political Affairs, Department of State, he was Acting Associate Chief, February–April 1945, and Associate Chief, April 1945–March 1947, interlapping with his post as Acting Chief, July–October 1945 and November 1945–January 1946.

Bunche was appointed by President Truman as US Commissioner, Anglo-American Caribbean Commission, September 1945–June 1947. At the request of Secretary-General Trygve Lie he began service in the United Nations as Director, Division of Trusteeship, in 1946. In June 1947, the confrontation between the Arabs and the Jews in Palestine brought him to the most important assignments of his career. He was first appointed assistant to the UN Special Committee on Palestine, then Principal Secretary of the UN Palestine Commission. This commission was charged with seeing to the activation of the partition approved by the UN General Assembly. In early 1948 the fighting between the Arabs and the Israelis became severe and Count Bernadotte was appointed as mediator with Bunche as his chief aide. Four months later Bernadotte was assassinated and Bunche was named acting mediator. After 11 months of nearly continuous negotiating, Bunche secured the necessary signatures for armistice agreements between the State of Israel and the Arab states.

He served as delegate or adviser at many conferences: twice in the US delegation at the Institute of Pacific Relations—once in Mont Tremblant, Canada, in 1942 and in Hot Springs, Virginia, in 1945. He was a member of the Secretariat, Pacific Council meeting, Atlantic City, 1944; Assistant Secretary to the US delegation at the Dumbarton Oaks Conference in 1944, and adviser to two International Labour Organization Conferences, in Philadelphia, 1944, and in Paris, 1945, At the First Session, General Assembly, UN, in London, 1946, he was Technical Adviser, Trusteeship, in the US Delegation. He served as Technical Expert, Trusteeship, to the US Delegation, UNCIO, San Francisco in 1945.

Bunche was Special Assistant to the Representative of the Secretary-General, UN Special Committee on Palestine, June–September 1947, and Principal Secretary, UN Palestine Commission, December 1947–May 1948. He was Principal Secretary and Personal Representative of the Secretary-General with the UN Mediator on Palestine, May–September 1948 and Acting UN Mediator on Palestine, September 1948–August 1949. He directed peacekeeping efforts in Suez in 1956, in the Congo, 1964, and Cyprus, 1964.

He wrote *A World View of Race* in 1937, and numerous articles on colonial policy, trusteeship, race relations, and minority problems.

He was awarded the Spingarn Prize by the NAACP in 1949; Four Freedoms Award, 1951; Peace Award of Third Order of St. Francis, 1954; Golden Key Award, 1962; US Presidential Freedom Award, 1963. During the three years following his return from Palestine he was given over 30 honorary degrees.

He married Ruth Ethel Harris in 1930; they had one son and two daughters. He continued his career in the UN: from 1955 to 1967 he served as Under-Secretary for Special Political Affairs, and from 1968 to 1971 as Under-Secretary-General. He died on December 9, 1971.

See also: Articles: *Arab–Israeli Conflict: Peace Plans and Proposals*

Bibliography

Bunche R 1968 *A World View of Peace*. Kennikat Press, Port Washington, New York

Hamilton T A 1930 Peacemaker extraordinary. *Américas* 2 (November): 12–15

Ross I 1950 Dr. Bunche of the U.N. *American Mercury* 70 (April): 473–79

RUTH C. REYNOLDS

Leon Jouhaux

(1951)

The 1951 Nobel Prize for Peace was awarded to Leon Jouhaux, a long-time leader in the French labor movement, as the person "who has worked most or best for promoting brotherhood among the peoples of the world, and for abolition or reduction of standing armies, and for the establishment and spread of peace congresses." The only labor leader ever to be awarded the Peace Prize, this was a recognition of Jouhaux's lifetime of unceasing work toward the accomplishment of all of Alfred Nobel's stipulations for the award of the Prize. He based his life's work on the premise that the removal of social and economic inequalities, both within nations and between nations, was the most important means of combating war. Jouhaux worked for 45 years through the International Federation of Trade Unions, the International Labour Organization, the League of Nations, the United Nations, and the European Movement to bring about a social environment capable of sustaining a society in which war would no longer be possible. Jouhaux called the

award a recognition of the "importance and steadfastness of the pacifist efforts of trade unionists."

Jouhaux participated in his first strike in 1900. The occasion must have been poignant for the 20-year-old, for the cause was protesting the use of white phosphorus, a substance which had disabled his father after years of working in a match factory. The month-long strike led to the abolition of the use of the toxic material, and to Jouhaux's dismissal for his part in the strike as recording secretary. His union later secured his reinstatement.

Already he showed attributes of a leader, with impressive industriousness, organizing ability, a strong personality, and the ability to speak persuasively. He became interested in pursuing a possible relationship between labor unions and peace. His labor union, Confédération Générale du Travail [General Confederation of Labor], known as CGT, held biannual congresses. As early as 1898 it had gone beyond questions of organization and corporate claims and had taken its stand in favor of general disarmament. Jouhaux was impressed by its tenets calling war a calamity and armed peace ruinous to the people who must shoulder the burden of its support with money that would be better spent on serving humanity.

In 1906 Jouhaux was appointed representative of his union at the congress of that year. There the delegates considered replying to declarations of war with a declaration of a revolutionary general strike. Nor did the trade unions confine themselves to passing motions at congresses. They established international liaisons and supported every policy furthering the cause of justice and understanding between nations.

In 1909 Jouhaux became secretary-general of the CGT, a position he held until 1949. "The trade-union movement was emerging from its infancy," Jouhaux said, "with an aim to protect and extend the rights and interests of the wage earners, and," he emphasized, "*to achieve international fraternity and solidarity.*" The CGT pitted its full strength against the war it saw impending, joining with laborers from other nations, including Germany, in declaring that war offered no solution to the problems facing them.

Jouhaux recalled that the First World War did not end their quest; rather, it intensified their passion for pacifism. They began to lay plans for participation in the peace which would come. Jouhaux was editor of *La Bataille Syndicaliste* [The Syndicalist Battle], the principal organ of the CGT, and he encouraged the CGT to call for arms limitation, international arbitration, and an end to secret treaties.

In 1916 at the Leeds Conference he presented a report which laid the foundation for the International Labour Organization (ILO). The ILO was subsequently established as part of the Treaty of Versailles following the war in recognition of the goal of peace between classes as well as peace between nations. Its masterstroke was its policy of "tripartism" which gave representation alike to workers, employers, and governments, providing a unique opportunity for greater understanding between the three groups through the invaluable context of working together. Through the ILO the work of Jouhaux and the labor unions had materialized into the only worldwide organization in existence in which international cooperation is the business of workers and their employers as well as governments. Jouhaux became a perennial labor delegate to this specialized agency whose goal was to create an infrastructure of peace.

In 1919 the trade unions organized the Fédération Syndicale Internationale [International Federation of Trade Unions] better known as FSI (succeeded by the World Federation of Trade Unions in 1945) with Jouhaux becoming its first vice-president. It acquired a membership of over 20 million. Its activities included offering concrete help to workers throughout the world: the Austrian workers escaped famine as a result of the many trainloads of supplies sent by various trade unions; and the FSI intervened on behalf of the Russian workers, sending three representatives to live in Russia supervising the distribution of food and medicines sent by the Federation.

Nor did the Federation limit itself to mitigating the cruel consequences of war. Its program emphasized worldwide economic and social stability. Jouhaux declared that "it is not distorting history to say that it was largely through the efforts and propaganda of our International Federation that the government of the USSR was recognized by the majority of the great powers." He pointed to the proposals ultimately put before the League of Nations; the majority had their inception in congresses of this international labor organization. Between 1925 and 1928 he was a French delegate to the League of Nations.

In the 1930s he and the CGT were a linchpin in the Socialist Front Populaire, fighting Franco, Laval, and Hitler, and in a reversal of his usual policy, he worked alongside the communists.

Jouhaux wrote four books in his field. Of particular distinction was his treatise on disarmament, *Le Désarmament*. But the opposing forces were gathering, and in the fall of 1939 Europe again became enveloped in war. After the fall of France in 1940, Jouhaux joined the Resistance movement (for which he received the Medal of the French Resistance after the war), but in 1941 he was captured by the Germans and interned first at Evaux-les-bains (Creuse) until December of that year and then deported to a German concentration camp. From there he was rescued in 1945.

Upon liberation he immediately resumed peace work; he was a French delegate to the United Nations, and vice-chairman, and then chairman, of the French Economic Council, a governmental official advisory board on economic matters. Through these offices he was able to keep alive before the French government and before the world his basic tenet that no peace can be established and maintained in the absence of a sound economic foundation.

From the time of the 1906 congress of the CGT, Jouhaux had worked on the principle of union independence from political parties. When he returned he found that the CGT had become infiltrated by communists who practiced a strong political involvement. Jouhaux sought to preserve the integrity and independence of the CGT, but when forced to share the secretaryship with the communist Benoit Frachon he found himself in intense friction with the communist determination to sabotage the Marshall Plan through French labor. Jouhaux led the noncommunist members out of the CGT, their numbers estimated at over a million, and formed the anticommunist Force Ouvrière [Workers' Force] in December 1947.

"The free trade-union movement is called on to play an essential part in the fight against international crisis and for the advent of true peace," Jouhaux said. For the worker, Jouhaux stood for the safeguarding of civil liberties, specifically the right of all citizens to hold their own opinions on the great questions of moral, philosophical, political, and economic import and to express them freely. He said this must not be merely theoretical, but that democracy must offer every individual effective opportunities, pointing out that "One who must be constantly preoccupied with his own subsistence cannot be an alert citizen."

For the welfare of the international community he would have the organized working class take an active part in the construction of Europe. "We want to make Europe simply a peninsula of the vast Eurasian Continent, where for thousands of years war has been the only way to resolve conflicts between peoples. We want Europe to be a peaceable community, united, despite and within its diversity, in a constant and ardent struggle against human misery."

Jouhaux called on the labor movement to play an essential part in the fight against international crisis and for the advent of peace. "The scope of the task is enormous, matched only by its urgency," he said.

Biography

Leon Jouhaux was born in Paris on July 1, 1879. His father, a veteran of the Commune of Paris, was an activist for the workers' welfare at the match factory where he was employed. Jouhaux was forced at 11 to leave his elementary school and augment the family income. Efforts to return for interrupted intervals were abandoned by his fourteenth year because of the family's impoverishment. Throughout his life Jouhaux worked at his education and ended on a university level.

Jouhaux participated in his first strike at the age of 21. Based on protest over the dangerous use of white phosphorus in a match factory, the strike was successful in bringing about its ban. Fired for his participation as recording secretary in the strike, and forced to find employment where he could, Jouhaux was reinstated through the efforts of his union, the Confédération Générale du Travail, known as CGT, and in 1906 he was appointed as the CGT's representative at its biannual congress. In 1909 he was elected its secretary-general, a post he held until 1947.

An ardent internationalist, and convinced that war brought intense misery and no solutions, Jouhaux fought all his life to bring the workers of the world into participation both in efforts to prevent war and in the peace treaties which followed the two world wars. He called for arms limitations, worker participation through peace congresses, international arbitration, as well as the more usual trade union functions of defending the civil and economic rights of the workers. To this end he edited *La Bataille Syndicaliste*, the newspaper of the CGT; participated at the Leeds Conference in 1916 where he played a principal role in laying the foundation for the International Labour Organization (ILO); was influential in getting the ILO incorporated in the Treaty of Versailles, and served as perennial French delegate to that organization; and served as a member of the French delegation to the League of Nations from 1925 to 1928. He was the first vice-president of the International Federation of Trade Unions.

After the fall of France in the Second World War he joined the Resistance movement, subsequently being captured and interned by the Germans until the end of the war in 1945. He received the Medal of the French Resistance in 1946. Upon his return to the CGT he found differing philosophies between himself and the communist members regarding the union's political independence an impossible barrier to surmount, and left the central organization of the CGT along with other leaders to form the Force Ouvrière [Workers' Force]. Jouhaux also served as a member of the French delegation to the United Nations. He was elected president of the International Council of the European Movement in 1949. His published works include: *Organisation Internationale du Travail, Le Désarmement, La fabrication privée des armes,* and *Le mouvement syndical en France.* He died on April 28, 1951.

Bibliography

American Federationist 1954 Leon Jouhaux. 61(6): 23
Time 1951 Nobel Prizewinner. 58 (November 19): 34

RUTH C. REYNOLDS

Albert Schweitzer

(1952)

In presenting the 1952 Nobel Peace Prize to Albert Schweitzer, Gunnar Jahn, chairing the Nobel Committee, said that Schweitzer "will never belong to any one nation. His whole life and all his work are a message addressed to all men, regardless of nationality or race. . . . Mankind yet searches for something which will allow people to believe that one day they will enjoy the reign of peace and goodwill."

Albert Schweitzer remarked upon this quest in his Nobel lecture: "The idea that the reign of peace must come one day has been given expression by a number of peoples . . . The originality I claim is . . . the intellectual certainty that the human spirit is capable of creating in our time a new mentality, an ethical mentality. Inspired by this certainty, I too proclaim this truth in the hope that my testimony may help to prevent its rejection as an admirable sentiment but a practical impossibility. Many a truth has lain unnoticed for a long time, ignored simply because no one perceived its potential for becoming reality."

Abert Schweitzer's life is an embodiment of truths revealed to him, as he put it, by "growing into" the ideals that were a part of his childhood and youth. The son of a Lutheran pastor, Schweitzer grew up in the presbytery of a small village in Alsace with a brother and three sisters in a warm and harmonious family. His happy childhood is attested to by his return to that village on every occasion possible when returning to Europe on fund-raising visits from Africa.

Schweitzer began the study of the piano when he was five, the organ at eight. By the time he was nine he was able to substitute for the parish organist at church services. It was an auspicious start to the career of a brilliant musician who would one day study under the legendary Charles Marie Widor, with fee waived because of unique promise, and who was destined to become an organist of distinction.

Qualities that were discernible in the child became the basic foundation of his later life despite all the experience and extensive education which followed. Chairman Jahn recounted an experience in Schweitzer's childhood which illustrates the ethical personality that was developing within the boy. An elderly Jew who occasionally passed through the village became a target for ridicule from the boys. The old man responded to their goading with only a gentle smile. That smile overpowered Albert Schweitzer, and he took great care thereafter to greet the old man with respect.

This quality in the child flowered into a deep compassion for every living thing, Jahn said. It became a voice within the young Schweitzer which gave him no peace: did he who had enjoyed such a happy childhood and youth have the right to accept all this happiness as a matter of course? The natural right to happiness and all the suffering prevailing in the world merged in his mind and brought forth a decisive direction to his future work. It became steadily clearer to Schweitzer that those who enjoy many of the good things of life should in return repay to others no less than they have received. We should all share the burden of life's suffering.

Meantime, as these principles were maturing in Schweitzer's mind, he started his studies at Strasbourg in the theological college of St. Thomas. In 1896, at the age of 21, while still a student, Schweitzer arrived at a lifetime decision: he would allow himself the following nine years in which to study philosophy and theology and to pursue his music, and thereafter he would pledge his life to easing the suffering of humanity.

In those nine years he completed his licentiate (a degree higher than the doctorate in German universities) with a thesis on Immanuel Kant's views on religion; he studied the organ, again with Widor in Paris; he became first a *Privatdozent* in theology at the University of Strasbourg in 1900, and in 1903 he was appointed the principal of the theology faculty there. He wrote *The Mystery of the Kingdom of God* and *Quest of the Historical Jesus*. At the same time he was writing a major biography of Bach and becoming a world-renowned interpreter of Bach's music. His work on the building of organs written during this period remains a classic in that field.

Distinguished careers in music, theology, philosophy, and education were open to him when, in his twenty-ninth year, he read an appeal from the French Protestant Missionary Society in Paris asking for help for the Negroes in French Equatorial Africa. For Schweitzer, the appeal was his long-awaited answer to the place of fulfillment of his pledge.

The missionaries were asking for a doctor, however, as well as a missionary. To qualify for the post, Schweitzer spent the next seven years studying medicine. His new profession held a unique attraction for Schweitzer: "For years I had used the word. My new occupation would be not to talk about the gospel of love, but to put it into practice," he said.

While pursuing his medical studies he served as curate at the church of St. Nicholas in Strasbourg, he gave concerts on the organ, conducted a heavy correspondence, and examined the teaching of St. Paul, especially that of dying and being born again "in Jesus Christ." It resulted in a book, *Paul and His Interpreters,* published in 1912. That same year he resigned his position as curate and married Helene Bresslau; the daughter of a scholar, and a scholar herself, she trained as a nurse in order to share her husband's life in Africa.

By now the Paris Missionary Society had become wary of Schweitzer's unorthodox views and barred him from preaching at the station. But they accepted him as a medical doctor. The site for the hospital was at Lambarene, on the Ogooue River. A few miles from the Equator, it is in the jungle, its climate among the world's worst, with days of merciless heat and clammy nights and seasonal torrential rains. The two Schweitzers were to meet with leprosy, dysentery, elephantiasis, sleeping sickness, malaria, yellow fever, plus the more usual diseases, and with only a broken-down chicken-coop for their first hospital. The natives flocked by foot, by improvised stretcher, and by dugout canoe for medical attention.

Schweitzer had just begun to clear the jungle for building a hospital when the First World War broke out. As German citizens the Schweitzers were interned as prisoners of war, but during the nine months before their internment they had treated 2,000 native patients.

Internment gave Schweitzer the opportunity to start writing the two-volume *The Philosophy of Civilization,* his masterwork in ethics. Schweitzer's ethical system is boundless in its domain. He summarized it once by saying, "A man is ethical only when life, as such, is sacred to him, that of plants and animals as that of his fellow men, and when he devotes himself helpfully to all life that is in need of help." Crystallized within the phrase "reverence for life," its applications are far reaching. The concept "does not allow the scholar to live for science alone, even if he is very useful to the community in so doing," Schweitzer explained. "It does not permit the artist to exist only for his art, even if it gives inspiration to many . . . it demands from all that they should sacrifice a portion of their own lives for others."

When Schweitzer was released from internment in 1918 he was gravely ill, and it was not until 1924 that he was able to return to Africa. From that date on he lived the rest of his life in Africa, with sporadic visits to Europe to raise funds for the hospital at Lambarene.

The *New York Times*, in a long and respectful obituary of Schweitzer, voiced a criticism of this period too often heard not to require an answer:

> . . . there was undisputed grandeur in his view that a man is ethical only when life is sacred to him. Such idealism underlay Schweitzer's hospital at Lambarene. His desire to bring Western medicine and healing to the jungle was grand, even heroic, in 1913. Less admirable were his treatment of Africans as children, his autocracy and his refusal to keep step

with medical gains. His hospital was rickety, dirty and way out of date; yet it was invariably crowded, whereas a sleek and gleaming one nearby had bed-space to spare.

The Gabonese preferred Schweitzer because he seemed part of the landscape, because he was a pioneer, because he cared when few white men did. These facts, not his faults, are his true measure.

Schweitzer did not leave Africa to accept his Peace Prize. But he regarded the award as a mandate to address the issues of peace, and he honored this obligation with a stirring written message:

> Let us dare to face the situation. Man has become superman. He is a superman because he not only has at his disposal innate physical forces, but he also commands, thanks to scientific and technological advances, the latent forces of nature . . . however, the superman suffers from a fatal flaw. He has failed to rise to the level of superhuman reason which should match that of his superhuman strength. He requires such reason to put this vast power to solely reasonable and useful ends, and not to destructive and murderous ones. Because he lacks it, the conquests of science and technology become a mortal danger to him rather than a blessing.

Schweitzer deplored that we are becoming inhuman to the extent that we become "supermen." We have learned to tolerate that people are killed en masse, and in that resignation we are guilty of inhumanity. He said the horror of this should shake us out of our lethargy so that we can direct our hopes and our intentions to the coming of an era in which war will have no place. This we can accomplish, he declared, only through a change in spirit. He said the League of Nations and the United Nations were both doomed to fail in a world in which there was no prevailing spirit directed toward peace. Only when an ideal of peace is born in the minds of the peoples of the world will the institutions set up to maintain this peace effectively fill that function.

We may well ask if the spirit is capable of achieving the changes that must be made. Schweitzer answered that we must not underestimate its power, the evidence of which can be seen throughout the history of humankind. The humanitarianism which is the origin of all progress toward some form of higher exercise is the child of this spirit. He said, "All that we have ever possessed of true civilization, and indeed all that we still possess, can be traced to a manifestation of this spirit . . . But the situation today is such that it must become reality in one way or another; otherwise mankind will perish."

Biography

Albert Schweitzer was born on January 14, 1875, in Kayserburg, Alsace, one of five children of Louis Schweitzer and Adele Schillinger Schweitzer. Raised in a presbytery in Gunsbach by loving and liberal parents, he developed early a sensitivity to those around him which transcended empathy and embraced a profound sense of personal responsibility. Highly gifted in music, he started learning the piano at five, the organ at eight, and by nine could substitute for the parish organist when needed. He studied under the eminent organist, Charles Marie Widor, and became an organist of note, particularly as an interpreter of Bach.

Schweitzer studied theology at the University of Strasbourg on a Goll Scholarship, taking his licentiate (a degree slightly higher than that of the doctorate in German universities) in 1900 and continuing on at Strasbourg as acting principal of the theological college. In 1902 he received the post of *Privatdozent*, and in 1903 he was appointed to the office of principal of the theological college. From 1903 to 1905 he worked on his *Quest of the Historical Jesus* and began a biography of Bach. He also wrote an influential treatise on the art of organ building.

When he was 21 he entered into a pledge that he would spend the next nine years in the study and writing of theology and philosophy, and in his pursuit of music; thereafter he would give the remainder of his life to the direct service of humanity.

In response to an appeal for a medical missionary, Schweitzer, in his thirtieth year, began to fulfill his pledge by entering the study of medicine, which he financed through giving lectures and organ concerts. In 1912 he married Helene Bresslau, who left her own scholarly pursuits to train as a nurse. With money raised from Alsatian churches and concerts, the Schweitzers left for the tropical community of Lambarene. During the nine months they served there before they were interned as alien citizens upon the outbreak of the First World War they treated 2,000 native patients.

During his internment Schweitzer became severely ill, but recovered and continued to orient his activities around the day he might return to Africa. He wrote *On the Edge of the Primeval Forest*; he gave concerts, he traveled and gave lectures. During 1922 and 1923 he wrote the two volumes of his great philosophical work, *The Decay and Restoration of Civilization* and *Civilization and Ethics*. He took advanced courses in obstetrics and dentistry, and attended lectures at the Institute for Tropical Hygiene in Hamburg. In 1924 he returned to Lambarene, and began construction of a new building two miles upstream in 1925. Except for trips to provide funding for the hospital, Lambarene became Schweitzer's permanent home, and by the early 1960s he had expanded the medical facilities to over 70 buildings. It became his habit to spend parts of his nights writing, and thus he continued to increase the legacy of theological and ethical thought he left to the world.

Schweitzer believed that the abdication of thought has been a decisive factor in the decay of civilization. In his own life he continued in his quest for the ultimate ethical values, and suddenly the phrase "reverence for life" came to him, crystallizing his search of many years. Schweitzer said, "A man is ethical only when life, as such, is sacred to him, and when he devotes himself helpfully to all life that is in need of help."

Honorary degrees were conferred upon Schweitzer from Prague, Oxford, St. Andrews, Edinburgh, and Zurich.

Albert Schweitzer died in his Lambarene hospital on September 5, 1965. In a posthumous tribute, us President Johnson wrote: "The world has lost a truly universal figure. His message and his example, which have lightened the darkest years of this century, will continue to strengthen all those who strive to create a world living in peace and brotherhood."

Bibliography

Christian Century 1965 Albert Schweitzer. 82(37): 1116–17

RUTH C. REYNOLDS

George Marshall

(1953)

In 1953, for the first time in the history of the Nobel Peace Prize, the award went to a professional soldier. The choice of thus honoring General George Catlett Marshall was met with intense criticism. Many felt that his position as Chief of Staff of the United States Army during the time of the development and use of the atomic bombs eliminated him forever from the roll call of peacemakers. George Marshall acknowledged this position with neither surprise nor rancor, saying that his experiences with the tragedies of war had left him deeply moved to find some means or method of avoiding another calamity of war.

The Peace Prize was not given to Marshall for what he accomplished during the war, the Nobel Committee said, explaining, "Nevertheless, what he has done after the war for peace is a corollary to this achievement, and it is this great work for the establishment of peace which the Nobel Committee has wanted to honor."

The wisdom General Marshall learned in his military career was a clear and passionate conviction that the overriding lesson of the last world war must be to recognize that another such war is now impossible. And when in 1947 Marshall accepted President Truman's appointment as Secretary of State, it was because he believed that he had come to understand some of the causes of war, and he intended to remove those causes insofar as it would fall within his power to do so.

Within his military experience Marshall developed two traits: one the insatiable desire to learn, to know, to understand, and the second his keen and wide-awake interest in the welfare of the individuals for whom he was responsible, be they soldier or civilian. Both of these traits nurtured the spiritual and social evolution of his mind. He displayed this eagerness to find out about his fellow human beings under his care early in his career when, at the age of 21, he was made commanding officer of some of the small and utterly lonely outposts in the Philippines. While there he made a study of the language, customs, and mentality of the Filipinos.

During the period between the wars Marshall was stationed in Tientsin for three years. And just as in the Philippines, where he had become an authority on their history and culture, so he applied himself to the language, both spoken and written, of the Chinese people and studied their history and culture. He was the only US officer who could examine Chinese witnesses who appeared before him without the use of an interpreter.

During the Depression when soldiers' pay was so low that it rendered a hardship on soldiers with families, Marshall taught his troops to raise chickens and hogs and tutored them in vegetable gardening. He instituted a lunch-pail system whereby each member of a soldier's family could have a meal-in-a-pail for 15 cents. Marshall and his wife ate the same fare so there would be no note of condescension. It was a true Marshall Plan in microcosm.

Marshall's military career might well be encapsulated by recounting an event fairly early in his army life, and one near its close. The first occurred in 1916 when a camp where he had been in charge of the training program closed. The commanding officer was required to make an efficiency report on his officers. When asked the routine question, "Would you desire to have Marshall under your immediate command in peace and in war?" Lt. Colonel Johnson Hagood said, "Yes, but I would prefer to serve *under his command* . . . In my judgement there are not five officers in the army so well qualified as he to command a division in the field." The second event followed the Allied victory in the Second World War.

Henry Stimson, US Secretary of War, said to Marshall in the presence of 14 generals and high officials, "I have seen a great many soldiers in my lifetime, and you, Sir, are the finest soldier I have ever known."

General Marshall was the first career soldier appointed US Secretary of State. He came with a wealth of background. As Chief of Staff he had taken part in the conference at sea between President Roosevelt and Winston Churchill which resulted in the Atlantic Charter. He assisted Roosevelt, Churchill, and the Combined Chiefs of Staff at a meeting which set up principles of unity of command in the Far East. Other conferences, some attended by Stalin and Chiang Kai-shek, have historical significance— at Casablanca, Quebec, and Yalta. He was with President Truman on a special mission to China, then in the throes of civil war. The following year, on February 12, 1947, he became Secretary of State.

In some of his early actions as Secretary of State he recommended aid to European displaced persons, continuance of relief abroad after termination of United Nations Relief and Rehabilitation Administration (UNRRA), and recommendations to Congress for proposals to permit the United States to join the UN International Refugees Organization. He supported the Stratton bill to admit 400,000 European displaced persons into the United States.

On June 5, 1947, at Harvard University commencement exercises, the new Secretary of State revealed his "Marshall Plan," later officially named the European Recovery Program (ERP). Dean Acheson (1961), a later Secretary of State, recalled the formation of the Marshall Plan. He said Marshall was determined that European recovery should come from and be devised by the Europeans themselves. The United States' role would be to help those who energetically and cooperatively helped themselves. There were many critics, Acheson recalled, but he said the plan would never have succeeded without the decision Marshall made.

Acheson recalled that Marshall also insisted that the offer should be made to all of Europe and not merely to Western Europe. To the storm of protests that "The Russians, if included, would sabotage the plan," and that "Congress would never appropriate the money," Marshall remained adamant in his stand. If Europe was to be divided more deeply and more lastingly than it was already, Moscow had to do it, not Washington.

Upon Marshall's invitation, Bevin, Molotov, and Bidault met in Paris to discuss Marshall's suggestions. In July, 16 European nations, including the

United Kingdom and France, met at the Paris Economic Conference on the ERP. The Soviet Union and its satellite nations boycotted the meetings, but Marshall held fast to his original plan described in his Harvard speech: "Our policy is directed not against any country or doctrine, but against hunger, poverty, desperation and chaos... Any government that is willing to assist in the task of recovery, will find full cooperation." Marshall thought it logical that the United States should do whatever it could to assist in the return of normal economic health over the world, without which, he was convinced, there could be no political stability and no assured peace. He insisted that political passion and prejudice should play no part.

"Your work stands," Chairman Jahn said to Marshall at the award ceremony. "Your intention was to create in the economic field a cooperation between the nations, embracing the whole of Europe, because you meant that unless people are free from fear, poverty and distress, there will be no sound foundation for a lasting peace. You did not know that some countries should not be willing to accept the help offered to them... it is the greatest example the world has seen of help given from one people to others and a true expression of brotherhood between nations."

In his Nobel lecture Marshall warned that millions who live under subnormal conditions are coming to a realization that they may aspire to a fair share of the God-given rights of human beings: "If we act with both wisdom and magnanimity, we can guide these yearnings of the poor to a richer and better life through democracy... but we must understand that these democratic principles do not flourish on empty stomachs."

Marshall deplored that in the past "we have walked blindly, ignoring the lessons of the past, with the tragic consequences of two world wars and the Korean struggle as a result." He urged that schools accept the responsibility for educating toward peaceful security, both in terms of its development and of its disruption. They must be taught as far as possible without national prejudices. They must learn to seek out the factors which favor peace. Marshall declared, "I am certain that a solution of the general problem of peace must rest on broad and basic understanding on the part of free peoples... and on a spiritual regeneration which would reestablish a feeling of good faith among men."

Biography

George Catlett Marshall was born on December 31, 1880, in Uniontown, Pennsylvania, son of George Catlett Marshall, a prosperous businessman, and Laura Bradford Marshall. He graduated in 1901 from the Virginia Military Institute as Senior First Captain of the Corps of Cadets, voted to the highest cadet rank at the institute by his classmates. He was commissioned a second lieutenant in the US Army and attached to the Thirtieth Infantry stationed in the Philippine Islands, where he remained for 22 months. After several years' duty in the West and on the West Coast he was selected to attend the Infantry–Cavalry School at Fort Leavenworth, Kansas, of which he was a senior honor graduate in 1907. He was next assigned to study at the Army Staff College, where he headed his class and to which he returned as instructor for two years following his graduation. Beginning in 1913 he again saw duty in the Philippines.

When the United States entered the First World War, Marshall accompanied the first convoy of the First Division to France, where he proved himself to be an outstanding tactician, and ended as Chief of Staff of the Eighth Army Corps. His rise in the army continued in meteoric fashion: by the opening of the Second World War, at the recommendation of General Pershing, President Roosevelt bypassed 20 major and 14 brigadier generals to make Marshall General of the Army, with five-star rank.

From 1941 General Marshall was one of the members of the policy committee guiding the atomic studies of US and British scientists. A member also of the Combined Chiefs of Staff of the United States and the United Kingdom, maintaining liaison with the Soviet Union through an Allied Military Mission to Moscow, and with China by the Allied Military Council at Chungking, Marshall exercised an important influence on United Nations strategy.

Many of his tasks were diplomatic: he was present at the conference at sea leading to the Atlantic Charter, and at conferences at Casablanca, Quebec, Cairo–Teheran, Yalta and Potsdam.

At his own request Marshall secured his release from duty as Chief of Staff and was appointed "Special representative of the President to China, with the personal rank of Ambassador." As a means of preventing famine, creating employment, and helping to institute a democratic government, Marshall recommended a loan to China. He was called back to the United States to assume the cabinet position of Secretary of State under President Truman in 1947. At his first press conference, in February 1947, he declared that the international control of atomic energy and the general issues involved in preserving the peace must be solved before any discussions on worldwide disarmament would be valid.

In other early actions he recommended aid to European displaced persons and continuance of relief abroad after termination of the United Nations Relief and Rehabilitation Administration (UNRRA). With Dean Acheson, Eisenhower, and others, Marshall formulated the "Truman Doctrine" (see Articles: *Truman Doctrine*), a "simple, declarative statement of New United States policy" to prevent the imposition of totalitarian regimes on European nations.

On June 5, 1947, he unveiled his Marshall Plan, officially named the European Recovery Program (ERP) before a Harvard University commencement audience. He described the plan as "not directed against any country or doctrine, but against hunger, poverty, desperation, and chaos. Its purpose would be the revival of a working economy in the world so as to permit the emergence of political and social conditions in which free institutions can exist." He required the European countries to design their own plans for using the monetary aid so that this would be a European plan. He insisted that all countries be included, and the Soviet Union's boycott of the 16-country meeting in Paris to implement ERP, was its own choice.

At the United Nations, Secretary Marshall proposed that the veto not be used in peaceful settlement of disputes and in the admission of new members in order to prevent its abuse. He also proposed the establishment of a continuous-session, all-nation interim committee on peace security which would "consider disputes at the request of the Security Council or individual states, recommend special General Assembly sessions it deemed necessary, and determine whether this little assembly should be made permanent." The plan for the "Little Assembly" was accepted later by General Assembly delegates with some modifications. Mar-

shall also supported the Stratton bill to admit 400,000 European displaced persons into the United States.

For one year during the Korean War he served as Secretary of Defense, from which position he resigned in September 1951.

Marshall received the Distinguished Service Medal for his service in the First World War, its Oak Leaf Cluster for Second World War duty, and many other medals, both from his own country and from France, the United Kingdom, the Soviet Union, Italy, Morocco, and various Latin American countries. He also received numerous honorary degrees.

Marshall married Elizabeth Carter Coles in 1902. Three years after her death in 1927, he married Katherine Boyce Tupper Brown. Although Marshall wrote no diaries or personal records, Katherine Tupper Marshall's *Together: Annals of an Army Wife*, written in 1946, presents an informal biography of General Marshall and herself.

General George C. Marshall died on October 16, 1959.

Bibliography

Acheson D 1961 General of the Army George Catlett Marshall. *Sketches from Life of Men I Have Known*. Harper, New York, pp. 147–66
Marshall K 1946 *Together: Annals of an Army Wife*. Tupper and Love, New York

RUTH C. REYNOLDS

United Nations High Commissioner for Refugees (UNHCR) (1954, 1981)

Through the ages the giving of sanctuary has become one of the noblest of human traditions. The 1954 and 1981 Nobel Peace Prizes were awarded to the Office of the United Nations High Commissioner for Refugees (UNHCR) in recognition of its sustained work toward ensuring the rights of refugees—people without political power, existing on the sufferance of strangers, who by 1981 numbered over 10 million individuals.

In presenting the 1954 award, the Nobel Committee said, "This is work for peace, if to heal the wounds of war is to work for peace, if to promote brotherhood among men is to work for peace. For this work shows us that the unfortunate foreigner is one of us; it teaches us to understand that sympathy with other human beings, even if they are separated from us by national frontiers, is the foundation upon which a lasting peace must be built."

The two awards honored a tradition long familiar to Norwegians through the work of their countryman, Fridtjof Nansen. An explorer, scientist and statesman, he devoted his life after the First World

War to administering humanitarian aid to refugees. In 1921 the League of Nations appointed him High Commissioner for Refugees, and for the leadership, vigor, and spirit he brought to the office he received the Peace Prize in 1922. After his death the momentum of his work continued through what was known simply as "the Nansen Office." In 1938 the Nansen Office joined the select group of Nobel Prize winners, creating a chain of tradition which leads to the UNHCR.

The Nansen award barely preceded the Second World War, which created unprecedented numbers of uprooted men, women, and children. At the war's end 44 nations joined to create the United Nations Relief and Rehabilitation Administration (UNRRA). Its task was to help with the voluntary repatriation of over 7 million persons during the following two years. For the many other refugees who could not, or did not wish to, return to their countries, another temporary body, the International Refugee Organization, was created, and it organized the resettlement of more than 1.5 million refugees.

These were the forerunners of the UNHCR, organizations which met specific problems created by the devastating world wars of the twentieth century. But it had become clear that not all the problems of refugees could be solved with their services, and the General Assembly of the United Nations decided to establish the Office of the United Nations High Commissioner for Refugees. With ill-fated optimism it was created for only three years, after which time its need would be subject to review. UNHCR, 31 years old when it received its second award of the Peace Prize, was still not officially a permanent body. But its services remained essential as violations of human rights and armed conflicts continued to afflict the world.

High Commissioner Hartling called UNHCR's expanding tasks "keeping pace with history in the making," as more than 100 new countries gained independence, sometimes in violent circumstances. Increasing international conflicts motivated the Commission to develop intermediary skills in order to act in behalf of refugees caught in the cross currents between powers.

As a means of establishing minimum standards for the treatment of refugees, a universally binding instrument was created at the 1951 Geneva Convention, followed by a supplementary protocol in 1967. The UNHCR was assigned the task of verifying that the 90 acceding countries each passed national legislation fully complying with these instruments, and further verifying that such legislation had been effectively implemented.

Hartling listed a portion of the Commission's accomplishments: its most gratifying service for the great majority of refugees has been assisting them to return to their homes. In 1954 Dr. Van Heuven Goedhart gave a haunting definition of "home." "Home is more than just a roof over the refugee's head," he said. "It is the all-embracing term for a series of elements which together constitute an individual's independence, and therefore his freedom and dignity."

This basic concept is costly to execute; it requires much organization. It can involve wide-ranging operations when refugees without funds or employment return to empty, or even destroyed, homes.

The first large-scale repatriation operation took place in 1962 with the return of 250,000 Algerians who had fled to Morocco and Tunisia during strife in their own country. In 1972 10 million refugees returned to their homes in their newly independent state, Bangladesh, after months spent in relief camps in India. That same year UNHCR helped bring back over 150,000 Sudanese refugees. In 1973 UNHCR assisted in one of history's largest airlift population exchanges when it organized a two-way movement of large numbers of people between Bangladesh and Pakistan.

In Africa, with the independence in 1974 of territories formerly under Portuguese administration, hundreds of thousands of refugees were assisted in returning to their homes in Guinea–Bissau, Mozambique, and Angola. Similar efforts on behalf of other refugees in Africa returning to their countries following independence intensified in 1975. By 1981 the numbers of people from Southeast Asia, Afghanistan, and the Horn of Africa who had received assistance from the Commission had swollen to proportions defying easy counting; estimates ranged from three to five million.

Countries accepting refugees without the means to care for them became a problem. The very presence of refugees can become threatening for the host countries, causing suspicion and political unrest; food supplies and economic resources can be severely strained. The refugees, deprived of support, having nothing, are helpless. "This is where concerned national and international efforts can bring stability to a situation fraught with danger," Hartling said. The UNHCR can encourage a decisive display of international cooperation in which programs of considerable magnitude can be planned, financed, and implemented to provide for refugees and ultimately lead to their self-sufficiency. Hartling cited Tanzania as an excellent example of such a program. "When refugees came from Rwanda and Burundi," he said, "we cleared up the bush, put up a refugee camp, gave them seeds and tools and they lived there. After some time, they took care of themselves. Today, thirty-six thousand of them have their own village—not a camp. They are no longer refugees. They are naturalized Tanzanians."

The Nobel Committee of 1981 singled out for praise UNHCR's work with the "boat people" from Vietnam, who, together with refugees from Laos and Cambodia, had been fleeing to other countries throughout Southeast Asia since 1975. Since 1977 UNHCR had assisted in the resettlement of more than 700,000 Asian refugees at the time of its 1981 Peace Prize award.

Serious political problems began to challenge the ingenuity of UNHCR as the chief host country, the United States, questioned whether the continuing migration was truly based on political necessity. The US government suggested it could result from the lure of better economic possibilities for refugees in the

United States. For UNHCR, balancing the demands of major contributors, of communist opponents and of countries like Thailand that have not signed the UN Covenant on Refugees is a difficult task.

During its first 30 years UNHCR had helped some 25 million people, but Commissioner Hartling estimated that at the time of the second award there were still about 10 million refugees throughout the world. With the later population upheavals a new cooperation was observed as both private enterprises and governments joined with UNHCR to carry out some of the largest population movements in history.

In dealing with the countries which the refugees are leaving, as well as the host countries receiving them, UNHCR has used diplomatic channels, offering its good offices as arbitrator between governments with differing interests to safeguard. The consideration of the refugees themselves has been UNHCR's guiding principle. Nobel Committee Chairman Sanness summarized this well: "The Office of the United Nations High Commissioner for Refugees is a bridge linking the world community conceived as a community of states, and the world community conceived as a community of men and women."

As they made the awards, the Committees on each occasion expressed their appreciation for all UNHCR had done for these "painful legacies of war." Looking toward a future still fraught with problems, they asked it to continue "to carry the flaming torch that Fridtjof Nansen once lit."

History

In 1948 the UN General Assembly established the International Refugee Organization to provide legal and political protection for refugees. At that time the greatest number of refugees were Europeans displaced by the Second World War. Three years later the agency was renamed the Office of the United Nations High Commissioner for Refugees (UNHCR). Minimum standards for refugees laid down by the 1951 Geneva Convention and supplemented by a 1967 protocol form the legal basis for UNHCR. It is UNHCR's role to assist in their implementation. For its vigorous and successful program, UNHCR won its first Nobel Peace Prize in 1954.

The growth of UNHCR's task reflects the upheavals and increasing violence following the Second World War. At UNHCR's inception in 1951 there were 51 countries in the world; at the time of its second award in 1981 there were 154. The High Commissioner for Refugees protects people who cross international borders without a passport. The UN has decreed that such people have protection, and the High Commissioner for Refugees becomes their ambassador. To this end, UNHCR has offices in 90 countries. Secondly, the UNHCR supplies relief. But its long-range purpose is to assist toward establishing self-sufficiency, either through refugees returning home or establishing them in a host country.

UNHCR is strictly nonpolitical: its doctrine is humanitarian. Its funding comes mainly from 20 countries, chiefly from the Western bloc, but with modest assistance from the Eastern bloc also. By 1981 it had assisted over 25 million refugees, but it estimated there remained 10 million in need of help at that time.

High Commissioners who have served in the past are: C. J. Van Heuven Goedhart (1951–56), Auguste R. Lindt (1956–60), Felix Schnyder (1961–65), and Prince Sadruddin Aga Kahn (1965–76). Poul Hartling, a former Prime Minister of Denmark, was named High Commissioner in 1977 and has remained in that post since that time.

Bibliography

Hartling P 1981 An inside look at agency that won Nobel Peace Prize (Interview). *U.S. News and World Report* 91(October 26): 55–56

Shawcross W 1981 The fourth world: Who's minding the refugees? *The Nation* 233 (November 28): 571–73

Time 1981 Timely honor. 118 (October 26): 55

RUTH C. REYNOLDS

Prize Not Awarded
(1955–56)

Lester Pearson
(1957)

Lester Bowles Pearson, the first Canadian to be awarded the Nobel Peace Prize, won the honor in 1957 because of the "powerful initiative, strength and perseverance he has displayed in attempting to prevent or limit war operations and to restore peace," the Nobel Committee said. Called "the diplomat of the atomic age," Pearson was an internationalist. "The scientific and technological discoveries that have made war so infinitely more terrible for us are part of the same process that has knit us all so much more closely together," he said. "Today, less than ever, can we defend ourselves by force, for there is no effective defense against the all-destroying effect of nuclear missile weapons . . . Peace must surely be more than this trembling rejection of universal suicide . . . "

"The best defense is not power," Pearson maintained, "but the removal of the causes of war and international agreements which will put peace on a stronger foundation than terror of destruction." Pearson's visionary diplomacy rested on the solid foundation of his study of history, first at the University of Toronto and then at Oxford. He taught history for four years at Toronto.

His first years served in the government in the Department of External Affairs also enhanced his preparation for his later role as diplomat as he gathered wide experience and broadened his outlook. During this time he attended numerous international conferences, among them the Hague Conference on International Law, the Geneva World Disarmament Conference, and meetings of the League of Nations.

From 1935 to 1941 he served in the Office of the High Commissioner for Canada, which placed him in London and extended his sphere of experience to include Europe. He returned to Canada to accept the post of Assistant Undersecretary of State for External Affairs. The following year he went to Washington as Canadian minister.

During the early years of the Second World War he joined those who were starting to build a structure of peace long before the end of the war. In 1943 he made a strong contribution to a conference in Hot Springs held to plan for the distribution of the world's food, and from which came the constitution for the Food and Agriculture Organization (FAO). He was reported as responsive and intelligent, with a flair for working out effective compromises between opposing viewpoints.

Pearson spoke at the close of that conference: "We at this Conference know, and we have shown, what science could do if harnessed to the chariot of construction. Man's fears have, however, harnessed it also to another chariot, that of atomic obliteration. On that chariot race, with science driven by both contestants, all our hopes and fears . . . are concentrated."

It was abundantly clear which chariot Pearson was driving. He took part in organizing the United Nations Relief and Rehabilitation Administration (UNRRA) to reestablish the economies of war-ravaged countries, and to take care of displaced persons inevitably following in the wake of war. Pearson undertook this task because he believed in a better world for humankind. "UNRRA must not merely do its job well," he said, "it must do it so well that it will give heart and courage to the governments who, slowly but steadily, are building up the international structure of peace . . . "

Pearson became Secretary of State for External Affairs in 1948, and during the nine years he held this position his chief contributions to international affairs were accomplished through the United Nations. He negotiated, and guided through the General Assembly, the plan that established the State of Israel (thereby earning Israel's Medallion of Valor).

He drafted the speech used by his Prime Minister, Louis St. Laurent, proposing the establishment of the North Atlantic Treaty Organization (NATO). Pearson headed the Canadian delegation to NATO in 1951–52. He would have liked to have seen it expanded beyond a defensive alliance to include cooperation among NATO countries covering political, economic, and cultural fields. "No person, no nation, no group of nations can view with comfort the prospects for a world where peace rests primarily on the deterrent effect of collective military strength and regional political unity . . . Even adequate collective force for defense is no final solution," he said.

When the bitter Arab–Israeli conflict over Palestine came to the UN he participated in the resolution of the UN committee that the United Kingdom should give up its mandate over Palestine, and that the country should be divided into an Arab and a Jewish state. Also as Secretary of State for External Affairs, he played a major part in the Korean truce of 1953.

Pearson's skill as a diplomat reached its zenith when Nasser nationalized the Suez Canal and the ensuing conflict was brought before the Security Council of the UN. Before a solution could be resolved, Israel marched into Egypt, and the next day the United Kingdom and France bombed Egyptian airfields. The action split the Western Alliance, brought on a crisis in the Commonwealth, and posed a threat of a new world war. The Security Council could do nothing in the face of the British and French vetos. Pearson began working on a plan of compromise. He also drafted and submitted a resolution for a neutral international UN peacekeeping force to supervise the cessation of hostilities. The favorable outcome of his work marked the UN's first successful peace move. "It may well be said that the

Suez crisis was a victory for the United Nations and for the man who contributed more than anyone else to save the world at that time. That man was Lester Pearson," Nobel Chairman Jahn declared.

A colleague once described Pearson's talents as a negotiator: "He sits down with a person from another country without ingrained hostility or prejudice or superiority." Although the Soviet Union twice blocked his nomination for Secretary-General of the UN, a Russian paid him a rare compliment. "I always listen with great attention to the Canadian delegate," Andrei Y. Vishinsky said, "because he often says what others may think but are afraid to say."

In his Nobel lecture, Pearson alone of all the Laureates brought up the powerful psychological attraction war holds for humankind. He quoted a Canadian psychiatrist, Dr. G. H. Stevenson:

> People are so easily led into quarrelsome attitudes by some national leaders. A fight of any kind has a hypnotic influence on most men. We men like war. We like the excitement of it, its thrill and glamor, its freedom from restraint. We like its opportunities for socially approved violence. We like its economic security and its relief from the monotony of civilian toil. We like its reward for bravery, its opportunities for travel, its companionship of men in a man's world, its intoxicating novelty. And we like taking chances with death. This psychological weakness is a constant menace to peaceful behavior. We need to be protected against this weakness and against the leaders who capitalize on this weakness.

Pearson's answer was twofold: people should face the fact that the consequences of nuclear war would hold none of war's previous attractions; and the peoples of the world should learn to know each other. He especially addressed the two Superpowers, pointing out that Western fears of the Soviet Union have been partly based on a lack of understanding and information about the people of that country. Similarly, the Soviet people, whom Pearson believed wished for peace, were in fear of the West. "How can there be peace without people understanding each other, and how can this be possible if they don't know each other?" he asked, adding that while contact can mean friction as well as friendship, more contact and freer communication would overcome this. "I can find nothing to say for keeping one people malevolently misinformed about others," he said. Quite to the contrary, Pearson urged that countries encourage contact between their citizens and those of other countries. To at least permit this he regarded as

"an acid test for the sincerity of protestations for better relations between peoples."

"We are now emerging into an age," he said, "when different civilizations will have to learn to live side by side in peaceful interchange, learning from each other, studying each other's history and ideals, art and culture, mutually enriching each other's lives. The only alternative in this overcrowded little world is misunderstanding, tension, clash and—catastrophe."

Pearson found hope in humanity's history: "The fact is," he said, "that to every challenge given by the threat of death and destruction, there has always been the response from free men: 'It shall not be' . . . May it be so again . . . as we face the awful and the glorious possibilities of the nuclear age."

Biography

Lester Bowles Pearson was born in Toronto, Canada, on April 23, 1897, the son of the Reverend Edwin Arthur Pearson and Annie Sarah Bowles Pearson. He attended schools in Toronto, Peterborough, and Hamilton, and graduated from the University of Toronto with a history degree. During the First World War he enrolled in the ambulance corps overseas, and then in the Royal Flying Corps, from which he was invalided home in 1918. He returned to England and earned a master's degree in history at Oxford. He then joined the faculty at the University of Toronto.

In 1928 Pearson joined the government service in the new Department of External Affairs. He was an adviser or delegate at the following: the London Naval Conference and the Conference on the Codification of International Law at The Hague, The Royal Commission on Wheat Futures, the Imperial Conference on Economic Cooperation, the Geneva Disarmament Conference, the League of Nations, and the International Commission on Commodity Prices.

In 1935 Prime Minister William Lyon McKenzie King appointed him to the Canadian High Commissioner's Office in London, first as a secretary, then as a counselor. In 1941 he returned to Ottawa as Assistant Undersecretary of State at the Department of External Affairs. He went to Washington as Canadian minister–counselor the following year, and became the Canadian Ambassador three years later.

Pearson believed that the United Nations represented the world's best chance for peace, and he contributed to its planning stage with the Food and Agriculture Organization (FAO) and the United Nations Relief and Rehabilitation Administration (UNRRA). He was senior adviser to the Canadian delegation at San Francisco in 1945 when the UN was launched. During the next 11 General Assemblies Pearson was a potent force in balancing the influence exerted by the United States and the United Kingdom through his participation in the UN's most important committee handling political and security questions. He was elected president of the General Assembly in 1952, also the year he presided over the North Atlantic Treaty Organization Council in Lisbon.

While Secretary of State for External Affairs, Pearson shared responsibility for the partition of Palestine in 1947. He played a major part in the Korean truce of 1953.

On April 22, 1963, Pearson was sworn in as the fourteenth Prime Minister of Canada. The *New York Times* described his five-year administration as "impressive," even though his Liberal Party was a few seats short of a majority. He brought in a national pension plan and a family assistance program. He broadened old-age security benefits, laid the foundations for the present National Free Medical Service, and inaugurated a massive study of French–English bilingualism and biculturism.

Pearson accumulated many awards and honors during his long service to his country and to the world. He was made an officer of the Order of the British Empire in 1935, and was admitted to the Privy Council of Canada in 1948.

The government of Israel awarded him its Medallion of Valor. He held more than 20 honorary LL.D degrees, from universities in Canada, the United States, the United Kingdom and other countries. Pearson wrote two books, *Democracy in World Politics* (1955) and *Diplomacy in the Nuclear Age* (1959).

On August 22, 1925, he married Maryon Elspeth Moody. They had a son, Geoffrey Arthur Holland and a daughter, Patricia Lillian Hannah.

Lester Bowles Pearson died on December 27, 1972, in his home near Ottawa, Canada.

Bibliography

New York Times Biographical Edition 1972 Lester Pearson dies at 72. 3 (July–December): 2230–31
Time 1963 A new leader. 81 (April 19): 33–37

RUTH C. REYNOLDS

Dominique Pire

(1958)

The Nobel Committee awarded the Peace Prize for 1958 to Father Dominique Pire for his tireless efforts to help refugees to leave their camps and return to a life of freedom and dignity. "Father Pire's work is known to all of us in Western Europe," the Committee said. "We have read of this man who, on his own initiative, has set himself the task of rescuing the handicapped refugees, the 'Hard Core,' the residue. These are the old and infirm who remained in the camps, doomed to stay there without hope of a brighter future, men for whom our hard, ruthless world . . . has had no further use."

Father Pire was guided by the principle that "each refugee is a being of infinite worth, who deserves all our attention, all our love, whatever his nationality, his religion, his learning, his moral misery." He was imbued "with the certainty of the deep unity of the human race. Newton said, 'Men build too many walls and not enough bridges.' " Pire claimed to be nothing more than "a man looking at his brothers and trying hard to get men to look at *their* brothers."

Pire had an early acquaintance with the inhumanity of war. During the First World War, he saw his grandfather shot by the Germans, and the four-and-a-half year old boy fled with his family to France. They returned four years later to find their home in ruins.

When Pire was 18 he entered the Dominican monastery of LaSarte in Huy, a small town in Belgium. There he began studies which would take him to the Dominican University in Rome. He

gained a Doctorate of Sacred Theology eight years later. He returned to the monastery in Huy to teach, and there he remained all his life. He also served as curé to the impoverished agricultural laborers of LaSarte.

After the Second World War, in addition to these duties, Father Pire began setting up camps for Belgian and French refugee children. On one fateful day in 1949 he heard a US United Nations Relief and Rehabilitation Administration (UNRRA) official describing the plight of Europe's displaced refugees. "It was such a heartbreak," recalled Pire, "that it suddenly seemed to me that there was nothing I could do—except do everything I could to remedy all that." He began to act that evening, writing to the 47 names the UN official had given him when Pire asked what he might do. He visited displaced persons (DPS) camps. He learned that of the eight million DPS stranded by the war there remained 150,000 refugees whom no country would have. He witnessed their squalid, unhygienic surroundings and lack of privacy. He saw men who no longer hoped for work, women who had lost their dream of a home. "They were people who had been sitting for twelve years on their suitcases in a railway station, waiting for a train that would never come," Pire said.

Father Pire tried to obtain information about the refugees which would lead him to their former friends. He hoped to assist in reestablishing contact with them and to help the refugees to find new friends willing to start a sustained relationship, usually through letters. From this came a "sponsoring" movement which in nine years, by the time of Pire's Nobel award, had grown to 18,000 persons, each "sponsoring" families of refugees with Pire's simple formula of a little time, some packages and money, and much love.

He began a bimonthly newspaper, named "Hard Core," in poignant salute to the refugees' plight. He delivered hundreds of lectures, in person, on radio, and on television, to raise funding. With the money he began to help refugees leave the camps. First, he attended to the problem of the old people. In four years he founded four homes for elderly refugees. There they were encouraged to call on forgotten skills like sewing and embroidering, to earn the sweet taste of independence through the sale of the fruits of their labor. Once forgotten and helpless, now they could look forward to care for the rest of their waning lifetimes. One woman wrote to Father Pire, "I feel that spiritual values are the most important things in our earthly lives, and that without them life itself is so full of sadness that it is scarcely worth living . . . Thank you for comforting me and for having made the last years of my life the best. I face the end . . . with serenity."

Father Pire found that the displaced "suffer from a 'rusting of the soul,' from a total uprooting, not only from their own countries, but from the society of men." Material help alone offered no cure for their malady. Pire's answer was to build "European villages," groups of about 20 houses near a city. Not *in* the city, where they could turn into ghettos, but "a neighborhood glued onto a city." The first of these villages was constructed in 1956 at Aachen (Aix-la-Chapelle) in the Federal Republic of Germany. There its 200 residents, rescued from their encampments, could set up housekeeping in family units. Father Pire believed that people must again know the pride of a clean home with curtains at the window, and be able again to look with hope toward earning their livelihood, before the "weight of the odor and noise" of the DP camps would fall away.

The year after receiving the Nobel Prize, Father Pire widened his crusade with an association called "Open Heart to the World." It included a University of Peace established at Huy where people of all opinions and conceptions could join together to engage in dialogue. Its sessions throughout the year, ranging from two days to two weeks, welcomed anyone interested in pursuing the subject of peace.

In 1960 Father Pire began a project of an "Island of Peace" in East Pakistan, where, in Moslem terrain, a team trained in tropical medicine and agron-

omy began a program designed eventually to establish a self-sufficient community. Forty thousand inhabitants developed an agricultural settlement there, based on the plan that with the end of the training project the entire program would be turned over to the initiative of the local inhabitants. A second peace island was opened in Kalakaddu, Madras, India, in the early 1960s.

Father Pire's work became formalized into a master organization, known as "Aid to Displaced Persons and European Villages." It has self-governing national sections in the Federal Republic of Germany, Austria, Belgium, France, Luxembourg, and Switzerland. There are national secretariats in Denmark, Italy, and the Netherlands. Because the work is supported by private contributions "from the hearts of men," the movement became popularly called "Europe of the Heart."

As Pire expanded his work to an international scope the programs remained rooted in his initial projects. World Friendships is an agency that encourages fraternal dialogue carried on through correspondence by people of different heritages; in 1958 it had about 6,500 participants. World Sponsorships administrates material help from people on a person-to-family basis, emphasizing education of children; it has about 400 enrolled "godparents." More and more displaced persons were rescued from their lives in the camps as the village project progressed; over a thousand refugees began renewed lives in seven villages throughout Europe.

In his Nobel address Pire shared the experiences of many of the refugees who had corresponded with him. Like Anne Frank, whose portrait hung in his office to keep before him an example of courage, Father Pire practiced sharing the riches of the heart. He told his audience that Aid to Displaced Persons is a means for the individual to act toward peace. While the common citizen feels he has little say in the great political questions, "he has every say and every opportunity to put words into practice on the Displaced Persons problem." And this can start a potent path toward peace. What one man cannot do alone, the love of many may achieve. Father Pire believed that no surer road to peace exists than the one that starts from little islands and oases of genuine kindness, constantly growing in number and being continually joined together "until one day they will ring the world."

When he accepted the Nobel Peace Prize Father Pire had made a pledge: "I should like to use the moral credit of the Nobel Peace Prize in such a way that when I die this credit will return to you, not only whole and intact, but increased, augmented by the way in which I have used it, so that later on, your successors will be able to offer in the Nobel Peace Prize even greater moral credit, because your 1958 laureate has borne it well." His pledge is fulfilled; his words now stand as a memorial.

Biography

Dominique Georges Henri Pire was born in Dinant, Belgium, on February 10, 1910. He was the son of a civic official, Georges Pire. At the age of 18 he entered the Dominican monastery of LaSarte in Huy, Belgium, and took the name Henri Dominique. He took his final vows on September 23, 1932. He continued his studies in the Dominican University in Rome, was ordained in 1934, and received his doctorate in theology in 1936. After studying the social sciences for a year at the University of Louvain (Leuven), Belgium, he returned to the Huy monastery to teach sociology and moral philosophy.

In 1938 he began his long service to the unfortunate by founding the Mutual Family Aid Service and the Open Air Camps for children. During and after the Second World War the stations were more than just camps, they were missions feeding thousands of Belgian and French children. During the war the Reverend Father Pire was a chaplain to the resistance movement, an agent for the intelligence service, and a participant in the underground escape system for downed Allied flyers. For his efforts he was awarded the Military Cross with Palms, the Resistance Medal with Crossed Swords, the War Medal, and the National Recognition Medal.

In addition to his duties as curé of LaSarte, Father Pire decided early in 1949 to study the refugee problem. He visited refugees in Austria, wrote *Du Rhin au Danube avec 60,000 D.P.,* and founded the Aid to Displaced Persons organization. Pire approached his work with refugees on three different levels. He found 18,000 Europeans to sponsor refugee families by sending them letters of encouragement and parcels with needed supplies. He established four homes for aged refugees. Recognizing that the younger refugees needed to have a home, the opportunity to gain economic independence, and circumstances amenable to achieving psychological wholeness, he conceived the idea of building small villages for refugees on the outskirts of cities. He constructed seven of these villages through private donations.

In 1957 the Aid to Displaced Persons organization became the Aid to Displaced Persons and European Villages, an international charitable association, with self-governing bodies in 10 European states.

After receiving the Nobel Peace Prize in 1958 Father Pire established The Heart Open to the World. This organization now sponsors the University of Peace at Huy, World Friendships, World Sponsorships, and Islands of Peace.

Throughout his 32 years of service promoting the dignity and brotherhood of humanity, Father Pire lived simply in the Huy monastery. He died at the age of 58 in the Louvain (Leuven) Roman Catholic Hospital on January 30, 1969.

Bibliography

America 1958 Nobel Prize winner. 100 (November 22): 230
America 1963 Pere Pire's peace corps. 109 (October 5): 373
New York Times 1969 Dominique Pire is dead at 58; Priest won Nobel Peace Prize. January 31, p. 39
Time 1958 Belgium "open on the world." 72 (November 24): 24

RUTH C. REYNOLDS

Philip Noel-Baker

(1959)

The 1959 Nobel Prize for Peace was awarded to Philip John Noel-Baker for a lifetime of support to the League of Nations and the United Nations, and in recognition of his sustained and tireless efforts dedicated to disarmament. "I do not think it an exaggeration to say that he has had some share in practically all the work that has been carried out to promote international understanding in its widest sense," the chairman of the Nobel award committee, Gunnar Jahn, said. "The dark years of this century in Europe started in 1914 and they are still with us. Throughout this span of time, for forty-five years, Philip John Noel-Baker has dedicated his efforts to the service of suffering humanity, whether in time of war or in the intervals between wars. But above all else, his efforts to prevent war breaking out have been tireless and ceaseless."

Noel-Baker was born in 1889 into a family of a long line of Quakers, and he grew up under the influence of parents who worked selflessly in behalf of London's poor. His father, Joseph Allen Baker, was a Member of Parliament between 1900 and 1918, and worked indefatigably to forge links between peace efforts throughout the world. Noel-Baker honored the example set by his father and his Quaker heritage through a lifetime devoted to study, teaching, writing, legislating, and organizing for peace.

His schooling began at a Quaker school in York, continuing at Haverford College in Pennsylvania, and from 1908 to 1912 at Cambridge University.

There he took honors in history and in economics at King's College in 1910 and 1912 respectively. In 1911 and 1913 he was named the Whewell Scholar in International Law. Following his completion of a degree in international law, he continued his studies at the Sorbonne and in Munich during the year preceding the First World War. He mastered six languages—German, Greek, French, Italian, Norwegian, and Spanish.

It was Chairman Jahn's opinion that Noel-Baker's academic discipline can be observed throughout his lifetime's work: "In all he has said and written, he has never succumbed to the temptation of making a statement that was not well-founded on meticulous documentation."

In 1914 Noel-Baker accepted the post of vice-principal of Ruskin College at Oxford, but when the First World War broke out, as a Quaker he served in the ambulance corps on the Belgian, French, and Italian fronts, receiving several decorations. At the close of the war he immediately turned his efforts to the cause of peace, serving as principal assistant to Lord Robert Cecil (Peace Prize Winner of 1937) on the committee which drafted the League of Nations Covenant at the Peace Conference in Paris. In 1920 he began his work as adviser to Fridtjof Nansen in Nansen's tremendous humanitarian work throughout the world in the wake of the First World War, and later in the League of Nations. But his principal efforts in the early 1920s were as a member of the Secretariat of the League and principal assistant to Sir Eric Drummond, first secretary-general of the League. From 1922 to 1924 he was private secretary to the British representative on the League's Council and Assembly, after which he returned to England to become first Cassell Professor of International Relations at the University of London.

He entered politics in 1929 and was elected as Labour Member of Parliament for Coventry. He was a member of Britain's delegation to the 1929–30 sessions of the League of Nations Assembly, and served from 1929 to 1931 as parliamentary private secretary to Foreign Secretary Arthur Henderson (Peace Prize winner of 1934) who chaired the Disarmament Conference.

Subsequently, representing Derby and Derby South, Noel-Baker was elected to the National Executive Committee of the Labour Party in 1937. In 1942 he accepted a post in Churchill's wartime government, and in 1945, when Attlee came to power, served in a number of ministerial posts. But his work as a member of the British government covered a great deal more: it was Noel-Baker who directed negotiations with India, Ireland, and Newfoundland, and Chairman Jahn credited him with a large role in the successful issue of negotiations with India on the question of independence.

He was in charge of British preparatory work for the United Nations. Bringing his wealth of experience from the League of Nations, he exerted considerable influence, laying groundwork for various sections of the United Nations such as the Food and Agriculture Organization (FAO) and the International Refugee Organization (IRO). He supported the regulation of traffic in arms, atomic control, economic aid for refugees, and the reintroduction of the Nansen "passport." Noel-Baker participated actively in the work of the United Nations Relief and Rehabilitation Administration (UNRRA), and represented the United Kingdom in the World Health Organization (WHO) and the UN Economic and Social Council.

He was a prolific writer. Chairman Jahn praised Noel-Baker's books for their timeless value: "All that Noel-Baker has written reflects his tremendous depth of knowledge, and the soundness, shrewdness, and eminent common sense of his views give his books a value far beyond the age in which they were written."

Jahn called Philip Noel-Baker "the man who possesses the greatest store of knowledge on the subject of disarmament and who best knows the difficulties involved." His book *The Arms Race—A Programme for World Disarmament* summarized a lifetime of research and experience. All the attempts made to reach agreement on disarmament since the First World War were traced, and Noel-Baker described the repeated efforts to find an acceptable system of control. He believed that up to 1955, the Soviet attitude was responsible for the lack of success in this area, but he was particularly critical about what he calls the "Western volte face" of May 10, 1955, when the Western powers, under the leadership of US Secretary of State Harold Stassen, backed away from agreement after the Soviet Union had fully accepted the Western disarmament proposals, including inspection. What Noel-Baker calls "a moment of hope" slipped away, never to be regained.

In his Nobel lecture Noel-Baker pleaded for disarmament as the supreme issue standing before the international community. He ruled out "limited war" as now obsolete. "Some people honestly believe that small steps will be easier to take than large ones," he said. "I prefer the words of John Stuart Mill: 'Against a great evil, a small remedy does not produce a small result; it produces no result at all.' "

Noel-Baker thought the greatest danger facing humanity to be the incredibly fatalistic apathy of people. He asserted that governments, general staffs, and peoples simply have not grasped what modern armaments mean—the very employment of the word "defense" to describe modern military preparations is an extreme example of a language which no longer serves reality. "For every nation disarmament is the safest and most practicable system of defense," he declared.

In his definitive *The Arms Race*, Noel-Baker wrote, "No one who has closely followed disarmament negotiations since 1919 is likely to be guilty of facile optimism about the prospect of peace. But no one who understands the present arms race should be guilty of facile pessimism, which is by far the graver fault. Defeatism about the feasibility of plans for disarmament and ordered peace has been the most calamitous of all the errors made by democratic governments in modern times."

Biography

Noel-Baker was born Philip John Baker in England on November 1, 1889, son of Joseph Allan Baker and Elizabeth Moscrip, descendants from a long line of Quakers. (Noel-Baker took his wife's surname, Noel, in combination with his own.) His father, a humanitarian and pacifist, held a seat on the London County Council from 1895 to 1907 and in the House of Commons from 1905 to 1918. Noel-Baker followed in the Quaker tradition, striving to help his fellows without regard to race or creed, and labored to build a world without violence or war.

He began his college studies at Haverford College in Pennsylvania, and continued at Cambridge from 1908 to 1912. There he took honors in history and economics tripos in 1910 and 1912 respectively. In 1911 and 1913 he was named the Whewell Scholar in International Law. Following his completion of a degree in international law at Cambridge, he studied at the Sorbonne and in Munich.

At the outbreak of the First World War, Noel-Baker was vice-principal of Ruskin College, Oxford, but he subsequently served in the ambulance corps on the Western Front.

Noel-Baker not only excelled in his academic studies, but also starred as an athlete, becoming president of the athletic club at Cambridge and running in the 1912 Stockholm Olympics. This was an interest he followed intermittently for many years; he won the silver medal in the 1500 meter run in the 1920 games at Antwerp and captained the British track team that year and in the 1924 games at Paris.

From 1920 to 1922 he was a member of the League of Nations Secretariat. In 1920 he also began assisting Fridtjof Nansen as an adviser, first in Nansen's humanitarian work in alleviating the suffering following in the wake of war, and later when Nansen represented Norway in the League. From 1922 to 1924 he served as private secretary to the British representative on the League's Council and Assembly. From 1924 to 1929 he was the Cassell Professor of International Relations at London University. From 1929 to 1931 he was a member of the British delegation to the League's Assembly. He worked with Arthur Henderson, Chairman of the Disarmament Commission, from 1931 to 1933. He recalled his League experience and wrote of further research in *The Geneva Protocol for the Pacific Settlement of International Disputes*; *The League of Nations at Work*; *Disarmament*; and *Disarmament and the Coolidge Conference*.

From 1936 to 1942 Noel-Baker was a member of the Opposition in the House of Commons, but accepted the office of Joint Parliamentary Secretary to the Minister of War Transport offered by Winston Churchill in 1942. In the Attlee government in 1945 he began serving successively as Minister of State in the Foreign Office, Secretary of State for Air, Secretary of State for Commonwealth Relations, and Minister of Fuel and Power. When the Labour Party lost power he joined the shadow cabinet, becoming vice-president of the foreign affairs group in 1961 and chairman in 1964.

At the close of the Second World War Noel-Baker helped with preparatory work for the United Nations much as he had with the League of Nations. As a delegate to the Food and Agriculture Conference in Canada he helped make the FAO a viable service organization in the UN. He helped draft the UN Charter in San Francisco in 1945, and sat as a member of the British delegation in 1946. In the General Assembly he supported the International Refugee Organization (IRO) and sought regulation in arms traffic and atomic control. He helped with the reintroduction of the Nansen passport so vital to refugees without a country, and he supported financial aid for refugees.

In the 1950s Noel-Baker returned to academic life. In 1958 he published *The Arms Race: A Programme for World Disarmament*, summarizing the results of extensive research and personal experiences. It won the Albert Schweitzer Book Prize in 1961.

Noel-Baker was made a life peer in 1977 as Baron Noel-Baker of Derby, the city he represented in the Commons for many years.

Philip John Noel-Baker died on October 8, 1982.

Bibliography

Christian Century 1959 Disarmament advocate wins Peace Prize. 76(46): 1332–33

Russell E 1960 Philip Noel-Baker. *Int. Relations* 2(1): 1–2

RUTH C. REYNOLDS

Albert Lutuli

(1960)

Albert John Lutuli,[1] Zulu Chief and African patriot, the 1960 recipient of the Nobel Peace Prize, declared that the award had, for him, a threefold significance:

> On the one hand, it is a tribute to my humble contribution to efforts by democrats on both sides of the color line to find a peaceful solution to the race problem .... On the other hand, the award is a democratic declaration of solidarity with those who fight to widen the area of liberty in my part of the world ... From yet another angle, it is welcome recognition of the role played by the African people during the last fifty years to establish, peacefully, a society in which merit and not race would fix the position of the individual in the life of the nation.

Lutuli was born into a heritage of tribal leadership. His grandfather was a chief of the Zulu tribe in Groutville; the title was passed to one of his sons. Lutuli was born around 1898 in Rhodesia. His father died when Lutuli was a young child, and Lutuli was raised in Groutville, where his devoted mother, Mtonya Gumede, saw to her young son's education, beginning at the local Congregationalist mission (primary) school. From there Lutuli progressed to a boarding school, the Ohlange Institute, and then to a teachers' training program at a Methodist institution in Edendale in 1917. After teaching there for two years he went on to complete a teachers' training course at Adams College on a scholarship. It was there that he accepted a teaching post as one of two Africans to join the staff.

Lutuli's Christian background remained a powerful force in his life, and he merged his inheritance of Zulu culture with the ethics of European Christianity to achieve a patient, persistent stance in his struggle for the dignity of his people. A fellow Christian remarked, "To him, nonviolence is a thing of the spirit, not one simply of organized protests and demonstrations" (Blaxall 1961). A leader of immense dignity, Lutuli earned a respect which transcended political and geographic boundaries; he personified before the world the black South African's struggle to end oppression and to participate in Africa's social revolution and its entrance into the family of nations in the role of peacemaker.

For 15 years Lutuli found fulfillment as an educator, and among his subjects was the history of the Zulu people. In 1935 he was invited by the members of the Zulu community to assume the functions of Chief of the Abasemakholweni tribe. It was with some hesitation that he left the security and the tranquility of an educator's life. The salary of the Chief is paid by the state, a fact that was later to have great significance for Lutuli because this gave the state the power of dismissal. When he took over as tribal chief, Lutuli devoted much time to working with his 5,000-strong tribe, performing the judicial function of a magistrate, the mediating function of an official acting as representative of his people, and at the same time as representative of the central government. He worked toward the betterment of his people's economic status—he taught them how to improve their sugar-cane fields, for instance—and he endeavored to help them blend their Zulu culture with Christian teaching. During those years he and his wife raised and educated their seven children.

But the forces of oppression in South Africa were accelerating. "There is nothing new in South Africa's apartheid ideas," Lutuli explained, "but South Africa is unique in this: the ideas not only survive in our modern age, but are stubbornly defended, extended, and bolstered up by legislation at the time when, in the major part of the world, they are now largely historical and are either shamefacedly hidden behind concealing formulations, or are being scrapped." And the South African government participates in the oppression. "The brotherhood of man is an illegal doctrine, outlawed, banned, censured, proscribed and prohibited; ... to work, talk or campaign for the realization in fact and deed of the brotherhood of man is hazardous, punished with banishment, or confinement without trial, or imprisonment." With white minority power resting on a heavily armed military, Lutuli said an effective democratic channel to peaceful settlement of the race problem had never, during a 300-year-relationship, existed.

In 1944 Lutuli sought such a channel through the African National Congress (ANC), an organization founded in 1912 by nonwhite Africans who had obtained a higher education. Their purpose was to use their talents toward democratic political development. Lutuli brought his customary zeal and strong

---

1. Lutuli preferred the spelling of his name used here, although "Luthuli," a commonly used spelling, may be a closer phonetic rendering.

leadership to the organization, and after holding lesser offices, in 1952 he was elected its president, an office he held until the Congress was banned in 1960.

At first the ANC tried to influence political development by means of petitions and deputations to the authorities, but when their attempts were met with ever more restrictive laws, the organization took stronger action based on boycotts, defiance campaigns, and strikes. It was here that Lutuli asserted his powerful influence toward nonviolent resolution, balancing the more defiant fringe who wanted a South Africa that was an entirely nonwhite state.

"How easy it would have been in South Africa for the natural feelings of resentment at white domination to have been turned into feelings of hatred and a desire for revenge . . . ," he remarked. A black racism could have developed equal to that of their oppressors to counter the white arrogance. Lutuli asserted that it was no accident that this had not happened. "It is because, deliberately and advisedly, we discarded the chance of an easy and expedient emotional appeal. Our vision has always been that of a nonracial, democratic South Africa which upholds the rights of all who live in our country to remain there as *full* citizens, with equal rights and responsibilities," he said.

The government ordered Lutuli to either withdraw from the Congress or give up his position as tribal chief. Lutuli refused to comply with either request, declaring to the Native Affairs Department in Pretoria that a chief, by Zulu tradition, was first of all a leader of his people and only secondarily a functionary of the government. "I only pray to the Almighty to strengthen my resolve," he said, "for the sake of the good name of our beloved country, the Union of South Africa, to make it a true democracy and a true union in form and spirit . . ." The government ordered him deposed and forbade his visiting any of the major towns or cities of the Union of South Africa for 12 months. But as a gesture of confidence in Lutuli, the ANC nonetheless elected him president–general a month later, and this position he held until the organization was outlawed in 1960.

The Nobel Committee Chairman, Gunnar Jahn, commented on this period. "It was first and foremost for the work he carried on during these years, from the 1940's to the present, that we honor him today . . . If the nonwhite people of South Africa ever lift themselves from their humiliation without resorting to violence and terror, then it will be above all because of the work of Lutuli . . ."

Lutuli was cruelly harassed for his activities. Repeated travel bans were imposed; in 1956 he was charged with treason and held in custody for nearly a year until the charges were dropped. Since his home exile started in 1959, visitors were reportedly barred to him, including the Nobel Prize investigators and the British Prime Minister Harold Macmillan (*Life* 1961). His travel ban was lifted for a brief 10-day period to allow him to attend the Nobel Prize award ceremony.

Lutuli was killed in an accident in July 1967 at the age of 69. He left a legacy of pioneering work toward an Africa now still visionary: "In a strife-torn world, tottering on the brink of complete destruction by man-made nuclear weapons, a free and independent Africa is in the making," Lutuli told his award audience. "Acting in concert with other nations, she is man's last hope for a mediator between the East and West, and is qualified to demand of the great powers to turn the swords into ploughshares," he declared.

"Africa's qualification for this noble task is incontestable, for her own fight has never been and is not now a fight for conquest of land, for accumulation of wealth or domination of peoples, but for the recognition and preservation of the rights of man and the establishment of a truly free world for a free people."

Biography

Albert John Lutuli (1898?–1967) was heir to a tradition of Zulu tribal leadership. His grandfather was chief of a small tribe at Groutville in the Umvoti Mission Reserve near Stanger, Natal. His father became a Christian missionary and spent most of his later years in the Matabele missions of Rhodesia. His father died when Lutuli was a small child.

His devoted mother, Mtonya Gumede, supported his education and he completed his teachers' training course in 1917. After spending two years as principal of an intermediate school he completed a Higher Teachers' Training course at Adams College, attending on a scholarship. Upon graduating he became one of two African faculty members at the college. He spent the next 15 years in education, his political activity confined to a deep interest in bettering the education available to black children. In 1927 he married a fellow teacher, Nokukhanya Bhengu. They had seven children.

After considering the call of his tribe for two years, Lutuli assumed the position of tribal chief, a position salaried by the state. He continued to display his tremendous zeal and patience as he worked for the progress and welfare of the 5,000 people in his tribe.

But the restrictions imposed by the Union of South Africa on its nonwhite population became increasingly severe. Lutuli's concern for the tribe expanded to encompass all black South Africans. In 1944 he joined the African National Congress (ANC), an organization founded in 1912 to obtain legal enfranchisement and human rights for all South Africans, inviting members of other racial groups who also believed in human brotherhood to join them in this work. In 1945 he was elected to the Committee of the Natal Province Division of the ANC, and in 1951 he became president of the division.

In 1952 he joined with other ANC leaders in organizing nonviolent activities to protest discriminatory laws. He was ordered by the South African government either to withdraw from the Congress or to relinquish his position as tribal chief. Lutuli refused to do either and was dismissed from his post as tribal chief. One month later he was elected president–general of the ANC, a position he held until the government banned the organization in 1960.

The government sought to limit his effectiveness by restricting his movement with repeated travel bans throughout his term of office. He was charged with high treason in 1956 but the charges were dropped in 1957. He was arrested in 1960 for publicly burning his travel pass after demonstrators against the Pass Law were massacred in Sharpeville. Although Lutuli had been outspoken in his stand against violence, and had advocated the peaceful enfranchisement of black South Africans, the ANC was banned after the Sharpeville incident.

The ban confining him to a radius of 15 miles from his home was lifted one final time for a 10-day period so that he and his wife might attend the Nobel Peace Prize ceremonies in Oslo.

Though the ban on Lutuli also included prohibiting his publishing any work, the continued respect accorded him throughout the world was reflected by a number of honors: the South African Colored People's Congress nominated him for president, the National Union of South African Students made him its honorary president, the students of Glasgow University voted him their rector, and the New York City Protestant Council conferred an award on him.

In July 1967, at the age of 69, Lutuli died in an accident near his home.

Bibliography

Blaxall A 1961 Honor deserved. *Christian Century* 78 (November 22): 1408–09

Life 1961 A prize for a Zulu Chief. 51 (November 17): 77–86

RUTH C. REYNOLDS

Dag Hammarskjöld
(1961)

The Nobel Committee awarded the Peace Prize for 1961 posthumously to Dag Hammarskjöld. As Secretary–General, with finesse and patience, this gifted diplomat molded the United Nations into a dynamic instrument for the realization of an organized international community. He challenged those countries which he observed clinging to outdated concepts of national sovereignty, and opened before them vistas of cooperative interchange which would transcend coexistence by balance of power and establish a lasting basis for peace.

In his final report which he wrote to the General Assembly on August 17, 1961, he deplored the philosophy of member states which advocated sovereignty with armed competition, a philosophy at total variance with the needs of a world of ever-increasing interdependence; and he outlined ways through the United Nations in which they could develop international cooperation. A month later he was killed in the line of duty. His report now stands as his last testament.

Dag Hammarskjöld worked with the same quiet strength he observed in his father: "A man of firm convictions does not ask, and does not receive, understanding from those with whom he comes into conflict. A mature man is his own judge. In the end, his only firm support is being faithful to his own convictions," Hammarskjöld said, in speaking of his father before the Swedish Academy as he took the seat left vacant there by his father's death.

Dag Hammarskjöld was the youngest of four sons born to Agnes Almquist Hammarskjöld and Hjalmar Hammarskjöld, Prime Minister of Sweden, member of the Hague Tribunal, governor of Uppland, and chairman of the Board of the Nobel Foundation. Hammarskjöld described the influence of his parents: "From generations of soldiers and government officials on my father's side I inherited a belief that no life was more satisfactory than one of selfless service to your country—or humanity. This service requires a sacrifice of all personal interests, . . . the courage to stand up unflinchingly for your convictions. From scholars and clergymen on my mother's side I inherited a belief that, in the very radical sense of the Gospels, all men were equals as children of God."

Both at school and at the Uppsala University his career was one protracted academic triumph, C. P. Snow tells us in his *Variety of Men* (1967 p. 209): "A whole class above the rest; in fact, a whole class above anyone for years past; he was not only as clever as a man can reasonably be, but fanatically hard-working (as he stayed all his life)." During that time Hammarskjöld began the mastery of German, French, and English which reached such fluency that in later years a baffled diplomat, after listening to Hammarskjöld practicing the diplomat's art of tactful obfuscation, pronounced him "the only man alive who can be totally incomprehensible with complete fluency in four languages." He was equally capable in discoursing on poetry, from the German Hermann Hesse to the American Emily Dickinson, and on music and painting, and in later years, in indulging in sophisticated dialogue on Christian theology. He was also a competent athlete and enjoyed skiing and gymnastics.

His degrees were in economics and law, as were his early professional posts, and he devoted 31 years to Swedish financial affairs, Swedish foreign relations, and global international affairs. He served as secretary of the Bank of Sweden in 1935, and as undersecretary of the Department of Finance of the Swedish government from 1936 to 1945. From 1941 to 1948, overlapping the undersecretaryship for four years, he was placed at the head of the Bank of Sweden.

Hammarskjöld worked in the Ministry of Social Welfare with his eldest brother Bo, and gained a reputation as an international financial negotiator for his part with the United Kingdom in the postwar economic reconstruction of Europe, for his reshaping of the United States–Swedish trade agreement, for his participation in the Marshall Plan, and through his leadership on the Executive Committee of the Organization for European Economic Cooperation. It is entirely logical that his introduction to the Swedish Ministry of Foreign Affairs was by way of becoming its financial adviser. From there he became the deputy foreign minister, with cabinet rank. In foreign affairs he followed a policy of international economic cooperation.

Hammarskjöld's initial role in the United Nations was as Sweden's delegate in 1949 and again from 1951 to 1953. Following more than two years of disagreement over a successor for Trygve Lie, Hammarskjöld was elected Secretary–General in 1953, receiving 57 votes out of 60. "Ironically," the *New York Times* (1961) observed, "the big powers had selected Mr. Hammarskjöld ... because they believed he would be content to be the efficient administrator and avoid a politically controversial role." But as he accepted the position, Hammarskjöld said he was not advocating a "passive role" for the Secretary–General, but an active one— "active as an instrument, a catalyst, an inspirer" (*New York Times*, April 2, 1953). In Snow's words, "He was a symbol of a longing for reason in world politics—a longing felt by masses of people in small

countries, and by many in great ones" (Snow 1967 p. 216).

His first major triumph came in 1955 when he made a dramatic flight to Beijing and succeeded in negotiations for the release of 15 US airmen from the People's Republic of China. But he also suffered defeats. In 1956 the United Nations did not succeed in getting representatives into Budapest after Soviet tanks crushed the Hungarian revolt. It was not for lack of typical Hammarskjöldian drive. He would work all day and into the night on occasions of stress. But after 10 UN resolutions and numerous personal efforts on Hammarskjöld's part, it became one of his disappointments that, in his own words, fell "in between the honesty of striving and the nullity of result."

During the next six years he was involved in struggles on three of the world's continents. He approached them through what he called "preventive diplomacy," and in doing so established more independence and effectiveness within the post of Secretary–General itself. In the Suez Canal crisis of 1956 he exercised his own personal brand of diplomacy with the nations involved, as well as working with many others in the UN. Hammarskjöld surprised many people by the force of his attack on Israel, the United Kingdom, and France for their invasion of Egypt following the seizure of the canal by Egypt's President Nasser. Under pressure from the United Nations and from the United States, they withdrew their forces. This was the first occasion of the use of the UN Emergency Force (UNEF)—indeed, the first international force mobilized by *any* international organization.

When Hammarskjöld accepted a second term he underscored his determination to maintain his office as an independent force and to act without political dictation from any state. Rolf Edberg, the Swedish Ambassador to Norway, who accepted the posthumous award to Dag Hammarskjöld, said of his compatriot, "[He] was much concerned with the awakening and fermenting continent which was to become his destiny. He once said that the next decade must belong to Africa or to the atom bomb. He firmly believed that the new countries have an important mission to fulfill in the community of nations ... Africa was to be the great test for the philosophy he wished to see brought to life through the United Nations."

In 1959 Hammarskjöld toured 21 African lands and came away impressed by the political maturity of many of the leaders he had met. He also came away convinced that financial and economic aid on a huge scale had to be found for those countries. It was on the occasion of the UN intervention in the Congo that he incurred the full force of Soviet attacks upon his leadership. With the decision of the Security Council, for the first time the UN used armed force to intervene actively in the solution of a problem involving the termination of colonial rule. Belgium was ordered to withdraw its troops from Congo territory, and the Secretary–General was authorized in consultation with the Congo government to provide whatever military aid might prove necessary until the country's own forces were in a position to carry out their functions. The UN force was to function as a noncombatant peace force; there was to be no intervention in disputes involving internal policy. This, however, did not meet the expectations of the Congo, which had visualized the UN forces expelling the Belgian troops. The UN assumption was that Belgium would comply with the order of the Security Council and withdraw her troops from the Congo. But this Belgium failed to do. While Hammarskjöld sought to attain Belgium's peaceful compliance with its promise to leave, the Congo leader, Patrice Lumumba, appealed to Khrushchev for Soviet aid. The Soviet campaign against Hammarskjöld peaked with the angry speech of Premier Khrushchev in the Assembly. He upbraided the Secretary–General for not having used military force in support of Lumumba, and demanded that Hammarskjöld be replaced by a three-member executive representing the Western, Soviet, and neutral camps. The Congo crisis had become entangled in the East–West conflict.

The Nobel Committee's Gunnar Jahn said of this occasion, "All that occurred cannot be given here; but an examination of the available documents covering this period will establish that it was the United Nations alone that worked to realize the establishment of the Republic of the Congo as an independent nation, and that the man who above all others deserves the credit for this is Dag Hammarskjöld."

Hammarskjöld himself answered Khrushchev's demand with the calm reply that he would remain in his job as long as "they wished"—referring to the small states and middle-ranking powers. And he added: "It is not Soviet Russia or any of the Great Powers that need the vigilance and protection of the UN; it is all the others." But he was not destined to live long enough to see the crisis brought to a conclusion. On September 18, 1961, he died in an airplane accident on the way to a meeting which he hoped would bring an end to the fighting in the Congo between the Katanga troops and the UN forces.

In his diary Hammarskjöld wrote, after he had been Secretary–General for a couple of years, "In our era, the road to holiness necessarily passes through the world of action." C. P. Snow (1967 p. 214) secularized Hammarskjöld's religious idiom: "The statement has a deep meaning for many twentieth century men. In our world, can a man feel even remotely reconciled to himself unless he has tried to do what little he can in action? That is a question which has required an answer of many of us; it is a part of the condition of modern men ... Hammarskjöld was speaking for our time: he knew it better than most."

Biography

Dag Hjalmar Agne Carl Hammarskjöld was born on July 29, 1905, in Jonkoping, Sweden, the youngest of four sons of Hjalmar L. and Agnes Almquist Hammarskjöld. He was descended from a family of statesmen and military men dating back to the Swedish knight, Peder Hammarskjöld, who was titled by Charles IX in 1610. His father was a famous jurist, a university professor, and during the First World War, Sweden's Prime Minister.

Hammarskjöld earned the Swedish equivalent of a B.A. and M.A. and a law degree from Uppsala University between 1925 and 1930. He held the post of secretary of the Swedish Government Committee on Unemployment 1930–34, for one year, 1933, concurrently with an associate professorship of political economics at the University of Stockholm, and the following year he received his degree of doctor of philosophy with a major in political economy from Uppsala. His thesis was titled *Konjunkturspridnisigen: en teoretisk och historisk undersokning* (A Theoretical and Historical Survey of Market Trends).

He served as undersecretary of the Department of Finance of the Swedish Government between 1936 and 1945. Concurrently, beginning in 1937, he joined the advisory board of the Swedish government as its counselor on the economic status and affairs of the country, holding this position until 1948. He was simultaneously chairman of the board of governors of the Bank of Sweden and member of the Board of Foreign Exchange from 1941 to 1948, having joined the latter in 1940.

Hammarskjöld was a delegate for the Swedish government in negotiations with the United States and the United Kingdom on the postwar economic reconstruction of Europe, the discussions lasting between 1944 and 1948. He entered the diplomatic service in 1946 as specialist in finance for the Swedish Foreign Office, during which time he explained the Swedish import bans to protesting US State Department officials. His ultimate base of argument was on favoring "a postwar necessity" and a "farsighted means of restoring the European economy."

Hammarskjöld participated in the organization meeting for the Marshall Plan in 1947, and served as his country's chief delegate to the Organization for European Economic

Cooperation (OEEC) in 1948 and as vice-chairman of its executive committee in 1948–49. He became Assistant Foreign Minister in 1949 and predicted in January 1950 that Sweden would surmount its postwar economic deficit "in two years" and become sufficiently solvent to aid neighboring countries. He became Deputy Foreign Minister and a member of the Swedish Cabinet in 1951, and chairman of an organization comprising Scandinavian countries and the United Kingdom with the purpose of promoting economic cooperation between these countries (UNISCAN) in 1950.

Hammarskjöld began his distinguished service in the UN as Sweden's delegate in 1949 and 1951–53. He became vice-chairman of the Swedish delegation to the UN General Assembly in 1953, and the next year he headed the delegation. In April 1953 he was elected Secretary–General of the UN by a vote of 57 of the 60 member states of the General Assembly. He stated that he was not advocating a "passive role" for the Secretary–General, but an active one "as an instrument, a catalyst, and an inspirer." He was as good as his word, personally negotiating the release of US soldiers captured by the Chinese in the Korean War, and actively seeking resolution to problems of the Middle East throughout his stay in office, including the Suez Canal crisis of 1956 during which the UN's Emergency Force (UNEF) was first commissioned and used.

With his second term, which began in 1958, he expressed keen interest in Africa, touring 21 African lands in 1959. With the eruption of the crisis in the Congo, an open break between the East and West seemed imminent as the Soviet Union castigated Hammarskjöld for failing to use the United Nations Emergency Force to expel Belgian troops, while Hammarskjöld sought to attain Belgium's peaceful compliance with its promise to leave. The Soviet Union demanded his resignation in favor of a tripartite leadership divided between East, West, and a neutral country. Hammarskjöld replied that it was not the Soviet Union, nor any of the Great Powers, which stood in need of the protection of the UN, but the smaller nations, and he would stay in his job as long as the small states and middle-ranking powers wished.

On September 17, 1961, Dag Hammarskjöld was killed in an airplane accident on the way to a meeting between the Katanga troops and the UN forces which he hoped would bring an end to the fighting in the Congo. Among his collected papers of autobiographical and introspective comments there were many references to death. In one of these he said, "The only value of a life is its content—*for others.* . . . Therefore, how incredibly great is what I have been given, and how meaningless what I have to 'sacrifice.'"

Bibliography

Hammarskjöld D 1964 *Markings*. Faber and Faber, London/ Knopf, New York
New York Times 1961 Hammarskjöld greatly extended UN's scope through leadership and personal initiatives. September 19
Snow C P 1967 Dag Hammarskjöld. *Variety of Men*. Charles Scribner's Sons, New York, pp. 201–23

RUTH C. REYNOLDS

Linus Pauling

(1962)

The award of the 1962 Nobel Peace Prize to Linus Pauling was in recognition that, with the opening of the atomic age, scientists had become a vital force in humankind's struggle to achieve a peaceful existence. "It is Linus Pauling's highly ethical attitude to life— the deepest driving force within him— that drew him into the fight against nuclear weapons," the Nobel Committee said, and continued, "Through his campaigning he has manifested the ethical responsibility that science, in his opinion, bears for the fate of mankind, today and in the future . . ."

Born in 1901, the young Linus showed early signs of his intellectual gifts. It sent his father inquiring about some appropriate titles for a nine-year-old boy. "He has read all the books in sight," the bewildered parent wrote to the editor of the *Portland Oregonian*. "All the books in sight" included his father's *United States Pharacopeia* and the *Dispensatory of the United States of America*.

The following year Pauling's father died. A retired neighbor befriended the young boy and acted as a guiding spirit to a young mind bursting beyond the ordinary boundaries of boyhood. Under his neighbor's warm and watchful interest, Pauling learned Greek to supplement his Latin, and also to speak German fairly well. He delighted in independent pursuits like learning chess from the *Encyclopaedia Britannica*. But his greatest joy centered on the makeshift laboratory his elderly friend provided out of discarded equipment from a nearby dental college. There Pauling indulged an early love for science.

As he grew into adolescence, Pauling's mind never fitted into conventional molds. Taking all the mathematics and science he could in his first three-and-a-half years of high school, he left without a diploma owing to a misunderstanding regarding graduation requirements, and the following fall, at 16, he entered Oregon State College. There his education continued, individualistic in style, formidable in scope. The possibility of understanding chemical activity as a submolecular process excited Pauling. Years later he looked back upon that period and wrote, "I was simply entranced by chemical phenomena, by the reactions in which substances disappear, and other substances, often with strikingly different properties, appear, and I hoped to learn more and more about this aspect of the world. It has turned out, in fact, that I have worked on this problem year after year, throughout my life."

Oregon State College gave up any thought of guiding the explosions of his mind, allowing him to take whatever courses he wished when he chose to. He was given the run of the laboratories for experiments he devised to test the validity of what he read.

The First World War had created a shortage of teachers, and in his senior year Pauling was assigned to teach the freshman chemistry class to women undergraduates. The event proved fateful for Pauling, not principally for its demonstration of his extraordinary ability, but because of his ablest student, Ava Helen Miller. Beautiful and bright, she entered his life, and soon his heart, and in just six weeks after their first meeting they were engaged. During his first year at graduate school she became his wife and thereafter his cherished partner until her death in 1981.

Following Pauling's Ph.D. *summa cum laude* at the California Institute of Technology (CIT) he studied on a Guggenheim Fellowship in Europe, where he extended his knowledge in the field of physics, fascinated with the new theory of quantum mechanics. At 26, Pauling became the youngest member on the CIT faculty. He discovered a great joy in teaching young students eager to learn. In later years, as he became a world-renowned professor, Pauling never lost this delight and continued always to teach a course in freshman chemistry.

During these early years of research his first interest was in physical chemistry. The perception and insight that would result in his classic essay *The Nature of the Chemical Bond* came to Pauling in one of those extraordinary intellectual leaps characteristic of his style. "I worked at my desk nearly all that night," Pauling recalled, "I was so full of excitement I could hardly write." In 1954 he earned the Nobel Prize in Chemistry for his "research into the nature of the chemical bond and its application to the elucidation of the structure of complex substances."

Pauling's formal studies had been centered on inorganic chemistry, but true to his individualistic style, when organic chemistry and biology came into his area of interest he set about mastering them. He

acquired an encyclopedic breadth of information on proteins. With insatiable curiosity he investigated amino acids present in hemoglobin. This led him to blood cell abnormalities and his discovery that sickle-cell anemia is a hemoglobinopathy. He pioneered in the relationship between molecular abnormality and heredity, the chemical basis of mental retardation, and the mechanism of anesthesia. With their critical implications to medicine, this research brought Pauling honors from a new field: the Thomas Addis medal from the American Nephrosis Society, the John Phillips Medal for Contributions to Internal Medicine, the Rudolf Virchow Medal for Medical Research, and the Modern Medicine Award for 1963.

Pauling became a scientist of world renown. William Stuckey called Pauling an "almost extraterrestrially brilliant scientific prophet . . . who gave the 20th century its ruling theory on how elements bond themselves into molecules, paved the way for the discovery of the form and function of DNA, ... revealed the distortion in hemoglobin that gives sickle-cell anemia its name." Professor Jonathon Singer, a member of the National Academy of Sciences, and creator of the most accurate chemical picture of a cell membrane, remarked, "He was the most brilliant man I ever met . . . The forty years of Pauling contributions to chemistry and medicine make up perhaps the single most profound and enlightening body of research an American, perhaps *anyone*, ever put together." The British journal *New Scientist* in 1978 ranked him with Newton, Madame Curie, and Einstein in a list of the 20 most important scientists of all time. His honors include more than 40 national and international awards and medals, and 40 honorary degrees, including the prestigious MA from Oxford.

But as the Second World War raged through its tragic five years, it was bringing Pauling ever closer to the event that would draw him from his beloved world of molecules, atoms, and subatomic particles. During that war Pauling worked on rocket fuels for the navy and developed a powder that could shoot a rocket off at high speed. Learning of an urgent need for an oxygen meter in submarines and airplanes, in one week he designed, constructed, and delivered an instrument that would warn crews when the oxygen content was dropping to the danger level. (This is still being used by doctors to measure the oxygen content of the blood during anesthesia.) With his associate, Daniel Campbell, Pauling made a synthetic plasma to replace blood. These services brought him the Presidential Medal for Merit.

With the dropping of the two atomic bombs at the war's end, suddenly science and politics formed a totally different kind of bond for Pauling to ponder. It was to change his life forever. Catalysts to his reaction were Albert Einstein and Ava Helen Pauling. Einstein said, "The atomic bomb has altered profoundly the nature of the world as we know it, and the human race consequently finds itself in a new habitat to which it must adopt its thinking . . . There is no defense in science against the weapon which can destroy civilization. Our defense is in law and order . . ." Ava Helen Pauling put it more succinctly: "What good will science do if the world is destroyed, Linus?" she asked.

Pauling determined to fit himself for the role of a responsible scientist–citizen. As he had once independently studied the fields of biology and medicine, he now turned his attention to international affairs. "I estimate that my independent studies in the field of international affairs are equivalent to several years of full time work," he once replied to a reporter who asked why he presumed to opinions in that field when Secretary of State Rusk did not attempt comments in biochemistry or nuclear physics.

In 1946, at Einstein's request, Pauling joined six other scientists in the Emergency Committee of Atomic Scientists. Their purpose was to inform the public of what they, as scientists, knew about the new atomic age and the unprecedented dangers it posed for humankind.

In company with Ava Helen, Pauling went on hundreds of lecture tours. "Nobel had wanted to invent a substance or a machine with such terrible power of mass destruction that war would thereby be made impossible forever," Pauling told his audiences. Nobel's wish now appeared as prophecy fulfilled. "The energy released in the explosion of this bomb was greater than that of all the explosives used in all of the wars that have taken place during the entire history of the world, including the First and Second World Wars," he said.

Now that war had seemingly been rendered impossible, Pauling was working toward a world he described as "in metamorphosis from its primitive period of history, when disputes between nations were settled by war, to its period of maturity, in which war will be abolished and world law will take its place." But the hope humankind had cherished of an age of peace that would follow the war gave way to a "balance of terror" in which an escalating armaments race became the guardian of peace.

Pauling threw all his energies against the development of more terrible weapons. His aim was above all to prevent the hydrogen bomb, and he sought to do this by educating his fellow citizens about its capacity for catastrophe. "This bomb," he declared, "may have a destructive effect, a hundred, a thousand, nay ten thousand times greater than that of the bombs dropped on Hiroshima and Nagasaki." He made this warning as early as 1947, and subsequent tests with the hydrogen bomb proved the validity of his predictions.

"It is not necessary," he said, "that the social and economic systems in Russia be identical with that in the United States in order that these two great nations can be at peace with one another." The only essential requirements are mutual respect and mutual recognition that "war has finally ruled itself out as arbiter of the destiny of humanity." He wrote to both the US and the Soviet governments, throwing his prestigious weight against development of the hydrogen bomb. But the arms race had created an atmosphere that deafened the ears of the public and the centers of political power alike. It began to threaten freedom of speech, and Pauling's passport was revoked.

Both the United States and the Soviet Union created and tested hydrogen bombs, the United States in 1952, and the Soviet Union in 1953. "There does not seem to be any theoretical limit to the size of these weapons," Pauling observed, and he and Mrs. Pauling continued with their tireless crusade of education.

In July 1955 Pauling was one of the 10 signatories to the Russell–Einstein Manifesto. The Mainau Declaration, also of July 1955, included 52 Nobel Prize winners among its signatories, most of whom were scientists. Presenting themselves as scientists of different countries, different creeds, and different political persuasions, they said it was with horror that they watched science giving humankind the means to destroy itself. Acknowledging that on a temporary basis the balance of mutual fear was now acting as a deterrent, they dismissed as a dangerous delusion any hope for a permanent sense of safety within such a system. "All nations must come to the decision to renounce force as a final resort of policy. If they are not prepared to do this, they will cease to exist," the declaration read.

Pauling's knowledge of genetics provided authenticity to his estimates of the frightening toll of leukemia and bone cancer among the living children, and of the malformations possible in children yet unborn, with each atmospheric bomb test carried out.

Albert Schweitzer issued a Declaration of Conscience in Oslo on April 24, 1957. The following month Pauling wrote the Scientists Bomb-Test Appeal, which within a few months was signed by 11,021 scientists from 49 countries. The Paulings presented the Appeal to Dag Hammarskjöld, Secretary-General of the United Nations, declaring that it represented the feelings of the great majority of the scientists of the world. But the paranoia gripping the country seemed to block reception of unwelcome information. The Senate Internal Security Committee appeared able only to fear the hand of communists behind his estimated statistics. Under the threat of contempt of Congress they demanded to know who helped gather the signatures. Pauling, perceiving the vilification he himself was receiving, feared a like danger to those who had helped him and refused to answer. He openly and willingly answered all other questions. He reiterated what anyone who had known him had long ago observed: Pauling was not a man to be bound by doctrinaires and counterdoctrinaires. "Nobody tells me what to think," he said, and freely denied having ever been a communist. Senators Dodd and McCarthy had on this occasion overstepped even the bounds granted them by the paranoic fears gripping the country, and the Senate Committee dropped the proceedings.

October 10, 1963, the day of Pauling's 1962 Nobel award deferred from the previous year—an award he declared Ava Helen Pauling shared—was a time of double celebration. With a stroke of timing exquisitely tinged with justice, the Limited Test Ban Treaty became effective on the same day. It presented a powerful rebuttal to the strange reception Pauling's own country rendered the award. For the first time ever the US ambassador did not attend the December ceremony of a US Nobel Prize winner. The press stood divided: "A Weird Insult from Norway," headlined *Life* magazine, while the prestigious *Bulletin of Atomic Scientists* editorialized to its small but informed readership its pleasure, "as fellow Americans, that the Norwegian Parliament has now given this special recognition to his role as scientist–citizen." Pauling gave a calm reception to criticism. "New views have always been greeted as heretic,"he once reminded a reporter.

Characteristically, Pauling recommends seeking information. "We must have research for peace," he contends in his book *No More War!* "It would embrace the outstanding problems of morality. The time has come for man's intellect, his scientific method, to win over the immoral brutality and irrationality of war and militarism.... Now we are forced to eliminate from the world forever this vestige of prehistoric barbarism, this curse to the human race."

Pauling still divides his time between his scientific pursuits and peace. Much of his research is in maximizing human health. But in his work for peace he battles the greatest health hazard of all.

At his Nobel award ceremony the Committee Chairman paid tribute to Pauling's legacy to humankind: "Should he, through his tireless efforts, have contributed—if only a little—to restoring to science its ideals, then Linus Pauling's campaign will in itself have been of such value that we living today cannot even appreciate the full extent of the debt we owe him."

Biography

Linus Carl Pauling was born in 1901 in Portland, Oregon, son of Herman William Pauling, a pharmacist, and Lucy Isabelle Darling Pauling. After primary and secondary schools in Condon and Portland, he attended Oregon Agriculture College (now Oregon State University). Receiving a BS in chemical engineering in 1922, he then went to California Institute of Technology (CIT), where he studied chemistry, physics, and mathematics, taking a Ph.D. *summa cum laude* in 1925. He married Ava Helen Miller in 1923. Following his doctorate he went to Europe on a Guggenheim Fellowship to study quantum physics. In 1927 he returned to CIT, where he became the youngest member on the faculty. During the 1930s and 1940s his development leading to his classic work, *The Nature of the Chemical Bond,* was responsible for the valence-bond theory's dominance of chemistry.

Pauling's interest in, and mastery of, biological sciences led to study of the hemoglobin molecule, and from there to an encyclopedic knowledge of proteins. His interest was attracted to serology through Karl Landsteiner, the discoverer of blood types. First he worked on problems of immunology, but shifted his attention during the Second World War to practical applications, which resulted in his finding an artificial substitute for blood serum. He went on to invent an oxygen detector, first used for military application, but eventually a permanent tool for anesthesiologists. He also developed a powder that could shoot a rocket off at high speed, and for these services he was awarded the Presidential Medal of Merit.

After the war Pauling became interested in sickle cell anemia, and he discovered that hemoglobinopathy was caused by a single amino-acid anomaly in one of the polypeptide chains. While at Oxford as a guest professor in 1948, he discovered the alpha helix.

In 1954 he received the Nobel Prize for Chemistry for his research into the nature of the chemical bond and its applications to the elucidation of the structure of complex substances.

With the coming of the atomic age, and the resulting arms race, Pauling became increasingly disturbed about the fallout resulting from nuclear bomb testing. In 1958 Ava Helen and Linus Pauling organized an anti-bomb-test petition signed by over 11,000 scientists around the world, and they presented this to Dag Hammarskjold, Secretary-General of the United Nations. Pauling was then called before the Senate Internal Security Commission to account for the signatures collected. He willingly answered all questions regarding himself, but refused to divulge the names of others involved.

Also in 1958, the first edition of his book *No More War!* was published. He and his wife gave hundreds of lectures, wrote papers and letters, and attended conferences to strengthen the peace movement over the world. For this activity Pauling was awarded the deferred 1962 Nobel Peace Prize on October 10, 1963, the same day as the Limited Test Ban Treaty between the United States and the Soviet Union entered into force.

Pauling left CIT to go to the Center for Study of Democratic Institutions, where he continued his double activities in science and peace. In the former discipline his close-packed spheron theory provided an explanation of nuclear properties, including asymmetric fission.

In 1967 Pauling became research professor of chemistry at the University of California in San Diego, where he researched the molecular basis of memory and published a paper on orthomolecular psychiatry. He spent the early 1970s at Stanford University, and in 1973 founded the Linus Pauling Institute in Palo Alto. Pauling's interest has since centered on nutrition, and particularly vitamin C. In 1970 he published the controversial *Vitamin C and the Common Cold*, and with Ewan Cameron, *Cancer and Vitamin C*. He has published over 500 scientific papers on molecules, hemoglobin, protein, immunology, anesthesiology, sickle cell anemia, and human nutrition.

His honors include more than 40 national and international awards and medals, and 40 honorary degrees (including a diploma from his high school and an M.A. from Oxford).

Dr. and Mrs. Pauling's four children are Linus, Jr., a psychiatrist practicing in Hawaii, Peter, a chemist at the University of London, Linda, a graduate of Reed College, who is married to Barclay Kamb, professor of geophysics at the California Institute of Technology, and Crellin, a biochemist and geneticist at the University of California at Riverside.

Acknowledgment: The author thanks Dr. Robert Paradowski, of the Rochester Institute of Technology, from whose biography of Dr. Pauling appearing in *No More War!* much material was drawn.

Bibliography

Bendiner E 1983 The passions and perils of Pauling. *Hospital Practice* 18(4): 1–12

Bulletin of Atomic Scientists 1963 The Pauling Prize: A welcome honor from Norway. 19 (December): 18

Life 1963 A weird insult from Norway. 55 (October 25): 4

Pauling L 1963 Pauling's position [letter]. *Harpers* 227 (October): 6

Pauling L 1983 *No More War!* Dodd, Mead, New York

Stuckey W 1976 Plain Harold and Linus superstar. *Science Digest* August, pp. 25–35

Wasowicz L 1985 Linus Pauling: America's brilliant scientific maverick still fighting the establishment. *Ames Daily Tribune Weekender Edition* January 19, p. B9

RUTH C. REYNOLDS

Red Cross

(1963)

see *Henri Dunant and the Red Cross*
(*1901*)   (*1917, 1944, 1963*)

Martin Luther King, Jr.

(1964)

In 1964 the Nobel Peace Prize was awarded to the American civil rights leader, the Reverend Martin Luther King, Jr. King called the award "a recognition of nonviolence as the answer to the crucial political and moral question of our time—the need for man to overcome oppression and violence without resorting to violence and oppression." He asked to share it with "those devotees of nonviolence who have moved so courageously against the ramparts of racial injustice ... the real heroes of the freedom struggle, they are the noble people for whom I accept the Nobel Peace Prize."

King had read correctly the Nobel Committee's thinking. "It was not because he led a racial minority in their struggle for equality that Martin Luther King achieved fame," Chairman Jahn said in presenting the award ... "King's name will endure for the way in which he has waged his struggle." Jahn observed that "Martin Luther King is the first person in the Western world to have shown us that a struggle can be waged without violence."

Martin Luther King, Jr. spent his youth in the Southern United States, the son of a Baptist minister. His father's efforts to shield his children from the humiliations of racial discrimination could not fully protect them from the community's relentless lessons in inequality. They left an indelible mark on the young Martin King.

King studied for the ministry in the North, where discrimination still existed in social practices but was not sanctioned by law, nor as pervasive as in the South. While studying at Boston he met and married Coretta Scott, a talented young music student from Alabama. After he took his doctorate degree in divinity at Boston University in 1955, the young couple returned to Montgomery, where King served as minister at the Dexter Avenue Baptist Church. They found their black community in sharp division over the issue of human rights: some cloaked their feelings in apathy; some were fearful of the personal consequences of speaking out. Even the clergy was divided, as some ministers felt their pastoral duties lay outside secular movements. In 1955, after the failure of an attempt to unite the blacks, King said, "The tragic division in the Negro community could be cured only by some divine miracle."

Later that year "the divine miracle" began with Rosa Parks, an exhausted black woman who refused to give up her seat to a white male on an Alabama bus. Her subsequent arrest sparked the unifying protest that had been lacking. A bus boycott was started. King was elected chairman of the organization which was forming to conduct the boycott. He recalls in his book, *Stride for Freedom*, his reluctance to accept. He was beginning to question the moral rectitude of conducting a boycott when he recalled a line in Thoreau's essay *Civil Disobedience*: "We can no longer lend our cooperation to an evil system." Thoreau's words answered King's inner doubts.

King also entertained a practical doubt that the people would unite behind a boycott. The next morning when he looked out of his window and saw buses absolutely empty of Negro passengers, this doubt, too, was answered. This was the beginning of a civil rights movement that was to sweep the South.

The young King (he was 26 at the time) led a boycott lasting 382 days when no blacks used the buses in Montgomery. They carpooled or walked, some as many as 12 miles a day. One black woman summarized why such a grueling regime could be followed by so many for so long: "My feets is tired," she said, "but my soul is rested" (quoted in Lipsky 1966 p. 199).

The boycott brought the first victory in civil rights for the black community. But King knew that freedom was something they would have to earn over and over again. His own life was changed: he became not only minister to the Baptist church in Alabama, but a moral leader whose pulpit expanded over the Western world. Between 1957 and 1968 King traveled over six million miles and gave over 2,500 lectures and speeches; during this time he wrote five books and numerous articles. He led the massive protest in Birmingham, Alabama, as the world gazed on through television screens or read accounts in graphically illustrated papers. The result King called "a coalition of conscience" and he wrote his inspiring manifesto *Letter from a Birmingham Jail*. He planned drives for voter registrations, and directed the nonviolent march to Washington, DC, where he delivered a masterful address, *I Have a Dream*. He talked with President Kennedy and campaigned for President Johnson. He was awarded honorary degrees, and named Man of the Year by *Time* magazine in 1963.

All this was accomplished in the midst of 20 arrests, at least four assaults, uncounted insults and threats to his life, and the personal grief he felt with the suffering of his people. It is a measure of the man that he did not dwell on this brutality and humiliation in his Nobel lecture; he spoke of it only in illustrating the practice of nonviolence, commending his people for "taking suffering upon themselves instead of inflicting it on others."

Instead he addressed in his lecture the larger problems facing humankind worldwide; problems rooted, he said, in our "poverty of spirit which stands in glaring contrast to our scientific abundance." On this occasion King proved himself a leader not just of a section of humankind in the United States, but of humankind everywhere.

"This problem of spiritual and moral lag, which constitutes modern man's chief dilemma, expresses itself in three larger problems which grow out of man's ethical infantilism," King said. "Each of these problems, while appearing to be separate and isolated, is inextricably bound to the other. I refer to racial injustice, poverty and war."

American racial injustice he saw as only one manifestation of a wider, global problem. We are leaving colonialism behind, he said. Likewise the specter of poverty must be abolished: ". . . if man is to redeem his spiritual and moral lag, he must go all out to bridge the social and economic gulf between the haves and the have nots of the world . . . There is nothing new about poverty. What is new is that we have the resources to get rid of it."

King said that man's proneness to war is still a fact. "Wisdom born of experience should tell us that war is obsolete . . . but we shall not have the will, the courage and the insight to deal with such matters . . . unless we are prepared to undergo a mental and spiritual reevaluation . . . ," he warned.

Martin Luther King was assassinated in his thirty-ninth year as he was preparing to lead a peaceful protest march in sympathy with the garbage workers in Memphis, Tennessee. He left behind a legacy which merges with that of Gandhi. "Gandhi," he once said, "was probably the first person in history to lift the love of Jesus above mere interaction between individuals to a powerful and effective social force."

Biography

Martin Luther King, Jr. was born in Atlanta, Georgia, on January 15, 1929, the son of a Baptist minister. His primary and secondary schooling took place in Atlanta, where he learned bitter lessons about inequality as did all black children.

He studied for the ministry at Crozer Theological Seminary, where he won the Plafker Award as the outstanding student and the J. Lewis Crozer Fellowship for graduate studies. One of six Negroes in a class of 100, King was elected president of the class. He took his B.D. in 1951 and continued his studies at Harvard in 1952–53 and at Boston University where he took a Ph.D. in the field of systematic theology in 1955. During his studies King became deeply influenced by India's Gandhi. He once said that from his Christian background he gained his ideals, and from Gandhi his operational techniques.

During this time he met and married Coretta Scott, a music student studying in Boston. In 1954 they returned to Montgomery where he took a post as pastor while finishing his doctoral dissertation. King observed with regret that the black community seemed hopelessly divided on issues of human rights, many seemingly ground to an apparent helplessness by continual and brutal oppression.

All this changed when a tired black woman, Rosa Parks, refused to relinquish her seat to a white man on a Mont-

gomery bus. Her arrest ignited a vital spark in the black community, and united, they arose to the occasion with a 382-day boycott of Montgomery buses. King accepted leadership of the Montgomery Improvement Association, the organization administering the boycott.

King's deep Gandhian convictions on the efficacy of nonviolence met and passed severe tests as his home was bombed and he and the community were harassed. Out of the victory of the boycott there grew a resistance movement throughout the South which coalesced in the Southern Christian Leadership Conference in 1957. King became its president. His pastorate was expanded over the entire South, and his voice heard over the world as he traveled nearly 800,000 miles and made 208 speeches that year.

King inspired nonviolent civil disobedience, and he led protest marches before the eyes of the world via television and wide media coverage as the marchers were set upon by dogs, water hoses, and arresting police. From his own arrest and incarceration following the Birmingham March came King's classic statement on the struggle for civil rights, *Letter from a Birmingham Jail*.

The march on Washington in behalf of the civil rights bill pending in the US Congress was followed by a partial victory in Congress of a bill King described as going far toward solving problems, but "not far enough." This march will be forever commemorated by King's famous "I Have a Dream" speech.

By 1964 when King's endorsement supported the election of President Johnson, many honors had come to him: He had received honorary doctorate degrees from Chicago Theological Seminary, Morgan State College, Central State College, Boston University, Howard University, Lincoln University, University of Bridgeport, Bard College, Keuka College, Springfield College, Wesleyan University, Yale University, and the Jewish Theological Seminary. He had been honored by Willy Brandt, by Lutheran Bishop Dibelius, and by an audience with Pope Paul VI.

King led a massive voter registration effort, and he continued to lead protest marches. His assassination on April 4, 1968, was on the eve of just such a march scheduled to take place in Memphis, Tennessee.

Martin Luther King, Jr. left four children, a grieving widow, and a world deprived of a vitally needed leader.

Bibliography

King M Jr. 1965 Toward brighter tomorrows. *Ebony* 20 (March): 34–47

Lipsky M 1966 *The Quest for Peace*. Barnes and Co., South Brunswick

RUTH C. REYNOLDS

United Nations Children's Fund (UNICEF)
(1965)

The Nobel Peace Prize for 1965 was awarded to the United Nations Children's Fund (UNICEF) in recognition of its promotion of community among nations. UNICEF's Zena Harman, chairwoman of its executive board, said she thought Alfred Nobel would have approved of the choice of this award. She asserted that today's children are a central factor in the strategy for peace and survival.

The accomplishments of UNICEF over the two decades preceding its award earned it a worldwide acceptance of the Nobel Committee's decision. But its initial acceptance was far from unquestioned. Originally UNICEF was envisaged as purely a temporary measure to solve the postwar crises facing Europe's many helpless children. Nobel Committee Chairwoman Lionaes recalled her experiences as a Norwegian delegate to the UN where many delegates maintained that the UN, as a political forum, was not justified in dealing with such a "minor" peripheral problem as aid to children. "It was a blessing for UNICEF and the millions of children it took to its heart from that very first day of its existence that it had a leader like Mr. Maurice Pate," she said. Pate served from its founding in 1946 until his death in 1965. "He was UNICEF's never slumbering conscience," Lionaes recalled, " . . . he never allowed formalities to impede him in his work . . . he recruited his fellow-workers from among those who were prepared uncompromisingly to pursue the policy of compassion."

When UNICEF tackled its first assignment of aiding the children of war-torn Europe it found children in that bitter winter of 1947 undernourished, ill, many homeless, and clothed only in rags. UNICEF calculated the number of such children at 20 million and mounted an unprecedented relief campaign, furnishing six million children and mothers with a meal a day.

As the economic reconstruction of Europe proceeded, within four or five years its countries were able to resume care of their own children. But it quickly became apparent that there were millions of children in the newly developing countries of Asia, Africa, and Latin America who were sick, starving, and dying. Harman described their plight: "abandoned in the backwash of history, left behind in the surge of time." By 1950 these helpless victims had forced the UN General Assembly to the recognition

that UNICEF could no longer be considered an emergency measure; it would be a permanent necessity for many decades.

The task facing UNICEF was overwhelming. Priorities had to be established. Malnutrition reigned over much of these countries; in its wake diseases such as malaria, trachoma, tuberculosis, and yaws carried off the weakened children. Ignorance threatened to lock future generations of children in the same tragic cycle unless an educated generation were created to free them. Although need has always been in sad excess over the means to meet it, with the help of the World Health Organization (WHO), the Food and Agriculture Organization (FAO) and the United Nations Educational, Scientific, and Cultural Organization (UNESCO), UNICEF began a patient, ongoing, dedicated inroad into these problems. But even these combined UN organizations could never have done this work on their own, nor would it have been appropriate for them to try to do so. They worked in countries whose governments solicited their aid, making contributions not less than that of UNICEF itself. While the aid given usually consisted of technical assistance, goods, and equipment which had to be purchased with foreign currency, the receiving country made its contribution in the form of its own products, local personnel, transport services, or however it could. The interest generated by UNICEF's program for children became so great that the contribution of governments comprised two and one-half dollars for every UNICEF dollar. Thus the very aid itself acted as a successful spur to self-help.

Long-range projects were launched for encouraging the production of foodstuffs rich in protein by creating dairies, and building factories to produce dried milk, by building industries to process fishmeal, all in preparation for the time when regions could take over the balanced feeding of their own children.

Indonesia exemplifies UNICEF's successful eradication of a painful and widely spread disease. Yaws attacked an estimated ten million throughout that land when it gained independence in 1950. Together with the World Health Organization, UNICEF succeeded in liberating whole villages from this scourge; and Harman stated with confidence that in a few years' time the eradication of yaws would be complete in Indonesia.

Harman related an example in Mexico where UNICEF together with other organizations in the UN helped the people to help themselves; they called on 2,800 men who, on foot, on horseback, and in motorboats, traversed the length and breadth of the country disinfecting three million houses with DDT in the course of 1960 alone. Not a single death due to malaria was reported that year. Agricultural production also rose.

In 1961 an important shift in policy occurred. It became apparent that despite all the assistance UNICEF and other UN organizations had provided, the statistical need kept apace, indeed leapt ahead. For due to the resulting rise in population growth, without solutions made at the base root of problems, real achievement would continue to elude them.

A growing interest in developing countries for intelligent planning in their economies reflected their grasp of the problem. "And yet," Harman reflected in her Nobel lecture, "maybe these words of Nehru contain a dangerous truth: 'In one way or another in all our thinking on development plans for factory plant and machinery, we lose sight of the fact that, in the last resort, development depends on the human factor.' It is this fundamental viewpoint that prompts UNICEF's efforts to ensure that the interests of the children are safeguarded in the development plans now being drawn up." These plans included both the education of the children themselves and the education of the adults in local training programs.

"UNICEF aid comes marvelously alive in the field," Executive Director H. Labouisse said, "when you see a whole pilot region raising its standards simultaneously in education, nutrition, sanitation and health, with everyone lending a hand, from the local teachers and doctors to the poorest families of the jungle villages." Labouisse outlined the broad plans for use of the Nobel Prize. UNICEF would establish a fund for the training of personnel in fields serving children in the developing countries. It hoped to train specialists, leaders for the future.

The statistics representing the first 25 years of UNICEF activity are impressive: 71 million children were examined for trachoma and 43 million were treated; 425 million were examined for yaws and 23 million were treated; 400 million were vaccinated against tuberculosis; countless millions were protected from malaria, and 415,000 were discharged as cured of leprosy. Supplementary materials and articles of clothing have been dispensed in billions—quite apart from emergency aid to hundreds of thousands of victims of floods, earthquakes, and other natural disasters.

In the training program, 12,000 health centers and several thousand maternity wards have been established in 85 countries; help has been given for providing equipment for 25,000 teacher-training schools, 56,000 primary and secondary schools, 965 vocational schools, 31 schools for training vocational instructors, 600 schools for training dietary personnel; equipment has been supplied for 4,000 nutrition centers and community gardens, and for 9,000 school gardens and canteens.

Nobel Chairwoman Lionaes told the award audience that in the long-term view no economic development is possible unless the growth of a healthy and enlightened generation of children is given priority in the plans for development. "Today the people of the developing countries are fully alive to their own misery; and they are determined to leave it behind," she said. "They contemplate the riches of the West—our surplus food, our fantastic technology, the health . . . all our material well-being—they compare this with the misery of their own children. This contrast creates a dangerous tension-factor, which threatens the peace of the world.

"The aim of UNICEF is to spread a table, decked with all the good things that Nature provides, for all the children of the world. For this reason the organization is a peace-factor of great importance."

History

UNICEF was established by the United Nations General Assembly on December 11, 1946, as an emergency measure for rendering aid to postwar children following the Second World War, and it originally used the phrase "Emergency Funds" in its title. Its first aid went principally to war-torn Europe, providing food, clothing, and health care for children. It clothed five million children, vaccinated eight million against tuberculosis, rebuilt food facilities, and fed millions of children.

In 1951 UNICEF was recognized as a permanent organization and dropped the "Emergency" from both name and plans for the future, dedicating itself to long-range projects eradicating disease, educating and assisting local peoples to achieve as much of this as possible. It equipped for, and educated in, the agricultural techniques for production of high protein foods.

By 1961 a firm connection had been established between the welfare of a nation, the chances for diminished tensions between nations, and the care given to children. The necessity was recognized for a generation of well-fed, well-educated children before historical bondage to the past could be broken and replaced with planning for a successful future. UNICEF accordingly increased its education and training programs.

Although the achievements of UNICEF, cooperating with other UN agencies, were impressive up to 1965, with disease diminished, malnutrition reduced, and education programs begun, the needs of millions of children continued to far outpace the means for addressing them. This was especially painful in the face of unlimited sums spent on weaponry worldwide.

Bibliography

Life 1965 Nobel Peace Prize for the Love of Children. pp. 30–36
The New Yorker 1965 The Peace Prize. November 6, pp. 44–47

RUTH C. REYNOLDS

Prize Not Awarded
(1966–67)

René Cassin
(1968)

The 1968 Nobel Peace Prize was awarded to the distinguished French jurist, René Cassin, principal author of the UN *Declaration of the Rights of Man*, in recognition of his "respect for human worth, irrespective of nationality, race, religion, sex or social position . . . for his contribution to the protection of the rights of man, as set forth in the Universal Declaration of Human Rights."

After receiving a doctorate degree in juridical, economic, and political sciences, Cassin had just begun a career as counsel in Paris when with the outbreak of the First World War he was mobilized into the infantry. This proved a turning point in his life. He sustained an abdominal wound which hampered him for the rest of his life, and which deepened his horror of war. "That war put its indelible and unmistakable stamp on me," he said in his Nobel lecture. It was not the battlefield experience, nor the suffering that followed, which so marked him. "It was the agonized perception of the lasting and wasteful consequences of war," he said.

It was characteristic of the innate fairness of this eminent jurist that he not only insisted upon compensatory aid to those wounded in the war, but that he also provided for their human dignity, designing the program to include the tools the wounded would need for their reentry into the mainstream of society —artificial limb banks, professional retraining programs, and loans for establishing small businesses.

For France's youngest war victims, the 800,000 orphans, Cassin saw to it that the nation stepped into the place of the lost parents, and these children were brought up and educated under the special protection of their country.

Cassin was not content with providing aid after the war's end. He wished to honor those sacrifices made in that long and terrible struggle that had promised to be "the war to end war." He organized the International Confederation of Disabled Veterans [Conférence Internationale des Associations des Multilés et d'Anciens Combattants (CIAMAC)] to enable veterans to participate in the creation of an international climate that would sustain peace. From 1925 to 1939 these disabled men—ally and adversary alike—joined together to fight for peace through increased communication, understanding, and disarmament. They worked together until violence and Fascism enveloped Hitler's Germany, and the invasion of Poland cut off all hope of salvaging peace.

In the Second World War which followed, when France fell before the German onslaught, Cassin was the first civilian to join General de Gaulle's Free French government administered from London. He was appointed Secretary of the Council of Defense which laid the groundwork for the military endeavors of the Free French, and Commissioner for Justice and Public Education in the General's provisional government. He drafted all of the legal texts of his incipient government and conducted difficult negotiations with the British authorities regarding the legal status of the Free French, which culminated in the Churchill–de Gaulle accord.

At the close of the Second World War, the revelation of the murderous depravity unleashed upon an entire ethnic group, a genocide of proportions the world had never before experienced, created urgent motivation to bring about preventive measures against it ever happening again. The United Nations therefore included a Commission on Human Rights in its Charter. Mrs. Eleanor Roosevelt chaired the Commission, and Cassin paid tribute to the patience which she brought to the complex and difficult task. Cassin was vice-chairman of the Committee and it was he who drew up the Declaration.

While the United Nations Charter did mention promoting human rights, the problem facing the Commission was the total lack of any definition of these rights. The vocabulary which would be appropriate in Western cultures for such a definition—freedom, equality, cultural and economic rights—may have starkly different meanings in other cultures. A striking example was offered by Nobel Committee Chairwoman Lionaes in her presentation speech: "We [Europeans] can readily agree on what we mean by 'the woman's legal position in society,' " she said. "But how is it interpreted by the people in those parts of the world where a woman's value is equated with four camels?"

The Commission, composed in the beginning of 18 members of different nationalities and diverse occupations, took two years to formulate the first section of the Declaration of Human Rights, called "Universal Human Rights," in a version which everyone could accept at the UN General Assembly in Paris in 1948. Although this portion of the three-part Charter of Human Rights does not have a juridically obligatory character, Cassin called it "a historical event of the first magnitude . . . the first document of an ethical sort that organized humanity has ever adopted, and precisely at a time when man's power over nature became vastly increased . . . " Also of first order importance, Cassin said, "is its universality: it applies to all human beings without any discrimination whatever . . . "

The second and third portions of the Charter Cassin called "difficult" and "time consuming." The first difficulty concerned whether the rights of people to self-determination should be a principle of a political and essentially collective nature; and should be included with rights exercised by the individual, either separately or communally. Cassin attributed its solution to the movement toward decolonization and the libertarian principles which followed the Second World War.

The second difficulty, which included substantive provision on the obligations of the state and their respective measures of application, was debated before the UN General Assembly for 18 years. In part the slow pace was set by the arrival each year of newly independent nations, each one of which had to form an opinion. But that explanation is only par-

tially valid, Cassin said. The most powerful cause was the desire of certain powers to put off for as long as possible the discussion of the—what he called "paradoxically quite modest"—enforcement measures voted by the Commission on Human Rights, which those powers considered encroachments on the sovereignty of the state.

In 1966 the final unanimous vote came, Cassin said, only because on the eve of the International Human Rights Year it would have been inconceivable to have prolonged the filibuster. Moreover, a heavy price had been paid. "The implementation measures . . . especially those of the Covenant concerning civil and political rights, were considerably weakened," he said.

Is there reason to be satisfied? Cassin considered the question in his Nobel lecture. He answered that the Charter provides the vehicle for safeguarding human rights, however tragically far the reality of today seems from the goal. But he observed that "ultimately, of course, the organizing of peace . . . presupposes tremendous efforts to modify through education some longstanding mental attitudes, to work toward limitation of armaments, to manifest solidarity with the hungry . . . "

He warned, "Emotional factors and especially the sense of justice must not be left to those who pervert them to the service of hate and destruction . . . "

"The time has come," Cassin said in conclusion, "to proclaim that, for the establishment of peace and human dignity, each of us must work and fight to the last." These words well summarize René Cassin's long and illustrious life.

Biography

René Samuel Cassin was born on October 5, 1887, in Bayonne in Southern France, son of Henri Cassin, a merchant, and his wife, Gabrielle Dreyfus Cassin. His promising legal career started in Paris following a doctorate degree in juridical, economic, and political sciences. It was interrupted by the First World War when he was mobilized into the infantry.

During the war he sustained a wound which modified his life, hampering him physically but greatly enriching him spiritually. His experience led him to use his considerable talents in behalf of the wounded of that long and terrible conflict. He saw first to compensatory aid, and from there to the aid they needed in order to reenter the mainstream of life: from artificial limbs to career counseling and training. Moreover, under his direction France assumed responsibility for the security and education of 800,000 war orphans.

Cassin established, with fellow veterans, the International Confederation of Disabled Veterans [Conférence Internationale des Associations des Mutilés et d'Anciens Combattants (CIAMAC)], an organization whose purpose was to unite soldiers from all sides, ally and adversary together, in cooperative work toward a permanent peace. CIAMAC was sustained from 1925 until Hitler's Germany invaded Poland and began the irreversible events leading to the Second World War.

With the fall of France in the early days of that war, Cassin joined de Gaulle in the Free France government administered from London, acting as Commissioner for Justice and Education. With the liberation of France he became president of the Council of the National School of Administration [Conseil de l'École Nationale d'Administration] (1945), and 15 years later he served as president of the French National Overseas Center of Advanced Studies [Centre National des Hautes-Études de la France d'Outre-mer]. Also after the war, Cassin became vice-president of the Council of State, France's administrative high court (1944–60), and later head of the Constitutional Council (1960–70).

Cassin was vice-chairman, with Mrs. Eleanor Roosevelt as chairwoman, of the Commission for Human Rights in the United Nations (1946–53), and from that time on he alternated as vice-chairman or chairman until 1959. During this period he was writing and engineering the passage of the Declaration of Human Rights, a procedure that spanned a total of 18 years and ultimately disappointed Cassin, and many others, for its lack of implementation and funding for enforcement. On five different occasions from 1946 to 1968 he served as French delegate to the Assembly of the United Nations. He was one of the founders of the United Nations Educational, Scientific, and Cultural Organization (UNESCO).

Cassin has left a rich heritage in the judiciaries of France and Europe: he served as president of the Court of Arbitration at The Hague from 1950 to 1960, and as a member of the International Institute of Human Rights in Strasbourg (1959–65) and its president (1965–68), during which time he joined the American Jewish Committee in the sponsorship of a conference which was ultimately to influence the Helsinki Declaration of 1975.

He received numerous honors and awards, and held honorary D.C.L. degrees from Oxford, Mainz, Jerusalem, and Brandeis.

Besides the *Declaration of the Rights of Man*, his publications include *Law on Contracts, Inheritance and Family, International Law and Relations, Domicile, Status of Companies in France, The Council of State, The League of Nations, The United Nations,* and *Human Rights.*

René Cassin married Simone Yzomard in 1917. She died in 1969. In 1975 he married Ghislaine Bru, whom he had met in the Free French headquarters in London in the Second World War.

He died on February 20, 1976.

See also: Articles: *International Bill of Human Rights*

Bibliography

International Labour Review 1969 Tribute to René Cassin, Nobel Peace Prize winner. 99(2): 209–10

RUTH C. REYNOLDS

International Labour Organization (ILO)
(1969)

In his will, Alfred Nobel stated that the Peace Prize was to be awarded to the person who had done the most to promote fraternity among nations. Mrs. Aase Lionaes, Chairwoman of the Nobel Committee, said it was with this consideration in mind that the 1969 Peace Prize was awarded to the International Labour Organization (ILO). "It is the international activity of ILO through 50 years that in my opinion makes it a worthy Peace Prize winner," she said.

In his Nobel lecture, David Morse, Director–General of ILO, traced the history of that international development. ILO was conceived within the Versailles Peace Treaty ending the First World War. That war had acted as a powerful leveler between the classes. The working classes had fought and suffered side by side with the upper classes; and consequently, at the war's end, trade unions demanded that workers should participate in the discussions of the peace treaty. Moreover, the architects of the Versailles Treaty had before them the example of the Russian Revolution, and they realized that the treaty should accommodate not only peace among nations, but peace between classes as well.

The Peace Conference established an international committee which included delegates not only from governments, but also from employers and from employees. Called "tripartism," this was the most daring and the most valuable innovation of the ILO constitution. "Universal and lasting peace can be established only if it is based upon social justice," declared the preamble to the ILO's constitution.

The preceding decades had brought profound economic and social change in Europe; industrialization in particular had led to an unprecedented growth of the economic power of European nations and to fierce competition between them, a competition ultimately contributing to the outbreak of war. Similarly, industrialization had led to the emergence of a large industrial working class which was often in open conflict with the established order. Alfred Nobel himself warned in 1892 of the dangers of an impending social revolution, of a "new tyranny . . . lurking in the shadows," and of its threat to world peace; Frédéric Passy, winner of the first Nobel Peace Prize in 1901, stressed the need for governments to ensure international stability through social reforms if international peace was to be preserved.

Therefore the peace movement was becoming inextricably linked with a movement for international action to promote improved conditions of labor. ILO was the product of currents of reformist and socialist thought and action in the nineteenth and early twentieth centuries in Europe, and it mirrors within its internal structure an accommodation to these changes. The demands of the workers for effective international action have often conflicted with their governments' views, which saw ILO as an instrument for strengthening the stability of the sovereign nation–state. "In spite of the political calamities, failures and disappointments of the past half century, ILO has patiently, undramatically, but not unsuccessfully, worked to build an *infrastructure of peace*," Morse declared. "It has provided the world with a meeting ground, an instrument for cooperation and for dialogue among very different interests, at times when men were more disposed to settle their differences by force than by talk. . . .

"If the ILO had done nothing more than offer the world a forum for tripartite discussion, it would have already rendered a great service to the cause of peace," Morse told his award ceremony audience. At the time of its inception, the idea of tripartism was hardly known even at national levels, and its implications have been far reaching. "It resulted in trade unions and organizations of employers acquiring a position at home which they would not otherwise have had. It gave the world a new approach to the resolution of social conflict, an approach based on dialogue . . .

"Its tripartite structure has also enabled it to broaden the scope of cooperation between countries. The ILO is still the only world-wide organization where international cooperation is the business not only of diplomats and government representatives, but also of the representatives of employers and workers. It thus provides opportunities for contacts and for greater understanding within the three

groups . . . it is only in the ILO that free enterprise employers meet regularly with managers of state enterprises in Socialist countries," Morse explained.

The second great principle of ILO is its universality. This organization has struggled towards a goal of universal membership in the belief—stated in the preamble to its constitution—that "the failure of any nation to adopt humane conditions of labour is an obstacle in the way of other nations which desire to improve conditions in their countries." In 1944, in Philadelphia, a declaration was adopted that "poverty anywhere constitutes a danger to prosperity everywhere."

It would be fair to question whether this is idealism beyond hope of implementation. Four months before the announcement of the award of the Peace Prize, ILO celebrated its fiftieth anniversary, and upon that occasion a conservative US journal, *Business Week* (June 1969) devoted a major article to the question, "Should US business support the ILO?" The conclusion reached was that there were many reasons for a positive answer; that ILO is not run as a lobby for labor interests, even though it deals with labor topics, but "speaks with several voices—government, worker and employer." The author found it regrettable that most US business ignores ILO. Director–General Morse is convinced that searching out causes will ultimately contribute to wiser action. Therefore he has supported the Institute for Labor Studies set up in Geneva in 1960. It receives a third of its funds from ILO. Presently it is coordinating a vast research program on worker participation in industry.

Another ILO operation is the Center for Advanced Technical and Vocational Training. It tailors its instructions to the level of sophistication in the country involved. Still another project being discussed for the future is a top-level management seminar between Soviet and American experts.

ILO has made major contributions to international law, proving that moral persuasion and moral pressure can be effective instruments to secure the observance of the rule of law at the international level. It also offers technical assistance to developing countries. "Many developing countries are so weak, politically and economically, and so lacking in social cohesion and stability," Morse observed in his Nobel lecture, "they could offer little resistance to subversion or aggression by an ambitious outside power. To provide these countries with the resources, the technical and managerial know-how, and the institutional and administrative framework which are essential for viable nationhood in the modern world . . . seems to me an essential aspect of the problem of peace-building in the modern world. And it is for this reason that the ILO gives top priority in its work today to the strengthening of developing nations."

Morse enumerated many of the unresolved problems facing ILO: an uneven distribution of their help so that rural areas lag behind in assistance. "We shall encourage the use of labour-intensive techniques of agricultural and industrial production wherever it is economically feasible to do so," he said. There remains the plight of those desperately poor who live outside a closed circle of affluence; the racial or religious minorities, the migrant workers, those in slum areas, elderly people. Morse observed that the ILO must address problems of discrimination; it must work for greater freedom, for greater participation of workers in decisions affecting their welfare. "The task," he said, "is far from finished . . . but there has been a growing recognition of the need for a truly world-wide solidarity in the fight against poverty and injustice with the aim of building a more peaceful world . . .

"The ILO has given the world the concept of the industrial dialogue," Morse said. "In the years to come it must seek to broaden the scope, and increase the substance of that dialogue . . . it will continue to seek to promote social evolution by peaceful means, to identify emerging social needs and problems and threats to social peace . . ." He pledged to devote the ILO to defusing what Nobel Laureate Frédéric Passy (1901) had warned were "dangerous explosives in the hidden depths of the community," making possible the building of a truly peaceful world order based on social justice.

Beneath the foundation stone in the ILO's office in Geneva lies a document on which is written: "*Si vis pacem, cole justitiam*"—if you desire peace, cultivate justice.

History

The International Labour Organization (ILO) was created in 1919 by Part XIII of the Versailles Peace Treaty ending the First World War. It grew out of nineteenth- and twentieth-century labor and social movements which created widespread demands for social justice. In 1946, after the demise of the League of Nations, the ILO became the first specialized agency associated with the United Nations. The original membership of 45 countries in 1919 had grown to 150 by May 1983.

ILO's tripartite policy of giving equitable voice to representatives of workers and employers and government is unique among world organizations. The annual International Labour Conference, the ILO deliberative body, is composed of four representatives from each member country: two government delegates, one worker and one employer delegate, all working independently.

The ILO has three major tasks: first, the adoption of international labor standards, called "Conventions and Recommendations," which contain guidelines on child labor, protection of women workers, hours of work, rest and holidays, labor inspection, vocational guidance and training, social security protection, housing, occupational safety, and protection of migrant workers. They also cover basic human rights, such as freedom of association, collective bargaining, and the abolition of forced labor and of discrimination in employment.

Second, technical cooperation to assist developing nations. More than half of ILO's resources are devoted to such programs. ILO's ultimate goal is a World Employment Program, designed to help countries provide employment and training opportunities to growing populations.

Third, standard setting and technical cooperation are backed by extensive research, training, education, and publications programs. The ILO is a major source of publications and documentation on labor and social matters.

The ILO's six Directors–General read as follows: Albert Thomas (1919–32) of France; Harold B. Butler (1932–38) of the United Kingdom; John G. Winant (1938–41) of the United States; Edward J. Phelan (1941–48) of Ireland; David A. Morse (1948–70) of the United States; Wilfred Jenks (1970–) of the United Kingdom.

Bibliography

Business Week 1969 Should U.S. business support the ILO? June 14, pp. 68–72

Lucal J 1969 The Church and the ILO. *America* 120 (May 31): 644–46

RUTH C. REYNOLDS

Norman Borlaug
(1970)

The Nobel Peace Prize for 1970 was awarded to the agronomist Norman Ernest Borlaug because, the Nobel Committee said, "more than any other single person of his age, he has helped to provide bread for a hungry world. We have made this choice in the hope that providing bread will also give the world peace."

Borlaug began his crusade against famine as a geneticist and plant pathologist with the Rockefeller Foundation at a research station in Campo

Atizapan, Mexico, where he began a momentous series of cross-breeding experiments that developed strains of wheat which increased the yields in Mexico sixfold since his start there in 1944. "I am impatient and do not accept the need for slow change and evolution to improve the agriculture and food production of the emerging countries," he once wrote. "I advocate instead a 'yield-kick, or a yield blast-off.' There is no time to be lost considering the magnitude of the world food and population problem." During the many years he has worked in Mexico he has collaborated with scientists from other countries, adapting wheat to the particular needs of the region in which it is grown. In India, for example, where he introduced the stocky wheat better able to support the rapid growth and heavier yields of grain, the annual yield soared from 12 million tons in 1965 to 21 tons in 1970. West Pakistan (now Pakistan) also planted the strain, and in five years also nearly doubled its yield.

Although Borlaug is a scientist with an M.S. and Ph.D. in plant pathology, he prefers field work to academic life. The hunger that afflicts a major share of the human family stimulated his ingenuity, and as director of the Rockefeller Foundation's wheat breeding program he set out in the 1950s to develop a dwarf wheat that could perform well in the varied conditions to be found in Mexico. He amassed germ plasm from Japan, the United States, Australia, and Columbia, and then began growing two alternate crops of wheat each year at sites with contrasting climatic and environmental conditions. The combination of the widely chosen ancestry of his seeds and the varying "laboratory" fields in which they were developed resulted in a dwarf wheat with wide adaptability to differing conditions. Borlaug pioneered in this work in geographic adaptability of cereals; before this, most cereal varieties grew well only under conditions similar to those under which they were first bred.

As a result of his innovative measures Borlaug became known as the "father of the Green Revolution." In his Nobel lecture Borlaug introduced some qualifications to be considered within that popular term. "Perhaps the term 'green revolution,' as commonly used, is too premature, too optimistic, or too broad in scope," he said. "Too often it seems to convey the impression of a general revolution in yields per hectare and in total production of all crops throughout vast areas comprising many countries . . .

"These implications both oversimplify and distort the facts. The only crops which have been appreciably affected up to the present time are wheat, rice and maize. Yields of other important cereals, such as sorghums, millets, and barley, have been only slightly affected; nor has there been any appreciable increase in yield or production of the pulse or legume crops which are essential in the diets of cereal-consuming populations."

Borlaug cautioned that there are no miracles in agricultural production, no elixir to cure all the accumulated ills of a stagnant, traditional agriculture. The importation of new seeds and new technology to developing countries must be backed by a crop-production campaign strategy wherein the government's economic policies would be tailored to assure the farmer a fair price for grain, and to guarantee that the fertilizers, insecticides, weedkillers, and machinery needed would be available. Traditional methods of threshing grain with bullocks, followed by winnowing, must be replaced by thousands of small threshing machines to accommodate the greatly increased harvest. Borlaug also cautioned against inadequate planning wherein some farmers, able to use the new seeds, would increase their net incomes up to fourfold, while those unable to use the new seeds for lack of water, or lack of credit to buy the equipment necessary to use the new techniques, would have to market their small yields in an economy adjusted to sharp increases in total harvests. The "Green Revolution" must be accompanied by equivalent and political breakthroughs. There must be, for instance, effective ways of distributing the additional food to vast underprivileged masses who have little or no purchasing power.

Borlaug emphasized that world leaders needed to tackle the problem of population control. The new wheats and the high-yielding rices being developed, together with continuing research toward increased protein contents, can only buy time. If corresponding means for stabilizing world populations are not developed at the same time, Borlaug warned that the "Green Revolution" would achieve only a "temporary success in man's war against hunger and deprivation, a breathing space in which to deal with the 'population monster,' and the subsequent environmental and social ills that too often lead to conflict between men and between nations.

"And yet I am optimistic for the future of mankind," Borlaug said in closing his lecture, "for in all biological populations there are innate devices to adjust population growth to the carrying capacity of the environment. Undoubtedly, some such device exists in man, but so far it has not asserted itself to bring into balance population growth and the carrying capacity of the environment on a worldwide scale. It would be disastrous for the species to continue to increase our human numbers madly until such devices take over . . . ”

Borlaug continued: “Since man is potentially a rational being, however, I am confident that within the next two decades he will recognize the self-destructive course he steers along the road of irresponsible population growth and will adjust the growth rate to levels which will permit a decent standard of living for all mankind . . . he may still see Isaiah’s prophesies come true: ‘and the desert shall rejoice, and blossom as the rose . . . And the parched ground shall become a pool, and the thirsty land springs of water . . . ’ ” (Isaiah 35: 1,7).

Biography

Norman Ernest Borlaug was born in Cresco, Iowa, on March 25, 1914. Educated in Iowa primary and secondary schools, he attended the University of Minnesota where he took a B.S. in 1937, an M.S. in 1939 and a Ph.D. in 1942. He originally studied forestry, and went on to work for the US Forestry Service at stations in Massachusetts and Idaho. But it was as an agriculturist, using the tools of genetics and plant pathology, that he became a pioneer in the increased production of cereal crops over the world.

Following his masters degree and doctorate in plant pathology Borlaug served as microbiologist on the staff of the duPont de Nemours Foundation, where he was in charge of research on industrial and agricultural bactericides, fungicides, and preservatives. In 1944 he accepted an appointment as geneticist and plant pathologist for the Cooperative Wheat Research and Production Program, a joint undertaking of the Rockefeller Foundation and the Mexican Government. Twenty years later Borlaug was awarded an honorary doctoral degree for the impressive results he achieved in improving wheat production, especially in the developing countries. In 1959 he became Assistant Director of the Rockefeller Foundation and Director of the Inter-American Wheat Research and Production Program, and in 1964 Director of the Wheat Program of the International Center for Maize and Wheat Improvement Center.

His success in Mexico paved the way for him to implement his practical humanitarian vision. Known by this time as the architect of the “Green Revolution,” Borlaug arranged to put the new cereal strains into extensive production to help feed the world’s hungry people. From Mexico, Borlaug went to other countries with large underfed populations to help them improve the yield of their food crops. At the invitation of the Food and Agriculture Organization he went to Pakistan in 1959, where he persuaded the authorities not only to import the new variety of wheat seeds, but to adopt appropriate technology in its use.

Borlaug is also concerned with the problems of population explosion, the control of which is essential no matter what the food supply. He sees the “Green Revolution” as a means for buying time until essential sociopolitical problems of equitable food distribution are resolved and the population brought to numbers commensurate with the support capacities of the Earth.

Borlaug has won recognition and awards from all over the world: he is a foreign member of the Royal Swedish Academy of Agriculture and Forestry (1971), and of the Indian Natural Science Academy (1973); an honorary member of the Acad. Nacional de Agronomia y Veterinaria de Argentina, and of the N.I. Vaviloti Acad. (USSR); an Honorary Fellow of the Indian Society of Genetics and Plant Breeding (1968); an Honorary D.Sc. (Punjab Agric. Univ., 1969; Royal Norwegian Agricultural College, 1970; Michigan State University, 1971; University of Florida, 1973; and others). He was given the Medal of Freedom in 1977 and holds numerous Mexican awards.

Borlaug married Margaret G. Gibson in 1937. They have a son and a daughter.

Bibliography

Brown L 1970 Nobel Peace Prize: Developer of high-yield wheat receives award. *Science* 170 (October 30): 518–19

RUTH C. REYNOLDS

Willy Brandt

(1971)

The Nobel Peace Prize for 1971 was awarded to Willy Brandt, then Chancellor of the Federal Republic of Germany, in recognition of the “reconciliatory hand he extended across the old enemy frontiers.” If Brandt’s gesture toward peace is accepted, the Nobel Committee said that “Willy Brandt will live in our history as the great German chancellor of peace and reconciliation.”

Brandt is often thought of as a Berliner, but he became a Berliner only after the Second World War. He was born Herbert Ernst Karl Frahm in the Lubeck workers’ district of St. Lorenz. A poverty-ridden childhood instilled in him a deeply ingrained reverence for human dignity and social justice. He was greatly influenced by his grandfather, an ardent Social Democrat.

At 13 he was granted a scholarship to high school, where his talent for journalism quickly surfaced. While still in his teens he was writing articles for the local Social Democratic paper using the name "Willy Brandt."

In the 1930s, with the ominous rise of the Nazi Party, the young journalist was known as a member of a group openly hostile to the Nazis. When Hitler came to power Frahm escaped to Norway using his assumed name "Willy Brandt." There he learned Norwegian and began to write for trade-union magazines, keeping in touch with the socialist underground in Germany. When the Germans invaded Norway he again fled, this time to Sweden. "I was a two-fold immigrant: a German who had fled to Norway, and a Norwegian who had escaped to Sweden," Brandt recalls.

After the war he was assigned to cover the Nuremberg Trials for Scandinavian Social Democratic Party newspapers. In 1946 the Norwegian Foreign Minister asked Brandt to join the country's diplomatic service, and sent him to Berlin as press attaché with the rank of major attached to the Norwegian military mission. He found Berlin covered with deep craters and mountains of rubble, its people hungry, suffering from the cold, despairing. In 1947 he made an important decision: he relinquished the personal and material privileges he enjoyed with a Norwegian diplomatic passport and applied for renaturalization.

He began to work first for a free Berlin because he was convinced that the defeat of Berlin carried in it the germ of a defeat for any hope of peace in Europe. He regarded Berlin as a microcosm of the East–West problem. Willy Brandt was destined to become its mayor.

The Nobel Committee commented on his leadership: "As Mayor of Berlin, at a time when the city was menaced by political pressures which eventually crystallized in the form of the Berlin Wall of 1961, Willy Brandt was, in critical situations, proof of a moderation and a courage, often a despairing courage, which saved Berlin from the risks of an immense catastrophe."

Brandt shared with Chancellor Adenauer the conviction that the next step was to "talk to the Russians," taking care to preserve and nourish the Federal Republic's ties to the Western bloc. The building of the Berlin Wall in August 1961 was a powerful factor in persuading Brandt of the urgent need to press for a policy of reconciliation. Under international law the Wall was illegal. Brandt saw that as Mayor he would have to walk a delicate path between legal claim and brute force. But he had become convinced that an approach must be tried, no matter what the risks. His policy of reconciliation, Ostpolitik, with the German Democratic Republic, the Soviet Union, Poland, and other members of the Soviet bloc led to an agreement on the renunciation of force between Bonn and Moscow. Brandt asserted that peace was needed not just in the sense of freeing a situation from conflict, but also as a prerequisite for the cooperative effort that must be made for solving problems. "It is not enough to pronounce peace-loving intentions, we must also actively endeavor to organize peace," he said. He had faith that peace is self-reinforcing; that where people work together, helping one another, trust will develop with time.

Brandt discussed the events of 1961 and 1962 in his Nobel lecture: "As Mayor of Berlin, I experienced how critical situations influence our thinking. I knew, though, that steadfastness serves the cause of peace." Recalling the Berlin Wall, with its "absurd division of what had remained intact of the whole organism of a metropolis," he said that passionate protests were justified and necessary, but they did not alter the situation. The Wall remained; people had to learn to live with it. He pursued every opportunity to open up fences, to create paths for people to cross borders *legally*.

In 1966 Brandt became Foreign Minister in Kurt Kiesinger's coalition government. He announced the policy of unequivocal safeguarding of peace as the common denominator to all actions. "Everyone must ask himself what specific contribution he should make," he said, and he made this the cornerstone of procedures in the Federal Republic of Germany.

Brandt's critics called his Ostpolitik "naive" and "risky," but Brandt declared his experience with coexistence had not vindicated these apprehensions. "Realistic self-confidence need not fear contact with the political and ideological antagonist; the uncertainty of the present time must not be permitted to make us uncertain too. What was the point," he asked, " of getting in touch with the other side without being prepared to speak? Speaking surely also means negotiating and being open to conciliation, not unilateral concessions. An active peace policy will remain for a long time to come the test of our intellectual and material vitality."

In 1969 Brandt became Chancellor in a new coalition between the Social Democrats and Liberals. Convinced that a strong Western Europe was necessary before confrontation could successfully be turned into collaboration with Eastern Europe, one of his first official acts was to persuade France to begin talks with the United Kingdom on expanding the European Common Market, and he encouraged other nations to join.

In his policy of détente with the communist bloc countries of Eastern Europe and with the Soviet Union, Brandt was always prepared to accept new relationships and new understandings provided his communist negotiators did not force him into violating good relationships with the North Atlantic Treaty Organization (NATO) and the West. He exercised great patience in his efforts to improve relations with the government of the German Democratic Republic. "Short steps are better than no steps at all," he said.

Chancellor Brandt argued persistently for a sense of proportion, resolution, and endurance, holding them to be essential to the transition from classical power politics to the businesslike peace policy that his government sought. Actively practicing a peace-oriented policy means a change, he stressed, from the imposition of one-sided views to the balancing of differing interests.

There are strong forces in opposition to the organization of peace, Brandt warned. Like freedom, peace is no original state which existed from the start; we shall have to make it, he asserted. "To achieve this, we shall have to know more about the origin of conflicts ... learning is in our world the true credible alternative to force."

Willy Brandt closed his Nobel lecture with some observations about the contemporary human condition: "Today we know how rich and at the same time how limited Man is in his possibilities. We know him in his aggression and in his brotherliness. We know that he is capable of applying his inventions for his own good, but also of using them to destroy himself ... I believe in active compassion and therefore in Man's responsibility. And I believe in the absolute necessity of peace ... Under the threat of mankind's self-destruction, co-existence has become a question of the very existence of man. Co-existence becomes not one of several acceptable possibilities, but the only chance of survival ... May all those who possess the power to wage war have the mastery of reason to maintain peace."

Biography

Born Herbert Ernst Karl Frahm on December 13, 1913, in Lubeck, son of Martha Frahm, Willy Brandt was educated through high school in Lubeck. He began a distinguished

career as a journalist at an early age, writing for the Social Democratic paper under the name "Willy Brandt" while still in Lubeck. He continued writing in Norway, to which he escaped upon the coming of Hitler to power in Germany in 1933. He participated in German and Norwegian resistance movements during the Second World War. At the close of the war he served in Berlin as Norwegian Press Attaché. He decided upon renaturalization, keeping the name Willy Brandt. He rose swiftly within the Social Democratic Party becoming Secretary to the Executive Committee, 1948–49, member of the Executive Committee, 1950–63, Deputy Chairman of the SPD, 1954–58, and Chairman in 1958. He became Mayor of Berlin in 1957, serving until 1966. He was a member of the Federal Parliament (Bundestag), 1949–57, and again from 1969; and in 1966 he was appointed Minister of Foreign Affairs and Vice-Chancellor. He was elected Chancellor in 1969 and served until 1974. He was President of the Socialist International, 1976, a member of the European Parliament from 1979 to 1983, and Chairman of the Committee on Development Issues, which produced the influential Brandt Reports, 1977–79. The reports of the commission, to which Brandt's name was attached, were published as: *North–South: A Programme for Survival,* 1980 and *Common Crisis: North–South: Co-operation for World Recovery,* 1983. He has been awarded honorary degrees from Pennsylvania University (1959), Maryland University (1960), Harvard University (1963), Oxford University (Hon. DCL, 1969) and Leeds University (1982). He was given the Reinhold Niebuhr Award (1972), the Aspen Institute for Humanistic Studies Prize (1973), and the B'nai Brith Gold Medal (1981). A prolific writer, his publications include: *Krigen i Norge* (1945), *Ernst Reuter* (with R. Lowenthal, 1957), *Von Bonn nach Berlin* (1957), *My Road to Berlin* (1960), *The Ordeal of Co-Existence* (1963), *Begegnung mit Kennedy* (1964), *A Peace Policy for Europe* (1968), *Peace and Politics, 1960–1975* (1978), *Links und Frei* (1982).

He married Rut Hansen in 1948; they divorced in 1980. He married Brigitte Seebacher in 1983. He is the father of three sons and one daughter.

See also: Articles: *Ostpolitik*; *North–South Conflict*

Bibliography

Brandt W 1972 Let me speak of peace policy in our time. Nobel lecture delivered at Oslo, December 11, 1971. *Vital Speeches* 38(7): 229–35

Nation 1972 The two Germanys: Lurching toward confrontation. 214(15): 461–63

The New Republic 1971 Hectoring Herr Brandt. 164(4): 7–8

Wechsberg J A 1974 *The New Yorker* January 14, 1974: 35–57

RUTH C. REYNOLDS

Prize Not Awarded

(1972)

Henry Kissinger

(1973)

The 1973 Nobel Peace Prize went to Le Duc Tho and Henry Kissinger, who had been working for nearly four years toward negotiating a ceasefire in Vietnam. The award proved controversial. Le Duc Tho refused the prize, objecting that peace in Vietnam had still not been completely achieved. Two of the five members of the Peace Prize Committee resigned in protest. Ripples of concern surrounded the choice of Henry Kissinger because his announcement "peace is at hand," made just before the US November elections, was followed in the next month by heavy US bombing in Vietnam. Ceasefire was achieved, however, on January 23.

The Nobel Committee made their award in recognition of the sustained efforts of Kissinger and Le Duc Tho to find a common policy favorable to establishing a way forward to peace. "No one," the Committee acknowledged, "could know whether this road would be followed; but they had lit a torch on the long and difficult road to peace among men." They had been, the Committee said, responsible politicians at the center of events, seeking the use of negotiation rather than war, intent on finding solutions to controversies rather than military victory.

This principle has been central in Henry Kissinger's philosophy as scholar and statesman. In his doctoral thesis he examined the protracted period of peace in Europe following 1814. While many historians explain these 100 years without war in terms of a military balance of power wherein no country was sufficiently strong to seek domination, Kissinger stressed the international order that existed in that period. Within an agreed set of rules, states dealt with their stresses on set principles of behavior. Although there were political systems which differed widely, as there are now, with the Great Powers swayed by conflicting interests, they respected the principles and rules through which they could prevent their differing systems and interests leading to war.

The circumstances in which Le Duc Tho and Henry Kissinger sought to negotiate were in opposite circumstances, during the pressures created by an ongoing, long, costly war. Meeting in secret for over three years, the diplomats found a formula to exchange war prisoners and to end the domestically unpopular involvement of US troops without the appearance of the United States abandoning an ally.

It is in recognition of these efforts of Henry Kissinger and Le Duc Tho to lead the contesting nations toward peace through increased understanding and in the hope of the Committee that the award might act as an effective spur toward renewed and conclusive negotiations that the Nobel award for peace was made.

Kissinger was born in Germany in 1923. His family fled from Nazi Germany in 1938, so it was as an adolescent that the young Kissinger arrived in the United States. Naturalized as a citizen in 1943, he began a three-year service in the US Army Counter-Intelligence Corps. From 1946 to 1949 he was a captain in the Military Intelligence Service.

Kissinger quickly distinguished himself as a student and attended Harvard on a series of scholarships. This was the beginning of a long and distinguished career at Harvard, where he taught in the Department of Government and at the Center for International Affairs. During the next 15 years he served in many posts, often simultaneously: he was Associate Director of the Center, Study Director of Nuclear Weapons and Foreign Policy at the Council of Foreign Relations, Director of the Special Studies Project for the Rockefeller Fund, Director of the Harvard International Seminar, and Director of the Harvard Defense Studies Program.

In 1968 Kissinger accepted an appointment as adviser to the President on national security affairs. As chief foreign policy adviser to President Nixon he initiated the Strategic Arms Limitation Talks (SALT) in 1969.

Kissinger prepared the way for President Nixon's visit to the People's Republic of China in 1972 and the opening of diplomatic relationships with that country through a number of unpublicized trips. He accompanied President Nixon to Moscow in 1972, an occasion that created a marked improvement in Soviet–US relations. By this time he was engaged in the intensive, protracted one-to-one negotiations with Le Duc Tho which culminated in a ceasefire in early 1973. In 1973 he became Secretary of State following the resignation of William P. Rodgers. He played a major role in Nixon's policy of disengaging US troops and replacing them by South Vietnamese. He gave diplomatic assistance in the resumption of diplomatic relations between the United States and Egypt, making a whirlwind tour of the capitals of Middle East countries and entering into consultation with the Soviet leader, Brezhnev. In February 1974 he announced from Cairo the resumption of diplomatic relations between the United States and Egypt, which had been severed for six years, and the reopening of the Suez Canal.

Secretary Kissinger has often been called a "realist." In his acceptance message to the Nobel Committee, Kissinger addressed this attitude: "To the realist, peace represents a stable arrangement of power; to the idealist, a goal so preeminent that it conceals the difficulty of finding the means to its achievement. But in this age of thermonuclear technology, neither view can assure man's preservation. Instead, peace, the ideal, must be practised. A sense of responsibility and accommodation must guide the behavior of all nations. Some common notion of justice can and must be found, for failure to do so will bring only more 'just' wars."

Secretary Kissinger's schedule as conciliator was unremitting. But his heavy schedule did not preclude a fine sense of the delicacy of his mission. In his acceptance speech as Nobel Laureate, Kissinger remarked, "Our experience has taught us to regard peace as a delicate, ever-fleeting condition, its roots too shallow to bear the strain of social and political discontent. We tend to accept the lessons of that experience and work toward those solutions that at best relieve specific sources of strain, lest our neglect allow war to overtake peace."

Bernt Ingvaldsen, Vice-President of the Committee, said it was interesting to follow Kissinger's development from doctoral dissertation to the long and patient negotiation leading to the ceasefire in Vietnam. "The views he has evolved testify to a mind free from prejudice, an analytical ability to learn the lessons of history, and constructive imagination."

Biography

Henry Alfred Kissinger was born in Furth, Germany, on May 27, 1923. He emigrated to the United States with his family in flight from Nazi Germany in 1938. He was naturalized as a citizen in 1943, and entered the US Army Counter-Intelligence Corps where he served as captain from 1946 to 1949. He earned his B.A. *summa cum laude* from Harvard, followed by an M.A. in 1950 and a Ph.D. in 1954. He taught at Harvard in the Department of Government and at the Center for International Affairs. He was Associate Director of the Center, 1957 to 1960; Study Director of Nuclear Weapons and Foreign Policy at the Council of Foreign Relations, 1955 to 1956; Director of the Special Studies Project for the Rockefeller Fund, 1956 to 1958; and Director of the Harvard International Seminar, 1951 to 1971.

Kissinger has served as consultant to a wide variety of officials and agencies: the Department of State, the US Arms Control and Disarmament Agency, Rand Corporation, National Security Council, Weapons Systems Evaluation Group of the Joint Chiefs of Staff, Operations Coordinating Board, and the Director of the Psychological Strategy Board and Operations Research Office. A Guggenheim Fellow, he also received the 1958 Woodrow Wilson Prize for the best book in the fields of government, politics, and international affairs. In 1973 he received the American Institute for Public Service Award, the International Platform Association Theodore Roosevelt Award, the Veterans of Foreign Wars Dwight D. Eisenhower Distinguished Service Medal, and the Hope Award for International Understanding.

While assistant to the President for National Security Affairs, Kissinger negotiated arrangements for President Nixon's trips to both the People's Republic of China and the Soviet Union. He accompanied the President on these trips, which proved important occasions, resulting in improvement in US relations with both countries. In 1972 he entered into negotiations with Le Duc Tho, seeking to achieve peace in Vietnam, and this resulted in a ceasefire in 1973. A visit to Moscow to see the Soviet leader, Brezhnev, followed by a tour of seven Middle East capitals, led to the signing of a ceasefire between Egypt and Israel. In 1974 full-scale diplomatic relations were resumed between the United States and Egypt after six years, and the Suez Canal was reopened. Kissinger remained as Secretary of State under President Ford until the 1977 elections. Since that time, following Ford's election defeat, Kissinger has been Professor of Diplomacy in Georgetown University, since 1977; Counselor to the Center for Strategic and International Studies, Georgetown University, since 1977; Contributing Analyst for ABC news, since 1983; and Senior Fellow, Aspen Institute, since 1977. In 1983, he became Chairman of the National Bipartisan Committee on Central America.

Kissinger's other honors include the American Institute for Public Service Award, 1973, American Legion Distinguished Service Medal, 1974, Wateler Peace Prize, 1974, Presidential Medal of Freedom, 1977, among many other awards and prizes. His publications include: *Nuclear Weapons and Foreign Policy* (1956); *A World Restored: Castlereagh, Metternich and the Restoration of Peace 1812–22* (1957); *The Necessity for Choice: Prospects of American*

Foreign Policy (1961); *The Troubled Partnership: A Reappraisal of the Atlantic Alliance* (1965); *American Foreign Policy* (3 essays) (1969); *White House Years* (1979); *For the Record* (1981); *Years of Upheaval* (1982); *International House* (1984); and numerous articles on US foreign policy, international affairs, and diplomatic history.

Henry Kissinger married Nancy Maginnes in 1974. He has a son and a daughter, Elizabeth and David, from a former marriage.

RUTH C. REYNOLDS

Le Duc Tho

(1973)

The decision to award the 1973 Nobel Peace Prize to the two negotiators, Henry Kissinger and Le Duc Tho, who had been working for nearly four years toward achieving a ceasefire in Vietnam proved a controversial one. One of the two winners, Le Duc Tho, refused the prize with the objection that peace in Vietnam eluded them still. Two out of the five members of the Peace Prize Committee resigned in protest. Controversy raged around the choice of Henry Kissinger when his announcement "peace is at hand," made just prior to the US November elections, was followed in December by heavy US bombing in Vietnam. Ceasefire eventually came about on January 23 of the following year.

The Nobel Committee explained that their decision was based on the persistent efforts made by Kissinger and Le Duc Tho to find a promising course of action likely to lead the way to peace. "No one," Mrs. Aase Lionaes, Chairwoman of the Committee, acknowledged, "could know whether this road would be followed; but they had lit a torch on the long and difficult road to peace among men."

The Nobel Committee was under no illusion that peace had been attained. But Mrs. Lionaes called attention to precedents for their decision under such circumstances. Ralph Bunche had received the prize for his contribution in negotiating a ceasefire between Israel and the Arab states. Later, that ceasefire had been superseded by open war in the Middle East. Still, the principle behind Bunche's award and, likewise, the award offered Secretary Kis-

singer and Le Duc Tho remained intact: they were responsible politicians at the heart of the search for a negotiated peace, rather than military victory seeking to resolve bitterly divisive issues through discussion, not war.

It is in recognition of the efforts of Henry Kissinger and Le Duc Tho to start the nations of today toward peace through increased understanding and negotiation that the Nobel award for peace was made.

Biography

Le Duc Tho was born in what is now Vietnam in 1912. As a teenager, he joined an anti-French revolutionary youth movement, and by the age of 17 he was a member of Indochina's Communist Party.

Reports differ on whether Le Duc Tho, who had been frequently incarcerated by the colonial government during his youth, spent all of the Second World War in prison, or whether he escaped and spent some of that time with Ho Chi Minh in China.

Following the war he went south to participate in the successful war of independence from the French. He returned to North Vietnam and became a member of the Politburo and Secretary of the Vietnam Workers' Party. He was a chief negotiator in seeking a ceasefire from the military conflict and ultimately to create peace in Vietnam. He signed the ceasefire without the satisfaction of feeling that true peace had been obtained in that country. On that basis he refused the offered Nobel Peace Prize.

RUTH C. REYNOLDS

Sean MacBride

(1974)

Sean MacBride, winner with Eisaku Sato of the 1974 Nobel Peace Prize, has devoted much of his life to the advancement of human rights. With endless skill and devotion, this Peace Prize Laureate has been prominent in the introduction of human rights legis-

lation and in its implementation in countries the world over.

MacBride had addressed problems of peace and human rights as journalist, lawyer, and distinguished member of the Irish government. In his youth he participated in Ireland's struggle for independence, and it proved a lasting influence. He gave up a career as a journalist to study law, a profession which better equipped him for taking up battle against the injustices he observed around him.

For sometime he worked in the Irish government, entering the Dáil Éireann (Irish National Assembly) in 1947 and remaining for 11 years. During the period 1948–51 he served as Ireland's Foreign Minister. The Council of Europe was then drafting the European Convention on Human Rights with the view to securing worldwide protection for human rights, and MacBride played a dominant role in guiding this convention to a successful conclusion. This proved to be the beginning of a battle against the twin forces of violence and injustice which he was to wage over much of the world, acting sometimes in the capacity of public servant, often as a private citizen.

From 1961 to 1974, as a fearless and vigorous leader of Amnesty International, he brought that organization from infancy to a position of respect and efficacy throughout the world community. Sometimes he combined the role of leader and field worker, his areas of activity ranging over Africa, Asia, and America. He fought injustice in many forms, exposing persecution and torture, seeking the release of prisoners incarcerated without trial or defense.

MacBride has emphasized the importance of extending and enforcing the legislative obligations to protect human rights. He was active as Secretary-General within the International Commission of Jurists during many of the years when he was also working for Amnesty International. In the Commission of Jurists a number of leading jurists from various countries worked to issue valuable publications and to operate in cooperation with the United Nations.

During this time, in September 1967, he participated in a Nobel symposium in Oslo. There he launched the idea of establishing a convention among the nations of East Europe for the protection of fundamental freedoms. He hoped that through regional agreements it would be possible to bring about a network of progress. He also worked in behalf of the UN's Declaration of Human Rights. It should, he felt, become an effective instrument through the establishment of a universal Human Rights Court with authority to act in behalf of individuals needing its protection. MacBride is of the opinion that no state can claim absolute national

sovereignty where universally accepted principles of justice are concerned.

MacBride possesses an abiding faith in the power of the individual to participate in the cause of justice. Much of the work of Amnesty International is accomplished by volunteers. During the UN's Human Rights Year in 1968 he took the initiative in setting up a joint committee for the various nongovernmental organizations working for justice. MacBride himself was pressed into command, and he applied his skill as a practical administrator to impressive effect.

In accord with his philosophy of meeting a problem by actively working toward solutions, MacBride has toiled within the International Peace Bureau (IPB), holding various positions of trust within that organization, to seek preventative measures against the greatest perpetrator of injustice and suffering of all, modern warfare.

At the time of the Peace Prize award MacBride was facing a new and demanding task as the UN's High Commissioner for Namibia. It is no surprise that such a man, steeped in the problems of injustice as practiced by the individual, by the nation, and by clusters of nations, should be an eloquent orator on the subject. He opened his Nobel lecture somberly: "It is nearly with a feeling of despair that I come to your beautiful country . . . despair partly because we are living in a world where war, violence, brutality and ever increasing armament dominate the thinking of humanity; but more so because humanity itself gives the appearance of having become numbed or terrified by its own impotence in the face of disaster."

MacBride observed that this threat of nuclear catastrophe and the growing menace against human rights have a common denominator. Both reflect a disintegration of ethics and morality. "The stupendous scientific and material revolution has changed practically every factor in our ecology and society," he asserted. "Perhaps as a result, or coincidental with it, there has taken place a near collapse of public and private morality in practically every sector of human relationships. The previously existing standards of public and private morality may have left a lot to be desired, but at least they existed . . . now they have ceased to be either accepted or observed.

"It is a rule of international law that weapons and methods of warfare which do not discriminate between combatants and civilians should never be used. . . . The bombing of hospitals and civilian targets was outlawed. All these principles and standards have suddenly vanished. . . . The use of the most cruel, terrible and indiscriminate weapon of all time is not even outlawed . . . One frightening aspect of this particular breakdown in our public standards of morality has been the comparative silence of many of the established guardians of humanitarian law. . . . Governments go to war directly or by proxy without declaring war. In these undeclared wars, civilians—men, women and children—are bombed and massacred indiscriminately; chemical agents are used to destroy humans, animals and crops. Prisoners are not only ill-treated, but are tortured systematically in a manner worse than at any barbaric period of history. . . . Secret services are used to assassinate political opponents or to provoke internal dissension in another country or to procure the overthrow of a democratically elected government."

MacBride further said that in earlier wars soldiers fought out of a belief in the defense of family and nation. "But in a war using hydrogen bombs, everything man might propose to defend will perish with him." MacBride defined the overriding obligation of the atomic age: "Peace has to be the DESPERATE IMPERATIVE of humanity," he declared.

MacBride drew his Nobel lecture to a close with the encouraging observation that the technology of the last 30 years may have brought the means which could enable us to protect ourselves, with mass media and higher standards of literacy and education. When we use these tools, we can attain a much greater degree of influence for public opinion in the world than it has ever enjoyed in the past.

He reminded his audience that it was US and world public opinion which forced the United States to withdraw from Vietnam. It was the first time ever that a country at war had been stopped in its tracks by public opinion. MacBride said also (perhaps optimistically) that the same thing is happening in the Soviet Union in regard to human rights and the right to intellectual freedom.

Cautioning that great vigilance will be needed to keep the press and mass media from control by governments or financial interests, MacBride encouraged the nongovernmental sector to use the media constructively. He stressed the importance of voluntary organizations. "In recent years the nongovernmental organizations have been playing an increasingly important role. They are virtually the only independent voices that are heard and that can alert public opinion. They are the only bodies possessing the necessary independence and initiative to restore some faith and idealism in our world."

He encouraged women to seek more prominent roles. "I have found that women have a much better understanding of the imperatives of peace and are much less easily 'taken in' by the specious arguments of experts or diplomats," he observed.

Sean MacBride ended his lecture with a clarion call to the private citizen: "If disarmament can be achieved it will be due to the untiring selfless work of the non-governmental sector," he said. "It is more urgent than ever before. The signpost just ahead of us is 'Oblivion.' The march on this road can be stopped, " MacBride urged, "if public opinion uses the power it now has."

Biography

Sean MacBride was born on January 26, 1904, in Paris, son of Major John MacBride and Maud Gonne MacBride; and was educated in Paris and subsequently at university in Dublin. He took an active part in Irish independence as a young man, suffering imprisonment several times. In 1926 he married Catalina Buford; their daughter, Anna, was born in 1927. MacBride worked as a journalist for many years before being called to the bar in 1937. He founded the Republican Party (Clann na Poblacon) in 1946; and was elected to the Irish Parliament (Dáil Éireann) in 1947, retaining his seat for the next 11 years.

MacBride held numerous posts both within the Irish government and with outside organizations: while a member of the Irish Parliament he was Minister for External Affairs 1948–51, Vice-President of the Organization for European Economic Cooperation 1948–51, and President of the Committee of Ministers of Council of Europe in 1950. He became Secretary–General of the International Commission of Jurists in 1963, and Consultant to the Pontifical Commission Justice and Peace (Iustitia et Pax). He chaired three organizations: the Amnesty International Executive, the Special Committee of the International Non-Governmental Organizations on Human Rights, and the Executive International Peace Bureau. He was president of this organization at the time of his Peace Prize award.

Also current to the time of his award, MacBride was Vice-Chairman of the Congress of World Peace Forces (Moscow, 1973) and Vice-President of the Continuing Committee of the World Federation of United Nations Associations (WFUNA).

He was elected by the General Assembly of the United Nations in 1973 to the post of United Nations Commissioner of Namibia with the rank of Assistant Secretary–General of the United Nations, a position he was also holding at the time of the award.

MacBride has been accorded many honors: elected to the International Gaelic Hall of Fame in 1974; Man of the Year, Irish United Societies, 1975; Lenin International Prize for Peace, 1977; American Medal of Justice, 1978; International Institute of Human Rights Medal, 1978; LLD College of St. Thomas, Minnesota, 1975, Guelph University of Canada, 1978; Trinity College, Dublin, 1978, University of Cape Coast, 1978; and D.Litt. Bradford University, 1977.

His publications include: *Civil Liberty* (pamphlet, 1948); *Our People—Our Money* (1951).

See also: *Amnesty International (1977)*

Bibliography

Time 1974 What price glory? 104 (October 21): 18

RUTH C. REYNOLDS

Eisaku Sato

(1974)

Alfred Nobel expressed a hope that dynamite would bring about the permanent cessation of war "a great deal more rapidly than peace congresses would ever succeed in doing." Fifty years later the creators of the atomic bomb likewise believed the unparalleled power of the bomb would force assurance of no future military use of atomic energy. The two recipients of the 1974 Nobel Peace Prize, Sean MacBride and Eisaku Sato, bear witness, each in contrasting ways, to the disillusion of these expectations. Eisaku Sato had experienced nuclear warfare practiced against his country and had seen the specter of planetary annihilation which it introduced to the planet.

In awarding the Peace Prize for 1974 to Eisaku Sato, the Nobel Committee wished to emphasize the important role the Japanese people had played in promoting close and friendly cooperation with other nations under his leadership as Prime Minister. The Committee took note of Sato's development and implementation of the doctrine that Japan shall never own, produce, or acquire nuclear arms. It is important, the Committee said, that under his leadership Japan signed a pact on the nonproliferation of nuclear arms in February 1970. The Committee observed the heartening precedent Prime Minister Sato had provided for sustained, successful use of dialogue and negotiation on the part of a leader of a major power.

Sato became Prime Minister of Japan in 1962, following 14 years in the House of Representatives and various governmental posts of responsibility. In his Nobel lecture Sato told his audience, "It is only natural that for any statesman at the helm of any government, the question of his country's security should be a concern of the utmost importance.

"Upon assuming the reins of government, I adopted, always conscious of the importance of the role of the United Nations, a policy of following a formula of collective security based on the Charter of the United Nations for the maintenance of my country's security."

Reminding his audience that in the nuclear age the common task confronting all countries is to find the means to survive, Sato said that as Prime Minister he had established the doctrine that Japan will not manufacture nuclear weapons, possess them, or bring them into the country. Also under Sato's administration, the Japanese government supported and signed the nuclear Non-Proliferation Treaty.

Sato, convinced of the possibility of peaceful negotiation between two democratic countries with sound economies, sought the return of the Pacific islands of Ogasawara and Okinawa from the United States. He hoped thereby to relax tensions in Asia, where many of the world's divided, unstable countries exist. His ultimate goal was global in scope: the creation of conditions amenable to world peace. His specific task proved complex. He recalled that the negotiations were not easy, but he finally saw the realization of his goal. The territories were returned through diplomatic negotiations. This accomplishment stands as a rare event in world history.

Sato recited to his Nobel audience a phrase which had long been a favorite saying of his: "Here I stand and there stand you: but we remain friends." Thus he encapsulated the philosophy within which he sought to develop a good neighbor policy in Asia. When challenged by difficulties, he said that he always conducted himself with the utmost sincerity and remained always open to dialogue.

The normalization of relations with Korea testified to the extent of his success in stabilizing an insecure area of Asia. Against a background of hostility, and despite the division within Korea, the spirit of mutual cooperation and the realistic advantage to be found in friendship between close neighbors brought about the highly desirable Treaty on Basic Relations between Japan and the Republic of Korea.

Sato described to his Nobel audience three nonnuclear principles which express the determination of the Japanese people to achieve peace: "First, we need the creation of international safety standards. Research and development in the peaceful use of nuclear energy should be carried on under common worldwide regulations that take the environment into account. Next, an international agreement on the exchange and allocation of nuclear fuel will have to be concluded ... it would be most desirable to establish a system where, under the terms of an agreement concluded for the exchange and allocation of nuclear fuel, such fuels would be placed under the control of an international agency." Lastly, Sato recommended international cooperation in research and development on nuclear fission, deploring the inadequate progress made toward the peaceful uses of atomic energy. He felt it was clear that narrow-minded nationalism was hampering progress in the peaceful utilization of atomic energy.

"All peoples should be united in positive efforts to make peace a reality and to strengthen the foundations on which that peace rests so as to secure for all humanity progress and a better life," Sato concluded. "For my part, I shall devote myself to increasing still my people's capacity to contribute to the well-being of the international community, and to obtaining the world's understanding for such efforts."

Biography

Eisaku Sato was born on March 27, 1901, in Tabuse, Yamaguchi Prefecture, Japan. Educated in German juris-prudence at Tokyo Imperial University (now Tokyo University), he passed the senior civil service examinations and joined the Ministry of Railways. In 1948 he first entered the political world as Chief Cabinet Secretary of the second Yosida Cabinet, an appointed post. The next year he was elected to the House of Representatives, following which he held many government and party posts: Chairman of the Policy Affairs Research, member of the Council of the Liberal Party, Secretary-General of the Liberal Party, Minister of Postal Services and Telecommunications, concurrently Minister of Construction and Minister of State in charge of Hokkaido Development, Chairman of the Executive Council of the Liberal Democratic Party, Minister of Finance, Minister of International Trade and Industry, Minister of State in Charge of Science and Technology, Minister of State in Charge of the 18th Olympic Games. In 1964 he became President of the Liberal Democratic Party and Prime Minister, a post he held until June 1972.

Eisaku Sako married Hiroko Sato in 1926. They had two sons, Ryutaro and Shinji.

President Sato died on June 3, 1975.

Bibliography

Time 1974 What price glory? 104 (October 21): 18

RUTH C. REYNOLDS

Andrei Sakharov

(1975)

The Nobel Peace Prize for 1975 was awarded to Andrei Dimitriyevich Sakharov for his fearless personal commitment in upholding the fundamental principles for peace between men. "Uncompromisingly and with unflagging strength, Sakharov has fought against the abuse of power and all forms of violation of human dignity, and he has fought no less courageously for the idea of government based on the role of law," Mrs. Aase Lionaes told the award ceremony audience. "In this way, in a particularly effective manner and under highly difficult conditions, he has enhanced respect for the values that rally all true peace lovers."

Something of these difficult conditions were reflected in the Soviet Union's refusal to allow Sakharov to attend the ceremony on the grounds that he had possession of secret military information, although he had done no research since his fall from grace in 1968.

Andrei Sakharov's evolution from a pinnacle position in the Soviet scientific community as "Father of the Soviet hydrogen bomb" to a Nobel Laureate, and "fearless combatant for peace among men," is a story of an unfolding social conscience. "I had money ... title, and everything which my work entitled me to have. But I had a very tragic feeling," Sakharov said of his years as an atomic scientist working on development of nuclear arms. Though the work of his group also included harnessing nuclear power for peaceful purposes in industry, Sakharov said that the tragedy which befell Hiroshima and Nagasaki distressed him "both as an atomic physicist and simply as a man of the Planet Earth."

In his book, *Sakharov Speaks*, he describes his changing way of thinking: "Beginning in 1957 (not without the influence of statements on this subject made throughout the world by such people as Albert Schweitzer, Linus Pauling, and others), I felt myself responsible for the problem of radioactive contamination from nuclear explosions." He was frank with the authorities about his convictions, hoping to generate a free and open exchange of opinion. In this he met with disappointment, although Sakharov

338

believes that his views did influence the Soviet decision to join with the United States in an agreement in 1963 on a ban on nuclear testing.

Between 1953 and 1962, much of what happened was connected with the development of nuclear weapons and with the preparations for and realization of the nuclear experiments, he said. "At the same time I was becoming ever more conscious of the moral problems inherent in this work. In and after 1964, when I began to concern myself with the biological issues, and particularly from 1967 onwards, the extent of the problems over which I felt uneasy increased to such a point that in 1968 I felt a compelling urge to make my views public." That year he wrote his famous essay, *Progress, Peaceful Coexistence, and Intellectual Freedom*, based on the belief that socialism and capitalism would eventually converge, and that a workable world government could become a reality. His growing fear of nuclear war motivated his writing this early essay, and he wrote it from a global point of view, appealing to responsible citizens worldwide. It was published abroad in 1968.

At that time, as a socialist, Sakharov was optimistic about the progress within his own country both toward lessening restrictions upon the citizens within its borders, and increased Soviet cooperation internationally. But he had misjudged the period of relative liberalism which he thought had arrived in the Soviet Union, and looking back he came to assess the context within which he wrote it as one of isolation in a highly privileged scientific milieu, without contact with the community outside. That same year Soviet tanks rolled into Czechoslovakia amidst a new wave of repression in the Soviet Union. Sakharov's security clearance was revoked and he was dismissed from his research position and assigned to the Physics Institute of the Academy of Scientists.

As Sakharov's life changed, his outlook expanded. Along with his long-time concern with global problems, he now confronted personal and human ones. His intimate contact with the daily life of the ordinary Soviet citizen propelled him into a commitment for an intense struggle in their behalf, a commitment which he openly indicated in letters to the authorities demanding reforms.

"From 1970 onwards," Sakharov said, "the defence of human rights and the defence of the victims of political trials became all-important to me." He founded the "Committee for Human Rights" that year, forming a committee with friends and fellow scientists. They labored to achieve the following aims while attempting to work within the framework of the law: the abolition of secret trials, a new press law ensuring that people would have full information, reforms in the prison system, the amnesty of political prisoners, the abolition of the death penalty, open frontiers, and a ban on the use of psychiatric institutes for political ends.

Sakharov's ideas on the conditions necessary for peace and détente have found an echo in the "Agreement on Security and Cooperation" in Europe. Signed in Helsinki on August 1, 1975, by 35 different nations, it was an endorsement of the leading states of the world that human rights are an essential factor in détente between nations. Sakharov's Nobel lecture, read by his wife, Elena Bonner Sakharov, opened with the declaration, "Peace, progress, human rights—these three goals are insolubly linked to one another: it is impossible to achieve one of these goals if the other two are ignored. This is the dominant idea that provides the main theme of my lecture.

"I am convinced that international confidence, mutual understanding, disarmament, and international security are inconceivable without an open society with freedom of information, freedom of conscience, the right to publish, and the right to travel and choose the country in which one wishes to live.

"I am likewise convinced that freedom of conscience, together with other civil rights, provides the basis for scientific progress and constitutes a guarantee that scientific advances will not be used to despoil mankind, providing the basis for economic and social progress."

Sakharov strongly recommended against any attempt to reduce the tempo of scientific and technological progress. "In actual fact all important aspects of progress are closely interwoven; not one of them can be dispensed without a risk of destroying the entire setup of our civilization. Progress is indivisible," he warned.

He pleaded for a proportional and simultaneous military deescalation for all countries, with attention to finding some solution to the economic and social problems involved.

Sakharov took the rare opportunity afforded to him through his Nobel lecture to speak of the repressions in the Soviet Union, thus opening a window upon that area of information so restricted to the Western world. He honored by name many Soviet compatriots who had suffered prison, banishment, and other deprivations as punishment for following their conscience, and begged to share his Nobel honors with them, and with the many who yet remain unnamed.

Sakharov addressed the problem of disarmament, defining it as one of the central problems of our present age. "It is imperative," he said, "to promote confidence between nations, and carry out measures of control with the aid of international inspection groups. This is only possible if détente is extended to the ideological sphere, and it presupposes greater social openness."

He concluded his lecture with some prerequisites he deemed essential for peace: "We need reform, not revolution. We need a pliant, pluralist, tolerant community, which selectively and tentatively can bring about a free, undogmatic use of the experiences of all social systems. What is détente? What is rapprochement? We are concerned not with words, but with a willingness to create a better and more friendly society, a better world order."

No Peace Prize Laureate has re-created so closely the dynamics behind the original decision by Alfred Nobel to create a prize for peace as has Sakharov. Nobel's invention of dynamite led Nobel to an acute awareness of the development in weaponry he had made possible, and he thought much about the consequences for humanity, ultimately giving of effort and money toward the prevention of its use. Sakharov, inventor of the hydrogen bomb, likewise became haunted by what his discovery might mean to humanity, and he, too, has made all the efforts within his power toward prevention of its use. His was a singularly appropriate award.

Biography

Andrei Dimitriyevich Sakharov was born in Moscow in 1921. He studied physics at Moscow State University, and attracted considerable attention at an early age with the publication of a number of scientific papers. In 1945 Sakharov joined the P. N. Lebedev Physics Institute in Moscow, where he worked with Igor Tamm, the specialist on quantum mechanics and subsequent winner (in 1958) of the Nobel Prize for Physics. Under Tamm's guidance, Sakharov obtained his doctorate in physical and mathematical sciences in 1947—a formidable achievement at such an early age in the Soviet Union.

During the years 1948–56, Sakharov was engaged almost exclusively in nuclear research as a member of a team of scientists engaged in the development of nuclear arms. A virtual press blackout was imposed on these activities; but such was the extent of his achievements that in 1953 Sakharov became the youngest scientist ever to be elected to the prestigious Soviet Academy of Sciences. He became a member of the American Academy of Sciences in 1945, of the National Academy of Sciences in 1972, and a Foreign Associate of the Academie des Sciences in 1981. In 1968, however, a significant change occurred in his status and way of life. In that year he published his famous essay on *Progress, Peaceful Coexistence, and Intellectual Freedom*; and these statements presaged the role he was later to play as a critic of his society. In addition to the Nobel Peace Prize, he has received the following honors: the Eleanor Roosevelt Peace Award, 1973, Cino del Duca Prize, 1974, Reinhold Niebuhr Prize, Chicago University, 1974, Fritt Ord Prize, 1980. Married to Elena Bonner, they have one son and one daughter. In addition to scientific works, his publications are: *Progress, Peaceful Coexistence, and Intellectual Freedom* (1968), *Sakharov Speaks* (1974), *My Country and the World* (1975), and *Alarm and Hope* (1979).

Bibliography

Sakharov A D 1968 *Progress, Peaceful Coexistence, and Intellectual Freedom*. Norton, New York

Sakharov A D 1975a *My Country and the World*. Knopf, New York

Sakharov A D 1975b The need for an open world. *Bull. At. Sci.* 31(9): 8–9

Sakharov A D 1978 *Alarm and Hope*. Knopf, New York

Science 1975 Letter to Izvestiya. 190 (December 19): 1152–53

Shapley D 1975 Sakharov: Scientists welcome award of Nobel Peace Prize. *Science* 190 (October 24): 358–59

York H F 1981 Sakharov and the nuclear test ban. *Bull. At. Sci.* 37(9): 33–37

RUTH C. REYNOLDS

Mairead Corrigan and Betty Williams

(1976)

Two women shared the Nobel Peace Prize for 1976. Given retroactively in 1977, the Prize honored Betty Williams and Mairead Corrigan, co-founders of the Northern Ireland Peace Movement, who, the Nobel Committee said, "have shown us what ordinary people can do to promote the cause of peace . . . They never heeded the difficulty of their task, they merely tackled it because they were so convinced that this was precisely what was needed." The Committee expressed admiration that these two women, without talk of "ingenious theories, of shrewd diplomacy or pompous declarations," unleashed in their war-torn country a fervent desire for peace lying latent in thousands of hearts. Out of this grew a peace movement, and, the Committee concluded, "with poignant simplicity and confidence they have accepted responsibility for what they started."

It was a campaign born in a moment of carnage on a street in Belfast. In August 1976 a British soldier shot the driver of an Irish Republican Army (IRA) get-away car. The driver, Danny Lennon, was killed instantly, and the out-of-control vehicle slammed into a mother and her three small children. The children died instantly, their mother was gravely injured. Violent death has become familiar in Northern Ireland, a community long-divided by hatred and sectarian bitterness. In 1969 a student-led civil rights movement sparked the simmering hostility into violence. The Provisional wing of the IRA, committed to an armed struggle for a united, Catholic Ireland, and the Ulster Defence Association (UDA), implacable opponents of the IRA in their commitment to a separate Protestant Ulster, engaged in such violent exchanges that in desperation the British government stepped in and imposed direct rule from London backed up by martial law. Yet senseless, sudden death continued: some 1,700 people were killed in the following seven years, and the citizens seemed too numbed to protest at the horror permeating their lives.

Betty Williams witnessed the horrific accident in August 1976 and the deaths of the three young children, and in that moment she was overwhelmed with a passionate determination to end the bloodshed. Galvanized into action, she went from door to door begging her neighbors to join her in demonstrating for an end to the violence. Her appeal touched a spontaneous, emotional response, and 200 people rallied around her. One of the first to join her was Mairead Corrigan, aunt of the dead children.

In that first week the two women, with Ciaran McKeown, a journalist, founded the "Movement of the Peace People." One week later 10,000 people—Protestants and Catholics—marched the streets of Belfast. To the cries of "treason" and "traitor" hurled at them by agitators from both sides, they replied, "We condemn all violence whether it is from the UDA, the IRA, or the British Army."

The two women acknowledged that they were facing a long-range and complex task. Betty Williams described the nature of the tenacious Irish conflict in an interview: "Most wars are wars of insanity. But ours is doubly insane, because we're fighting over something they call 'faith': Catholic and Protestant. We live on an absolutely beautiful land, and we cultivate it with our blood" (*Christian Century* 1977).

Though Ireland has long been locked into the warring factions Betty Williams describes, and though reason would declare that the use of arms could never bring about a lasting peace, no-one had seemed capable of suggesting a viable alternative. The "two women of peace from Ulster" challenged this deadlock. "We know that this insane and immoral imbalance of priorities cannot be changed overnight; we also know that it will not be changed without the greatest struggle," they conceded.

In her Nobel lecture Mrs. Williams called for "an incessant struggle to get the human race to stop wasting its vast resources on arms, and start investing in the people who must live out their lives on the planet we share, east and west, north and south. And that struggle must be all the greater because it has to be an unarmed, nonviolent struggle, and requires more courage and more persistence than the courage to squeeze triggers or press murderous buttons. Men must not only end war, they must begin to have the courage not to even prepare for war."

"We have to think, and think hard, but if we do not have compassion before we even start thinking, then we are quite likely to start fighting over theories," Mrs. Williams said. "We are divided on the surface of this planet by physical barriers, emotional barriers, ideological barriers, barriers of prejudice and hatreds of every kind . . . yet the whole human family can be united by compassion." She said that now the moment in history has come when, for very survival, compassion and understanding must be given "pride of place over the vainglorious adventures that lead to war."

The Nobel Committee acknowledged the perilous challenge facing the two women, "But," the Committee said, "one incontrovertible fact remains: they took the first courageous step along the road to peace. They did so in the name of humanity and love of their neighbour: someone had to start forgiving."

"We admire Betty Williams and Mairead Corrigan for tackling so fearlessly the perilous task of leading the way into no-man's land, in the cause of peace and reconciliation . . . a courageous, unselfish act that proved an inspiration to thousands, that lit a light in the darkness, and that gave fresh hope to people who believed that all hope was gone."

Biographies

Mairead Corrigan was born in January, 1944, in Belfast, one of eight children of Mr. and Mrs. Andrew Corrigan. Educated at St. Vincent's Primary School, Belfast, and at Miss Gordon's Commercial College, she worked from the age of 16 in various positions as a shorthand typist. She volunteered in Catholic Organizations establishing clubs for physically handicapped children and for teenagers, and she worked in preschool play groups. She was also a visitor to internees in Long Kesh Prison. On August 10, 1976 her sister's three children were crushed by a runaway car driven by an IRA man who had been shot by British soldiers on the streets of Belfast. A week later, as the outcome of a spontaneous and emotional response, she co-founded the Community of Peace People with Mr. Ciaran McKeown and Mrs. Betty Williams. She has been prominent in the Peace Movement since that time, and was Chairman of the Peace People Organisation, 1980–81. She has been awarded the Carl Von Ossietzky Medal for Courage from the Berlin section of the International League of Human Rights, an Honorary Doctor of Law from Yale University, and the Norwegian People Peace Prize, 1976. In September 1981, Mairead Corrigan married Mr. Jackie Maguire, her former brother-in-law. Mr. Maguire's wife, Ann, Miss Corrigan's sister, committed suicide in 1980.

Betty Williams was born in May, 1943, in Belfast to Mr. and Mrs. Smyth. She was educated at St. Teresa's Primary School in Belfast and St. Dominic's Grammar School and worked as an office receptionist. She married Mr. Ralph Williams on June 14, 1961, and they had a son, Paul, and a daughter, Deborah. In August 1976, following the tragic death of a neighbor's three small children, crushed on the streets of Belfast by a car driven by an IRA member who had been shot by British troops, Betty Williams co-founded the Northern Ireland Peace Movement. She has received the Carl Von Ossietzky Medal for Courage from the Berlin section of the International League of Human Rights, an Honorary Doctor of Law from Yale University, and the Norwegian People Peace Prize, 1976. In February 1980, after falling out with her co-founders, Betty Williams resigned from the executive committee and ceased to be associated with the Peace Movement. In October 1982, she married Mr. Jim Perkins in Florida.

Bibliography

Christian Century 1977 Good news from Norway. 94(34): 973–74

Keerdoja E 1978 Ulster's women of peace. *Newsweek* 91: 18

Kennedy R S, Klotz-Chamberlin P 1977 Northern Ireland's 'guerrillas of peace': An interview with Betty Williams and Nancy McDonnell. *Christian Century* 94(25): 746–48

Time 1977 Two Peace Prizes from Oslo. 110(17): 54

Willenson K, Collings A 1977 Two women of Ulster. *Newsweek* 90: 61

RUTH C. REYNOLDS

Amnesty International

(1977)

Amnesty International received the 1977 Nobel Peace Prize, in an award ceremony shared with the initiators of the Northern Ireland Peace Movement, Mairead Corrigan and Betty Williams, who were receiving the 1976 Peace Prize retroactively. With these awards the Nobel Committee expressed its conviction that peace is more than merely abstinence from war; it also embodies such basic human rights as freedom of thought, freedom of conscience, and freedom of religion or faith.

In his acceptance speech for Amnesty International, Mumtaz Soysal expressed gratification with this recognition that a just society is a precondition to a peaceful world. The awareness of this must not grow dim. "Each violation," Soysal explained, "can set in motion a trend toward the debasement of human dignity. From individuals to groups, from groups to nations, from nations to groups of nations, in chain reaction a pattern is set of violence and repression. . . . This must never be allowed to start and the place to stop it is at the level of the individual. . . . Therefore, the protection of the rights of the individual to think freely, to express himself freely, to associate freely with others and to disseminate his thoughts is essential to the preservation of world peace."

These freedoms are interlocked with the economic and social conditions necessary to make them possible. Therefore the aim of economic and social development is to work always towards the ultimate end that individuals are made more free, more able to express and fulfill themselves, more able to contribute to humanity. Soysal explained that where there are communities composed of individuals who are free in this fullest sense there is less likelihood of exploitation of the weaker by the strong. This applies whether for a social class, or a nation, or a group of nations. Therefore promotion of human rights in the fullest possible sense is directly related to the preservation of lasting peace.

The world community stands at a tragic distance from this picture. Information obtained by Amnesty International shows that human rights are violated in all parts of the world, in all major regions, and in all political or ideological blocs.

By the beginning of 1985 there were 3,430 Amnesty International groups in 55 countries—almost 200 more groups than the year before. There were over

500,000 members, supporters and subscribers with sections in 45 countries.

A total of 4,668 prisoners were adopted as prisoners of conscience or were being investigated as possible prisoners of conscience. During 1984, 1,655 new cases were taken up and 1,516 prisoners re ased.

Amnesty International issued 319 urgent action appeals on behalf of individuals or groups of prisoners in 67 countries. Of these, 104 were prompted by reports of torture, 22 were made on medical grounds, 67 were issued because of legal concerns, 57 related to extrajudicial executions or "disappearances" and 58 were on behalf of people under sentence of death. (*Amnesty International Report* 1985 p. 359)

Hopeful situations where there have been substantial releases of political prisoners are more than outweighed by deteriorating situations in other parts of the world. In Latin America some countries' security forces have been used as instruments for political murder. Government-sanctioned torture is still practiced. The list of crimes deemed punishable by the death penalty is growing, and the rate of execution is high, especially in Africa and Asia. Long-term banishments are secretively imposed without the basic right of trial. In some instances the laws and court procedures make a mockery of justice.

A great many people have been seized with a sense of horror that is paralyzing, the Nobel Committee noted, but Amnesty International, far from shrinking into the impotence of discouragement, has stepped up its efforts to ensure that governments in all countries should feel morally obligated to abide by the United Nations Universal Declaration on Human Rights.

Amnesty International had its inception in 1960 in a compartment of a train in London, where a British lawyer, Peter Benenson, happened to read an account of two Portuguese students who were being sentenced to long internment in prison for making critical remarks of Salazar's regime. At that moment Benenson decided he would try to do something for the two young men. Gathering together some friends, he organized a letter-writing campaign. What they began so modestly on that day developed into a movement that is renowned today for its worldwide befriending of prisoners. Its early years of rapid growth were administrated under the skillful leadership of 1974 Peace Prize Laureate Sean MacBride.

Called "the conscience of the world" by many, Amnesty International works for the release of prisoners who are incarcerated for their opinions and have made no use of violence or incited others to do so. These it calls "prisoners of conscience."

In behalf of all prisoners anywhere, Amnesty International works for basic rights: that they be accorded fair trial, openly and with legal defense, and if convicted, that prisoners be guaranteed humane treatment. As violence escalates over the world, Amnesty works rigorously to expose torture or cruel, inhumane treatment, to the end that public opinion and censure can be brought to bear against such practices.

An important tool which Amnesty International has guarded carefully since its inception is its own meticulous neutrality. It is committed to political and geographic impartiality. Nor will it accept donations which could compromise its freedom of activity. This absolute neutrality is the *sine qua non* if it is to maintain credibility.

The people in Amnesty work within groups. Relatively small groups "adopt" prisoners from a country other than their own. With the help of the head office in London these groups trace, help, and seek to secure the release of prisoners of conscience. Wherever possible the adopting group develops a close relationship with the prisoners they seek to help. They write the prisoners letters. They help their families. They seek ways to boost morale, so the forgotten and banished can shed their fear that no-one cares. They expose prisoners' plight in any way possible. The groups organize letter writing, flooding government officials with mail. They demonstrate and use any form of media exposure open to them in behalf of the prisoners. Often release has resulted simply because they have become a nuisance in a situation which has been operating under the cloak of secrecy. The avalanche of mail bombarding officials at all levels can create an untenable annoyance to a government.

Amnesty International never claims responsibility for winning a prisoner's release. As Secretary-General Martin Ennals explained, "No government likes to be told they have done something under duress."

It is clear, the Nobel Committee noted, that the organization's future will depend to a large extent upon its audience with fair-minded people worldwide. At the Belgrade Conference held to negotiate a follow-up on promises made in the Helsinki Agreements to promote human rights, a number of nations maintained that for one country to call attention to a violation of human rights in another country constitutes interference in the internal affairs of that country. Chairwoman Lionaes, speaking for the Nobel Committee, refused to believe that a ruse of this nature would be countenanced by international opinion, holding that human rights recognize no national boundaries.

What have been the results of Amnesty International's activity? At the time of the award, of some 16,000 prisoners aided since 1961, 10,600 had been released. Other factors may well have contributed to these results, but it is a fair reflection on the scope of Amnesty's work. However, statistics cannot adequately measure what hope might mean to an inmate sunk in the depths of despair. No accounting can establish the weight of impact that the defense of human dignity against torture, violence, and degradations has upon the cause of peace in this world.

"This work to protect human dignity," the Committee said in awarding Amnesty International the Peace Prize, "is not a sacrifice we make for others: it is important that all of us should understand that in this age we must act accordingly in recognition of the earnest appeal contained in Aleksandr Solzhenitsyn's words:

> You're defending yourself—
> Your future is at stake."

History

Amnesty International was founded by a London lawyer, Peter Benenson, in 1961. Sean MacBride, Nobel Peace Prize Laureate of 1974, was its Chairman from 1961 to 1975, leading it from its simple start as a letter-writing campaign on behalf of two unfairly imprisoned students in Portugal to a world-renowned organization working against many aspects of injustice. Amnesty International works for the release of prisoners jailed because of political or religious beliefs, and in behalf of the basic rights and humane treatment of all prisoners everywhere. It also opposes capital punishment.

Their method is exposure of the prisoners' plight through flooding members of governments and influential citizens with mail, and through use of any media open to them. The governments often react to the annoyance thus created by releasing the prisoners. At the time of the Amnesty International Nobel Peace Prize award in 1977, out of 16,000 prisoners in whose behalf they had worked over 10,000 had been released. By the beginning of 1985 there were 3,430 Amnesty International groups in 55 countries. It had over 500,000 members, supporters, and subscribers, sections in 45 countries, and 21 languages were spoken (*Amnesty International Report* 1985 p. 359).

Bibliography

Amnesty International Report 1985 Amnesty International Publications, London

Christian Century 1977 Good news from Norway. 94 (October 26): 973–74

Christian Century 1984 Events and people: Rights abuses continue. 101 (November 14): 1057–58

Newsweek 1977 The world's conscience. 90 (October 24): 61

Stempf T 1984 Getting away with murder. *America* 151 (October 24): 166–68

Time 1977 Two Peace Prizes from Oslo. 110 (October 24): 54

RUTH C. REYNOLDS

Menachem Begin

(1978)

The 1978 Nobel Peace Prize was awarded to Prime Minister Menachem Begin of Israel and President Anwar al-Sadat of Egypt in recognition of the foundation they laid for future peace by opening negotiations between their one-time enemy countries and preparing a pathway toward nonviolent solutions in the Middle East.

The Nobel Committee pronounced their award to be without precedent in many ways: "Never has the Nobel Committee considered it apposite to award the Peace Prize to statesmen from the troubled and sadly devastated Middle East," Chairwoman Lionaes declared. "Never has the Prize been closely associated with agreements such as the two Camp David agreements. Never has the Peace Prize expressed a greater or more audacious hope—a hope of peace for the people of Egypt, for the people of Israel, and for all the peoples of the strife-torn and war-ravaged Middle East."

Israel and Egypt lie in the cradle of civilization, inheritors of a turbulent history. Juxtapositioned between the birthplaces of Islam, Judaism, and Christianity, their soil is regarded by followers of each religion as a divinely established birthright. The cultures of the Middle East are diverse, and differing economic interests often clash. Its countries are ravaged by schisms, prey to foreign domination and wars.

Menachem Begin was born in a country also fraught with tensions. In 1913 his birthplace, Poland, was in the grip of unparalleled anti-Semitism. The persecution he witnessed early in life crystallized Begin's determination to see the restoration of the ancient Jewish homeland. Both of his parents and his only brother were killed in the Nazi Holocaust.

Begin's youthful years were turbulent. Twice he was imprisoned: first during his law school years, when he took part in a demonstration for the right of persecuted Jews to emigrate to Palestine; and again in Lithuania, where the Soviets intercepted his family's flight to Palestine and he was sentenced to eight years of forced labor in a Siberian prison camp.

The German attack on the Soviet Union provided the circumstances for Begin's release. He was pressed into service in a new Polish army that the Soviets hoped to deploy in the struggle against Nazism, and was posted to Transjordan, and from there, in 1942, he made his way to Palestine. There he again found Jews denied the means of escape from the threat of extermination at the hands of the Nazis—this time through restrictions on immigration imposed by Great Britain. Begin demanded an open door for Jewish refugees, throwing his energy into opposing the devastating restrictions. His subsequent leadership of the Irgun, an underground combatant organization calling for the independence of Palestine as a Jewish state, brought him a reputation as a terrorist and a price of £30,000 on his head. Commanding a small but well-disciplined force that numbered never more than 2,000 activists, Begin planned and directed a guerrilla campaign against the British that has become what *Current Biography* (1977) termed "something of a classic in the annals of wars of liberation."

In 1948 the State of Israel was founded with the help of the United Nations, and Begin with his former Irgun associates created the Herut ("Freedom") political party, which was radically opposed to the Israeli Labour Party, Mapai, led by Ben Gurion. The creation of this new state exacerbated the long-standing conflict between the Jews and the Arabs, and four wars have since been fought between them. It was against this background of resentment and hostility that Begin, as newly elected Prime Minister of Israel, accepted Sadat's diplomatic overture and invited the charismatic leader of Israel's ancient "enemy" country to speak before the Israeli Knesset (Parliament).

Years of bitter hostility between the two countries with only brief intervals of truce now stood challenged by the two new leaders who dared to propose a visionary program to establish a permanent peace. Begin described the philosophy that had led him to that momentous occasion: "If through your efforts and sacrifices you win liberty, and with it the pros-

pect for peace, then work for peace because there is no mission in life more sacred."

In his pursuit of that dream, Begin recalled, "We went any place, we looked for any avenue, we made any effort to bring about negotiations between Israel and its neighbors, negotiations without which peace remains an abstract desire ... in peace, the Middle East will become invigorated and transformed."

With his invitation to Sadat, Begin made a promise: "You will be received with respect and cordiality." And indeed he was. "We knew and learned that we have differences of opinion," Begin recalled. "But whenever we remember those days of Jerusalem we say, always, that they were shining, beautiful days of friendliness and understanding."

The two leaders forged a mutual pledge: "No more war. No more bloodshed. We shall negotiate and reach agreement." Their daring leadership provided the way to the historic agreements at Camp David.

"Admittedly, there were difficult times," Begin told his Nobel award ceremony audience. "Let nobody forget that we are dealing with a conflict of more than sixty years with its manifold tragedies. These we must put behind us in order to establish friendship and make peace the beauty of our lives.

"The President of the United States, Mr. Jimmy Carter, unforgettably invested unsparing effort, untiring energy and great devotion in the peace-making process ... If, because of all these efforts, President Sadat and I have been awarded the Nobel Peace Prize, let me from this rostrum again congratulate him."

Nobel Chairwoman Lionaes also recognized Henry Kissinger's role in bringing about the Camp David meetings. "We recall his energetic attempts to get the belligerent parties in the so-called Yom Kippur War to come together in a peace conference in Geneva," she told the Nobel audience. The conference resulted in agreement between Egypt and Israel on a number of important points, and provided the basis for the meeting at Camp David.

Begin summarized their achievement there. "Despite all the differences, we found solutions for problems, agreed on issues, and the Framework for Peace was signed. The path leading to peace was paved."

The Nobel Committee acknowledged that "time-consuming negotiations" on the Israeli-occupied territories of the West Bank, Gaza, and the Golan Heights remained for the future. Their award at this time was based upon recognition that Sadat and Begin had played key roles in creating a vigorous quest for peace between two former enemies.

The Committee commended their long-sustained efforts: "Both men were born in a century marked by global wars and gigantic revolutions, both of them have been active in the mainstream of history ... from their earliest years both identified with the fate of their countries, both have fought and suffered in prison and in labor camp, for the sovereignty of their native land and for the freedom of man.

"Their lives have crossed in an act of peace that may well usher in a new era, a future of material renewal and peace, not only for their two respective countries, but for the entire Middle East."

In his Nobel lecture Prime Minister Begin expanded this vision: "Perhaps the very capability for total destruction of our little planet—achieved for the first time in the annals of mankind—will one day, God willing, become the origin, the cause and the prime mover for the elimination of all instruments of destruction from the face of the earth. And ultimate peace, prayed for and yearned for by previous generations, will become the portion of all nations."

Biography

Menachem Begin was born in the Polish city of Brest-Litovsk (now part of the Soviet Union), son of Wolf Begin and Hassia Kossovsky Begin. Educated at the gymnasium in Brest-Litovsk, he went on to study law at the University of Warsaw, taking a Master of Jurisprudence degree in 1935. As a student, Begin was co-founder of the Jewish Student Defense Unit; and in 1929 had joined Birit Trumpeldor (or BCTK), a militant youth organization associated with the Revisionist wing of the World Zionist Organization. After graduating, he served first as General Secretary of the Czechoslovakian branch (1936–38) before becoming commander of the Polish Betar in 1939. When the Soviet Union annexed Lithuania, his Betar role stamped him as "unreliable" to the communist regime and he was arrested and sentenced to eight years as a slave laborer in the Arctic wasteland.

After the German attack on the Soviet Union, Begin was released to serve in the new Polish army that the Soviets hoped to deploy in the struggle against Nazism, and was posted to Transjordan. From there, he made his way into Palestine where he became commander of the Irgun Zvai Leumi (National Fighting Organization associated with the Revisionist faction). His opposition to the British refusal to an open door for all escapees from Hitler's Europe and immediate political independence for a Jewish state won him a price of £30,000 on his head.

Commanding a small but well-disciplined force that never numbered more than 2,000 activists, Begin planned and directed a guerrilla campaign against the British. He gained a reputation for ruthlessness and was condemned as a terrorist by the British.

When the State of Israel became a reality in 1948 Begin founded a new political party, Herut, in opposition to Ben Gurion. As Chairman of Herut he won a seat in the Israeli Knesset (Parliament) in the first election and was an active member thereafter. In 1977 he became the sixth Prime Minister of Israel. Declaring that the main goal of his government was peace, he called for direct talks with the heads of Egypt, Jordan, and Syria, and expressed hope for strengthened ties with the United States, France, and the Soviet Union. One of his first official actions was to authorize the granting of asylum to 66 Vietnamese refugees picked up at sea by an Israeli ship.

Begin was reelected Prime Minister in national elections in 1981, and remained in office until his retirement in 1983.

Menachem Begin married Aliza Arnold in Poland in 1939 and they have one son, Benyamin, two daughters, Hassia and Leah, and several grandchildren. Begin is the author of an autobiography, *HaMered* (1950), *Be-Leilot Levanim* (1953), *White Nights* (1957), describing his wartime experiences in Europe, and *The Revolt* (1964), which has been read worldwide in many languages, and numerous articles.

See also: Articles: *Camp David Accords*

Bibliography

Deming A, Martin D C, DeFrank T M 1978 A timely award? *Newsweek* 92 (November 6): 67–68, 71
Feld B T 1978 Norwegian prophecy or a gamble for peace? *Bull. Atomic Sci.* 34(10): 5
O'Hare J A 1978 Of many things. *America* 139(15): inside cover
Time 1978 Alone in Oslo. 112 (December 18): 44

RUTH C. REYNOLDS

Anwar al-Sadat

(1978)

The 1978 Nobel Peace Prize was shared by Anwar al-Sadat, President of Egypt, and Menachem Begin, Prime Minister of Israel, in recognition of their creation of two frame agreements on peace, one in the Middle East and one between Egypt and Israel.

The Nobel Committee said that three precedents were established in the history of the Nobel Peace Prize by these two choices. Never before had the Prize gone to statesmen from the Middle East, never before had the prize honored agreements such as the two reached at Camp David, and never before, the Committee stated, "has the Peace Prize expressed a greater or more audacious hope—a hope of peace for the people of Egypt, for the people of Israel, and for all the peoples of the strife-torn and war-ravaged Middle East."

The history of the Middle East covers 6,000 years, during which the juxtaposition of diverse cultures, civilizations, and religions has given rise to many longlasting tensions. Islam, Judaism, and Christianity all revere its soil as the birthplace of their belief. The economic interests of the Middle East, positioned as it is at the junction of Asia, Europe, and Africa, have long been entangled, making for a history of continuous foreign invasions.

Such is the legacy which influenced Anwar Sadat early in life. His country's struggle for freedom from British subjugation dominated Sadat's aspirations during his youth. He entered a military career with the dream of throwing off the British yoke, and he was destined to play a vital part in achieving that dream.

Sadat began life in humble circumstances. Born on December 25, 1918, he was one of 13 children in a devout and loving Moslem family, and grew up in a small village in the Nile Delta. He paid high tribute to the childhood he spent there: "Everything I experienced in Mit Abul-Kum made me happy." His boyhood feeling of oneness with nature and closeness with family created a sense of balance between himself, the soil, and his family which brought a sense of inner harmony important to Sadat all his life. "I first felt that inner peace in my village where I still have my roots, deep in the soil of the Nile Valley," he said. "But I really found this peace in Cell 54, a bare damp room in Cairo Central Prison where I spent 18 months for revolutionary activity. I was in solitary, where I could not read or write or listen to the radio.... Suffering builds up a human being and gives him self knowledge."

Along with his school friend, Gamal Abdel Nasser, Sadat became an army officer, and together they formed a secret group of officers in 1939 devoted to freeing Egypt from foreign domination. Hoping to weaken Britain's hold on his country by cooperating with her enemy during the Second World War, Sadat attempted collusion with the Germans. The attempt proved ill-fated, and for this activity he was stripped of his officer's rank and imprisoned in 1942.

Reinstated in the army in 1950, Sadat played a supporting role to his friend Nasser in the Egyptian revolution which led to the overthrow of King Farouk. During the 18 years of Nasser's presidency which followed, Sadat became intimately acquainted with his country's problems through service in a wide range of posts: as cabinet minister, Secretary-General of the Islamic Conference, Speaker of the National Assembly, editor of the government newspaper, and finally, in 1969, Vice-President.

Sadat was the only member of the original revolutionary officers' group not purged by the suspicious dictator–president. He enjoyed the confidence of Nasser and understood well how the revolution had fallen sadly short of establishing democratic practices. When he became President in September 1970 following Nasser's fatal heart attack, Sadat devoted his energies to addressing this failure.

Sadat's sudden "October war" against Israel in 1975 he described in his autobiography, *In Search of Identity*, as a "paradoxical necessary prelude to any kind of lasting peace in the Middle East.... It was for us in Egypt a historic transformation from despair to hope, from complete lack of self-confidence to the regaining of confidence. After the cease-fire we initiated an ambitious program of building and reconstruction ... constant military preparation had plunged our economy to below zero.... Despite these obstacles, we succeeded in restoring our economic path from total isolation to an open-door policy.

"And since that time we have worked wholeheartedly for peace," he said. It was after that struggle, when lasting peace seemed elusive to all efforts, that Sadat sent a message to Prime Minister Begin of Israel expressing interest in coming to address the Israeli Knesset (Parliament). When Begin responded with an invitation immediately, President Sadat startled the world, his fellow countrymen included, by his unprecedented trip to Jerusalem in 1977. "I made that trip because I was convinced that we owe it to this generation and the generations to come not to leave a stone unturned in our pursuit of peace," he said.

Nobel Committee Chairwoman Lionaes commented on that remarkable event: "During the thirty preceding years the peoples of the Middle East have on four separate occasions been the victims of warfare, and there seemed no prospect of peace. President Sadat's great contribution to peace was that he had the sufficient courage and foresight to break away from this vicious circle.

"His decision to accept Prime Minister Menachem Begin's invitation of November 17th, 1977, to attend a meeting of the Israeli parliament on November 19th was an act of great courage, both from a personal and from a political point of view. This was a dramatic break with the past and a courageous step forward into a new age."

With this forward step, Sadat and Begin created a diplomatic climate conducive to their meeting at Camp David in September 1978. There, two major peace documents were created: "A Framework for Peace in the Middle East," and the "Framework for the Conclusion of a Peace Treaty Between Egypt and Israel," which established broad areas of compromise and made arrangements for difficult areas of conflict to be negotiated in the future.

Chairwoman Lionaes referred to an important third personage in the Camp David setting. "The masterbuilder responsible for the bridge that had to be built between Egypt and Israel in order that these two one-time enemy nations should have any opportunity of coming together ... was the President of the United States, Jimmy Carter." Sadat concurred, opening his Nobel lecture saying "Recognition is due to a man of the highest integrity, President Jimmy Carter, whose signal efforts to overcome obstacles in the way of peace deserves our keenest appreciation."

The Committee, although admitting that difficult problems dealing with the Israeli-occupied territories of the West Bank, Gaza, and the Golan Heights had been left for future negotiations, gave high praise to the effort made and the progress achieved: "Meanwhile, the world must be allowed to share in the happiness of the people of Egypt and Israel, that, for the first time since the re-establishment of the state of Israel in 1948, an agreement has successfully been reached which, on a long term basis, provides a genuine opportunity for peace in an area over which the shadow of war had hovered for so long."

Had President Sadat been allowed to pursue his goal, the future for establishment of permanent peace between Egypt and Israel would seem promising in the hands of a leader who could say during his historic first appearance before the Israeli Knesset: "Any life lost in war is the life of a human being, irrespective of whether it is an Arab or an Israeli.

"The wife who becomes widowed is a human being, entitled to live in a happy family, Arab or Israeli.

"Innocent children, deprived of paternal care and sympathy are all our children, whether they live on Arab or Israeli soil, and we owe them the responsibility of providing them with a happy present and a bright future.

"For the sake of all this, for the sake of protecting the lives of all our sons and brothers; for our socie-

ties to produce in security and confidence; for the development of man, his well-being and his right to share in an honourable life; for our responsibility toward the coming generations, this is our conception of peace which I repeat today ..."

Biography

Anwar al-Sadat was born on December 25, 1918, in Talah Monufiya, a village in the Nile Delta. One of 13 children in a devout Moslem family, he attended a local religious primary school and a secondary school in Cairo. As a student in Abbassia Military Academy in 1936 he met Gamal Abdel Nasser. After graduation in 1938, Sadat and Nasser formed the Free Officers Committee, a group intent on liberating Egypt from foreign control.

Sadat's attempt to overthrow the British yoke by conspiring with the Germans in 1942 resulted in his imprisonment. Escaping in 1944, he again incurred imprisonment after a series of attacks against pro-British officials. Released from prison, he worked once more with Nasser in the Free Officers Committee, ultimately deposing Farouk in the Egyptian revolution to bring Nasser to the presidency. As a trusted friend, Sadat worked in various posts under Nasser's authoritarian rule: editor of the government paper, *Al Jumhuriya* and *Al Tahrir* (1955–61); Chairman of the Afro–Asian Solidarity Council (1961); member of the Presidential Council (1962–64). In 1964–66 and 1969–70 he served as Vice-President, which placed him in the role of successor to the presidency upon the death of Nasser in 1970. As President, Sadat liberalized the government within Egypt and worked for an Arab Socialist Union in his foreign policy, a policy which was dominated by the desire to lay down roots for lasting peace.

Anwar al-Sadat was assassinated on October 6, 1981, by members of a violent fundamentalist Moslem sect. His death was mourned by his devoted family, by his countrymen, and by people the world over who valued his role in bilateral negotiations between Egypt and Israel designed to bring a peaceful solution to age-old conflicts in the Middle East.

See also: Articles: *Camp David Accords*

Bibliography

Deming A, Martin D C, DeFrank T M 1978 A timely award? *Newsweek* 92 (November 6): 67–68, 71
Feld B T 1978 Norwegian prophecy or a gamble for peace? *Bull. Atomic Sci.* 34(December): 5
Sadat A 1978 *In search of identity*. Harper and Row, New York
Time 1978 Alone in Oslo. 112 (December 18): 44

RUTH C. REYNOLDS

Mother Teresa

(1979)

Mother Teresa of Calcutta received the Nobel Peace Prize for 1979. Over the years the Nobel Committee for the Peace Prize has rewarded diverse virtues. The nominees range from the idealist, who visualizes the creation of a world where war has become obsolete, to the pragmatist, who finds a workable alternative to presently threatening conflicts. Other choices have honored those who have addressed the abuses and deprivations which errant humanity imposes upon itself. With Mother Teresa we see the pure in heart recognized. Her message transcends nationalities and creeds; her spirit soars across common frailties and speaks to an innate commonality in the human species. She daily ministers through recognition of the potential for fundamental good in humanity without which the hope of peace would falter for us all. Seeing Christ in every human being, making each individual sacred, she tells us that every service each of us can offer to the other becomes a means of experiencing God in all of us.

Mother Teresa was born Agnes Gonxha Bojaxhiu, daughter of Albanian parents in Skopje, in what is now Yugoslavia, on August 27, 1910. By the time she was 12 she knew she wanted to become a nun, and at 18 she took her first vows in an Irish order, the Sisters of Loretto, in which she taught for 20 years in a fashionable school for the daughters of prosperous families of Calcutta. Within this sheltered environment she sensed deeply the suffering and poverty of the destitute nearby, and the poor ultimately became her calling.

In 1948 Mother Teresa received permission to leave her teaching order and she answered the call of the "poorest of the poor," working without funds and starting with an open-air school for homeless children. Two years later she was granted permission to start a new religious order, the Society of the Missionaries of Charities, with canonical sanction. She took Indian citizenship.

Testimony to the success of Mother Teresa's work on the one hand is the picture familiar over much of the world of a beloved nun dressed in a coarse white sari ministering in the streets of India to the sick and dying, child and adult alike; and on the other hand statistics tell of the impressive growth of her order to 158 branches, with 1,800 nuns and 12,000 co-workers including lay doctors and brethren trained in the healing arts. But even on such a scale, achievement itself does not account for the decision made by the Nobel Committee.

Chairman John Sanness said that while the Committee took note of the success of Mother Teresa's Missionaries of Charity, still their admirable record has been but one out of many others also meriting respect. The ingredient within Mother Teresa's success which was decisive for the Committee is the spirit which has permeated her work, he said. "This has been Mother Teresa's fundamental contribution to the Order she has created and run. This it is that explains both why so many people would flock to join the Order, and the interest and respect she has encountered throughout the world. This springs," he stressed, "from Mother Teresa's own fundamental attitude to life and her very special personality."

"The hallmark of her work has been respect for the individual and the individual's worth and dignity. The loneliest and the most wretched, the abandoned lepers, the destitute and the dying, have been received by her and her Sisters with warm compassion, devoid of condescension, and based on the reverence for Christ in man.

"Better than anyone else she has managed to put into practice the recognized fact that gifts given *de haut en bas*, where the recipient has a feeling of one-sided and humiliating dependence on the giver, may prove so hurtful to the recipient's dignity as a human being that it may well breed bitterness and animosity . . ." He said that Mother Teresa teaches that the person who, in the accepted sense, is the recipient is also the giver. And it is the recipient who gives the most. This principle underlies all that she does.

In her Nobel lecture Mother Teresa described powerfully and poignantly her respect and admiration for those she serves: "The poor people are very great people. They can teach us so many beautiful things." She told of a woman whom she picked up from the streets "in a most terrible condition." Mother Teresa ministered to her "with all that my love can do. I put her in bed, and there was such a beautiful smile on her face. She took hold of my hand, as she said only: 'Thank you' and she died.

"I could not help but examine my conscience before her, and I asked what would I say if I was in her place. And my answer was very simple. I would have tried to draw a little attention to myself, I would have said I am hungry, that I am cold, that I am dying ... but she gave me her grateful love. And she died with a smile on her face."

She described the transcendent purity she witnessed in a man whom the Order picked up from the drain half-eaten with worms and brought to the home: "He said 'I have lived like an animal in the street, but I am going to die like an angel, loved and cared for.' And it was so wonderful to see the greatness of that man who could speak like that, who could die like that without blaming anybody, without cursing anybody, without comparing anything. 'Like an angel'–this is the greatness of our people," Mother Teresa told the award audience. "We may be doing social work in the eyes of the people, but we are really contemplatives of the world," she said.

Violence has no place in Mother Teresa's view of the world. And the violence she finds cruelest of all is that which is practiced against the smallest and most helpless of victims, the unborn child. She pronounced abortion to be "the greatest destroyer of peace today because it is a direct war, a direct killing —direct murder by the mother herself." Mother Teresa offers concrete alternatives. For those unwanted children who are already conceived, her Order offers adoption. "We will find that child a home," promises this woman who calls being unwanted the cruelest disease that can scourge the life of a human being. The Order also teach natural family planning to the people of the street.

Mother Teresa closed her Nobel address with instructions to her audience, each one, to remember "God loves me, and I have an opportunity to love others as He loves me, not in big things, but in small things with great love." Then, she promised, "you become a burning light in the world of peace."

An Indian journalist wrote recently that "the Sisters with their serene ways, their saris, their knowledge of local languages ... have come to symbolize not only the best in Christian charity, but also the best in Indian culture and civilization, from Buddha to Gandhi, the great saints, the seers, the great lovers of humanity with boundless compassion and consideration ... what Shakespeare called the 'quality of mercy'."

"Mother Teresa's most astonishing and bewildering characteristic is her lack of any sense of indignation," reported an interviewer from the London *Observer* (Polly Toynbee, October 3, 1971). "Mother Teresa reminds one sharply that in the teachings of Christ there is no rage and indignation, no burning desire to change the horrifying injustices of a society that allows such poverty; like it or not, there is only the injunction to love and turn the other cheek."

Regarding socially militant Catholic dissidents, such as the Berrigan brothers, she told Toynbee: "If they feel this is the way they must serve Him, that is between them and God ... I am called to help the individual, to love each poor person, not to deal with institutions."

Chairman Sanness said Mother Teresa's view of the dignity of humankind has built a bridge across the gulf that exists between the rich nations and the poor nations. "Politics have never been her concern, but economic, social and political work with these same aims are in complete harmony with her own life's work."

Sanness quoted the President of the World Bank, Robert McNamara, whose words describe those of Mother Teresa's qualities being honored in the decision of the Committee: "Mother Teresa deserves Nobel's Peace Prize because she promotes peace in the most fundamental manner, by her confirmation of the inviolability of human dignity."

Biography

Mother Teresa was born in Skopje in what is now Yugoslavia on August 27, 1910. She was born Agnes Gonxha Bojaxhiu, one of three children of an Albanian peasant family. By the age of 12 she knew she had a calling, and at 18 she left home to join the Sisters of Loretto, an Irish order with a mission in Calcutta; and trained at Loretto institutions in Dublin and in Darjeeling. After 20 years of teaching wealthy children at St. Mary's High School in Calcutta, she responded to "a call within a call" and left her order to minister to the "poorest of the poor." In 1948, after three months of intensive medical training under the American Medical Missionary Sisters in Patna, she established the Missionaries of Charity, in order to work among and minister to the inhabitants of the Calcutta slums. Her first school was in the open air, but her work swiftly attracted both financial donations and volunteer workers—many of whom came to dedicate their lives to the work of the Missionaries of Charity. By 1979 the Order had grown to nearly 200 branches in 24 countries throughout the world. In 1952 the Order opened the Nirmal Hriday, a home for dying destitutes. In 1957 the missionaries began special treatment for lepers, including the opening of a colony for lepers in 1964 in West Bengal. In 1969 the International Association of Co-Workers of Mother Teresa was affiliated to the Missionaries of Charity. Following this, Missionaries of Charity houses were opened in Jordan, in the East End of London and New York City's Harlem. Through the Missionaries of Charity, Mother Teresa has established more than 50 schools, orphanages, and homes for the poor in India and in other countries.

Mother Teresa has been accorded the following honors: the Pope John XXIII Peace Prize (1971); Templeton Foundation Prize (1973); Bharat Ratna (Star of India) (1980); Hon. DD, Cambridge (1977); Hon. OBE (1978); Hon. Dr., Med., Catholic University of Sacred Heart, Rome (1981), Catholic University of Louvain (1982); Hon. Citizen of Assisi (1982); Hon. OM (1983); and Presidential Medal of Freedom (1985). She is the author of a book, *Gift for God* (1975).

Bibliography

Kearney V S 1972 Of many things. *America* 127(December): inside cover
Muggeridge M 1971 *Something Beautiful for God: Mother Teresa of Calcutta.* Collins, London

RUTH C. REYNOLDS

Adolfo Pérez Esquivel
(1980)

The 1980 Nobel Peace Prize was awarded to Adolfo Pérez Esquivel, a devout Argentine Roman Catholic layman and human rights activist, in recognition of his efforts in behalf of peace and justice throughout Latin America. "He is an untiring and consistent champion of the principle of non-violence in the struggle for social and political liberty," the Nobel Committee said. "He has lit a light in the dark, a light which, in the opinion of our Committee, should never be allowed to be extinguished."

Pérez Esquivel's intense commitment to the cause of human rights and nonviolent methods was fueled by the wave of terror that swept over many countries in Latin America, including his own country, Argentina. For Pérez Esquivel, nonviolence involves much more than passively accepting the world as it is. For him it is a strategy in a struggle to change the world, using means that will not stifle the good intentions and the results one aims to achieve.

After graduating from the National School of Fine Arts of Buenos Aires and La Pija in 1956, Pérez Esquivel pursued a successful and politically detached career as a sculptor and Professor of Art for the next 15 years. His sculptures are to be seen in various public places in Argentina. In 1974 he relinquished his teaching post at the Manuel Belgrano National School of Fine Arts in Buenos Aires in order to devote all his time and energy to the work of coordinating the activities of the various nonviolent elements in Latin America under the organization Servico Paz y Justicia (Service for Peace and Justice). Pérez Esquivel served as its secretary–general. On their behalf, he travelled tirelessly throughout Central and Latin America. During a trip to Brazil in 1975 he was briefly jailed; and he was arrested again in Ecuador the following year. In 1976 he initiated an international campaign aimed at persuading the United Nations to establish a Human Rights Commission, and in this connection a document was drawn up recording breaches of human rights in Latin America. "Unjust structures must be changed," Pérez Esquivel declared. He also called for the trial or release of the 6,000 *desaparecidos*, Argentinians who have disappeared during the past years of dictatorial rule, many of whom are now assumed dead. Among these were many people unacquainted with the ways of terrorists, including journalists who not only knew too much of the regime's contraventions of human rights, but who were anxious to publish what they knew.

In the midst of this frightening repression, Pérez Esquivel remained unflinchingly true to his principles of open, nonviolent protest. He paid a price for his public denunciations of Argentine government atrocities. In 1977 when he went to a police station to renew his passport following a trip to visit European human rights activists, he was arrested. Without legal charge, or even an interrogation, the regime held him for 14 months and tortured him in ways that he refuses to discuss in detail. He said that constant prayer and the performance of yoga exercises whenever possible helped him to resist the attempt to break his morale. "When you experience this extreme situation of being between life and death, you try to understand what Christ said on the cross: 'Father, forgive them, for they don't know what they are doing,'" Esquivel recalls. "But I thought that, yes, these people *did* know what they were doing.... What I discovered little by little was that what the torturers did not know was that they were persons, and that we were persons. They had lost their identities."

His harrowing experience did not distract Pérez Esquivel from the larger picture of deprivation and tragedy that go hand-in-hand with poverty. "You cannot talk solely of human rights in terms of torture and imprisonment and killing," he said. "True, this is the gravest aspect. But we must also look at the case of the peasant who has no land and is dying of hunger." Pérez Esquivel believes that poverty is the cause of most of Latin America's problems because poverty breeds violence which leads to repression. In turn, repression causes more poverty. Servico Paz y Justicia seeks to break this cycle by helping peasants get land and by supporting workers in their fight for better conditions.

Pérez Esquivel likewise champions the use of nonviolence in relations between nations. He has, for instance, warned of the danger of an escalation of the territorial conflict between Argentina and Chile. Commenting on their recurring border problems, he said that countries which share common historical and cultural roots as do these two must resolve their differences in a manner that is just for both populations. He saw that the people were practically ignorant of what their governments were doing, and along with Msgr. Jime de Navares and 1976 Nobel Peace Laureate Mairead Corrigan, Servico Paz y Justicia set about informing the people and campaigning in support of the papal mediation of the conflict.

Although such activities have political implications, Pérez Esquivel avoids alignment with specific political groups. "For us," he has explained, "the aim of politics should be the search for the common good in a society. In this sense, our activity is political. But if we are talking about party politics, that is a different matter ... we have no political preference. Our work is oriented towards a wider dimension, in all sectors."

His organization is ecumenical, and no-one is excluded on religious grounds. The Church itself has yet to decide upon its own role. Miguel Amador, writing for the *Christian Century* (1980), reported that the hierarchy of Argentina's Roman Catholic Church followed the news about the award by announcing that the Service for Peace and Justice organization was not to be confused with the Pontifical Commission on Justice and Peace and/or the Argentine Commission on Justice and Peace, which is under the Bishops' Conference. Though some Catholic parishes and some Protestant churches are staunch supporters of Servico Paz y Justicia, and though some Roman Catholic bishops have publicly acknowledged and congratulated the Peace and Justice organization, Amador reports that most of them have kept silent. "Equally accomplices in silence," he said, "are the Protestant and Orthodox churches ... as of this writing, no pronouncements have appeared from any of the major Protestant churches, or from any of the centers of theological study."

Professor Sanness, Nobel Committee Chairman, said that the Christian teaching in which Servico Paz y Justicia is rooted, in spite of the presence of resistance from the orthodoxy, forged new links between the Church and the broad masses of the people.

"This means that clergy and laymen must undertake fresh obligations within the community. The Church must not be content merely to carry out its ritual functions—baptism, mass, funerals," he said. "At a minimum, society is expected not to reconcile itself to conditions that make it impossible for men and women to gain respect for their human dignity or to accord this respect to others ... this is where people like Pérez Esquivel take their place in the social struggle."

Sanness pointed to the differences that exist between the many countries of Latin America, some poorer than Argentina, many with deeper historical sources of friction between sections of their populations, some of them smaller and more helpless. "Nevertheless," he said, "the Committee is of the opinion that Adolfo Pérez Esquivel has a message that is valid for the whole of Latin America....

"It is our hope that his work will bear fruit in his own country, that it will hearken to his voice and break out from the vicious circle of terror and counter-terror, of anarchy and reaction, setting an example to the whole of Latin America....

"These fundamental principles are supported by many excellent spokesmen in numerous countries, men who may be better known than Esquivel," he said. "The reason his voice reached all the way from Latin America to the Norwegian Nobel Committee was not because of its strength, but because of its purity and clarity."

Biography

Adolfo Pérez Esquivel was born in Buenos Aires in 1931. Educated as an architect and sculptor, after graduating from the National School of Fine Arts of Buenos Aires and La Pinta in 1956, Pérez Esquivel pursued a nonpolitical career as a sculptor and Professor of Fine Art for the next 15 years. His sculpture is shown in permanent collections in the Buenos Aires Museum of Modern Art, the Museum of Fine Arts, Cordoba, and the Fine Arts Museum in Rosario. Then, in 1974, he relinquished his teaching post at the Argentine National School of Fine Arts to accept leadership in the work of coordinating the activities of the various nonviolent protest groups in Latin America.

Pérez Esquivel works through the organization Servico Paz y Justicia, an organization dedicated to assisting rural workers to get land and to help trade unions protect rights of workers through, among other ways, legal aid, and he founded their journal, *Paz y Justicia*. As General Coordinator of Servico Paz y Justicia, he travelled extensively throughout Latin America in support of various groups dedicated to the advancement of human rights and to the principles of militant nonviolence. In 1977 he was imprisoned without trial or opportunity for defense. While in prison he was denied all legal rights and severely tortured.

After 14 months he was released subject to various restrictions, including a further period of house arrest. Since 1980 he has been allowed to resume his activities, including travel to coordinate international efforts towards human rights. He is cofounder of the Ecumenical Movement for Human Rights of Argentina, and is President of the Permanent Assembly for Human Rights.

Pérez Esquivel has been awarded the Pope John XXIII prize, and membership of the Pax Christi Organization (1977).

He married his wife Amanda in 1956; they have three sons, the oldest of whom, Leonardo, is active in Servico Paz y Justicia.

Bibliography

Amador M 1980 Silent accomplices. *Christian Century* 97(39): 1180–81
Brecher J, Rohter L 1980 Peace Prize: 'Why him?' *Newsweek* 96 (October 27): 78
Lundy M 1980 An interview: Adolfo Pérez Esquivel. *America* 143(21): 427–30

RUTH C. REYNOLDS

United Nations High Commisioner for Refugees (UNHCR)

(1981)

see *United Nations High Commisioner for Refugees* (*UNHCR*) (*1954, 1981*)

Alfonso Garcia Robles

(1982)

The 1982 Nobel Peace Prize was awarded to Alva Myrdal and Alfonso Garcia Robles, two diplomats who had labored long and effectively for disarmament. Though both had long been revered within arms control and peace organizations, they were without the worldwide renown associated with many of the previous winners. Garcia Robles and Myrdal had both worked for the UN Disarmament Commission in Geneva. The choice seemed a recognition by the Nobel Committee of the widespread efforts being made for disarmament by diplomats and international civil servants who labor in the background.

The Committee stated, "In today's world the work to promote peace, disarmament and the brotherhood of mankind is carried on in different ways.... There is the patient and meticulous work undertaken in international negotiations on mutual disarmament, and there is also the work of the numerous peace movements with their greater emphasis on influencing the climate of public opinion...."

Alfonso Garcia Robles has spent his life in public service, working with constant emphasis on creating means to solving international relationships without the use of violence. After studying law he joined Mexico's foreign service in 1939. As State Secretary in the Ministry of Foreign Affairs he served as delegate to the 1945 San Francisco Conference which founded the United Nations. He has been the Permanent Representative of Mexico to the Committee on Disarmament in Geneva. As Mexico's Director–General for Europe in the late 1950s he played a central role in the Law of the Sea Conferences.

In 1962, while Ambassador to Brazil, he was introduced to the idea of making Latin America a nuclear free zone. This concept gained an invaluable advocate in Garcia Robles. Following the Cuban crisis of 1962 he persuaded Mexico to start efforts toward the creation of a non-nuclear Latin America. His years of negotiation resulted in 22 nations signing the Treaty of Tlatelolco (1967), which barred nuclear weapons from their territories. As of August 1982, 15 years later, the number of signatory states stood at 25, of which 22 are already parties to the treaty (see Articles: *Nuclear Weapon Free Zones*).

In his Nobel lecture Garcia Robles pointed out that the Latin American nuclear weapon free zone "has the privilege of being the only one in existence which covers densely inhabited territories. Outside it, only in Antarctica, the Outer Space and the sea bed are similar prohibitions in force."

The preamble of the treaty describes its fundamental aims. They are concrete and important: the people of participating countries are spared from squandering their limited resources on nuclear armaments. In offering protection against possible nuclear attacks on their territories, this treaty also makes a significant contribution toward preventing the proliferation of nuclear weapons. It creates a pathway toward general and complete disarmament.

Garcia Robles says that when countries declare their land a nuclear free zone they are making a realistic statement about the destructive power inherent in nuclear arms. He believes they are taking action upon their recognition that nuclear arms are not defensive weapons, but a threat to the human race and to the planet.

Garcia Robles thought it worth noting that the "Final Document" approved by the first special session of the UN General Assembly devoted to disarmament, meeting in May and June of 1978, contained several declaratory statements of striking similarity to the Treaty of Tlatelolco, written 16 years previously. Both strongly urge the containment of nuclear weapons whose existing arsenals "attack the integrity of the human species and ultimately may render the whole earth uninhabitable." Garcia Robles played a central role in the session and was instrumental in the successful adoption of the "Final Document."

He recommended to the Nobel Committee that when awarding the Peace Prize in the future the highest priority be given to the contribution which the candidates, be they individuals or nongovernmental organizations, have made to disarmament. "The time has come," he said, "to seek security not in weapons, but in disarmament."

Garcia Robles's lifetime of work and accomplishment finds eloquent expression in the reasons the Committee gave for their two choices for the 1982 Peace Prize: "Putting across truth about nuclear arms has been, and still is, the prime concern of this year's Peace Prize Winners. They have clearly shown that the work of promoting peace and disarmament must be carried on at several levels. . . . The challenge facing peace workers is not to be found in a single universal question-and-answer, but in peaceful solutions to a host of conflicts, and in the exertion to achieve peace on many different levels.

"They know—better than most people—what it means to make intense efforts to find constructive proposals . . . they know how vital it is that negotiations on disarmament should be conducted on the basis of down-to-earth realism and on the assumption of give-and-take between the great powers."

Bernard Feld, of the *Bulletin of Atomic Scientists*, endorsed the choices of Myrdal and Garcia Robles for the Peace Prize award in an editorial (December 1982) which places into global context the unique contribution made by these two disarmament negotiators: "Between them the winners represent the vast but usually silent and unrepresented majority of humankind, whose stake in avoiding a nuclear war between the major industrial powers is as great as that of the direct protagonists.

"Never has the urgency been greater for the nuclear giants to recognize that, whatever their political and ideological differences, they have an overriding mutual interest in defusing their nuclear confrontation. But given the self-righteous arrogance of many of our leaders, it is necessary to propel them toward the negotiating table by overwhelming pressures, not only from within their own countries but from the rest of the world as well.

"For their part in raising the level of understanding of and the pressure for action on nuclear disarmament and peaceful accommodation, Alva R. Myrdal and Alfonso Garcia Robles have more than earned their award. By giving the prize to them, the Nobel Peace Prize Committee has not only honored the recipients and their cause: it has gone a long way toward vindicating its own mission as well."

Biography

Alfonso Garcia Robles was born in Zamora in Mexico in 1911. After studying law he entered his country's foreign service in 1939, where he held the following posts: Ambassador to Brazil, 1962–64, State Secretary in the Ministry of Foreign Affairs, 1974–70, Mexico's permanent representative in the United Nations, 1971–75, and Foreign Minister, 1975–76. Since 1977 he has been the Permanent Representative of Mexico to the Committee on Disarmament in Geneva. Garcia Robles played a crucial role in launching and implementing the agreement on a nuclear free zone in Latin America, culminating in the signing of the Tlatelolco Agreement in 1967. The effect of the agreement was to make Latin America the world's largest inhabited nuclear free zone. At the time of the award, however, some countries which signed had yet to implement it (Brazil, Argentina). He is currently Chairman of the UN's Disarmament Committee. His main priority, to which much of his work is directed, is to establish a world disarmament campaign.

He married Juana Maria Szyszlo in 1950. They have two sons.

Bibliography

Feld B T 1982 Nobel Peace Prize. *Bull. At. Sci.* 38 (December): inside cover
Newsweek 1982 A disarming Peace Prize. 100 (October 25): 88
Time 1982 Two disarming choices. 120 (October 25): 52

RUTH C. REYNOLDS

Alva Myrdal

(1982)

In its choices of Alva Myrdal and Alfonso Garcia Robles, the two winners of the 1982 Peace Prize, the Nobel Committee gave recognition and support to the peace movements which have been proliferating worldwide, all working in various ways to awaken public awareness of the suicidal nature of nuclear weapons. Both winners criticized the governments of the United States and the Soviet Union for escalating the arms race ever closer to Einstein's warning of "unparalleled catastrophe." Both had devoted their lives to seeking ways to promote effective protest.

The Chairman of the Nobel Committee, Egil Aarvik, observed that while humankind at large seems loath to face the threats of nuclear weapons, the first requirement for solutions to political problems is the moral courage to look these problems in the face. "It is such a temptation to shut one's eyes," he said. "It is as though the process of comprehension were obstructed. At some point we recoil, lacking the courage to know what we actually know. The truth . . . is so horrifying that it numbs our ability to comprehend it."

Alva Myrdal long displayed the courage to confront the truth. When she was asked by the Swedish Foreign Minister to become his special disarmament adviser in 1961 she became an expert on the subject, facing every aspect unflinchingly. She wrote *The Game of Disarmament: How the United States and Russia Run the Arms Race*, in which she provides a study of the two Superpowers and their rivalry in producing weapons which presently endanger the world, supported by expenditures ruinous to the world economy, draining resources from health, education, and housing and many other social programs worldwide (see Articles: *Disarmament and Development*).

Myrdal cautioned that peace movements cannot address overly ambitious goals like leading the way to eternal peace, or solving all disputes among nations. The economic and political roots of the conflicts are too strong, she said, and therefore immediate goals must be more modest. We must aim at preventing what, in the present situation, is the greatest threat to the very survival of humankind—the threat of nuclear weapons.

She was especially gratified that the award had gone to citizens representing two nations which are both denuclearized and nonallied. "The mass media call attention to this all too seldom, being one-sidedly concerned with the rivalry between the two superpower blocks," she said. "There are, after all, so many other countries in the world and most have refused to serve as hostages to the superpowers."

Myrdal spoke of the efforts of their two countries to refute objectively attempts by the nuclear weapon powers to conceal or give false explanation of actual facts. "We must exert ourselves to break through the wall of silence which, unfortunately, the great powers have erected to ward off the small powers' influence in the international debate," she warned.

She persuaded her government to underwrite the seismological Hagfors station. This station monitors independently and systematically even the smallest subterranean nuclear tests, using the most modern equipment, and publishes the results internationally, unhampered by any political considerations.

Under Myrdal's influence the Swedish government was persuaded to cover the costs of the Stockholm International Peace Research Institute. A vital purpose of these two organizations is to establish an international network for open verification of nuclear test explosions. The smaller nations can thereby exert more influence on disarmament negotiations than they have previously done.

Myrdal saw a strong correlation between collective military violence and personal violence. She was convinced that the militarization permeating society was eroding basic ethical values. The exercise of force by various nations plays an ominous role in maintaining what Myrdal called the "weaponry and violence cult of our age." She asserted that the mass media exacerbated the problems of violence, affecting not only the countries in which the media were created, but also the Third World countries to which much of the media were imported.

Bernard Feld, writing for the *Bulletin of Atomic Scientists* (1982) endorsed the choices of Myrdal and Garcia Robles for the Peace Prize in an editorial which succinctly summarized their unique contributions: "Between them the winners represent the vast but usually silent and unrepresented majority of humankind, whose stake in avoiding a nuclear war between the major industrial powers is as great as that of the direct protagonists.

"Never has the urgency been greater for the nuclear giants to recognize that, whatever their political and ideological differences, they have an overriding mutual interest in defusing their nuclear confrontation. But given the self-righteous arrogance of many of our leaders, it is necessary to propel them toward the negotiating table by overwhelming pressures, not only from within their own countries, but from the rest of the world as well.

"For their part in raising the level of understanding of and the pressure for action on nuclear disarmament and peaceful accommodation, Alva R. Myrdal and Alfonso Garcia Robles have more than earned their award. By giving the prize to them, the Nobel Peace Prize Committee has not only honored the recipients and their cause: it has gone a long way toward vindicating its own mission as well."

Biography

Alva Myrdal was born in Uppsala in 1902. She graduated from university in 1924 and married Gunnar Myrdal the same year. The couple have made major contributions in the field of social welfare separately and together. In 1974 Gunnar Myrdal won the Nobel Prize in Economics.

In 1943 Mrs. Myrdal was appointed to the Government Commission on International Post-War Aid and Reconstruction. In 1949 she headed the UN's section on welfare policy. In 1955 she was appointed Swedish ambassador to India. In 1962 she served as Sweden's representative to the Geneva disarmament conference. That same year she became a Social Democrat member of Parliament, and in 1967 a member of the Cabinet. Her many articles and books have brought much insight and influence to the current disarmament debate. She won the Federal Republic of Germany's Peace Prize in 1970, the Albert Einstein Peace Prize in 1981, and the People's Peace Prize (awarded by political and pacifist organizations in Norway) in the same year.

Alva Myrdal died on February 2, 1986.

Bibliography

Feld B 1982 Nobel Peace Prize. *Bull. At. Sci.* 38 (December): inside cover
Newsweek 1982 A disarming Peace prize. 100 (October 25): 88
Time 1982 Two disarming choices. 120 (October 25): 52

RUTH C. REYNOLDS

Lech Walesa

(1983)

The Nobel Committee awarded the Peace Prize for 1983 to Lech Walesa of Poland in recognition of his continuing struggle, in the face of very powerful opposition, for the recognition of basic human rights. Though Walesa's struggle essentially centered on the right of Polish workers to establish their own trade unions, his campaigning, carried out at great personal sacrifice, engaged the attention and the support of people far beyond his own country. In making this award, the Nobel Committee said that Walesa's defense of workers' rights in Poland was something more than a domestic Polish issue. Walesa's contribution is of essential importance in the historical campaign to establish the freedom of organization as a universal human right. "This workers' movement, known as 'Solidarity' has come," the Committee said, "to represent the determination to resolve conflicts and obliterate disagreement through peaceful negotiation, where all involved meet with a mutual respect for one another's integrity."

Lech Walesa would agree: he insists the struggle must be nonviolent. "We can effectively oppose violence only if we ourselves do not resort to it," he has said. He, too, sees the struggle in a global context: "The civil and human rights sought by Solidarity are the ideals not just of Polish workers, but of people everywhere," he said. "In many parts of the world the people are searching for a solution that would link the two basic values: peace and justice. The two are like bread and salt for mankind." The Committee Chairman, Egil Aarvik, called this ideal "A burning torch which Walesa has lifted unarmed . . . . The word, the spirit and the thought of freedom and human rights were his weapons."

Looking back upon the genesis of Solidarity, the first sign of the free trade union forming on the Baltic Coast came quietly, unobserved by most of the outside world. In January 1979 an underground bimonthly, *The Worker of the Coast,* edited by Walesa, signaled the embryonic stirring of a new movement among the Polish workers. It was followed in July by a charter of workers' rights. With Walesa as one of the signatories, the charter asked for an end to censorship, an eight-hour day, improved job safety conditions, higher wages, and the legalization of the right to strike. Its most important statement presented the basic concept in Solidarity: "Strikes are useful short-term weapons, but free and independent trade unions are necessary to ensure that the gains won through a strike are not later lost. Only they will give us an equal footing in negotiations, a power the authorities cannot ignore."

In his award lecture (read in Oslo by his wife, Danuta Walesa, because Walesa feared that if he attended the award ceremony himself he would not be allowed back into Poland), Walesa traced the charter's precedents, going back to his boyhood: "I belong to the generation of workers who, born in the villages and hamlets of rural Poland, had the opportunity to acquire education and find employment in industry, becoming in the course conscious of their rights and the importance of society.

"These were the years of awakening aspirations of workers and peasants, but also years of many wrongs, degradation and lost illusions," he said. During these years periodic workers' protests were brutally suppressed. In 1956 the desperate struggle in Poznan for bread and freedom was forcefully put down by the authorities. Among the victims was a 13-year-old boy. A similar response was met with in 1970 during protest demonstrations in the Gdansk Shipyard, and again in 1976 during the strike of workers at Ursus and Radom. Walesa (who at this time was fired for his participation in the labor movement) not only was convinced of the justness of the working people's demands and aspirations, but also became persuaded of the urgent need for their solidarity.

In the following years Walesa lived inconspicuously, providing for his family as best he could despite successive job losses and jailings resulting from his labor activities. Meanwhile, a deteriorating economy in Poland placed new deprivations upon its citizens. Poland overextended itself in an effort to modernize industry, running up high international debts. Also, in an attempt to right the balance of trade and build up buying power with the West, it increased its export of goods, including meat products, which consequently exacerbated food shortages at home.

In July 1980 the Polish government doubled meat prices. Scattered work stoppages followed. On August 14 the Lenin Shipyard was seized by strikers. Among their demands was the reinstatement of three dismissed workers, including Walesa. Scaling the fence, Walesa joined the workers and became the leader of the strike. It was a leap destined to carry his movement far beyond the shipyards into the pages of history. Walesa declared that the settlement of that strike, the Gdansk Agreement, "stands out as a great charter of the rights of the working people which nothing can ever destroy ... it shall remain the model and the only method to follow, the only one

that gives a chance of finding a middle course between the use of force and a hopeless struggle," he said.

"Our firm conviction that ours is a just cause, and that we must find a peaceful way to attain our goals gave us the strength and the awareness of the limits beyond which we must not go .... Solidarity as a trade union movement did not reach for power, nor did it turn against the established constitutional order," Walesa declared. It was a shared cause among Poland's workers. "Lying at the root of the social agreements of 1980 are the courage, sense of responsibility, and the solidarity of the working people," Walesa said. He further reflected, "I think it marked also the road to be taken by the authorities, if they think of a state governed in cooperation and participation of all citizens."

Even allowing for the considerable tact exercised by Walesa it is obvious that the Solidarity campaign would greatly alarm the rulers of the Soviet bloc because Solidarity stood as an implicit contradiction of the Communist Party's claim to be the sole legitimate representative of the working class. Walesa was careful not to make this contradiction explicit, and steered a course designed to satisfy Polish workers without provoking Soviet intervention. He seemed to know instinctively just how far he could go in challenging the authorities without inviting disaster.

But his caution and tact were not shared by all members of the movement. Less pragmatic workers called for a referendum on Poland's communist government and the country's alliance with the Soviet Union. The authorities imposed martial law, Solidarity was outlawed, and Walesa interned for 11 months.

In June 1981, on the invitation of the Polish government, Pope John Paul II paid a papal visit to Poland during which he met with both the Polish Prime Minister, General Jaruzelski, and Walesa. The Pope spoke repeatedly of the need for national reconciliation and for responsible dialogue, asserting that "the working people in Poland—and everywhere—have this right because the working man is not a mere tool of production, but the subject which throughout the process of production takes precedence over capital."

At the time the Peace Prize was awarded to Walesa, Solidarity had become a forbidden organization. Walesa, reinstated at the shipyards in Gdansk, remains guardedly optimistic. Asked if he thought Solidarity could work within the government's Patriotic Front for National Rebirth, Walesa replied, "They are Poles like myself and probably know what the words honor and dignity mean. I don't want to isolate myself in anger. I will search for all possible solutions" (*Newsweek,* June 20, 1983).

Chairman Aarvik observed at the award ceremony, "Walesa cannot be presented as a victor at the end of a struggle full of sacrifice. His chosen course was not as short and easy as that. And it could seem that the goals he set himself are just as distant still.

"But is Lech Walesa really silent today? Is he completely without victory? Has his cause suffered defeat? Many are of the opinion that his voice has never been stronger nor reached further than it does now. The electrician from Gdansk, the carpenter's son from the Vistula Valley has managed to lift the banner of freedom and humanity so high that the whole world can once again see it . . . the future will recognise his name among those who contributed to humanity's legacy of freedom."

Biography

One of eight children of Boleslaw and Feliksa Walesa, Lech Walesa was born on September 29, 1943, in Popowo during the German occupation of Poland in the Second World War. He was educated in primary and technical schools. As an electrician he began work in the Lenin Shipyard in Gdansk in 1966. He married Danuta Walesa in 1969; they have four sons and three daughters.

In 1970 during the circumstances which led to Gomulka's replacement by Gievak as Party Secretary, Walesa was a member of a 27-strong action committee at the Lenin yards. As a result of his activities as shop steward, he was dismissed in 1976 and thereafter relied on temporary jobs to earn a living. When in the summer of 1980 there were further disturbances among shipyard workers, Walesa was helped into a protest meeting and seized the leadership by proposing that the workers occupy the shipyard. He subsequently became Chairman of the National Co-ordinating Committee of the Independent Autonomous Trade Union (known as Solidarity). The activites of Walesa, a devout Catholic, were supported by the Catholic Church, and in January 1981 he was received by Pope John Paul II—a fellow Pole—in Rome.

When General Jaruzelski became Prime Minister in February 1981 the relationship between Solidarity and the authorities worsened, and in December 1981 martial law was declared. The leadership of Solidarity was arrested, including Walesa, and he was interned for 11 months. He was released in November 1982 and has since been reinstated at the Lenin Shipyards in Gdansk.

Walesa has received numerous honorary awards and recognitions, including: Dr. honoris causa, Alliance College (1981), Providence College (1981), University of Columbia (1981), Catholic University (1981), MacMurray College (1982), Harvard University (1983), St. Denis University, Paris (1982). He was named "Man of the Year," by: *Financial Times* (1980), *The Observer* (1980), *Die Welt, Die Zeit* (1981), *L'Express* (1981), and *Le Soir* (1981). He was awarded the Freedom Medal, Philadelphia, Medal of Merit, Congress of Polish Community in USA (1981), Free World Prize, Norway (1982), Social Justice Award (1983), among other honors and prizes.

Bibliography

O'Hare J A 1983 Of many things. *America* 148 (January 1–8): inside cover

Singer D 1983 Honor the man—and the movement. *Nation* 237(13): 393–94

Stanglin D 1983a Walesa: We will keep trying. An interview with Walesa. *Newsweek* 101 (June 20): 42

Stanglin D 1983b Walesa on his struggle. *Newsweek* 102 (October 17): 34

Willey F, Stanglin D 1983 Poland's man of peace. *Newsweek* 102 (October 17): 33–34

RUTH C. REYNOLDS

Desmond Tutu
(1984)

The 1984 Nobel Peace Prize was awarded to South Africa's Bishop Desmond Tutu. "He is representative of the best in us all," the Nobel Committee said, and its hope was that the award would direct attention to his role as a unifying leader in the campaign to solve South Africa's apartheid problem by peaceful means. In a situation that courts violence and disaster it is all the more remarkable, Chairman Aarvik commented, that a peaceful alternative exists. It rests in large part on the shoulders of Bishop Tutu, whose campaign is waged with the weapons of the spirit and reason: truth, freedom, and justice. The Committee sees Bishop Tutu as a hope for the future, for the country's white minority as well as the black majority. "Desmond Tutu is an exponent of the only form for conflict solving which is worthy of civilized nations," the Committee declared.

In his Nobel lecture Bishop Tutu described the precarious balance between peaceful and violent resolution that exists in South Africa: "Our people are rapidly despairing of a peaceful resolution in South Africa. Those of us who still speak 'peace' and 'reconciliation' belong to a rapidly diminishing minority."

The struggle for democracy and justice has touched Tutu's life in many decisive ways. Growing up in Johannesburg, he learned sympathy for the weak and the underprivileged. Here too he met the man who probably exercised the strongest influence on his formative years, Father Trevor Huddleston, then serving as parish priest in the black slum of Sophiatown. The son of a teacher at a Methodist school, Tutu also taught at mission schools. In 1957 the government took over these institutions, installing a system of Bantu (black) education so inferior that he felt compelled to resign.

Tutu judged that he could best help his people through the church. "It just occurred to me," he has said, "that, if the church would have me, the profession of priest would be a good way of helping my people." He studied in theological colleges in South Africa and London, and was ordained in 1962. For several years he worked for the World Council of Churches' Theological Education Fund, and in 1976 he was elected Anglican Bishop of Lesotho. It was in 1978 that his appointment as the first black to direct the South African Council of Churches plunged him into a leadership role opposing apartheid. With 18 member denominations and 13 million members, of whom 80 percent are black, the South African Council of Churches (SACC) is one of the most eloquent and important voices of opposition to apartheid. Indeed, the Nobel Committee included the South African Council of Churches in the "gesture of support" it hoped to make with the Peace Prize award.

Bishop Tutu has been a fearless and dynamic leader of this council. Courageously he has opposed injustice, and is frequently found at the front of processions demonstrating against the government and its policies. He has maintained that in a situation such as exists in South Africa the church has to be political. "Not party political," he stipulates, "but morally political." His goal of a democratic and just society without racial segregation would seem reasonable throughout much of the world. But he struggles in the reality of a social order which has deported three million human beings from their homes, stripping them of personal possessions, and transporting them to an empty veld with just a tent and a sack of maize as their means of survival.

Bishop Tutu described their plight before the award audience. In pursuance of apartheid's ideological racist dream, hundreds of thousands of families have been dumped in the Bantustan homeland resettlement camps. "I say 'dumped' advisedly;" Bishop Tutu explained, "only things or rubbish is dumped, not human beings. Apartheid has, however, ensured that God's children, just because they are black, should be treated as if they were things, and not as of infinite value created in the image of God." These

dumping grounds, designated by the South African government as "tribal homelands," are far from where work and food can be procured easily. Children starve, suffering from the often irreversible consequences of malnutrition. This happens to them not accidentally, the Bishop declared, but by deliberate government policy.

He told of the tragic plight of many of the fathers to the towns, where they labor 11 months of the year separated from their families in a desperate effort to send back support. This, he said, is just a part of the cost of apartheid in human suffering. Apartheid is upheld by a complex mesh of draconian laws: security legislation which permits the indefinite detention of persons without access to family, doctor, or lawyer. Some are held in solitary confinement; some die mysteriously in detention. Laws which uphold the forced population removals, the Bantu education system which educates children for serfdom, the migratory labor system—all are part of a repressive and unjust system. "We see before us a land bereft of much justice, and therefore without peace and security," Bishop Tutu said. "Unrest is endemic, and will remain an unchanging feature of the South African scene until apartheid, the root cause of it all, is finally dismantled.. . .

"I have spoken extensively about South Africa," he said, "first because it is the land I know best, but because it is also a microcosm of the world and an example of what is to be found in other lands in differing degree. Where there is injustice, invariably peace becomes a casualty.. . . Because there is global insecurity, nations are engaged in a mad arms race, spending billions of dollars wastefully on instruments of destruction when millions are starving."

He does not confine his observations on ethics for those at home. To the US business community he said recently, "What we have to say to those who invest in South Africa is that your investment is a moral as well as an economic issue.. . . This is our last peaceful chance. My fears are the fears of many that we could very well have a blood bath. It is for everyone to speak out—business, bishops, everybody."

Tutu has said that the only true hope for a peaceful solution would come through holding a national convention of the real leaders, black and white. But the whites will do this only under pressure. "It is up to the international community to exert pressure on the South African government," he said, "especially economic pressure.. . . This is our last chance for change because if that doesn't happen . . . it seems the bloodbath will be inevitable." Here Tutu is echoing a request for sanctions made 25 years ago by

Zulu Chief Albert Lutuli, recipient of the 1960 Nobel Peace Prize.

No-one can remain impartial in a situation of injustice and oppression, Tutu asserts. "To be impartial and not to take sides is indeed to have taken sides already. It is to have sided with the status quo." He urges the international community to disinvest from South Africa: International economic pressure against the regime "is the only alternative to violence," he declared.

Bishop Tutu calls himself only a part of a mass movement of South African blacks seeking fundamental change. He graciously shared his award with his compatriots. He addressed the crowd that welcomed him in Johannesburg after the announcement of his prize: "This award is for you, your mothers who sit at railway stations trying to eke out an existence selling potatoes, selling mealies.... This award is for you, the three-and-a-half-million of our people who have been uprooted and dumped as if you were rubbish.... It is for you who, down through the ages, have said that you seek to change this evil system peacefully; for you who have marched against the pass laws peacefully and who, unarmed, have been shot, mown down, and killed. With this award, the world is saying it recognized that you have been peace-loving to a fault."

Chairman Aarvik also honored the black South Africans' patient and courageous seeking out of non-violent solutions. The award should be seen as "a renewed recognition of the courage and heroism shown by black South Africans in their ... peaceful ... struggle against apartheid," he said. It was the Committee's decision "in recognition ... that it is this alternative vision which must succeed, that the South African Bishop, Desmond Tutu, has been selected as this year's Prize Laureate."

Biography

Desmond Mpilo Tutu was born on October 7, 1931, in Klerksdorp, Transvaal. His parents were Zachariah Tutu, a teacher in a Methodist school, and Aletta Tutu. After graduation from Johannesburg Bantu High School he earned a teacher's diploma at Pretoria Bantu Normal College (1953) and a B.A. at the University of South Africa (1954). He immediately took a teaching position at Johannesburg Bantu High School, where he stayed for one year. In 1955 he began teaching at Munsieville High School in Krugersdorp, and married Leah Nomalizo; they have four children, Trevor Thamsanqa, Theresa Thandeka, Naomi Nontombi, and Mpho Andrea. In 1958 the government installed a Bantu education system abhorrent to Tutu because of its inferiority, and he left teaching. He entered St. Peters Theological College, Rosettenville, Johannesburg, for Ordina-

tion Training and earned a Licentiate in Theology in 1960. He was ordained as Priest in 1961. From 1962 to 1965 he was part-time curate at St. Alban's, Golder's Green, London, obtaining his B.D. (honors) in 1965, and his Master's in Theology, both from King's College, London, in 1966. He was part-time curate at St. Mary's, Bletchingley, Surrey, 1965–66.

Between 1967 and 1969 he served on the Staff of the Federal Theological Seminary, Alice, Cape, and as Chaplain at the University of Fort Hare. From 1970 to 1972 he served as lecturer in the Department of Theology, University of Botswana, Lesotho and Swaziland, Roma, Lesotho. Between 1972 and 1975 he was Associate Director of the Theological Education Fund of the World Council of Churches based in Bromley, Kent, where he served as honorary curate of St. Augustine's, Grove Park. In 1975 he was made Dean of Johannesburg; in 1976, Bishop of Lesotho. In 1978 he was appointed General Secretary of the South African Council of Churches. In 1985 he was appointed Bishop of Johannesburg.

Bishop Tutu has earned many awards and honorary degrees: he was elected Fellow of King's College, London (1978), awarded an Honorary Doctorate of Divinity from the General Theological Seminary, USA (1978), an Honorary Doctorate of Civil Law from Kent University, England (1978), and an Honorary Doctorate of Laws from Harvard, USA (1979). He received the Prix d'Athene (Onassis Foundation) in 1980, an Honorary Doctorate of Theology from Ruhr University, Bochum (1981), an Honorary Doctorate of Sacred Theology, Columbia University (1982). He was designated a member of the International Social Prospects Academy (1983), and given the Family of Man Gold Medal Award (1983). In 1984 he received an Honorary Doctorate of Law from Claremont Graduate School, and an Honorary Doctorate of Sacred Theology from Dickinson College, the Martin Luther King, Jr. Humanitarian Award of Annual Black American Heroes and Heroines Day, an Honorary Doctorate of Divinity from Aberdeen University, Scotland, and Doctor of Human Letters, Howard University, United States. His publications include *Crying in the Wilderness* (1982), *Hope and Suffering* (1983), and various articles and reviews.

Bibliography

America 1984 Prophets of South Africa. p. 266
Canine C, Underwood A 1984 A parable—and a Peace Prize. *Newsweek* 104 (October 29): 89
Commonweal 1984 Gifts seen and heard. 101(21): 645–46
Howell L 1984 Antiapartheid Bishop awarded Peace Prize. *Christian Century* November 14, pp. 1054–55
New York Times 1984 Bishop Tutu given Nobel Prize in Oslo ceremony. December 11
Pohl K I 1985 The ethics of disinvestment. *Christian Century* 102(31): 759–60
Progressive 1984 The Bishop's message. 48(12): 11
Tutu D 1983 *Hope and Suffering*. Eerdmans, Grand Rapids, Michigan

RUTH C. REYNOLDS

International Physicians for Prevention of Nuclear War (IPPNW)
(1985)

The Nobel Peace Prize for 1985 was awarded to the International Physicians for Prevention of Nuclear War (IPPNW). The Nobel Committee stated in its announcement that the IPPNW had "performed a considerable service to mankind by spreading authoritative information and by creating an awareness of the catastrophic consequences of atomic warfare." The award was made just prior to the first summit meeting to be held between the United States and the Soviet Union since Ronald Reagan became US President. In this long interval, tensions had heightened and the arms race had accelerated between the two countries, bringing closer the possibility of a nuclear disaster. Nobel Chairman Egil Aarvik linked the choice of the Committee to these upcoming talks: "If this award has any message, it is for the two superpowers to come up with results," he said.

The Committee's decision voices a conviction that nuclear war presents an overall threat to the Earth's peoples, and that ideologically opposed nations must work together to prevent such a disaster despite all disagreements, large and small, between them. The IPPNW is founded on this single, overriding premise. Its co-presidents, American cardiologist Bernard Lown of Harvard's School of Public Health and Soviet cardiologist Eugene Chazov of the National Cardiological Research Center in Moscow, emphasized this in their message to the 1985 IPPNW Congress: "Combating the nuclear threat has been our total and exclusive preoccupation," they said. They attributed their success largely to an insistent avoidance of association with problems that have embittered relations between the Superpowers, resisting being sidetracked to other issues for any reason.

This organization comes from a distinguished and responsible lineage. In 1961 a group of physicians in Cambridge, Massachusetts, became concerned over the health effects of atmospheric testing of nuclear weapons and alarmed over the growing US confidence in a fallacious civil defense program. They felt these things to be an increasing hazard to the health of their community, and ultimately a threat to the peoples of the Earth. They founded Physicians for Social Responsibility (PSR), whose purpose was twofold: to create an education program, acquainting themselves as physicians with the problems of nuclear age, and to seek preventive measures against the major health hazard therein.

In 1973 a quite different event took place. The problem of sudden death from cardiovascular causes brought together physicians from the East and West to participate in collaborative studies on this health problem. In the resulting series of visits and exchanges of information between US and Soviet physicians, two of the participating cardiologists, Lown and Chazov, began to see the possibility of similar cooperation in facing a potentially far greater health problem—the threat to all life lying within a possible nuclear disaster. Their mutual concern led to a Geneva meeting in December 1980 between three Soviet and three US physicians. There they generated a set of resolutions that became the basis for the founding of IPPNW: they would restrict their focus to preventing nuclear war, and to this end they would involve both Eastern and Western bloc nations and seek to circulate the same factual information about nuclear war throughout the world. Acknowledging that many things divided them politically and ideologically, they agreed not to allow these issues to become divisive. Thus IPPNW provides a model for international cooperation, finding common ground and issuing prescriptions that transcend political and cultural boundaries. Since that day in late 1980, IPPNW has gained a membership of 135,000 physicians in 41 countries. With a large supportive lay membership, they have helped penetrate the fog of psychic denial, persuading millions of people, for the first time, to confront the "unthinkable" reality of nuclear war. They have convinced a large public that there can be no useful medical response to the horrors of blast, fire, and radiation that would come in its wake.

The physicians also deplore the long-term effects on health and welfare imposed by the arms race itself: "Its cost is not only the vast sums being diverted to armaments in a world where tens of thousands of human beings die each day of treatable diseases. The cost is also in the great psychological damage that is occurring, particularly to young people and children who fear they will have no future."

How is one to explain the growing awareness of the unprecedented danger which exists side by side with a persistant refusal to resist that danger? How can one explain that, notwithstanding the education of millions about the consequences of nuclear war, we are still addicted to a nuclear fix?

Chazov and Lown offer an answer and suggest a solution. One fundamental reason for such a calamitous impasse, they say, relates to the fostering of the image of an all-powerful and unscrupulous adversary. In thousands of years of human history the fixed response has been to gather rocks, muskets, and napalm, and now it is to increase nuclear arsenals. To reverse this behavior pattern it is not enough to make apocalyptic predictions, however well-founded, however persuasively put. The enemy stereotypes must be dissipated.

IPPNW has fostered opportunities for a free-flowing dialogue between physicians of the two contending power blocs. One of the main planks of their program has been to eradicate "image of the enemy" stereotyping by promoting closer personal contacts between representatives of the two nations and by better education about each other's countries.

In 1985 IPPNW expanded its platform to include support toward a substantial shift of funding from the nuclear arms race to the health needs of developing countries, especially those of children. Lown and Chazov explained: "We need to set examples and venture imaginatively to harness medical talent East and West for resolution of global health problems. Leading world experts from the USA, USSR and the World Health Organization will detail a program for immunizing children in the Third World against six diseases that claim more than 4 million lives annually and cripple as many."

"We physicians do not accept the inevitability of nuclear conflict," Drs. Lown and Chazov asserted at the close of the 1985 IPPNW Congress. "We reject subverting technology for genocidal weapons rather than employing the fruits of science for improving the quality of life. We meet here because of our abiding faith in human reason and because we hold dear the concept that what humanity creates, humanity can control....Let us pledge—as physicians and world citizens—to work tirelessly toward eradicating the greatest public health threat of all time."

IPPNW embodies the professional tradition of physicians' organizing themselves in favor of life. The great nineteenth-century physician and scientist Rudolf Virchow foresaw that this tradition must embrace societal responsibility: "Should medicine ever fulfill its great ends, it must enter into the larger political and social life of our time, it must indicate the barriers which obstruct the normal completion of the life cycle and remove them. Should this ever come to pass, medicine, whatever it may then be, will become the common good of all." IPPNW has indeed proven Virchow's vision prophetic.

Biography

In December 1980 three US and three Soviet physicians met in Geneva to found the International Physicians for the Prevention of Nuclear War (IPPNW). The three US physicians were members of the Physicians for Social Responsibility (PSR), an activist group organized in 1961 to educate themselves, their fellow physicians, and their patients about the hazards to health and life itself posed by the nuclear testing being done at that time, and to educate the public about the fallacy of civil defense as a means of preserving life in the event of nuclear warfare. PSR remains the US affiliate of IPPNW.

The IPPNW quickly gained worldwide support. Within months of its inception, doctors from 11 countries attended IPPNW's first annual meeting. At the time of the 1985 annual meeting the membership had grown to 135,000 with 41 countries represented. Its co-presidents are Bernard Lown, a cardiologist from Harvard's School of Public Health, and Eugene Chazov, a cardiologist from the National Cardiological Research Center in Moscow.

IPPNW has been a one-issue organization, seeking only to prevent nuclear war. In 1985, however, an adjunctive plan was adopted wherein IPPNW cooperates with the World Health Organization in the immunization of children in the Third World against six diseases that claim more than four million lives annually and cripple an equal number.

See also: Articles: *Nuclear Winter*

Bibliography

Abrams H L 1984 Medical resources after nuclear war. *J. Am. Med. Assoc.* 252(5): 653–58

Boyer P 1985 Physicians confront the apocalypse—The American medical profession and the threat of nuclear war. *J. Am. Med. Assoc.* 254(5): 633–43

Bruwer A 1985 The nuclear weapons freeze and a cancer metaphor.—A physician's view. *J. Am. Med. Assoc.* 254(5): 657–58

Cassel C K, Jameton A 1982 Medical responsibility and thermonuclear war: An analysis of medical responsibility. *Annals of Internal Med.* 97: 426–32

Chalmers T C, Lown B, Chazov E 1984 Physicians should contribute to preventing nuclear war (Letter). *J. Am. Med. Assoc.* 252(5): 625

Day B, Waitzkin H 1985 The medical profession and nuclear war—A social history. *J. Am. Med. Assoc.* 254(5): 644–51

Bulletin of Atomic Scientists 1985 Nobel for physicians. 41(11): 2

Gunby P 1980 Sudden death brings East and West together. *J. Am. Med. Assoc.* 243(3): 215–15

Hiatt H H 1984 The final epidemic—Prescriptions for prevention. *J. Am. Med. Assoc.* 252(5): 635–38

Jennet C, Starr M 1985 A prescription for peace. *Newsweek* October 21, p. 56

Liebow A A 1965 Encounter with disaster: A medical diary on Hiroshima. *Yale J. Biol. Med.* 38:62–239

Lifton R J 1985 Hiroshima and ourselves. *J. Am. Med. Assoc.* 254(5): 621–32

Litwin M S 1985 Physician's group seeks nuclear arms ban. *J. Am. Med. Assoc.* 254(5): 586–91

Lown B, Chazov E 1985 Cooperation not confrontation: The imperative of a nuclear age. *J. Am. Med. Assoc.* 254(5): 655–57

Lundberg G D 1983 Hiroshima. *J. Am. Med. Assoc.* 250(5): 617

Lundberg G D 1985 Prescriptions for peace in a nuclear age. *J. Am. Med. Assoc.* 254(5): 660–61

Southgate M T The shadow of Hiroshima: Two diaries. *J. Am. Med. Assoc.* 252(5): 667–68

Ziparyn T, Goldsmith M F 1985 Physicians' antinuclear war group expanding to include child health. *J. Am. Med. Assoc.* 254(5): 585–87

RUTH C. REYNOLDS

Elie Wiesel

(1986)